ORGB

STUDENT TESTED, FACULTY APPROVED

THE ORGB SOLUTION

Every 4LTR Press solution includes:

Visually Engaging Textbook

Online Study Tools

Tear-out Review Cards

Interactive eBook

STUDENT RESOURCES:
- Interactive eBook
- Auto-Graded Quizzes
- Flashcards
- Games & Crossword Puzzles
- PowerPoint® Slides
- Videos
- E-Lectures
- Cases & Exercises
- KnowNOW!
- Self-Assessments
- Career Transitions
- Review Cards

INSTRUCTOR RESOURCES:
- All Student Resources
- Engagement Tracker
- First Day of Class Instructions
- LMS Integration
- Custom Options through 4LTR+ Program
- Instructor's Manual
- Test Bank
- PowerPoint® Slides
- Instructor Prep Cards

Students sign in at **www.cengagebrain.com**

Instructors sign in at **www.cengage.com/login**

AUGUST 2010
Engagement Tracker launches, giving faculty a window into student usage of digital tools.

1 out of every 3 (1,400) schools has adopted a 4LTR Press solution.

4LTR Press adds eBooks in response to a 10% uptick in digital learning preferences.

NOVEMBER 2010
750,000 students are IN.

 A+

Third party research confirms that 4LTR Press digital solutions improve retention and outcomes.

IN 2011
60 unique solutions across multiple course areas validates the 4LTR Press concept.

CourseMate
Students access the 4LTR Press website at 4x's the industry average.

APRIL 2011
1 out of every 2 (2,000) schools has a 4LTR Press adoption.

IN 2011
2,000

AUGUST 2011
Over 1 million students are IN.

We're always evolving. Join the 4LTR Press In-Crowd on Facebook at www.facebook.com/4ltrpress

2012 AND BEYOND

SOUTH-WESTERN
CENGAGE Learning

ORGB3

Debra L. Nelson, Oklahoma State University
James Campbell Quick, University of Texas, Arlington

SVP, Learning Acquisitions & Solutions Planning: Jack W. Calhoun

Vice President, 4LTR Press: Neil Marquardt

Publisher: Erin Joyner

Executive Editor: Scott Person

Developmental Editor: John Choi, B-Books, Ltd.

Product Development Manager, 4LTR Press: Steven E. Joos

Associate Project Manager, 4LTR Press: Pierce Denny

Sr. Project Manager: Michelle Lockard

Editorial Assistant: Megan Fischer

Marketing Manager: Jon Monahan

Marketing Manager, 4LTR Press: Courtney Sheldon

Marketing Coordinator: Julia Tucker

Sr. Marketing Communications Manager: Jim Overly

Production Director: Amy McGuire, B-Books, Ltd.

Sr. Content Project Manager: Tamborah Moore

Media Editor: Rob Ellington

Manufacturing Planner: Ron Montgomery

Production Service: B-Books, Ltd.

Rights Acquisitions Specialist: Deanna Ettinger

Photo Researcher: Charlotte Goldman

Text Permissions Researcher: Melissa Tomaselli, PreMediaGlobal

Sr. Art Director: Tippy McIntosh

Internal Designer: Joe DeVine, Red Hangar Design

Cover Design: KeDesign, Mason, OH

Cover Image: © iStockphoto.com

For product information and technology assistance, contact us at **Cengage Learning Customer & Sales Support, 1-800-354-9706.**

For permission to use material from this text or product, submit all requests online at **www.cengage.com/permissions**. Further permissions questions can be emailed to **permissionrequest@cengage.com**.

Library of Congress Control Number: 2011944036

Student Edition ISBN-13: 978-1-133-19119-3
Student Edition ISBN-10: 1-133-19119-3

South-Western
5191 Natorp Boulevard
Mason, OH 45040
USA

Cengage Learning products are represented in Canada by Nelson Education, Ltd.

For your course and learning solutions, visit **www.cengage.com**. Purchase any of our products at your local college store or at our preferred online store **www.CengageBrain.com**.

Cover and Page i Photography Credits:
Inside Front Cover: ©iStockphoto.com/sdominick, ©iStockphoto.com/Alexsl, ©iStockphoto.com/A-Digit; Page i: ©iStockphoto.com/CostinT, ©iStockphoto.com/photovideostock, ©iStockphoto.com/Leontura; Back Cover: ©iStockphoto.com/René Mansi

Printed in the United States of America
1 2 3 4 5 6 7 15 14 13 12 11

Brief Contents

Part 1
Introduction   2

Chapter 1   Organizational Behavior and Opportunity   2
Chapter 2   Challenges for Managers   16

Part 2
Individual Processes and Behavior   36

Chapter 3   Personality, Perception, and Attribution   36
Chapter 4   Attitudes, Emotions, and Ethics   54
Chapter 5   Motivation at Work   74
Chapter 6   Learning and Performance Management   90
Chapter 7   Stress and Well-Being at Work   106

Part 3
Interpersonal Processes and Behavior   124

Chapter 8   Communication   124
Chapter 9   Work Teams and Groups   142
Chapter 10   Decision Making by Individuals and Groups 158
Chapter 11   Power and Political Behavior   176
Chapter 12   Leadership and Followership   192
Chapter 13   Conflict and Negotiation   210

Part 4
Organizational Processes and Structure   228

Chapter 14   Jobs and the Design of Work   228
Chapter 15   Organizational Design and Structure   244
Chapter 16   Organizational Culture   262
Chapter 17   Career Management   278
Chapter 18   Managing Change   296

Notes   313
Index   345

Contents

Part 1

Introduction   2

©Eric Audras/PhotoAlto Agency RF Collections/Getty Images

Chapter 1
Organizational Behavior and Opportunity 2

Human Behavior in Organizations   3
   Understanding Human Behavior   4
   Interdisciplinary Influences   4
Behavior in Times of Change   5
The Organizational Context   6
   Organizations as Open Systems   6
The Formal and Informal Organization   7
Diversity of Organizations   8
Change Creates Opportunities   9
   Global Competition in Business   10
   Customer Focused for High Quality   10
   Behavior and Quality at Work   11
   Managing Organizational Behavior in Changing
      Times   12
Learning About Organizational Behavior   13
   Objective Knowledge   13
   Skill Development   14
   Application of Knowledge and Skills   15

Chapter 2
Challenges for Managers   16

Competing in the Global Economy   17
   Social and Political Changes   18
   Cultural Differences   19
Cultural Differences and Work-Related Attitudes   20
   Individualism versus Collectivism   20
   Power Distance   20
   Uncertainty Avoidance   22
   Masculinity versus Femininity   22
   Time Orientation   22
   Developing Cross-Cultural Sensitivity   22
The Diverse Workforce   23
   Ethic Diversity   23
   Gender Diversity   24
   Age Diversity   25
   Ability Diversity   26
   Valuing Diversity   26
   Diversity's Benefits and Problems   27
Ethics, Character, and Personal Integrity   28
   Consequential Theories of Ethics   28
   Rule-Based Theories of Ethics   29
   Character Theories of Ethics   29
   Cultural Relativism   29
Ethical Dilemmas Facing the Modern Organization   29
   Employee Rights   29
   Sexual Harassment   30
   Organizational Justice   30
   Whistle-Blowing   31
   Social Responsibility   31
   Codes of Ethics   31
Technological Innovation and Today's Workforce   32
   Alternative Work Arrangements   33
   Impact of Technology on Management   34
   Helping Employees Adjust to Technological
      Change   35

Part 2

Individual Processes and Behavior   36

Chapter 3
Personality, Perception, and Attribution   36

Individual Differences and Organizational Behavior   37

   Skills and Abilities   38
Personality and Organizations   38
   Trait Theory   38
   Integrative Approach   40

Personality Characteristics in Organizations   40
Proactive Personality   42
Application of Personality Theory in Organizations   42
Common Personality Measurement Tools   42
Carl Jung and the Myers-Briggs Type Indicator®
Instrument   43
Social Perception   46
Characteristics of the Perceiver   48
Characteristics of the Target   48
Characteristics of the Situation   49
Barriers to Social Perception   49
Impression Management   51
Attribution in Organizations   52
Internal and External Attributions   52
Attributional Biases   53

Chapter 4
Attitudes, Emotions, and Ethics   54

Attitudes   55
The ABC Model   55
Cognitive Dissonance   56
Attitude Formation   57
Attitudes and Behavior   57
Work Attitudes   58
Job Satisfaction   58
Organizational Citizenship versus Workplace Deviance   60
Organizational Commitment and Job Satisfaction   62
Persuasion and Attitude Change   63
Source Characteristics   63
Target Characteristics   63
Message Characteristics   63
Cognitive Routes to Persuasion   63
Emotions and Moods at Work   64
Emotions   64
Moods   65
Emotional Contagion at Work   65
Emotional Intelligence   65
Emotional Labor   65
Ethical Behavior   66
Factors That Affect Ethical Behavior   67
Values   68
Locus of Control   70
Machiavellianism   70
Cognitive Moral Development   70

Chapter 5
Motivation at Work   74

Motivation and Work Behavior   75
Internal Needs   75
External Incentives   76
Maslow's Need Hierarchy   77
Theory X and Theory Y   78
ERG Theory   78
McClelland's Need Theory   78
Need for Achievement   79
Need for Power   79
Need for Affiliation   79
Herzberg's Two-Factor Theory   80
Motivation Factors   81
Hygiene Factors   82
Critique of the Two-Factor Theory   82
Two New Ideas in Motivation   82
Eustress, Strength, and Hope   82
Positive Energy and Full Engagement   83
Social Exchange and Equity Theory   84
Demands and Contributions   84
Adams's Theory of Inequity   85
The Resolution of Inequity   85
New Perspectives on Equity Theory   85
Expectancy Theory of Motivation   87
Motivational Problems   87
Motivation and Moral Maturity   88
Cultural Differences in Motivation   88

Chapter 6
Learning and Performance Management   90

Behavioral Models of Learning in Organizations   91
Classical Conditioning   91
Operant Conditioning   92
Reinforcement Theory   92
Social and Cognitive Theories of Learning   94
Bandura's Social Learning Theory   94
Cognitive Theories of Learning   95
Goal Setting at Work   95
Characteristics of Effective Goals   95
Goals Increase Work Motivation and Task
Performance   96
Goals Reduce Role Stress, Conflict, and Ambiguity   97
Goals Improve Performance Evaluation   97
Performance: A Key Construct   97
Performance Management   97
Defining Performance   98
Measuring Performance   98
Performance Feedback   99

360-Degree Feedback   100
   Developing People and Enhancing Careers   100
   Key Characteristics of an Effective Appraisal
     System   101
Rewarding Performance   101
   Individual versus Team Reward Systems   102
   The Power of Earning   102
Correcting Poor Performance   102
   Performance and Kelley's Attribution Theory   103
   Coaching, Counseling, and Mentoring   104

Chapter 7
Stress and Well-Being at Work   106

What Is Stress?   107
Four Approaches to Stress   107
   The Homeostatic/Medical Approach   108
   The Cognitive Appraisal Approach   108
   The Person-Environment Fit Approach   108

   The Psychoanalytic Approach   108
The Stress Response   109
Sources of Work Stress   109
Work Demands   110
Nonwork Demands   112
The Consequences of Stress   112
   Positive Stress   112
   Individual Distress   113
   Organizational Distress   114
Individual Differences in the Stress-Strain
   Relationship   115
   Gender Effects   115
   Type A Behavior Pattern   116
   Personality Hardiness   116
   Self-Reliance   117
Preventive Stress Management   117
   Organizational Stress Prevention   118
   Individual Prevention   120
   Comprehensive Health Promotion   122

Part 3
Interpersonal Processes and Behavior   124

©iStockphoto.com/Jacob Wackerhausen

Chapter 8
Communication   124

Interpersonal Communication   125
   An Interpersonal Communication Model   125
   Reflective Listening   126
Communication Skills for Effective Managers   129
   Expressiveness   129
   Empathy and Sensitivity   129
   Persuasiveness   130
   Informative Managing Style   130
Barriers and Gateways to Communication   130
   Gender Differences   130
   Cultural Diversity   131
   Language   131
Civility and Incivility   132
   Consequences of Incivility   132
   Blessings of Civility   132
   Defensive and Nondefensive Communication   132

   Defensive Communication at Work   133
   Defensive Tactics   133
   Nondefensive Communication   133
Nonverbal Communication   134
   Proxemics   134
   Kinesics   136
   Facial and Eye Behavior   136
   Paralanguage   136
Positive, Healthy Communication   136
Communicating through New Technologies and Social
   Media   137
   Written Communication   137
   Communication Technologies   138
   How Do Communication Technologies Affect
     Behavior?   138

Chapter 9
Work Teams and Groups   142

Groups and Work Teams   143
Why Work Teams?   144
   Benefits to Organizations   144
   Social Benefits to Individuals   144
Group Behavior   145
   Norms of Behavior   145
   Group Cohesion   145
   Social Loafing   146
   Loss of Individuality   146
Group Formation and Development   146
   Group Formation   146
   Stages of Group Development   147
   Punctuated Equilibrium Model   148
   Characteristics of a Mature Group   148
Task and Maintenance Functions   150

Factors That Influence Group Effectiveness   151
    Work Team Structure   151
    Work Team Process   151
    Diversity   152
    Creativity   153
Empowerment and Self-Managed Teams   154
    Empowerment Skills   154
    Self-Managed Teams   154
Upper Echelons: Teams at the Top   155
    Diversity at the Top   155
    Multicultural Top Teams   156

©RubberBall Productions/theAgencyCollection/Jupiterimages

Chapter 10
Decision Making by Individuals and Groups   158

The Decision-Making Process   159
Models and Limits of Decision Making   161
    Rational Model   161
    Bounded Rationality Model   161
    Z Model   162
    Escalation of Commitment   162
Individual Influences on Decision Making   163
    Risk and the Manager   163
    Personality, Attitudes, and Values   164
    Intuition   164
    Creativity   165
The Group Decision-Making Process   168
    Advantages and Disadvantages of Group Decision
        Making   168
    Limits of Group Decision Making   168
    Techniques for Group Decision Making   171
    Factors in Selecting the Appropriate Technique   172
    Special Decision-Making Groups   172
Diversity and Culture in Decision Making   173
Participation in Decision Making   173
    The Effects of Participation   174
    Foundations for Participation and Empowerment   174
    What Level of Participation?   175

Chapter 11
Power and Political Behavior   176

The Concept of Power   177
Forms and Sources of Power in Organizations   178

    Interpersonal Forms of Power   178
    Intergroup Sources of Power   179
Using Power Ethically   180
    Positive versus Negative Power   181
Symbols of Power   182
    Kanter's Symbols of Power   182
    Kanter's Symbols of Powerlessness   183
    Korda's Symbols of Power   183
Political Behavior in Organizations   183
    Influence Tactics   184
    Political Skill   186
Managing Political Behavior in Organizations   187
    Managing Up: Managing the Boss   188
    Sharing Power: Empowerment   189

©John Lund/Drew Kelly/Blend Images/Jupiterimages

Chapter 12
Leadership and Followership   192

Leadership versus Management   193
Early Trait Theories   194
Behavioral Theories   195
    Foundational Behavioral Research   195
    The Leadership Grid: A Contemporary Extension   196
Contingency Theories   198
    Fiedler's Contingency Theory   198
    Path-Goal Theory   200
    Vroom-Yetton-Jago Normative Decision Model   200
    The Situational-Leadership® Model   201
Recent Leadership Theories   201
    Leader-Member Exchange   201
    Inspirational Leadership   204
Emerging Issues in Leadership   205
    Emotional Intelligence   205
    Trust   206
    Gender and Leadership   206
    Servant Leadership   207
    Abusive Supervision   207
Followership   207
    Types of Followers   207
Guidelines for Leadership   208

Chapter 13
Conflict and Negotiation   210

The Nature of Conflicts in Organizations   211
    Importance of Conflict Management Skills for the
        Manager   211

Functional versus Dysfunctional Conflict   211
Diagnosing Conflict   212
Causes of Conflict in Organizations   213
Structural Factors   213
Personal Factors   214
Forms of Group Conflict in Organizations   215
Interorganizational Conflict   215
Intergroup Conflict   216
Intragroup Conflict   216
Individual Conflict in Organizations   216
Types of Intrapersonal Conflict   216

Managing Intrapersonal Conflict   218
Managing Interpersonal Conflict   218
Conflict Management Strategies and Techniques   221
Ineffective Techniques   222
Effective Techniques   222
Conflict Management Styles   224
Avoiding   225
Accommodating   225
Competing   225
Compromising   226
Collaborating   227

Part 4
Organizational Processes and Structure   228

©iStockphoto.com/Orlando Rosu

Chapter 14
Jobs and the Design of Work   228

Work in Organizations   229
The Meaning of Work   229
Jobs in Organizations   230
Traditional Approaches to Job Design   231
Scientific Management   231
Job Enlargement/Job Rotation   232
Job Enrichment   233
Job Characteristics Theory   233
Alternative Approaches to Job Design   235
Social Information Processing   236
Ergonomics and Interdisciplinary Framework   236
International Perspectives on the Design of Work   237
Work Design and Well-Being   239
Contemporary Issues in the Design of Work   240
Telecommuting   240
Alternative Work Patterns   241
Technology at Work   242
Skill Development   243

Chapter 15
Organizational Design and Structure   244

Key Organizational Design Processes   245

Differentiation   247
Integration   248
Basic Design Dimensions   249
Five Structural Configurations   250
Simple Structure   251
Machine Bureaucracy   251
Professional Bureaucracy   251
Divisionalized Form   252
Adhocracy   252
Contextual Variables   252
Size   252
Technology   253
Environment   254
Strategy and Goals   256
Forces Reshaping Organizations   257
Life Cycles in Organizations   258
Globalization   258
Changes in Information-Processing Technologies   259
Demands on Organizational Processes   259
Emerging Organizational Structures   260
Factors That Can Adversely Affect Structure   261

Chapter 16
Organizational Culture   262

Levels of Organizational Culture   263
Artifacts   264
Values   267
Assumptions   267
Functions of Organizational Culture   267
The Relationship of Culture to Performance   268
The Strong-Culture Perspective   268
The Fit Perspective   268
The Adaptation Perspective   268
The Leader's Role in Shaping and Reinforcing
Culture   269
What Leaders Pay Attention To   269
How Leaders React to Crisis   269
How Leaders Behave   269
How Leaders Allocate Rewards   269
How Leaders Hire and Fire Individuals   270

Organizational Socialization   270
    The Stages of the Socialization Process   270
    Outcomes of Socialization   272
Assessing Organizational Culture   272
    Organizational Culture Inventory   272
    Kilmann-Saxton Culture-Gap Survey   273
    Triangulation   273
Changing Organizational Culture   273
Challenges to Developing a Positive, Cohesive
    Culture   274
    Merger or Acquisition   274
    Developing a Global Organizational Culture   275
    Developing an Ethical Organizational Culture   275
    *Developing a Culture of Empowerment and
        Quality   275*

©Corbis/Jupiterimages

Chapter 17
Career Management   278

Occupational and Organizational Choice Decisions   280
    Preparing for the World of Work   280
    Occupational Choice   280
Organizational Choice and Entry   282
Foundations for a Successful Career   284
    Becoming Your Own Career Coach   284
    Emotional Intelligence and Career Success   284
The Career Stage Model   285
The Establishment Stage   286
    Psychological Contracts   286
The Advancement Stage   287
    Career Paths and Career Ladders   287
    Finding a Mentor   288
    Dual-Career Partnerships   290
    Work-Home Conflicts   291
The Maintenance Stage   293
    Sustaining Performance   293
    Becoming a Mentor   293
The Withdrawal Stage   293
    Planning for Change   293
    Retirement   294
Career Anchors   294

©Thinkstock/Jupiterimages

Chapter 18
Managing Change   296

Forces for Change in Organizations   297
    External Forces   298
    Internal Forces   300
The Scope of Change   300
    The Change Agent's Role   301
Resistance to Change   302
    Major Reasons People Resist Change   302
    Managing Resistance to Change   303
Lewin's Model for Managing Change   305
Determining the Need for Organization Development
    Interventions   306
    Diagnosis and Needs Analysis   307
Group-Focused Techniques for OD Intervention   307
    Survey Feedback   307
    Management by Objectives   308
    Product and Service Quality Programs   308
    Team Building   308
    Process Consultation   309
Individual-Focused Techniques for OD Intervention   309
    Skills Training   310
    Leadership Training and Development   310
    Executive Coaching   310
    Role Negotiation   311
    Job Redesign   311
    Health Promotion Programs   311
    Career Planning   312

Notes   313
Index   345

Organizational Behavior and Opportunity

LEARNING OUTCOMES

1 Define *organizational behavior.*

2 Identify four action steps for responding positively in times of change.

3 Identify the important system components of an organization.

4 Describe the formal and informal elements of an organization.

5 Identify factors that contribute to the diversity of organizations in the economy.

6 Describe the opportunities that change creates for organizational behavior.

7 Demonstrate the value of objective knowledge and skill development in the study of organizational behavior.

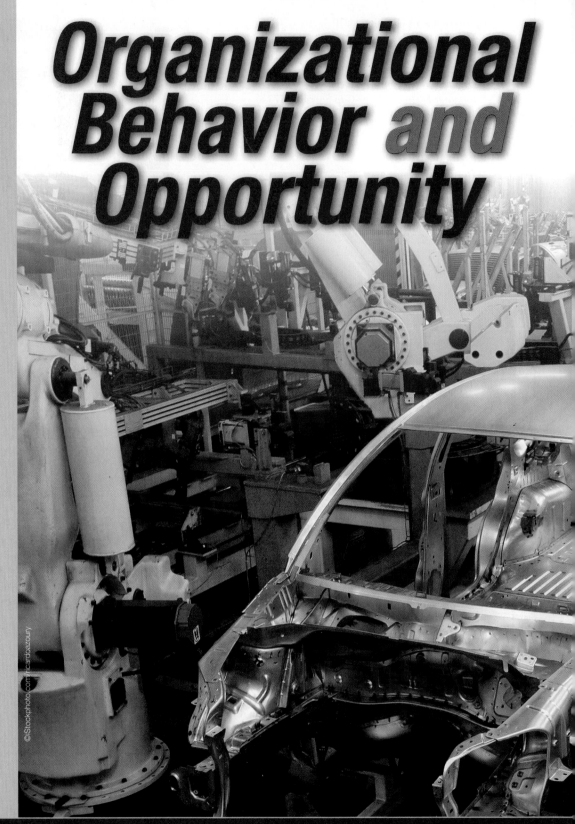

©iStockphoto.com/ricardoazoury

❝Organizations have been described as clockworks, but they often seem like snake pits.❞

After You Finish This Chapter Go to **Page 15** for **Study Tools**

Human Behavior in Organizations

Human behavior in organizations is complex and often difficult to understand. Organizations have been described as clockworks in which human behavior is logical and rational, but they often seem like snake pits to those who work in them.[1] The clockwork metaphor reflects an orderly, idealized view of organizational behavior devoid of conflict or dilemma because all the working parts (the people) mesh smoothly. The snake pit metaphor, on the other hand, conveys the daily conflict, distress, and struggle in organizations. Each metaphor reflects reality from a different perspective—the organization's versus the individual's. The snake pit metaphor expresses the dark side of human behavior, which is seen at its extreme in cases of air rage and workplace violence. In contrast, the clockwork metaphor expresses the view of organizations as healthy and productive systems in which individuals have a clear sense of the shared vision and values, are personally invested in outcomes, feel that their contributions are significant, and receive support and respect from the organization's leadership.[2]

This chapter serves as an introduction to the complex subject of organizational behavior. The first section provides an overview of human behavior in organizations, its interdisciplinary origins, and its responses to change. The second section presents an organizational context within which behavior occurs. The third section highlights the **opportunities** that exist in times of **change** and **challenge** for people at work.[3] The fourth section addresses the ways people learn about organizational behavior and explains how the text's pedagogical features relate to the various

opportunities

Favorable times or chances for progress and advancement.

change

The transformation or modification of an organization and/or its stakeholders.

challenge

The call to competition, contest, or battle.

3

learning styles. The final section presents the plan for the book.

We can define **organizational behavior** as the study of individual behavior and group dynamics in organizations. The study of organizational behavior is primarily concerned with the psychosocial, interpersonal, and behavioral dynamics in organizations. However, organizational variables that affect human behavior at work are also relevant to the study of organizational behavior. These organizational variables include jobs, the design of work, communication, performance appraisal, organizational design, and organizational structure.

Understanding Human Behavior

The vast majority of theories and models of human behavior fall into two basic categories: that of an internal perspective and that of an external perspective. The internal perspective looks at workers' minds to understand their behavior. It is psychodynamically oriented, and its proponents understand human behavior in terms of the thoughts, feelings, past experiences, and needs of the individual. The internal perspective explains people's actions and behavior in terms of their histories and personal value systems. The idea of this perspective is that internal processes of thinking, feeling, perceiving, and judging lead people to act in specific ways; therefore, people are best understood from the inside and their behavior is best interpreted alongside their thoughts and feelings. The internal perspective has given rise to a wide range of motivational and leadership theories.

The external perspective, on the other hand, focuses on factors outside the person to understand behavior, that is, external events, consequences, and environmental forces. This perspective excludes consideration of a person's history, feelings, thoughts, and personal value system in interpreting actions and behavior. Thus, it has given rise to an alternative set of motivational and leadership theories, which are covered in Chapters 5 and 12. The internal and external perspectives offer alternative explanations for human behavior. For example, the internal perspective might say Mary is an outstanding employee because she has a high need for achievement, whereas the external perspective might say it is because she is extremely well paid for her work. Kurt Lewin combined both perspectives with his claim that behavior is a function of both the person and the environment.[4]

Internal Perspective

External Perspective

Interdisciplinary Influences

Organizational behavior is a blended discipline that has grown out of contributions from numerous earlier fields of study. The sciences of psychology, sociology, engineering, anthropology, management, and medicine have each contributed to our understanding of human behavior in organizations.

Psychology, the science of human behavior, developed during the closing decades of the nineteenth century. Psychology traces its origins to philosophy and the science of physiology. One of the most prominent early psychologists, William James, held a degree in medicine (MD). Since its beginnings, psychology has branched into a number of specialized fields, including clinical, experimental, military, organizational, and social psychology. Organizational psychology frequently overlaps with organizational behavior; for instance, both investigate work motivation.[5] Johnson & Johnson, Valero Energy, and Chaparral Steel all used psychological research on American military personnel from the World War I era to develop their sophisticated personnel selection methods.[6]

Sociology, the science of society, has contributed greatly to our knowledge of group and intergroup dynamics. Because sociology takes society rather than the individual as its point of departure, sociologists focus on the variety of roles within a society or culture, the norms and standards of behavior in groups, and the consequences of compliant and deviant behavior. Individuals have a role set that is determined by their social position, and roles affect how people interact within organizations. The Professional Role Behaviors Survey, for example, studied how the roles of various medical practitioners changed during hospital restructuring and these changes influenced organizational behavior and culture.[7]

Engineering is the applied science of energy and matter. It enhances our understanding of the design of work. Frederick Taylor took basic engineering ideas and applied

©iStockphoto.com/Pali Rao

[Ergonomics]

One way that the study of medicine has influenced organizational behavior is the field of ergonomics, the study of the design and fit of tools for work. Ergonomics is primarily concerned with how people fit with their working environment, and how to make that environment as comfortable and efficient as possible. Anyone with a full-time job can tell you that even for healthy people, sitting behind a desk, staring at a computer screen for eight hours a day is physically difficult. Your eyes get strained, your wrists get sore or numb, your back goes stiff, and your shoulders and neck get tight, all of which makes it hard to concentrate on the task at hand. For that reason, a number of companies such as GeekDesk and Anthro have created adjustable desks. At the touch of a button, the desks can be raised or lowered, allowing the user to stand or even walk around the desk. These desks alleviate the stress of staying in one position all day and can help workers be more creative and efficient with their time.

SOURCE: F. Manjoo, "Can't Stand to Sit Too Long? There's a Desk for That," *New York Times*, April 21, 2010, http://www.nytimes.com/2010/04/22/technology/personaltech/22basics.html, accessed June 10, 2011.

©m42/ZUMA Press/Newscom

them to human behavior at work, influencing the early study of organizational behavior.[8] With his engineering background, Taylor placed special emphasis on human productivity and efficiency in work behavior. Job preparation and performance shifted from a long apprenticeship and a creative, problem-solving approach to work to training in and automated performance of simplified tasks. A study published in 1990 showed that Taylor's notions of performance standards and differential piece-rate systems were still shaping organizational goal-setting programs at Black & Decker, IBM, and Weyerhaeuser at that time.[9]

Anthropology, the science of human learned behavior, is especially important to our understanding of *organizational culture*. In fact, anthropological research has been used to examine the effects of efficient organizational cultures on organizational performance[10] and the ways pathological personalities may lead to dysfunctional organizational cultures.[11] In one case study, Schwartz used a psychodynamic, anthropological mode of inquiry to explore corporate decay at General Motors and NASA.[12]

Management, originally called *administrative science*, is the study of overseeing activities and supervising people in organizations. It includes the design, implementation, and management of various administrative and organizational systems. March and Simon take the human organization as their point of departure to investigate administrative practices that enhance the effectiveness of the system.[13] Management is the first discipline to take the modern corporation as the unit of analysis, a viewpoint that distinguishes its contribution to the study of organizational behavior.

Medicine, the applied science of treating diseases to enhance an individual's health and well-being, focuses on both physical and psychological health as well as industrial mental health.[14] As modern care defeats acute diseases, medical attention is shifting to more chronic diseases such as hypertension and to issues involved in occupational health and well-being.[15] These trends have contributed to the growth of corporate *wellness programs* such as Johnson & Johnson's "Live for Life Program." Moreover, *ergonomics* has gained increasing attention as a way to prevent medical problems resulting from poor design of workstations, resulting in the loss of billions of dollars from higher healthcare costs and lower worker productivity.[16] Such costs can be cut nearly in half by implementing the results of medical research into better workplace design.[17]

LEARNING OUTCOME **2**

Behavior in Times of Change

Early research of individuals and organizations in the midst of environmental change found that people often experience change as a threat and respond by relying on well-learned and dominant forms of behavior.[18] That is, people often become rigid and reactive in the midst of change, rather than open and responsive. This behavior works well in the face of gradual, incremental

anthropology
The science of human learned behavior.

management
The study of overseeing activities and supervising people in organizations.

medicine
The applied science of healing or treating diseases to enhance an individual's health and well-being.

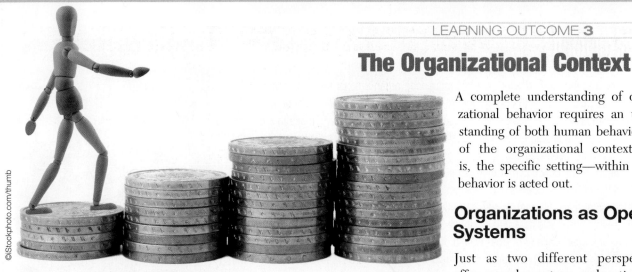
©iStockphoto.com/thumb

The Organizational Context

A complete understanding of organizational behavior requires an understanding of both human behavior and of the organizational context—that is, the specific setting—within which behavior is acted out.

Organizations as Open Systems

Just as two different perspectives offer complementary explanations for human behavior, two views shape complementary explanations of organizations. Organizations are open systems of interacting components, including people, tasks, technology, and structure. These internal components also interact with components in the organization's task environment.

Today, the corporation is the dominant organizational form for much of the Western world, but other organizational forms have dominated other societies. Religious organizations, such as the temple corporations of ancient Mesopotamia and the churches in colonial America, can often dominate society.[23] So can military organizations, such as the clans of the Scottish Highlands and the regional armies of the People's Republic of China.[24] All of these societies are woven together by family organizations, which themselves may vary from nuclear and extended families to small, collective communities.[25] The purpose and structure of religious, military, and family organizational forms varies, but people within different organizations often behave alike. In fact, early discoveries about power and leadership in work organizations were remarkably similar to findings about power and leadership within families.[26]

Because organizations are so varied in function, manufacturing products such as aircraft components or delivering services such as money management, for example, we must first understand the open system components of an organization and its task environment in order to see how the organization performs.

Accordingly, Katz and Kahn in one study, and Leavitt in another, established open system frameworks for understanding organizations.[27] The four major internal components are task, people, technology, and structure. These four components, along with the organization's inputs, outputs, and key elements in the task environment, are depicted in Figure 1.1. The **task** of the organization is its mission, purpose, or goal for existing. The **people** are the human resources of the organization.

---

change. However, rigid and well-learned behavior may be a counterproductive response to significant change, such as outsourcing. Prompted by dramatic advances in the Internet and networking technology, outsourcing has been unavoidable in much of American industry.[19] Yet factors such as employee attrition and the potential for data loss have caused many companies to modify their outsourcing strategies to keep both talent and information within the organization.[20] Big changes disrupt people's habitual behavior and force them to learn new skills, often creating discomfort and discontent. To such employees, Eric Brown, CEO of Johnson Products Company, Inc., recommends looking for the positive opportunities in change and viewing challenge as a good rather than bad experience. His action steps for adapting to change are to (1) have a positive attitude, (2) ask questions, (3) listen to the answers, and (4) be committed to success.[21]

Success is never guaranteed, however, and change sometimes results in failure. Some of the world's greatest leaders, such as Winston Churchill, experienced dramatic failures before they achieved lasting success. It was their capacity to learn from the failure and to respond positively to new opportunities that helped them overcome early setbacks. Knowing this, one venture capitalist with whom the authors have worked likes to ask an executive who is seeking to build a business to tell him about his or her greatest failure. He wants to hear how the executive responded to the failure and what he or she learned from the experience.

So change carries both the risk of failure and the opportunity for success; our behavior often determines the outcome. Moreover, success can come through the accumulation of small wins and through the use of microprocesses, as has been found with middle managers engaged in institutional change.[22]

task
An organization's mission, purpose, or goal for existing.

people
The human resources of an organization.

FIGURE 1.1 An Open-Systems View of Organization

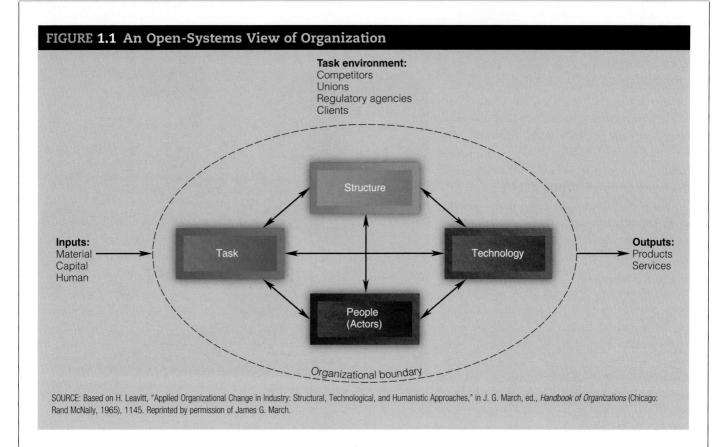

Task environment:
Competitors
Unions
Regulatory agencies
Clients

Structure

Inputs:
Material
Capital
Human

Task

Technology

Outputs:
Products
Services

People
(Actors)

Organizational boundary

SOURCE: Based on H. Leavitt, "Applied Organizational Change in Industry: Structural, Technological, and Humanistic Approaches," in J. G. March, ed., *Handbook of Organizations* (Chicago: Rand McNally, 1965), 1145. Reprinted by permission of James G. March.

The **technology** is the wide range of tools, knowledge, and/or techniques used to transform inputs into outputs. The **structure** involves the systems of communication, authority and roles, and workflow.

In addition to these major internal components, the organization as a system also has an external task environment composed of different constituents such as suppliers, customers, and federal regulators. Thompson describes the task environment as that element of the environment related to the organization's degree of goal attainment, or its basic task.[28] A number of organizations are using or considering the use of Twitter as a way of networking into elements of their task environments.[29] For example, NASA uses Twitter to update followers on the status of upcoming shuttle flights.

The organization system works by taking inputs, converting them into throughputs, and delivering outputs to its task environment. *Inputs* are the human, informational, material, and financial resources used by the organization. *Throughputs* are the materials and resources as they are transformed by the organization's technology component. Once the transformation is complete, they become *outputs* for customers, consumers, and clients. The actions of suppliers, customers, regulators, and other elements of the task environment affect the organization and the behavior of people at work. For example, Caterpillar's survival was threatened by its total dependence on one large utility for its outputs when a tornado destroyed the only plant in the company that produced high-pressured

couplings necessary to build its various types of equipment. Caterpillar's inability to produce this part threatened to grind global production to a halt. Managers solved the problem in the short run by collecting parts from warehouses and outsourcing them from other vendors, and in the long run by diversifying their supply chain.[30] Transforming inputs into high-quality outputs is critical to every organization's success.

LEARNING OUTCOME 4

The Formal and Informal Organization

The open systems view of organizations suggests that they are designed like clockwork (recall the clockwork metaphor described at the beginning of this chapter), with a neat, precise, interrelated functioning. The **formal organization** is the official, legitimate, and most visible part of the organization, and this is the part that enables people to think of organizations in logical and rational ways. The snake pit metaphor mentioned earlier originates from the study of

technology
The tools, knowledge, and/or techniques used to transform inputs into outputs.

structure
The systems of communication, authority and roles, and workflow.

formal organization
The official, legitimate, and most visible part of the system.

the **informal organization**, which is unofficial and less visible. The **Hawthorne studies**, conducted during the 1920s and 1930s, first suggested the importance of the informal elements. During the "interview study," the third of the four Hawthorne studies, the researchers began to fully appreciate the informal elements of the Hawthorne Works as an organization.[31] The formal and informal elements of the organization are depicted in Figure 1.2.

Since the formal and informal elements of an organization can sometimes conflict, we must understand both. Such conflicts erupted in many organizations during the early years of the twentieth century and were embodied in the union–management strife of that era. Sometimes these formal–informal conflicts escalated into violence. For example, supervisors at the Homestead Works of U.S. Steel during the 1920s were issued pistols "just in case" they felt it necessary to shoot unruly, dangerous steelworkers. However, during that same era, the progressive Eastman Kodak company provided financial backing for employees' neighborhood communities, such as Meadowbrook in Rochester, New York. Kodak's concern for employees and attention to informal issues made unions unnecessary within the company.

The informal elements of the organization are often points of diagnostic and intervention activities in organizational development, though the formal elements must always be considered because they provide the context for the informal.[32] It is the informal elements involving people's feelings, thoughts, and attitudes about their work that most affect their behavior and performance, but individual behavior plays out in the context of both the formal and informal elements of the system, becoming, in the process, organizational behavior. Employees' moods, emotions, and dispositions all influence critical organizational outcomes such as job performance, decision making, creativity, turnover, teamwork, negotiation, and leadership.[33]

informal organization

The unofficial and less visible part of the system.

Hawthorne studies

Studies conducted during the 1920s and 1930s that suggested the importance of the informal organization.

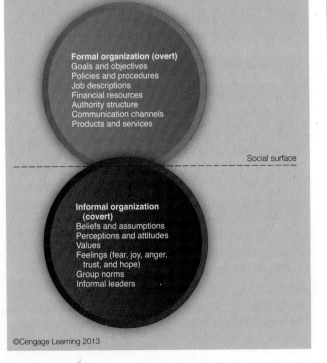

FIGURE **1.2** Formal and Informal Organization

Formal organization (overt)
Goals and objectives
Policies and procedures
Job descriptions
Financial resources
Authority structure
Communication channels
Products and services

Social surface

Informal organization (covert)
Beliefs and assumptions
Perceptions and attitudes
Values
Feelings (fear, joy, anger, trust, and hope)
Group norms
Informal leaders

©Cengage Learning 2013

©Eric Audras/PhotoAlto Agency RF Collections/Getty Images

LEARNING OUTCOME **5**

Diversity of Organizations

Most attempts at explaining or predicting organizational behavior rely heavily on factors within the organization and give less weight to external environmental considerations.[34] Yet organizational behavior always occurs in the context of a specific organizational setting, so students can benefit from being sensitive to that industrial context and from developing an appreciation for the diversity of various organizations.[35] In this vein, we will focus on six organizations throughout the text.

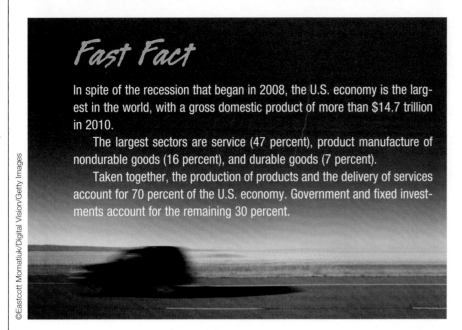

Fast Fact

In spite of the recession that began in 2008, the U.S. economy is the largest in the world, with a gross domestic product of more than $14.7 trillion in 2010.

The largest sectors are service (47 percent), product manufacture of nondurable goods (16 percent), and durable goods (7 percent).

Taken together, the production of products and the delivery of services account for 70 percent of the U.S. economy. Government and fixed investments account for the remaining 30 percent.

Large and small organizations operate in each sector of the economy: the private, manufacturing, service, government, and nonprofit sectors. In the pivate sector are a great variety of organizations that play an important role in the economy. The manufacturing sector includes the production of basic materials, such as steel, and the production of finished products, such as automobiles and electronic equipment. The service sector includes transportation, financial services, insurance, and retail sales. The government sectors, which provide essential infrastructure, and nonprofit organizations are important to our collective well-being because they meet needs that aren't addressed by other sectors.

Hundreds of small, medium, and large organizations contribute to the economic health and human welfare of the United States. Throughout this book, we provide examples from a variety of organizations to help you develop a greater appreciation for your own organization and for others in the diverse world of private business enterprises and nonprofit organizations.

LEARNING OUTCOME
6

Change Creates Opportunities

Global competition, which is a leading force driving change at work, has increased significantly during the past few decades, especially in industries such as banking, finance, and air transportation. As a result, change has accelerated and, with it, both opportunities and risks. Corporate competition creates performance and cost pressures, changes that have a ripple effect on people and their behavior at work. Although one such risk for employees is the marginalization of part-time professionals, good management practice can ensure their integration.[36] Furthermore, although competition may lead to downsizing and restructuring, it also provides the opportunity for revitalization.[37] And small companies don't necessarily lose in this competitive environment. Scientech, a small power and energy company, needed to enhance its managerial talent and service quality to meet the challenges of growth and big-company competitors, and it consequently improved its performance. Thus competition spurred its increased success.

Product and service quality are the major ways that companies can win in a competitive environment. IBM, Control Data Services, Inc., Northwest Airlines (now Delta), and Southwest Airlines all used problem-solving skills to achieve high-quality products and services in their attempts to deal with competitive forces. Change in the coffee industry has been a key stimulus for both Caribou Coffee and Starbucks as they innovate and improve.

Too much change, however, leads to chaos, and too little change leads to stagnation. Also, winning in a competitive industry can be a transient victory; staying ahead of the competition requires constant change.

[Nintendo Wins with Wii]

In 1985 Nintendo revolutionized the video game market with the introduction of the Nintendo Entertainment System. By 2000, however, the company saw its market share of U.S. hardware sales decline by 50 percent as competitors such as Sony and Microsoft introduced incredibly powerful systems and games saturated with increasingly lifelike graphics. Spending billions of dollars on game development became a standard in the industry, and Nintendo needed to rethink how it was competing. Top managers decided to build something simple, economically priced, and enjoyable for the whole family. The result was the Wii, a game console controlled by a motion-sensitive wireless handheld controller. Although the decision was risky when it was made, thinking in a new way about the controller and the console has paid off handsomely for Nintendo. Demand for the Wii outstripped supply for more than a year after the console's 2006 launch, and as of 2009 more than 50 million units had been sold. Aided by top-selling applications such as *Wii Play* and *Wii Fit*, the Wii has reversed nearly 20 years of declining Nintendo console sales.

SOURCE: J. Gaudiosi, "Why Wii Won," *Business 2.0* 8 (May 2007): 35–37.

THE UNITED STATES AND CHINA

China has moved quickly to become a key player in the global economy, attracting foreign investment and becoming a member of the World Trade Organization. The economic health of China is important for multinational firms in the United States, the health of the global environment, and security and stability in East Asia. Both countries have much to gain from cooperation. The challenges of globalization are, however, illustrated by the points of tension that must be addressed, including the bilateral trade deficit, the status of Taiwan, and especially human rights.

SOURCE: S. Chen and C. Wolf, Jr., *China, the United States, and the Global Economy* (RAND, 2001).

Global Competition in Business

Managers and executives in the United States face radical change in response to increased global competition. According to noted economist Lester Thurow, this competition is characterized by intense rivalry between the United States, Japan, and Europe in core industries.[38] As a result, all categories of employees face increased pressure to be productive and to add value to the firm. Moreover, corporate warfare and competition make employment uncertain for people in companies or industries that pursue cost-cutting strategies to achieve economic success. The global competition in the automotive industry among Japanese, U.S., and European car companies exemplifies the intensity that other industries can expect in the future.

Some people feel that the future must be the focus in coming to grips with this international competition, whereas others believe we can deal with the future only by studying the past.[39] Global, economic, and organizational changes have dramatic effects on the study and management of organizational behavior.

Customer Focused for High Quality

Global competition has challenged organizations to become more customer focused, to meet changing product and service demands, and to exceed customers' expectations of high quality. Quality has the potential to give organizations in viable industries a competitive edge against international competition. By aiming to be number one in experience, for example, Caribou Coffee competes with a customer-focused, high-quality approach.

Quality has become a rubric for products and services of high status. *Total quality* is defined in many ways.[40] *Total quality management (TQM)* is the total dedication to continuous improvement and to customers, so that the customers' needs are met and their expectations exceeded.

This customer-oriented philosophy of management has important implications for virtually all aspects of organizational behavior. Quality cannot be optimized, because customer needs and expectations are always changing, but it is embedded in highly successful organizations. Part of what has catapulted Toyota to the top of the auto industry is its attention to quality and detail throughout the organization. Even though TQM consulting has experienced a boom-to-bust cycle, the main concepts underlying its initial rise in popularity are here to stay.

Quality improvement enhances the probability of organizational success in increasingly competitive industries. One study of 193 general medical hospitals examined seven TQM practices and found them positively related to the financial performance of the hospital.[41] Indeed, quality improvement is an enduring feature of an organization's culture and of the economic competition we face today. It leads to competitive advantage through customer responsiveness, results acceleration, and resource effectiveness.[42] In evaluating quality improvement ideas for people at work, three key questions should be asked: (1) Does the idea improve customer response? (2) Does the idea accelerate results? (3) Does the idea increase the effectiveness of resources? A "yes" answer means the idea should be implemented to improve quality.

Six Sigma is a philosophy for company-wide quality improvement developed by Motorola and popularized by General Electric. Characterized by its customer-driven approach, its emphasis on using quantitative data to make decisions, and its priority of saving money,[43] it has evolved into a high-performance system for executing business strategy. Part of its quality program is a twelve-step problem-solving method specifically designed to lead a Six Sigma "Black Belt" to significant improvement within a defined process. It tackles problems in four

According to a 2011 J.D. Power and Associates customer satisfaction study, the three highest-quality smartphone manufacturers are (1) Apple, (2) HTC, and (3) Motorola.

©iStockphoto.com/Maxim Tupikov

phases: (1) measure, (2) analyze, (3) improve, and (4) control. In addition, it forces executives to align the right objective and targets, and it forces quality improvement teams to mobilize for action in order to accelerate and monitor sustained improvement. Six Sigma is set up so that that it can be applied to a range of situations, from manufacturing settings to service work environments. Table 1.1 contrasts Six Sigma and TQM.

TABLE 1.1 Contrasting Six Sigma and Total Quality Management	
SIX SIGMA	**TOTAL QUALITY MANAGEMENT**
Executive ownership	Self-directed work teams
Business strategy execution system	Quality initiative
Truly cross-functional	Largely within a single function
Focused training with verifiable return on investment	No mass training in statistics and quality
	Return on investment
Business results oriented	Quality oriented

SOURCE: M. Barney, "Motorola's Second Generation," *Six Sigma Forum Magazine* (May 2002): 13.

Any quality control method has some success and some failure, and some methods may work better in a given organization than others due to differences in organizational culture. One study, with a strong emphasis on exploring statistical modeling techniques, compared Six Sigma to two other methods for quality improvement (specifically, Taguchi's methods and the Shainin system) and found it to be the most complete strategy of the three.[44] On the other hand, statistical data on the actual economic effect of Six Sigma is lacking, and the method has come under some critique.[45] It is important for managers to consider which of a variety of options is best for their organization.

Behavior and Quality at Work

Whereas total quality may draw on reliability engineering or just-in-time management, total quality improvement can succeed only when employees have the skills and authority to respond to customer needs.[46] Total quality has important direct effects on the behavior of employees at all levels in the organization, not just on employees working directly with customers. Thus, chief executives can advance total quality by engaging in participative management, being willing to change things, focusing quality efforts on customer service (not cost cutting), including quality as a criterion in reward systems, improving the flow of information regarding quality-improvement successes or failures,

Quality is a customer-oriented philosophy of management with important implications for virtually all aspects of organizational behavior.

Hot Trend

Developed by and for the manufacturing industry, Six Sigma is a quality and management trend with staying power. The fundamental goal of Six Sigma is to increase quality by reducing the variation between manufactured parts. To achieve Six Sigma, an organization must only incur 3.4 defective or nonstandard parts per million. It's easy to see why companies across a wide range of industries are implementing Six Sigma techniques: the goal of stratospheric perfection is motivating and actually measurable.

and being actively and personally involved in quality efforts. While serving as chairman of Motorola, George Fisher emphasized the behavioral attributes of leadership, cooperation, communication, and participation as important elements in the company's Six Sigma program.

Quality improvement is crucial to competitive success. The U.S. Department of Commerce sponsors an annual award in the name of Malcolm Baldrige, former secretary of commerce in the Reagan administration, in order to recognize companies excelling in quality improvement and management. The Malcolm Baldrige National Quality Award examination evaluates an organization in seven categories: leadership, information and analysis, strategic quality planning, human resource utilization, quality assurance of products and services, quality results, and customer satisfaction.

According to George H. W. Bush, "Quality management is not just a strategy. It must be a new style of working, even a new style of thinking. A dedication to quality and excellence is more than good business. It is a way of life, giving something back to society, offering your best to others."[47]

Quality is one watchword for competitive success. Organizations that do not respond to customer needs find their customers choosing alter-native product and service suppliers who are willing to exceed customer expectations. Keep in mind, however, that total quality isn't a panacea for all organizations, and it doesn't guarantee unqualified success.

Managing Organizational Behavior in Changing Times

Over and above the challenge of quality improvement to meet international competition, managing organizational behavior during changing times is challenging for at least four other reasons: (1) the increasing globalization of organizations' operating territory, (2) the increasing diversity of organizational workforces, (3) the continuing demand for higher levels of moral and ethical behavior at work, and (4) continuing technological innovation with its companion need for skill enhancement.

Each of these four issues is explored in detail in Chapter 2 and highlighted throughout the text as they appear intertwined with contemporary organizational practices. For example, the issue of women in the workplace concerns workforce diversity and at the same time overlaps with the globalization issue. Gender roles are often defined differently in various cultures, and sexual harassment often plagues organizations in the United States, Europe, Israel, and South Africa.

Learning is challenging and fun because we are all different.

LEARNING OUTCOME **7**

Learning about Organizational Behavior

The study of organizational behavior is based on scientific knowledge and applied practice. It involves abstract ideas, such as valence and expectancy in motivation, as well as concrete matters, such as observable behaviors and medical symptoms of distress at work. Therefore, learning about organizational behavior includes at least three activities, as shown in Figure 1.3. First, the science of organizational behavior requires the mastery of a certain body of **objective knowledge**. Objective knowledge results from research, experimentation, and scientific observation. Second, the practice of organizational behavior requires **skill development** based on knowledge and an understanding of oneself in order to master the abilities essential to success. Third, both objective knowledge and skill development must be applied in real-world settings.

Learning can be challenging and fun if student diversity is addressed in the learning process, when students have more options and can take greater responsibility as coproducers.[48] Teaching and learning styles should be aligned carefully, and educators should be aware that teaching is no longer merely verbal and visual, but has now become virtual.[49] If you are a visual learner, use charts, maps, PowerPoint slides, videos, the Internet, notes, or flash cards, and write things out for visual review. If you are an auditory learner, then listen, take notes during lectures, consider taping them so you can fill in gaps later, review your notes frequently, and recite key concepts out loud. If you are a tactile learner, trace words as you are saying them, write down facts several times, and make study sheets.

Objective Knowledge

In any field of study, objective knowledge is developed through basic and applied research. Since the early research on scientific management, research on organizational behavior has continued to provide objective knowledge involving theories, conceptual models, and various research findings. In this book, the objective knowledge in each chapter is reflected in the supporting notes. Mastering the concepts and ideas that come from these notes enables you to discuss intelligently topics such as motivation, performance, leadership,[50] and executive stress.[51]

We encourage instructors and students of organizational behavior to think critically about the objective knowledge that has been gained in the study of organizational behavior. Only by engaging in critical thinking can one question or challenge the results of specific research or consider how such research should be applied in a particular work setting. Rote memorization does not prepare students to appreciate the complexity of specific theories or the intricacies of interrelated concepts, ideas, and topics. Critical thinking, by contrast, enables students to identify inconsistencies and limitations in the current body of objective knowledge.

Critical thinking, based on knowledge and understanding of basic ideas, leads to inquisitive exploration and is a key to accepting

FIGURE 1.3 Learning about Organizational Behavior

Learning Activity

- Mastery of basic objective knowledge
- Development of specific skills and abilities
- Application of knowledge and skills

©Cengage Learning 2013

objective knowledge
Knowledge that results from research and scientific activities.

skill development
The mastery of abilities essential to successful functioning in organizations.

©J&L Images/Photodisc/Getty Images

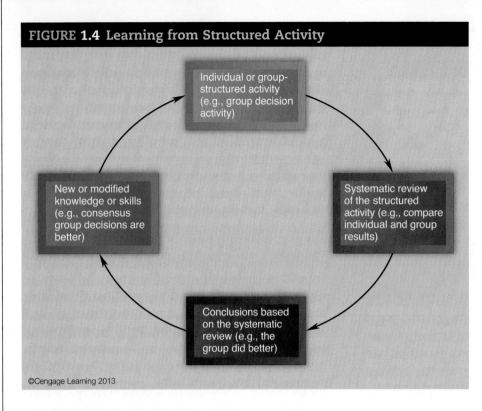

Individual or group-structured activity (e.g., group decision activity)

Systematic review of the structured activity (e.g., compare individual and group results)

Conclusions based on the systematic review (e.g., the group did better)

New or modified knowledge or skills (e.g., consensus group decisions are better)

©Cengage Learning 2013

work; (4) systems behavior and performance skills, such as cause–effect relationships; and (5) technology utilization skills, such as trouble-shooting. Many of these skills, such as decision making and information management, are directly related to the study of organizational behavior.[53] The Department of Labor's 21st Century Workforce Initiative offers workshops and online resources to assist people in acquiring the knowledge and skills to be employable in a rapidly changing economy.[54]

Developing skills is different from acquiring objective knowledge because it requires structured practice and feedback. A key function of experiential learning is engaging the student in individual or group activities that are systematically reviewed, leading to new skills and understandings. However, objective knowledge acquisition and skill development are interrelated, as shown in Figure 1.4. The student engages in an individual or group-structured activity and then systematically reviews that activity, gaining new or modified knowledge and skills.

If skill development and structured learning occur in this way, there should be an inherently self-correcting element to learning because of the modification of the student's knowledge and skills over time.[55] To ensure that skill development does occur and that the learning is self-correcting as it occurs, three basic guidelines must be followed.

the responsibility of coproducer in the learning process. A questioning, probing attitude is at the core of critical thinking. The student of organizational behavior should evolve into a critical consumer of knowledge related to organizational behavior—one who is able to intelligently question the latest research results and distinguish plausible, sound, new approaches from fads that lack substance or adequate foundation. Ideally, the student of organizational behavior develops into a scientific, professional manager who is knowledgeable in the art and science of organizational behavior.

Skill Development

Learning about organizational behavior requires doing as well as knowing. Furthermore, the development of skills and abilities requires that students be challenged by the instructor and by themselves. The "What about You?" features on the Chapter Review Cards give you a chance to learn about yourself, challenge yourself, and apply what you are learning.

The U.S. Department of Labor tries to ensure that people acquire the necessary skills to be successful in the workplace.[52] The essential skills identified by the department are (1) resource management skills, such as time management; (2) information management skills, such as data interpretation; (3) personal interaction skills, such as team-

©iStockphoto.com/thesuperph

First, students must accept responsibility for their own behavior, actions, and learning. This is key to the coproducer role in the learning process. A group cannot learn for its members. Members must accept responsibility for what they each individually do and learn. Denial of responsibility helps no one, least of all the learner.

Second, each student must actively participate in the individual or group-structured learning activity. Structured learning is not passive; it is active. In group activities, everyone suffers if just one person adopts a passive attitude. All must actively participate.

Third, each student must be open to new information, new skills, new ideas, and experimentation. This does not mean that students should be indiscriminately open. It does mean that students should have nondefensive, open attitudes so that they can learn and adjust to new ideas.

Application of Knowledge and Skills

Understanding organizational behavior includes an appreciation and understanding of working realities as well as of science and of oneself. One of the advantages of structured, experiential learning is that a person can explore new behaviors and skills in a comparatively safe environment. Fortunately, losing your temper in a classroom activity and learning about the potentially adverse impact on other people will have dramatically different consequences from losing your temper with an important customer in a tense work situation. Thus, learning spaces that offer the interface of student learning styles with institutional learning environments give learners safe spaces to engage their brains to form abstract hypotheses, to actively test these hypotheses through concrete experiences, and to reflectively observe the outcomes in behavior and experience.[56] The ultimate objective of skill application and experiential learning is that one transfers the process employed in learning from structured activities in the classroom and learning spaces to learning from unstructured opportunities in the workplace.

> **Learning about organizational behavior requires doing as well as knowing.**

Although organizational behavior is an applied discipline, students are not "trained" in organizational behavior. Rather, they ares "educated" in organizational behavior and are coproducers in learning. The distinction between these two modes of learning is found in the degree of direct and immediate applicability of either knowledge or skills. As an activity, training ties objective knowledge or skill development more directly to specific applications. By contrast, education enhances a person's residual pool of objective knowledge and skills that may then be selectively applied later—sometimes significantly later—when the opportunity presents itself. Hence, education is consistent with the concept of lifelong learning. Especially in a growing area of knowledge such as organizational behavior, the student can think of the first course as the outset of lifelong learning about the subject.

Log in to the **CourseMate** for **ORGB3** at **www.cengagebrain.com** to:

* Review **Key Terms Flash Cards** online
* Play **Beat the Clock** and **Quiz Bowl** to master concepts
* Complete **web quizzes** to prepare for exams
* Watch the video on **Holden Outerwear** and from **In Good Company** for examples, then test yourself with a quick quiz
* Work through the **"What about You?"** and **Ethical Dilemma** exercises to see how you would handle various situations that organizations face on a daily basis

2

Challenges for Managers

LEARNING OUTCOMES

1 Describe the factors that affect organizations competing in the global economy.

2 Explain how cultural differences form the basis of work-related attitudes.

3 Describe the challenges and positive influences diversity brings to today's business environment.

4 Discuss the role of ethics, character, and personal integrity in the organization.

5 Explain five issues that pose ethical dilemmas for managers.

6 Describe the effects of technological advances on today's workforce.

©iStockphoto.com/Andrew Rich

❝ What major challenges must managers overcome in order to remain competitive? ❞

Key challenges that managers face today stem from the fact that business is increasingly global in scope.[1] Globalization is driven by the spread of economic logics centered on freeing, opening, deregulating, and privatizing economies to attract investment as well as technological innovations that are revolutionizing communication.[2] The resulting challenges for managers can be viewed as both opportunities and threats.

Chief executive officers of U.S. corporations have cited four challenges managers must overcome in order to remain competitive: (1) globalizing the firm's operations to compete in the global village; (2) leading a diverse workforce; (3) encouraging positive ethics, character, and personal integrity; and (4) advancing and implementing technological innovation in the workplace.[3]

LEARNING OUTCOME **1**

Competing in the Global Economy

Only a few years ago, business conducted across national borders was referred to as *international* activity, a term implying that the individual's or the organization's nationality is held strongly in consciousness.[4] *Globalization*, by contrast, suggests that the world is free from national boundaries and is borderless.[5] U.S. workers now compete with workers in other countries. Organizations from other countries, such as the auto manufacturers Honda, Toyota, Nissan, and Daimler Benz, are establishing subsidiaries in the United States.

Similarly, what were once called *multinational organizations* (organizations that did business in several countries) are now referred to as **transnational organizations**, indicating that the global viewpoint supersedes national issues.[6] Transnational organizations such as 3M, Dow Chemical, and Coca-Cola operate worldwide across long distances and employ a multicultural mix of workers.

transnational organization

An organization in which the global viewpoint supersedes national issues.

After You Finish
This Chapter
Go to **Page 35**
for **Study Tools**

Social and Political Changes

Social and political upheavals have led organizations to change the way they conduct business as a result of thinking globally. Toyota, for example, is one Japanese company thinking big, thinking globally, and thinking differently by learning to speak to the 60-million-strong Generation Y, or "millennials."[7]

Business ventures in China have become increasingly attractive to U.S. companies. One challenge U.S. managers have tackled is understanding the Chinese way of doing business, ways that have been shaped by the Communist Party, socialism, feudalistic values, and *guanxi* (building networks for social exchange). Once *guanxi* is established, individuals can ask favors of each other with the expectation that the favor will be returned. Thus, many Chinese use *guanxi*, or personal connections, to conduct business or obtain jobs.

The concept of *guanxi* is not unique to China. There are similar concepts in many other countries, including Russia and Haiti. It is a broad term that can mean anything from strongly loyal relationships to ceremonial gift-giving, sometimes seen as bribery. *Guanxi* is more common in societies with underdeveloped legal support for private businesses.[8]

Americans can learn to build their own *guanxi* in order to interact effectively with Chinese managers.

guanxi

The Chinese practice of building networks for social exchange.

©iStockphoto.com/Carmen Martínez Banús

This would involve understanding the Chinese chain of command and negotiating slow, general agreements. Using the foreign government as a local franchisee may be effective in China. For example, KFC's operation in China is a joint venture between KFC (60 percent) and two Chinese government bodies (40 percent).[9]

The opening of trade barriers is a third issue that affects organizations competing in a global economy. In 1993 the European Union integrated fifteen nations into a single market by removing trade barriers. At that time, the member nations of the European Union were Austria, Belgium, Denmark, Finland, France, Germany, Greece, Ireland, Italy, Luxembourg, the Netherlands, Portugal, Spain, Sweden, and the United Kingdom. By 2007 Bulgaria, Cyprus, the Czech Republic, Estonia, Hungary, Latvia, Lithuania, Malta, Poland, Romania, Slovakia, and Slovenia had also joined. Europe's integration provides many opportunities for U.S. organizations to engage 494 million potential customers. Companies such as Ford Motor Company and IBM, which entered the market early with wholly owned subsidiaries, were able to capitalize on their much-anticipated head start.[10] Competition within the European Union will intensify, however, as will competition from Japan and the former Soviet nations.

The United States, Canada, and Mexico dramatically reduced trade barriers with the North American Free Trade Agreement (NAFTA), which took effect in 1994. Organizations found promising new markets for their products, and many companies located plants in Mexico to take advantage of low labor costs. Prior to

NAFTA, Mexico placed heavy tariffs on U.S. exports. The agreement immediately eliminated many of these tariffs and provided that the remaining tariffs be phased out over time.

Given these changes, managers must think globally and adopt a long-term view. Entering global markets requires long-term strategies.

Cultural Differences

One key for any company competing in the global marketplace is to understand diverse cultures. Whether managing culturally diverse individuals within a single location or managing individuals at remote locations around the globe, organizations must appreciate the differences among cultures. Edgar Schein suggests that to understand an organization's culture or, more broadly, any culture, one should dig below the surface of visible artifacts and uncover the basic underlying assumptions at the core of the culture.[11]

Microcultural differences (i.e., differences within cultures) are key to our understanding of the global work environment.[12] One such difference is the gap between generations, which Toyota, as previously mentioned, is addressing by learning to speak to the 60-million-strong "millennial" Generation Y.[13]

When considering differences among cultures, symbols are extremely important, as they can generate misunderstanding or inhibit communication if they are interpreted incorrectly. Consider the thumbs-up sign, which means approval in the United States but is an obscene gesture in Australia. Consider also the Windows icon representing a manila file folder, which is meaningless to Europeans who have never used such folders.[14]

Do cultural differences translate into differences in work-related attitudes? To answer this question, the pioneering Dutch researcher Geert Hofstede, with his colleagues, surveyed 160,000 managers and employees of IBM working in sixty different countries. Thus, the researchers were able to study individuals from the same company in the same jobs but living in different

FIGURE 2.1 Hofstede's Dimensions of Cultural Differences

Individualism ⟷ Collectivism

High power distance ⟷ Low power distance

High uncertainty avoidance ⟷ Low uncertainty avoidance

Masculinity ⟷ Femininity

Long-term orientation ⟷ Short-term orientation

SOURCE: Reprinted with permission of Academy of Management, P.O. Box 3020, Briarcliff Manor, NY 10510-8020. *Cultural Constraints in Management Theories.* G. Hofstede, *Academy of Management Executive* 7 (1993). Reproduced by permission of the publisher via Copyright Clearance Center, Inc.

countries. They found that national culture explains more differences in work-related attitudes than do age, gender, profession, or position within the organization. Five dimensions of cultural differences that formed the basis for work-related attitudes were identified (Figure 2.1).[15]

Management careers have taken on a global dimension in that working in transnational organizations may give managers the opportunity to work in other countries. **Expatriate managers**, those who work in a country other than their home country, benefit greatly from knowledge of cultural differences.

International executives are executives whose jobs have international scope, whether they have an expatriate assignment or deal with international issues. What kind of competencies should an individual develop in order to prepare for an international career? Some key competencies are integrity, insightfulness, risk taking, courage to take a stand, and ability to bring out the best in people. Learning-oriented attributes of international executives include cultural adventurousness, flexibility, openness to criticism, desire to seek learning opportunities, and sensitivity to cultural differences.[16] Further, strong human capital generally has a positive effect on internationalization.[17] Notice that all these qualities are based upon core competencies and the ability to learn from experience.

expatriate manager

A manager who works in a country other than her or his home country.

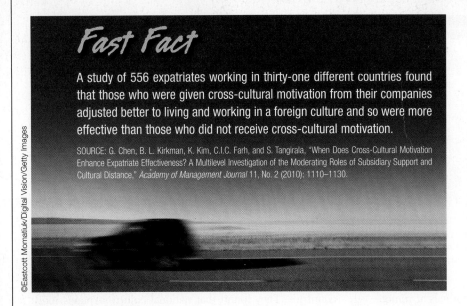

Fast Fact

A study of 556 expatriates working in thirty-one different countries found that those who were given cross-cultural motivation from their companies adjusted better to living and working in a foreign culture and so were more effective than those who did not receive cross-cultural motivation.

SOURCE: G. Chen, B. L. Kirkman, K. Kim, C.I.C. Farh, and S. Tangirala, "When Does Cross-Cultural Motivation Enhance Expatriate Effectiveness? A Multilevel Investigation of the Moderating Roles of Subsidiary Support and Cultural Distance," *Academy of Management Journal* 11, No. 2 (2010): 1110–1130.

Because workplace customs vary widely, understanding cultural differences becomes especially important for companies that are considering opening foreign offices. It is wise to do the research in advance. Consulate offices and companies operating within the foreign country provide excellent information about national customs and legal requirements. Table 2.1 presents a business guide to cultural differences in three countries: Japan, Mexico, and Saudi Arabia.

Another reality affecting global business practices is the cost of layoffs in other countries. As the economy has become more global, downsizing has presented challenges worldwide. For example, dismissing a forty-five-year-old middle manager with twenty years of service and a $50,000 annual salary varied in cost from a low of $13,000 in Ireland to a high of $130,000 in Italy.[18] Laying off this manager in the United States would have cost approximately $19,000. The wide variability in costs stems from the various legal protections that certain countries give workers. In Italy, laid-off employees must receive a "notice period" payment (one year's pay if they have nine years or more of service) plus a severance payment (based on pay and years of service). U.S. companies operating overseas often adopt the European tradition of training and retraining workers to avoid overstaffing and potential layoffs. Appreciating the customs and rules for doing business in another country is essential to global success.

individualism

A cultural orientation in which people belong to loose social frameworks, and their primary concern is for themselves and their families.

collectivism

A cultural orientation in which individuals belong to tightly knit social frameworks and depend strongly on extended families or clans.

power distance

The degree to which a culture accepts unequal distribution of power.

Cultural Differences and Work-Related Attitudes

Hofstede's work has implications for work-related attitudes. We'll now take a closer look at how his five dimensions of cultural differences are manifest in a variety of countries.

Individualism versus Collectivism

In cultures where **individualism** predominates, the social framework is loose, and employees put loyalty to themselves and their families ahead of loyalty to their company and work group. Cultures characterized by **collectivism**, on the other hand, are tightly knit social frameworks in which individual members depend strongly on others and group decisions are valued and accepted.

North American and European cultures are individualistic in orientation. Managers in Great Britain and the Netherlands, for example, emphasize and encourage individual achievement. By contrast, in collectivist cultures such as Israeli *kibbutzim* and Japan, people view group loyalty and unity as paramount. Collectivistic managers seek to fit harmoniously within the group and encourage their employees to do the same. The world's regions are patterned with varying degrees of this cultural difference.

Power Distance

Power distance relates to the acceptance of unequal distribution of power. In countries with a high power distance, bosses are afforded more authority, which is seldom bypassed, titles are used, and formality is the rule. Managers and employees in such countries see one another as fundamentally different kinds of people. India, Venezuela, and Mexico all demonstrate high power distance.

In societies with low power distance, people believe in minimizing inequality. People at various power levels in these countries are less threatened by and more willing to trust one another. Managers and employees judge each other on a basis of equality. Managers are given authority only if they have expertise. Employees frequently bypass the boss in order to get work done in countries with a low power distance, such as Denmark and Australia.

TABLE 2.1 Business Guide to Cultural Differences

COUNTRY	APPOINTMENTS	DRESS	GIFTS	NEGOTIATIONS
Japan	Punctuality is a necessity. It is considered rude to be late.	Conservative dress is the norm for men and women in large to medium companies, though pastel shirts are common. One may be expected to remove shoes in temples and homes, as well as in some ryokan (inn) style restaurants. In that case, slip-on shoes should be worn.	Important part of Japanese business protocol. Gifts are typically exchanged among colleagues on July 15 and January 1 to commemorate midyear and the year's end, respectively.	Business cards (*meishi*) are an important part of doing business and key for establishing credentials. One side of your card should be in English and the other in Japanese. It is an asset to include information such as membership in professional associations.
Mexico	Punctuality is not always as much of a priority. Nonetheless, Mexicans are accustomed to North Americans arriving on time, and most Mexicans in business, if not government, will try to return the favor.	Dark, conservative suits and ties are the norm for most men. Standard office attire for women includes dresses, skirted suits, or skirts and blouses. Femininity is strongly encouraged in women's dress.	Not usually a requirement in business dealings though presenting a small gift will generally be appreciated as a gesture of goodwill. If giving a gift, be aware that inquiring about what the receiver would like to receive may offend.	Mexicans avoid directly saying "no." A "no" is often disguised in responses such as "maybe" or "we'll see." You should also use this indirect approach in your dealings. Otherwise, your Mexican counterparts may perceive you as being rude and pushy.
Saudi Arabia	It is customary to make appointments for times of day rather than precise hours. The importance Saudis attach to courtesy and hospitality can cause delays that prevent keeping to a strict schedule.	The only absolute requirement of dress code is modesty. For men, this means covering everything from navel to knee. In public, women are required to cover everything except the face, hands, and feet by wearing an *abaya* (standard black cloak) and headscarf.	Should only be given to the most intimate of friends. For a Saudi to receive a present from a lesser acquaintance is so embarrassing that it is considered offensive.	Business cards are common but not essential. If used, the common practice is to have both English and Arabic printed on same side so that neither language is perceived as less important by being on the reverse of same card.

SOURCE: Adapted from information obtained from business culture guides accessed online at http://www.executiveplanet.com.

In cultures with low power distance, managers are more likely to consult employees and work with them to achieve harmonious results.

tender.[19] Money and possessions are very important in this viewpoint, and performance is what counts. Achievement is admired. Cultures characterized by traditional **femininity** emphasize relationships and concern for others. Men and women are expected to assume both assertive and nurturing roles. Quality of life is very important, and people and the environment are emphasized.

Time Orientation

Cultures also differ in **time orientation**. A culture's values may be oriented toward the future (long-term orientation) or toward the past and present (short-term orientation).[20] In China, which has a long-term orientation, values such as thrift and persistence, which look toward the future, are emphasized. Russians generally have a short-term orientation and particularly value respect for tradition (past) and meeting social obligations (present).

Developing Cross-Cultural Sensitivity

In today's multicultural environment, it is imperative that organizations help their employees recognize and appreciate cultural differences. One way companies do this is through cultural sensitivity training. IBM's cultural sensitivity program, Global Citizens Portfolio, consists of flexible spending accounts employees can use to enhance their training and in turn benefit the company.[21] Another way to develop sensitivity is by using cross-cultural task forces or teams. The Milwaukee-based GE Medical Systems Group (GEMS), with 19,000 employees working worldwide, has developed a vehicle for bringing managers from each of its three regions (the Americas, Europe, and Asia) together to work on a variety of business projects. Their Global Leadership Program forms several work groups made up of managers from various regions and has them work together on important projects, such as worldwide employee integration, to increase employees' sense of belonging throughout the GEMS international organization.[22] Because cultural differences are constantly in flux, it is important for managers to foster up-to-date knowledge of relevant cultural trends.

The globalization of business affects all parts of the organization, but particularly human resource manage-

Uncertainty Avoidance

Cultures with high **uncertainty avoidance** are concerned with security and tend to avoid conflict. People in such cultures tend to seek consensus in an effort to moderate the threat of life's inherent uncertainty. Cultures with low uncertainty avoidance tolerate ambiguity better. People are more willing to take risks and are more comfortable with individual differences. Conflict is seen as constructive, and people accept dissenting viewpoints. Accordingly, Norwegians and Australians value job mobility because they have low uncertainty avoidance; Japan and Italy are characterized by high uncertainty avoidance, and, not surprisingly, their cultures emphasize career stability.

Masculinity versus Femininity

In cultures characterized by traditional **masculinity**, assertiveness and materialism are valued. Men, the idea goes, should be assertive, tough, and decisive, whereas women should be nurturing, modest, and

uncertainty avoidance
The degree to which a culture tolerates ambiguity and uncertainty.

masculinity
A cultural orientation in which assertiveness and materialism are valued.

femininity
A cultural orientation in which relationships and concern for others are valued.

time orientation
Whether a culture's values are oriented toward the future (long-term orientation) or toward the past and present (short-term orientation).

WHAT ABOUT CULTURE?

H ofstede found the United States to be the most individualistic country of any he studied. It ranked among the countries with weak power distance, and its level of uncertainty avoidance indicated a tolerance of uncertainty. The United States also ranked as a masculine culture with a short-term orientation. These values have shaped U.S. man-

agement theory, so Hofstede's work casts doubt on the universal applicability of U.S. management theories. Because these dimensions vary widely, management practices should be adjusted to account for cultural differences. Managers in transnational organizations must learn as much as they can about other cultures in order to lead their culturally diverse organizations effectively.

ment. Human resource managers must adopt a global view of human resource planning, recruitment and selection, compensation, and training and development. This means that they must possess a working knowledge of the legal systems in various countries as well as of global economics, culture, and customs. Not only do HR managers prepare U.S. workers to live outside their native country, but they also help foreign employees interact with U.S. culture. Global human resource management is a complex field, one that is critical to organizations' success in the global marketplace.

LEARNING OUTCOME **3**

The Diverse Workforce

Cultural differences contribute a great deal to the diversity of the workforce, but other forms of diversity are important as well. **Diversity** encompasses all forms of difference among individuals, including culture, gender, age, ability, religion, personality, social status, and sexual orientation. Largely because of demographic changes in the working population, diversity has garnered increasing attention in recent years. Managers feel that deal-

ing with diversity is a paramount concern for two reasons: first, they need to motivate diverse work groups, and, second, they must communicate with employees who have different values and language skills.

Several demographic trends are affecting organizations. By the year 2020, the workforce will be more culturally diverse, more female, and older than ever. Thus, workforce demographic change and diversity are critical challenges for the study and management of organizational behavior.[23] The theories of motivation, leadership, and group behavior based on research in a workforce of one composition may not be applicable in a workforce of a very different composition.[24] This may be especially problematic if ethnic, gender, and/or religious differences lead to conflict between leaders and followers in organizations. Still another factor in diversity involves individuals with disabilities, as recent legislation and new technologies have helped more such people enter the workforce. Hence, learning to work together with an open mind is an increasingly important skill. Alcon Laboratories, the Swiss-owned and Fort Worth–based international company whose mission is to improve and preserve eyesight, is an example of the kind of organization that offers diversity training to help employees learn to work together.

Ethnic Diversity

The globalization of business is not the only force promoting cultural and ethnic diversity in the workplace. Changing domestic demographics also affect organizations' cultural diversity. By 2020, minorities will constitute more than one-half of the new entrants to the U.S. workforce. Yet African Americans and Hispanic Americans are overrepresented in declining occupations, thus limiting their opportunities. Further, African Americans and

diversity

All forms of difference among individuals, including culture, gender, age, ability, religion, personality, social status, and sexual orientation.

lenge and risk. The challenge is to harness the wealth of differences provided by cultural diversity. The risk is that prejudices and stereotypes may prevent managers and employees from developing synergies to benefit the organization. Diversity of the workforce was a major factor in the innovation that drove the dot-com boom in Silicon Valley, illustrating that the benefits of a diverse workforce make good management of these challenges and risks important.[26]

Gender Diversity

The number of women in the labor force increased from 31.5 million in 1970 to 65 million in 2008. This increase in women employees accounts for almost 60 percent of the overall expansion of the entire U.S. labor force for this period. In 2007, women made up more than 46 percent of the labor force.[27] In 2009, 70 percent of new workplace entrants were women and/or people of color.

Women are better prepared to contribute in organizations than ever before, because they earn 49 percent of all doctorates, 60 percent of master's degrees, and 58 percent of all undergraduate degrees.[28] But their share of authority and compensation is not increasing commensurately with their education and participation in the workforce. Not only has there been little recent increase in the number of women CEOs, but the number of women positioned to move into top jobs has also dropped. Half of the male workforce occupy line positions, compared to only one-quarter of women in business.[29] American Express is an exception to the rule. Rated one of the top companies for women in 2007 by *Pink* magazine, American Express not only places women in top positions, it trains them for advancement.[30] Nonetheless, median weekly earnings for women persist at a level of 81 percent of their male counterparts' earnings.[31] Because benefits are tied to compensation, women also receive fewer benefits.

Hispanic Americans tend to live in a few large cities that are facing severe economic difficulties and high crime rates. Minority workers are less likely to be prepared because they are less likely to have had satisfactory schooling and on-the-job training, which will likely put them at a disadvantage within organizations. It need not be this way. For example, Coca-Cola has made substantial progress on diversity by monitoring its human resource systems, and companies such as Motorola already recognize and meet these needs by focusing on basic skills training.[25]

In sum, the globalization of business and changing demographic trends present organizations with a culturally diverse workforce, creating both challenge

glass ceiling

A transparent barrier that keeps women from rising above a certain level in organizations.

The **glass ceiling** is a transparent barrier that keeps women from rising above a certain level in organizations. In the United States, it has been rare to find women in positions above middle management.[32] Although growth in opportunities for women to attain executive positions has recently stagnated, the situation is improving for women in the boardroom. One study found no substantive increase in female corporate board members between 1996 and 2002, although this increased in 2007.[33] The ultimate glass

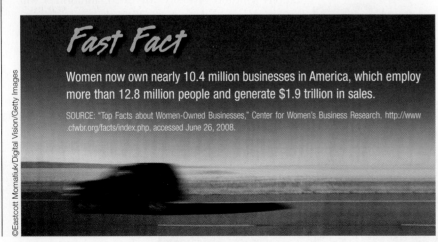

Fast Fact

Women now own nearly 10.4 million businesses in America, which employ more than 12.8 million people and generate $1.9 trillion in sales.

SOURCE: "Top Facts about Women-Owned Businesses," Center for Women's Business Research, http://www.cfwbr.org/facts/index.php, accessed June 26, 2008.

CAN WOMEN WORK AND HAVE A LIFE?

How to balance work with other life commitments such as family and personal growth is a key issue on the minds of women and the companies they work for. Western women have typically adopted the provider role and are often still responsible for home management, child care, and sometimes care for their elderly parents.

Because of their multiple roles, women frequently experience conflicts between work and home. They struggle to manage logistics, avoid burnout, and find good mentors as well as time for themselves. Companies and governments in the United States and abroad are placing greater emphasis on support systems and alter-native structures to help women create balance in their lives, and investors are increasingly looking to companies who offer flexibility and support. Flexible work schedules enabled by technology, child care, elder care, and work-site health promotion programs assist working women in managing the stress of their lives.

SOURCES: D. L. Nelson and M. A. Hitt, "Employed Women and Stress: Implications for Enhancing Women's Mental Health in the Workplace," in J. C. Quick, L. R. Murphy, and J. J. Hurrell, Jr., eds., *Stress and Well-Being at Work* (Washington, D.C.: American Psychological Association, 1992): 164–177; S. Riss, "This Is How She Does It," *Working Mother* (June/July 2008): 19–23; E. McDargh, "Work-Life Balance Issues Loom Large across the Globe: Work-Life Balance Isn't Just Making News. It's Also Become a Criterion for Investment," *Arkansas Business* (May 12, 2008).

ceiling may well be the professional partnership. While women account for 30 percent of legal professionals, they account for only 17 percent of the partners.[34]

On a global basis, the leadership picture for women is improving. For example, the number of female political leaders has grown dramatically worldwide in recent decades. In the 1970s there were only five such leaders. In the 1990s, twenty-one female leaders came into power, and today women around the world are leading major global companies. Note, however, these global female business leaders do not come predominantly from the West. In addition, a large number of women have founded entrepreneurial businesses.

Removing obstacles to women's success presents a major challenge for organizations. If they do not help the increasing numbers of female employees achieve their potential, they risk underutilizing the talents of half the U.S. workforce. Therefore, it is wise for organizations to develop policies that promote equity in pay and benefits, to encourage benefit programs of special interest to women, and to provide equal starting salaries for jobs of equal value. Corporations that shatter the glass ceiling share several practices:

1. Upper managers demonstrate support for the advancement of women.

2. Leaders incorporate practices into their diversity management programs to ensure that women perceive the organization as attractive.[35]

3. Women are represented on standing committees addressing key strategic business issues and are targeted for participation in executive education programs.

4. Systems are put in place to identify women with high potential for advancement.[36]

Companies such as IBM and Ernst & Young work for diversity not only by offering excellent programs for advancing and developing women executives, but also judge supervisors based on their active support for such endeavors.[37]

Age Diversity

The graying of the U.S. workforce is another source of workplace diversity. Aging baby boomers (those individuals born between 1946 and 1964) contributed to the rise of the median age in the United States to thirty-six in the year 2000—six years older than at any other time in history. The number of middle-aged Americans is rising dramatically, while the numbers of younger workers and older workers (over age sixty-five) are declining. People over age sixty-five will comprise 13 percent of the population in 2010, and 20 percent of the population by 2030.[38]

This change in worker profile has profound implications for organizations. The job crunch among middle-aged workers will intensify as companies seek flatter organizational structures and eliminate middle-management jobs. Older workers are often higher paid, and companies that employ large numbers of aging baby boomers may find these pay scales a handicap to competitiveness.[39] Paid volunteerism, however, can be a draw to younger generations.[40] Conversely, a more experienced, stable, reliable, and healthier workforce can pay dividends to companies. A recent study showed that age diversity among employees in Western companies had a positive impact on profitability.[41] The baby boomers are well trained and educated, and their knowledge is a definite asset to organizations.

The aging workforce is increasing intergenerational contact at work.[42] As organizations flatten, workers traditionally segregated by old corporate hierarchies find themselves working together. Four generations are cooperating: *the silent generation* (people born from 1930 through 1945), a small group that includes most organizations' top managers; *the baby boomers* (people born from 1946 through 1964), whose substantial numbers give them a strong influence; *the baby bust generation*, popularly known as *Generation X* (those born from 1965 through 1976); and the subsequent generation, tentatively called *Generation Y, millenials*, or *the baby boomlet* (those born after 1976).[43] The millenials often bring new challenges to the workplace because of their early access to technology and their continuing connection to parents.[44]

The differences in attitudes and values among these four generations can be substantial, and managers struggle to integrate their workers into a cohesive group. Most leadership positions are currently held by members of the silent generation. Baby boomers tend to (1) regard the silent generation as complacent (2) strive for moral rights in the workplace, and (3) take a more activist position regarding employee rights. The baby busters, newer to the workplace, are often impatient, want short-term gratification, and value a greater balance between family and work. They scorn the achievement orientation and materialism of the baby boomers. Members of Generation Y, on the other hand, place high importance on independence and creativity, and are less inclined to settle for work that is not in line with their values.

Younger workers may have false impressions of older workers, viewing them as resistant to change, unable to learn new work methods, less physically capable, and less creative than younger employees. Research indicates, however, that older employees are more satisfied with their jobs, more committed to the organization, and more internally motivated than their younger cohorts.[45] Research also indicates that direct experience with older workers reduces younger workers' negative beliefs.[46] Motivating aging workers and helping them maintain high levels of contribution to the organization is a key task for managers.

Ability Diversity

Employees with different abilities present yet another form of diversity. Individuals with disabilities are an underutilized human resource. An estimated 50 million individuals with disabilities live in the United States, and their unemployment rate is estimated to exceed 50 percent.[47] Nevertheless, they have entered the workforce in greater numbers since the Americans with Disabilities Act went into effect in the summer of 1992. The act defines a person with a disability as "anyone possessing a physical or mental impairment that substantially limits one or more major life activities."[48] Under this law, employers are required to make reasonable accommodations to permit workers with disabilities to perform jobs. The act's protection encompasses a broad range of illnesses that produce disabilities, including acquired immune deficiency syndrome (AIDS), cancer, hypertension, anxiety disorders, dyslexia, blindness, and cerebral palsy, to name only a few.

Some companies recognized the value of employing workers with disabilities long before the legislation. In 1981, McDonald's created McJOBS, a corporate plan to recruit, train, and retain individuals with disabilities that has hired more than 9,000 mentally and physically challenged individuals.[49] Its participants include workers with visual, hearing, or orthopedic impairments; learning disabilities; and developmental disabilities. McJOBS holds sensitivity training sessions with managers and crew members before workers go onsite to help workers without disabilities understand what it means to be a worker with a disabling condition. Most McJOBS workers start part time and advance according to their abilities and the opportunities available.

Valuing Diversity

Diversity involves more than culture, gender, age, ability, and personality. It also encompasses religion, social status, and sexual orientation. These diversity types lend heterogeneity to the workforce.

Managers must combat prejudice and discrimination to manage diversity. *Prejudice* is an attitude, whereas

[Walking Assistance]

An invention from Israeli entrepreneur Amit Goffer may soon change the way paralyzed individuals live and work. His device, the ReWalk, is a high-tech set of leg braces that is outfitted with motion sensors, motorized joints, and a computer that allows paraplegics (people with paralyzed legs) to walk. When it detects subtle movements in the arms and shoulders, the ReWalk provides motion to the leg braces, allowing the user to walk, stand, squat, and even ascend and descend stairs.

SOURCE: "Revolutionary Exoskeleton That Helps Wheel-Chair Bound Walk to Go on Sale in UK," *The Daily Mail* (April 2, 2011) http://www.dailymail.co.uk/health/article-1374067/Robot-trousers-gives-paraplegics-power-walk-sale-UK.html, accessed June 10, 2011.

discrimination describes behavior. Both diminish organizational productivity in that they present obstacles to promoting and compensating good workers fairly. The potential for unfair treatment increases as the workforce becomes increasingly diverse. Combating stereotypes is essential. For example, a recent study revealed that male bosses sometimes hold certain stereotypes that negatively influence their interaction with female employees of color.[50] Open communication can help clarify misperceptions and clear the way for advancement.

Diversity helps organizations in many ways. Some organizations recognize the potential benefits of aggressively working to increase the diversity of their workforces. Yum! Brands' Kentucky Fried Chicken (KFC) tries to attract and retain female and minority-group executives. A president of KFC's U.S. operations said, "We want to bring in the best people. If there are two equally qualified people, we'd clearly like to have diversity."[51]

In an effort to understand and appreciate diversity, Alcon Laboratories developed a diversity training class called Working Together. The course takes advantage of two key ideas. First, people work best when they are valued and when diversity is taken into account. Second, when people feel valued, they build relationships and work together as a team.[52] Even majority-group managers may be more supportive of diversity training if they appreciate their own ethnic identity. One evaluation of diversity training found that participants preferred training with a traditional title and a broad focus.[53] Further,

women were found to react more positively to diversity training than were men. A conclusion from the evaluation was that companies should measure the effects of training so they can monitor its positive payoffs.

Managing diversity helps companies become more competitive, but effective diversity management involves more than simply being a good corporate citizen or complying with affirmative action.[54] Managing diversity requires a painful examination of employees' hidden assumptions. Biases and prejudices about people's differences must be uncovered and dealt with so that differences can be celebrated and used to their full advantage.

Diversity's Benefits and Problems

Although diversity has the potential to enhance organizational performance, it may pose some problems as well. Table 2.2 summarizes the main benefits and problems with diversity at work. The first main benefit of diversity management is that it helps firms attract and retain the best available human talent. The companies topping the lists of the best places to work are usually excellent at managing diversity. A second benefit is that diversity aids marketing efforts. Just as workforces are diversifying, so are markets. A diverse workforce, therefore, can improve a company's marketing plans by drawing on insights from various employees' cultural backgrounds. Third, diversity promotes creativity and innovation. The most innovative companies, such as Hewlett-Packard, deliberately build diverse teams to foster creativity. Fourth, diversity improves problem

TABLE 2.2 The Benefits and Problems of Diversity	
Benefits	*Problems*
• Attracts and retains the best talent	• Resistance to change
• Improves marketing efforts	• Lack of cohesiveness
• Promotes creativity and innovation	• Communication problems
• Results in better problem solving	• Interpersonal conflicts
• Enhances organizational flexibility	• Slower decision making

consequential theory
An ethical theory that emphasizes the consequences or results of behavior.

solving. Diverse groups bring more expertise and experience to bear on problems and decisions, and they encourage higher levels of critical thinking. Fifth, diversity enhances organizational flexibility because it makes an organization challenge old assumptions and become more adaptable. These five benefits add up to competitive advantage for companies with well-managed diversity.

We must also recognize diversity's potential problems. Five problems are particularly notable: resistance to change, lack of cohesiveness, communication problems, interpersonal conflicts, and slower decision making. People are attracted to and more comfortable with others like themselves. Thus, it stands to reason that workers may resist diversity efforts when they are forced to interact with others unlike themselves. Managers should be prepared for this resistance rather than naively assuming that everybody supports diversity. Another difficulty with diversity is the issue of cohesiveness, that invisible "glue" that holds a group together. Cohesive groups have higher morale and better communication, but diverse groups take longer to achieve cohesiveness, so they may also take longer to develop high morale.

Another obstacle to performance in diverse groups is communication. Culturally diverse groups may encounter special communication barriers. Misunderstandings can lower work group effectiveness by creating conflict and hampering decision making.[55]

corporate citizens.[56] For many many organizations, however, unethical conduct sometimes occurs despite their best attempts to prevent such problems. The toughest problems for managers to resolve include employee theft, environmental issues, comparable worth of employees, conflicts of interest, and sexual harassment.[57]

Ethical theories help us understand, evaluate, and classify moral arguments; make decisions; and then defend conclusions about what is right and wrong. Ethical theories can be classified as consequential, rule based, or character theories.

Consequential Theories of Ethics

Consequential theories of ethics emphasize the consequences or results of behavior. John Stuart Mill's *utilitarianism*, a well-known consequential theory, suggests that the consequences of an action determine whether it is right or wrong.[58] "Good" is the ultimate moral value, and we should maximize good effects for the greatest number of people. But do good ethics make for good business?[59] Right actions do not always produce good consequences, and good consequences do not always follow right actions. And how do we determine the greatest good, whether short-term or long-term consequences? Using the "greatest number" criterion may mean that minorities (less than 50 percent) are excluded in evaluating the morality of actions. An issue that matters to a minority but not to the majority might be ignored. These are but two of the dilemmas raised by utilitarianism.

Corporations and business enterprises tend to subscribe to consequential ethics, partly due to the persuasive arguments of the Scottish political economist and moral philosopher Adam Smith.[60] He believed that the self-interest of human beings is God's providence, not the government's. Smith set forth a doctrine of *natural liberty*, presenting the classical argument for open-market competition and free trade. Within this framework, people should be allowed to pursue what is in their economic self-interest, and the natural efficiency of the marketplace will then serve the well-being of society.

Ethics, Character, and Personal Integrity

Managers frequently face ethical dilemmas and tradeoffs. Merck & Company is an example of a company that manages ethical issues well, and its emphasis on ethical behavior has consistently earned it a place on *Business Ethics'* list of top 100

ETHICAL BEHAVIOR

PROFIT AT ANY COST

©iStockphoto.com/Geoffrey Holman

Rule-Based Theories of Ethics

Rule-based theories of ethics emphasize the character of the act itself, not its effects, in arriving at universal moral rights and wrongs.[61] Moral rights, the basis for legal rights, are associated with such theories. In a theological context, the Bible, the Talmud, and the Koran are rule-based guides to ethical behavior. Immanuel Kant worked toward the ultimate moral principle in formulating his *categorical imperative*, a universal standard of behavior.[62] Kant argued that individuals should be treated with respect and dignity and that they should not be used as a means to an end. He argued that we should put ourselves in the other person's position and ask if we would make the same decision if we were in that person's situation.

Character Theories of Ethics

Virtue ethics, of which **character theories** of ethics are a type, offer an alternative to understanding behavior in terms of self-interest or rules. Character theories of ethics emphasize the character of the individual and the intent of the actor instead of the character of the act itself or its consequences. These virtue-ethics theories are based on an Aristotle's view of ethics, which focused on an individual's inner character and virtuousness rather than outward behavior. Thus, the good person who acted out of virtuous and right intentions was one with integrity and ultimately good ethical standards. Robert Solomon is the best-known advocate of this Aristotelian approach to business ethics.[63] He advocates a business ethics theory centered on the individual within the corporation, emphasizing personal virtues as well as corporate roles. Solomon's six dimensions of virtue ethics are community, excellence, role identity, integrity, judgment (*phronesis* in Greek), and holism. Further, the virtues summarize the ideals defining good character. These include honesty, loyalty, sincerity, courage, reliability, trustworthiness, benevolence, sensitivity, helpfulness, cooperativeness, civility, decency, modesty, openness, gracefulness, and many others.

Cultural Relativism

Cultural relativism contends that there are no universal ethical principles and that people should not impose their own ethical standards on others. Local standards guide ethical behavior. Cultural relativism encourages individuals to operate under the old adage of "When in Rome, do as the Romans do." Unfortunately, people who adhere strictly to cultural relativism may avoid difficult ethical dilemmas by denying their own accountability.

> " People need ethical theories to guide them through complex, difficult, and often confusing moral choices and ethical decisions.

Ethical Dilemmas Facing the Modern Organization

People need ethical theories to guide them through complex, difficult, and often confusing moral choices and ethical decisions. Contemporary organizations experience a wide variety of ethical and moral dilemmas. In this section, we address employee rights, sexual harassment, organizational justice, and whistle-blowing. We conclude with a discussion of social responsibility and codes of ethics.

Employee Rights

Managing the rights of employees at work creates many ethical dilemmas in organizations. Drug testing, free speech, downsizing and layoffs, and due process are but a few of the employee rights issues managers face.

These dilemmas include privacy issues related to technology. Many feel that computerized monitoring constitutes an invasion of privacy. Using employee data from computerized information systems presents many ethical concerns. New software allows employers to tap into their employees' address books and e-mail contacts to obtain new potential clients and discern who in the company might be best suited to approach them.[64] Safeguarding the employee's right to privacy while preserving access to the data for those who need it forces managers to balance competing interests.

The reality of AIDS in the workplace also illustrates the difficulties managers face in balancing various interests. Managers may face a conflict between the rights of HIV-infected workers and the rights of their coworkers who feel threatened. But laws protect HIV-infected workers. The Americans with Disabilities Act (ADA) requires employees to treat HIV-infected workers as disabled individuals and to make reasonable accommodations for them. But ADA cannot encompass all of the ethical dilemmas involved.

rule-based theory
An ethical theory that emphasizes the character of the act itself rather than its effects.

character theory
An ethical theory that emphasizes the character, personal virtues, and intent of the individual.

Confidentiality may also present challenges. Employers are not required to make concessions to coworkers, but they are obligated to educate, reassure, and provide emotional support to coworkers. Some employees with HIV or AIDS fear stigmatization or reprisals and do not want to reveal their condition to their coworkers. Management should discuss the ramifications of trying to maintain confidentiality and should assure the affected employee that every effort will be made to prevent negative consequences for him or her in the workplace.[65]

How does a manager protect the dignity of the HIV-infected employee and preserve the morale and productivity of the work group when so much prejudice and ignorance surround this disease? Many organizations, such as Wells Fargo, believe the answer is education.[66] Wells Fargo has written an AIDS policy to address confidentiality, employee socialization, coworker education, and counseling.

Sexual Harassment

According to the Equal Employment Opportunity Commission, sexual harassment is unwelcome verbal or physical sexual attention that affects an employee's job conditions or creates a hostile working environment.[67] Supreme Court rulings tend to blame companies when managers create a sexually hostile working environment. Sexual harassment is more likely to occur in some organizations than in others—for example, in male-dominated workplaces.[68] In some organizations, employees risk their jobs by complaining of sexual harassment or are not taken seriously, and perpetrators are rarely punished. Managers can defend themselves by demonstrating that they took action to eliminate workplace harassment and that the complaining employee did not take advantage of company procedures to deal with harassment. Even the best sexual harassment policy, however, will not absolve a company when harassment leads to firing, demotions, or undesirable working assignments.[69]

There are three types of sexual harassment. *Gender harassment* includes crude comments or behaviors that convey hostility toward a particular gender. *Unwanted sexual attention* involves unwanted touching or repeated pressures for dates. *Sexual coercion* consists of implicit or explicit demands for sexual favors by threatening negative job-related consequences or promising job-related rewards.[70] Recent theory has focused attention on the aggressive behavior of sexual harassers.[71]

Sexual harassment costs the typical *Fortune* 500 company $6.7 million per year in absenteeism, turnover, and lost productivity. Valeant Pharmaceuticals International paid out millions to settle four sexual harassment complaints against former CEO Milan Panic. Plaintiffs may now sue for compensatory and punitive damages in addition to back pay. And these costs do not take into account the negative publicity sexual harassment cases may attract. Moreover, victims of sexual harassment who do not report the problem are less satisfied with their work, supervisors, and coworkers and may psychologically withdraw at work. They may suffer poorer mental health and even exhibit symptoms of post-traumatic stress disorder in conjunction with the harassment experience. Some victims report alcohol abuse, depression, headaches, and nausea.[72]

Several companies have created comprehensive sexual harassment programs. Atlantic Richfield (ARCO), owned by British Petroleum and a player in the male-dominated energy industry, has a handbook on preventing sexual harassment that includes phone numbers of state agencies where employees can file complaints. The openness seems to work. Lawsuits rarely happen at ARCO. When employees make sexual harassment complaints, the company investigates thoroughly. ARCO fired the captain of an oil tanker for sexually harassing coworkers.

Organizational Justice

Organizational justice also generates moral and ethical dilemmas at work. **Distributive justice** concerns the fairness of outcomes individuals receive. For example, during former President George H. W. Bush's 1992 visit, Japanese CEOs questioned the distributive justice of keeping American CEOs' salaries so high while many companies were struggling and laying off workers.

Procedural justice concerns the fairness of the process by which outcomes are allocated. The ethical questions in procedural justice examine the process by which an organization distributes its resources. Has the organization used the correct procedures in allocating resources? Have the right considerations, such as competence and skill,

©iStockphoto.com/Don Bayley

[Protection for Whistle-Blowers]

One reason that many people refrain from reporting violations in their companies is the fear of retaliation. They worry that they could be harassed, ridiculed, or worse, fired, for going to the authorities. The Sarbanes-Oxley Act, passed by U.S. Congress in 2002, provides legal protection for whistle-blowers in three ways. First, it requires publicly held companies to set up a structure through which employees can make anonymous reports about potential criminal activities. Second, it makes it illegal to harass, demote, suspend, threaten, or fire an employee who makes a report. The penalties for such actions range from heavy financial penalties to ten years in prison.

SOURCE: "Sarbanes Oxley Act 2002," http://www.soxlaw.com.

been brought to bear in the decision process? And have the wrong considerations, such as race and gender, been excluded from the decision process? One study of work scheduling found that advance notice and consistency, two dimensions of procedural justice, reduced voluntary turnover.[73] Some research suggests cultural differences in the effects of distributive and procedural justice.[74]

Whistle-Blowing

Whistle-blowers are employees who inform authorities of wrongdoings by their companies or coworkers. Depending on their situations, whistle-blowers may be perceived as either "public heroes" or "vile wretches." Those seen as heroes generally report serious and high-magnitude ethical breaches widely perceived as abhorrent.[75] Others may see the whistle-blower as a wretch if they feel the act of whistle-blowing is more offensive than the situation reported.

Whistle-blowing is a powerful influence on corporate America because committed organizational members sometimes engage in unethical behavior in an intense desire to succeed. Organizations can manage whistle-blowing by explaining the conditions that are appropriate for disclosing wrongdoing. Clearly delineating wrongful behavior and the appropriate ways to respond are important organizational actions.

Social Responsibility

Corporate **social responsibility** is an organization's obligation to behave ethically in its social environment. Ethical conduct at the individual level can translate into social responsibility at the organizational level. Multiple stakeholders in society expect organizations to engage in socially responsible actions.

Current concerns include protecting the environment, promoting worker safety, supporting social issues, and investing in the community, among others. Some organizations, such as IBM, loan executives to inner-city schools to teach science and math. Some companies have even

tried to build a brand around social responsibility, such as the Just Coffee Cooperative, which sponsors trips to coffee-producing regions in order to build customer loyalty to the cause and their brand.[76] Firms that are seen as socially responsible have a competitive advantage in attracting applicants.[77] American Apparel, however, tried to build a brand around the fact that they produce garments locally rather than in foreign sweatshops but found that, as attractive as its ethics might have been to customers, sex appeal was more effective in actually selling its product.[78]

Codes of Ethics

Most mature professions guide their practitioners' actions and behavior with codes of ethics. For example, the Hippocratic oath guides doctors. A profession's code of ethics becomes a standard against which members can measure themselves in the absence of internalized standards.

No universal code of ethics or oath exists for business as it does for medicine. However, Paul Harris and four business colleagues who founded Rotary International in 1905 addressed ethical and moral behavior by developing the four-way test shown in Figure 2.2. Now used in more than 166 nations by 1.2 million Rotarians, this test focuses the questioner on key ethical and moral questions.

Beyond the individual and professional level, corporate culture is another excellent starting point for addressing ethics and morality. Sometimes regulations

whistle-blower
An employee who informs authorities of the wrongdoings of her or his company or coworkers.

social responsibility
The obligation of an organization to behave ethically in its social environment.

FIGURE 2.2 The Four-Way Test

**The Four-Way Test
of What We Think, Say, or Do**

1. Is it the TRUTH?

2. Is it FAIR to all concerned?

3. Will it build GOODWILL and better friendships?

4. Will it be BENEFICIAL to all concerned?

©Cengage Learning 2013

articulate a corporation's ethics. For example, the Joint Ethics Regulation (DOD 5500.7-R, August 1993) specifies the ethical standards that all U.S. military personnel must follow. In other cases, corporate ethics appear as a credo. Johnson & Johnson's credo, shown in Figure 2.3, helped hundreds of employees ethically address criminal tampering with Tylenol products.

Individual codes of ethics, professional oaths, and organizational credos must all be anchored in a moral, ethical framework because ethical theories are the only way to question and improve our current standards. However, even though a universal right and wrong may exist, it would be hard to agree upon a single code of ethics to which all individuals, professions, and organizations can subscribe.

organizations avoid technology fads and bandwagons, instead pioneering the application of carefully selected technologies.[81]

The Internet has radically changed organizations' communication and work performance. By integrating computer, cable, and telecommunications technologies, businesses have learned new ways to compete. For example, Kmart takes advantage of the Internet through BlueLight.com for online retailing, thereby drastically reducing its investments in inventories. Networked organizations conduct business anytime and anywhere, which is essential in the global marketplace.

The Internet and electronic innovation have made surveillance of employees more widespread. Companies need to balance the use of spyware, monitoring of employee e-mails and websites, and video monitoring systems with respect for employee rights to privacy. Clearly written policies spelling out the company's approach to monitoring employees can help

LEARNING OUTCOME **6**

Technological Innovation and Today's Workforce

In addition to globalization, diversity, and ethics, a fourth challenge that managers face is technological innovation. **Technology** consists of the intellectual and mechanical processes used by an organization to transform inputs into products or services that meet its goals. Managers must adapt to rapidly changing technology and ensure its optimum use in their organizations. Their ability to incorporate new technologies into their organizations can make or break economic growth.[79] Although the United States still leads the way in developing new technologies, it lags behind in using them productively in workplace settings.[80] Great

technology

The intellectual and mechanical processes used by an organization to transform inputs into products or services that meet its goals.

FIGURE 2.3 The Johnson & Johnson Credo

We believe our first responsibility is to the doctors, nurses, and patients, to mothers and all others who use our products and services. In meeting their needs everything we do must be of high quality. We must constantly strive to reduce our costs in order to maintain reasonable prices. Customers' orders must be serviced promptly and accurately. Our suppliers and distributors must have an opportunity to make a fair profit.

We are responsible to our employees, the men and women who work with us throughout the world. Everyone must be considered as an individual. We must respect their dignity and recognize their merit. They must have a sense of security in their jobs. Compensation must be fair and adequate, and working conditions clean, orderly, and safe. Employees must feel free to make suggestions and complaints. There must be equal opportunity for employment, development and advancement for those qualified. We must provide competent management, and their actions must be just and ethical.

We are responsible to the communities in which we live and work and to the world community as well. We must be good citizens—support good works and charities and bear our fair share of taxes. We must encourage civic improvements and better health and education. We must maintain in good order the property we are privileged to use, protecting the environment and natural resources.

Our final responsibility is to our stockholders. Business must make a sound profit. We must experiment with new ideas. Research must be carried on, innovative programs developed and mistakes paid for. New equipment must be purchased, new facilities provided, and new products launched. Reserves must be created to provide for adverse times. When we operate according to these principles, the stockholders should realize a fair return.

SOURCE: "Our Credo," http://www.jnj.com/wps/wcm/connect/c7933f004f5563df9e22be1bb31559c7/jnj_ourcredo_english_us_8.5x11_cmyk.pdf?MOD=AJPERES.

managers walk the fine line between respecting employees' privacy and protecting the interests of the organization. Furthermore, managers with excellent interpersonal skills can go beyond intense employee performance monitoring to ensure high productivity, commitment, and appropriate behavior from employees.

One fascinating technological change is the development of **expert systems**, computer-based applications that use a representation of human expertise in a specialized field of knowledge to solve problems. Expert systems can be used in many ways, including providing advice to nonexperts, providing assistance to experts, replacing experts, and serving as a training and development tool in organizations.[82] They are used in medical decision making, diagnosis, and medical informatics.[83] Anheuser-Busch has used an expert system to assist managers in ensuring that personnel decisions comply with antidiscrimination laws.[84]

Robots, another technological innovation, were invented in the United States. Although advanced research on **robotics** is still conducted here, Japanese organizations lead the world in the use of robotics. Organizations in the United States have fewer total robots than were added in 1989 alone in Japan.[85] Whereas Japanese workers are happy to let robots take over repetitive or dangerous work, American employees worry that they will be replaced by labor-saving robots.[86] The main reason for the reluctance of U.S. organizations to use robots is their slow payout. Robotics represents a big investment that does not pay off in the short term. Japanese managers are more willing to evaluate the effectiveness of robotics technology with a long-term horizon in view.

It is tempting to focus only on the positive side of technology, but a little realism is in order. Some firms that have been disappointed with costly technologies are electing to *de*-engineer: 42 percent of information technology projects are abandoned before completion, and half of all technology projects fail to meet managers' expectations. Pacific Gas and Electric (part of PG&E Corporation) spent tens of millions of dollars on a new IBM-based system. Then deregulation hit the utility industry, allowing customers to choose among utility companies. Keeping up with multiple suppliers and fast-changing prices was too much for the massive new system, and it was scrapped in favor of a new project using the old first-generation computer system that is being updated and gradually replaced. Because, as in this case, some innovations fail to live up to expectations, managers have to handle both revolutionary and evolutionary approaches to technological transitions.[87]

Telecommuting gives employees flexibility and helps companies reduce costs and increase productivity.

©iStockphoto.com/Mustafa Deliormanli

Alternative Work Arrangements

Technological advances have prompted the advent of alternative work arrangements, or the nontraditional work practices, settings, and locations that are now supplementing traditional workplaces. One alternative work arrangement is **telecommuting**, or electronically transmitting work from a home computer to the office. IBM was one of the first companies to experiment with the notion of installing computer terminals at employees' homes and having employees work at home. By telecommuting, employees gain flexibility, save the commute to work, and enjoy the comforts of being at home. Telecommuting also has disadvantages, however, including distractions and lack of opportunities to socialize with other workers. Despite these disadvantages, telecommuters still feel "plugged in" to the communication system at the office. Studies show that telecommuters often report higher satisfaction with office communication than do workers in traditional office environments.[88]

Telecommuting offers a number of advantages to both employers and employees, and an estimated 28 million Americans telecommute. Cost reductions are an obvious motivator for companies to encourage telecommuting. Since 1991, AT&T has gained $550 million in cash flow by eliminating office space and reducing overhead costs. Telecommuting also increases

expert system
A computer-based application that uses a representation of human expertise in a specialized field of knowledge to solve problems.

robotics
The use of robots in organizations.

telecommuting
Electronically transmitting work from a home computer to the office.

productivity by letting companies access workers with key skills regardless of their locations and gives them an advantage in hiring and keeping talented employees who find the flexibility of working at home very attractive. The environment also benefits from telecommuting, as less driving means cleaner air and reduces the contribution to global warming.[89]

Satellite offices comprise another alternative work arrangement. In a satellite office system, large facilities are broken into a network of smaller workplaces located near employees' homes. Satellites are often located in comparatively inexpensive cities and suburban areas. They usually have simpler furnishings than the more centrally located offices. Satellites can save a company as much as 50 percent in real estate costs and can attract employees who do not want to work in a large urban area, thus broadening the pool of potential employees.[90]

These alternative work arrangements signal a trend toward *virtual offices*, in which people work anytime, anywhere, and with anyone. The concept suggests work occurring where people are, rather than people coming to work. Information technologies make connectivity, collaboration, and communication easy. Critical voicemails and messages can be delivered to and from the central office, a client's office, the airport, the car, or home. Wireless Internet access and online meeting software such as WebEx allow employees to participate in meetings anywhere at any time.

Impact of Technology on Management

Technological innovation affects the very nature of the management job. Managers who once had to coax workers back to their desks from coffee breaks now find that they need to encourage workers mesmerized by new technology to take more frequent breaks.[91] Working with a computer can be stressful, both physically and psychologically. Long hours at computer terminals can cause eye strain, neck and back strain, and headaches. In addition, workers accustomed to the fast response time of the computer come to expect the same from their coworkers and scold coworkers when they fail to match the computer's speed and accuracy. New technology, combined with globalization and intensified business pressures, has created *extreme workers*, pushing up the ranks of workaholics.[92] These extreme workers pay a price in relationships, other dimensions of a full, rich life, and increased stress.

Computerized monitoring provides managers with a wealth of information about employee performance but holds great potential for misuse. In particular, the telecommunications, airline, and mail-order merchandise industries make wide use of systems that secretly monitor employees' interactions with customers. Employers praise such systems for improving customer service; workers, however, react to secret scrutiny with higher levels of depression, anxiety, and exhaustion. Bell Canada evaluated operators using a system that tabulated average working time with customers. Operators found the practice highly stressful and sabotaged the system by giving callers wrong directory-assistance numbers rather than taking the time to look up the correct ones. Bell Canada now uses average working-time scores for entire offices rather than for individuals.[93] If managed well, of course, technology can benefit the company. Google, with this in mind, gives its employees freedom to choose which technologies they use. While this strategy costs more, it leads to increased productivity.[94]

New technologies and rapid innovation place a premium on a manager's technical skills. Managers must

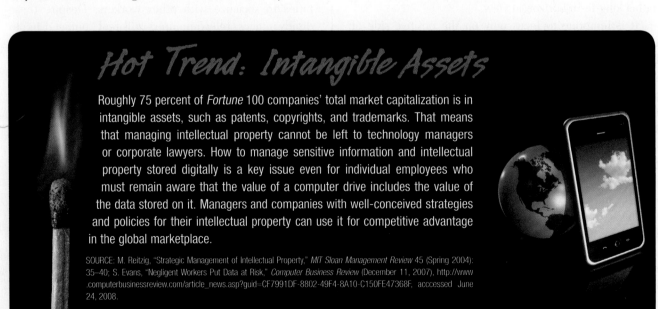

Hot Trend: Intangible Assets

Roughly 75 percent of *Fortune* 100 companies' total market capitalization is in intangible assets, such as patents, copyrights, and trademarks. That means that managing intellectual property cannot be left to technology managers or corporate lawyers. How to manage sensitive information and intellectual property stored digitally is a key issue even for individual employees who must remain aware that the value of a computer drive includes the value of the data stored on it. Managers and companies with well-conceived strategies and policies for their intellectual property can use it for competitive advantage in the global marketplace.

SOURCE: M. Reitzig, "Strategic Management of Intellectual Property," *MIT Sloan Management Review* 45 (Spring 2004): 35–40; S. Evans, "Negligent Workers Put Data at Risk," *Computer Business Review* (December 11, 2007), http://www.computerbusinessreview.com/article_news.asp?guid=CF7991DF-8802-49F4-8A10-C150FE47368F, acccessed June 24, 2008.

develop technical competence in order to gain workers' respect. Computer-integrated manufacturing systems, for example, require managers to use participative management styles, open communication, and greater technical expertise to be effective.[95] In a world of rapid technological innovation, managers must focus on helping workers manage the stress of their work. They must take advantage of the wealth of information available to motivate, coach, and counsel workers rather than to stringently control or police them.

Helping Employees Adjust to Technological Change

Most workers understand the benefits of modern technologies: innovation has improved working conditions and increased the availability of skilled jobs. Technology is also bringing disadvantaged individuals into the workforce. Microchips, for example, have dramatically increased opportunities for workers with visual impairments. Information can be decoded into speech using a speech synthesizer, into Braille using a hard-copy printer, or into enlarged print visible on a computer monitor.[96] Engineers at Carnegie Mellon University have developed PizzaBot, a robot that individuals with disabilities can operate using a voice-recognition system.

Despite these and other benefits of new technology in the workplace, however, employees may still resist change. Technological innovations change employees' work environments, generating stress. Also, many workers react negatively to change that they feel threatens their work situation. Often their fears center around loss—of freedom, of control, of the things they like about their jobs.[97] Consequently, they may fear diminished quality of work life along with increased pressure. Further, employees may fear being replaced by technology or being displaced into jobs of lower skill levels.

Managers can take several actions to help employees adjust to changing technology. Encouraging workers' participation in early phases of decisions regarding technological changes is important. Individuals who participate in planning for the implementation of new technology learn about the potential changes in their jobs and are less resistant to the changes. Workers' input in early stages can smooth the transition into new ways of performing work.

Managers should also keep in mind the effects that new technology has on the skill requirements of workers. Many employees support changes that increase the skill requirements of their jobs because increased skill requirements often lead to increased job autonomy, responsibility, and (potentially) pay. Whenever possible, managers should select technology that increases workers' skill requirements.

Providing effective training is essential. Training helps employees perceive that they control the technology rather than being controlled by it. The training should be designed to match workers' needs and should increase workers' sense of mastery of the new technology.

A related challenge is to encourage workers to invent new uses for existing technology. **Reinvention** is the creative application of new technology.[98] Individuals who explore the boundaries of a new technology can personalize the technology, adapt it to their own job needs, and share this information with others in their work groups.

Managers must lead organizations to adopt new technologies more humanely and effectively. Technological changes are essential for earnings growth and for expanded employment opportunities, and the adoption of new technologies is a critical determinant of U.S. competitiveness in the global marketplace.

reinvention

The creative application of new technology.

Log in to the **CourseMate** for *ORGB3* at **www.cengagebrain.com** to:

※ Review **Key Terms Flash Cards** online

※ Play **Beat the Clock** and **Quiz Bowl** to master concepts

※ Complete **web quizzes** to prepare for exams

※ Watch the video on **Theo Chocolate** and from *Lost in Translation* for examples, then test yourself with a quick quiz

※ Work through the **"What about You?"** and **Ethical Dilemma** exercises to see how you would handle various situations that organizations face on a daily basis

Personality, Perception, and Attribution

LEARNING OUTCOMES

1 Describe individual differences and explain why they are important in understanding organizational behavior.

2 Articulate key personality traits and explain how they influence behavior in organizations.

3 Discuss how personality theories may be applied in organizations.

4 Define *social perception* and explain the factors that affect it.

5 Identify five common barriers to social perception and explain the difficulties they cause.

6 Explain the attribution process and how attributions affect managerial behavior.

©Yagi Studio/Digital Vision/Jupiterimages

❝Individuals are unique in terms of their skills, abilities, personalities, perceptions, attitudes, emotions, and ethics.❞

Individual Differences and Organizational Behavior

Over the next two chapters, we'll explore the concept of **individual differences**. Individuals are unique in terms of their skills, abilities, personalities, perceptions, attitudes, emotions, and ethics. Hence, individual differences represent the essence of the challenge of management. Managers must often work with people who possess a multitude of varying characteristics, so the more managers understand individual differences, the better they can work with others.

The basis for understanding individual differences stems from Kurt Lewin's early contention that behavior is a function of the person and the environment.[1] He expressed this idea in an equation: $B = f(P, E)$, where B = behavior, P = person, and E = environment. Lewin's idea has been developed further by the **interactional psychology** approach.[2] Basically, this approach says that we must know something about the person and something about the situation in order to understand human behavior. There are four basic propositions of interactional psychology:

1. Behavior is a function of continuous, multidirectional interaction between the person and the situation.
2. The person is active in this process, both changing his or her situations and being changed by them.
3. People vary in many characteristics, including cognitive, affective, motivational, and ability factors.
4. Two aspects of a situation are important: the objective situation and the person's subjective view of the situation.[3]

individual differences
The way in which factors such as skills, abilities, personalities, perceptions, attitudes, values, and ethics differ from one individual to another.

interactional psychology
The psychological approach to understanding human behavior that involves knowing something about the person and about the situation.

After You Finish This Chapter Go to **Page 53** for **Study Tools**

37

FIGURE **3.1** Variables Influencing Individual Behavior

Personality and Organizations

©Cengage Learning 2013

The interactional psychology approach points out the need to study both persons and situations. The *person* consists of individual elements such as personality, perception, attribution, attitudes, emotions, and ethics. The *situation* consists of the environment the person operates in, including the organization, work group, personal life situation, job characteristics, and other environmental influences. The effect of personal and environmental differences on organizational behavior is shown visually in Figure 3.1. In this chapter, we'll address skills and abilities, personality, perception, and attribution. Chapter 4 will deal with attitudes, emotions, and ethics.

Skills and Abilities

Many skills and abilities influence work outcomes. Nearly 100 years ago, Charles Spearman introduced the concept of *general mental ability (GMA)* as a measure of an individual's innate cognitive intelligence.[4] GMA, which includes a person's skills and abilities, is the single best predictor of work performance across many occupations and across different cultures.[5]

What makes an individual behave consistently in a variety of situations? **Personality** is the relatively stable set of characteristics that influences an individual's behavior and lends it consistency. Although researchers debate what determines personality, we conclude that it has several origins. One determinant is heredity. Researchers have found that identical twins who were separated at birth and raised in very different situations nevertheless shared personality traits and job preferences. In fact, about half of the variations in traits such as extraversion, impulsiveness, and flexibility were shared by identical twins who grew up separately.[6] Thus, genes appear to influence personality.

Environment also determines personality, shaping it through family influences, cultural influences, educational influences, and other environmental factors. Two major theories of personality are the trait theory and the integrative approach. Each theory has influenced the study of personality in organizations.

Trait Theory

Some early personality researchers believed that we must break down behavior patterns into a series of observable traits in order to understand individuals. According to **trait theory**, the combination of these traits forms an individual's personality. Gordon Allport, a leading theorist, saw traits as broad, general guides that lend consistency to behavior.[7] Thousands of traits have been identified over the years. Raymond Cattell, another prominent theorist, identified sixteen traits that formed the basis for differences in individual behavior. He described traits in binary pairs such as self-assured/apprehensive, reserved/outgoing, and submissive/dominant.[8]

One popular personality classification involves the "Big Five." These traits (described in Table 3.1) include extraversion, agreeableness, conscientiousness, emotional stability, and openness to experience.[9] The Big Five are broad, global traits associated with behaviors at work. For example, from preliminary research, we know that introverted and conscientious employees are less likely to be absent from work.[10]

personality

A relatively stable set of characteristics that influence an individual's behavior.

trait theory

A personality theory that advocates breaking down behavior patterns into a series of observable traits in order to understand human behavior.

TABLE 3.1 The Big Five Personality Traits

Extraversion	The person is gregarious, assertive, and sociable (as opposed to reserved, timid, and quiet).
Agreeableness	The person is cooperative, warm, and agreeable (rather than cold, disagreeable, and antagonistic).
Conscientiousness	The person is hardworking, organized, and dependable (as opposed to lazy, disorganized, and unreliable).
Emotional stability	The person is calm, self-confident, and cool (as opposed to insecure, anxious, and depressed).
Openness to experience	The person is creative, curious, and cultured (rather than practical with narrow interests).

SOURCES: P. T. Costa and R. R. McCrae, *The NEO-PI Personality Inventory* (Odessa, Fla.: Psychological Assessment Resources, 1992); J. F. Salgado, "The Five Factor Model of Personality and Job Performance in the European Community," *Journal of Applied Psychology* 82 (1997): 30–43.

Individuals with high agreeableness tend to rate others more leniently on peer evaluations, while those with high conscientiousness tend to be tougher raters.[11] Extraverts tend to have higher salaries, receive more promotions, and be more satisfied with their careers.[12] Across many occupations, conscientious people are more motivated and perform better than others.[13]

But different patterns of the Big Five traits are related to high performance in different occupations and work situations. For customer service jobs, individuals high in emotional stability, agreeableness, and openness to experience perform best. Managers with emotional stability and extraversion are top performers.[14] Recent research results indicate that the minimum level of agreeableness and the mean levels of conscientiousness and openness to experience in a work team have a strong effect on overall team performance.[15] Studies have also shown that an extreme amount of any trait harms organizations. Interestingly, highly conscientious and emotionally stable individuals perform worse on the job than those with more moderate levels of both traits.[16] The reasons could be that very conscientious individuals may be overly rigid, inflexible, and compulsive, paying too much attention to small details at the expense of larger goals. Similarly, very high levels of emotional stability may result in extreme over-control of emotions, making a person less socially competent than those who have more moderate levels of this personality trait.

The Big Five framework is helpful for understanding cultural differences and has held up well when applied to Western cultures, particularly among Spanish and Mexican populations.[17] But it remains to be seen whether or not the Big Five traits will emerge in studies of non-Western cultures.[18] Personality traits are also relevant to *cultural intelligence*, which, in the workplace, means how we adapt to cultural differences.[19]

But the trait approach has many critics. Some theorists argue that simply identifying traits is not enough, because personality is dynamic and never completely stable. Further, early trait theorists tended to ignore the influence of situations.[20] The trait theory also tends to ignore process—that is, how we get from a trait to a particular outcome.

Hot Trend: Personality Matters

Does your personality affect life outcomes? In a recent comprehensive review of research on the Big Five personality model, researchers found that the answer seems to be a resounding yes. Extraverts, for example, are happier, more satisfied with romantic relationships, and less likely to be depressed. Agreeable individuals are less likely to have heart disease, and more likely to have a positive leadership style. Conscientious people are healthier, enjoy greater occupational success, and are less likely to engage in criminal or antisocial behaviors. Emotionally stable individuals experience greater job satisfaction, commitment, and occupational success. Those who are open to new experiences tend to choose occupations that involve creative and artistic skills, but they are also more likely to engage in substance abuse.

SOURCE: D. J. Ozer and V. Benet-Martínez, "Personality and the Prediction of Consequential Outcomes," *Annual Review of Psychology* 57 (2006): 401–421.

©iStockphoto.com/narvikk

©Stocktrek/Digital Vision/Getty Images

Integrative Approach

In response to the criticisms of trait theory, researchers have taken a broader, more **integrative approach** to the study of personality.[21] This integrative approach focuses on both personal dispositions and situational variables as combined predictors of behavior. *Dispositions* are the tendencies of an individual to respond to situations in consistent ways. They include emotions, cognitions, attitudes, expectations, and fantasies.[22] Influenced by both genes and experiences, dispositions can be modified.

A recent study of how personality affects status offers a good example of how an integrative approach can be applied to better understand organizations. The study looked at a variety of personality variables that affected not only the actual status held by an individual, but how that individual perceived his or her status as well as how the person's status was viewed by others. The most important variable was leadership identity, though the leader's self-perception was determined largely by emotional stability and agreeableness. Meanwhile, extraversion and conscientiousness most affected how the leader was perceived by others.[23]

Personality Characteristics in Organizations

Managers should learn as much as possible about personality in order to understand and better relate to their employees, which is why we devote much attention to the subject of personality in this text. While researchers have identified hundreds of personality characteristics, we have selected a few with particularly strong influences on individual behavior in organizations. *Core self-evaluation (CSE)* involves a broad set of personality traits that articulates an individual's concept of himself or herself.[24] CSE is concerned with people's locus of control, self-esteem, generalized self-efficacy, and emotional stability. It predicts both goal-directed behavior and performance, even in non–U.S. cultures (e.g., Japan).[25] All these aspects of CSE will be examined shortly. In addition to the traits associated with CSE, we will consider the personality traits of self-monitoring and positive/negative affect.

Can managers predict the behavior of their employees from their personalities? Not completely. Recall that the interactional

psychology model (Figure 3.1) requires both dispositional and situational variables to predict behavior. As we consider the following personality variables, then, keep in mind that they are only one piece of the personality puzzle.

When weighing the role of situation, it is important to understand that situations vary in strength. **Strong situations** overwhelm the effects of individual personalities. These situations are interpreted in the same way by different individuals, evoke agreement on the appropriate behavior in the situation, and provide cues to appropriate behavior. For example, at performance appraisal sessions, employees know to listen to their bosses and to contribute when asked to do so this is a strong situation.

Weak situations are open to many interpretations. They provide few cues to appropriate behavior and no obvious rewards for any particular behavior. Individual personalities thus have a greater influence in weak situations than in strong situations. An informal meeting without an agenda might be a weak situation. Because organizations present combinations of strong and weak situations, personality affects behavior more in some situations than in others.[26]

Following are explanations of the various aspects of personality involved in CSE plus the traits of self-monitoring and positive/negative affect. Locus of control, self-efficacy, self-esteem, and the effects of emotional stability together constitute the core self-evaluations. CSE is a strong predictor of both job satisfaction and job performance, next only to GMA.[27]

Locus of Control An individual's generalized belief about internal (self) versus external (situation or others) control is called **locus of control**. People who believe they control what happens to them have an internal locus of control, whereas people who believe that circumstances or other people control their fate have an external locus of control.[28] In an organization, people with an internal locus of control (called *internals*) often report higher job satisfaction, exhibit superior job performance, are more likely to assume managerial positions, and tend to prefer participative management styles more than those with an external locus of control (*externals*).[29]

Internals and externals have similar positive reactions to being promoted, including high job satisfaction, job involvement, and organizational commitment. However, internals remain happy long after the promotion, whereas externals' joy over the promotion is short-lived. This might occur because externals do not believe their own performance led to the promotion.[30]

Knowing about locus of control can prove valuable to managers. Because internals believe they control what happens to them, they will want to exercise control in their work environments. Internals don't react well to

integrative approach
The broad theory that describes personality as a composite of an individual's psychological processes.

strong situation
A situation that overwhelms the effects of individual personalities by providing strong cues for appropriate behavior.

locus of control
An individual's generalized belief about internal control (self-control) versus external control (control by the situation or by others).

close supervision, so managers should give them considerable voice in how work is performed. Externals, by contrast, may appreciate more structured work settings and prefer not to participate in decision making.

Self-Efficacy People's **general self-efficacy** is their overall view of themselves as being able to perform effectively in a wide variety of situations.[31] Employees with high general self-efficacy have more confidence in their job-related abilities and other personal resources (e.g., energy, influence over others, etc.) that help them function effectively on the job. People with low general self-efficacy often feel ineffective at work and may express doubts about performing new tasks well. Previous success or performance is one of the most important determinants of self-efficacy. People who trust their own efficacy tend to attempt difficult tasks, persist in overcoming obstacles, and experience less anxiety when faced with adversity.[32] Because they are confident in their capability to provide meaningful input, they value the opportunity to participate in decision making.[33] High self-efficacy has also been related to higher job satisfaction and performance.[34]

Another form of self-efficacy, called *task-specific self-efficacy*, describes a person's belief that she or he can perform a specific task. ("I believe I can do this sales presentation today.") In contrast, general self-efficacy is broader. ("I believe I can perform well in just about any part of the job.")

Self-Esteem **Self-esteem** is an individual's general feeling of self-worth. Individuals with high self-esteem have positive feelings about themselves, perceive themselves to have strengths as well as weaknesses, and believe their strengths are more important than their weaknesses.[35] Individuals with low self-esteem view themselves negatively. They are more strongly affected by what other people think of them, and they compliment individuals who give them positive feedback while cutting down people who give them negative feedback.[36]

Evaluations from others affect our self-esteem. You might be liked for who you are, or you might be liked for your achievements. Being liked for who you are is more stable, and people with self-esteem stemming from this type of reaction from other people are usually able to be less

Fast Fact

Individuals with high levels of CSE perform better on their jobs, are more successful in their careers, are more satisfied with their jobs and lives, report lower levels of stress and conflict, cope more effectively with setbacks, and better capitalize on advantages and opportunities.

SOURCE: T. A. Judge and C. Hurst, "How the Rich (and Happy) Get Richer (and Happier): Relationship of Core Self-Evaluations to Trajectories in Attaining Work Success," *Journal of Applied Psychology* 93 (2008): 849–863.

defensive and more honest with themselves. Being liked for your achievements is more unstable; self-esteem resulting from this type of reaction waxes and wanes depending on the magnitude of achievements.[37]

Self-esteem affects attitudes and behavior in organizations. People with high self-esteem perform better and are more satisfied with their jobs.[38] They tend to seek out higher-status jobs.[39] A work team made up of individuals with high self-esteem is more likely to succeed than a team with low or average self-esteem.[40]

High self-esteem, however, can be too much of a good thing. People with inflated self-esteem may brag inappropriately when they find themselves in stressful situations.[41] Very high self-esteem may also lead to overconfidence and relationship conflicts.[42] Such individuals may shift their social identities to protect themselves when they do not live up to some standard. For example, if Denise outperforms Teresa on a statistics exam, Teresa may convince herself that Denise is not really a good person to compare herself with because Denise is an engineering major and Teresa is a physical education major. Teresa's high self-esteem protects her

general self-efficacy
An individual's general belief that he or she is capable of meeting job demands in a wide variety of situations.

self-esteem
An individual's general feeling of self-worth.

from this unfavorable though, in truth, valid comparison,[43] which might otherwise prompt her to improve her knowledge of statistics.

Self-esteem may be strongly affected by situations. Success tends to raise self-esteem, whereas failure lowers it. Managers should thus encourage employees to raise their self-esteem by giving them appropriate challenges and opportunities for success.

Self-Monitoring

Self-monitoring—the extent to which people base their behavior on cues from other people and situations—has a huge impact on behavior in organizations.[44] High self-monitors pay attention to what is appropriate in particular situations and to the behavior of other people, and they behave accordingly. Low self-monitors, by contrast, pay less attention to situational cues and act from internal states instead. As a result, low self-monitors behave consistently across situations. High self-monitors, because their behavior varies with the situation, appear more unpredictable and less consistent but in practice are actually more effective at work because they respond appropriately to changes in the organizational situation. For example, one study of managers at a recruitment firm found that high self-monitors were more likely to offer emotional help to people dealing with work-related anxiety. Low self-monitors, on the other hand, were unlikely to offer such emotional support.[45]

According to our research, high self-monitors get promoted because they accomplish tasks by meeting the expectations of others and because they seek out central positions in social networks.[46] They are also more likely to use self-promotion to make others aware of their skills and accomplishments.[47] However, the high self-monitors' flexibility may not be suited for every job, and the tendency to move may not fit every organization.[48]

Because high self-monitors base their behavior on cues from others and from the situation, they demonstrate higher levels of managerial self-awareness. This means that, as managers, they assess their own workplace behavior accurately.[49] Managers who are high self-monitors are also good at reading their employees' needs and changing the way they interact with employees.[50]

We can further speculate that high self-monitors respond more readily to work group norms, organizational culture, and supervisory feedback than do low self-monitors, who adhere more to internal guidelines for behavior ("I am who I am"). In addition, high self-monitors may support the trend toward work teams because they can easily assume flexible roles.

Positive/Negative Affect

Individuals who focus on the positive aspects of themselves, other people, and the world in general are said to have **positive affect**.[51] In contrast, those who accentuate the negative in themselves, others, and the world are said to possess **negative affect** (also called *negative affectivity*).[52] Individuals with positive affect are more satisfied with their jobs.[53] They are also more likely to help others at work and engage in more organizational citizenship behaviors.[54] Employees with positive affect have fewer absentee days.[55] Positive affect has also been linked to more life satisfaction and better performance across a variety of life and work domains.[56] Individual affect influences the work group as well. Positive individual affect produces positive team affect, which promotes cooperation and reduces conflict.[57] In particular, leader affectivity influences the affectivity of his or her subordinates. Thus, positive affect is a definite asset in work settings. Managers can encourage it by allowing people to participate in decision making and by providing pleasant working conditions.

Proactive Personality

Proactive personalities identify opportunities and act on them; they show initiative, take action, and persevere until they effect change. People who are not proactive fail to identify, let alone seize, opportunities to effect change.[58] Proactivity has been positively related to job performance, career success, and job search success.[59] Additionally, leaders who identify themselves as proactive are viewed as more charismatic by their subordinates.[60]

LEARNING OUTCOME 3

Application of Personality Theory in Organizations

To apply personality theories in their organizations, managers first must measure the personalities of their organizations' members. Projective tests, behavioral measures, and self-report questionnaires can all be used to measure personality.

Common Personality Measurement Tools

During **projective tests**, individuals are shown a picture, abstract image, or photo and are asked to describe what they see or to tell a story about it. The rationale behind

---

self-monitoring
The extent to which people base their behavior on cues from other people and situations.

positive affect
An individual's tendency to accentuate the positive aspects of herself or himself, other people, and the world in general.

negative affect
An individual's tendency to accentuate the negative aspects of himself or herself, other people, and the world in general.

projective test
A personality test that elicits an individual's response to abstract stimuli.

projective tests is that each individual responds to the stimulus in a way that reflects his or her unique personality. The Rorschach ink blot test is commonly used to assess personality.[61] Like other projective tests, however, it has low reliability. The individual being assessed may look at the same picture and see different things at different times. In addition, the assessor might apply her or his own biases in interpreting the information about the individual's personality.

Behavioral measures of personality examine an individual's behavior in a controlled situation. We might assess a person's sociability, for example, by counting the number of times he or she approaches strangers at a party. The behavior is scored to produce an index of personality. Some potential problems with behavioral measures include the observer's ability to stay focused and the way the observer interprets the behavior. Additionally, some people behave differently when they know they are being observed.

The most common method of assessing personality is the **self-report questionnaire**. An individual responds to a series of questions, usually in an agree/disagree or true/false format. One of the more widely recognized questionnaires is the *Minnesota Multiphasic Personality Inventory (MMPI)*, a comprehensive test assessing a variety of traits that can help diagnose several neurotic or psychotic disorders. Another self-report questionnaire, the *NEO Personality Inventory*, measures the Big Five traits. Self-report questionnaires also suffer from potential biases. It is difficult to view your own personality objectively. People often answer the questionnaires in terms of how they want to be seen rather than as they really are.

Carl Jung and the Myers-Briggs Type Indicator® Instrument

Another approach to applying personality theory in organizations is the Jungian approach and its measurement tool, the *Myers-Briggs Type Indicator® (MBTI)*. This instrument was developed to measure ideas about individual differences advocated by the Swiss psychologist Carl Jung. Many organizations use the MBTI instru-

A Rohrshach ink blot, like the one shown here, is a commonly used projective test.

ment, and we will focus on it as an example of how some organizations use personality concepts to help employees appreciate diversity.

Jung built his work on the notion that people are fundamentally different, but also fundamentally alike. His classic treatise *Psychological Types* proposed that the population was made up of two basic types—Extraverted types and Introverted types.[62] He went on to identify two types of Perceiving (Sensing and Intuition) and two types of Judgment (Thinking and Feeling). Perceiving (how we gather information) and Judging (how we make decisions) represent the two universal basic mental functions.

Jung suggested that human similarities and differences could be understood by combining preferences. We prefer and choose one way of doing things over another. We are not exclusively one way or another; rather, we have a preference for Extraversion or Introversion, just as we have a preference for right-handedness or left-handedness. Jung's type theory argues that no preferences are better than others. Differences are to be understood, celebrated, and appreciated.

During the 1940s, the mother–daughter team of Katherine Briggs and Isabel Briggs Myers became fascinated with individual differences among people and with Jung's work. They developed the **Myers-Briggs Type Indicator® (MBTI) instrument** to put Jung's type theory into practical use. The MBTI instrument is used extensively in organizations as a basis for understanding individual differences. More than 2 million people complete the instrument per year in the United States, and it is frequently used by *Fortune* 500 companies.[63] The MBTI instrument has been used in career counseling, team

behavioral measures
Personality assessments that involve observing an individual's behavior in a controlled situation.

self-report questionnaire
A common personality assessment that involves an individual's responses to a series of questions.

Myers-Briggs Type Indicator® (MBTI) instrument
An instrument developed to measure Carl Jung's theory of individual differences.

building, conflict management, and understanding management styles.[64]

The Preferences There are four scale dichotomies in type theory: extraversion/introversion, sensing/intuition, thinking/feeling, and judging/perceiving. Table 3.2 shows these preferences. The combination of these preferences makes up an individual's psychological type.

Extraversion/Introversion The Extraversion/Introversion preference represents where you find energy. Jung's theory holds that the Extraversion/Introversion preference reflects the most important distinction among individuals. The Extraverted type (E) is energized by interaction with other people. The Introverted type (I) is energized by time alone. Extraverted types typically have a wide social network, whereas Introverted types have a more narrow range of relationships. As articulated by Jung, this preference has nothing to do with social skills. Many introverts have excellent social skills but prefer the internal world of ideas, thoughts, and concepts. Extraverts represent approximately 49 percent of the U.S. population, and introverts represent about 51 percent, indicating a fairly even split.[65] Our U.S. culture rewards and nurtures extraverts. In work settings, extraverts prefer variety and do not mind being interrupted by phone calls or visits. They communicate freely but, on the negative side, may say things that they regret later.

Introverts prefer to concentrate quietly and think things through privately. They are detail oriented and do not mind working on a project for a long time; but they dislike telephone interruptions and may have trouble recalling names and faces.

Sensing/Intuition The Sensing/Intuition preference represents perception or information-gathering. The Sensing type (S) pays attention to information gathered through the five senses and to what actually exists. The Intuitive type (N) pays attention to a "sixth sense" and to what could be rather than to what actually

Extraversion

Being energized by interaction with other people.

Introversion

Being energized by spending time alone.

Sensing

Gathering information through the five senses and focusing on what actually exists.

Intuition

Gathering information through a "sixth sense" and focusing on what could be.

Thinking

Making decisions in a logical, objective fashion.

Feeling

Making decisions in a personal, value-oriented way.

TABLE 3.2 Type Theory Preferences and Descriptions

EXTRAVERSION	INTROVERSION
Outgoing	Quiet
Publicly expressive	Reserved
Interacting	Concentrating
Speaks, then thinks	Thinks, then speaks
Gregarious	Reflective
SENSING	**INTUITION**
Practical	General
Specific	Abstract
Feet on the ground	Head in the clouds
Details	Possibilities
Concrete	Theoretical
THINKING	**FEELING**
Analytical	Subjective
Clarity	Harmony
Head	Heart
Justice	Mercy
Rules	Circumstance
JUDGING	**PERCEIVING**
Structured	Flexible
Time oriented	Open ended
Decisive	Exploring
Makes lists/uses them	Makes lists/loses them
Organized	Spontaneous

SOURCE: Modified and reproduced by special permission of the Publisher, CPP, Inc., Mountain View, CA 94043 from Introduction to Type®, Sixth Edition by Isabel Briggs Myers. Copyright 1998, 2011 by CPP, Inc. All rights reserved. Further reproduction is prohibited without the Publisher's written consent.

exists.[66] Approximately 70 percent of people in the United States are Sensing types.[67]

At work, Sensing types prefer specific answers to questions and can be frustrated by vague instructions. They like jobs yielding tangible results and would rather use established skills than learn new ones. Intuitive types like solving new problems and are impatient with routine details. They enjoy learning new skills more than actually using them. They tend to think about several things at once and may appear absentminded. They like figuring out how things work just for the fun of it.

Thinking/Feeling The Thinking/Feeling preference describes the way we prefer to make decisions. The Thinking preference (T) makes decisions in a logical, objective fashion, whereas the Feeling preference (F) makes decisions in a personal, value-oriented way. The general U.S. population is divided 40/60 on the Thinking/Feeling type preference respectively. But, interestingly, the majority of

CAN AN INTROVERT BE CEO?

A prevalent belief in the business world is that to be CEO, an individual must be outgoing, animated, and eager to network. Must a person be naturally extroverted to reach the upper echelon of a corporation? Bill Gates, Warren Buffett, and Steven Spielberg might say no. All three are introverts, as are 40 percent of all American CEOs. Another notable introvert is Brenda Barnes, CEO of Sara Lee. Formerly heading up Starwood Hotels and PepsiCo's North American operations, Barnes took a four-year sabbatical to spend time with her three children. She returned to the workforce as Sara Lee's COO, becoming CEO in 2005. Upon returning, Barnes felt compelled to demonstrate that individuals returning from time away still have much to offer corporate America. "There's a large pool of women who chose to leave the workforce," she says. "But it doesn't mean they lost their brains."

Since Barnes became CEO, Sara Lee Corp. initiated Returnships, a program designed to aid both male and female professionals in returning to the workforce after having been away for a number of years. In the program, applicants are granted flexible, paid internships of four to six months before they must commit to full-time positions. Barnes is further transforming Sara Lee by refocusing its product portfolio and attempting to move the values of the company's corporate culture toward integrity and teamwork.

One of Barnes's key leadership strengths is listening to her employees, a skill that introverts are particularly good at. Other skills that introverts bring to the CEO position include thinking carefully before speaking and the capacity for reflective, creative thought. Remember that the trait of introversion relates only to energy, not social skills. Introverts are refreshed and energized by time alone, which the position of CEO can often accommodate.

©John Gress/Reuters/Landov

SOURCES: A. Fisher, "Job Hunting for Introverts," *Fortune* (February 13, 2009) http://money.cnn.com/2009/02/11/news /economy/Introverts.fortune/; D. Winston, "A Woman CEO's View," *Forbes* (March 17, 2009) http://www.forbes.com/2009/03/17 /work-life-ceo-leadership-careers-imbalance .html?partner-whiteglove_google.

males are Thinking types, whereas the majority of females are Feeling types. It is the one preference in type theory that has a strong gender difference. Thinking types tend to analyze decisions, while Feeling types sympathize. Thinking types try to be impersonal, whereas Feeling types base their decisions on how the outcome will affect the people involved.

In work settings, Thinking types tend to show less emotion. They also tend to be less comfortable with others' emotional expressions and respond more readily to other people's thoughts. They tend to be firm minded and like putting things into a logical framework. Feeling types, by contrast, are comfortable with emotion in the workplace. They enjoy pleasing people and receiving frequent praise and encouragement.

Judging/Perceiving

The **Judging/Perceiving** dichotomy reflects one's orientation to the outer world. The Judging preference (J) loves closure. They prefer to lead planned, organized lives and like making decisions. On the other hand, Perceivers (P) prefer flexible and spontaneous lives and like to keep options open. Imagine two people, one with a preference for Judging and the other for Perceiving, going out for dinner. J asks P to choose a restaurant, and P suggests ten alternatives. J just wants to decide and get on with it, whereas P wants to explore all the options.

Judging types love getting things accomplished and delight in checking off completed tasks on their calendars. Perceiving types generally adopt a wait-and-see attitude, collecting new information instead of drawing conclusions. Perceiving types are curious and welcome new information. They may start many projects without finishing them.

The Sixteen Types

The preferences combine to form sixteen distinct types, as shown in Table 3.3 on pages 46 and 47. For example, the ESTJ type has Extraversion, Sensing, Thinking, and Judging preferences. ESTJs see the world as it is (S); make decisions objectively (T); and like structure, schedules, and order (J). Combining these qualities with their preference for interacting with others makes them ideal managers. ESTJs are dependable, practical, and able to get any job done. They are conscious of the chain of command and see work as a series of goals to be reached by following rules and regulations. They may have little tolerance for disorganization and have a high need for control. Research results from the *MBTI Atlas* show that most of the 7,463 managers studied were ESTJs.[68]

The MBTI instrument has been found to have good reliability and validity as a measurement instrument for identifying type.[69] There are no good or bad types; each has its own strengths and weaknesses. Type influences learning style, teaching style, and choice of occupation. A study of the MBTI types

Judging

Preferring closure and completion in making decisions.

Perceiving

Preferring to explore many alternatives with flexibility and spontaneity.

TABLE 3.3 Characteristics Frequently Associated with Each Type

	SENSING TYPES		INTUITIVE TYPES	
Introverted Types	**ISTJ** Quiet, serious, earn success by thoroughness and dependability. Practical, matter-of-fact, realistic, and responsible. Decides logically what should be done and works toward it steadily, regardless of distractions. Takes pleasure in making everything orderly and organized—work, home, and life. Values traditions and loyalty.	**ISFJ** Quiet, friendly, responsible, and conscientious. Committed and steady in meeting obligations. Thorough, painstaking, and accurate. Loyal, considerate, notices and remembers specifics about people who are important, concerned with how others feel. Strives to create an orderly and harmonious environment at work and at home.	**INFJ** Seeks meaning and connection in ideas, relationships, and material possessions. Wants to understand what motivates people and is insightful about others. Conscientious and committed to firm values. Develops a clear vision about how best to serve the common good. Organized and decisive in implementing his or her vision.	**INTJ** Has an original mind and great drive for implementing ideas and achieving goals. Quickly sees patterns in external events and develops long-range explanatory perspectives. When committed, organizes a job and carries it through. Skeptical and independent, has high standards of competence and performance for self and others.
	ISTP Tolerant and flexible, quiet observer until a problem appears, then acts quickly to find workable solutions. Analyzes what makes things work and readily gets through large amounts of data to isolate the core of practical problems. Interested in cause and effect, organizes facts using logical principles, values efficiency.	**ISFP** Quiet, friendly, sensitive, and kind. Enjoys the present moment, and the immediate environment. Likes to have his or her own space and to work within a selected time frame. Loyal and committed to personal values and to people who are important to him or her. Dislikes disagreements and conflicts, does not force opinions or values on others.	**INFP** Idealistic, loyal to values and to people who are important to him or her. Wants an external life that is congruent with values. Curious, quick to see possibilities, can be a catalyst for implementing ideas. Seeks to understand people and to help them fulfill their potential. Adaptable, flexible, and accepting unless a value is threatened.	**INTP** Seeks to develop logical explanations for everything that interests him or her. Theoretical and abstract, interested more in ideas than in social interaction. Quiet, contained, flexible, and adaptable. Has unusual ability to focus in depth to solve problems in area of interest. Skeptical, sometimes critical, always analytical.

of engineering students at Georgia Tech determined that STs and NTs were more attracted to engineering. Es and Fs were more likely to withdraw from engineering courses.[70] Type can also determine an individual's decision-making and management styles.

How Companies Use MBTI Recent studies have focused on the relationship between type and specific managerial behaviors. The Introverted type (I) and the Feeling type (F), for example, appear to be more effective at participative management than their counterparts, the Extraverted type and the Thinking type.[71] Companies such as AT&T, ExxonMobil, and Honeywell use the MBTI instrument in their management development programs to help employees understand the different viewpoints of others in the organization. The MBTI instrument can also be used for team building, and resources are available to help managers learn how to do so effectively.[72] Hewlett-Packard and Armstrong World Industries use the MBTI instrument to show teams that diversity and differences lead to successful performance.

social perception

The process of interpreting information about another person.

Managers value type theory for its simplicity and accuracy. But information from the MBTI instrument can be misused in organizational settings.[73] Some inappropriate uses include labeling one's coworkers, claiming results as a convenient excuse that one simply can't work with a particular coworker, and avoiding responsibility for learning to work flexibly with others. Although personality type is not an excuse for inappropriate behavior, if used well, type theory helps managers develop interpersonal skills. It also helps in building teams that capitalize on individuals' strengths and foster appreciation of individual team members' differences.

LEARNING OUTCOME **4**

Social Perception

Perception is another psychological process that creates individual differences. As the primary vehicle through which we come to understand ourselves and our world, perception adds meaning to information gathered via the five senses of touch, smell, hearing, vision, and taste. Virtually all management activities rely on perception. Here, we focus specifically on **social perception**, or

TABLE 3.3 Concluded

SENSING TYPES		INTUITIVE TYPES	
ESTP	**ESFP**	**ENFP**	**ENTP**
Flexible and tolerant, takes a pragmatic approach focused on immediate results. Finds theories and conceptual explanations boring. Wants to act energetically to solve the problem. Focuses on the here and now, spontaneous, enjoys each moment that he or she can be active with others. Enjoys material comforts and style. Learns best through doing.	Outgoing, friendly, and accepting. Exuberant lover of life, people, and material comforts. Enjoys working with others to make things happen. Brings common sense and a realistic approach to his or her work and makes work fun. Flexible and spontaneous, adapts readily to new people and environments. Learns best by trying a new skill with other people.	Warmly enthusiastic and imaginative. Sees life as full of possibilities. Makes connections between events and information very quickly, and confidently proceeds based on the patterns he or she sees. Wants a lot of affirmation from others, and readily gives appreciation and support. Spontaneous and flexible, often relies on his or her ability to improvise and verbal fluency.	Quick, ingenious, stimulating alert, and outspoken. Resourceful in solving new and challenging problems. Adept at generating conceptual possibilities and then analyzing them strategically. Good at reading other people. Bored by routine, will seldom do the same thing the same way, apt to turn to one new interest after another.
ESTJ	**ESFJ**	**ENFJ**	**ENTJ**
Practical, realistic, matter-of-fact. Decisive, quickly moves to implement decisions. Organizes projects and people to get things done, focuses on getting results in the most efficient way possible. Takes care of routine details. Has a clear set of logical standards, systematically follows them and wants others to do so also. Forceful in implementing plans.	Warmhearted, conscientious, and cooperative. Wants harmony in the environment, works with determination to establish it. Likes to work with others to complete tasks accurately and on time. Loyal, follows through even in small matters. Notices what others need in their day-to-day lives and tries to provide it. Wants to be appreciated for who he or she is and for his or her contribution.	Warm, empathetic, responsive, and responsible. Highly attuned to the emotions, needs, and motivations of others. Finds potential in everyone, wants to help others fulfill their potential. May act as a catalyst for individual and group growth. Loyal, responsive to praise and criticism. Sociable, facilitates others in a group, and provides inspiring leadership.	Frank, decisive, assumes leadership readily. Quickly sees logical and inefficient procedures and policies, develops and implements comprehensive systems to solve organizational problems. Enjoys long-term planning and goal setting. Usually well informed, well read, enjoys expanding knowledge and passing it on to others. Forceful in presenting ideas.

Extraverted Types

NOTE: I = Introversion; E = Extraversion; S = Sensing; N = Intuition; T = Thinking; F = Feeling; J = Judging; and P = Perceiving.

the process of interpreting information about another person.

The *selection interview* highlights the importance of perception. The consequences of a bad match between an individual and the organization are devastating for both parties, so accurate data must be gathered. First interviews are typically brief, and the candidate is usually one of many seen by an interviewer during a day. The interviewer often makes an accept or reject decision in the first four to five minutes based on her or his perception of the candidate.[74]

Another aspect of the importance of perception was shown by a study that found increased conflict related to perceptions of dissimilarity in values between CEOs and top management teams. Even if, in reality, there was no difference in values, the mere perception of differences increased conflict. This study highlights the importance of managers paying attention to how their employees perceive organizational decisions, since their perceptions will influence their behavior.[75]

Perception is often culturally determined. Based on our cultural backgrounds, we tend to perceive things in certain ways. Read the following sentence:

Finished files are the result of years of scientific study combined with the experience of years. Now quickly count the number of *Fs* in the sentence. Individuals who speak English as a second language see all six *Fs*. Most native English speakers report that there are three *Fs* because they are culturally conditioned to ignore unimportant words like *of*.[76] Culture can affect our interpretation of the data we gather as well as the meaning we add to it. In other words, our culture can affect our social perception. Valuing diversity, including cultural diversity, has been

> **Your individual social perception determines the way that you see your peers.**

recognized as a key to international competitiveness, so managers need good social perception skills.[77]

Three major categories of factors influence our perception of others: characteristics of ourselves as perceivers, characteristics of the target person we are perceiving, and characteristics of the situation in which the interaction takes place. Figure 3.2 models social perception.

Characteristics of the Perceiver

Several characteristics of the perceiver can affect social perception. One such characteristic is *familiarity* with the target (the person being perceived). When we are familiar with someone, we have multiple observations on which to base our impressions. Familiarity does not always mean accuracy, however. Sometimes, when we know a person well, we tend to screen out information that is inconsistent with our beliefs about that person. This is a particular danger in performance appraisals.

The perceiver's *attitudes* also affect social perception. Suppose you are interviewing candidates for a very important position in your organization—a position that requires negotiating contracts with suppliers, most of whom are male. You may feel that women are not capable of holding their own in tough negotiations. This attitude will doubtlessly affect your perceptions of the female candidates you interview. Male bosses' attitudes about women of color—for example, that they are not open to feedback or avoid challenges—can create misperceptions that limit job performance and opportunities in the workplace. The effects of such attitudes can, however, be mitigated, and stronger relationships can be built by creating forums for open discussion of social perception.[78]

Mood can have a strong influence on the way we perceive someone.[79] We think differently when we are happy than we do when we are depressed. We also remember information that matches our mood state better than information that is inconsistent with it. When in a positive mood, we form more positive impressions of others. When in a negative mood, we tend to evaluate others unfavorably.

Another factor that can affect social perception is the perceiver's *self-concept*. An individual with a positive self-concept tends to notice positive attributes in another person. In contrast, a negative self-concept can lead a perceiver to pick out negative traits in another person. The better we understand ourselves, the more accurate our perceptions of others.

Cognitive structure, an individual's pattern of thinking, also affects social perception. Some people tend to perceive physical traits such as height, weight, and appearance more readily. Others focus on central traits, or personality dispositions. Cognitive complexity allows a person to perceive multiple characteristics of another person rather than attending to just a few traits.

Characteristics of the Target

Characteristics of the target (the person being perceived) influence social perception in various ways. *Physical appearance* plays a big role in our perception of others. The perceiver will notice physical features such as height, weight, estimated age, race, and gender. Clothing says a great deal about a person. Blue pinstriped suits, for example, suggest banking or Wall Street. Perceivers tend to notice physical appearance characteristics that contrast with the norm, that are intense, or that are new or unusual.[80] A loud person, one who dresses outlandishly, a very tall person, or a hyperactive child will be noticed because he or she contrasts with what is commonly encountered. Novel individuals such as newcomers or minorities also attract attention.

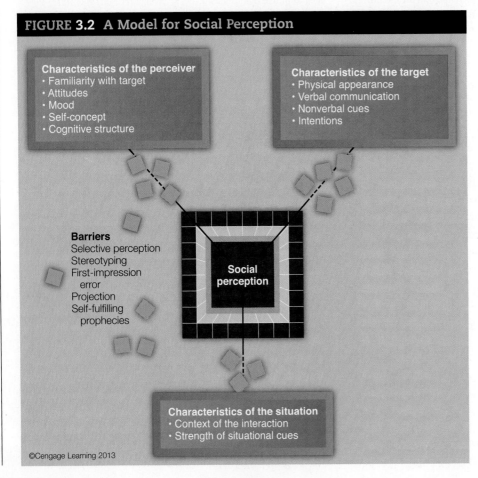

FIGURE 3.2 A Model for Social Perception

Characteristics of the perceiver
- Familiarity with target
- Attitudes
- Mood
- Self-concept
- Cognitive structure

Characteristics of the target
- Physical appearance
- Verbal communication
- Nonverbal cues
- Intentions

Barriers
Selective perception
Stereotyping
First-impression error
Projection
Self-fulfilling prophecies

Social perception

Characteristics of the situation
- Context of the interaction
- Strength of situational cues

©Cengage Learning 2013

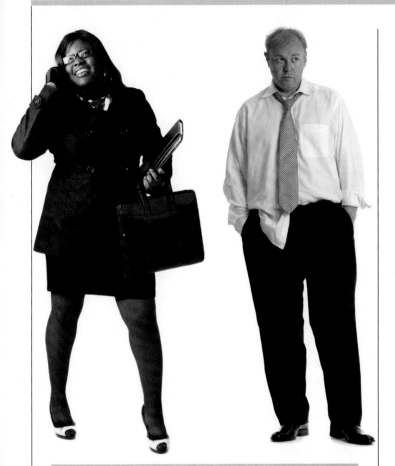

The way you dress influences how people perceive you.

Physical attractiveness often colors our entire impression of another person. Interviewers rate attractive candidates more favorably and award them higher starting salaries.[81] But people who are perceived as physically attractive face some nonbeneficial stereotypes as well.

Verbal communication from a target affects our perception of him or her. We listen to the topics discussed and his or her tone of voice and accent, and we make judgments based on this input.

Nonverbal communication conveys a great deal of information about the target. Eye contact, facial expressions, body movements, and posture all are deciphered by the perceiver in an attempt to form an impression of the target. Awareness of cultural differences is particularly important when it comes to nonverbal communication, as some nonverbal signals mean very different things in different cultures. The "okay" sign in the United States (forming a circle with the thumb and forefinger) is an insult in South America. Facial expressions, however, seem to have universal meanings. Individuals from different cultures can recognize and decipher expressions the same way.[82]

The *intentions* of the target are inferred by the perceiver who observes the target's behavior. We may see our boss appear in our office doorway and think, "Oh no! She's going to give me more work to do." Or we may perceive that her intention is to congratulate us on a recent success. In any case, the perceiver's interpretation of the target's intentions affects the way the perceiver views the target.

Characteristics of the Situation

The situation in which the interaction between the perceiver and the target takes place, the *social context*, also influences perception. Meeting your professor in his or her office affects your impression differently than meeting your professor in a local restaurant would. Social context is very important in Japan. Business conversations after working hours or at lunch are taboo. If you try to talk business during these times, you may be perceived as rude.[83]

The *strength of situational cues* also affects social perception. As we discussed earlier in the chapter, some situations provide strong cues about appropriate behavior. In these situations, we assume that the individual's behavior can be accounted for by the situation and may not reflect the individual's disposition. This is the **discounting principle** in social perception.[84] For example, you may encounter an automobile salesperson who has a warm and personable manner, asks about your work and hobbies, and seems genuinely interested in your taste in cars. Yet, you probably cannot assume that this behavior reflects the salesperson's personality because of the influence of the situation. This person is trying to sell you a car and probably treats all customers in this manner.

Barriers to Social Perception

It would be wonderful if all of us had accurate social perception skills. Unfortunately, barriers often prevent us from perceiving others accurately. Five barriers to social perception are selective perception, stereotyping, first-impression error, projection, and self-fulfilling prophecies.

Selective perception is our tendency to prefer information that supports our viewpoints. Individuals often ignore information that threatens their viewpoints. Suppose, for example, that a sales manager is evaluating the performance of his employees. One employee does not get along well with colleagues and rarely

discounting principle
The assumption that an individual's behavior is accounted for by the situation.

selective perception
The tendency to select information that supports our individual viewpoints while discounting information that threatens our viewpoints.

[Fighting Selective Perception]

When Dave Sokol took over as the CEO of NetJets, a company that operates partial ownership and rental of private jets, he found a disaster—$1.9 billion in debt, $711 million lost the previous year, and a hangar full of unsold planes. He decided to take immediate action to revive the company, selling old planes (even at a loss), canceling orders for new ones, and laying off employees. He even cut costs by canceling the company's annual poker tournament in Las Vegas and no longer allowing free flights for celebrities. All of these moves were met with severe resistance from senior managers who were used to an organization that was entrepreneurial in spirit and focused on short-term success rather than long-term planning. They were not used to having to think about the company's services and costs or the long-term impact of inflation, fuel prices, inventory, or changing markets.

SOURCE: B. Dumaine, "Buffett's Mr. Fix-It," *Fortune* (August 16, 2010); 78–86; M. M. Rose, "NetJets Returns to Profit in the First Quarter," *The Columbus Dispatch* (April 22, 2010) http://www.dispatch.com/live/content/business/stories/2010/04/22/netjets-returns-to-profit-in-first-quarter.html, accessed August 22, 2010.

completes sales reports on time. This employee, however, generates the most new sales contracts in the office. The sales manager may ignore the negative information, choosing to evaluate the salesperson only on contracts generated. The manager is exercising selective perception.

A **stereotype** is a generalization about a group of people. Stereotypes reduce information about other people to a workable level so that it can be compiled efficiently. Stereotypes become even stronger when they are shared with and validated by others.[85] Some stereotypes are accurate and serve as useful perceptual guidelines, but, of course, many are inaccurate and do much harm, generating false impressions that may never be tested or changed.

In multicultural work teams, members often form impressions of foreign coworkers based on stereotypes before getting to know them as individuals. Asians, for example, are sometimes pushed toward career choices that fit with a stereotype that Asians excel at math and science, setting aside what a particular individual's strengths and talents may actually be. Stereotypes such as these can compromise the productivity of the work team, lower morale, and result in limited opportunities for individuals. The more accurate information employees have about their coworkers and their backgrounds, however, the less likely stereotypes are to play a role in how individuals are perceived both in terms of group dynamics and individual advancement.[86]

Attractiveness is a powerful stereotype. We assume that attractive individuals are also warm, kind, sensitive, poised, sociable, outgoing, independent, and strong. However, a study of romantic relationships showed that most attractive individuals do not fit the stereotype apart from possessing good social skills and being popular.[87] Some individuals may seem to us to fit the stereotype of attractiveness because our behavior elicits from them behavior that confirms the stereotype. Consider, for example, a situation in which you meet an attractive fellow student. Chances are that you respond positively to this person because you assume she or he is warm, sociable, and so on. Even though the person may not possess these traits, your positive response may bring out these behaviors in the person. Thus, your interaction may be channeled to confirm the stereotype.[88]

Stereotyping pervades work life. When an individual's behavior contrasts with a stereotype of his or her group, he or she is treated more positively (given more favorable comments or pats on the back). For example, a female softball player might receive more applause for a home run hit than a male teammate because some people may stereotype women as less athletic than men and hold female players to a lower standard. Either way, the contrast is still part of stereotyping.[89]

First impressions are lasting impressions, so the saying goes. We tend to remember what we perceive first about a person, and sometimes we are quite reluctant to change our initial impressions.[90] **First-impression error**, also known as *primacy effect*, occurs when we observe a very brief bit of a person's behavior in our first encounter and infer that this behavior reflects what the person is really like. Such primacy effects can be particularly dangerous in interviews, given that we form first impressions quickly and that these impressions may be the basis for long-term employment relationships.

What factors do interviewers rely on when forming first impressions? Perceptions of the candidate, such as whether they like the person, whether they trust the person, and whether or not the person seems credible, all influence the interviewer's decision. Something as seemingly unimportant as the pitch of your voice can leave a lasting impression.

Speakers with lower vocal pitch are believed to be more competent, more dominant, and more assertive than those with higher voices. Men whose voices are high enough that they sound feminine are judged the least favorably of all by interviewers. This finding is ironic, given that research has found that students with higher vocal pitch tend to earn better grades.[91]

stereotype

A generalization about a group of people.

first-impression error

Forming lasting opinions about an individual based on initial perceptions.

Projection, also known as the *false-consensus effect*, causes inaccurate perceptions of others. When we project, we assume that our own beliefs and values are commonly held and normative and overestimate the number of others who share them. People who are different are viewed as unusual and even deviant. Projection occurs most often when you surround yourself with others similar to you. You may overlook important information about others when you assume we are all alike and in agreement.[92]

Self-fulfilling prophecies, also called the *Pygmalion effect*, interfere with social perception in that our expectations affect the way we interact with others such that we provoke the very response we expect. Early studies of self-fulfilling prophecy were conducted in elementary school classrooms. Teachers were given bogus information that some of their pupils had high intellectual potential. These pupils were chosen randomly; there were really no differences among the students. Eight months later, the "gifted" pupils scored significantly higher on an IQ test. The teachers' expectations elicited growth from these students because they had given them tougher assignments and more feedback on their performance.[93]

A manager's expectations of an individual affect both the manager's behavior toward the individual and the individual's response. For example, suppose your initial impression is that an employee has the potential to move up within the organization. Chances are you will spend a great deal of time coaching and counseling the employee, providing challenging assignments, and grooming the individual for success. Managers can harness the power of the Pygmalion effect to improve productivity in the organization simply by expecting positive results from a group of employees.[94]

Impression Management

Most people want to make favorable impressions on others. This is particularly true in organizations where individuals compete for jobs, favorable performance evaluations, and salary increases. The process by which individuals try to control the impressions others have of them is called **impression management**. Individuals use several techniques to control others' impressions of them.[95]

Some impression management techniques are *self-enhancing*. Name-dropping, or mentioning an association with important people in the hope of improving one's image, is often used. Controlling one's appearance is another self-enhancing technique for impression management. Individuals dress carefully for interviews because they want to "look the part" in order to get the job. Self-descriptions, or statements about one's characteristics, are used to manage impressions as well.

Another group of impression management techniques are *other-enhancing*. They focus on the individual on whom one is trying to make an impression rather than on oneself. People often use flattery and favors to win approval. Agreeing with someone's opinion can create a positive impression. People with disabilities, for example, often use other-enhancing techniques. They may feel that they must take it upon themselves to make others comfortable interacting with them. Impression management techniques help them prevent potential avoidance by others.[96]

Research results indicate that job candidates who engage in impression management by self-promoting performed better in interviews, were more likely to obtain site visits with potential employers, and were more likely to be hired.[97] In addition, employees who engage in impression management are rated more favorably in performance appraisals than those who do not.[98]

©Marcin Balcerzak/Shutterstock.com

projection
Overestimating the number of people who share our own beliefs, values, and behaviors.

self-fulfilling prophecy
Allowing expectations about people to affect our interaction with them in such a way that those expectations are fulfilled.

impression management
The process by which individuals try to control the impressions others have of them.

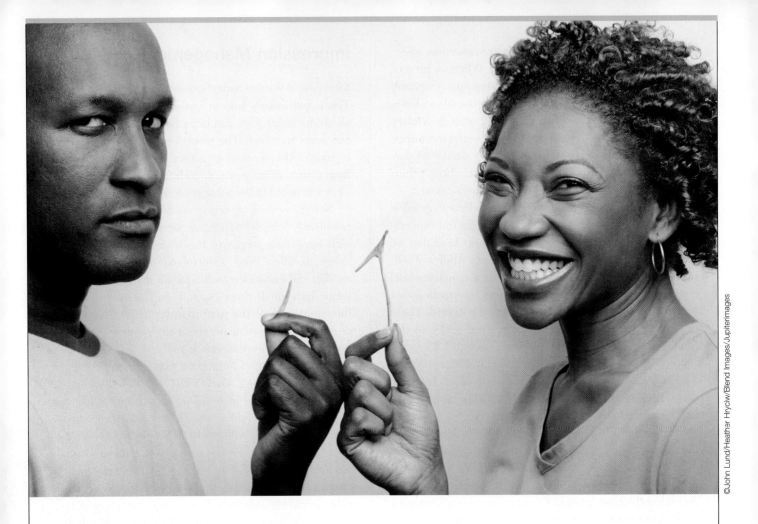

So impression management does seem to influence others' impressions. As long as the impressions conveyed are accurate, this process benefits organizations. If the impressions are found to be false, however, the result is a strongly negative overall impression. Furthermore, excessive impression management can lead to the perception that the user is manipulative or insincere.[99]

LEARNING OUTCOME 6

Attribution in Organizations

Human beings are innately curious. We want to know *why* people behave the way they do. We also seek to understand and explain our own behavior. **Attribution theory** explains how we pinpoint the causes of our own behavior (and therefore our performance) and that of other people.[100]

Internal and External Attributions

We can attribute events to an internal source of responsibility (something

attribution theory
A theory that explains how individuals pinpoint the causes of their own and others' behavior.

Luck or skill?

within the individual's control) or an external source (something outside the individual's control). Suppose you perform well on an exam. You might say you aced the test because you are smart or because you studied hard; this internal attribution credits your ability or effort. Alternatively, you might make an external attribution for your performance by saying it was an easy test or that you had good luck.

Attribution patterns differ among individuals.[101] Achievement-oriented individuals attribute their success to ability and their failures to lack of effort—both internal causes. Failure-oriented individuals attribute their failures to lack of ability and may develop feelings of incompetence (or even depression) as a result.[102] Women managers are less likely to attribute their success to their own ability. This may be because they are adhering to social norms that compel women to be modest or because they believe that success has more do to with hard work than ability.[103]

Attribution theory has many applications in the workplace. The way you explain your own behavior affects your motivation. If you believe careful preparation and rehearsal led to your successful presentation, you're likely to take credit for the performance and to have a sense of self-efficacy about future presentations. If, however, you believe that you were just lucky, you may not be motivated to repeat the performance because you believe you had little influence on the outcome.

Lots of attributions are made during employment interviews when candidates are asked to explain the causes of previous performance. Candidates want to give interviewers reasons to hire them ("I work well with people, so I'm looking for a managerial job"). Research shows that successful candidates make different attributions for negative outcome than unsuccessful ones. Successful candidates are willing to make internal attributions for negative events. Unsuccessful candidates blame negative outcomes on things beyond their control, giving interviewers the impression that they failed to learn from the event and that they will likely blame others when something goes wrong in the workplace.[104]

Attributional Biases

The attribution process may be affected by two very common problems: The first is the tendency to make attributions to internal causes when focusing on someone else's behavior, known as the **fundamental attribution error**.[105] The other error, **self-serving bias**, occurs when focusing on one's own behavior. Individuals tend to make internal attributions for their own successes and external attributions for their own failures.[106] In other words, when we succeed, we take credit for it; when we fail, we blame the situation on other people.

Both biases were illustrated in a study of healthcare managers asked to cite the causes of their employees' poor performance.[107] The managers claimed that internal causes (their employees' lack of effort or lack of ability) explained their employees' poor performance. When the employees were asked to pinpoint the cause of their own performance problems, they blamed a lack of support from the managers (an external cause), which illustrates self-serving bias.

There are cultural differences in these two attri-

bution errors. In fatalistic cultures, such as India, people tend to believe that fate is responsible for much that happens. People in such cultures tend to emphasize external causes of behavior.[108] In China, people are taught that hard work is the route to accomplishment. When faced with either a success or a failure, Chinese individuals first reflect on whether they tried hard enough or whether their attitude was correct. Thus, in analyzing a cause, they first look to their own effort.[109]

The way individuals interpret the events around them has a strong influence on their behavior. People in general try to understand the causes of behavior so they can predict and control future behavior, and managers certainly do this. Hence, they use attributions in all aspects of their jobs. Especially in evaluating performance and rewarding employees, managers must determine the causes of behavior and a perceived source of responsibility.

Attribution theory explains how performance evaluation judgments can lead to differential rewards. A supervisor attributing an employee's good performance to internal causes such as effort or ability may give a larger raise than a supervisor attributing the good performance to external causes like help from others or good training. Managers are often called on to explain their own actions as well, and in doing so they make attributions about the causes of their own behavior. We continue our discussion of attributions in Chapter 6.

fundamental attribution error
The tendency to make attributions to internal causes when focusing on someone else's behavior.

self-serving bias
The tendency to attribute one's successes to internal causes and one's failures to external causes.

Log in to the **CourseMate** for *ORGB3* at **www.cengagebrain.com** to:

✳ Review the **Key Terms Flash Cards** online

✳ Play **Beat the Clock** and **Quiz Bowl** to master concepts

✳ Complete **web quizzes** to prepare for exams

✳ Watch the video on **Theo Chocolate** and from *Because I Said So* for examples, then test yourself with a quick quiz

✳ Work through the **"What about You?"** and **Ethical Dilemma** exercises to see how you would handle various situations that organizations face on a daily basis

Attitudes, Emotions, and Ethics

LEARNING OUTCOMES

1 Explain the ABC model of an attitude.

2 Describe how attitudes are formed.

3 Identify sources of job satisfaction and commitment.

4 Distinguish between organizational citizenship and workplace deviance behaviors.

5 Identify the characteristics of the source, target, and message that affect persuasion.

6 Discuss the definition and importance of emotions at work.

7 Contrast the effects of individual and organizational influences on ethical behavior.

8 Identify the factors that affect ethical behavior.

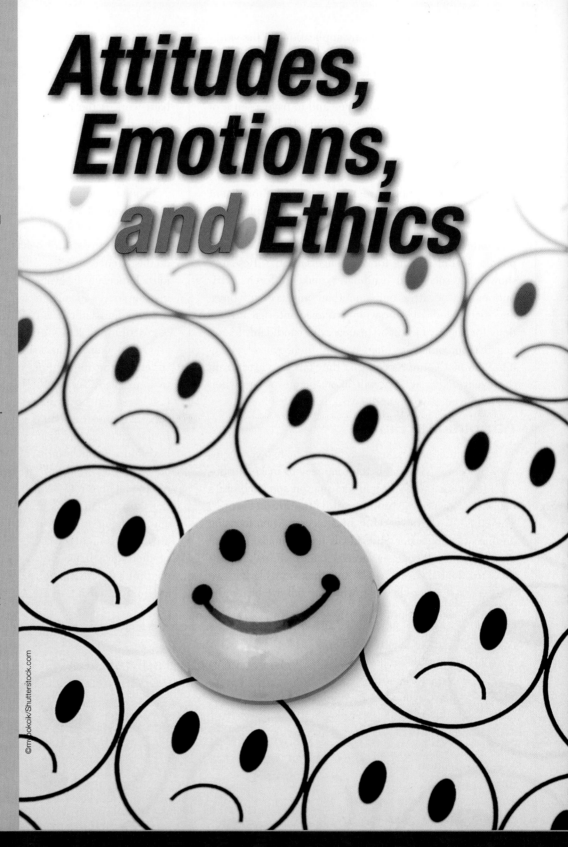

©mmbokcik/Shutterstock.com

"We may be supportive, passive, or hostile, depending on our attitude."

After You Finish
This Chapter
Go to **Page 72**
for **Study Tools**

Attitudes

An **attitude** is a psychological tendency expressed when we evaluate a particular entity with some degree of favor or disfavor.[1] Since we respond favorably or unfavorably toward many things such as coworkers, our own appearance, or politics, we have attitudes toward many things. Attitudes are closely linked to behavior in general, so they are an important factor in organizational behavior. Managers complain about workers with "bad attitudes" and conduct "attitude adjustment" talks. Poor performance attributed to "bad attitude" can often stem from lack of motivation, minimal feedback, lack of trust in management, or other problems. On the positive side, recognition and praise from colleagues and supervisors can positively impact an individual's attitudes and job performance.[2]

Thus, managers should understand the antecedents to attitudes as well as their consequences. They also need to understand the different components of attitudes, how attitudes are formed, the major attitudes that affect work behavior, and how to use persuasion to change attitudes.

The ABC Model

An individual does not have an attitude until he or she responds to an entity (person, object, situation, or issue) on an affective, behavioral, or cognitive basis. We can break attitudes down into three components, as depicted in Table 4.1 on the next page. These three components compose what we call the *ABC model* of an attitude.[3]

Affect is the emotional component of an attitude. It refers to an individual's feeling about something or someone. Statements such as "I like this" or "I prefer that" reflect the affective component of an attitude. Affect can be measured by self-report questionnaires as well as physiological indicators such

attitude

A psychological tendency expressed by evaluating something with a degree of favor or disfavor.

affect

The emotional component of an attitude.

as blood pressure, which show emotional changes by measuring physiological arousal.

The second component is *behavioral intent* toward an object or person. Here, it is important to note that a behavioral intent may not actually lead to a particular behavior. But often it does. Our attitudes toward women in management, for example, may be inferred from observing the way we treat a female supervisor. We may be supportive, passive, or hostile, depending on our attitude. The behavioral component of an attitude is measured by observing behavior or by asking a person about behavior or intentions.

The third component of an attitude, *cognition* (thought), reflects a person's perceptions or beliefs. Cognitive elements are evaluative beliefs measured by attitude scales or by asking about thoughts. The statement "I believe Japanese workers are industrious" reflects the cognitive component of an attitude.

The ABC model shows that we must assess all three components to understand an attitude. Suppose, for example, you want to evaluate your employees' attitudes toward *flextime* (flexible work scheduling). You would want to determine how they feel about the policy (affect), whether they would participate in it (behavioral intention), and what they think about it (cognition). The most common method of attitude measurement, however, is the attitude scale, which measures only the cognitive component.

Cognitive Dissonance

As rational beings, people prefer consistency (consonance) between their attitudes and behavior. Anything that disrupts this consistency causes tension (dissonance), which motivates individuals to change either their attitudes or their behavior to maintain consistency. The tension produced by a conflict between attitudes and behavior is **cognitive dissonance**.[4]

Suppose, for example, a salesperson is required to sell damaged televisions for the full retail price without revealing the damage to customers. She believes, however, that this is unethical, which creates a conflict between her attitude (concealing information from customers is unethical) and her behavior (selling defective TVs to uninformed customers). Uncomfortable with the dissonance, she will try to resolve the conflict. She might change her behavior by refusing to sell the defective TV sets. Alternatively, she might rationalize that the defects are minor and that the customers won't be harmed by not knowing about them. These are attempts by the salesperson to restore equilibrium between her attitude and behavior, thereby eliminating the tension from cognitive dissonance.

Managers need to understand cognitive dissonance because employees often find themselves in situations in which their attitudes conflict with their behavior. Employees who display sudden shifts in behavior may be attempting to reduce dissonance. Some employees find the conflicts between strongly held attitudes and required work behavior so uncom-

TABLE 4.1 The ABC Model of an Attitude

	COMPONENT	MEASURED BY	EXAMPLE
A	Affect	Physiological indicators Verbal statements about feelings	I don't like my boss.
B	Behavioral intent	Observed behavior Verbal statements about intentions	I want to transfer to another department.
C	Cognition	Attitude scales Verbal statements about beliefs	I believe my boss plays favorites at work.

SOURCE: Adapted from M. J. Rosenberg and C. I. Hovland, "Cognitive, Affective, and Behavioral Components of Attitude," in M. J. Rosenberg, C. I. Hovland, W. J. McGuire, R. P. Abelson, and J. H. Brehm, eds., *Attitude Organization and Change* (New Haven, Conn.: Yale University Press, 1960). Copyright 1960 Yale University Press. Used with permission.

©iStockphoto.com/Peter Borman

cognitive dissonance
A state of tension produced when an individual experiences conflict between attitudes and behavior.

A salesperson who tries to sell a damaged product for full price may experience cognitive dissonance.

fortable that they leave the organization to escape the dissonance.

Attitude Formation

Attitudes are learned. Our responses to people and issues evolve over time. Two major influences on attitudes are direct experience and social learning.

Direct experience with something strongly influences attitudes toward it. How do you know that you like biology or dislike math? You have probably formed these attitudes from experience studying the subjects. Research has shown that attitudes derived from direct experience are stronger, held more confidently, and more resistant to change than attitudes formed through indirect experience.[5] These attitudes are powerful because of their availability; they are easily accessed and active in our cognitive processes.[6] When attitudes are available, we can call them quickly into consciousness.

In **social learning**, the family, peer groups, religious organizations, and culture shape an individual's attitudes indirectly.[7] Children adopt certain attitudes when their parents reinforce attitudes they approve. This is evident from the fact that very young children express political preferences similar to those held by their parents. Later, peer pressure molds attitudes through group acceptance of individuals who express popular attitudes and through sanctions, such as exclusion from the group, placed on individuals who espouse unpopular attitudes. Substantial social learning occurs through *modeling*, in which individuals acquire attitudes by observing others. After overhearing other individuals expressing opinions or watching them engage in behaviors that reflect an attitude, the observer adopts the attitude.

Culture also plays a definitive role in attitude development. Consider, for example, the contrast in the North American and European attitudes toward vacation and leisure. The typical vacation in the United States is two weeks. In Europe, longer vacations are the norm. In some countries, *holiday* means everyone taking a month off. The European attitude is that an investment in longer vacations is important to health and performance.

Attitudes and Behavior

The correspondence between attitude and behavior has concerned organizational behaviorists and social psychologists for quite some time. Can attitudes predict behaviors such as being absent from work or quitting your job? Some studies suggested that they can, because attitudes and behavior are closely linked, while others found no relationship at all. Researchers also focused on when attitudes predict behavior and when they do not. Attitude–behavior correspondence depends on five things: attitude specificity, attitude relevance, timing of measurement, personality factors, and social constraints.

Individuals possess both general and specific attitudes. You may favor a woman's right to reproductive freedom (a general attitude) and prefer pro-choice political candidates (a specific attitude) without attending pro-choice rallies or donating to Planned Parenthood. That you don't perform these behaviors appears to weaken the link between your attitude and behaviors. However, given a choice between a pro-choice and an anti-abortion political candidate, you will probably vote for the pro-choice candidate. In this case, your attitude seems quite predictive of your behavior. The more specific the attitude, the stronger is its link to behavior.[8]

Another factor that affects the attitude–behavior link is relevance.[9] Attitudes that address an issue in which we have some self-interest are more relevant for us, and our subsequent behavior is consistent with our expressed attitude. Consider a proposal to raise income taxes for those earning $150,000 or more. If you are a student,

social learning
The process of deriving attitudes from family, peer groups, religious organizations, and culture.

LEARNING FROM OBSERVING A MODEL

For an individual to learn from observing a model, four processes must take place:
1. The learner must focus attention on the model.
2. The learner must retain what was observed from the model. Retention is accomplished in two basic ways:
   - The learner "stamps in" what was observed by forming a verbal code for it.

- The learner forms a mental image of himself or herself behaving like the model, what is known as *symbolic rehearsal*.
3. The learner must reproduce the behavior through practice.
4. The learner must be motivated to learn from the model.

[Delighted Employees, Extraordinary Sales]

Working at a call center might not be your idea of a dream job, but for call center representatives at online shoe store Zappos.com, it's still a prized position. From bloggers to warehouse workers, Zappos employees across the board report significantly above average job satisfaction. Among the company's core values is a drive to "create fun and a little weirdness," which culminates in office parades, pajama parties, and happy hours. Employees have access to fully paid medical and dental benefits, free food and drinks, flexible work hours, and a nap room at Zappos's Henderson, Nevada, headquarters. When employees consult the company's full-time life coach, they sit on a red velvet throne. Zappos CEO Tony Hsieh believes that a productive work environment begins with a positive corporate culture and a focus on employee contentment—workers can't provide great customer service if they're dissatisfied with their work. After a four-week training session, new Zappos employees are offered $2,000 to quit. This policy helps to ensure cultural cohesion by granting an acceptable exit to those who can't assimilate into the company culture. Fewer than 3 percent accept the offer. There is evidence that Zappos's employees-first strategy is paying off. Seventy-five percent of purchases are from repeat customers, and since its founding in 1999, the company has grown to be the biggest online shoe store. Zappos grossed more than $1 billion in 2008, and in 2009 was bought by online retailer Amazon.com for $940 million in stock and cash. Zappos employees received a separate $40 million in cash and restricted stock units in the sale. With continuing leadership from Hsieh and his employees-first business model, Zappos is poised to continue its growth under the banner of Amazon.

SOURCES: M. Borden, "#20 Zappos," *Fast Company* (February 11, 2009), http://www.fastcompany.com/fast50_09/profile/list/zappos; J. O'Brien, "Zappos Knows How to Kick It," *Fortune* (February 2, 2009), 55–58; N. Wingfield, "Amazon Opens Wallet, Buys Zappos," *The Wall Street Journal* (July 23, 2009), http://online.wsj.com/article/SB124829443610573361.html, accessed July 29, 2009.

you may not find the issue of great personal relevance. Individuals in that income bracket, however, might find it highly relevant. Their attitude toward the issue would be strongly predictive of whether they would vote for the tax increase.

The timing of the measurement is still another factor affecting attitude–behavior correspondence. The shorter the time is between the attitude measurement and the observed behavior, the stronger the relationship. For example, voter preference polls taken close to an election are more accurate than earlier polls.

Personality factors also influence the attitude–behavior link. One personality disposition that affects the consistency between attitudes and behavior is *self-monitoring*. Recall from the discussion of personality characteristics in Chapter 3 that low self-monitors rely on their internal states when making decisions about behavior, while high self-monitors are more responsive to situational cues. Low self-monitors therefore display greater correspondence between their attitudes and behaviors.[10] High self-monitors may display little correspondence between their attitudes and behavior because they behave according to signals from others and from the environment.

Finally, *social constraints* affect the relationship between attitudes and behavior.[11] The social context provides information about acceptable attitudes and behaviors.[12] New employees in an organization are exposed to the attitudes of their work group.[13] A newcomer from Saudi Arabia may hold a negative attitude toward women in management because this attitude prevails in his home culture. He sees, however, that his work group members respond positively to their female supervisor. His own behavior may therefore be compliant because of social constraints even though it is inconsistent with his attitude and cultural belief system.

Work Attitudes

Attitudes at work are important because, directly or indirectly, they affect work behavior. Chief among the things that negatively affect employees' work attitudes are demanding jobs over which employees have little control.[14] A study concerned with how to prevent turnover in nursing found that commitment to the profession was one factor, but nurses' attitudes were significantly affected by whether or not they had flexibility in their schedules, could get enough time off, and had opportunities to learn new skills and advance. A major factor was the tension between patient care and hospital profits. The nurses in this study said that they felt called to make a difference in their patients' lives, but sometimes worried they could not offer patients adequate care and attention due to competing interests.[15] In contrast to the nursing situation in that study, another study found that a positive psychological climate was enough to generate positive attitudes and good performance in various jobs.[16]

LEARNING OUTCOME **3**

Job Satisfaction

Job satisfaction is a pleasurable or positive emotional state resulting from the appraisal of one's job or job experiences.[17] It has been treated both as a general attitude and as satisfaction with five specific dimensions of the job: pay, the work itself, promotion opportunities, supervision, and coworkers.[18]

An individual may hold different attitudes toward various aspects of a job. For example, an employee may like her

job satisfaction

A pleasurable or positive emotional state resulting from the appraisal of one's job or job experiences.

YAHOO! DOWN AND OUT

When several industry analysts started to speculate that Yahoo! would be at risk of a takeover if the company didn't cut costs or divest assets, employee morale plummeted. Low morale precipitated a mass exodus of experienced managers—including top executives and engineers—taking with them years of know-how. To make matters worse, decision making was slow due to an entrenched bureaucratic organizational structure, and employees complained about the lack of passion from their CEO, Terry Semel, who ultimately lost his job because of the severity of morale problems at Yahoo!

SOURCES: R. D. Hof, "Even Yahoo! Gets the Blues." *Business Week* (2007): 37; M. Helft, "Can She Turn Yahoo into, Well, Google?" *The New York Times* (July 1, 2007), http://www.nytimes.com, accessed July 2, 2008.

job responsibilities but be dissatisfied with the opportunities for promotion. Characteristics of individuals also affect job satisfaction.[19] Those with high negative affectivity are more likely to be dissatisfied with their jobs. Challenging work, valued rewards, opportunities for advancement, competent supervision, and supportive coworkers are dimensions of the job that can lead to satisfaction. What may surprise you is that pay is only marginally related to job satisfaction, as well-paid individuals are only trivially more satisfied with their jobs than low-paid individuals.[20]

There are several measures of job satisfaction. One of the most widely used measures comes from the *Job Descriptive Index (JDI)*. This index measures the specific facets of satisfaction by asking employees to respond "yes," "no," or "cannot decide" to a series of statements describing their jobs. Another popular measure is the *Minnesota Satisfaction Questionnaire (MSQ)*.[21] This survey also asks employees to respond to statements about their jobs using a five-point scale that ranges from very dissatisfied to very satisfied. Figure 4.1 presents some sample items from each questionnaire.

Managers and employees believe that happy or satisfied employees are more productive at work. Most of us feel more satisfied than usual when we believe that we are performing better than usual.[22] But research on the relationship between job satisfaction and performance has shown it to be more complex than that. If job satisfaction always improved performance, then the manager's job would simply be to keep workers happy.

Although this may be the case for certain individuals, research has shown that job satisfaction for most people is only one of several causes of good performance. Another view holds that good performance causes satisfaction, yet some high performers are not satisfied with their jobs. It

---

FIGURE 4.1 Sample Items from Satisfaction Questionnaires

Job Descriptive Index

Think of the work you do at present. How well does each of the following words or phrases describe your work? In the blank beside each word given below, write

Y	for "Yes" if it describes your work
N	for "No" if it does NOT describe it
?	if you cannot decide

WORK ON YOUR PRESENT JOB:

_____ Routine
_____ Satisfying
_____ Good

Think of the majority of the people who you work with now or the people you meet in connection with your work. How well does each of the following words or phrases describe these people? In the blank beside each word, write

Y	for "Yes" if it describes the people you work with
N	for "No" if it does NOT describe them
?	if you cannot decide

COWORKERS (PEOPLE):

_____ Boring
_____ Responsible
_____ Intelligent

Minnesota Satisfaction Questionnaire

1 = Very dissatisfied
2 = Dissatisfied
3 = I can't decide whether I am satisfied or not
4 = Satisfied
5 = Very satisfied

On my present job, this is how I feel about:

_____ The chance to work alone on the job (independence)
_____ My chances for advancement on this job (advancement)
_____ The chance to tell people what to do (authority)
_____ The praise I get for a good job (recognition)
_____ My pay and the amount of work I do (compensation)

SOURCES: The Job Descriptive Index is copyrighted by Bowling Green State University. The complete forms, scoring key, instructions, and norms can be obtained from the JDI Office, Department of Psychology, Bowling Green State University, Bowling Green, OH 43403. Minnesota Satisfaction Questionnaire from D. J. Weiss, R. V. Davis, G. W. England, and L. H. Lofquist, *Manual for the Minnesota Satisfaction Questionnaire* (University of Minnesota Vocational Psychology Research, 1967).

Managers and employees believe that happy or satisfied employees are more productive at work.

©iStockphoto.com/Andresr

is important to consider all of the potential variables when considering job satisfaction.[23]

The lack of a clear relationship between satisfaction and performance can be explained by the intervening role of rewards. Employees who receive valuable rewards are more satisfied. In addition, employees who receive rewards that are contingent on performance (the higher the performance, the larger the reward) tend to perform better. Rewards thus influence both satisfaction and performance. The key to influencing both satisfaction and performance through rewards is that the rewards are valued by employees and are tied directly to performance.

[With the Aid of Ethics]

Johnson & Johnson, manufacturer of Tylenol, Band-Aids, Splenda, and Listerine, is the fifth most valuable and sixth most profitable company in the *Fortune* 500. Beyond its impressive array of popular brands, Johnson & Johnson's market success can be attributed to strict observance of the company credo (recall Figure 2.3). While many companies boast ethical codes or statements, few truly rely on these codes to govern behavior. Johnson & Johnson, however, adheres to the principles and ethical responsibilities explicated in its credo.

In 1982, a handful of Extra Strength Tylenol capsules were poisoned with cyanide, resulting in seven deaths. While the crime was never solved, Johnson & Johnson's immediate response, including a nationwide recall, was widely praised by the media. In 2007, Johnson & Johnson turned itself in to the SEC for possible violations of the Foreign Corrupt Practices Act. These deft actions, based on the tenets of the credo, are often heralded as crowning moments in the history of public relations.

Johnson & Johnson CEO Bill Weldon travels around the world to talk with employees moving into new leadership positions about proper application of the credo in executive decisions. He does so using a high-tech artificial knee built by Johnson & Johnson's medical devices group. These open dialogues help company leaders keep the credo in mind as they make judgments and manage workers. The secret to Johnson & Johnson's success is not just the company's credo—it's the steadfast application of the credo's principles in everyday decisions.

SOURCE: G. Colvin and J. Shambora, "J&J: Secrets of Success," *Fortune* (May 4, 2009), 117–119.

LEARNING OUTCOME **4**

Organizational Citizenship versus Workplace Deviance

Job satisfaction encourages **organizational citizenship behavior (OCB)**—behavior that is above and beyond the call of duty. Satisfied employees are more likely to help their coworkers, make positive comments about the company, and refrain from complaining when things at work go poorly.[24] Going beyond the call of duty is especially important to organizations using teams, as employees in teams depend on extra help from each other to get things accomplished.

Satisfied workers are more likely to want to give something

back to the organization—that is, to engage in OCBs because they want to reciprocate their positive experiences.[25] Often, employees may feel that their OCBs are not recognized because they occur outside the confines of normal job responsibilities, but they do indeed influence performance evaluations. Employees who help others, suggest innovations, and develop their skills receive higher performance ratings.[26]

OCBs can be directed at different facets of an organization, determined according to individual attitudes. For example, affect tends to direct OCBs toward other people, while cognition directs OCBs toward the organization.[27]

Individuals who identify strongly with the organization are more likely to perform OCBs.[28] High self-monitors, or individuals who base their behavior on cues from the situation, are also more likely to perform OCBs.[29] One study found that individual workers were more likely to offer OCBs when doing so was the norm among other team members. The impact of one worker's OCBs can thus spread throughout an entire department.[30]

Researchers have found a strong link between job satisfaction and organizational performance, although, as mentioned earlier, the relationship between the two factors is more complex than one might think. Nevertheless, overall, companies with satisfied workers have better performance than companies with dissatisfied workers.[31] This may be due to the more intangible elements of performance, such as OCB, that contribute to organizational effectiveness but aren't necessarily captured by measuring individual job performance.

Job satisfaction connects to other important outcomes. Dissatisfied workers are more likely to skip work and quit their jobs, driving up the cost of turnover. Furthermore, dissatisfied workers report more psychological and medical problems than do satisfied employees.[32]

One factor that leads to dissatisfaction at work is a misfit between an individual's values and the organization's values, or a lack of *person–organization fit*. People who feel that their values don't mesh with the organization's values experience job dissatisfaction and eventually leave the organization.[33]

Like all attitudes, job satisfaction is influenced by culture. A recent study of job satisfaction rates in forty-nine countries found a close link between job characteristics and job satisfaction in countries with higher incomes, higher individualism, and lower power distance than in countries with lower incomes, lower individualism (higher collectivism), and higher power distance.[34] As employees from different cultures may have differing job expectations, there may be no single prescription for increasing the job satisfaction of a multicultural workforce. Researchers found in China's hotel and restaurant industry that high-performance human resource practices such as promotions from within, flexible job assignments, long-term results-oriented appraisals, and job security fostered service-oriented OCBs. Such OCBs were in turn linked to lower turnover and higher productivity at the organizational level.[35]

When employees are dissatisfied with their jobs, they are more likely to engage in **workplace deviance behavior (WDB)**, which is defined as any voluntary, attitude-driven, counterproductive behavior that violates organizational norms and causes some degree of harm to organizational functioning. Examples of such behavior

> **workplace deviance behavior (WDB)**
>
> Any voluntary counterproductive behavior that violates organizational norms and causes some degree of harm to organizational functioning.

[Deviance at Galleon]

Pressure to engage in unethical business practices was intense at Galleon Group, a hedgefund where stock traders were pushed to get illegal inside information about company performance that gave them an advantage in buying and selling stocks. For example, according to the Securities and Exchange Commission, Galleon paid an analyst at a San Francisco investment firm who illegally told them, before public statements were released, what Google's quarterly profits would be. Once, when Google's profits unexpectedly decreased, Galleon shorted the stock, that is, bet that Google's stock would decrease in price, and earned $9 million on the trade. Galleon's aggressive investment goals led its senior managers and traders to berate, punish, and fire analysts who couldn't produce inside information. A former Galleon trader said, "Get an edge or you're gone."

SOURCES: G. Zuckerman, D. Clark, and S. Pulliam, "Colleagues Finger Billionaire—Galleon Founder Pushed Hard for Stock-Trading Tips; 'Get an Edge or You're Gone,'" *The Wall Street Journal* (October 19, 2009), A1. So far, nineteen of the twenty-six defendants associated with Galleon's insider trading scandal have plead guilty; S. Pulliam and M. Rothfield, "Plea Deals Ramp up Pressure in Galleon," *The Wall Street Journal* (January 27, 2011), C1.

©iStockphoto.com/g_studio

include gossiping about coworkers, sabotaging others' projects, and theft from the company or colleagues.[36] Negative events in the business world, such as downsizing and technological insecurities, are generally considered responsible for spikes in workplace deviance. Layoffs, for example, may inspire employees to develop negative attitudes, to feel anger and hostility toward the organization, and to retaliate. Even when an employee keeps her job but believes the procedure used to determine the layoff is unfair, she may still take revenge against the manager.[37] Perceived unfairness at work is a major cause of deviance, sabotage, and retaliation. Managers must prevent and manage WDB to keep it from harming performance, and one way to do that is to encourage positive attitudes among employees.

Organizational Commitment and Job Satisfaction

The strength of an individual's identification with an organization is known as **organizational commitment**. There are three kinds of organizational commitment: affective, continuance, and normative. **Affective commitment** is an employee's intention to remain in an organization because of a strong desire to do so. Affective commitment encompasses loyalty and a deep concern for the organization's welfare based on three factors: a belief in the goals and values of the organization, a willingness to put forth effort on behalf of the organization, and a desire to remain a member of the organization.[38]

organizational commitment
The strength of an individual's identification with an organization.

affective commitment
Organizational commitment based on an individual's desire to remain in an organization.

continuance commitment
Organizational commitment based on the fact that an individual cannot afford to leave.

normative commitment
Organizational commitment based on an individual's perceived obligation to remain with an organization.

Continuance commitment is an employee's tendency to remain in an organization because he cannot afford to leave.[39] Sometimes employees believe that they will lose a great deal of their investments in time, effort, and benefits if they leave. **Normative commitment** is a perceived obligation to remain with the organization. Individuals who experience normative commitment stay with the organization because they feel they should.[40]

Certain organizational conditions, such as participation in decision-making and job security, encourage commitment. And so do job characteristics such as autonomy, responsibility, role clarity, and interesting work.[41] Affective and normative commitments are related to lower rates of absenteeism, higher quality of work, increased productivity, and overall performance.[42] Managers should encourage affective commitment in particular because committed individuals expend more task-related effort and are less likely to leave the organization.[43]

Managers can increase affective commitment by communicating their appreciation of employees' contributions and concern for employees' well-being.[44] Affective commitment also increases when the organization and employees share the same values and when the organization emphasizes values like moral integrity, fairness, creativity, and openness.[45] Negative experiences at work, such as perceived age discrimination, diminish affective commitment.[46]

ETHICS AT NORTEL

Visitors to Nortel's website at http://www.nortel.com/corporate/community/ethics/guide.html can download a comprehensive document, called "Code of Business Conduct," that establishes very specific ethical standards on topics ranging from bribes and kickbacks to expense vouchers and illegal copying of software. For example, most businesspeople believe that it is wrong to take bribes or other gifts from a company that wants your business. Therefore, one of Nortel's ethical guidelines is "Directly or indirectly offering or receiving any gift or entertainment that might be perceived to improperly influence a business interaction violates our commitment to maintaining objectivity and transparency in our relationships." And just to be sure there's no confusion over what constitutes a gift, the guidelines spell things out explicitly: "Certain types of gifts may not be given to or received from persons doing business or seeking to do business with Nortel: Cash, gift certificates, or any other cash equivalent; Stock, stock options, or 'friends and family stock'; Discounts not generally available to the public."

SOURCE: "Code of Business Conduct," (2009), p.13, http://www.nortel.com/corporate/community/ethics/collateral/nn104800-110309.pdf.

Persuasion and Attitude Change

The days of command-and-control management, in which executives simply told employees what do to, are over. Modern managers must instead aim to change employee attitudes and thus need to be skilled in the art of persuasion.[47] Through persuasion, one individual (the source) tries to change the attitude of another person (the target) in regard to a certain issue (the message). Certain characteristics of the source, target, and message affect the persuasion process.

Source Characteristics

Three major characteristics of the source affect persuasion: expertise, trustworthiness, and attractiveness.[48] A source who is perceived as an expert is particularly persuasive. Testimonials, for example, are the third most effective technique in advertising, after corporate responsibility and emotional appeal. Endorsers of a product are effective when they are perceived as trustworthy, attractive, or similar to the consumer, or when they represent an image the consumer would like to adopt.[49]

Target Characteristics

Individuals with low self-esteem are more likely to change their attitudes in response to persuasion than are individuals with high self-esteem. Individuals who hold very extreme attitudes are more resistant to persuasion, and people who are in a good mood are easier to persuade.[50] Undoubtedly, individuals differ widely in their responsiveness to persuasion. Managers must recognize these differences and realize that their attempts to change attitudes may not be universally accepted.

Message Characteristics

Suppose you want to persuade your employees that an unpopular policy is a positive change. Should you present one side of the issue or both sides? Given that your employees are already negatively inclined toward the policy, you will have more success in changing their attitudes if you present both sides. This shows support for one side of the issue while acknowledging that another side does exist. Moreover, refuting the other side rather than ignoring it makes it harder for the targets to hang on to their negative attitudes.

Persuasion is a delicate skill. Undisguised deliberate attempts at changing attitudes may drive employees' attitudes in the opposite direction. This is most likely to occur when the target of the persuasive communication feels her or his freedom is threatened.[51] Less threatening approaches are less likely to elicit negative reactions. The emotional tone of the message is also important. Messages framed with the same emotion as that felt by the receiver are more persuasive.[52]

Cognitive Routes to Persuasion

The source, target, and message characteristics are weighed differently in the two cognitive routes to persuasion, the central route and the peripheral route, as shown in the *elaboration likelihood model* of persuasion in Figure 4.2 on the next page.[53] The routes are differentiated by the amount of elaboration, or scrutiny, that the target is motivated to give to the message.

The *central route* to persuasion involves direct cognitive processing of the message's content. In this route, individuals think carefully about issues that are personally relevant. The listener may nod his head at strong arguments and shake his head at weak ones.[54] Logical and convincing arguments are needed to change attitudes by this route.

In the *peripheral route* to persuasion, the individual is not motivated to pay much attention to the message's content because she is distracted or perceives the message as personally irrelevant. Instead, she is persuaded by characteristics of the persuader such as expertise, trustworthiness, and attractiveness. The individual may also be persuaded by statistics, the number of arguments presented, or the method of presentation—none of which relate to the actual content of the message.

The elaboration likelihood model shows that the target's level of involvement with the issue is important. That involvement also determines which route to persuasion will be more effective. In some cases, attitude change comes about through both the central and the peripheral routes. To cover all of the bases, managers should structure the content of their messages carefully, develop their own effective persuasive attributes, and choose a method of presentation that will appeal to the audience.[55]

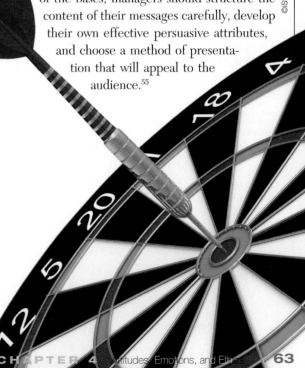

©iStockphoto.com/iLexx

FIGURE 4.2 The Elaboration Likelihood Model of Persuasion

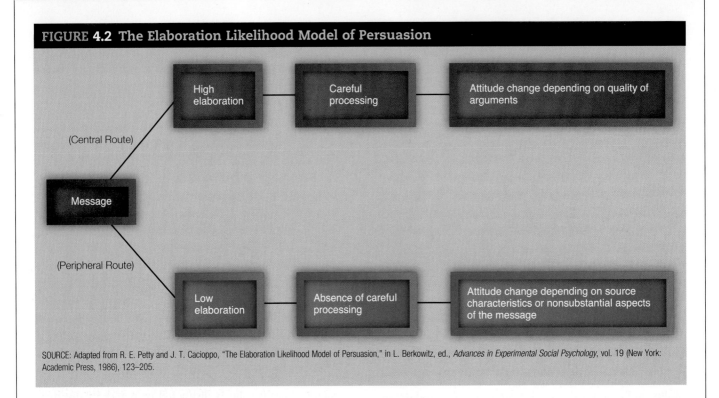

SOURCE: Adapted from R. E. Petty and J. T. Cacioppo, "The Elaboration Likelihood Model of Persuasion," in L. Berkowitz, ed., *Advances in Experimental Social Psychology*, vol. 19 (New York: Academic Press, 1986), 123–205.

Emotions and Moods at Work

Emotions are discrete and fairly short-lived feelings that have a specific, known cause. An emotion like anger, for example, may arise because a colleague was rude to you. Or you may feel happy because you got a promotion. *Moods*, on the other hand, are typically classified as positive or negative and are made up of various emotions. Moods typically last longer than emotions and don't have a specific cause. Traditional management theories did not place a premium on studying the effects of employees' moods and emotions because they were thought to be bad for rational decision making at work. Ideas about management centered around the stereotypical ideal employee who kept his emotions in check and behaved in a totally rational, nonemotional manner. Research has proven that emotions and cognitions are intertwined and that both are normal parts of human functioning and decision making.[56]

emotions
Mental states that include feelings, physiological changes, and the inclination to act.

Emotions

Emotions (e.g., anger, joy, pride, hostility) are short-lived, intense reactions to an event. Employees have to cope with both positive and negative events at work on a daily basis, and these events, in turn, lead to emotions. When events at work are positive and goals are being met, employees experience positive emotions. But when events at work are perceived as negative, the opposite can be true.[57] Emotions, in turn, impact both work attitudes and work behaviors.[58]

Events that threaten or thwart the achievement of goals cause negative emotions, which then threaten job satisfaction and commitment. Positive emotions produce better cognitive functioning, physical and psychological health, and coping mechanisms.[59] Individuals differ in their capacity to experience both positive emotions (e.g., happiness, pride) and negative emotions (e.g., anger, fear, guilt).[60] People who experience positive emotions tend to do so repeatedly.[61] Overall, people who experience positive emotions are more successful across a variety of life domains and report higher life satisfaction. Negative emotions, on the other hand, lead to unhealthy coping behaviors and lowered cardiovascular function and physical health.[62]

Moods

Moods are feeling states that are more enduring than emotions and have no clear cause. Moods are one level above emotions since they are made up of a variety of emotions. Individuals experiencing a strongly positive mood at work feel excited, enthusiastic, and peppy, while individuals experiencing a less positive mood feel dull and sluggish. Individuals experiencing a negative mood at work feel distressed, hostile, or jittery, while those experiencing a less negative mood are calm and relaxed.[63]

Moods may be particularly important in the workplace because they last longer than emotions. Positive moods at work lead to better work performance and OCBs and decrease deviance.[64] Negative moods lead to more turnover intentions and absenteeism.[65] Interestingly, negative moods also increase altruistic behavior and subsequently improve the mood of the altruistic individuals.

Emotional Contagion at Work

Emotions have far-reaching influence on workplace behavior. They drive employee decision making and are even used as a manipulative tool to ensure desired outcomes from conflicts or negotiations.[66] The influence of emotion at work is extended by **emotional contagion**, which is the dynamic process through which emotions are transferred from one person to another, either consciously or unconsciously, through nonverbal channels.

Emotions need to be managed at work because they spread easily. Emotional contagion occurs primarily through nonverbal cues and the basic human tendency to mimic each other's facial expressions, body language, speech patterns, vocal tones, and even emotions. Contagion affects any job involving interpersonal interaction. Positive emotions that travel through a work group due to emotional contagion produce cooperation and task performance.[67] The opposite occurs when negative emotions destroy morale and performance.

When organizations and their employees experience change and/or huge losses, they may struggle to recover. Good leaders can

©BananaStock/Jupiterimages

help by using compassion to heal and rebuild employee morale.[68] Organizations need to give employees a comfortable place to share their mutual grief and trauma. These issues can be resolved by caring leaders who are willing to share their emotions with employees.

Emotional Intelligence

Emotional intelligence (EI) is the ability to recognize and manage emotion in oneself and in others. EI is made up of several types of abilities: perceiving, understanding, facilitating, and regulating emotion.[69] This type of intelligence is thought to be an important ability for many types of jobs and to be a fundamental aspect of leadership (see Chapter 12 for more information). It seems to facilitate job performance in a sequential fashion. Having the ability to perceive emotions allows one to better understand emotions, which then increases emotion regulation. Being able to regulate your emotion, in turn, helps as you display appropriate emotions in the workplace, which allows you to perform better at work.[70] Emotional intelligence helps you avoid amygdala hijacks, in which the emotional brain runs away with the rational brain. Jet Blue flight attendant Steven Slater's famous rant and exit from the airplane is a well-documented example of an amygdala highjack. Such losses of self-control, if frequent or extreme enough, can cost you your career!

Although self-report measures are often used to measure EI, they are not always accurate, since individuals do not always have a good perspective as to their own abilities. Another way to measure EI is an ability-based measure similar to an IQ test that attempts to test an individual's actual ability in each of the four EI categories rather than asking individuals to assess their own abilities.

Emotional Labor

It is clear that moods and emotions impact employees and organizations a great deal. Positive moods and emotions bring about positive outcomes. This can be particularly true for highly interpersonal jobs like

emotional contagion
A dynamic process through which the emotions of one person are transferred to another, either consciously or unconsciously, through nonverbal channels.

customer service representatives, flight attendants and, oftentimes, professors, who are expected to express positive emotions and suppress any anger or hostility they may be feeling. *Emotional labor* is the work that employees do to control their feelings and expression of emotions in the workplace and is a type of emotion regulation.[71]

Often organizations have specific rules regarding emotional expression called *display rules*. There are two primary types of emotional labor used to meet these display rules: deep acting and surface acting. *Deep acting* involves attempting to feel the emotion one is displaying. Picturing a beautiful mountain vista or thinking about a pleasant memory are examples of deep acting. *Surface acting* is faking an emotion to meet the display rules. Surface acting causes *emotional dissonance*, or a discrepancy between one's felt emotion and one's expressed emotion. Surface acting can result in negative outcomes such as burnout, negative mood, and work withdrawal. Deep acting, in general, seems to have positive consequences and has been related to positive mood at work as well as high-quality customer service performance and reduced burnout.[72]

LEARNING OUTCOME **7**

Ethical Behavior

Ethics is the study of moral values and moral behavior. **Ethical behavior** involves acting in ways consistent with one's personal values and the commonly held values of the organization and society.[73] Paying attention to ethical issues pays off for companies. In the early 1990s, James Burke, then CEO of Johnson & Johnson, put together a list of companies committed to ethics. The group included Johnson & Johnson, Coca-Cola, Gerber, Kodak, 3M, and Pitney Bowes. A recent study showed that over a forty-year period, the market value of these organizations grew at an annual rate of 11.3 percent, as compared to 6.2 percent for the Dow Jones industrials as a whole.[74] Doing the right thing can have a positive effect on an organization's performance.[75]

Ethical behavior in firms can also lead to practical benefits, particularly by attracting new talent. Firms with better reputations attract more applicants, creating a larger hiring pool, and evidence suggests that respected firms can choose higher-quality applicants.[76] For example, Timberland's strong value system helps the company attract and recruit the best talent and maintain a solid reputation with investors.

Failure to handle situations ethically can hurt companies. Employees who are laid off or terminated are very concerned about the quality of treatment they receive. Honestly explaining the reasons for the dismissal and preserving the dignity of the employee will reduce the likelihood of employees initiating a claim against the company. One study showed that less than 1 percent of employees who felt the company was being honest filed a claim. More than 17 percent of those who felt the company was being less than honest filed claims.[77] Conversely, ethical actions can be a boon to organizations. Australia's former prime minister, Kevin Rudd, apologized publicly for the ill treatment of Aborigines on the part of the national government. Even before the issue of financial compensation was addressed, this action built trust and hope among Australians of all races.[78]

[Greenwashing]

As environmentalism grows in popularity, so do "green" products and services. Companies eager to reap the benefits of recent buying trends are transitioning to sustainable business practices and producing more environmentally sound products. But the green public images of some companies are not quite consistent with their actions. *Greenwashing* refers to the practice of establishing a false or misleading environmentally friendly image in order to sell products, appease critics and regulators, and attract talent and investors. In the early 1990s, facing market pressure and pending regulations, Mobil Chemical produced a plastic trash bag containing starch and advertised it as biodegradable. In actuality it was only *photo*degradable, which means little when most plastic trash bags end up buried in landfills. Mobil faced lawsuits from seven states and the Federal Trade Commission. Although the company denied guilt, noting the lack of a national standard for the meaning of "biodegradable," they had to pay $150,000 in damages. A 2009 study concluded that greenwashing is on the rise, and is most prevalent in the marketing of children's products, cosmetics, and cleaning products. In all three industries, ambiguous labeling and advertising are used to mislead consumers about products' actual ecological impact.

SOURCE: M. Whellams and C. MacDonald, "What Is Greenwashing, and Why Is it a Problem?," *Business Ethics*, http://www.businessethics.ca/greenwashing/, accessed July 2, 2008; "Mobil: Develop National Degradability Standard," *Discount Store News* (July 2, 1990), http://infotrac-college.thomsonlearning.com, accessed July 2, 2008; "Mobil Settles on Hefty Bags," *The New York Times* (June 28, 1991), http://infotrac-college.thomsonlearning.com, accessed July 2, 2008; "The Seven Sins of Greenwashing—Greenwashing Report 2009," TerraChoice Environmental Marketing Inc., http://sinsofgreenwashing.org/findings/greenwashing-report-2009, accessed July 27, 2009.

ethical behavior

Acting in ways consistent with one's personal values and the commonly held values of the organization and society.

Unethical behavior by employees can affect individuals, work teams, and even the organization. Organizations thus depend on individuals to act ethically. For this reason, more and more firms are starting to monitor their employees' Internet usage. Although some employees complain that this monitoring violates their privacy, the courts tend to disagree, arguing that companies have the right to monitor employees' use of company-owned hardware and software.

Michael Smyth was fired from his job with Pillsbury Company after employees read inflammatory comments he made in several e-mails to his supervisor. Smyth sued for wrongful termination, claiming that the firm had violated his right to privacy after telling employees their e-mail would remain confidential. Despite these promises, the court ruled that Smyth had no reasonable expectation of privacy while using the firm's equipment. Further, it said, Smyth's right to privacy was outweighed by the firm's need to conduct business in a professional manner. Only future court cases will clarify where a firm's effort to monitor potentially unethical behavior actually violates its own ethical code.[79] Nonetheless, today's high-intensity business environment only increases the need for strong ethics programs.

Managers often struggle to align the ideal of ethical behavior with the reality of everyday business practices. Violations of the public's trust are costly. When Mattel recalled 20.5 million toys that were manufactured in China because they contained lead, its public image suffered greatly. The company attempted to undo the damages through a national advertising campaign.[80] Firms can experience lower accounting returns and slow sales growth for as long as five years after having been convicted of illegal corporate behavior.[81]

Individuals face complex ethical issues at work. A one-week review of *The Wall Street Journal* revealed more than sixty articles dealing with ethical issues in business.[82] As

Table 4.2 suggests, few of these issues are clear-cut. They depend on the specifics of the situation, and their interpretation depends on the characteristics of the individuals examining them. Consider lying, for instance. Many business people tell white lies. Is this acceptable? The perception of what constitutes ethical versus unethical behavior in organizations varies among individuals.

LEARNING OUTCOME **8**

Factors That Affect Ethical Behavior

Two sets of factors—individual characteristics and organizational factors—influence ethical behavior.[83] In this section, we'll look at the individual influences on ethical behavior. Ethical decision making requires three qualities of individuals:[84]

1. The competence to identify ethical issues and evaluate the consequences of alternative courses of action.

TABLE 4.2 Ethical Issues from One Week in the Life of *The Wall Street Journal*

1. Stealing	Taking things that don't belong to you
2. Lying	Saying things you know aren't true
3. Fraud and deceit	Creating or perpetuating false impressions
4. Conflict of interest and influence buying	Bribes, payoffs, and kickbacks
5. Hiding or divulging information	Concealing information that another party has a right to know or failing to protect personal or proprietary information
6. Cheating	Taking unfair advantage of a situation
7. Personal decadence	Aiming below excellence in terms of work performance (e.g., careless or sloppy work)
8. Interpersonal abuse	Behaviors that are abusive of others (e.g., sexism, racism, emotional abuse)
9. Organizational abuse	Organizational practices that abuse members (e.g., inequitable compensation, misuses of power)
10. Rule violations	Breaking organizational rules
11. Accessory to unethical acts	Knowing about unethical behavior and failing to report it
12. Ethical dilemmas	Choosing between two equally desirable or undesirable options

SOURCE: Kluwer Academic Publishers, by J. O. Cherrington and D. J. Cherrington, "A Menu of Moral Issues: One Week in the Life of *The Wall Street Journal*," *Journal of Business Ethics* 11 (1992): 255–265. Reprinted with kind permission of Springer Science and Business Media.

2. The self-confidence to seek out different opinions about the issue and decide what is right in terms of a particular situation.

3. Tough-mindedness—the willingness to make decisions when all that needs to be known cannot be known and when the ethical issue has no established, unambiguous solution.

Which individual characteristics lead to these qualities? According to our model, they are value systems, locus of control, Machiavellianism, and cognitive moral development. Figure 4.3 illustrates these, as well as the organizational influences, which we will examine throughout the remainder of the book.

Values

Different values generate different ethical behaviors. **Values** are enduring beliefs that a specific mode of conduct or end state of existence is personally or socially preferable to an opposite or converse mode of conduct or end state of existence.[85] This definition was proposed by Rokeach, an early scholar of human values. As individuals grow and mature, they learn values, although these may change as an individual develops a sense of self. Cultures, societies, and organizations shape values. Parents and other respected role models influence value development by providing guidance about what is right and wrong. Like general beliefs about right and wrong, values form the basis for ethical behavior. Though values vary widely among individuals, we use them to evaluate our own behavior and that of others.

Instrumental and Terminal Values
Rokeach distinguished between two types of values: instrumental and terminal. **Instrumental values**

shape the acceptable behaviors that can be used to achieve some goal or end state. Instrumental values identified by Rokeach include ambition, honesty, self-sufficiency, and courage. **Terminal values** influence the goals to be achieved or the end states of existence. Rokeach identified happiness, love, pleasure, self-respect, and freedom among the terminal values. Table 4.3 gives a complete list of instrumental and terminal values. Terminal and instrumental values work in concert by providing individuals with goals to strive for and acceptable ways to achieve those goals.

Americans' rankings of instrumental and terminal values have been remarkably stable over time.[86] The highest ranked instrumental values were honesty, ambition, responsibility, forgiveness, open-mindedness, and courage. The highest ranked terminal values were world peace, family security, freedom, happiness, self-respect, and wisdom.

Age also affects values. Baby boomers' values contrast with those of the baby busters, who are beginning to enter the workforce. The baby busters value family life and time off from work and want to balance work and home life. This contrasts with the more driven, work-oriented value system of the boomers. The baby boomers place a huge emphasis on achievement values at work. Their successors in Generations X and Y are markedly different. Generation X values self-reliance, individualism, and balance between family and work life. Generation Y values freedom in scheduling and embraces a work-to-live mind-set rather than the live-to-work approach of the baby boomers.[87]

Work Values
Work values influence individuals' perceptions of right and wrong on the job.[88] Four work

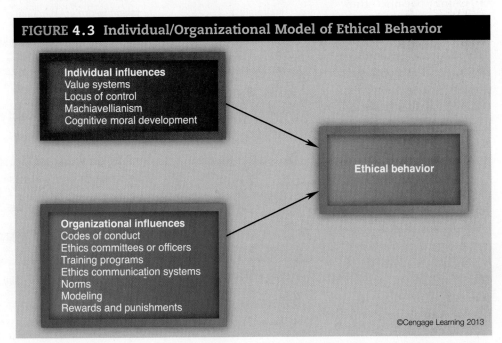

values
Enduring beliefs that a specific mode of conduct or end state of existence is personally or socially preferable to an opposite or converse mode of conduct or end state of existence.

instrumental values
Values that shape the acceptable behaviors that can be used to achieve some goal or end state.

terminal values
Values that influence the goals to be achieved or the end states of existence.

FIGURE 4.3 Individual/Organizational Model of Ethical Behavior

Individual influences
Value systems
Locus of control
Machiavellianism
Cognitive moral development

Ethical behavior

Organizational influences
Codes of conduct
Ethics committees or officers
Training programs
Ethics communication systems
Norms
Modeling
Rewards and punishments

©Cengage Learning 2013

TABLE 4.3 Instrumental and Terminal Values

INSTRUMENTAL VALUES		
Honesty	Ambition	Responsibility
Forgiveness	Open-mindedness	Courage
Helpfulness	Cleanliness	Competence
Self-control	Affection/love	Cheerfulness
Independence	Politeness	Intelligence
Obedience	Rationality	Imagination
TERMINAL VALUES		
World peace	Family security	Freedom
Happiness	Self-respect	Wisdom
Equality	Salvation	Prosperity
Achievement	Friendship	National security
Inner peace	Mature love	Social respect
Beauty in art and nature	Pleasure	Exciting, active life

SOURCE: Adapted with the permission of The Free Press, a Division of Simon & Schuster, Inc., from *The Nature of Human Values* by Milton Rokeach. Copyright © 1973 by The Free Press. Copyright renewed © 2001 by Sandra Ball-Rokeach. All rights reserved.

values are achievement, concern for others, honesty, and fairness.[89] *Achievement* is a concern for the advancement of one's career; it drives people to work hard and seek opportunities to develop new skills. *Concern for others* is shown in caring, compassionate behaviors such as encouraging others or helping them with difficult tasks. These behaviors also constitute organizational citizenship. *Honesty* is providing accurate information and refusing to mislead others for personal gain. *Fairness* means remaining impartial while recognizing different points of view.

Individuals rank these values in terms of their relative importance in their work lives.[90] Employees who share their supervisor's values are more satisfied with their jobs and more committed to the organization.[91] Values also have profound effects on job choice. Although traditionally pay and advancement potential have had the strongest influences on job choice decisions, one study found that

three other work values—achievement, concern for others, and fairness—had greater influence.[92] This means that organizations recruiting job candidates should pay careful attention to individuals' values and to the messages their organizations send about company values.

Cultural Differences in Values

Organizations facing the challenges of an increasingly diverse workforce and a global marketplace must understand culture's influence on values. Doing business in a global marketplace often means encountering a clash of values among different cultures. Consider loyalty, for example. In Japan, loyalty means "compassionate overtime." Even when you have no work yourself, you should stay late to provide moral support for your peers who are working late.[93] In contrast, Koreans value loyalty to the person for whom one works.[94] In the United States, family and other personal loyalties are held above loyalty to the company or one's supervisor.

Cultures differ in the individual contributions they value at work. Collectivist cultures like China and Mexico value a person's contributions to relationships in the work team. By contrast, individualist cultures (the United States, the Netherlands) value a person's contribution to task accomplishment. Both collectivist and individualist cultures, however, value rewards based on individual performance.[95] Iran's collectivist managers demonstrate little tolerance for ambiguity, high need for structure, and willingness to sacrifice for the good of society—all values they derive from Islam, which promotes belonging, harmony, humility, and simplicity.[96]

Values also affect individuals' views of what constitutes authority. French managers value authority as a right of office and rank. Their behavior reflects this value, as they tend to exercise power based on their position in the organization. By contrast, managers from the Netherlands

MEASURING SUSTAINABILITY

One way to assess a company's values regarding sustainability is to examine the *Dow Jones Sustainability Index* ratings. Since 1999, the DJSI has measured the financial and sustainability performance of companies all over the world. Companies that are listed on the index are those that show a strong commitment to maintaining sustainable practices, while those companies that do not operate in a sustainable or ethical manner are removed from the index. Air France was recently named in the index as the sector leader

in travel and leisure for six years running. The company has publically and boldly committed to reduce CO_2 emissions through its climate action plan. It routinely partners with environmental groups such as the World Wildlife Fund and GoodPlanet on a variety of issues, including combating deforestation in Madagascar.

SOURCE: T. Jones, "Survey Finds Big Business Lacking in Social Responsibility," *Australian Broadcasting Corporation* (October 13, 2003), http:// www.abc.net.au/lateline/content/2003 /s966137.htm; RepuTex, http://www.reputex.com.au.

value group inputs to decisions and expect employees to challenge and discuss their decisions.[97]

We may be prone to judging the value systems of others, but we should resist this tendency. Tolerating diverse values can help us understand other cultures. Value systems of other nations are not necessarily right or wrong—they are merely different.

Locus of Control

Another individual influence on ethical behavior is locus of control. Recall from Chapter 3 that individuals with an internal locus of control believe that they control events in their lives and that they are responsible for their own experiences. Those with an external locus of control believe that outside forces such as fate, chance, or other people control what happens to them.[98]

Internals are more likely than externals to take personal responsibility for the consequences of their ethical or unethical behavior. Externals are more apt to believe that external forces caused their ethical or unethical behavior. Research has shown that internals make more ethical decisions than do externals.[99] Internals also are more resistant to social pressure and are less willing to hurt another person even if ordered to do so by an authority figure.[100]

Machiavellianism

Machiavellianism also influences ethical behavior. Niccolò Machiavelli was a sixteenth-century Italian statesman famous for writing *The Prince*, a guide for acquiring and using power.[101] He suggested that manipulating others was the best way to achieve power. **Machiavellianism**, then, is a personality characteristic involving one's willingness to do whatever it takes to get one's own way.

A high-Mach individual operates from the notion that it is better to be feared than loved. High-Machs tend to be deceitful, have a cynical view of human nature, and care little for conventional notions of right and wrong.[102] They are skilled manipulators, relying on their persuasive abilities. Low-Machs, in contrast, value loyalty and relationships. They are less willing to manipulate

Machiavellianism
A personality characteristic involving one's willingness to do whatever it takes to get one's own way.

cognitive moral development
The process of moving through stages of maturity with regard to making ethical decisions.

others for personal gain and are concerned with others' opinions.

High-Machs believe that the desired ends justify any means, so they feel it's fine to manipulate others in order to achieve a goal.[103] They are emotionally detached from other people and focus on the objective aspects of situations. High-Machs are also more likely to engage in ethically questionable behavior.[104] Employees can counter Machiavellian individuals by focusing on teamwork instead of one-on-one relationships where high-Machs have the upper hand. Making interpersonal agreements public reduces their susceptibility to Machiavellian manipulation.

Cognitive Moral Development

An individual's level of **cognitive moral development** also affects ethical behavior. Psychologist Lawrence Kohlberg proposed that as individuals mature, they move through a series of six stages of moral development (Figure 4.4).[105] With each successive stage, they become less dependent on other people's opinions of right and wrong and less self-centered (focusing less on their own interests). At higher levels of moral development, individuals are concerned with broad principles of justice and with their self-chosen ethical principles. Kohlberg's model focuses on the decision-making process

FIGURE 4.4 Kohlberg's Stages of Cognitive Moral Development

Level I	Premoral	Reward, punishment, self-interest
Level II	Conventional	Expectations of other people and society
Level III	Principle	Universal values and personal ethical principles

©Cengage Learning 2013

and on how individuals justify ethical decisions. His cognitive developmental theory explains how people decide what is right and wrong and how the decision-making process changes through interaction with peers and the environment.

Cognitive moral development occurs at three levels, each consisting of two stages. At Level I, called the *premoral level*, a person's ethical decisions are based on rewards, punishments, and self-interest. In Stage 1, people obey rules to avoid punishment. In Stage 2, people obey rules only if it is in their immediate interest to do so.

At Level II, the *conventional level*, people focus on the expectations of others. In Stage 3, individuals try to live up to the expectations of people close to them. In Stage 4, they broaden their perspective to include the laws and norms of the larger society. They fulfill duties and obligations to contribute to society.

At Level III, the *principled level*, universal values determine what is right. The individual sees beyond laws, rules, and the expectations of other people. In Stage 5, individuals are aware that people have diverse value systems. They uphold their own values even if others disagree. Individuals in Stage 5 make decisions based on principles of justice and rights. For example, someone who decides to picket an abortion clinic just because his religion bans abortion is not a Stage 5 individual. A person who arrives at the same decision through a complex decision process based on justice and rights may be a Stage 5 individual. The key is the process rather than the decision itself. In Stage 6, the individual follows self-selected ethical principles. Stage 6 individuals act according to their own self-selected ethical principles, even when these principles conflict with a law.

As individuals mature, their moral development passes through these stages in an irreversible sequence. Research suggests that most adults are in Stage 3 or 4. Most adults thus never reach the principled level of development (Stages 5 and 6).

Kohlberg's model of cognitive moral development has been supported by a great deal of research since it was proposed more than thirty years ago. Individuals at higher stages of development are less likely to cheat, more likely to engage in whistle-blowing, and more likely to make ethical business decisions.[106]

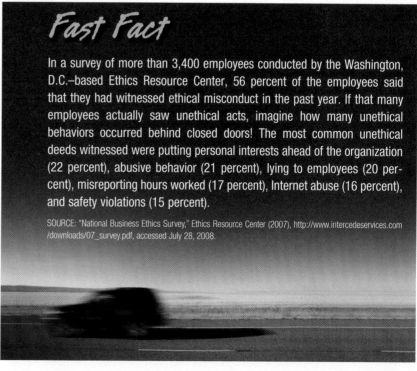

Fast Fact

In a survey of more than 3,400 employees conducted by the Washington, D.C.–based Ethics Resource Center, 56 percent of the employees said that they had witnessed ethical misconduct in the past year. If that many employees actually saw unethical acts, imagine how many unethical behaviors occurred behind closed doors! The most common unethical deeds witnessed were putting personal interests ahead of the organization (22 percent), abusive behavior (21 percent), lying to employees (20 percent), misreporting hours worked (17 percent), Internet abuse (16 percent), and safety violations (15 percent).

SOURCE: "National Business Ethics Survey," Ethics Resource Center (2007), http://www.intercedeservices.com/downloads/07_survey.pdf, accessed July 28, 2008.

But Kohlberg's model has also been criticized. Carol Gilligan, for example, argues that the model does not take gender differences into account. Kohlberg's model was developed from a twenty-year study of eighty-four boys.[107] Gilligan contends that women's moral development follows a different pattern, one based not on individual rights and rules but on responsibility and relationships. Women and men face the same moral dilemmas but approach them from different perspectives—men from the perspective of equal respect and women from the perspective of compassion and care. But researchers who reviewed the research on these gender differences concluded that the differences may not be as strong as Gilligan originally suggested.[108]

In general, though, evidence supports the idea that men and women view ethics differently. A large-scale review of sixty-six studies found that women were more likely than men to perceive certain business practices as unethical. Young women were more likely than young men to see breaking the rules and acting on insider information as unethical. Both sexes agreed that collusion, conflicts of interest, and stealing are unethical. It takes about twenty-one years for this gender gap to disappear. Men seem to become more ethical with more work experience; the longer they are in the workforce, the more their attitudes resemble those held by women. That said, age and experience are related for both sexes. Experienced workers of either sex are more likely to think that lying, bribing, stealing, and colluding are unethical.[109]

Individual differences in values, locus of control, Machiavellianism, and cognitive moral development all influence ethical behavior in organizations. Organizations might use this knowledge to promote ethical behavior by hiring individuals who share the organization's values or hiring only internals, low-Machs, and individuals at higher stages of cognitive moral development.

Log in to the **CourseMate** for *ORGB3* at **www.cengagebrain.com** to:

* Review **Key Terms Flash Cards** online
* Play **Beat the Clock** and **Quiz Bowl** to master concepts
* Complete **web quizzes** to prepare for exams
* Watch the video on **Mitchell Gold + Bob Williams** and from *The Emperor's Club* for examples, then test yourself with a quick quiz
* Work through the **"What about You?"** and **Ethical Dilemma** exercises to see how you would handle various situations that organizations face on a daily basis

Such strategies, however, obviously present both practical and legal problems.

Training may be a safer way to use this knowledge. Evidence suggests that training can increase cognitive moral development. Organizations could help individuals move to higher stages of moral development by providing educational seminars. That said, values, locus of control, Machiavellianism, and cognitive moral development are fairly stable in adults.

The best way to use the knowledge of individual differences may be to recognize that they help explain why ethical behavior differs among individuals and to focus managerial efforts on creating a work situation supporting ethical behavior.

Most workers are responsive to external influences. They do not act as independent ethical agents, but look to their organization for guidance. Managers can offer such guidance by exercising the organizational influences listed in Figure 4.3. They can encourage ethical behavior through codes of conduct, ethics committees, ethics communication systems, training, norms, modeling, and rewards and punishments, as shown in Figure 4.3. We discuss these areas further in Chapter 16.

4LTR Press solutions are designed for today's learners through the continuous feedback of students like you. Tell us what you think about ORGB and help us improve the learning experience for future students.

YOUR FEEDBACK MATTERS.

Complete the Speak Up survey in CourseMate at www.cengagebrain.com

 Follow us at www.facebook.com/4ltrpress

photo.com/mustafahacalak | © Cengage Learning 2013

Motivation at Work

LEARNING OUTCOMES

1 Define *motivation* and articulate different views of how individuals are motivated at work.

2 Explain Maslow's hierarchy of needs and its two main modifications.

3 Discuss how the needs for achievement, power, and affiliation influence an individual's behavior in the workplace.

4 Describe the two-factor theory of motivation.

5 Explain two new ideas in human motivation.

6 Describe the role of inequity in motivation.

7 Describe the expectancy theory of motivation.

8 Describe the cultural differences in motivation.

©iStockphoto.com/Enrico Fianchini

A comprehensive approach to understanding motivation, behavior, and performance must consider all three elements of the work situation and how they interact.

After You Finish This Chapter Go to **Page 88** for **Study Tools**

Motivation and Work Behavior

Motivation is the process of arousing and sustaining goal-directed behavior. Motivation theories attempt to explain and predict observable behavior. They may be broadly classified into internal, process, and external theories. *Internal theories* of motivation give primary consideration to variables within the individual that lead to motivation and behavior. Maslow's hierarchy of needs is a good example of an internal theory. *Process theories* of motivation, such as expectancy theory, emphasize the nature of the interaction between the individual and the environment. *External theories* of motivation focus on the elements in the environment, including the consequences of behavior, as the basis for understanding and explaining people's behavior at work. Any single motivation theory explains only a small portion of the variance in human behavior, so researchers have developed many alternative theories to account for unexplained behavior. A comprehensive approach to understanding motivation, behavior, and performance must consider three elements of the work situation—the individual, the job, and the work environment—and how these elements interact.[1]

Internal Needs

Philosophers and scholars have theorized for centuries about human needs and motives. During the past century, researchers have focused on motivation in a business context.[2] Max Weber, an early German sociologist, argued that the meaning of work lies not in the work itself but in its deeper potential for contributing to a person's ultimate salvation.[3] Weber, and later Milton Blood, understood this *Protestant ethic*, with its foundations in Calvinist thought, as the fuel for human industriousness. The Protestant ethic encouraged hard work on the grounds that prosperous workers were more likely to find a place in heaven.

Sigmund Freud proposed a more complex motivational theory,

motivation

The process of arousing and sustaining goal-directed behavior.

75

suggesting that a person's organizational life was founded on the compulsion to work and the power of love.[4] He emphasized the unconscious mind's influence on human motivation. **Psychoanalysis** is Freud's method for delving into the unconscious mind to better understand a person's motives and needs. Thus, the psychoanalytic approach can help explain irrational and self-destructive behaviors such as suicide or workplace violence.[5] Analyzing a person's unconscious needs and motives can help us understand such traumatic work events. The psychoanalytic approach also helps explain deviant behavior in the workplace.

Freud's thought served as the basis for subsequent *need theories* of motivation. Research suggests that people's deeper feelings transcend culture, with most people caring deeply about the same few things. Factors that make employees motivated and loyal to the organization include fair compensation and the trust and respect of their supervisors. Individuals also generally want to see a match between their personal ethics and those of the organization as well as a match between their skills and the job.[6] Intrinsic motivation nonetheless varies by the individual.[7] Managers who are more supportive and less controlling appear to elicit more intrinsic motivation from their employees.

External Incentives

Most economic assumptions about human motivation emphasize financial incentives. The Scottish political economist and moral philosopher Adam Smith argued that a person's **self-interest** was determined by God, not the government.[8] Smith laid the cornerstone for the free enterprise system of economics when he formulated the "invisible hand" and the free market to explain the motivation for individual behavior. The "invisible hand" refers to the unseen forces of a free market system that shape the most efficient use of people, money, and resources for productive ends. Smith assumed that people are motivated by self-interest for economic gain to provide the necessities and conveniences of life. Thus, employees are most productive when motivated by self-interest.

The more collective wealth an economy can produce, the better individuals can fulfill their self-interest. Techonology and labor efficiency are two ways of promoting greater collective wealth. Technology is crucial to Smith's view, because he believed that the productivity of a nation's labor force determines its wealth. Therefore, a more efficient and effective labor force yields greater abundance for the nation. Technology acts as a force multiplier for the productivity of labor.[9]

Frederick Taylor, the founder of *scientific management*, also examined labor efficiency and effectiveness.[10] His goal was to change the relationship between management and labor from one of conflict to one of cooperation.[11] Taylor believed the basis of the conflict was the division of the profits. Instead of continuing this conflict, labor and management should work together to enlarge total profits.

Early organizational scholars assumed that people were motivated by self-interest and economic gain. Consequently, they developed differential piecerate systems of pay emphasizing external incentives. Modern management practices, such as employee recognition programs, flexible benefit packages, and stock ownership plans, stem from Smith's and Taylor's original theories. They emphasize external incentives, which may take either strictly economic form or more material form, such as "outstanding employee" plaques. Whataburger has developed the WhataGames in which

[**Meeting Employee Needs**]

A great way to motivate employees is to meet various needs that they have through incentive and benefits programs. Employees at S.C. Johnson, a manufacturer of cleaning products, can use a concierge service to mail packages, send flowers, pick up groceries, and even take their cars in for an oil change. Amgen, a biotech company, gives its employees three weeks of paid vacation per year, as well as seventeen paid holidays, nearly double other businesses. At Netflix, meanwhile, employees are given unlimited vacation days, and no one keeps track of how many days workers are in or out of the office. When employees of the Miller Brewing Company need a place to unwind after work, they can head to Fred's Pub, a bar located in the company's facilities that serves twenty different kinds of beer—for free.

SOURCE: A. Greene, "9 Companies with the Best Perks," *Woman's Day* (April 26, 2010), http://www.womansday.com/Articles/Lifestyle /9-Companies-with-the-Best-Perks.html, accessed February 15, 2011.

psychoanalysis

Sigmund Freud's method for delving into the unconscious mind to better understand a person's motives and needs.

self-interest

What is in the best interest of and benefit to an individual.

©Polka Dot Images/Jupiterimages

While pay incentives have positive effects on productivity, recent studies suggest that social and interpersonal rewards also play important roles.

©iStockphoto.com/DNY59

the best employees compete for bragging rights and medals.[12] This training-and-loyalty exercise reduces turnover and builds commitment.

Some approaches, however, suggest that economic motives alone are not sufficient and need to be combined with other external motives. The Hawthorne studies, mentioned in Chapter 1 as the first to recognize informal aspects of an organization, also studied what motivates people to be productive. They confirmed the positive effects of pay incentives on productivity but also demonstrated the importance of social and interpersonal motives.[13] Other people constitute yet another external motive. Executives have recently championed "enlightened" self-interest. Self-interest is concern for one's own needs; enlightened self-interest recognizes others' interests as well.

In still other approaches, external and internal motivations are combined. Psychological ownership considers both psychological needs and external incentives to motivate workers. One study of 800 managers and employees in three different organizations found that "feelings of ownership" of an organization increased organizational citizenship behavior.[14]

LEARNING OUTCOME 2

Maslow's Need Hierarchy

Abraham Maslow, a psychologist, proposed a theory of motivation that went beyond just physical and economic needs to emphasize psychological and interpersonal needs as well. The core of Maslow's theory is a hierarchy of five "need" categories.[15] Although he recognized that factors other than one's needs (for example, culture) determine behavior, his theory focused on specifying people's internal needs. As shown in Figure 5.1, Maslow labeled the five levels of his *need hierarchy* as physiological needs, safety and security needs, love (social) needs, esteem needs, and the need for self-actualization. He conceptually derived the five need categories from the early thoughts of William James and John Dewey, coupled with the psychodynamic thinking of Sigmund Freud and Alfred Adler.[16]

One distinguishing feature of Maslow's need hierarchy is the *progression hypothesis*, which suggests that as one level of need is met, a person progresses to the next higher level of need as a source of motivation. Hence, people progress up the hierarchy as they successively gratify each level of need. Maslow understood the lowest level of ungratified needs to motivate behavior, although some research has challenged this view.[17]

Managers can make the most of Maslow's need hierarchy for success in their teams by recognizing that each individual has a unique set of needs and therefore gearing incentives to meet various needs. An ergonomic work space, for example, can fill physiological needs by making an employee comfortable in the work space. The need for security might be filled by a good retirement plan. Some

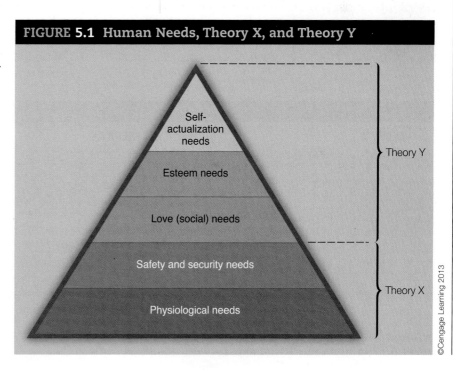

FIGURE 5.1 Human Needs, Theory X, and Theory Y

©Cengage Learning 2013

employees have a high need for social interaction, and opportunities for after-work tennis or racquetball may fill those needs. Needs for status and self-actualization can be filled by opportunities to work with higher-ups or to work on projects that particularly suit the individual's skills and interests.[18]

Theory X and Theory Y

Maslow's need hierarchy has been applied to organizational behavior in two key ways. Douglas McGregor strove to explain motivation by grouping the physiological and safety needs as "lower order" needs and the social, esteem, and self-actualization needs as "upper order" needs. According to McGregor's theory, managers can make one of two sets of assumptions about an individual depending on what factors motivate his or her behavior. McGregor's **Theory X** assumptions are appropriate for employees motivated by lower order needs, while **Theory Y** assumptions apply to employees motivated by higher order needs. These assumptions are listed in Table 5.1, and have been mapped onto Maslow's hierarchy, from which they derive, in Figure 5.1.[19]

McGregor understood the responsibility of management to be the same under both sets of assumptions. Specifically, "Management is responsible for organizing the elements of productive enterprise—money, materials, equipment, people—in the interest of economic ends."[20] Theory Y assumptions have inspired employee participation programs, and *Fortune* 1000 corporations use employee involvement to encourage high performance achievements.[21] Whole Foods founder and CEO John Mackey relies on Maslow's hierarchy of needs in motivating employees.[22]

ERG Theory

Clayton Alderfer recognized Maslow's contribution to understanding motivation, yet believed that the original need hierarchy didn't accurately identify and categorize human needs.[23] He proposed the **ERG theory** of motivation, which grouped human needs into only three basic categories: existence, relatedness, and growth.[24] Alderfer classified Maslow's physiological and physical safety needs in an *existence need* category. The interpersonal safety, love, and interpersonal esteem needs were reclassified in a *relatedness need* category. Finally, a *growth need* category encompassed Maslow's self-actualization and self-esteem needs.

ERG theory also supplemented Maslow's original progression hypothesis with a *regression hypothesis*. Alderfer's regression hypothesis suggests that when people are frustrated by their inability to meet needs at the next higher level in the hierarchy, they regress to the next lower category of needs and intensify their desire to gratify those needs. Hence, ERG theory explains both progressive need gratification and regression when people face frustration.

McClelland's Need Theory

A second major need theory of motivation focuses on personality and learned needs. Henry Murray developed a long list of motives and manifest needs in his early studies of personality.[25] Inspired by Murray's work, David McClelland identified three learned, or acquired, needs,

---

Theory X

A set of assumptions managers might apply to individuals who are motivated by lower order needs.

Theory Y

A set of assumptions managers might apply to individuals who are motivated by higher order needs.

ERG theory

A theory that organizes human needs into the categories of existence, relatedness, and growth.

TABLE 5.1 McGregor's Assumptions about People

THEORY X	THEORY Y
> People are by nature indolent. That is, they work as little as possible. > People lack ambition, dislike responsibility, and prefer to be led. > People are inherently self-centered and indifferent to organizational needs. > People are by nature resistant to change. > People are gullible and not very bright, the ready dupes of the charlatan and the demagogue.	> People are not by nature passive or resistant to organizational needs. They have become so as a result of experience in organizations. > The motivation, the potential for development, the capacity for assuming responsibility, and the readiness to direct behavior toward organizational goals are all present in people. Management does not put them there. It is a responsibility of management to make it possible for people to recognize and develop these human characteristics for themselves. > The essential task of management is to arrange conditions and methods of operation so that people can achieve their own goals best by directing their own efforts toward organizational objectives.

called **manifest needs** because they are easily perceived.[26] These are the needs for *achievement*, *power*, and *affiliation*. Some individuals have a high need for achievement, while others have a moderate or low need for achievement. The same is true for the other two needs. A manager may have a strong need for power, a moderate need for achievement, and a weak need for affiliation. Different needs are dominant in different people, and each need has different implications for people's behavior. Companies such as American Express recognize the importance of such diverse employee needs by creating and maintaining family-friendly policies.

Need for Achievement

The **need for achievement** encompasses excellence, competition, challenging goals, persistence, and overcoming difficulties.[27] People with a high need for achievement thus seek performance excellence, enjoy difficult and challenging goals, persevere, and are competitive. The *Murray Thematic Apperception Test (TAT)*, a projective test such as those discussed in Chapter 3, was used as an early measure of the achievement motive. It was further developed by McClelland and his associates, although it has been criticized, and alternative instruments have been developed.[28]

McClelland found that people with a high need for achievement perform better than those lacking such a need. Such individuals share these three characteristics: First, they set goals that are moderately difficult, yet achievable. Second, they like to receive feedback on their progress toward these goals. Third, they do not like having external events or other people interfere with their progress toward the goals.

In addition, high achievers (1) often hope and plan for success: (2) may be quite content to work alone or with other people, whichever is more appropriate to their task; and (3) like being very good at what they do so, accordingly, tend to develop expertise and competence in their chosen endeavors. The need for achievement is consistent across countries for adults who are employed full-time, but researchers have found international differences in the tendency for achievement.[29] Achievement tendencies are highest in the United States, an individualistic culture, and lowest in collectivist societies such as Japan and Hungary.[30]

Need for Power

The **need for power** includes the desire to influence others, the urge to change people or events, and the wish to make a difference in life. The need for power is interpersonal because it involves influence over other people. McClelland distinguishes between *socialized power*, which is used for the benefit of many, and *personalized power*, which is used for individual gain. The former is a constructive force, while the latter may be a very disruptive or even destructive force.

According to McClelland's research, the best managers have a very high need for socialized power as opposed to personalized power.[31] They are concerned for others; have an interest in organizational goals; and want to be useful to the larger group, organization, and society. For example, the CEO of Management Sciences for Health, Jonathan D. Quick, MD, displayed a high need for interactive, or socialized, power on the McClelland need profile while showing a very low need for imperial power, both of which are strong positive traits.

Need for Affiliation

The **need for affiliation** is an urge to establish and maintain warm, close, intimate

©iStockphoto.com/Neustockimages

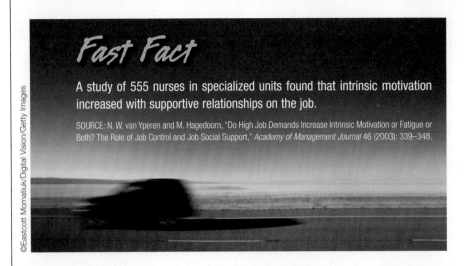

Fast Fact

A study of 555 nurses in specialized units found that intrinsic motivation increased with supportive relationships on the job.

SOURCE: N. W. van Yperen and M. Hagedoorn, "Do High Job Demands Increase Intrinsic Motivation or Fatigue or Both? The Role of Job Control and Job Social Support," *Academy of Management Journal* 46 (2003): 339–348.

relationships with others.[32] People with a high need for affiliation are motivated to express their emotions to others and expect them to do the same in return. They find conflicts disturbing and are strongly motivated to work through any such barriers to closeness. The need for relationships is important not only in McClelland's theory, but in each of the theories we have discussed so far.

Over and above these three needs for achievement, power, and affiliation, Murray's manifest needs theory also included the need for autonomy. This is the desire for independence and freedom from constraints. People with a high need for autonomy prefer to work alone and to control the pace of

motivation factor

A work condition that satisfies the need for psychological growth.

their work. They dislike bureaucratic rules, regulations, and procedures.

Figure 5.2 shows the parallel structures of Maslow's, McGregor's, Alderfer's, and McClelland's theories of motivation.

LEARNING OUTCOME **4**

Herzberg's Two-Factor Theory

In developing his *two-factor theory of motivation*, Frederick Herzberg departed from need-based theories and examined the experiences that satisfied or dissatisfied people at work.[33] Herzberg's original study included 200 engineers and accountants in western Pennsylvania during the 1950s. He asked them to describe two important incidents at their jobs: one that was very satisfying and made them feel exceptionally good at work and another that was very dissatisfying and made them feel exceptionally bad.

Herzberg and his colleagues believed that people had two sets of needs—one based on avoiding pain and one stemming from the desire for psychological growth. Conditions in the work environment would affect one or the other of these two needs. Work conditions related to satisfaction of the need for psychological growth were labeled **motivation factors**. Work conditions related to dissatisfaction caused by discomfort or pain were labeled

FIGURE **5.2** Need Theories of Motivation

	Maslow	McGregor	Alderfer	McClelland
Higher order needs	Self-actualization		Growth	Need for achievement
	Esteem — Self / Interpersonal	Theory Y		Need for power
	Belongingness (social and love)		Relatedness	Need for affiliation
Lower order needs	Safety and security — Interpersonal / Physical	Theory X		
	Physiological		Existence	

FIGURE 5.3 The Motivation–Hygiene Theory of Motivation

Hygiene factors: Job dissatisfaction	Motivation factors: Job satisfaction
	Achievement
	Recognition of achievement
	Work itself
	Responsibility
	Advancement
	Growth
Company policy and administration	
Supervision	
Interpersonal relations	
Working conditions	
Salary*	
Status	
Security	

*Because of its ubiquitous nature, salary commonly shows up as a motivation as well as a hygiene factor. Although primarily a hygiene factor, it also often takes on some of the properties of a motivator, with dynamics similar to those of recognition for achievement.

SOURCE: Reprinted from F. Herzberg, *The Managerial Choice: To Be Efficient or to Be Human* (Salt Lake City: Olympus, 1982). Reprinted by permission.

hygiene factors. Motivation factors relate to job satisfaction, and hygiene factors relate to job dissatisfaction, as shown in Figure 5.3.[34]

Motivation Factors

Job enrichment involves building motivation factors into a job and, according to Herzberg, creates job satisfaction. In his original research, Herzberg identified motivation factors as responsibility, achievement, recognition, advancement, and the work itself. When these factors are present, they improve a worker's effort and performance. Figure 5.3 shows that salary is also a motivational factor in some studies. Acceptance of this idea has led many organizational reward systems to include financial benefits such as stock options as part of an employee's compensation package.

Motivation factors lead to positive mental health. They challenge people to

hygiene factor

A work condition that generates dissatisfaction due to discomfort or pain.

grow, contribute to the work environment, and invest themselves in the organization. The absence of these factors does not lead to dissatisfaction, but rather to feelings of neutrality. Motivation factors are the more important of the two sets of factors because they directly affect a person's drive to do a good job. When they are absent, a person lacks the motivation to perform well and achieve excellence.

Hygiene Factors

Hygiene factors are completely distinct from the motivation factors and are unrelated to the drive to achieve and do excellent work. While motivation factors create job satisfaction if present or feelings of neutrality if absent, absent or insufficient hygiene factors result in job dissatisfaction. Herzberg's hygiene factors include company policy and administration, technical supervision, interpersonal relations with one's supervisor, working conditions, salary, and status. Good hygiene factors cannot stimulate psychological growth or human development, but they are necessary to prevent job dissatisfaction.

When these hygiene factors are poor or absent, the dissatisfied employee complains about "poor supervision," "poor medical benefits," or whatever hygiene factor is poor. Many companies have initiated formal flextime policies to reduce dissatisfaction and persuade women leaders to come back to work.[35] Even in the absence of good hygiene factors, employees may still be very motivated to perform their jobs well if the motivation factors are present.

Two conclusions can be drawn. First, hygiene factors are important to a certain level, but unimportant beyond that threshold. Second, the presence of

eustress

Healthy, normal stress.

motivation factors is essential to enhancing employee motivation to excel at work.

Critique of the Two-Factor Theory

One criticism of Herzberg's theory concerns the classification of the two factors. Data have shown that a factor may not fit exclusively into either the hygiene or motivation categories. For example, employees generally classify pay as both a hygiene factor and a motivation factor. Second, the theory does not account for individual differences. Differences in age, sex, social status, education, or occupational level may influence the classification of factors. A third problem is that intrinsic job factors like the workflow process may be more important in determining satisfaction or dissatisfaction on the job. Finally, almost all of the supporting data for the theory come from Herzberg and his students using his peculiar *critical-incident technique*. These criticisms challenge and qualify the theory, yet do not invalidate it. Independent research found his theory valid in a government research and development (R&D) environment.[36] Herzberg's two-factor theory has important implications for the design of work, as we will discuss in Chapter 14.

Two New Ideas in Motivation

Two new ideas in motivation have emerged in the past decade. One centers on eustress, strength, and hope. This idea comes from the new discipline of *positive organizational behavior*. A second new idea centers on positive energy and full engagement, translating what was learned from high-performance athletes for the use of *Fortune* 500 executives and managers.

Eustress, Strength, and Hope

Eustress (called so for "euphoria + stress") is healthy, normal stress.[37] Stress is the energy we experience when confronted with a challenging or difficult situation. Such situations can produce *distress*, a negative response such as frustration or fear, which leads to unhealthy and unproductive results, or eustress, a positive response to challenges that generates energy and motivates an individual to achieve. Eustress leads us to invest in strengths, find meaning in work, display courage and principled action, and draw on positive emotions at work.[38] This positive perspective on organizational life encourages optimism, hope, and health for people at work. Instead of focusing on the individual's needs or the rewards or punishment meted out in the work environment, the idea of encouraging eustress is to focus on the individual's interpretation of or response to events. An assumption underlying eustress is that although things happen that are out of our control,

Hot Trend: Sleeping on the Job

Human resource manager Jackie Walsh recently approved the use of an innovative performance-enhancing technique at her company, toy manufacturer Worlds Apart. When employees feel fatigued or low on energy during the work day, they are free to take twenty-minute naps on inflatable mattresses provided by the company. The practice is not intended to replace a good night's sleep, nor does it grant employees two-hour siestas. *Power-napping* is an energy-recovery technique that has been practiced over the ages by accomplished and talented people, such as Lieutenant General George C. Patton.

While falling asleep at one's desk imposes poor posture (preventing appropriate relaxation and recovery), reclined napping, even for as few as fifteen minutes, reverses information overload and improves memory and performance. A number of progressive companies allow employees to retreat into special napping rooms for several hours so they can work late into the night. Some managers, however, criticize long midday naps for producing lethargy and interfering with the work-home balance. The Worlds Apart approach to napping is a focused strategy similar to high-performance athletes' use of short energy-recovery activities to achieve peak performance when fully engaged. Power-napping is a welcome reprieve at Worlds Apart, proving especially valuable to new parents and employees engaged in long stretches of work.

SOURCE: Staff, "Bizarre HR: A 20-Minute Nap Leaves Staff Perky and Motivated." *Human Resources* (May 2009): 11; "The National Institute of Mental Health Power-Nap Study," National Institutes of Health (July 1, 2002), http://www.nih.gov/news/pr/jul2002/nimh-02.htm, accessed July 20, 2009.

we can control our response to a situation. Thus, we can control distress by reframing our perspective on a situation. Eustress is a healthy and positive motivational force for individuals who harness its energy for productive work and organizational contributions.

Positive Energy and Full Engagement

The second new concept in motivation, Jim Loehr's *full engagement* idea, uses lessons learned from professional athletes.[39] The central tenets are that an individual should manage energy rather than

time and should strategically disengage from certain activities to balance the power of full engagement.[40] This approach suggests that individuals do not need to be activated by unmet needs but are already activated by their own physical, emotional, mental, and spiritual

[The Money in Motivation]

Kenexa is a leading human resources company in America. Its client list includes sixty *Fortune* 100 companies, such as Caterpillar, Time Warner, and Wells Fargo. Kenexa's success can be attributed to an understanding of both psychology and technology, which enable it to accurately and efficiently respond to employee needs. Kenexa recognizes that employees want to enjoy their work, and sometimes need inspiration to manage overwhelming dilemmas. The company utilizes interviews and surveys to evaluate workplace environments, including employees' anxieties. Based upon the data collected, Kenexa devises company-specific strategies that motivate and reassure employees while satisfying their needs. The benefits of deft human resources are not simply speculative—companies with higher employee satisfaction scores net 700 percent higher shareholder returns. In addition to bolstering motivation and job satisfaction, Kenexa works to inspire loyalty and pride in employees. Turnover, an expensive and frustrating phenomenon, is 21 percent lower among managers who express pride in their company. Understanding and responding to employees' needs is not just good for workers—it's good for the entire corporation.

SOURCE: K. Rockwood. "Employee Whisperer," *Fast Company* (November 2008): 72–73.

energy. Managers should therefore help individuals learn to manage their energy so that they can build positive energy and capacity for work.

Loehr's concept stresses the role of energy recovery in overall performance. Some individuals work best by putting forth productive energy for short periods and then taking time to rest and reenergize. This mimics the human body's potential to build or enhance its capacity, enabling the individual to sustain a high level of performance in the face of increasing work demands. Organizations with high levels of employee engagement have strong financial performance, even in volatile economic conditions.[41]

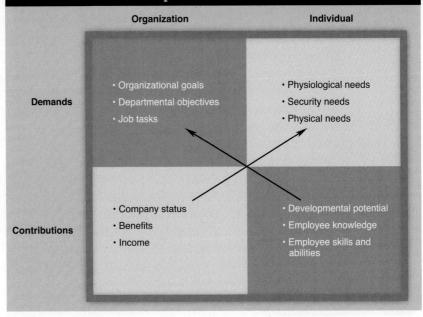

FIGURE **5.4** **The Individual–Organizational Exchange Relationship**

SOURCE: J. P. Campbell, M. D. Dunnette, E. E. Lawler, III, and K. E. Weick, Jr., *Managerial Behavior, Performance, and Effectiveness* (New York: McGraw-Hill, Inc., 1970). Reproduced with permission from McGraw-Hill, Inc.

LEARNING OUTCOME **6**

Social Exchange and Equity Theory

Equity theory is a social exchange process approach to motivation that focuses on the interaction between an individual and her environment. In contrast to needs theories based on internal motivation, equity theory is concerned with the social processes that influence motivation and behavior. Power and exchange are important considerations in understanding human behavior.[42] Accounting for such external factors, Amitai Etzioni developed three categories of exchange relationships that people have with organizations: committed, calculated, and alienated involvements.[43] Committed relations have high positive intensity, calculated relationships have low positive or low negative intensity, and alienated relationships have high negative intensity. Committed relationships may characterize a person's involvement with a religious group, and alienated relationships may characterize a person's incarceration in a prison. These three categories will be discussed further in Chapter 11.

Demands and Contributions

Calculated involvements are based on the notion of social exchange in which each party in the relationship demands certain things of the other and contributes accordingly to the exchange. Business partnerships and commercial deals are both calculated involvements. When both parties to the exchange benefit, the relationship has a positive orientation. When losses occur or conflicts arise, the relationship has a negative orientation. Figure 5.4 offers a model for examining calculated exchange relationships.

Demands Each party to the exchange makes demands on the other. The organization expresses its demands on the individual in the form of goal or mission statements, job expectations, performance objectives, and performance feedback. The individual expresses demands, or needs, in the form of expectations of the organization. Employee need fulfillment and the feeling of belonging are both important to a healthy exchange and to organizational membership.[44] These needs may be viewed from the perspective of Maslow, Alderfer, Herzberg, or McClelland. When employees are well taken care of by the company, they take care of the business even in very difficult times.

Contributions Just as each party to the exchange makes demands upon the other, each also contributes to the relationship. These contributions are the basis for satisfying the demands expressed by the other party. Employees satisfy organizational demands through a range of contributions, including their skills, abilities, knowledge, energy, professional contacts, and native talents. As people grow and develop over time, they are able to increasingly satisfy the range of demands and expectations placed upon them by the organization.

In a similar fashion, organizations contribute to the exchange relationship to meet individual needs. These contributions include salary, benefits, advancement opportunities, security, status, and social affiliation. Some organizations are richer in resources and better able to meet employee needs than other organizations. One of the concerns that both individuals and organizations have is whether the relationship is a fair deal or an equitable arrangement for both members of the relationship. Social exchange relationship perceptions are influenced by executive leadership style, organizational culture, and employment approach, which in turn have an effect on commitment and performance, though not organizational citizenship behavior (OCB), discussed in Chapter 4.[45]

Adams's Theory of Inequity

Ideas about social process and exchange advocated by Etzioni and others provide a context for understanding fairness, equity, and inequity in work relationships. Stacy Adams developed the idea that **inequity** in the social exchange process is a particularly important motivator. Adams's *theory of inequity* suggests that people are motivated when they find themselves in situations of inequity, or unfairness.[46] Inequity occurs when a person receives more or less than she believes she deserves based on her effort and/or contribution. Inequity creates tension, which in turn motivates a person to take action to resolve the inequity.

A perception of inequity arises when people consider their inputs (their contributions to the relationship) and their outcomes (the organization's contributions to the relationship) according to an input/outcome ratio, which they compare to that of a generalized "other," or *comparison other*. Figure 5.5 shows two inequity scenarios for a single situation, one negative and one positive. The negative inequity in (b) could occur, for example, if the comparison other earned a higher salary, while inequity in (c) could occur if the person had more vacation time, in both cases all else being equal. Although not illustrated in the example, nontangible inputs such as emotional investment and nontangible outcomes such as job satisfaction may enter into a person's equity equation.

Pay inequity has been a thorny issue for women in some companies. Eastman Kodak and other companies have made real progress in addressing the issue of pay equity.[47] Globalization also presents a challenge for pay equity. As organizations grow internationally, they may have trouble determining pay and benefit equity/inequity across national borders.

Adams considers a situation in which there is inequity in only one variable to be a first level of inequity. A more severe, second level of inequity would occur, for example, in a situation where the inputs of a person experiencing negative inequity, as in Figure 5.5(b), are also greater than those of the comparison other. Inequalities in one (inputs or outcomes) coupled with equality in the other (inputs or outcomes) are experienced as a less severe inequity than inequalities in both inputs and outcomes. One drawback of Adams's theory is that it does not provide a way of determining if some inputs or some outcomes are more important than others.

The Resolution of Inequity

Once a person establishes the existence of an inequity, she might use a number of strategies to restore equity. Adams's theory provides seven basic strategies for restoring equity: (1) alter the person's outcomes, (2) alter the person's inputs, (3) alter the comparison other's outcomes, (4) alter the comparison other's inputs, (5) change who is used as a comparison other, (6) rationalize the inequity, and (7) leave the organizational situation.

Each of the first four strategies could involve a wide variety of tactics. For example, if an employee has a strategy to increase his income by $11,000 per year to restore equity, the tactic might be a meeting between the employee and his manager concerning the issue of salary equity. Another tactic would be for the person to work with the company's compensation specialists.

The selection of a strategy and a set of tactics is a sensitive issue with possible long-term consequences. In this example, a strategy aimed at reducing the comparison other's outcomes may have the desired short-term effect of restoring equity but reduce morale and productivity in the long term. The equity theory does not include a hierarchy predicting which inequity-reduction strategy a person will or should choose, but it is nevertheless a reminder of the importance of fairness. One study found that workers who perceived compensation decisions as equitable displayed greater job satisfaction and organizational commitment.[48]

New Perspectives on Equity Theory

Equity theory has been revised in light of new theories and research. One important theoretical revision proposes three

inequity

A situation in which a person perceives that he or she is receiving less than he or she is giving or is giving less than he or she is receiving.

FIGURE 5.5 Equity and Inequity at Work

	Person		Comparison other
(a) Equity	$\dfrac{\text{Outcomes}}{\text{Inputs}}$	$=$	$\dfrac{\text{Outcomes}}{\text{Inputs}}$
(b) Negative Inequity	$\dfrac{\text{Outcomes}}{\text{Inputs}}$	$<$	$\dfrac{\text{Outcomes}}{\text{Inputs}}$
(c) Positive Inequity	$\dfrac{\text{Outcomes}}{\text{Inputs}}$	$>$	$\dfrac{\text{Outcomes}}{\text{Inputs}}$

©Cengage Learning 2013

Equality in pay is an important factor in motivation.

©iStockphoto.com/Kadir Barcin

types of individuals based on preferences for equity.[49] **Equity sensitives** prefer equity based on the originally formed theory. In other words, they want the relationship between their own input and output to be equal to that of their comparison other. Equity sensitivity contributes significantly to variation in free time spent working.[50] **Benevolents** are comfortable with an equity ratio less than that of their comparison other.[51] These people may be thought of as givers. **Entitleds** are comfortable only with an equity ratio greater than that of their comparison other.[52] These people may be thought of as takers.

Equity in pay is an important factor in motivation because pay is often thought to relate to a person's self-imposed performance expectations. But one study suggests that a person's organizational position also influences self-imposed performance expectations and may be a more important factor than pay.[53] Specifically, a two-level move up in an organization with no additional pay creates a higher self-imposed performance expectation than a one-level move up with modest additional pay. Similarly, a two-level move down in an organization with no reduction in pay creates a lower self-imposed performance expectation than a one-level move down with a modest decrease in pay.

Unfortunately, inequity and organizational injustice can also generate dysfunctional behavior.[54] More seriously, workplace injustice can trigger aggressive reactions that harm both individuals and the organization. Fortunately, only a small number of individuals respond to such unfairness through dysfunctional behavior.[55]

Increasing, decreasing, or constant experiences of inequity over time may have very different consequences for people.[56] Equity theory can help companies implement two-tiered wage structures such as the one used by American Airlines in the early 1990s. In a two-tiered system, one group of employees receives different pay and benefits than another group of employees. Such a system can, however, generate perceptions of inequity, especially where the value of equal pay for equal work is strongly

equity sensitive
An individual who prefers an equity ratio equal to that of his or her comparison other.

benevolent
An individual who is comfortable with an equity ratio less than that of his or her comparison other.

entitled
An individual who is comfortable with an equity ratio greater than that of his or her comparison other.

PAY INEQUITY

CEOs of companies that are listed on the S&P 500 make an average of $9.25 million per year, and the average CEO makes 319 times more than the average U.S. worker. To address this significant inequity in salaries, a number of companies have connected CEO pay to company performance. Jim Skinner, CEO of McDonald's, received an $11.5 million bonus on top of his $1.4 million salary because the company produced a 16 percent return for shareholders. Conversely, John Stumpf, the CEO of Wells Fargo, took a 6 percent pay cut, since his company lost $3 billion in revenue.

SOURCES: "Trends in CEO Pay," AFL-CIO, http://www.aflcio.org/corporatewatch/paywatch/pay/index.cfm, accessed August 11, 2010; G. Rudawsky, "McDonald's CEO's $17 Million Pay Tied to Performance," *DailyFinance* (April 10, 2010), http://www.dailyfinance.com/story/mcdonalds-ceos-17-million-pay-tied-to-performance/19434075, accessed February 15, 2010; "Wells Fargo CEO's Pay Cut to $17.56 Million," *The News Tribune* (March 22, 2011), http://www.thenewstribune.com/2011/03/22/1594796/wells-fargo-ceos-pay-cut-to-1756.html, accessed June 10, 2011.

held. Research suggests that unions and management may want to consider work location and employment status (part-time versus full-time) prior to implementing a two-tiered system.[57]

LEARNING OUTCOME **7**

Expectancy Theory of Motivation

In addition to individual needs and social exchange, motivation can also be explained in terms of an individual's perception of the performance process. Victor Vroom's *expectancy theory* of motivation is a cognitive process theory founded on two basic notions. First, Vroom assumes that people expect certain outcomes of behavior and performance, which may be thought of as rewards, or consequences of behavior. Second, people believe there is a correlation between the effort they put forth, the performance they achieve, and the outcomes they receive. Expectancy theory has been used in a wide variety of contexts, including test-taking motivation among students.[58]

The key constructs in the expectancy theory of motivation are the valence of an outcome, expectancy, and instrumentality.[59] **Valence** is the value, or importance, one places on a particular reward. **Expectancy** is the belief that effort leads to performance (for example, "If I try harder, I can do better"). **Instrumentality** is the belief that performance is related to rewards (for example, "If I perform better, I will get more pay"). Figure 5.6 models the expectancy theory notions of effort, performance, and rewards.

Valence, expectancy, and instrumentality all influence a person's motivation. The perceived relationship between effort and performance varies from person to person and from activity to activity. One person might believe that an increase in effort has a direct, positive effect on performance. Another person might have a very different set of beliefs about the link between effort and performance. In a similar fashion, people's beliefs about the link between performance and reward vary. From a motivation perspective, it is the person's belief about the relationships between these constructs that is important, not the actual nature of the relationship.

Managers can use expectancy theory to design *motivation programs*.[60] Sometimes called *performance planning* or *evaluation systems*, these motivation programs are meant to enhance a person's belief that effort will improve performance and therefore lead to better pay. Valence and expectancy are particularly important in establishing priorities for people pursuing multiple goals.[61]

Valence is the third key idea within the expectancy theory of motivation. Different people value different rewards. One person prefers salary to benefits, whereas another person prefers just the reverse. In fact, employees vary greatly with respect to the link between work and pay, as well as how much they value money.[62]

Motivational Problems

Expectancy theory attributes motivational problems to three basic causes: disbelief in a relationship between effort and performance, disbelief in a relationship between performance and rewards, and lack of desire for the rewards offered. If the motivational problem stems from the person's belief that effort will not improve performance, the solution lies in altering this belief. The person can be shown how an increase in effort or an alteration in the kind of effort put forth can be converted into improved performance.

If the motivational problem is related to the person's belief that performance will not result in rewards, the solution also lies in altering that belief. The person can be shown how an increase in performance or a somewhat altered form of performance will be converted into rewards. If, however, the motivational problem is related to the value placed on certain rewards, there are two possible solutions: to alter the value placed on the rewards or to alter the rewards themselves.

Research results on expectancy theory have been mixed.[63] The theory predicts job satisfaction accurately, but its complexity makes it difficult to test the full model, and the measures of instrumentality, valence, and expectancy have only weak validity.[64] In addition, measuring expectancy constructs is time consuming, and the values

valence
The value or importance one places on a particular reward.

expectancy
The belief that effort leads to performance.

instrumentality
The belief that performance is related to rewards.

FIGURE **5.6** An Expectancy Model for Motivation

Effort → Performance → Reward

Perceived effort–performance probability

Perceived performance–reward probability

Perceived value of rewards

"What are my chances of getting the job done if I put forth the necessary effort?"

"What are my chances of getting the rewards I value if I satisfactorily complete the job?"

"What rewards do I value?"

©Cengage Learning 2013

for each construct change over time for an individual. Finally, the theory assumes that the individual is totally rational and acts as a minicomputer, calculating probabilities and values. In reality, the theory may be more complex than the way people typically function.

Motivation and Moral Maturity

Expectancy theory predicts that people will work to maximize their personal outcomes. This is consistent with Adam Smith's idea of working for one's own self-interest. Both suggest that people work to benefit themselves alone. Expectancy theory cannot explain altruistic behavior. Therefore, it may be necessary to consider an individual's **moral maturity** in order to understand altruistic, fair, and equitable behavior. Moral maturity is the measure of a person's cognitive moral development, as discussed in Chapter 4. Morally mature people behave based on universal ethical principles, while morally immature people behave based on egocentric motivations.[65]

examining equity theory in cross-cultural contexts have suggested reexamining equity preferences, selection of referent others, and reactions to inequity.[69] Finally, expectancy theory may hold up well in cultures that value individualism but break down in more collectivist cultures that value cooperative efforts. In collectivist cultures, rewards are more closely tied to group and team efforts, and expectancy theory is ill-equipped to deal with such differences.

LEARNING OUTCOME **8**

Cultural Differences in Motivation

Most motivation theories in use today have been developed by and about Americans.[66] When researchers have examined the universality of these theories, they have found cultural differences, at least with regard to Maslow's, McClelland's, and Herzberg's theories. For example, while self-actualization is the pinnacle need for Americans in Maslow's need hierarchy, security may be the most important need for people in cultures with a high need to avoid uncertainty.[67] Although achievement is an important need for Americans, research suggests that other cultures do not value achievement as much as Americans do.

The two-factor theory has been tested in other countries as well. Results in New Zealand did not replicate the results found in the United States; supervision and interpersonal relationships were important motivators in New Zealand, as opposed to the importance of hygienic factors as in America.[68] Researchers

moral maturity
The measure of a person's cognitive moral development.

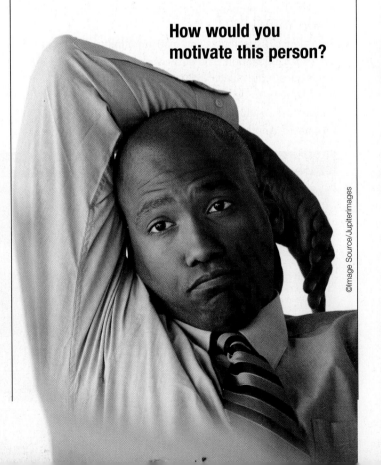

How would you motivate this person?

©Image Source/Jupiterimages

THE IN-CROWD

Share your 4LTR Press story on Facebook at www.facebook.com/4ltrpress for a chance to win.

To learn more about the In-Crowd opportunity 'like' us on Facebook.

Learning and Performance Management

LEARNING OUTCOMES

1 Describe behavioral theories of learning.

2 Describe social and cognitive theories of learning.

3 Explain how goal setting can be used to direct learning and performance.

4 Define *performance* and identify the tools used to measure it.

5 Explain the importance of performance feedback and how it can be delivered effectively.

6 Identify ways managers can reward performance.

7 List several strategies for correcting poor performance.

©iStockphoto.com/sextoacto

"Reinforcement and punishment are used to manage good and bad behavior."

Behavioral Models of Learning in Organizations

Learning is a change in behavior acquired through experience. It helps guide and direct motivated behavior. Learning may begin with the cognitive activity of developing knowledge about a subject, which then leads to a change in behavior. Alternatively, the behaviorist approach to learning assumes that observable behavior is a function of its consequences. Behaviorists argue that learning stems from classical and operant conditioning.

Classical Conditioning

Classical conditioning is the process of modifying behavior by pairing a conditioned stimulus with an unconditioned stimulus to elicit an unconditioned response. Its discovery is largely the result of Russian physiologist Ivan Pavlov's experimentation on animals (primarily dogs).[1] During the early 1900s, Pavlov's professional exchanges with Walter B. Cannon and other American researchers brought his ideas to prominence in the United States.[2]

Classical conditioning builds on the natural reaction of an unconditioned response to an unconditioned stimulus. In dogs, this might be the natural production of saliva (unconditioned response) in response to the presentation of meat (unconditioned stimulus). By presenting a conditioned stimulus (for example, a ringing bell) simultaneously with the unconditioned stimulus (meat), the researcher made the dog develop a conditioned response (salivation). After enough trials, the dog salivated at the sound of a bell, even when no meat was presented.

As demonstrated by B. F. Skinner, classical conditioning may occur similarly in humans.[3] For example, people working

learning
A change in behavior acquired through experience.

classical conditioning
Modifying behavior by pairing a conditioned stimulus with an unconditioned stimulus to elicit an unconditioned response.

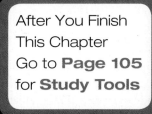

After You Finish This Chapter Go to **Page 105** for **Study Tools**

at a computer terminal may get lower back tension (unconditioned response) from poor posture (unconditioned stimulus). If they become aware of that tension only when the manager appears (conditioned stimulus), then they may develop a conditioned response (lower back tension) to the appearance of the manager.

But classical conditioning has limited applicability to human behavior in organizations for three reasons. First, humans are more complex than dogs and less amenable to simple cause-and-effect conditioning. Second, the behavioral environments in organizations are complex and not very amenable to single stimulus–response manipulations. Third, the human capacity for decision making can override simple conditioning.

Operant Conditioning

Operant conditioning is the process of modifying behavior by following specific behaviors with positive or negative consequences.[4] These consequences influence behavior through three strategies: reinforcement, punishment, and extinction. Management pioneer Fred Luthans and his colleagues used *organizational behavior modification (OBM)* to shape behavior in a variety of organizations.[5] OBM employs three types of consequences: financial reinforcement, nonfinancial reinforcement, and social reinforcement. A major review of OBM's influence in organizations found that it had significant and positive influence on task performance in both manufacturing and service organizations, but that the effects were most powerful in manufacturing organizations.[6] In a study of pay for performance, more productive employees chose performance-based compensation over fixed compensation when given a choice.[7] However, regardless of which pay scheme employees chose, all produced more under a pay-for-performance scheme. And while attitudes about pay for performance continue to vary according to cultural values, research suggests that its use may be rising cross-culturally.[8]

Reinforcement Theory

Reinforcement theory holds that reinforcement enhances desirable behavior, whereas punishment and extinction diminish undesirable behavior. This theory is central to the design and administration of organizational reward systems, which are a key factor in attracting and

Positive consequences, such as travel opportunities, have a significant impact on task performance.

©iStockphoto.com/Stephen Strathdee

retaining top employees. Strategic rewards help motivate behavior, actions, and accomplishments, all of which advance the organization toward specific business goals.[9] In addition to cash rewards such as bonuses, strategic rewards include training and educational opportunities, stock options, and recognition awards such as travel.

Reinforcement and punishment represent the positive and negative consequences of behavior. **Positive consequences** are the results that the person finds attractive or pleasurable. They might include a pay increase, bonus, promotion, transfer to a more desirable geographic location, or praise from a supervisor. **Negative consequences** are the results that the person finds unattractive or aversive. They might include disciplinary action, an undesirable transfer, a demotion, or harsh criticism from a supervisor. The recipient of the consequences defines them as positive or negative. Therefore, individual personality differences as well as gender and cultural differences may be important in their classification.

Following a specific behavior with a positive or negative consequence either reinforces or punishes that behavior.[10] Thorndike's *law of effect* states that behaviors followed by positive consequences are more likely to recur and behaviors followed by negative consequences are less likely to recur.[11] Figure 6.1 shows how positive and negative consequences may be applied or withheld in the strategies of reinforcement and punishment.

Reinforcement Reinforcement is a strategy to cultivate desirable behavior by either bestowing positive consequences or withholding negative ones. Positive reinforcement occurs when a positive consequence (like a bonus) follows a desirable behavior (like a successful business year). Marriott International provides positive reinforcement by honoring ten to twenty employees each year with its J. Willard Marriott Award of Excellence. Each recipient receives a medallion engraved with the words that express the basic values of the company: dedication, achievement, character, ideals, effort, and perseverance.

operant conditioning

Modifying behavior through the use of positive or negative consequences following specific behaviors.

positive consequences

Results of a behavior that a person finds attractive or pleasurable.

negative consequences

Results of a behavior that a person finds unattractive or aversive.

reinforcement

A strategy to cultivate desirable behavior by either bestowing positive consequences or withholding negative consequences.

FIGURE 6.1 Reinforcement and Punishment Strategies

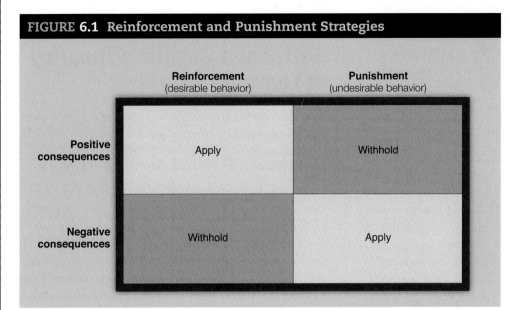

	Reinforcement (desirable behavior)	Punishment (undesirable behavior)
Positive consequences	Apply	Withhold
Negative consequences	Withhold	Apply

SOURCE: Table from *Organizational Behavior Modification* by Fred Luthans and Robert Kreitner. Copyright © 1985, p. 58 by Scott Foresman and Company and the authors. Reprinted by permission of the authors.

Negative reinforcement occurs when managers withhold a negative consequence after an employee demonstrates a desirable behavior. For example, a manager who reduces an employee's pay (negative consequence) if the employee comes to work late (undesirable behavior) refrains from doing so when the employee is on time (desirable behavior). The employee avoids the negative consequence (a reduction in pay) by exhibiting the desirable behavior (being on time to work).

When managers design organizational reward systems, they consider not only the type of reinforcement but also how often to provide it, according to continuous or intermittent schedules, as shown in Table 6.1.

Punishment

Punishment is a strategy to discourage undesirable behavior. One way to punish a person is to follow an

punishment
A strategy to discourage undesirable behavior by either bestowing negative consequences or withholding positive consequences.

TABLE 6.1 Schedules of Reinforcement

SCHEDULE	DESCRIPTION	EFFECTS ON RESPONDING
Continuous	Reinforcer follows every response.	1. Steady, high rate of performance as long as reinforcement follows every response 2. High frequency of reinforcement may lead to early satiation 3. Behavior weakens rapidly (undergoes extinction) when reinforcers are withheld 4. Appropriate for newly emitted, unstable, low-frequency responses
Intermittent	Reinforcer does not follow every response.	1. Capable of producing high frequencies of responding 2. Low frequency of reinforcement precludes early satiation 3. Appropriate for stable or high-frequency responses
Fixed Ratio	A fixed number of responses must be emitted before reinforcement occurs.	1. A fixed ratio of 1:1 (reinforcement occurs after every response) is the same as a continuous schedule 2. Tends to produce a high rate of response that is vigorous and steady
Variable Ratio	A varying or random number of responses must be emitted before reinforcement occurs.	Capable of producing a high rate of response that is vigorous, steady, and resistant to extinction
Fixed Interval	The first response after a specific period of time has elasped is reinforced.	Produces an uneven response pattern varying from a very slow, unenergetic response immediately following reinforcement to a very fast, vigorous response immediately preceding reinforcement
Variable Interval	The first response after varying or random periods of time have elapsed is reinforced.	Tends to produce a high rate of response that is vigorous, steady, and resistant to extinction

SOURCE: F. Luthans and R. Kreitner, *Organizational Behavior Modification* (Glenview, Ill.: Scott, Foresman, 1985). Copyright © by Scott Foresman and Company and the authors. Reprinted by permission of the authors.

©iStockphoto.com/Sean Locke

undesirable behavior with a negative consequence. For example, a professional athlete who is excessively offensive to an official (undesirable behavior) may be ejected from the game (negative consequence). The other way to punish a person is to withhold a positive consequence following an undesirable behavior. For example, a salesperson who puts little effort into his pitch (undesirable behavior) won't likely receive a large commission check (positive consequence).

Punishment sometimes has unintended results. Because punishment is discomforting to the individual being punished, it can bring about negative psychological, emotional, performance, or behavioral consequences (such as workplace deviance), especially when applied too often. Being aware of this potential consequence of a generalized negative response and decreased motivation to work better, some managers use the threat of punishment—rather than actually applying the punishment—to scare workers into greater effort whenever possible.[12]

Extinction An alternative to punishing undesirable behavior is **extinction**—a strategy to weaken a behavior by attaching no consequences (either positive or negative) to it. This strategy may require time and patience, but the absence of consequences eventually weakens a behavior. Extinction may be most effective when used in conjunction with the positive reinforcement of desirable behaviors. For example, complimenting a sarcastic colleague for constructive comments (reinforcing desirable behavior) while ignoring sarcastic comments (extinguishing undesirable behavior) may prove doubly effective. Extinction is not always the best strategy, however. In cases of dangerous or seriously undesirable behavior, punishment might better deliver a swift, clear lesson.

extinction
A strategy to weaken a behavior by attaching no consequences to it.

task-specific self-efficacy
An individual's internal expectancy to perform a specific task effectively.

Social and Cognitive Theories of Learning

In addition to behavorist theory, social and cognitive theories of learning have been proposed.

Bandura's Social Learning Theory

Albert Bandura's social learning theory offers a complementary alternative to Pavlov's and Skinner's behaviorist approaches.[13] Bandura asserts that learning occurs when we observe other people and model their behavior. Because employees look to their supervisors for acceptable norms of behavior, they are likely to pattern their own actions after the supervisor's. Central to Bandura's social learning theory is the notion of **task-specific self-efficacy**, an individual's internal expectancy to perform a specific task effectively. Individuals with high self-efficacy believe that they have the ability to get things done. Self-efficacy is higher in a learning context than in a performance context, especially for individuals with a high learning orientation.[14] There are four sources of task-specific self-efficacy: prior experiences, behavior models (witnessing the success of others), persuasion from other people, and assessment of current physical and emotional capabilities.[15] Evidence suggests that self-efficacy leads to high performance on a wide variety of physical and mental tasks.[16] Prior success can also enhance one's self-efficacy. For example, women who trained in physical self-defense increased their self-efficacy in self-defense and new tasks.[17]

Alexander Stajkovic and Fred Luthans drew on Bandura's ideas of self-efficacy and social learning to expand their original work in behavioral management and OBM into a comprehensive framework for performance management.[18] Bandura saw the power of social reinforcement, recognizing that financial and material rewards often follow or coincide with the approval of others,

> " Managers can empower employees and help them develop self-efficacy by providing job challenges, offering coaching and counseling, and rewarding employees' achievements.

TABLE 6.2 Personality Functions and Learning

PERSONALITY PREFERENCE	IMPLICATIONS FOR LEARNING BY INDIVIDUALS
Information Gathering	
Intuitors	Prefer theoretical frameworks. Look for the meaning in material. Attempt to understand the grand scheme. Look for possibilities and interrelations.
Sensors	Prefer specific, empirical data. Look for practical applications. Attempt to master details of a subject. Look for what is realistic and doable.
Decision Making	
Thinkers	Prefer analysis of data and information. Work to be fairminded and evenhanded. Seek logical, just conclusions. Do not like to be too personally involved.
Feelers	Prefer interpersonal involvement. Work to be tenderhearted and harmonious. Seek subjective, merciful results. Do not like objective, factual analysis.

SOURCE: From *Type Talk at Work* by Otto Kroeger and Janet Theusen, copyright © 1992 by Janet Theusen and Otto Kroeger. Used by permission of Delacorte Press, an imprint of The Random House Publishing Group, a division of Random House, Inc.

whereas punishments often follow social disapproval. Thus, Stajkovic and Luthans saw that self-efficacy and social reinforcement influence behavior and performance at work and have suggested that managers can be confident that employees with high self-efficacy will perform well.

Managers can empower employees and help them develop self-efficacy by providing job challenges, offering coaching and counseling for improved performance, and rewarding employees' achievements. Managers can also remove organizational barriers that stand in the way of employees making progress in meaningful work.[19] Given the increasing diversity of the workforce, managers may want to target their efforts toward women and minorities, who tend to have lower than average self-efficacy.[20]

Cognitive Theories of Learning

The cognitive approach to learning is based on the *Gestalt* school of thought and draws on Jung's theory of personality differences, discussed in Chapter 3. Recall the distinction between introverts (who need to study, concentrate, and reflect) and extraverts (who need to interact with other people). Introverts learn best alone, while extraverts learn best by exchanging ideas with others.

The personality functions of intuition, sensing, thinking, and feeling all have learning implications, which are listed in Table 6.2. Each person has a pre-ferred mode of gathering information and a preferred mode of evaluating and making decisions about that information. For example, an intuitive thinker may want to skim research reports about implementing total quality programs and then, based on hunches, decide how to apply the research findings to the organization. A sensing feeler may prefer viewing videos of interviews with people in companies that implemented total quality programs and then identify people in the organization most likely to be receptive to the approaches presented.

Goal Setting at Work

Goal setting is the process of establishing desired results that guide and direct behavior. Goal-setting theory is based on laboratory studies, field research experiments, and comparative investigations by Edwin Locke, Gary Latham, John M. Ivancevich, and others.[21] Goals crystallize the sense of purpose and mission that drives success.

Characteristics of Effective Goals

Various organizations define the characteristics of effective goals differently. As one example, Sanger-Harris, a former retail organization, used SMART goals. SMART stands for *Specific, Measurable, Attainable, Realistic,* and *Time-bound.* Specific and challenging goals focus attention on exactly what will be accomplished and inspire peak performance. People who set specific, challenging goals consistently outperform those with easy or unspecified goals, as Figure 6.2 on the next page shows. Subconscious thought may have a positive effect as well. Two studies of subconscious motivation found that goals that were ingrained but not explicitly expressed significantly enhanced task performance for difficult conscious goals, though not for easy goals.[22]

Measurable, quantitative goals provide opportunities for feedback about goal progress. Qualitative goals are also valuable. The Western Company of North America (now part of BJ Services Company) allows about 15 percent of a manager's goals to be of a qualitative nature.[23] An example of a qualitative goal is improving customer relations. To assess its progress, this qualitative goal might be quantified using measures like the number of complaints or the frequency of compliments.

goal setting
The process of establishing desired results that guide and direct behavior.

Time-bound goals enhance measurability. Many organizations work on standardized cycles of time, such as quarters or years. If there is any uncertainty about the time period of the goal effort, the time limit should be explicitly stated.

The prioritizing of goals allows efficient resource allocation. As time, energy, or other resources become available, a person can work through her list of goals in order of importance.[24] Priority helps direct a person's efforts and behavior.

Goal setting can serve three functions. First, it can increase work motivation and task performance.[25] Second, it can reduce stress caused by conflicting or confusing expectations.[26] Third, it can improve the accuracy and validity of performance evaluation.[27] Let's look at each of these functions in some detail.

Goals Increase Work Motivation and Task Performance

Goals often increase employee effort and motivation, which in turn improve task performance. The higher the goal is, the better the performance. People work harder to reach difficult goals. Figure 6.2 depicts this positive relationship.

Managers who use goal setting should ensure employee participation, supervisory commitment, and useful performance feedback. Participation encourages employees to accept and commit to the goal, two prerequisites to goal accomplishment. Employee participation is espe-

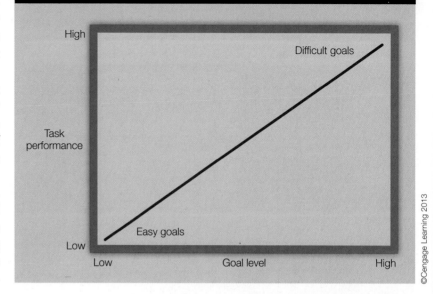

FIGURE **6.2** **Goal Level and Task Performance**

©Cengage Learning 2013

cially important in the accomplishment of difficult goals.[28] And when a difficult goal is assigned, acceptance and commitment are considered essential prerequisites to accomplishment.

Supervisory goal commitment reflects an organization's commitment to goal setting. Indeed, organizational commitment is a prerequisite for successful goal-setting programs such as *management by objectives (MBO)*, discussed shortly.[29] The organization commits to the program, and the supervisors and employees commit to its specific work goals.

The supervisor also provides employees with interim performance feedback on their progress toward goals. Such performance feedback is most useful for goals that are specific, and specific goals improve performance most when interim feedback is given.[30] When approached correctly, even negative performance feedback can improve performance.[31] For example, assume an insurance salesperson has a goal of selling $500,000 worth of insurance in six months but has sold only $200,000 after three months. During an interim performance feedback session, the supervisor helps the salesperson identify his problem—that he is not focusing his calls on the likeliest prospects—and gets him back on track to achieve his goal. Feedback is most helpful when it provides practical advice and is timely.

AGGRESSIVE GOALS

Hyundai used aggressive goals to find success in the U.S. auto market. When the company first sold cars in the United States, it had a reputation for being cheap, shoddy, and unreliable. In today's market, however, Hyundai has a sterling reputation for building high-quality, highly reliable cars that get rave reviews from journalists and consumers. It was able to achieve this reversal by setting aggressive goals and benchmarks for the quality of its cars. Now, Hyundai is again using an aggressive goal to set its path for the future. As announced by John Krafcik, CEO of Hyundai America, Hyundai's entire model line will average

fifty miles per gallon in fuel economy by the year 2025. Though Krafcik admits that the company may not yet know how it will precisely reach that goal, it does set a road map that has already guided significant amounts of research.

SOURCE: J. M. Amend, "Hyundai Sets 50-MPG Goal; Hunting for More Sonata Capacity," *Wards Automotive* (September 1, 2010), http://wardsautoworld.com/ar/auto_hyundai_sets_mpg, accessed June 20, 2011.

©Vox Productions LLC/Drive Images/Photolibrary

Goals Reduce Role Stress, Conflict, and Ambiguity

Goal setting also reduces the *role stress* associated with conflicting and confusing expectations because it clarifies the task–role expectations for employees. Supervisors, coworkers, and employees all provide task-related information. A fourteen-month evaluation found that goal setting reduced conflict, confusion, and absenteeism.[32]

Because goal setting improves role clarity, it generally improves communication between managers and employees.[33] This is why FedEx encourages managers to include communication-related targets in their annual MBO goal-setting process.[34]

Goals Improve Performance Evaluation

The third major function of goal setting is improving the accuracy and validity of performance evaluation. One of the best methods for this is **management by objectives (MBO)**—a goal-setting program based on interaction and negotiation between employees and managers.

According to Peter Drucker, who developed the concept of MBO over fifty years ago, the objectives-setting process begins with the employee writing an "employee's letter" to the manager. The letter explains the employee's general understanding of the scope of the manager's job as well as the scope of the employee's own job. The employee lays out a set of specific objectives to be pursued over the next six to twelve months, and after some discussion and negotiation, the manager and the employee finalize these items into a performance plan.

Drucker considers MBO a participative and interactive process. This does not mean that goal setting begins at the bottom of the organization. It means that goal setting is applicable to all employees; both lower-level organizational members and professional staff influence the goal-setting process.[35] Most goal-setting programs are designed to enhance performance, especially when incentives are associated with goal achievement.[36]

The two central ingredients in goal-setting programs are planning and evaluation. The *planning* component consists of organizational and individual goal setting, two essential and interdependent processes.[37] In planning, individuals and departments usually develop operational and tactical plans to support the corporate objectives. The idea is to formulate a clear, consistent, measurable, and ordered set of goals to articulate *what* to

> Goal setting can increase work motivatation and task performance, reduce stress, and improve the accuracy of performance evaluation.

do. Operational support planning then determines *how* to do it. The concept of *intention* encompasses both the goal (*what*) and the pathways that lead to goal attainment (*how*).[38]

The *evaluation* component of goal setting consists of interim reviews conducted by managers and employees and formal performance evaluation. The interim reviews are designed to help employees take self-corrective action. The formal performance evaluation occurs at the close of a reporting period, usually once a year. Effective performance reviews must be tailored specifically to the business, be reflective of what goes on internally, and be easily adapted to changes.[39]

Because goal-setting programs are somewhat mechanical by nature, they are most valuable and easily implemented in stable, predictable industrial settings. They are less useful in small, unpredictable organizations. Neither individual personality differences nor gender nor cultural differences appear to threaten the success of goal-setting programs, making them useful tools for a large, diverse workforce.[40]

LEARNING OUTCOME **4**

Performance: A Key Construct

Performance is most often called *task accomplishment*, the term *task* coming from Frederick W. Taylor's conception of a worker's required activity.[41] Some early management research found that performance standards and differential piece-rate pay inspired high levels of performance, while other early research found that stress improved performance up to an optimum point.[42] Hence, outcomes and effort are both important to good performance.

Predicting job performance has been a concern for over a century. Early World War I–era theories focused on intelligence and *general mental ability (GMA)*. Research has found GMA highly predictive of job knowledge in both civilian and military jobs.[43] But before job performance can be predicted, it must be defined.

Performance Management

Performance management is a process of defining, measuring, appraising, providing feedback on, and improving

management by objectives (MBO)

A goal-setting program based on interaction and negotiation between employees and managers.

performance management

A process of defining, measuring, appraising, providing feedback on, and improving performance.

©iStockphoto.com/Alex Gumerov

performance.[44] Defining performance in behavioral terms is an essential first step in the process. Done well, the performance management process leads to increased employee engagement, whereby workers know exactly what's expected of them and have the skills and abilities to meet those expectations.[45] Once defined, performance can be measured and assessed so that workers can receive feedback and managers can set goals to improve performance. Positive performance behaviors should be rewarded, and poor performance behaviors should be corrected.

Defining Performance

Managers must clearly define performance if their employees are to perform well at work. Most work performance is multidimensional. For example, a sales executive's performance will require administrative, financial, and interpersonal skills. Knowing the skills and behaviors needed to succeed in a position is a prerequisite to measuring and evaluating job performance.

Although different jobs require varying skills and behaviors, *organizational citizenship behavior (OCB)* spans many jobs. Recall from Chapter 4 that OCB is behavior above and beyond the call of duty. Employee involvement programs enhance OCB by engaging employees in the work environment.[46] OCB emphasizes collective performance rather than individual performance. It is but one of many dimensions to consider when defining the requirements of a specific job.

Performance appraisal is the evaluation of a person's performance. Accurate appraisals help supervisors fulfill their dual roles as evaluators and coaches. As the latter, a supervisor encourages growth and development. As the former, a supervisor makes judgments about employees' roles in the

performance appraisal
The evaluation of a person's performance.

organization. Keeping an employee's position within the company in mind lends greater contextual significance to the appraisal process.[47]

Performance appraisals give employees feedback on performance, identify their developmental needs, and influence promotion, demotion, termination, selection and placement decisions.

Measuring Performance

Ideally, actual performance matches measured performance, but this is actually seldom the case. Since operational performance generates more quantifiable data, it is easier to measure than managerial performance. Recent research measuring motivation for task performance has found that wording and context may influence the validity of direct self-reports.[48] Accuracy of self performance evaluations is also important. The more accurately that individuals evaluate their performance on a task, the better their performance on a subsequent task.[49]

Performance appraisal systems should improve the accuracy of measured performance and increase its parity with actual performance. The extent of their agreement is called the *true assessment*, as Figure 6.3 shows. Performance measurement problems such as deficiency, unreliability, and invalidity contribute to inaccuracy. *Deficiency* occurs when important aspects of a person's actual performance are overlooked. Unreliability results from poor-quality performance measures. *Invalidity* stems from inaccurate definition of the expected job performance.

Table 6.3, a sample of officer effectiveness reports from a nineteenth-century infantry company, demonstrates the bias of early performance appraisals. Even contemporary executive appraisals have a dark side, arousing the defenses of managers and executives. Addressing emotions and defenses is important to the effectiveness of appraisal sessions.[50] Some performance review systems lead to forced rankings of employees, which may be controversial or counterproductive. While a recent study found that supervisors were reluctant to give negative feedback overall, they were more likely to emphasize social factors when describing the performance of ethnic minorities.[51]

Many performance-monitoring systems use modern electronic technology to measure the performance of vehicle operators, computer technicians, and customer service representatives. For example, such systems might record the rate or the total number of keystrokes for a computer technician.

FIGURE 6.3 Actual and Measured Performance

Deficiency problem
Performance overlooked by the evaluator

Reliability problems
1. Situational factors affecting the evaluator, such as mood or timing of the evaluation

2. Disagreement between evaluators about methods

3. Temporary personal factors, such as fatigue or ill health of the person being evaluated

Validity problem
Poorly defined task performance causing invalidity

Deficiency — True assessment — Unreliability — Invalidity

Actual performance — Measured performance

SOURCE: Table from *The Air Officer's Guide*, 6th ed. Copyright © 1952 Stackpole Books. Used with permission.

Sometimes employees are unaware that their performance is being measured. What constitutes inappropriate electronic monitoring of an employee? The ethics of monitoring performance differ by culture. For example, firms in the United States and Sweden generally respect individual privacy more than those in Japan or China.

Goal setting and MBO are results-oriented performance appraisal methods that do not necessarily rely on modern technology. Like performance-monitoring systems, they focus on observable, verifiable results, instead of subjective, judgmental performance dimensions. Goals established during planning serve as the standard for measuring subsequent performance. However, managers who adhere rigidly to a results-oriented approach risk overlooking performance opportunities.

Performance Feedback

Feedback sessions create stress for both supervisors and employees. Early research at General Electric found, not surprisingly, that employees responded constructively to positive feedback but often responded defensively to critical or negative feedback. In response to a negative feedback, they shifted responsibility for the problem, denied it outright, or provided a wide range of excuses.[52] In a study of 499 Chinese supervisor–subordinate pairs, supervisors responded positively to employees who sought performance feedback if their motive was performance enhancement or improvement but not so positively if the employee's motive was to influence how their supervisor perceived them.[53]

Both supervisor and employee should try to make performance feedback a constructive learning experience, since feedback has long-term implications for the employee's performance and for the supervisor-employee working relationship. American Airlines follows three guidelines for providing evaluative feedback.[54] First, supervisors refer to specific, verbatim statements and specific, observable behaviors displayed by the employee. This specificity enhances the acceptance of the feedback while discouraging denial. Second, the feedback focuses on changeable behaviors, not intrinsic or personality-based attributes. Third, the session is planned ahead of time and the person who will receive the feedback is notified so that both parties can be ready.

Supervisors should start coaching and counseling sessions with something positive. Once the session is under way and rapport is established, the evaluator can introduce more difficult and negative material. No one is perfect, so everyone can learn and grow through performance feedback sessions. Critical feedback is the basis for improvement. Managers should

TABLE 6.3 Officer Effectiveness Reports, Circa 1813

Alexander Brown, Lt. Col., Comdg.—A good-natured man.
Clark Crowell, 1st Major—A good man, but no officer.
Jess B. Wordsworth, 2nd Major—An excellent officer.
Captain Shaw—A man of whom all unite in speaking ill. A knave despised by all.
Captain Thomas Lord—Indifferent, but promises well.
Captain Rockwell—An officer of capacity, but imprudent and a man of violent passions.
1st Lt. Jas. Kearns—Merely good, nothing promising.
1st Lt. Robert Cross—Willing enough, has much to learn, with small capacity.
2nd Lt. Stewart Berry—An ignorant unoffending fellow.
Ensign North—A good young man who does well.

SOURCE: J. C. Benton, *The Air Officer's Guide*, 6th ed. (Mechanicsburg, Penn.: Stackpole Books 1952). Copyright © 1952 Stackpole Books. Used with permission.

©iStockphoto.com/Skip O'Donnell

be aware, however, that although specific feedback can improve initial performance, it may also undermine the learning needed for later, more independent performance.[55]

360-Degree Feedback

Many organizations use **360-degree feedback**, which is based on multiple sources of information, to improve the accuracy of performance appraisals. Evidence suggests that including self-evaluations in this process makes evaluation interviews more satisfying, more constructive, and less defensive.[56] Some dislike the fact that self-evaluations often conflict with supervisory evaluations.[57] However, these disagreements are part of the full picture of the person's performance. The 360-degree feedback method provides a well-rounded view of performance from superiors, peers, followers, and customers.[58]

As an illustration of the benefits of a 360-degree feedback evaluation, consider a

360-degree feedback

A process of self-evaluation and evaluations by a manager, peers, direct reports, and possibly customers.

mid-level civilian executive working in a large military organization. The executive is positive, compliant, and deferential toward superiors but largely indifferent toward peers. With followers, he is tough and demanding, bordering on abusive. Without each of these perspectives, the executive's performance cannot be accurately assessed.

Adding a systematic coaching component can improve 360-degree feedback.[59] By focusing on enhanced self-awareness and behavioral management, feedback coaching improves performance, satisfaction, and commitment, and reduces turnover. Separating the performance feedback component from the management development component also improves the 360-degree method.[60] The feedback component contains quantitative feedback and performance measures, while the management development component emphasizes qualitative feedback and competencies for development.

Developing People and Enhancing Careers

Good performance appraisal systems develop people and enhance careers. They should explore individual growth needs and future performance. However, in order to coach and develop employees successfully, the supervisor must establish mutual trust. This means she must be vulnerable and open to challenge from the subordinate while maintaining responsibility for the subordinate's best interests.[61] Good supervisors are skilled, empathetic listeners who encourage employees to discuss their aspirations.[62] Employees must also take active responsibility for future development and growth. This might mean challenging the supervisor's ideas about future development and expressing their own

©Stockbyte/Getty Images

goals. Passive, compliant employees cannot accept responsibility for themselves or achieve full emotional development. Individual responsibility is a key characteristic of the culture of the steel manufacturer Gerdau Ameristeel. The company joke is that the company manages by "adultry" (pun intended). Gerdau Ameristeel treats people like adults and expects adult behavior from them.

Key Characteristics of an Effective Appraisal System

Effective performance appraisal systems have five key characteristics: validity, reliability, responsiveness, flexibility, and equitability. *Validity* means capturing multiple dimensions of a person's job performance. *Reliability* means collecting evaluations from multiple sources and at different times throughout the evaluation period. *Responsiveness* means allowing the person being evaluated to have some input. *Flexibility* means staying open to modification based on new information such as federal requirements. *Equitability* means evaluating fairly against established criteria, regardless of individual differences.

FedEx has incorporated a novel and challenging approach to evaluation in its blueprint for service quality. All managers at FedEx are evaluated by their employees through a survey-feedback-action system. Employees, in turn, evaluate their managers using a five-point scale on twenty-nine standard statements and ten local option ones. Low ratings suggest problem areas requiring management attention. One year the survey revealed that employees thought upper management was not paying attention to ideas and suggestions from people at their level. In response, CEO Fred Smith developed a biweekly employee newsletter to correct the problem.

Rewarding Performance

Performance appraisals can provide input for reward decisions. If companies celebrate "teamwork," "values," and "customer focus," they must reward behaviors demonstrating these ideas. Despite their importance, reward decisions are among the most difficult and complicated decisions managers make. They should remember that people do not simply work for money.[63] While pay and rewards for performance have value, so too do trust, fun, and meaningful work. In fact, some compensation professionals have advanced the idea of Total Rewards that include extrinsic rewards like compensation and benefits as well as intrinsic ones like work-life benefits, performance and recognition, and career-development opportunities.[64]

Reward and punishment decisions affect entire organizations, not just the people receiving the consequence. Reward allocation involves sequential decisions about which people to reward, how to reward them, and when to reward them. These decisions shape all employees' behavior, either directly or through vicarious learning, especially when new programs are implemented. People watch what happens to peers who make mistakes and adjust their own behavior accordingly.

Individual versus Team Reward Systems

While motivation and reward systems outside the United States are often group focused, many U.S. organizations use systems that are focused on rewarding employees as individuals.[65] These systems foster independent behavior and encourage creativity, problem solving, and distinctive

DOS AND DON'TS OF APPRAISALS

Employee appraisals can be a horrific time for both managers and employees. Done poorly, appraisals heap stress on employees, who are worried about how long they will be criticized and what the criticisms will be. Fortunately, appraisals don't need to be a source of frustration. They can be productive conversations about what an employee has done well and what he or she can improve on in the future. Jonathan Segal, a partner at the Duane Morris legal firm, provides a list of errors that savvy managers should avoid:

1. An appraisal that is late
2. Overevaluating the performance of an employee
3. Bringing up baggage from the past
4. Being inconsistent in applying standards
5. Being more favorable to employees who are similar to themselves
6. Stereotyping
7. Using labels rather than behaviors
8. Describing people in absolute terms (someone is all good or all bad)
9. Implying an employee's intent with statements like "You don't care!"
10. Talking about medical or personal leaves
11. Not making the evaluation a dialogue
12. Not setting or discussing goals

Reward systems shape productive behavior.

contributions to the organization. Different types of employees may prefer different rewards. For example, adventure seekers may prefer travel awards, while nesters prefer days off.[66]

Individual reward systems directly affect individual behavior and encourage competition within a work team.[67] Too much competition, however, may create a dysfunctional work environment. At the Western Company of North America (now part of BJ Services Company), individual success in the MBO program was tied too tightly to rewards, and individual managers became divisively competitive. Some managers took last-minute interdepartmental financial actions to meet their objectives. By doing so, they caused other managers to miss their objectives. These actions raise ethical questions about how far individual managers should go in serving their own self-interest at the expense of their peers.

Team reward systems solve the problems caused by individual competitive behavior in that they encourage cooperation, joint efforts, and the sharing of information and expertise. The collectivist orientations of Japanese and Chinese cultures position the individual as an element of the team, not as a separate individual.

Some organizations have experimented with individual and group alternative reward systems. At the individual level, these include skill-based and pay-for-knowledge systems that emphasize skills or knowledge possessed by an employee beyond the requirements for the basic job. At the group level, gain-sharing plans emphasize collective cost reduction by allowing workers to share in the gains achieved by reducing production costs. In such plans, everyone shares equally in the collective gain. Avnet, Inc., found that collective profit sharing improved performance. The most effective incentives are those that celebrate the group's accomplishments collectively rather than those that single out individuals.[68]

The Power of Earning

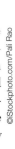

Both individual and team reward systems can shape productive behavior, so effective performance management boosts both individual and team achievements in an organization. Performance management and reward systems assume a demonstrable connection between performance and rewards—that is, that organizations get the performance they reward, not the performance they say they want.[69]

When there is no apparent link between performance and rewards, people may begin to believe they are entitled to rewards regardless of their performance. The notion of entitlement at work counteracts the *power of earning*.[70] People who believe they are entitled to rewards without earning them are not motivated to behave constructively. Merit raises in some organizations, for example, have come to be viewed as entitlements, thus reducing their positive value in the organizational reward system. Entitlement engenders passive, irresponsible behavior, whereas earning engenders active, responsible behavior. The power of earning rests on a direct link between performance and rewards. In order for employees not to feel entitled, this connection must be clearly apparent and quantifiable.[71]

LEARNING OUTCOME **7**

Correcting Poor Performance

Often a challenge for supervisors, correcting poor performance can be conceived as a three-step process. First, supervisors must identify the cause or primary responsibility for the poor performance. Second, if the primary responsibility is the employee's (and not the

[Give Them What They Want]

How should employees who do great work be rewarded? Many people think a big cash bonus might be the best reward. But, according to the consulting firm Globoforce, the rewards that are typically given out for good performance, like annual bonuses, promotions, or high-priced giveaways, don't actually do a very good job of motivating people. They found that what employees really wanted were smaller rewards, most worth less than $100, given more frequently, given to most of the employees, and given with a personal touch. Rather than a $5,000 bonus check sent through the mail, employees put more value on a $50 restaurant gift card that was given by the manager personally with a genuine "Thank you." So, when it comes to rewarding employees, it's not simply a matter of how much is given, but how it is given.

SOURCE: T. Demos, "Motivate without Spending Millions," *Fortune* (April 12, 2010), 37–38.

organization's) supervisors must determine the source of the personal problem. Third, they must develop a plan for correcting the poor performance.

A number of problems trigger poor performance. These include poorly designed work systems, poor selection processes, inadequate training and skills development, lack of personal motivation, and personal problems intruding on the work environment. Not all poor performance is self-motivated, though; some is induced by the work system. Therefore, a good diagnosis should precede corrective action, and work systems should be the first factor considered. It may be that an employee is subject to a work design or selection system that keeps him from exhibiting good performance.

If the poor performance can't be attributed to work design or organizational process problems, then supervisors should examine the employee. The problem may lie in (1) some aspect of the person's relationship to the organization or supervisor, (2) some area of the employee's personal life, or (3) a training or developmental deficiency. In the latter two cases, poor performance can be treated as a symptom rather than a motivated consequence. In such cases, identifying financial problems, family difficulties, or health disorders may help the employee solve problems before they become too extensive.

Poor performance may also stem from an employee's displaced anger or conflict with the organization or supervisor. In such cases, the employee may be unaware of the internal reactions causing the problem. Such angry motivations can generate sabotage, work slowdowns, and work stoppages. The supervisor might be attributing the cause of the problem to the employee while the employee is attributing it to the supervisor or organization. Supervisors must treat the poor performance as a symptom with a deeper cause and resolve the underlying anger or conflict.

Performance and Kelley's Attribution Theory

According to Harold Kelley's *attribution theory*, managers make attributions, or inferences, concerning employees' behavior and performance.[72] The attributions may not always be accurate. Supervisors and employees who share perceptions and attitudes tend to evaluate each other highly.[73] Those who do not share perceptions and attitudes are more likely to blame each other for performance problems.

Kelley's attribution theory proposes that individuals make attributions based on information gathered in the form of three informational cues: consensus, distinctiveness, and consistency.[74] **Consensus** is an informational cue indicating the extent to which peers in the same situation behave in a similar fashion. **Distinctiveness** is a cue indicating the degree to which an individual behaves

A lack of motivation often leads to poor performance.

the same way in other situations. **Consistency** is a cue indicating the frequency of behavior over time. We form attributions based on whether these cues are low or high.

Certain combinations of cues suggest an internal attribution, while other combinations suggest that the cause of the poor performance is external. Suppose you have received several complaints from customers regarding one of your customer service representatives, Niki. You have not received complaints about your other service representatives (low consensus). Reviewing Niki's records, you find that she also received customer complaints during her previous job as a sales clerk (low distinctiveness). The complaints have been coming in steadily for three months (high consistency). In this case, you would most likely make an internal attribution and conclude that the complaints must stem from Niki's behavior. The combination of low consensus, low distinctiveness, and high consistency suggests internal attributions.

Other combinations of these cues, however, point to external attributions. High consensus, high distinctiveness, and low consistency, for example, produce external attributions. Suppose one of your employees, Sanjay, is performing poorly on collecting overdue accounts. You find that the behavior is widespread within your work team (high consensus) and that Sanjay is performing

consensus

An informational cue indicating the extent to which peers in the same situation behave in a similar fashion.

distinctiveness

An informational cue indicating the degree to which an individual behaves the same way in other situations.

consistency

An informational cue indicating the frequency of behavior over time.

poorly only on this aspect of the job (high distinctiveness), and that most of the time he handles this aspect of the job well (low consistency). You will probably decide that something about the work situation caused the poor performance.

On the basis of the informational cues, the supervisor makes either an internal (personal) attribution or an external (situational) attribution. Internal attributions might include low effort, lack of commitment, or lack of ability. External attributions are outside the employee's control and might include equipment failure or unrealistic goals. These examples are illustrated visually in Figure 6.4. Be warned, however, that the process of determining the cause of a behavior is not always as simple and clear-cut as these examples suggest, because biases sometimes interfere.

Figure 6.5 presents an attribution model of supervisors' responses to poor performance. Supervisors may choose from a wide range of responses. They can, for example, express personal concern, reprimand the employee, or provide training. Supervisors who attribute the cause of poor performance to a person (an internal cause) will respond more harshly than supervisors who blame the work situation (an external cause). Supervisors should avoid both common attribution errors discussed in Chapter 3: the fundamental attribution error and the self-serving bias.

Coaching, Counseling, and Mentoring

Supervisors and coworkers are often more effective guides than formally assigned mentors from higher up in the organizational hierarchy.[75] Consequently, they have important coaching, counseling, and mentoring responsibilities to their subordinates. Success in the mentoring relationship depends on openness

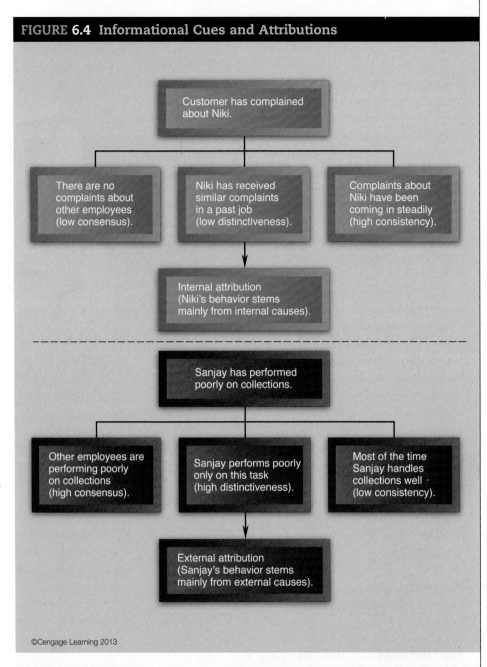

FIGURE **6.4** Informational Cues and Attributions

Customer has complained about Niki.

There are no complaints about other employees (low consensus).

Niki has received similar complaints in a past job (low distinctiveness).

Complaints about Niki have been coming in steadily (high consistency).

Internal attribution (Niki's behavior stems mainly from internal causes).

Sanjay has performed poorly on collections.

Other employees are performing poorly on collections (high consensus).

Sanjay performs poorly only on this task (high distinctiveness).

Most of the time Sanjay handles collections well (low consistency).

External attribution (Sanjay's behavior stems mainly from external causes).

©Cengage Learning 2013

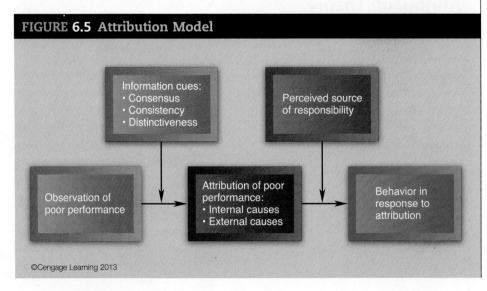

FIGURE **6.5** Attribution Model

Information cues:
• Consensus
• Consistency
• Distinctiveness

Perceived source of responsibility

Observation of poor performance

Attribution of poor performance:
• Internal causes
• External causes

Behavior in response to attribution

©Cengage Learning 2013

Hot Trend: Tri-Mentoring

Tri-mentoring is a targeted, peer-mentoring system that recognizes and encourages implicit learning in organizations. Employees learn from each other in the normal performance of daily tasks, regardless of their individual levels of competency. By formalizing the dissemination of tacit knowledge, tri-mentoring is beneficial not only to individuals, but to organizations. In traditional mentoring, a senior employee guides a junior. In tri-mentoring, three employees meet as equals to share implicit knowledge and build organizational capability. While groups of four or more can lead to problems in coordination and accord, tri-mentoring encourages flexibility, camaraderie, and healthy discussion. While the trio usually self-selects its members, managers provide direction and assess outcomes. Already in use at a number of corporations, tri-mentoring continues to grow in popularity for its efficacy.

SOURCE: D. Williams. "Tri-Mentoring: A New Spin on an Old Practice." *New Zealand Management* 56. No. 2 (March 2009): 28.

©Stocktrek/Digital Vision/Getty Images

and trust.[76] This relationship may help address performance-based deficiencies or personal problems.[77] In either case, supervisors can play a helpful role in employee problem-solving activities without accepting responsibility for the employees' problems. They may refer the employee to trained professionals.

Coaching and counseling are among the career and psychosocial functions of a mentoring relationship.[78] **Mentoring** is a work relationship that encourages development and career enhancement for people moving through the career cycle. Mentor relationships typically go through four phases: initiation, cultivation, separation, and redefinition. Mentoring offers protégés many career benefits.[79] The relationship can significantly enhance the early development of a newcomer and the midcareer development of an experienced employee. Some companies, such as IBM, offer mentoring at all levels of employment.[80] Peer relationships can also enhance career development.[81] Executive coaching is increasingly used to outsource the business mentoring functions. Informational, collegial, and special peers aid the individual's development by sharing information, career strategies, job-related feedback, emotional support, and friendship.

Log in to the **CourseMate** for *ORGB3* at **www.cengagebrain.com** to:

✳ Review **Key Terms Flash Cards** online

✳ Play **Beat the Clock** and **Quiz Bowl** to master concepts

✳ Complete **web quizzes** to prepare for exams

✳ Watch the video on **Barcelona Restaurant Group** and from *Take the Lead* for examples, then test yourself with a quick quiz

✳ Work through the **"What about You?"** and **Ethical Dilemma** exercises to see how you would handle various situations that organizations face on a daily basis

mentoring
A work relationship that encourages development and career enhancement for people moving through the career cycle.

Stress and Well-Being at Work

LEARNING OUTCOMES

1 Define *stress*, *distress*, and *strain*.

2 Compare four different approaches to stress.

3 Explain the psycho-physiology of the stress response.

4 Identify work and non-work causes of stress.

5 Describe the conse-quences of stress.

6 Discuss individual fac-tors that influence a person's response to stress and strain.

7 Identify the stages and elements of preventive stress management for individuals and organizations.

©iStockphoto.com/Robert Churchill

> **❝** *Stress is a great asset in managing legitimate emergencies and achieving peak performance.* **❞**

After You Finish
This Chapter
Go to **Page 122**
for **Study Tools**

What Is Stress?

Stress is an important topic in organizational behavior, due in part to its influence on competitive pressures that impact workers and managers alike. Poor leadership, work–family conflicts, and sexual harassment are among the leading causes of work stress.[1] Although experts do not always agree on its definition, **stress**, or the *stress response*, can be described as the unconscious preparation to fight or flee that a person experiences when faced with any demand.[2] A **stressor**, or demand, is a person or event that triggers the stress response. While stress is a neutral concept, it carries a negative connotation for some people, as though it should be avoided. This is unfortunate, because stress is a great asset in managing legitimate emergencies and achieving peak performance. **Distress**, or **strain**, refers to the adverse psychological, physical, behavioral, and organizational consequences that *may* occur as a result of stressful events.

Four Approaches to Stress

The *stress response* was discovered by Walter B. Cannon, a medical physiologist, early in the twentieth century.[3] Later, however, researchers defined stress differently than Cannon did, so we will review four different approaches to defining stress: the homeostatic/medical, cognitive appraisal, person–environment fit, and psychoanalytic approaches.

stress
The unconscious preparation to fight or flee that a person experiences when faced with any demand.

stressor
The person or event that triggers the stress response.

distress
The adverse psychological, physical, behavioral, and organizational consequences that may arise as a result of stressful events.

strain
Distress.

The Psychophysiology of Stress

In preparing to fight or flee, the body
1. Redirects blood to the brain and large-muscle groups
2. Increases alertness through improved vision, hearing, and other sensory processes
3. Releases glucose (blood sugar) and fatty acids into the bloodstream to sustain the body during the stressful event
4. Suppresses the immune system as well as restorative and emergent processes (such as digestion)

These four approaches to stress will give you a more complete understanding of what stress really is.

The Homeostatic/Medical Approach

When Walter B. Cannon first developed the concept of stress, he called it the *emergency response* or the *militaristic response*, arguing that it was rooted in "the fighting emotions." His early writings provide the basis for the *fight-or-flight* nomenclature. According to Cannon's *homeostatic/medical approach*, stress occurs when an external, environmental demand upsets an individual's natural steady-state balance, what he calls **homeostasis**.[4] Cannon believed the body was designed with natural defense mechanisms to keep it in homeostasis. He was especially interested in the role of the sympathetic nervous system in activating a person under stressful conditions.[5]

The Cognitive Appraisal Approach

Richard Lazarus was more concerned with the psychology of stress, emphasizing the psychological and cognitive aspects of the stress response in his *cognitive appraisal approach*.[6] Like Cannon, Lazarus saw stress as a result of a person–environment interaction, yet he emphasized the individual's cognitive appraisal in classifying persons or events as stressful or not. Individuals differ in their appraisals of events and people. Perception and cognitive appraisal are important processes in determining what is stressful. One study found higher instances of major depression when job demands were objectively assessed.[7] Another study found culture-specific differences in the perception of job stress between China and the United States.[8] American employees reported lack of control as a source of stress, while Chinese employees reported job evaluations as

a significant source. In addition to cognitive appraisal, Lazarus introduced the ideas of problem-focused and emotion-focused coping. The former emphasizes managing the stressor, while the latter emphasizes managing the response. Whether individuals use problem- or emotion-focused coping strategies depends on motivation. For example, students planning and preparing for exams would more likely use problem-focused coping.[9] Those who evaluate themselves positively and consider themselves capable and in control of their own lives tend to favor emotion-focused coping when faced with stressors.[10]

The Person–Environment Fit Approach

Robert Kahn was concerned with the social psychology of stress, so his *person–environment fit* approach emphasized the idea that confusing and conflicting expectations of a person in a social role create stress for that person.[11] He extended the approach to consider a person's fit in the environment. A good person–environment fit occurs when one's skills and abilities match a clearly defined, consistent set of role expectations. Stress occurs when the role expectations are confusing and/or conflict with one's skills and abilities. After a period of this type of stress, one can expect to experience symptoms of strain such as depression.

The Psychoanalytic Approach

Freudian psychoanalytic theory can help us understand the role of unconscious personality factors as causes of stress within a person.[12] Applying this *psychoanalytic* approach, Harry Levinson argued that two elements of the personality interact to cause stress. The first element is the **ego-ideal**—the embodiment of a person's perfect self. The second element is the **self-image**—how the person really sees herself, both positively and negatively. Although not sharply defined, the ego-ideal encompasses admirable attributes of parental personalities, desired and/or imaginable qualities, and the absence of any negative or distasteful qualities. Stress results from the discrepancy between the idealized self (ego-ideal) and the real self-image; the greater the discrepancy, the more stress a person experiences.

homeostasis
A steady state of bodily functioning and equilibrium.

ego-ideal
The embodiment of a person's perfect self.

self-image
How a person sees himself or herself, both positively and negatively.

©iStockphoto.com/endopack

The Stress Response

Whether activated by an ego-ideal/self-image discrepancy, a poorly defined social role, a cognitive appraisal suggesting threat, or a lack of balance, the resulting stress response is characterized by a predictable sequence of mind and body events. The stress response begins with the release of chemical messengers, primarily adrenaline, into the bloodstream. These messengers activate the sympathetic nervous system and the endocrine (hormone) system. These two systems work together to trigger four mind–body changes that prepare the person for fight or flight (see the feature, "The Psychophysiology of Stress" on the previous page).

As the body responds, the person shifts from a neutral posture to an offensive posture. The stress response can be very effective in preparing a person to handle legitimate emergencies through peak performance. Thus, it is neither inherently bad nor necessarily destructive.

Sources of Work Stress

Work stress is caused by factors in the work environment as well as by nonwork (external) pressures that spill over into the workplace. The two major categories of sources of both types of work stress are shown in Table 7.1. An example of an external pressure is when a working mother or father is called at work to come pick up a sick child from day care. One of the most complex work-related causes of stress is role conflict. An innovative study by Pam Perrewé and her colleagues examined the dysfunctional physical and psychological consequences of role conflict.[13] The researchers found political skill to be an antidote for role conflict, one of a range of preventive stress-management strategies discussed later in the chapter.

TABLE 7.1 Work and Nonwork Demands

WORK DEMANDS

Task Demands	Role Demands
Change	Role conflict:
Lack of control	Interrole
Career progress	Intrarole
New technologies	Person–role
Temporal pressure	Role ambiguity

Interpersonal Demands	Physical Demands
Emotional toxins	Extreme environments
Sexual harassment	Strenuous activities
Poor leadership	Hazardous substances
	Global travel

NONWORK DEMANDS

Home Demands	Personal Demands
Family expectations	Workaholism
Child-rearing/day care arrangements	Civic and volunteer work
Parental care	Traumatic events

©Cengage Learning 2013

THE HIDDEN DANGERS OF OFFICE WORK

While workers in construction and manufacturing jobs can easily identify on-site risks to their health and safety, office employees often consider their workspaces safe havens. However, many offices cause stress and other health problems in a number of unexpected ways. The close quarters of office buildings expose employees to influenza and other contagious diseases. While the spread of bacteria and viruses can be combated by regular hand washing, pathogens are difficult to contain entirely. Poor or abusive management causes psychological stress and can increase the risk of cardiovascular disorders. Working fifty-five or more hours a week exposes workers to the risk of diminished capacity in memory and mental tasks.

Working forty-one or fewer hours a week is considered healthy. In 2000, France instituted a thirty-five-hour workweek to increase productivity and quality of life. Computer work places the entire muscular-skeletal system under stress. Inadequately designed chairs and poor posture put stress on the lower vertebrae, while repetitive actions like typing can damage the upper arms and hands. Finally, inactive office work often results in a sedentary lifestyle, causing weight gain, fatigue, and depression. Although one shouldn't think of the office as a dangerous environment, a heightened awareness of stress-inducing risks will better prepare an individual to identify and alleviate stressors.

SOURCE: R. Sharp, "How Your Office Makes You Sick," *The Independent* (March 3, 2009).

Work Demands

Role demands include role ambiguity as well as role conflict. But there are also three other categories of work demands: task demands, interpersonal demands, and physical demands. Table 7.1 does not present an exhaustive list of work demands but rather aims to show major causes of work stress in each of the four major domains of the work environment.

Task Demands Dramatic changes at work lead to uncertainty in a person's daily tasks and activities, provoking on-the-job pressure and stress.[14] Globalization and large-scale business trends lead to change, as do smaller-scale shifts in company policy. In recent years, the global economic recession has led many companies to make stressful changes, such as downsizing. At least 20 million jobs were lost by the end of 2009 due to the crisis.[15] Even during periods of growth, when hundreds of thousands of jobs are created every month, there may be significant numbers of jobs lost within certain sectors of the U.S. economy. For those who do not lose their jobs, underemployment, monotony, and boredom may be problematic.

Technological innovation creates change and uncertainty for many employees, requiring additional training, education, and skill development. New technologies create both career stress and "technostress" for those who wonder if "smart" machines will replace them.[16] Although they enhance the organization's productive capacity, new technologies may be viewed as the enemy by workers who must ultimately learn to use them. This creates a real dilemma for management. Intended to make work easier and more convenient, information technology may have the paradoxical effect of incurring stress rather than relieving it.

Lack of control is another major task-related source of stress, especially in positions that are difficult and psychologically demanding. The lack of control may be caused by the inability to

> influence the timing of tasks and activities;

> select tools or methods for accomplishing the work;

> make decisions that influence work outcomes; or

> exercise direct action to affect the work outcomes.

Concerns over career progress and time pressures (or work overload) are two additional task demands triggering stress at work.

> New technologies create both career stress and "technostress" for those who wonder if "smart" machines will replace them.

Career stress has occurred in many organizations over the past two decades as middle-manager ranks have been thinned by mergers, acquisitions, and downsizing.[17] Leaner organizations, unfortunately, mean overload for the retained employees. Fewer people doing the same amount of work or more creates time pressure, a leading cause of stress often associated with work overload. Time pressure may also result from poor time-management skills. But not all task demands are negative. Challenge stressors that promote personal growth and achievement are positively related to job satisfaction and organizational commitment.[18]

Role Demands The social–psychological demands of the work environment may be every bit as stressful as task demands. Role stress may be particularly harmful to the job satisfaction and affective commitment of newcomers to the organization.[19] People encounter two major categories of role stress at work: role conflict and role ambiguity.[20] *Role conflict* results from inconsistent or incompatible expectations. The conflict may be an interrole, intrarole, or person–role conflict.

Interrole conflict is caused by opposing expectations related to two separate roles assumed by the same individual, such as employee and parent. For example, the employee with a major sales presentation due on Monday and a sick child at home Sunday night is likely to experience interrole conflict. Work–family conflicts such as these can lead individuals to withdrawal behaviors.[21] *Intrarole conflict* is caused by opposing expectations related to a single role. For example, the manager who presses employees for both very fast and high-quality work may be viewed at some point as creating a conflict for employees.

Ethics violations are likely to cause *person–role conflicts*. Employees expected to behave in ways that violate personal values, beliefs, or principles experience this type of conflict. Person–role conflicts and ethics violations create a sense of divided loyalty for an employee. For example, if a distributor tells an organic farmer to cut costs by using a synthetic pesticide, the farmer may find that his personal beliefs are compromised by his role as a producer. Organizations with high ethical standards, such as Johnson & Johnson, are less likely to create ethical conflicts for employees.

The second major cause of role stress is *role ambiguity*, which is the confusion a person experiences in relation to the expectations of others. Role ambiguity may be caused by misunderstanding what is expected, not knowing how to do it, or not knowing the result of failure to do it. For example, a new magazine employee asked to copyedit a manuscript may experience confusion because she mistakes copyediting for proofreading, she doesn't know what formatting style to use, or she doesn't know what will happen if she misses her deadline.

A twenty-one-nation study examined middle managers' experiences in role conflict, role ambiguity, and role overload. The results indicated that role stress varies more by country than it does by demographic and organizational factors. For example, non-Western managers experience less role ambiguity and more role overload than do their Western counterparts.[22] Another study, this time of 2,273 Norwegian employees, found that role conflict, role ambiguity, and conflict with coworkers increased under laissez-faire leadership, suggesting that a hands-off leadership style is destructive.[23] On the other hand, a study of U.S. military personnel found that when role clarity was high in a supportive work group, psychological strain was low.[24]

Interpersonal Demands

Emotional toxins, such as sexual harassment and poor leadership in the organization, are examples of interpersonal demands, often generated at work by abrasive personalities.[25] Another consequence of interpersonal demands can be *emotional dissonance*, which can spread through a work environment and cause a range of disturbances and stress.[26] Organizations are increasingly less tolerant of sexual harassment, a gender-related interpersonal demand that creates a stressful working environment for both the person being harassed and for others. The vast majority of sexual harassment is directed at women in the workplace and is a chronic, yet preventable problem.[27]

Poor organizational leadership and demanding managerial styles are leading causes of work stress for employees. But much depends on an employee's individual characteristics. Employees who feel secure under strong, directive leadership may be anxious under an open, self-directed style of management. Those comfortable with participative leaders may feel restrained by a directive style. In every case, however, trust is an important characteristic of the leader–follower interpersonal relationship, so a threat to a worker's reputation with his supervisor may be especially stressful.[28] Functional diversity in project groups

also causes difficulty in the establishment of trusting relationships. Lack of trust increases job stress, which in turn leads to lower cohesiveness within the group.[29]

Physical Demands

Extreme environments, strenuous activities, hazardous substances, and global travel create physical demands for people at work. One cross-cultural study that examined the effects of ambient temperature on role stress concluded that uncomfortable temperatures diminish human well-being, leading to the development of the term *sweatshop* for inhumane working conditions.[30] The unique physical demands of work are often occupation-specific, such as the risk of gravity-induced loss of consciousness for military pilots flying high-performance fighters or jet lag and loss of sleep for globetrotting CEOs.[31] Despite the fact that there are many positive aspects to business travel, the associated demands are increasingly recognized as sources of stress.[32]

Office work has its physical hazards as well. Noisy, crowded offices, such as those of some stock brokerages, can prove stressful, and even harmful. Working with a computer can also be stressful, especially if the ergonomic design of the workstation is not correct. Eyestrain, neck stiffness, and arm and wrist problems may result. Office designs that use partitions rather than full walls may create stress by offering little privacy and little protection from interruptions. *Stress audits* provide companies with detailed assessments of possible workplace stressors. Identification and alleviation of overlooked stress factors can save a company money and boost productivity.

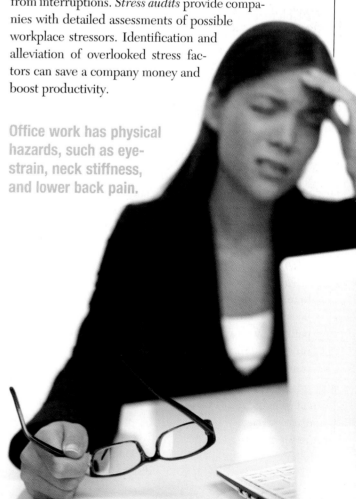

Office work has physical hazards, such as eyestrain, neck stiffness, and lower back pain.

Nonwork Demands

Nonwork demands also create stress, which may carry over into the work environment.[33] *Nonwork demands* may broadly be identified as impositions from an individual's personal life environment (home) and self-imposed restrictions.

Home Demands The wide array of home and family arrangements in contemporary American society has created great diversity in the arena of home demands. Traditional and non-traditional families may experience demands that create role conflicts or overloads that are difficult to manage. For example, the loss of good day care for children may be especially stressful for dual-career and single-parent families.[34] The tension between work and family may lead to a real struggle for balance in life. This struggle led Rocky Rhodes, cofounder of Silicon Graphics, to establish four priorities for his life: God, family, exercise, and work.[35] These priorities helped him reallocate his time for better balance in his life. Moreover, as a result of the maturing of the American population, an increasing number of people face the added demand of parental care. Even when a person dedicates herself to reducing stress by integrating opposing social and work-related roles into a balanced, "whole" identity, the process is not an easy one.[36]

Personal Demands Self-imposed personal demands are the second major category of nonwork demands identified in Table 7.1. **Workaholism**, a form of addiction, may be the most notable of these stress-inducing demands.[37] Some of the early warning signs of workaholism include overcommitment to work, inability to enjoy vacations and respites from work, preoccupation with work problems when away from the workplace, and insistence on working at home over weekends.

Another type of personal demand comes from civic activities, volunteer work, and organizational commitments to religious or public service organizations. These demands become more or less stressful depending on their compatibility with work and family life, and their capacity to provide alternative satisfactions for the individual. Finally, traumatic events, such as the devastating earthquake and tsunami in Japan in March 2011, are stressful for people who experience them.[38] Not all traumatic events are as catastrophic as natural disasters, of course, but job loss, failed exams, and romantic break-ups are all traumatic and may lead to distress if not addressed and resolved.

workaholism
An imbalanced preoccupation with work at the expense of home and personal life satisfaction.

Fast Fact

MYTH: People get used to noise and it doesn't affect them after a certain amount of time.

FACT: The body continues to release stress hormones and doesn't become inured to the noise.

The Consequences of Stress

Stress may be positive or negative. Positive stress can create a healthy, thriving work environment, while negative stress, or distress, can erode morale and performance.

Positive Stress

Some managers and executives thrive under pressure because they practice what world-class athletes already know—that bringing mind, body, and spirit to peak condition requires recovering energy, which is as important as expending energy.[39] Hence, world-class athletes and managers get high marks on any stress test because they use stress-induced energy in positive, healthy, and productive ways. The consequences of healthy, normal stress (*eustress*; see Chapter 5) include a number of performance and health benefits.[40] An organization striving for high-quality products and services needs a healthy workforce to support the effort. Eustress is a characteristic of healthy people; distress is not.

The *Yerkes-Dodson law*, shown in Figure 7.1, indicates that stress leads to improved performance up to an optimum point.[41] Beyond that point, stress has a detrimental effect on performance. Therefore, healthy amounts of stress are desirable to improve performance by arousing a person to action. The greatest performance benefits from stress are achieved in the midrange of the Yerkes-Dodson curve, and after that, as Joseph McGrath has suggested, increasing difficulty of the task is probably what causes performance to decline.[42] Thus, the stress response invokes heightened strength and physical force for limited periods of exertion. This is how stress provides a basis for peak performance in athletic competition, and it can do the same for any type of

FIGURE **7.1** Yerkes-Dodson Law

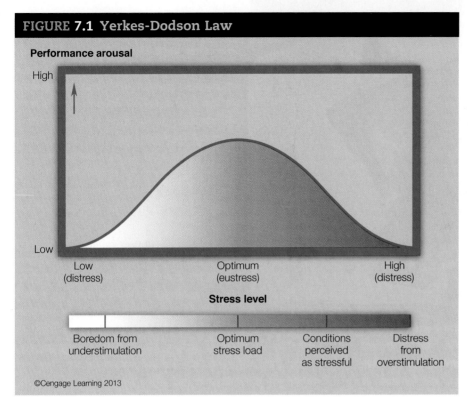

Performance arousal

High

Low

Low
(distress)

Optimum
(eustress)

High
(distress)

Stress level

Boredom from
understimulation

Optimum
stress load

Conditions
perceived
as stressful

Distress
from
overstimulation

©Cengage Learning 2013

job performance. In addition, psychological well-being reduces stress and thereby contributes positively to job performance.[43]

Specific stressful activities, including aerobic exercise, weight training, and flexibility training, improve health and enhance a person's ability to manage stressful demands or situations. Cannon argued that the stress response better prepares soldiers for combat.[44] In the outdoors, in survival or combat situations, stress provides one with the necessary energy boost to manage the situation successfully.

The various individual and organizational forms of distress often associated with the word *stress* are the result of prolonged activation of the stress response, mismanagement of the energy induced by the response, or unique vulnerabilities in a person. We next examine the forms of individual distress, and then the forms of organizational distress.

Individual Distress

An extreme preoccupation with work may result in acute individual distress. In its most extreme form,

individual distress can lead to a phenomenon described by the Japanese word *karoshi*, or death by overwork.[45] Work-related psychological disorders are among the ten leading health disorders and diseases in the United States, according to the National Institute for Occupational Safety and Health.[46] The most common symptoms of psychological distress are depression, burnout, and psychosomatic disorders—physical ailments with psychological origins. These psychological distresses usually lead to *emotional exhaustion*, a form of psychological fatigue caused by energy depletion.[47] Emotional exhaustion may also be caused by the requirement for sustained emotional expression on the job.[48] A recent study of 257 Australian police officers found that emotional exhaustion at work had the potential to spill over to home life, causing work–family conflict.[49]

Burnout is a psychological response to job stress that Christina Maslach characterizes along three dimensions: emotional exhaustion, depersonalization, and reduced perceptions of personal accomplishment. Emotional exhaustion is at the heart of the burnout experience. The conventional belief is that emotional drain leads to

[Eustress in Action]

A study examining the effects of challenge stressors and hindrance stressors was recently conducted throughout the Louisiana Office of Motor Vehicles. Responses from 215 employees and their direct supervisors were collected from sixty-one offices throughout the state. Challenge stressors include factors such as the amount of responsibility an employee is granted, time pressure, and the number of concurrent projects and/or assignments. Hindrance stressors include factors such as the degree to which politics rather than performance affects organizational decisions and bureaucracy's effect on action. The researchers hypothesized that challenge stressors would have a positive effect on talk performance, citizenship performance, and customer service performance. They postulated that hindrance stressors would have a negative effect on these three role-based performances.

The results of the study showed that hindrance stressors do indeed have a negative effect on performance, and challenge stressors have a positive effect, though it's moderated by organizational support. The researchers concluded that companies can benefit from challenges in the workplace if they work to alleviate hindrances and are supportive of employees. While most job stress research has focused on the negative consequences of work stressors, this study demonstrates that some stressors have benefits as well.

SOURCE: J. C. Wallace, B. D. Edwards, T. Arnold, M. L. Frazier, and D. M. Finch, "Work Stressors, Role-Based Performance, and the Moderating Influence of Organizational Support," *Journal of Applied Psychology* 94 (2009): 254–262.

©iStockphoto.com/Ed Hidden

reduced job performance, creating a direct link between burnout and performance. A study by the National Institute questions this assumption and suggests that the influence of motivation has been overlooked in understanding the burnout–performance relationship. Its authors believe that motivation is directly connected to the psychological processes of voluntary goal-directed action, specifically its arousal, direction, intensity, and persistence. Because motivation is considered a direct antecedent of performance, this study suggests that motivation mediates the burnout–performance relationship. Hence, their model is burnout-motivation-performance.[50]

Burnout is not the same as *rust-out*, which is a form of psychological distress caused by a lack of challenge, inspiration, and/or opportunity on the job.[51] For example, a fast-food line cook who has flipped burgers at minimum wage for three years may experience rust-out for all the previously mentioned reasons, resulting in apathy, resentment, and diminished performance.

A number of medical illnesses have a stress-related component.[52] The most significant are heart disease, strokes, backaches, peptic ulcers, and headaches. Ford Motor Company found that cardiovascular diseases, the leading cause of death in the United States since 1910, constituted only 1.5 percent of the medical incidents among 800 salaried employees at its headquarters but accounted for 29 percent of the reported medical costs.[53]

Behavioral problems are another form of individual distress. These problems include workplace aggression, substance abuse, and accidents. Workplace aggression may be triggered by perceptions of injustice in the workplace.[54] Interpersonal conflicts can be a form of nonphysical aggression. One study found that conflicts with workmates, neighbors, and other "non-intimates" account for about 80 percent of our bad moods.[55] Ethnic and cultural differences are too often a basis for interpersonal conflicts and may escalate into physical violence in the workplace. For example, some U.S. employees of Arab descent experienced ethnic slurs and bullying at work after the terrorist attacks of 9/11.

Substance abuse ranges from legal behaviors such as alcohol abuse, excessive smoking, and the overuse of prescription drugs to illegal behaviors such as heroin and cocaine use. The abuse of certain substances, such as tobacco and heroin, can lead to addiction—a physical and/or psychological dependency. Abuse and addiction are behavioral problems that can impair job performance and often lead to significant individual distress.

Accidents, both on and off the job, are still another behavioral form of distress that can sometimes be traced to work-related stressors. For example, an unresolved problem at work may preoccupy or distract an employee, causing an accident either at the office or on the road. These three forms of individual distress—psychological disorders, medical illnesses, and behavioral problems—cause a burden of personal suffering. They also cause a collective burden of suffering reflected in organizational distress.

Organizational Distress

Studies performed at the University of Michigan on *organizational stress* identified a variety of indirect costs of mismanaged stress for an organization, such as low morale, dissatisfaction, breakdowns in communication, and disruption of working relationships. Subsequent research at the Survey Research Center at Michigan established *behavioral costing guidelines*, which specify the direct costs of organizational distress.[56] New research suggests that even positive performance stereotypes can have an adverse effect on organizational health.[57] Three major costs of organizational distress are participation problems, performance decrements, and compensation awards.

Participation problems include absenteeism, tardiness, strikes and work stoppages, and turnover. In the case of absenteeism, the organization may compensate by hiring temporary personnel who take the place of the absentee, possibly elevating personnel costs. When considering turnover, a distinction should be made between

participation problem

A cost associated with absenteeism, tardiness, strikes and work stoppages, and turnover.

dysfunctional and functional turnover. *Dysfunctional turnover* occurs when an organization loses a valuable employee. Replacement costs, including recruiting and retraining, range from five to seven months of the individual monthly salary. *Functional turnover*, in contrast, benefits the organization by creating opportunities for new members, new ideas, and fresh approaches. Functional turnover occurs when an organization loses an employee who has little or no value to the organization; thus the loss of that employee is considered a positive result. The "up or out" promotion policy for members of some organizations is designed to create functional turnover.

Performance decrements are the costs resulting from poor quality or low quantity of production, grievances, and unscheduled machine downtime and repair. As in the case of medical illness, stress is not the only causal agent in these performance decrements. Stress does play a role, however, whether the poor quality or low quantity of production is motivated by distressed employees or by an unconscious response to stress on the job. Some employees in California have the option of taking a "stress leave" rather than filing a grievance against the boss.

Compensation awards are the organizational costs resulting from court awards for job distress.[58] In a federal lawsuit against Allstate, Frank Deus claimed that the company created a high-strain job for him that resulted in incapacitating depression.[59] A jury awarded him a $1.5 million judgment that was later overturned. Job stress–related claims have skyrocketed and threaten to bankrupt the workers' compensation system in some states, although claims and costs are down in other states.[60] Employers need not panic, because fair procedures go a long way toward avoiding legal liability, and legal rulings are setting realistic limits on employers' obligations.[61]

LEARNING OUTCOME 6

Individual Differences in the Stress–Strain Relationship

Individual differences play a central role in the stress–strain relationship. The *weak organ hypothesis* in medicine, also known as the *Achilles' heel phenomenon*, suggests that a person breaks down at her weakest point. Individual differences, such as gender and Type A behavior pattern, enhance vulnerability to strain under stressful conditions. Other individual differences, such as personality hardiness and self-reliance, reduce vulnerability to strain under stressful conditions. One study of personality and emotional performance found that individuals high

©Erik Isakson/Rubberball/Getty Images

on extraversion experienced elevated heart rates when asked to express personality-incongruent emotions such as anger, and that neuroticism was more generally associated with increased heart rate and poor performance.[62] Extraversion and neuroticism thus seem to affect the stress–strain relationship.

Gender Effects

While prevailing stereotypes suggest that women are the weaker sex, the truth is that the life expectancy for American women is almost six years longer than for American men. The "weaker sex" stereotype is further challenged by research in public accounting, which finds that female public accountants have no higher turnover rates than males even though they report more stress.[63] Moreover, research that finds women's behavioral responses to stress are not only different from men's responses, but that they are also strengths in women, rather than weaknesses.[64]

Some literature suggests that there are differences in the stressors to which the two sexes are subject.[65] For example, sexual harassment is a gender-related source of stress for many working women. Men sometimes experience sexual harassment as well, though, and are more likely than women to abuse alcohol as a coping mechanism. This may be because harassment is not a normative occurrence for men.[66]

There is substantive evidence that vulnerabilities constitute the important differences between the sexes.[67] Males are more vulnerable at an earlier age to fatal health problems such as cardiovascular disorders, whereas women report more nonfatal but long-term and disabling health problems. Although we can conclude that gender indeed creates

performance decrement
A cost resulting from poor quality or low quantity of production, grievances, and unscheduled machine downtime and repair.

compensation award
An organizational cost resulting from court awards for job distress.

TYPE A BEHAVIOR

TYPE B BEHAVIOR

a differential vulnerability between the two sexes, it may actually be more important to examine the differences *among* women or *among* men.

Type A Behavior Pattern

Type A behavior pattern is a combination of personality and behavioral characteristics that include competitiveness, time urgency, social status insecurity, aggression, hostility, and a quest for achievements. Type A behavior pattern is also labeled *coronary-prone behavior* because it is linked with coronary heart disease.[68] There are two primary hypotheses concerning which part of the Type A behavior pattern is lethal. One suggests that the problem is time urgency, while the other suggests that it is hostility and aggression. The weight of evidence suggests that hostility and aggression, not time urgency, are the lethal agents.[69]

The alternative to the Type A behavior pattern is the Type B behavior pattern. People with Type B personalities are relatively free of Type A behaviors and characteristics. Type B people are less coronary prone, but if they do have a heart attack, they do not appear to recover as well as those with Type A personalities. Organizations can also be characterized as Type A or Type B.[70] Type A individuals in Type B organizations and Type B individuals in Type A organizations experience stress related to a misfit between their personality type and the predominant type of the organization.

Type A behavior pattern
A complex of personality and behavioral characteristics, including competitiveness, time urgency, social status insecurity, aggression, hostility, and a quest for achievements.

personality hardiness
A personality characterized by commitment, control, and challenge and, hence, resistant to distress.

transformational coping
A way of managing stressful events by changing them into less subjectively stressful events.

[Type A Behavior Pattern Components]

1. Sense of time urgency (a kind of "hurry sickness").
2. The quest for numbers (success is measured by the number of achievements).
3. Status insecurity (feeling unsure of oneself deep down inside).
4. Aggression and hostility expressed in response to frustration and conflict.

Type A behavior can be modified. The first step is for Type A people to recognize that they are prone to the Type A pattern, and possibly, spend time with Type B individuals. Type B people often recognize Type A behavior and can help Type A individuals judge situations realistically. Type A individuals can also pace themselves, manage their time well, and try not to do multiple things at once. Focusing only on the task at hand and its completion rather than worrying about other tasks can help Type A individuals cope more effectively.

Personality Hardiness

People who have hardy personalities resist strain reactions when subjected to stressful events more effectively than do people who are not hardy.[71] The components of **personality hardiness** are commitment, control, and challenge. Commitment is an engagement with one's environment that leads to the experience of activities as interesting and enjoyable. Employees with high levels of commitment are less likely to leave the organization or experience promotion-related stress.[72] Control is an ability to influence the processes and outcomes of events that leads to the experience of activities as personal choices. Challenge is the conception of change as a stimulus to personal development, which leads to the welcome experience of new activities.

The hardy personality appears to use these three components actively to engage in transformational coping when faced with stressful events.[73] **Transformational coping** is the active process of modifying one's perception of an event in order to reduce stress. This is accomplished by viewing the event in broader terms, by altering the course and outcome through action, and/or by achieving greater understanding of the process. The alternative to transformational coping is *regressive coping*, characterized by a passive avoidance of events and decreased interaction with the environment. Regressive coping may lead to short-term stress reduction at the cost of healthy, long-term life adjustment.

Hardy	Not Hardy
Commitment	Alienation
Control	Powerlessness
Challenge	Threat

Self-Reliance

There is increasing evidence that social relationships have an important impact on health and life expectancy.[74] **Self-reliance**, a healthy, secure interdependent pattern of behavior, is a personality attribute strongly related to social relationships. The concept of self-reliance was originally based on *attachment theory*, a psychological approach to normal human development that identifies three distinct patterns of attachment.[75] Research suggests that these patterns become behavioral strategies during adulthood in professional as well as personal relationships.[76] A secure pattern of attachment and *interdependent* behavior results in self-reliance. The connection between self-reliance and the word *interdependent* may appear paradoxical, because a person appears independent while maintaining a host of supportive attachments.[77] But self-reliant people respond to stressful, threatening situations by reaching out to others appropriately. Indeed, self-reliance is a flexible, responsive strategy of forming and maintaining multiple, diverse relationships. Self-reliant people are confident, enthusiastic, and persistent in facing challenges. Their flexibility allows them to form healthy partner relationships that buffer work-related stress.[78]

Interpersonal attachment is emotional and psychological connectedness to another person. In contrast, the two insecure patterns of attachment are counterdependence and overdependence. **Counterdependence** is an unhealthy, insecure pattern of behavior that leads to separation in relationships with other people. When faced with stressful and threatening situations, counterdependent people withdraw. Counterdependence may be characterized as a rigid, dismissing denial of the need for other people in difficult and stressful times. Counterdependent people exhibit a fearless, aggressive, and active response to challenges, but they are not truly self-reliant.

Overdependence is also an unhealthy, insecure pattern of behavior. Overdependent people respond to stressful and threatening situations by clinging to other people in any way possible. Overdependence may be characterized as a desperate, preoccupied attempt to achieve a sense of security through relationships. Overdependent people exhibit an active but disorganized and anxious response to challenges. This quality prevents a person from being able to organize and maintain healthy relationships; therefore, it creates distress. Interestingly, both counterproductive and overdependence can be exhibited by military personnel who are experiencing adjustment difficulties during the first thirty days of basic training.[79] The recruits who have the most difficulty adjusting to new jobs demonstrate severe overdependence. They often find it difficult to function on their own during training.

Preventive Stress Management

Stress is an inevitable part of work and personal life. **Preventive stress management** is an organizational philosophy according to which people and organizations should take joint responsibility for promoting health and preventing distress and strain. This philosophy is rooted in public health practices first used in preventive medicine. A framework for understanding preventive stress management is presented in Figure 7.2 on the next page, which includes three stages of prevention that apply in a preventive medicine context as well as an organizational context.

Primary prevention is intended to reduce, modify, or eliminate the stress-causing demand or stressor. The idea behind primary prevention is to eliminate or alleviate the source of a problem. True organizational stress prevention is largely primary in nature, because it reduces the demands the organization places on the employee. **Secondary prevention** is intended to modify the individual's or the organization's response to a demand or

©Ljupco Smokovski/Shutterstock.com

self-reliance
A healthy, secure, interdependent pattern of behavior related to how people form and maintain supportive attachments with others.

counterdependence
An unhealthy, insecure pattern of behavior that leads to separation in relationships with other people.

overdependence
An unhealthy, insecure pattern of behavior that leads to preoccupied attempts to achieve security through relationships.

preventive stress management
An organizational philosophy according to which people and organizations should take joint responsibility for promoting health and preventing distress and strain.

primary prevention
The stage in preventive stress management designed to reduce, modify, or eliminate the demand or stressor causing stress.

secondary prevention
The stage in preventive stress management designed to alter or modify the individual's or the organization's response to a demand or stressor.

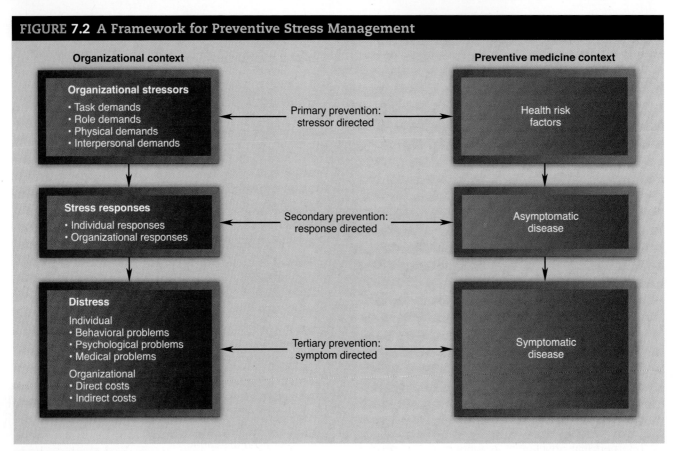

FIGURE 7.2 A Framework for Preventive Stress Management

Organizational context

Organizational stressors
- Task demands
- Role demands
- Physical demands
- Interpersonal demands

Stress responses
- Individual responses
- Organizational responses

Distress

Individual
- Behavioral problems
- Psychological problems
- Medical problems

Organizational
- Direct costs
- Indirect costs

Primary prevention: stressor directed

Secondary prevention: response directed

Tertiary prevention: symptom directed

Preventive medicine context

Health risk factors

Asymptomatic disease

Symptomatic disease

SOURCE: J. D. Quick, R. S. Horn, and J. C. Quick, "Health Consequences of Stress," *Journal of Organizational Behavior Management* 8, No. 2 (Fall 1986): 21. Reprinted by permission of (Taylor & Francis Ltd, http://www.tandf.co.uk/journals).

stressor. Employees must learn to manage the inevitable, unalterable work stressors and demands to avert distress and strain while improving health and well-being. **Tertiary prevention** is intended to heal individual or organizational symptoms of distress and strain. The symptoms may range from early warning signs (such as headaches or absenteeism) to more severe forms of distress (such as hypertension, work stoppages, and strikes). An innovative approach used by data recovery company DriveSavers bolsters treatment and prevention with a full-time grief counselor.[80] The stages of prevention can be applied to organizational prevention, individual prevention, and comprehensive health promotion.

Organizational Stress Prevention

Some organizations maintain low-stress, healthy environments, while others cultivate high-stress environments that may place their employees' health at risk. The experience of organizational justice and fairness is emerging as one contextual factor that leads to a positive, low-stress work environment.[81] One comprehensive approach to organizational health and preventive stress management was pioneered in the

U.S. Air Force by Colonel Joyce Adkins, who developed an Organizational Health Center (OHC) with the Air Force Materiel Command.[82] The OHC's goal is to keep workers happy, healthy, and on the job while increasing efficiency and productivity to their highest levels. This goal is achieved by focusing on workplace stressors, organizational and individual forms of distress, and managerial and individual strategies for preventive stress management. Adkins's comprehensive, organizational health approach addresses primary, secondary, and tertiary prevention. Most organizational prevention, however, is primary prevention, including job redesign, goal setting, role negotiation, and career management.

Two organizational stress prevention methods—team building and social support at work—are secondary prevention. We discuss team building in Chapter 9, but we should note here that under stress, team structure may influence team effectiveness. Specifically, teams experiencing quantitative demands are more effective when more tightly structured, while teams experiencing qualitative demands are more effective when more loosely structured.[83] Finally, companies such as Kraft Foods (a subsidiary of Altria Group, Inc.) and Hardee's Food Systems (part of CKE Restaurants, Inc.) have developed specific violence prevention programs to combat the rise in workplace violence. Violence in organizations is a cat-

tertiary prevention

The stage in preventive stress management designed to heal individual or organizational symptoms of distress and strain.

egory of dysfunctional behaviors that is often motivated by stressful events and whose negative consequences need to be prevented.[84]

Job Redesign The job strain model illustrated in Figure 7.3 suggests that the combination of stringent demands and restricted control leads to a high-strain job. A major goal in job redesign should be to increase worker control. In many cases, this reduces distress and strain without reducing productivity.

Increasing worker control is a strategy of preventive stress management that can be accomplished in a number of ways, the most common being to increase job decision latitude. Increased latitude might include greater authority over the sequencing of work activities, the timing of work schedules, the selection and sequencing of work tools, or the selection of work teams. A second objective of job redesign should be to reduce uncertainty and increase predictability in the workplace.

Goal Setting Preventive stress management can also be achieved through goal-setting activities. These activities are designed to increase task motivation while reducing role conflict and ambiguity. Goal setting focuses a person's attention while directing energy into a productive channel. Implicit in much of the goal-setting literature is the assumption that people participate in determining their work goals.

Role Negotiation The organizational development technique of role negotiation has value as a stress-management method because it allows individuals to modify their work roles.[85] Role negotiation begins with the definition of a focal role within the organizational context. The person in the focal role identifies the expectations understood for the role, and organizational supervisors specify their own expectations of the person in the focal role. A negotiation of integrated role expectation follows. In the process of such negotiation, points of confusion and conflict become opportunities for clarification and resolution. The final result of the role negotiation process should be a clear, well-defined focal role with which the incumbent and organizational members are all comfortable.

Social Support Systems Team building is one way to develop supportive social relationships in the workplace. However, team building is primarily task oriented, not socio-emotional, in nature. Although employees may receive much of their socio-emotional support from personal relationships outside the workplace, some socio-emotional support within the workplace is also necessary for psychological well-being.

Social support systems can be enhanced through the work environment in a number of ways. Interpersonal communication is the key to unlocking social support for preventive stress management.[86] Figure 7.4 on the next page identifies key elements in a person's work and nonwork social support system. These relationships provide emotional caring, information, evaluative feedback, modeling, and instrumental support.

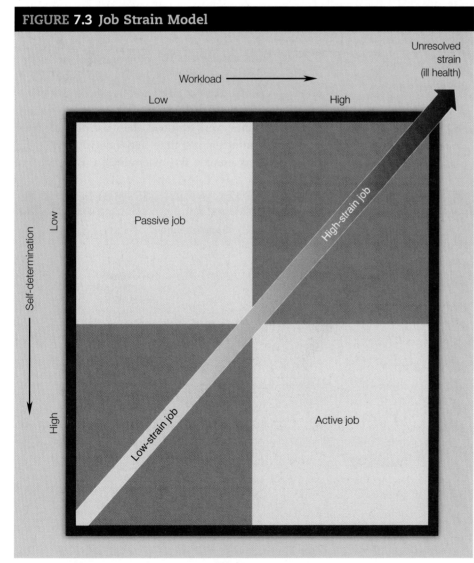

FIGURE 7.3 Job Strain Model

Workload — Low → High
Self-determination — Low → High
Passive job
Active job
Low-strain job
High-strain job
Unresolved strain (ill health)

SOURCE: Republished with permission of ABC-CLIO Inc., from *Work Stress: Health Care Systems in the Workplace*, J. C. Quick, R. S. Bhagat, J. E. Dalton, and J. D. Quick. © 1987; permission conveyed through Copyright Clearance Center, Inc.

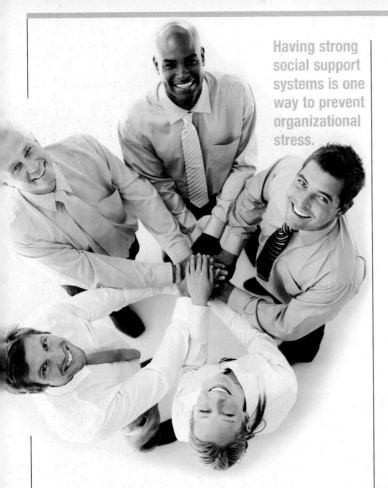

Having strong social support systems is one way to prevent organizational stress.

tive. It is usually learned over time, though some are predisposed to it. *Pessimism* is an alternative style of thought that focuses on the negative. It can lead to depression, health problems, and low levels of achievement. By contrast, positive thinking enhances physical health and achievement and decreases susceptibility to depression.

Positive thinking does not mean ignoring stressors and challenges. It means viewing them through a different lens. Optimistic people avoid distress by framing the difficult times in their lives as temporary, limited in scope, and often unavoidable. They face adversity with hope, and take credit for the good events in their lives, which they see as more pervasive and generalized. Optimists are also more motivated and more likely to use proactive coping skills to achieve goals and pursue development opportunities.[89] *Learned optimism* begins with identifying pessimistic thoughts and then distracting oneself from these thoughts or disputing them with evidence and alternative thoughts. It is one of the five dimensions of *positive organizational behavior (POB)*. The other four dimensions are confidence/self-efficacy, hope, subjective well-being/happiness, and emotional intelligence.[90]

Time Management Temporal pressure is one of the major sources of stress, as listed in Table 7.1. It applies to people both at work and in school. Symptoms of poor time management include constant rushing, missed deadlines, work overload, the sense of being overwhelmed, insufficient rest time, and indecision. Effective time managers employ the macro-level *GP³ method* of

Individual Prevention

Clinical research shows that individuals may use a number of self-directed interventions to help prevent distress and enhance positive well-being.[87] Such individual prevention can be of a primary, secondary, or tertiary nature. The *primary prevention* activities we discuss are learned optimism, time management, and leisure time activities. The *secondary prevention* activities we discuss are physical exercise, relaxation, and diet. The *tertiary prevention* activities we discuss are opening up and professional help.

Positive Thinking The power of *positive thinking* too often goes unappreciated. When one cultivates an optimistic frame of mind, bad life events are bathed in a positive light, preventing future and healing past distress.[88] An optimistic style of thought must be practiced habitually in order to be effec-

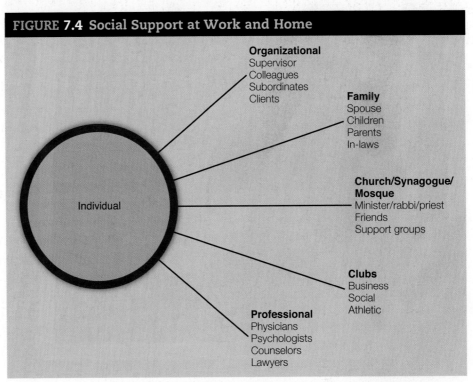

FIGURE 7.4 Social Support at Work and Home

Individual

Organizational
Supervisor
Colleagues
Subordinates
Clients

Family
Spouse
Children
Parents
In-laws

Church/Synagogue/ Mosque
Minister/rabbi/priest
Friends
Support groups

Clubs
Business
Social
Athletic

Professional
Physicians
Psychologists
Counselors
Lawyers

SOURCE: J. C. Quick, J. D. Quick, D. L. Nelson, and J. J. Hurrell, Jr., *Preventive Stress Management in Organizations* (Washington, D.C.: American Psychological Association, 1997), 198. Reprinted with permission.

time management.[91] The GP³ method is to (1) set *goals* that are challenging yet attainable; (2) *prioritize* these goals in terms of their relative importance; (3) *plan* for goal attainment through specific tasks, activities, scheduling, and delegation; and (4) *praise* oneself for specific achievements along the way. Setting concrete goals and prioritizing these goals are the most important first steps in time-management skills, ensuring that the most important work and study activities receive enough time and attention. This system of time management enables a person to track his success over time and goes a long way toward reducing unnecessary stress and confusion.

Leisure Time Activities People with a high need for achievement are often characterized by an unremitting urge to strive for excellence. Leisure time provides employees an opportunity for rest and recovery from strenuous activities at home and work. When asked what they do with their leisure time, many individuals say that they clean the house or mow the lawn. These activities are fine, as long as the individual gets the stress-reducing benefit of pleasure from them. Some say our work ethic is a cultural barrier to pleasure. We work longer hours, and two-income families are the norm. Leisure is increasingly a luxury among working people. The key to the effective use of leisure time is enjoyment. Leisure time can be used for spontaneity, joy, and connection with others in our lives. Although vacations can be a relief from job burnout, they may incur fade-out effects.[92] Hence, leisure time and vacations must be periodic, recurring activities.

Physical Exercise Different types of physical exercise are important secondary stress prevention activities for individuals. Colleges and universities often implement physical exercise through physical education classes, while military organizations implement it through fitness standards and regulated training. Kenneth Cooper, among others, has long advocated aerobic exercise to improve a person's responsiveness to stressful activities.[93] Research at the Aerobics Center in Dallas has found that aerobically fit people (1) have lower levels of adrenaline in their blood at rest; (2) have a slower, stronger heart beat; and (3) recover from stressful events more quickly.

Flexibility training is an important type of exercise because muscular contractions are associated with the stress response. One component of the stress response is the contraction of the flexor muscles, which prepares a person to fight or flee. Flexibility training enables a person to stretch and relax these muscles to prevent the accumulation of unnecessary muscular tension.[94] In addition, flexibility exercises help maintain joint mobility, increase strength, and play an important role in the prevention of injury.

Hot Trend: Stress Naps

A number of companies have found a rather simple solution to organizational stress: naps. They find that allowing employees to take short naps during the workday increases their energy, focus, and productivity, and reduces the amount of stress they feel (and cause others). At Google, employees can use a MetroNap Energy Pod, a futuristic chair with speakers that play soothing sounds, to take a quick, recharging nap. A number of New York–based companies like Hearst, Newsweek, and Time Warner have contracted with a local spa, Yelo, so that their employees can nap or get a quick massage. Airlines like Continental and British Airways, meanwhile, allow pilots on long international flights to take naps in a resting area while other pilots control the plane.

SOURCE: J. Hoffman, "Napping Gets a Nod at the Workplace," *Bloomberg Businessweek* (August 26, 2010), http://www.businessweek.com/magazine/content/10_36/b4193084949626.htm, accessed June 21, 2011.

Relaxation Training Herbert Benson was one of the first people to identify the relaxation response as the natural counterresponse to stress.[95] In studying Western and Eastern peoples, Benson found that Jews and Christians have elicited this response through their time-honored traditions of prayer, whereas those with backgrounds in Eastern religions have elicited it through meditation. The relaxation response does not require a theological or religious component, however. Reading, massage, and secular yoga practice can all elicit the relaxation response. If you have an "unwinding" ritual, you may already elicit the relaxation response regularly.

Diet Diet may play an indirect role in stress and stress management. Large amounts of sugar in one's diet can stimulate the stress response, and foods high in cholesterol can adversely affect blood chemistry. Good dietary practices contribute to overall health. In his nonsurgical, nonpharmacological approach to reversing heart disease, Dean Ornish proposes a very stringent "reversal diet" for individuals with identifiable blockage of the arteries.[96] He recommends a somewhat less stringent "prevention diet" as one of four methods for opening up the arteries of healthy individuals. Another element in his program is an emotional one—openness in relationships with other people.

Opening Up Traumatic, distress-inducing events are an unfortunate fact of life. One of the most therapeutic responses to such events is to confide in other people.[97] Discussing difficult experiences with another person is not always easy, but mental and physical heath improves through self-disclosure. Confessions need not be made in person, or to another person at all. Writing in a private diary and posting anonymously on the Internet are also therapeutic. In a study comparing those who wrote once a week about traumatic events with those who wrote about non-traumatic events, significant health benefits and reduced absenteeism were found in the first group.[98] Whatever form it takes, the process of opening up and confessing appears to counter the detrimental effects of stress.

Professional Help Confession and opening up may occur in professional healing relationships. Psychological counseling, career counseling, physical therapy, medical treatment, surgical intervention, and other therapeutic techniques are available to people who need help. *Employee assistance programs (EAPs)* may be very helpful in referring employees to appropriate caregivers. Even soldiers who experience battle stress reactions severe enough to take them out of action can experience healing through EAPs and then participate in subsequent combat missions.[99] The early detection of distress and strain reactions, coupled with prompt professional treatment, can be instrumental in averting permanent physical and psychological damage, such as posttraumatic stress disorder.

> " Mental and physical health improves through self-disclosure

Comprehensive Health Promotion

Whereas organizational stress prevention programs are aimed at eliminating health risks at work, comprehensive health promotion programs are aimed at establishing a "strong and resistant host" by teaching individual prevention and lifestyle change.[100] Physical fitness and exercise programs characterize corporate health promotion programs in the United States and Canada.[101] A health and wellness survey of accredited medical schools in the United States, Canada, and Puerto Rico found that these programs place significant emphasis on physical well-being and minor emphasis on spiritual well-being.[102] A new approach to comprehensive health promotion places emphasis on the organization and *organizational wellness*.[103] Still, social and cognitive processes are key considerations in the successful implementation of stress prevention programs.[104]

Johnson & Johnson developed a comprehensive health promotion program with a wide array of educational modules for individuals and groups. Each of these educational modules addresses a specific topic, such as Type A behavior, stress, diet (through cooperative activities with the American Heart Association), and risk assessment (through regular health evaluations for participants). Upon implementation of this health promotion program, Johnson & Johnson found that the health status of employees improved, even if they didn't participate in the program.

Log in to the **CourseMate** for *ORGB3* at **www.cengagebrain.com** to:

* Review **Key Terms Flash Cards** online
* Play **Beat the Clock** and **Quiz Bowl** to master concepts
* Complete **web quizzes** to prepare for exams
* Watch the video on **Modern Shed** and from *The Upside of Anger* for examples, then test yourself with a quick quiz
* Work through the **"What about You?"** and **Ethical Dilemma** exercises to see how you would handle various situations that organizations face on a daily basis

Effects of Stress on the Body

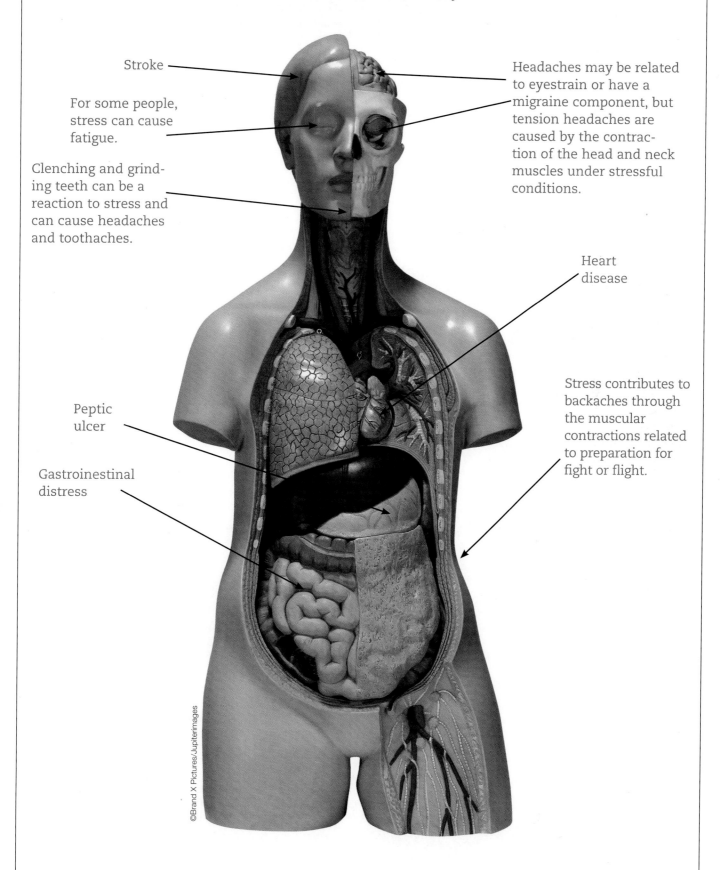

Stroke

For some people, stress can cause fatigue.

Clenching and grinding teeth can be a reaction to stress and can cause headaches and toothaches.

Headaches may be related to eyestrain or have a migraine component, but tension headaches are caused by the contraction of the head and neck muscles under stressful conditions.

Heart disease

Stress contributes to backaches through the muscular contractions related to preparation for fight or flight.

Peptic ulcer

Gastroinestinal distress

©Brand X Pictures/Jupiterimages

CHAPTER 8

Communication

LEARNING OUTCOMES

1 Describe the interpersonal communication process and the role of listening in the process.

2 Describe the five communication skills of effective supervisors.

3 Explain five communication barriers and the gateways through them.

4 Distinguish between civility and incivility, and defensive and nondefensive communication.

5 Explain the impact of nonverbal communication.

6 Explain positive, healthy communication.

7 Identify how new communication technologies and social media affect the communication process.

©istockphoto.com/Andreas Laubscher

" *Interpersonal communication is central to health and well-being, both at home and on the job.* **"**

After You Finish
This Chapter
Go to **Page 140**
for **Study Tools**

Interpersonal Communication

Communication evokes a shared, or common, meaning in another person. **Interpersonal communication** occurs between two or more people in an organization. It is central to health and well-being, both at home and on the job. Reading, listening, managing and interpreting information, and serving clients are among the interpersonal communication skills identified by the Department of Labor as necessary for success in the workplace.[1] In Chapter 7, we noted that interpersonal communication is the key to unlocking social support for preventive stress management.[2] It is also important in building and sustaining human relationships at work. Recent advances in information technology and data management cannot replace interpersonal communication. Figure 8.1 on the next page illustrates the key elements of interpersonal communication: the communicator, the receiver, the perceptual screens, and the message.

An Interpersonal Communication Model

The **communicator** is the person sending the message. The **receiver** is the person accepting the message. **Perceptual screens** are the windows through which we interact. The communicator's and the receiver's respective perceptual screens influence the quality, accuracy, and clarity of the message. They can allow the message to transmit smoothly, or they can cause static and distortion. Perceptual screens are built upon the sender's and receiver's individual

communication

The evoking of a shared or common meaning in another person.

interpersonal communication

Communication between two or more people in an organization.

communicator

The person sending a message.

receiver

The person accepting a message.

perceptual screen

A window through which one interacts with others. It influences the quality, accuracy, and clarity of the communication.

FIGURE 8.1 A Basic Interpersonal Communication Model

Feedback

Communicator

Message
• Context
• Affect

Receiver

Event X

Perceptual
screens

Perceptual
screens

©Cengage Learning 2013

attributes, such as age, gender, values, beliefs, past experiences, cultural influences, and individual needs. The degree to which these screens are open significantly influences both sent and received messages.

The **message** contains the thoughts and feelings that the communicator intends to evoke in the receiver. The message has two primary components. The *thought*, or conceptual component, of the message (its content) is contained in the words, ideas, symbols, and concepts chosen to relay the message. The *feeling*, or emotional component, of the message (its affect) is contained in the intensity, demeanor, and gestures of the communicator. The emotional component of the message adds overtones of joy, anger, fear, or pain to the conceptual component. This addition often enriches and clarifies the message.

Feedback may or may not be activated in communication. It occurs when the receiver provides the communicator with a response to the message. More broadly, feedback occurs when information is fed back to the sender that completes two-way communication.

The **language** of the message is important. *Language* is a broad term denoting the words, their pronunciations, and the methods of combining them used and understood by a group of people. Culture and situation dictate the specific language utilized in a message.

Data are the uninterpreted, unanalyzed elements of a message. **Information** is data with meaning to the person who interprets or analyzes them. Since messages are conveyed through a *medium*, such as a telephone or face-to-face discussion, they differ in **richness** according to the ability of that medium to transmit meaning to a receiver.[3] Table 8.1 compares different media with regard to data capacity and richness. Such attributes of communication media affect how influence-seeking behavior is generated and perceived in organizations.[4]

Reflective Listening

Even though it isn't explicitly noted in the communication model, good listening is paramount to effective communication. **Reflective listening** is the skill of carefully

---

message

The thoughts and feelings that the communicator is attempting to evoke in the receiver.

feedback

Information fed back that completes two-way communication.

language

The words, their pronunciations, and the methods of combining them used and understood by a group of people.

data

Uninterpreted and unanalyzed elements of a message.

information

Data that have been interpreted, analyzed, and have meaning to some user.

richness

The ability of a medium to convey meaning to a receiver.

reflective listening

Carefully listening to a message and immediately repeating it back to the speaker.

TABLE 8.1 Communication Media: Information Richness and Data Capacity

Medium	Information Richness	Data Capacity
Face-to-face discussion	Highest	Lowest
Telephone	High	Low
Electronic mail	Moderate	Moderate
Blog	Moderate	Moderate
Individualized letter	Moderate	Moderate
Personalized note or memo	Moderate	Moderate
Formal written report	Low	High
Flyer or bulletin	Low	High
Formal numeric report	Lowest	Highest

SOURCE: Adapted from E. A. Gerloff, "Information Richness: A New Approach to Managerial Behavior and Organizational Design" by R. L. Daft and R. H. Lengel in *Research in Organizational Behavior* 6 (1984): 191–233. Reprinted by permission of JAI Press Inc.

[Listen Up!]

While it's important that managers learn how to talk to their employees, it's just as important that managers take the time to listen to employees. By taking the time to hear what employees are saying about the workplace, managers can make the organization much more effective. HCL Technologies, an IT services firm located in India, hosts a site called U&I, which allows employees to post questions and complaints, and to respond to others' posts. The forum is completely uncensored, and many of the first postings were variants of "Why do you guys [management] suck?" "Why does your strategy suck?" and "Why aren't you living up to your ideals?" Though some managers were tempted to censor posts, employees saw U&I as a commitment to communication transparency and a way to hold management accountable to the decision it made. CEO Vineet Nayar also hosts a "My Problems" section on the U&I site, in which he describes various issues that company leadership was dealing with and asks employees at all levels to give him advice on how to handle them.

SOURCE: G. Hamel, "HCL: Extreme Management Makeover," *The Wall Street Journal* (July 6, 2010), http://blogs.wsj.com /management/2010/07/06/hcl-extreme-management-makeover, accessed August 20, 2010.

listening to a message and immediately repeating it back to the speaker. This technique helps the communicator clarify the intended message and correct inaccuracies or misunderstandings. Reflective listening emphasizes the role of the receiver, or audience, in interpersonal communication. Managers can use this technique to understand other people and help them solve problems at work.[5] Reflective listening better enables the listener to comprehend the communicator's meaning, reduce perceptual distortions, and overcome interpersonal barriers that lead to communication failures. Especially useful in problem solving, reflective listening can be learned in a short time. Given its positive effects on behavior and emotion in the corporate environment, reflective listening is a valuable skill to possess.[6]

Reflective listening can be characterized as personal, feeling oriented, and responsive.[7] First, it emphasizes the *personal* elements of the communication process. The reflective listener demonstrates empathy and concern for the communicator as a person, not an object. Second, reflective listening emphasizes the *feelings* communicated in the message—the receiver must pay special attention to the feeling component as she repeats the message. Third, reflective listening emphasizes a rational and considerate *response*. Receivers should distinguish their own feelings and thoughts from those of the speaker. In other words, the

conversation's focus must remain at all times on the ideas and emotions of the speaker in order for the receiver to effectively respond to them. A good reflective listener does not lead the speaker according to his own thoughts and feelings.

Reflective listening necessitates four levels of verbal response: affirming contact, paraphrasing expressed thoughts and feelings, clarifying implicit thoughts and feelings, and reflecting core feelings not fully expressed. Nonverbal behaviors, such as eye contact and silence, are also important in reflective listening. Each of these responses can be illustrated through an example: the interaction between a software engineer, who has just discovered a major problem in a large information system she is building for a difficult customer, and her supervisor.

Affirming Contact The receiver (in this case, the supervisor of the software engineer) affirms contact with the communicator (the software engineer) by making periodic statements such as "I see," "Okay," and "Yes, I understand." The purpose of an affirmation response is to communicate attentiveness, not necessarily agreement. Affirming contact is especially reassuring to a speaker in the early stages of expression, and even more so when there may be some associated anxiety or discomfort. As the problem is more fully explored and expressed, it is increasingly important for the receiver to employ other reflective responses.

Paraphrasing the Expressed After an appropriate length of time, the receiver (the supervisor in our example) might paraphrase the expressed thoughts and feelings of the speaker (the engineer). Paraphrasing is useful because it tells the speaker what the receiver heard and what the receiver's thoughts and feelings are about what he heard. This verbal response enables the speaker and receiver to build greater empathy, openness, and acceptance into their relationship while ensuring the accuracy of the communication process.

In the case of the software engineer, the supervisor may find paraphrasing the engineer's message particularly useful for both of them in developing a clearer understanding of the system problem. He might say, "I can tell that you're very upset about this problem. Even though you're not quite sure how it happened, it sounds like you have a few good leads." It is difficult to solve a problem until it is clearly understood.

Clarifying the Implicit People often communicate *implicit* thoughts and feelings—that is, thoughts and feelings that are not clearly or fully expressed—along with their explicitly expressed message. The receiver may or may not assume that this implicit component of the message is within the awareness of the speaker. For example, the software engineer may be anxious about how to approach a difficult customer with the system problem. This may be implicit in her discussion with her supervisor because of a previous discussion about this customer. If her feelings of anxiety are not expressed, the supervisor may want to clarify them. He might say, "You seem particularly stressed . . . were you worried about the client's reaction?" This would help the engineer shift the focus of her attention from the main problem, which is in the software, to the important issue of discussing the matter with the customer.

Reflecting Core Feelings Next, the receiver should look beyond the speaker's explicit and implicit messages to understand the speaker's *core feelings*, the speaker's deepest and most important emotions, beliefs, and values. If the software engineer had not been aware of any anxiety in her relationship with the difficult customer, her supervisor's ability to sense the tension and bring it to the engineer's awareness would exemplify the reflection of core feelings.

However, the receiver runs a risk of overreaching if a secure, empathetic relationship with the speaker has not already been established or if strongly repressed feelings are reflected back. Even if the receiver is correct, the speaker may not want those feelings brought to her awareness. Therefore, it is important to exercise caution and care in reflecting core feelings to a speaker.

Silence Long periods of silence may cause discomfort or embarrassment, but a certain amount of silence can help both speaker and listener in reflective listening. From the speaker's perspective, silence may be useful in moments of thought or confusion about how to express difficult ideas or feelings. The software engineer may need some patient silence from her supervisor as she thinks through what to say next. Listeners can use brief periods of silence to sort their own thoughts and feelings from those of the speaker. In the case of the software engineer's supervisor, any personal feelings toward the difficult customer should not intrude on the engineer's immediate problem. Silence provides time to identify and isolate the listener's personal responses and exclude them from the dialogue.

Eye Contact Eye contact is a nonverbal behavior that may promote openness in communication between two people. During a dialogue, the absence of appropriate eye contact tends to close communication. However, the presence of inappropriate eye contact can also hinder a relationship. Cultural and individual differences influence what constitutes appropriate and inappropriate eye contact. For example, direct eye contact initiated by women and children is discouraged in India. In fact, too much direct eye contact, regardless of the individual or culture, can have an intimidating effect.

Moderate direct eye contact communicates openness and affirmation without causing either speaker or listener to feel intimidated. Periodic aversion of the eyes allows for a sense of privacy and control, even in intense interpersonal communication. The software engineer and the supervisor make eye contact throughout their discussion, though each looks away periodically to ease the tension of intimacy.

One-Way versus Two-Way Communication Reflective listening encourages **two-way communication**, an interactive form of communication in which there is an exchange of thoughts, feelings, or both, and through which shared meaning often occurs. Problem solving and decision making are often examples of two-way communication. **One-way communication** occurs when a person sends a message to another person and no feedback, questions, or interaction follows. Giving instructions and giving directions are examples of one-way communication.

One-way communication tends to be efficient, although how efficient it is depends on the amount and complexity of information communicated and the medium chosen. Even though it is faster than two-way communication, one-way communication is often less accurate. This is especially true for complex tasks that require clarification for completion. When time and accuracy are both important to the successful comple-

two-way communication
An interactive form of communication in which there is an exchange of thoughts, feelings, or both.

one-way communication
Communication in which a person sends a message to another person and no feedback, questions, or interaction follows.

Two-way communication is an interactive form of communication.

©iStockphoto.com/Jacob Wackerhausen

tion of a task and two-way communication is not an option (such as in combat or emergency situations), extensive training prior to execution enhances accuracy and efficiency.[8] Firefighters and military combat personnel engage extensively in such training to minimize the need for communication during emergencies. These highly trained professionals rely on abbreviated one-way communication as shorthand for more complex information. However, this communication only works within the range of situations for which the professionals are specifically trained.

It is difficult to draw generalizations about individual preference for one-way or two-way communication. Communicators with a stronger need for feedback or who are comfortable with conflict or confusing questions may find two-way communication more satisfying. By contrast, receivers who believe that a message is straightforward may be satisfied with one-way communication and be impatient with lengthy two-way communication.

LEARNING OUTCOME 2

Communication Skills for Effective Managers

Interpersonal communication is a critical foundation for effective performance and individual well-being in organizations. Power is intertwined in the language of communication between managers and their employees.[9] This power dynamic is especially critical when leaders are articulating an organizational vision and attempting to achieve buy-in from employees.[10] One large study of managers in a variety of industries found that those with the most effective work units

engaged in routine communication with their employees, whereas the managers with the highest promotion rates engaged in networking activities with superiors.[11] A study of banking managers found that higher performing managers were more effective, less apprehensive communicators than lower performing managers.[12] Oral communication and managerial cooperation are important contextual performance skills that have positive effects on the psychosocial quality of the work environment.[13]

Research on manager–employee communication identifies five communication skills that distinguish good supervisors from bad ones.[14] A good supervisor is an expressive speaker, an empathetic listener, a persuasive leader, a sensitive person, and an informative manager. Some supervisors are effective without possessing all of these skills, however, and some organizations value one or two skills over the others. But because dyadic relationships are at the core of much organization-based communication, possessing all five skills makes a supervisor that much more effective in communicating to employees.[15]

Expressiveness

Effective supervisors express their thoughts, ideas, and feelings openly and aren't afraid to voice opinions in meetings. They tend toward extroversion. Supervisors who are not talkative or who tend toward introversion may at times leave their employees wondering what they're thinking about certain issues. Supervisors who speak out let the people they work with know where they stand, what they believe, and how they feel.

Empathy and Sensitivity

In addition to being expressive speakers, good supervisors are willing, empathetic, reflective listeners. Empathetic listeners are able to hear the emotional dimensions of the messages people send them, as well as the content of the ideas and issues. Good supervisors are approachable and willing to listen to suggestions and complaints. In a recent study of physicians, those with higher perceptions of control were more open in their communication, and patients found them more empathetic.[16]

Good supervisors are also sensitive to the feelings, self-images, and psychological defenses of their employees. They know how and when to communicate with employees to maximize psychological health. For example, employees' accomplishments, honors, and achievements should be announced in public, while criticism should be delivered in private. The best supervisors are sensitive to the self-esteem of others.

> *Good supervisors keep their employees well informed by appropriately and selectively disseminating information.*

Persuasiveness

All supervisors must exercise power and influence in organizations if they want to ensure high performance and achieve positive results. Effective supervisors tend to be persuasive leaders, distinguished by their use of persuasive language to influence others. They are not deceitful or autocratic—they encourage results earnestly instead of manipulating others.

Of course, sometimes emergencies and high-risk situations necessitate the abandonment of sensitive and subtle persuasion. In cases such as a fire at an oil rig or a life-threatening trauma in an emergency room, a supervisor must be direct and assertive.

Informative Managing Style

Finally, good supervisors keep their employees well informed by appropriately and selectively disseminating information. Failing to effectively filter information may lead to either information overload or a lack of sufficient information for task accomplishment. Good supervisors give advance notice of organizational changes and explain the rationale for organizational policies.

A person may become a good supervisor even in the absence of one of these communication skills. For example, a manager with special talents in planning, organizing, or decision making may compensate for a shortcoming in expressiveness or sensitivity. No matter their perceived skill level or effectiveness, when supervisors and employees engage in open communication and forward planning, they have a greater number of agreements about the employee's performance and behavior.[17]

LEARNING OUTCOME 3

Barriers and Gateways to Communication

Barriers to communication are factors that distort, disrupt, or even halt successful communication. They may be temporary and easily resolved or long-lasting and deeply rooted. Roughly 20 percent of all such barriers to communication can be prevented or solved by communication policy guidelines.[18] **Gateways to communication** are the openings that break down communication barriers. Awareness and recognition of communication barriers are the first steps in opening the gateways. Obvious barriers are physical separation (employees in different geographic locations or buildings) and status differences (related to the organizational hierarchy). Not so obvious are the barriers caused by gender differences, cultural diversity, and language.

Gender Differences

Communication barriers can be attributed in part to differences in conversational styles.[19] When individuals of different economic backgrounds converse, the receiver's understanding may not be the same as the speaker's meaning. In a similar vein, men and women tend to have different conversational styles. For exam-

---

barriers to communication
Factors that distort, disrupt, or even halt successful communication.

gateways to communication
Openings that break down communication barriers.

THE FAME METHOD

A fter it encountered employee trepidation during a difficult period of reorganization, drug manufacturer AstraZeneca resolved to teach its leadership teams how to properly engage apprehensive workers. The company developed a method of leadership communication called FAME: Focus, Articulate, Model, and Engage.

- First, leaders develop a clear *focus* for what they want employees to think, feel, and do in the midst of change.
- Second, leaders *articulate* that vision using words that employees can remember and repeat.
- Third, leaders *model* the behavior for employees, using their own communicatory strengths.
- Fourth, leaders *engage* employees, demonstrating to them how they fit into the bigger picture.

AstraZeneca found that the FAME method enables leaders to ease employee anxiety while developing their own styles of effective communication. Leadership communication is a learned skill that can make supervisors more self-aware and confident in their interactions with employees. This improves performance, morale, and business relationships across the board.

SOURCE: D. Walters and D. Norton, "Leadership Communication—The AstraZeneca Way," *Strategic Communication Management* 12 (Dec 2007/Jan 2008): 16–19.

ple, women often prefer to converse face to face, whereas men are comfortable conversing while sitting side by side, concentrating on a focal point in front of them. Hence, conversational differences may result in a barrier of communication between men and women. Male–female conversation is really cross-cultural communication. In a work context, one study found that female employees sent less information to their supervisors and experienced less information overload than did male employees.[20]

An important gateway through the gender barrier is the development of an awareness and appreciation of gender-specific differences in conversational style. These differences can enrich organizational communication and empower professional relationships.[21] A second gateway is to actively seek clarification of the person's meaning rather than freely interpreting meaning from one's own frame of reference.

Cultural Diversity

Culturally influenced values and patterns of behavior can be very confusing barriers to communication. Significant differences in work-related values exist among people in the United States versus those in Germany, the United Kingdom, Japan, and other nations.[22] These differences in value impact motivation, leadership, and teamwork in work organizations.[23] Habitual patterns of interaction can obstruct communication in any given culture. For example, the German culture places greater value on authority and hierarchical differences than does the United States. It is therefore more difficult for German workers to engage in open communication with their supervisors than it is for U.S. workers.[24]

When a person from one culture views people from another culture through the lens of a stereotype, she discounts the individual differences that exist within that foreign culture. For example, a stereotype of Americans common throughout Asia is that they are aggressive and arrogant, and thus insensitive and unapproachable. Stereotypes of Asians common throughout America are that they are studious, subservient, and assimilative. Individuals who depend

on the accuracy of cultural stereotypes may unknowingly create barriers in communicating with people from other cultures.

One gateway through the barrier of diversity is increasing cultural awareness and sensitivity. Further, companies can provide seminars for expatriate managers as part of their training for overseas assignments. Bernard Isautier, president and CEO of Petro Kazakstan, believes that understanding and communication are two keys to harmonious workplace diversity, an essential ingredient for success in international markets.[25] A second gateway is developing or acquiring a guide for understanding and interacting with members of other cultures. One approach to initiating diversity training is to describe a nation by way of a suitable metaphor.[26] For example, Irish pubs, the Spanish bullfight, and American football are consensually derived metaphors for culturally specific conversational styles that can enable those outside the culture to understand members within.

Language

Language can be another barrier to communication. Growing numbers of business men and women are bilingual or multilingual, but even subtle distinctions in dialects within the same language can be barriers. For example, the word *chemist* means a molecular scientist in the United States and a drugstore worker in Great Britain. Language barriers are created across disciplines and professional boundaries by technical terminology. Although acronyms and professional jargon may be very useful tools of communication within in a discipline, they may only serve to confuse and derail any attempt at clear understanding by those unfamiliar with the profession. When doing business, it's best to use simple, direct, declarative language. One should speak in brief sentences and employ terms or words already used by one's audience. As much as possible, one should speak in the language of the listener. Above all else, one should not use jargon or technical language except with those who are already familiar with it.

A *pharmacist* or a *chemist?*

Civility and Incivility

While **incivility** can create a barrier between people and jar people's emotions, **civility** may be a gateway to communication that smoothes troubled waters at work. Those who practice incivility are often called bullies, creeps, jerks, tyrants, tormentors, despots, backstabbers, egomaniacs, and even worse. There are, however, some instances in which incivility can have positive effects when it is strategically used. In this section, we examine the full range of consequences of incivility and the blessings of civility. In addition, we examine defensive and nondefensive communication that may spring from civil and uncivil communication behavior.

Consequences of Incivility

Workplace incivility can jar the emotions and cause a range of adverse outcomes both in the workplace and at home. Discourteousness, rudeness, impatience, and lack of respect are very common forms of incivility. The consequences of incivility depend on its source. Much incivility originates with superiors and those in powerful positions within the organization. This type of incivility is often tolerated even though it leads to a decline in satisfaction with the supervisor. Coworkers may display incivility too. As we would expect, someone subject to coworker incivility experiences less satisfaction with the coworker, and that may generalize to all coworkers. In addition, coworker incivility can trigger the perception of being treated unfairly at work and may even lead to depression. So the emotional and psychological adverse effects of coworker incivility are quite real along with additional costs from unfair treatment and depression.

Before rushing to judgment that all incivility is destructive, we need to point out that there is a place in the workplace for what may appear uncivil. Take, for example, swearing. Annoyance swearing is a problem because of the emotional jarring and stressful impact on others, often disrupting social support within a team as well as the team's well being. Social swearing, on the other hand, can be a stress release for an individual provided the language is not aimed at someone else.

It may even be something in which others can empathize and vicariously share while building relationships and camaraderie.

Blessings of Civility

The blessings of civility are found in its gracious and positive nature. Civil communication and behavior carry the potential to avoid hurt feelings, prevent harm and damage to working relationships, and contribute to well-being in the workplace. Civility should not be confused with the avoidance of difficult or complicated workplace issues, which must be confronted and addressed. There are several ways to create a more civil workplace: bring difficult issues out in the open, write things down before speaking, set enforcement guidelines for incivility, and be consistent in enforcing those guidelines. Civility ensures respect for the integrity and dignity of each and every member of the workplace.

Defensive and Nondefensive Communication

In the workplace, defensive language creates barriers between people, whereas nondefensive communication helps to open and deepen relationships.[27] **Defensive communication** includes aggressive, malevolent messages as well as passive, withdrawn messages. **Nondefensive communication** is assertive, direct, and powerful. Though it can be misinterpreted as aggressiveness, assertiveness is indeed nondefensive. Corporations today are increasingly engaged in situations such as courtroom battles and media exchanges that call for nondefensive language although they are particularly fertile ground for defensive communication.

Defensive communication leads to a wide range of problems, including injured feelings, communication barriers, alienation in working relationships, destructive and retaliatory behaviors, nonproductive efforts, and problem-solving failures. When such problems arise in organizations, people are prone to blame everyone

civility
Communication and behavior that respect the integrity and dignity of the individual.

incivility
Discourteous communication and rude behavior that are disrespectful, hurtful, or injurious.

defensive communication
Messages that are aggressive, malevolent, passive, or withdrawn.

nondefensive communication
Messages that are assertive, direct, and powerful.

[**Dealing with Defensive People**]

Catherine Crier gained extensive experience in defensive communication while serving as a trial lawyer and judge. She carried this knowledge over into a new career as a news anchor for CNN, ABC, Fox News, and Court TV. Her four basic rules of engagement are to

1. define the situation,
2. clarify the person's position,
3. acknowledge the person's feelings, and
4. bring the focus back to the facts.

else for what is not working.[28] Defensive reactions such as counterattack and sheepish withdrawal derail communication. These responses tend to lend heat, not light, to the process of communication. Defensive communication often evokes still more defensive communication.

Nondefensive communication, in contrast, provides a positive and productive basis for asserting and defending oneself against aggression without further damaging the communication process. An assertive, nondefensive style restores order, balance, and effectiveness in working relationships. Further discussion of nondefensive communication and defensive communication in the workplace follows.

Defensive Communication at Work

The two basic patterns of defensiveness are dominant defensiveness and subordinate defensiveness. Subordinate defensiveness is characterized by passive or submissive behavior. The psychological attitude of the subordinately defensive person is "You are right, and I am wrong." People with low self-esteem may be prone to this form of defensive behavior, as may people at lower organizational levels. Individuals who are subordinately defensive do not adequately assert their thoughts and feelings. Their input is likely to be lost, even if it is critical to organizational performance.[29] Passive-aggressive behavior is a form of defensiveness that begins as subordinate defensiveness and ends up as dominant defensiveness. It is behavior that appears very passive, though it actually masks underlying aggression and hostility.

In contrast, dominant defensiveness is characterized by overtly aggressive and domineering behavior. It is offensive in nature, sometimes culminating in verbal or physical harassment. The psychological attitude of the dominantly defensive person is "I am right, and you are wrong." People who are egotistical or overcompensating for low self-esteem may exhibit this pattern of behavior, as may people in higher-level positions within the organizational hierarchy.

Defensive Tactics

Defensive tactics are subversive actions that employ defensive communication.

Unfortunately, these tactics are common in many work organizations. Until defensiveness and defensive tactics are recognized for what they are at an organizational level, it is difficult to address them or respond to them in nondefensive ways. In many cases, defensive tactics raise ethical dilemmas for victims and their supervisors. At what point does simple defensiveness become unethical behavior? Consider the following defensive tactics.

Power plays are tactics used to control and manipulate others. Restricting the choices of employees, enforcing either/or conditions, intentionally ignoring or insulting others, bullying, and displaying overt aggression are all power plays. The underlying dynamic in power plays is that of domination and control. The aggressor attempts to gain the upper hand in the relationship by making the victim feel inferior and thus vulnerable to control.

Labeling is often used to portray another person as abnormal or deficient. Medical and legal labels are often used out of context for this purpose. The words "paranoid," "retarded," and "insane" have specific, clinical meanings that are discarded in defensive labeling. Similar to labeling is publicly raising doubts about a person's abilities, values, sexual orientation, or other personal aspects. This tactic breeds confusion and uncertainty, though it tends to lack the specificity and clarity of labeling.

Disseminating misleading information, a form of deception, is the selective presentation of information intentionally designed to produce an inaccurate impression in the listener's mind. This obfuscated information can be used to scapegoat or "pass the buck," which shifts responsibility for an error or problem to the wrong person. If information cannot be altered, defensive individuals may simply blame others for their own wrongdoing.

Finally, *hostile jokes* are a passive-aggressive defensive tactic. Because a jocular framing is used to mask aggressive and even overtly mean sentiments, hostile jokes often go uncited. They should not be confused with good humor, which is both therapeutic and nondefensive. Jokes made at the expense of others are destructive to self-esteem and workplace communication.

Nondefensive Communication

Nondefensive communication is a healthy alternative to defensive communication in working relationships. An individual who consistently communicates nondefensively may be characterized as centered, assertive, controlled, informative, realistic, and honest. Nondefensive communication is powerful because the speaker exhibits self-control and self-possession without rejecting the listener. It should be self-affirming without being self-aggrandizing—a sometimes difficult balance to maintain.

Converting defensive patterns of communication to nondefensive ones builds relationships at work. Behaviors that build relationships simultaneously reduce adverse responses, such as blame and anger, when negative events occur at work.[30]

To strengthen nondefensive patterns, the subordinately defensive person must learn to be more assertive. One way to do this is to report what one intends to do and invite confirmation instead of asking for permission to do something. Another way is to stop using self-deprecating phrases such as "I'm just following orders." One should drop the *just* and thereby convert the message into a self-assertive, declarative statement.

To strengthen nondefensive patterns, the dominantly defensive person must learn to be less aggressive. This may be especially difficult because it requires overcoming the sense of certitude. Those who are working to overcome dominant defensiveness should be particularly sensitive to feedback from others about their behavior. To change this behavior, one should stop giving and denying permission. Instead, one should give others free rein (except in situations where permission is essential to clearance or the security of the task). Alternatively, instead of becoming inappropriately angry, one should provide information about the adverse consequences of a particular course of action.

Nonverbal Communication

Whereas defensive and nondefensive communication focus on the language used in delivering a message, most of a message's meaning (an estimated 65 to 90 percent) is conveyed through nonverbal communication.[31] **Nonverbal communication** includes all elements of communication that do not involve words or language such as gestures and the use of space.[32] The four basic types of nonverbal communication that managers need to understand are proxemics, kinesics, facial and eye behavior, and paralanguage. Managers also need to understand that nonverbal communication is influenced by both psychological and physiological processes.[33]

The interpretation of nonverbal communication is specific to the context of the interaction and the actors. That is, the particular meaning of any nonverbal cue relies on its sender, receiver, and the environment in which the cue occurs. For example, some federal and state judges attempt to curb nonverbal communication in the courtroom. Though it may mean nothing outside the courtroom, some nonverbal behavior may unfairly influence jurors' decisions if displayed during a trial. Beyond the contextual element, nonverbal behavior is also culturally bound. (Recall from Chapter 2 the difference in meaning the "thumbs-up" sign has in Australia versus the United States.)

Proxemics

The study of an individual's perception and use of space, including territorial space, is called **proxemics**.[34] **Territorial space** refers to bands of concentric space radiating outward from the body. These bands are commonly known as *comfort zones*. Figure 8.2 illustrates the four zones of territorial space common to U.S. culture.

nonverbal communication
All elements of communication that do not involve words or language.

proxemics
The study of an individual's perception and use of space.

territorial space
Bands of concentric space radiating outward from the body.

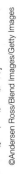

Most of a message's meaning is conveyed through elements of nonverbal communication, like gestures and facial expressions.

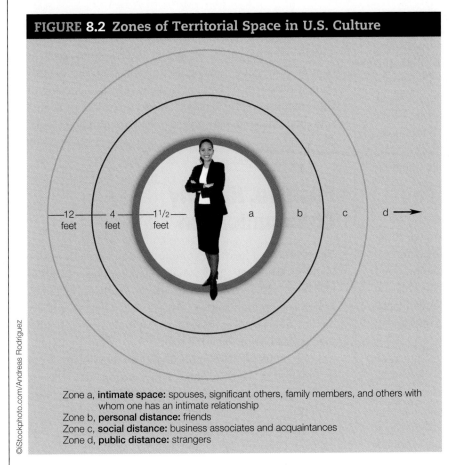

FIGURE 8.2 Zones of Territorial Space in U.S. Culture

—12— —4— —1½— a b c d →
feet feet feet

Zone a, **intimate space:** spouses, significant others, family members, and others with whom one has an intimate relationship
Zone b, **personal distance:** friends
Zone c, **social distance:** business associates and acquaintances
Zone d, **public distance:** strangers

©iStockphoto.com/Andreas Rodriguez

Territorial space varies greatly around the world. Both the sizes of comfort zones and their acceptable modes of interaction are culturally defined. And people often become uncomfortable when operating in territorial spaces different from those with which they are familiar.

According to leading proxemics researcher Edward Hall, Americans working in the Middle East tend to back away to a comfortable distance when conversing with Arabs because Arabs' comfortable conversation distance is closer than that of Americans. As a result, Arabs sometimes perceive Americans as cold and aloof. One Arab wondered, "What's the matter? Does he find me somehow offensive?"[35] The circumference of personal space tends to be larger in cultures with cool climates, such as the United States, Great Britain, and northern Europe, and smaller in cultures with warm climates, such as southern Europe, the Caribbean, India, and South America.[36]

Our relationships shape our use of territorial space. For example, we hold hands with or put an arm around significant others to pull them into *intimate space.* Conversely, we can use territorial space to shape our interactions. A four-foot-wide desk pushes business interactions into the *social distance* zone. Not comfortable with that definition of space, one SBC manager met with her seven first-line supervisors crowded around her four-foot desk, putting them elbow to elbow with each other. As a result of being placed in one another's intimate space, they appeared to act more like friends and frequently talked about their children, favorite television shows, and other personal concerns. When the manager moved the staff meetings to a larger room and thus relocated the supervisors into each others' social distance zones, the personal exchanges ceased, and they acted more like business associates again.

Seating dynamics, another aspect of proxemics, is the art of seating people in certain positions according to their purpose in communication. Figure 8.3 depicts some common seating dynamics. To encourage cooperation, one should seat the adjoining party beside oneself, facing the same direction. To facilitate direct and open communication, one should seat the other party across a corner of one's desk or in another place where he will be at right angles. This allows for more honest disclosure. To take a competitive stand with someone, one must position the person directly across from oneself. Suppose a manager holds a meeting around a conference table, and two of the attendees are disrupting the meeting by chatting loudly. Where should they be seated? If the manager places the two disruptive attendees on either side of herself, the argument should be stifled (unless one is so bold as to lean in front of the manager to keep chatting).

FIGURE 8.3 Seating Dynamics

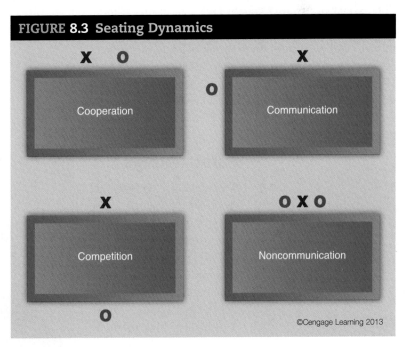

X O   X

Cooperation   O

                       Communication

X   O X O

Competition   Noncommunication

O

©Cengage Learning 2013

Kinesics

Kinesics is the study of body movement and posture.[37] Like proxemics, kinesics is bound to culture. With this in mind, we can interpret some common U.S. gestures. Rubbing one's hands together while inhaling sharply indicates anticipation. Stress is indicated by balled fists, clenched teeth, hand wringing, and rubbing the temples. Nervousness may be indicated by drumming fingers, pacing, or jingling coins in one's pocket. Kinesics also includes insulting gestures like giving someone "the finger."

Facial and Eye Behavior

The face is a rich source of nonverbal communication. Facial expression and eye behavior are used to communicate an emotional state, reveal behavioral intentions, and cue the receiver. It may even give unintended clues to emotions the sender is trying to hide.[38] Unintended facial movements can undermine the illusion of truthfulness, especially in stressful situations.[39]

Culture, environment, and specific actors must be taken into consideration when interpreting smiles, frowns, raised eyebrows, and other expressions. One study of Japanese and U.S. students illustrated the point. The students were shown a stress-inducing film, and their facial expressions were videotaped. When alone, the students had almost identical expressions. When in the presence of others, however, the Japanese students masked their facial expressions of unpleasant feelings much better than the American students did.[40]

As mentioned earlier, eye contact can enhance reflective listening. Along with smiling, eye contact is an easy way to express honesty and positive emotion.[41] However, eye contact must be understood in a cultural context. A direct gaze indicates dedication, truthfulness, and forthrightness in the United States. This may not be true in other cultures. For example, Barbara Walters was uncomfortable interviewing Libyan head of state Muammar al-Gaddafi because he refused to look directly at her. However, in Libya it is a serious offense for a man to look directly at a woman.[42] In many Asian cultures it is considered polite to bow in deference to a superior rather than to look in the supervisor's eyes.

Paralanguage

Paralanguage consists of variations in speech, such as pitch, loudness, tempo, tone, duration, laughing, and crying.[43] People make assumptions about the communicator by deciphering paralanguage cues. A female's high-pitched, breathy voice may lead coworkers to stereotype her as a "dumb blonde." Rapid, loud speech may be taken as a sign of nervousness or anger. Interruptions such as "mmm" and "okay" may be used to speed up the speaker so that the receiver can get in a few words. Clucking of the tongue and the "tsk-tsk" sound are used to shame someone. All these cues relate to how something is said.

LEARNING OUTCOME 6

Positive, Healthy Communication

The absence of heartfelt communication in relationships leads to loneliness and social isolation. This condition has been labeled **communicative disease** by James Lynch.[44] Communicative disease has adverse effects on the heart and cardiovascular system, and can ultimately lead to premature death. According to Lynch, the only cure for communicative disease is to reengage in thoughtful, heartwarming conversation with friends and loved ones. Yet, even though feelings may be more important to the communication process than cognition, a stable balance between the two is integral. This balance between head and heart is achieved when a person displays positive emotional competence and can maintain a healthy internal conversation between his thoughts and emotions.

Positive, healthy communication is an important aspect of *working together*—that is, cooperating to reach a shared goal—in both the interpersonal and intrapersonal

---

kinesics

The study of body movement and posture.

communicative disease

Loneliness and social isolation resulting from the absence of heartfelt communication in relationships.

©Digital Vision/Getty Images

settings.[45] Such communication requires trust and truthfulness. However, it does not exclude honest competition within the workplace, which in fact is consistent with the concept of working together. Sincere, well-managed competition can bring out the best in all those involved.

Healthy communication is at the core of personal integrity and managerial success, as is evident in the lives of most successful executives, including those in the executive branch of the U.S. government.[46] President Ronald Reagan was nicknamed "the great communicator" for his ability to connect with the American people. He conveyed strong ethical character, personal integrity, and simplicity in his communication. Reagan exemplified Lynch's concept of heartfelt communication, as his language in speeches and interviews seemed to stem from core values and sincere aspirations. Communication from the heart is communication anchored in personal integrity and ethical character.

Personal integrity is a product of emotional competence and a stable balance of head and heart, as mentioned earlier. Psychologist Karol Wasylyshyn has shown that one method of developing personal integrity is to coach an executive in developing her capacity to talk through challenging issues, both personally and professionally.[47] James Campbell Quick and Marilyn Macik-Frey developed a similar coaching program that works to cultivate executives' inner selves through deep, interpersonal communication.[48] This executive coaching model relies on what Lynch might call a "healing dialogue" between executive and coach. In addition to improving interpersonal communication between executives and employees, this model can enhance positive, healthy communication in a wider range of human relationships.

Fast Fact

According to researchers from Stanford's Graduate School of Business, there are a number of clues that can help people identify when their bosses are lying. First, lying bosses make more references to general knowledge using phrases like *as you know*. Second, they tend to overstate positive results by using words like *fantastic* instead of *good*. Third, they avoid using the word *I*, instead using *he, she, it*, or *they* more frequently. Bosses who lie also tend not to use vocal pauses like *um* or *er*, which suggests that they've been coached as to what to say.

SOURCE: "How to Tell When Your Boss Is Lying" *The Economist* (August 19, 2010), http://www.economist.com /node/16847818, accessed June 21, 2011.

©Eastcott Momatiuk/Digital Vision/Getty Images

Communicating through New Technologies and Social Media

Nonverbal behaviors can be important in establishing trust in working relationships, but modern technologies may challenge our ability to maintain that trust. Managers in today's business world have access to more communication tools than ever before. Lawyers and legal consultants use Facebook and Twitter to do background checks on potential jurors.[49] Brian J. Dunn, the CEO of Best Buy, uses social media to spot trends and communicate with customers and employees.[50] Information technology can encourage or discourage moral dialogue, and these types of conversations are central to addressing ethical issues at work.[51]

Written Communication

Even though many organizations are working toward paperless offices and paperless interfaces with their customers, written communication is far from dead—there are many types of written communication still necessary to business. Manuals and reports are generally the longest forms of written communication found in the office. Policy manuals are important in organizations because they establish guidelines for decision making and codes of conduct. Operations and procedures manuals explain how to perform various tasks and resolve problems that may occur at work. Reports, such as annual company finance reports, may summarize the results of a committee's or department's work or provide information on progress toward certain objectives.

Letters and memorandums (memos) are briefer than manuals and reports and are more frequently used in larger organizations. Letters are used to communicate formally with individuals and businesses outside the organization. They vary substantially in length and topic. Memos are also used for formal, internal communication within an organization. They are sometimes used as historical records of specific events or occurrences that individuals within the organization can refer back to later.

The shortest kind of written communication is the form, which may be used to collect information from constituencies inside or outside the organization.

Communication Technologies

Computer-mediated communication influences virtually all behavior in the work environment. E-mail, voice mail, instant messaging, and facsimile (fax) machines have been common in the business world for more than a decade. Recently, large information databases have become relatively commonplace. These databases provide a tremendous amount of information at the push of a button. An example of an information database is the electronic card catalog system used in university libraries throughout the world. These systems, sometimes linked with each other to form massive networks of data, store information about books' and journals' contents, distributions, and availability.

The newest technology to impact the work environment is the smartphone, which is nearly as ubiquitous at work as standard cell phones are in our personal lives. Smartphones combine the capabilities of advanced cell phones with PC-like applications and connectivity. Examples include the Apple iPhone, the HTC Thunderbold, and the Nokia N9. The smartphone's introduction was particularly transformative for sales jobs involving travel. While they are widely used, not all reactions to smartphones are positive. For example, one oil producer did not want his daily commute disturbed by outside interference—he used driving as a time for thought and relaxation. Some estimates suggest that using a phone while driving is as risky as driving while under the influence of alcohol. For this reason, some states have outlawed cell-phone talking or texting while driving a motor vehicle.

information communication technology (ICT)

An extensive category of new developments in interpersonal communication that allow fast, even immediate, access to information.

How Do Communication Technologies Affect Behavior?

Information communication technology (ICT) is an extensive category of new developments in interpersonal communication that allow fast, even immediate, access to information. E-mail, teleconferencing, and Wi-Fi are all classified as ICT. It can facilitate the instant exchange of information in minutes or seconds across geographic boundaries and time zones. With adequate ICT implementation, schedules and office hours become irrelevant in that considerations of time and distance that once beleaguered international and intranational business become far less important in the exchange. Given its impact on the way business is done, ICT has a significant influence on people's behavior.

Computer-mediated communication is impersonal in nature. Instant messaging, e-mail, and other forms of online communication can therefore depreciate the richness of personal interaction. Studies show that using these technologies may increase one's likelihood to flame—to make rude, needlessly argumentative or obscene comments by means of computer-mediated communication.[52] Employees' interpersonal skills such as tact and graciousness subside online, and managers tend to be more blunt when using electronic media. People who normally participate in discussions quietly and politely may become more intimate, impolite, or uninhibited when they communicate using computer conferencing or electronic mail.[53]

Another effect of computer-mediated communication is that the nonverbal cues we rely on to decipher a message are absent. Gesturing, touching, facial expressions, and eye contact are not possible, so the emotional aspect of the message is difficult to discern. Even in teleconferencing, where users can see each others' faces, it is often difficult to perceive nonverbal cues.[54] Clues to power such as organizational position and departmental membership may not be available, so the social context of the exchange is often altered.

Hot Trend: Tweeting for Turnout

More and more, companies are turning to social networking sites like Facebook and Twitter to track customer perceptions of products. On Facebook, companies can establish and monitor pages for specific products, marketing campaigns, public faces, or the companies themselves. On Twitter, companies can link to images and external websites in 140-character micro-blog posts. The direct line of communication facilitated by online corporate networking instills a sense of empowerment in customers. They can send messages and join product discussions on Facebook and follow up-to-the-minute news on Twitter. For companies, this online interaction translates to invaluable and cost-effective market research and advertising. Internally, social networking sites can be used to communicate efficiently and effectively. Employees can use Facebook to plan meetings and events, and to network with potential clients. Each of the 429 employees of the online retailer Zappos, including CEO Tony Hsieh, use Twitter accounts to follow breaking company news and keep in contact with each other and the outside world.

SOURCE: R. Donkin, "Irrational Resistance to Innovation," *Human Resources* (August 2008): 20.

Communication via technology also changes group dynamics by equalizing participation. As a result, charismatic or higher-status members may lose some power.[55] Studies of group decision making have shown that computer-mediated groups took longer to reach consensus than face-to-face groups. In addition, they were less cooperative, more uninhibited, and there was less influence from any one dominant person. Another study found that ICTs, especially e-mail and e-meetings, reduce tension caused by intercultural communication.[56] Groups that communicate via computer seem to experience a breakdown of social and organizational barriers.

The potential for information overload is particularly great when individuals are first introduced to new communication technologies. Both the sheer volume of information available and its speed of delivery are staggering. An individual can easily become overwhelmed by information and must learn to be selective about its access.

Many new technologies encourage multitasking.

While modern ICT may make work easier and increase employees' productivity, it can also prove precarious for managers. In the wake of mobile e-mail, instant messaging, and texting, managers are more accessible to coworkers, subordinates, and the boss today than they've ever been. Work can no longer be compartmentalized between the hours of 8:00 and 5:00.

Further, many new technologies encourage *polyphasic activity*, or multitasking (that is, doing more than one thing at a time). Managers can simultaneously make phone calls, send instant messages, and work on memos. Polyphasic activity has its advantages in terms of getting more done—but only up to a point. Paying attention to more than one thing at a time splits a person's attention and may reduce effectiveness at individual tasks. At its extreme, focusing on multiple tasks can become a destructive habit, making it psychologically difficult for a person to let go of work.

Finally, new technologies may make people less patient with face-to-face communication. The speed of electronic media may lead to expectations of acceleration in all forms of communication. However, if they spend too much time communicating online, individuals may come to miss social interaction with others, and may find their social needs unmet. Communicating via computer often means the end of small talk. In the name of speed, amenity is sacrificed for efficiency. Managers can use new technologies more efficiently and effectively by keeping in mind the suggestions presented in Table 8.2.

Log in to the **CourseMate** for *ORGB3* at **www.cengagebrain.com** to:

* Review **Key Terms Flash Cards** online
* Play **Beat the Clock** and **Quiz Bowl** to master concepts
* Complete **web quizzes** to prepare for exams
* Watch the video on **Plant Fantasies** and from *Friday Night Lights* for examples, then test yourself with a quick quiz
* Work through the **"What about You?"** and **Ethical Dilemma** exercises to see how you would handle various situations that organizations face on a daily basis

TABLE 8.2 Channel Etiquette			
Facebook	**Twitter**	**YouTube**	**LinkedIn**
• Take sensitive queries into a private sphere online or offline. • Remember all wall posts are public; don't write anything there that is not for wider consumption. • Ensure all updates are frequent and relevant but not too frequent. • Use language relevant to the channel and the target demographics. • Show appreciation and acknowledge positive comments. • Follow up and respond to any feedback.	• Begin with an introduction if used for outreach or active engagement. • Develop a tone of voice and personality. • Keep requests for re-tweets to a minimum. • Keep tweets as short and sweet as possible (less than 140 characters). • Avoid pure self-promotion Twitter is a knowledge-sharing and conversation channel.	• Develop a thick skin; many comments are not constructive, so do not take such comments to heart or argue, as defensive reactions will only fan the flames. • Use video replies, as these can be powerful and a good way to spread a message. • Acknowledge comments and thank those who are being positive about a brand.	• Join groups and contribute information about relevant experience. • Answer questions and contribute to share pages and communities. • Avoid asking for references unless the person is someone already known or if company has genuinely delivered great service. • Support unsolicited contacts with a full explanation of who is contacting and why; don't assume that contacts will view underlying profile.

SOURCE: Adapted from M. Ramsey, "Social Media Etiquette: A Guide and Checklist to the Benefits and Perils of Social Marketing," *Journal of Database Marketing and Customer Strategy Management* 17 (2010): 257–261.

USE THE TOOLS.

- Rip out the Review Cards in the back of your book to study.

Or Visit CourseMate to:

- Read, search, highlight, and take notes in the Interactive eBook
- Review Flashcards (Print or Online) to master key terms
- Test yourself with Auto-Graded Quizzes
- Bring concepts to life with Games, Videos, and Animations!

Go to CourseMate for ORGB to begin using these tools.
Access at **www.cengagebrain.com**

Complete the Speak Up survey in CourseMate at **www.cengagebrain.com**

Follow us at **www.facebook.com/4ltrpress**

Work Teams and Groups

LEARNING OUTCOMES

1 Define *group* and *work team*.

2 Explain the benefits organizations and individuals derive from working in teams.

3 Identify the factors that influence group behavior.

4 Describe how groups form and develop.

5 Explain how task and maintenance functions influence group performance.

6 Discuss the factors that influence group effectiveness.

7 Describe how empowerment relates to self-managed teams.

8 Explain the importance of upper echelons and top management teams.

©iStockphoto.com/Jacob Wackerhausen

"Work teams emphasize shared leadership, mutual accountability, and collective work products."

Groups and Work Teams

A **group** is formed when two or more people have common interests, objectives, and continuing interaction. **A work team** is a group of people with complementary skills who are committed to a common mission, performance goals, and approach for which they hold themselves mutually accountable.[1] All work teams are groups, but not all groups are work teams. Groups emphasize individual leadership, personal accountability, and exclusive work products. Work teams emphasize shared leadership, mutual accountability, and collective work products.

Work teams are task-oriented groups, though in some organizations the word *team* has a negative connotation for union members. Work teams make valuable contributions to the organization and are important to the need satisfaction of members.

Several kinds of work teams exist. Some are like baseball teams in that members have set responsibilities, others are like football teams in that members have coordinated action, and still others are like doubles tennis teams in that members have primary yet flexible responsibilities. Another analogy for work teams is that some operate like groundskeeping crews in that all members work synergistically toward a single goal.[2] Although each type of team may have a useful role in the organization, the individual expert should not be overlooked.[3] At the right time and in the right context, individual members must be allowed to shine.

Teams and groups do not all work face-to-face. Advanced computer and telecommunications technologies enable organizations to be more flexible through the use of *virtual teams*.[4] Organizations use

group

Two or more people with common interests, objectives, and continuing interaction.

work team

A group of people with complementary skills who are committed to a common mission, performance goals, and approach for which they hold themselves mutually accountable.

After You Finish This Chapter Go to **Page 156** for **Study Tools**

virtual teams to access expertise and the best employees around the world. Whether traditional or virtual, groups and teams continue to play a vital role in organizational behavior and performance at work.

Why Work Teams?

Teams are very useful in performing work that is complicated, fragmented, and/or more voluminous than one person can handle. Harold Geneen, while chairman of ITT, said, "If I had enough arms and legs and time, I'd do it all myself." Obviously, no one person in an organization can do everything by himself, not only because of the limitations of arms, legs, and time, but also expertise, knowledge, and other resources. However, individual limitations can be overcome through teamwork and collaboration. World-class U.S. corporations, such as Motorola Inc., are increasingly deploying work teams in their global affiliates to meet the competition and gain advantage.[5] Motorola's "Be Cool" team in the Philippines has a family atmosphere (and may even begin a meeting with a prayer), yet is committed to improving individual and team performance.

Benefits to Organizations

Teams make the most significant contributions to organizations when members can put aside individual interests in favor of unity. This joint action is called **teamwork**. Complex, collaborative work tasks and activities tend to require considerable amounts of teamwork. When knowledge, talent, and abilities are dispersed across numerous workers and require an integrated effort for task accomplishment, teamwork is often the only solution.

teamwork
Joint action by a team of people in which individual interests are subordinated to team unity.

[**Characteristics of a Well-Functioning, Effective Group**]

- The atmosphere tends to be relaxed, comfortable, and informal.
- The group's task is well understood and accepted by the members.
- The members listen well to one another; most members participate in a good deal of task-relevant discussion.
- People express both their feelings and their ideas.
- Conflict and disagreement are present and centered around ideas or methods, not personalities or people.
- The group is aware and conscious of its own operation and function.
- Decisions are usually based on consensus, not majority vote.
- When actions are decided, clear assignments are made and accepted by members of the group.

SOURCE: D. M. McGregor, *The Human Side of Enterprise* (New York: McGraw-Hill, 1960).

A recent movement toward team-oriented work environments has championed empowerment through collaboration rather than self-reliance and competition. Teams with experience working together may produce valuable innovations, and individual contributions within teams are valuable as well.[6] Larry Hirschhorn labeled this structure "the new team environment," founded on a significantly more empowered workforce in the industrial sectors of the American economy. (See Table 9.1 for a comparison of new and old environments.) In this new environment, teams must bring together members with different specialties and knowledge to work on complex problems. The ability to do so improves team performance and psychological well being.[7]

Social Benefits to Individuals

On an individual level, team or group members derive benefits from the collective experience of teamwork. These individual benefits are best organized into two cat-

TABLE 9.1 New Team Environment versus Old Work Environment	
NEW TEAM ENVIRONMENT	**OLD WORK ENVIRONMENT**
Person comes up with initiatives. Team has considerable authority to chart its own steps.	Person follows orders. Team depends on the manager to chart its course.
Members form a team because people learn to collaborate in the face of their emerging right to think for themselves. People both rock the boat and work together.	Members were a team because people conformed to direction set by the manager. No one rocked the boat.
People cooperate by using their thoughts and feelings. They link up through direct talk.	People cooperated by suppressing their thoughts and feelings. They wanted to get along.

SOURCE: L. Hirschhorn, *Managing in the New Team Environment: Skills, Tools, and Methods.* San Jose: Authors Choice Press, © 2002. Reprinted with permission.

©Corbis/Photolibrary

egories. One set of benefits accrues from achieving psychological intimacy, while the other comes from achieving integrated involvement.[8]

Psychological intimacy is emotional and psychological closeness to other team or group members. It results in feelings of affection and warmth, unconditional positive regard, opportunity for expression, security and emotional support, and nurturing. Failure to achieve psychological intimacy may result in feelings of emotional isolation and loneliness. This can be especially problematic for chief executives, who sometimes report experiencing loneliness "at the top." However, although psychological intimacy is valuable for emotional health and well-being, it need not necessarily be achieved in the work setting. Many executives satisfy their need for intimacy with a rich home life.

Integrated involvement is closeness achieved through tasks and activities. It results in enjoyment of work, social identity and self-definition, being valued for one's skills and abilities, opportunities for power and influence, conditional positive regard, and support for one's beliefs and values. Failure to achieve integrated involvement may result in social isolation. Whereas psychological intimacy is based more in emotion, integrated involvement is based in behavior and activity. Integrated involvement contributes to social psychological health and well-being.

LEARNING OUTCOME **3**

Group Behavior

Group behavior has been a subject of interest in social psychology for a long time, and many different aspects of group behavior have been studied over the years. We now look at four of those aspects: norms of behavior, group cohesion, social loafing, and loss of individuality. Group behavior topics related to decision making, such as polarization and groupthink, are addressed in Chapter 10.

Norms of Behavior

The standards that a work group uses to evaluate the behavior of its members are its **norms of behavior**. These norms may be written or unwritten, verbalized or not verbalized, implicit or explicit. As long as individual members of the group understand them, the norms can be effective in influencing behavior. They may specify what members of a group should do (such as a specified dress code) or not do (such as executives not behaving arrogantly with employees).

Norms may exist in any aspect of work group life. They may evolve informally or unconsciously, or they may arise in response to specific challenges, such as firefighters' disciplined behavior in responding to a three-alarm fire in a manner that protects the group.[9] *Morality norms* are more important than *competence norms* when it comes to making decisions about improving the status of one's work group.[10] *Performance norms* are among the most important group norms from the organization's perspective. Even when group members work in isolation on creative projects, they display conformity to group norms.[11] Group norms of cooperative behavior within a team can lead to members working for mutual benefit, which in turn facilitates team performance.[12] On the other hand, verbal expressions of negativity can be detrimental to team performance and a violation of group norms.[13] Organizational culture and corporate codes of ethics, such as Johnson & Johnson's credo (recall Figure 2.3), reflect behavioral norms expected within work groups. Finally, norms that create awareness of and help regulate emotions are critical to groups' effectiveness.[14]

Group Cohesion

The "interpersonal glue" that makes the members of a group stick together is **group cohesion**. Group cohesion can enhance job satisfaction for members and improve organizational productivity.[15] Highly cohesive groups are able to manage their membership better than work groups low in cohesion. In one study of 381 banking teams in Hong Kong and the United States, increased job complexity and task autonomy led to increased group cohesiveness, which translated into better performance.[16] A recent

---

psychological intimacy
Emotional and psychological closeness to other team or group members.

integrated involvement
Closeness achieved through tasks and activities.

norms of behavior
The standards that a work group uses to evaluate the behavior of its members.

group cohesion
The "interpersonal glue" that makes members of a group stick together.

study found that when there is a fit between the group's values and those of the organization, groups will report more cohesion and exhibit higher levels of organizational citizenship behavior (OCB).[17] In addition to improved performance, highly cohesive groups can lead to the maintenance of close relationships among the members. We will discuss group cohesion in further detail when we examine the common characteristics of well-developed groups.

Social Loafing

Social loafing occurs when one group member comes to rely on the efforts of other group members and fails to contribute her own time, effort, thoughts, or other resources to a group.[18] This may create a real drag on the group's efforts and achievements. Some scholars argue that social loafing, also known as *free riding*, is a rational response to feelings of inequity or situations in which individual efforts are hard to observe. However, it shortchanges the group, which loses potentially valuable resources possessed by individual members.[19]

One method for countering social loafing is a member self-evaluation system. If members must formally review their contributions to the group, they are less likely to loaf. Identifying individual contributions to the group product also counters loafing. If each group member is responsible for a specific input, an individual's failure to contribute will be noticed by everyone.

social loafing

The failure of a group member to contribute personal time, effort, thoughts, or other resources to the group.

loss of individuality

A social process in which individual group members lose self-awareness and its accompanying sense of accountability, inhibition, and responsibility for individual behavior.

Loss of Individuality

Social loafing may be detrimental to group achievement, but it does not have the potentially explosive effects of **loss of individuality**. Loss of individuality is a social process through which group members lose self-awareness and its accompanying senses of accountability, inhibition, and responsibility for individual behavior.[20] People may engage in morally reprehensible acts and even violent behavior as committed members of their group or organization when their individuality is lost. Loss of individuality was one of several contributing factors to the riot that destroyed sections of Los Angeles following the Rodney King verdict in April 1992. Yet loss of individuality is not always negative or destructive. The loosening of normal ego control mechanisms in the individual sometimes leads to prosocial behavior and even heroic acts in dangerous situations.[21]

LEARNING OUTCOME 4

Group Formation and Development

After its formation, a group goes through predictable stages of development. If each of the stages is successfully negotiated, the group emerges as a mature and tightly knit entity. One logical group development model proposed by Warren Bennis and Herbert Shepard delineates four stages following the group's formation: mutual acceptance, decision making, motivation and commitment, and control and sanctions.[22]

According to this group development model, a group addresses three issues: interpersonal issues, task issues, and authority issues.[23] The *interpersonal issues* include matters of trust, personal comfort, and security. Trust, in particular, is a key issue for any company in its working relationships. The *task issues* include the mission or purpose of the group, the methods the group employs, and the outcomes expected of the group. The *authority issues* include decisions about who is in charge, how power and influence are managed, and who has the right to tell whom to do what. This section addresses group formation, each stage of group development, and the characteristics of a mature group.

Group Formation

Formal and informal groups coalesce in organizations for different reasons. Formal groups

©iStockphoto.com/Matt Jeacock

are sometimes called *official* or *assigned* groups, and informal groups may be called *unofficial* or *emergent* groups. Formal groups such as project task forces, boards of directors, and temporary committees come together to perform specific tasks. An example of a formal group was the task force assembled by the University of Texas at Arlington to design the Goolsby Leadership Academy. Chaired by the associate dean of business, the task force was composed of seven members with diverse academic expertise and business experience. The task force established a five-year plan to inaugurate the select undergraduate program, which cultivates advanced leadership skills in its Goolsby Fellows and Associates.

Informal groups evolve in the work setting to gratify a variety of member needs not met by formal groups. For example, organizational members' inclusion and affirmation needs might be satisfied through informal athletic or specialized interest groups. Athletic teams representing a department, unit, or company may achieve semi-official status, such as the AT&T National Running Team that uses the corporate logo on its race shirts.

Diversity is an important consideration in the formation of groups, as it can enhance performance and lead to new ways of thinking. One study of gender diversity among U.S. workers found that men and women in gender-balanced groups had higher job satisfaction than those in homogeneous groups.[24] Organizations have been challenged to blend culturally and linguistically diverse peoples into effective work groups since America's founding. This task was especially demanding during the early years of the 1900s, when waves of immigrant workers arrived from numerous European nations.

In addition to ethnic, gender, and cultural diversity, there is interpersonal diversity, which may be indicated by different needs for inclusion, control of people and events, and affirmation from others. Successful interpersonal relationships are the basis of group effort, a key foundation for business success.

> "Diversity is an important consideration in the formation of groups.

Stages of Group Development

All groups go through stages of development, some more successfully than others. Mature groups are able to work through the interpersonal, task, and authority issues inevitable at the highest echelons of the business world. The path to maturity does not always go smoothly, however. Immature groups often experience personality clashes and other fault lines (that is, potential breaking points within the group) at various stages of development.[25]

The Five-Stage Model Bruce Tuckman's five-stage model of group development proposes that team behavior progresses through five stages: forming, storming, norming, performing, and adjourning.[26] These stages and their properties are illustrated in Figure 9.1.

Dependence on guidance and direction is the defining characteristic of the *forming* stage. At this point, team members are unclear about individual roles and responsibilities and tend to rely heavily on the leader to answer questions about the team's purpose, objectives, and external relationships. Moving from this stage requires that team members feel they are part of the team. During this time, it may also be beneficial for leaders to encourage team members to get to know each other on an interpersonal level before focusing on task performance.[27]

Team members compete for position in the *storming* stage. As the name suggests, this is a period of considerable conflict as power struggles, cliques, and factions within the group begin to surface. Clarity of purpose increases, but uncertainties still exist. This is also the stage in which members assess one another with regard to trustworthiness, emotional comfort, and evaluative acceptance. The group leader's coaching style is key during this stage of development, as team members may challenge her.

FIGURE 9.1 Tuckman's Five-Stage Model of Group Development

Forming	Storming	Norming	Performing	Adjourning
Little agreement Unclear purpose Guidance and direction	Conflict Increased clarity of purpose Power struggles Coaching	Agreement and consensus Clear roles and responsibilities Facilitation	Clear vision and purpose Focus on goal achievement Delegation	Task completion Good feeling about achievements Recognition

Organizational members' inclusion and affirmation needs can be satisfied through informal groups like company sports teams.

Agreement and consensus are characteristic of team members in the *norming* stage. It is during this period that roles and responsibilities become clear and are accepted. The group's focus will turn from interpersonal relations to decision making and task accomplishment. Insignificant decisions may be delegated to individuals or small teams, while larger decisions will be discussed and decided by the entire group. The group may address questions of authority, such as the necessity of a primary spokesperson and the delegation of roles within the group. Wallace Supply Company, an industrial distributor of pipes, valves, and fittings, found employee teams particularly valuable in raising and answering questions of authority.[28] The teams concluded that leadership ought to be facilitative and that certain responsibilities could be delegated to teams themselves.

As a team moves into the *performing* stage, it becomes more strategically aware of its mission and purpose. In this stage of development, the group has successfully worked through interpersonal, task, and authority issues and can stand on its own with little interference from the leader. Disagreements are resolved positively with necessary changes to structure and processes attended to by the team. A mature group is able to control its members through the judicious application of positive and negative sanctions based on the evaluation of specific behaviors. Recent research shows that evaluation biases stemming from liking someone operate in face-to-face groups but not in electronic groups, such as virtual teams.[29] Members at this stage do not need to be instructed but may ask for assistance from the leader in regard to personal or interpersonal development.

The final stage of group development is the *adjourning* stage. When the task is completed, everyone on the team can move on to new and different things. Team members retain a sense of accomplishment and feel good knowing that their purpose was fulfilled. The leader's role at this point is primarily to recognize the group's achievements. But unless the group is a task force or other informal team, most groups in organizations remain at the performing stage and do not disband as the adjourning stage suggests.

Punctuated Equilibrium Model

Though it is still highly cited in team and group research, Tuckman's model may be unrealistic from an organizational perspective. Research has shown that many teams experience relational conflicts at different times and in different contexts. Connie Gersick proposes that groups do not necessarily progress linearly from one step to another in a predetermined sequence but alternate between periods of inertia with little visible progress toward goal achievement. Progress is punctuated by bursts of energy as work groups develop. It is in these bursts that the majority of work is accomplished.[30] For example, a task force given nine months to complete a task may use the first four months to choose its norms, explore contextual issues, and determine how it will communicate. The final five months would then be dedicated to executing the task itself.

Characteristics of a Mature Group

A mature group has four characteristics: a clear purpose and mission, well-understood norms and standards of conduct, a high level of group cohesion, and a flexible status structure.

Purpose and Mission The group's purpose and mission may be assigned (as in the example of the Goolsby Leadership Academy task force) or emerge from within the group (as in the example of the AT&T National Running Team). In the case of an assigned mission, the group may embrace the mission as stated or reexamine, revise, or question it. The importance of mission is exemplified by IBM's Process Quality Management, which requires that a process team of no more than twelve people develop a clear understanding of the group's mission as the first step in the process.[31] The IBM approach demands that all members agree to go in the same direction. The mission statement is converted into a specific agenda, clear goals, and a set of critical success factors. Stating the purpose and mission in the form of specific goals enhances productivity and performance far more effectively than individual goal setting.[32]

Behavioral Norms *Behavioral norms*, which evolve over time, are well-understood standards of behavior within a group.[33] They are benchmarks against which team members are evaluated by other team members. Although some become written rules, such

©iStockphoto.com/cjmckendry

as an attendance policy or an ethical code, other norms remain informal, such as dress codes and norms about after-hours socializing. Additionally, behavioral norms may evolve around performance and productivity.[34] For example, productivity norms can influence the performance of sports teams in office leagues as well as in the professional realm.[35]

A group's productivity norm may or may not be consistent with the organization's productivity standards. A high-performance team sets productivity standards above organizational expectations; average teams set productivity standards consistent with organizational expectations; and noncompliant or counterproductive teams set productivity standards below organizational expectations, sometimes with the intent of damaging the organization or creating change. Usually, however, behavioral norms affect organizational culture in a beneficial way for all.

Group Cohesion Group cohesion enables a group to exercise effective control over its members in relation to its behavioral norms and standards. Among the threats to a group's cohesion are goal conflict, unpleasant experiences, and domination of a subgroup. Groups with low levels of cohesion have greater difficulty exercising control over their members and enforcing their standards of behavior; hence, they are more vulnerable to such threats. Specifically, work-related tensions and anxieties increase in highly cohesive teams and decrease in teams low in cohesion, as depicted in Figure 9.2. This relationship suggests that cohesion has a calming effect on team members.

In addition, actual productivity was found to vary significantly less in highly cohesive teams, making them much more predictable. The actual productivity levels, though, were primarily determined by the productivity norms within each work group. Thus, highly cohesive groups with high production standards were very productive, but highly cohesive groups with low productivity standards were unproductive despite their high level of cohesion. Nevertheless, no matter what the productivity was, member satisfaction, commitment, and communication were greater in highly cohesive groups.

Group cohesion is influenced by a number of factors, most notably time, size, the prestige of the team, external pressure, and internal competition. Usually cohesion

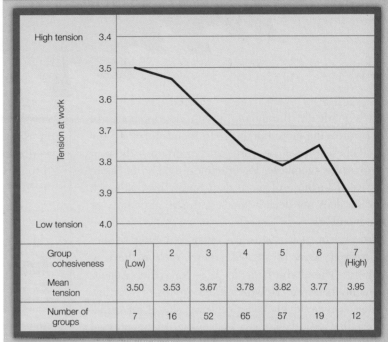

FIGURE 9.2 Cohesiveness and Work-Related Tension*

Group cohesiveness	1 (Low)	2	3	4	5	6	7 (High)
Mean tension	3.50	3.53	3.67	3.78	3.82	3.77	3.95
Number of groups	7	16	52	65	57	19	12

Note: Product–moment correlation is 0.28, and critical ratio is 4.20; the group cohesion–tension relationship is highly significant at the .001 level.

*The measure of tension at work is based on group mean response to the question "Does your work ever make you feel 'jumpy' or nervous?" A low numerical score represents relatively high tension.

SOURCE: S. E. Seashore, *Group Cohesiveness in the Industrial Work Group,* 1954. Research conducted by Stanley E. Seashore at the Institute for Social Research, University of Michigan. Reprinted by permission.

HAVING GOOD MEETINGS

Dan Rosensweig, CEO of Chegg, which rents textbooks online and by mail, has some basic strategies for keeping team meetings productive. First, they stick to the clock. That means starting on time and ending on time. Second, no technology. That means BlackBerrys and iPhones are off, and there's no Twitter, no Facebook, and no e-mail. Using these kinds of strategies to keep meetings focused can help make them more productive. As Rosensweig puts it, "Wherever you are, be all in."

SOURCE: D. Rosensweig, "Corner Office: Remember to Thank Your Star Players," interview by A. Bryant, *The New York Times* (July 9, 2010), http://www.nytimes.com/2010/07/11 /business/11corner.html?_r=1, accessed July 20, 2010.

Groups like the U.S. Navy Blue Angels are highly cohesive.

©Comstock Images/Jupiterimages

evolves gradually throughout group development. In other words, the more time a group spends together, the more cohesive it will be. Also, smaller groups—those of five or seven members, for example—tend to be more cohesive than those of more than twenty-five, although cohesion does not decline much with size after forty or more members.

Prestige or social status may enhance a group's cohesion as well. More prestigious groups, such as the U.S. Air Force Thunderbirds or the U.S. Navy Blue Angels, are highly cohesive. However, even groups of very low prestige may be highly cohesive as a result of other factors tending toward cohesion, such as the aforementioned factors of longer time together and smaller group size. Finally, external pressure and internal competition are two other factors influencing group cohesion. Although the mechanics' union, pilots, and other internal constituencies at Eastern Airlines had various differences of opinion, they all pulled together in a cohesive fashion in resisting Frank Lorenzo when he came in to reshape the airline before its demise. Whereas external pressures tend to enhance it, internal competition usually decreases cohesion within a team. One study found that company-imposed pressure disrupted group cohesion by increasing internal competition and reducing cooperative interpersonal activity.[36]

Status Structure Status structure is the set of authority and task relations among a group's members. It may be hierarchical or egalitarian, depending on the group. Successful resolution of the authority issue within a team results in a well-understood status structure of leader–follower relationships. Where leadership problems arise, it is important to find solutions and build team leader effectiveness.[37] Although groups usually have just one leader, teams tend to share leadership. For example, one person may be the team's taskmaster, who sets the agenda, initiates much of the work activity, and ensures that the team meets its deadlines. Another team member may take a leadership role in maintaining effective interpersonal relationships in the group. Hence, shared leadership is

status structure

The set of authority and task relations among a group's members.

task function

An activity directly related to the effective completion of a team's work.

very feasible in teams. An effective status structure results in role interrelatedness among group members.[38] Bill Perez and Bill Wrigley have promoted interrelatedness through a tag-team style of cooperation in leadership that has served the Wm. Wrigley Jr. Company well.

LEARNING OUTCOME 5

Task and Maintenance Functions

An effective group or team carries out various task functions to perform its work successfully and various maintenance functions to ensure member satisfaction and a sense of team spirit.[39] Teams that successfully fulfill these functions afford their members the potential for the social benefits of psychological intimacy and integrated involvement we discussed at the beginning of the chapter. Table 9.2 presents nine task and nine maintenance functions in teams or groups.

Task functions are those activities directly related to the effective completion of the team's work. For example, the task of initiating activity involves suggesting ideas, defining problems, and proposing approaches and/or solutions to problems. The task of seeking information involves asking for ideas, suggestions, information, or facts. A study of security analysts found that the quality of colleagues' work helped to improve and maintain the quality of individual member performance.[40] Effective teams have members who fulfill various task functions as they are required.

Different task functions vary in importance throughout the life cycle of a group. For example, during the engineering test periods for new technologies, the engineering team needs members who focus on testing the practical applications of suggestions and those who diagnose problems and suggest solutions. The effective use of task functions leads to the success of the group. In one case, the successful initiation and coordination of an emergency room team's activities by the senior resident saved the life of a knife wound victim.[41] The victim was stabbed one-quarter inch below the heart, and the team acted quickly to stem the bleeding, begin intravenous fluids, and monitor the victim's vital signs.

TABLE 9.2 Task and Maintenance Functions in Teams or Groups

TASK FUNCTIONS	MAINTENANCE FUNCTIONS
Initiating activities	Supporting others
Seeking information	Following others' leads
Giving information	Gatekeeping communication
Elaborating concepts	Setting standards
Coordinating activities	Expressing member feelings
Summarizing ideas	Testing group decisions
Testing ideas	Consensus testing
Evaluating effectiveness	Harmonizing conflict
Diagnosing problems	Reducing tension

©Cengage Learning 2013

Maintenance functions are those activities essential to the effective, satisfying interpersonal relationships within a group or team. Following another group member's lead may be as important as being a leader. Communication gatekeepers within a group ensure balanced contributions from all members. Because task activities build tension within teams or groups, tension-reduction activities are important to drain off negative or destructive feelings. In a study of twenty-five work groups over a five-year period, humor and joking behavior were found to enhance the social relationships in the groups.[42] The researchers concluded that performance improvements in the twenty-five groups indirectly resulted from improved relationships attributable to the humor and joking behaviors. Maintenance functions enhance togetherness, cooperation, and teamwork, enabling members to achieve psychological intimacy while furthering the success of the team. Jody Grant's supportive attitude and comfortable demeanor as chairman and CEO of Texas Capital Bancshares enabled him to build a vibrant bank in the aftermath of the great Texas banking crash. Grant was respected for his expertise *and* his ability to build relationships. Both task and maintenance functions are important for successful groups and teams.

LEARNING OUTCOME 6

Factors That Influence Group Effectiveness

Work team effectiveness in the new team environment requires management's attention to both work team structure and work team process.[43] In addition to how the team is structured and what the team does, diversity and creativity are emerging as two areas with significant impact on team performance.

Work Team Structure

Work team structure issues include goals and objectives, operating guidelines, performance measures, and role specification. A work team's goals and objectives specify what must be achieved, while the operating guidelines set the organizational boundaries and decision-making limits within which the team must function. The goal-setting process discussed in Chapter 6 applies to work teams, too. In addition to these two structural elements, the work team needs to know what performance measures are being used to assess its task accomplishment. For example, a medical emergency team's performance measures might include the success rate in saving critically injured patients and the average number of hours a patient is in the emergency room before being transferred to a hospital bed.

Finally, work team structure requires a clearly specified set of roles for the executives and managers who oversee the work of the team, for the work team leaders who exercise influence over team members, and for team members. These role specifications should include information about required role behaviors, such as decision making and task performance, as well as restrictions or limits on role behaviors, such as the limitations on managerial interventions in work team activities and decision making. Expectations as well as experience may be especially important for newcomer role performance in work teams.[44]

Work Team Process

Work team process is the second important dimension of effectiveness. Two of the important process issues in work teams are the managing of cooperative behaviors and the managing of competitive behaviors. Both sets of behaviors are helpful in task accomplishment, and they should be viewed as complementary. *Cooperative teamwork skills* include open communication, trust, personal integrity, positive interdependence, and mutual support. On the other hand, *positive competitive teamwork skills* include the ability to enjoy competition, play fair, and be a good

maintenance function
An activity essential to effective, satisfying interpersonal relationships within a team or group.

winner or loser; to have access to information for monitoring where the team and members are in the competition; and not to overgeneralize or exaggerate the results of any specific competition. In a study of reward structures in seventy-five four-member teams, competitive rewards enhanced speed of performance, while cooperative rewards enhanced accuracy of performance.[45]

Work team process issues have become more complex in the global workplace, where teams are composed of members from many cultures and backgrounds. This complexity is increased by the presence of virtual work teams operating on the global landscape. In addition to the process issues of cooperation, competition, and diversity, three other process issues are related to topics we discuss elsewhere in the text. These are empowerment, which is discussed in the next major section of this chapter; team decision making, which is discussed in Chapter 10; and conflict management and resolution, which are discussed in Chapter 13.

Diversity

Diversity also plays a large role in how effective work groups and teams are. Diversity in a group is healthy, and members may contribute to the collective effort through one of four basic styles: the contributor, the collaborator, the communicator, or the challenger.[46] The *contributor* is data driven, supplies necessary information, and adheres to high performance standards. The *collaborator* sees the

[**The Ten Golden Rules**]

In-depth case studies of successful virtual teams at Ogilvy & Mather, BP, and Nokia have led to ten golden rules to enhance the effectiveness of virtual teams.

1. Invest in an online resource where members can learn quickly about one another.
2. Choose a few team members who already know each other.
3. Identify "boundary spanners" and ensure that they make up at least 15 percent of the team.
4. Cultivate boundary spanners as a regular part of companywide practices and processes.
5. Break the team's work into modules so that progress in one location is not overly dependent on progress in another.
6. Create a website where a team can collaborate, exchange ideas, and inspire one another.
7. Encourage frequent communication.
8. Assign only tasks that are challenging and interesting.
9. Ensure the task is meaningful to the team and the company.
10. When building a virtual team, solicit volunteers as much as possible.

These rules come from successful experience, and any company implementing virtual teams should monitor the success and problems within their own work context.

SOURCE: L. Gratton, "Working Together…When Apart," *The Wall Street Journal* (June 16, 2007): R4.

big picture and is able to keep a constant focus on the mission and urge other members to join efforts for mission accomplishment. The *communicator* listens well, facilitates the group's process, and humanizes the collective effort. The *challenger* is the devil's advocate who questions everything from the group's mission, purpose, and methods to its ethics. Members may exhibit one or more of these four basic styles over a period of time. In addition, an effective group must have an *integrator*, especially when the group is a cross-functional one, where different perspectives carry the seeds of conflict.[47] However, cross-functional teams are not necessarily a problem. Effectively managing cross-functional teams of artists, designers, printers, and financial experts enabled Hallmark Cards to cut its new-product development time in half.[48]

Dissimilarity Recent research in diversity has focused on the effect of dissimilarity within a team. This issue is often studied in relation to social identity theory and self-categorization theory. Since creativity concerns new ideas, some amount of dissimilarity is necessary within a team in order for creativity, novelty, and innovation to blossom. Although creativity is discussed in

Diversity in a group is healthy.

©iStockphoto.com/Daniel Laflor

some detail in Chapter 10, we address it briefly here in the context of teams.

We defined diversity in Chapter 1 in terms of individual differences. Recent relational demography research finds that demographic dissimilarity influences employees' absenteeism, commitment, turnover intentions, beliefs, work group relationships, self-esteem, and OCB.[49] Thus, dissimilarity may have positive or negative effects in teams and on team members. Racial dissimilarity may also impact the extent to which team members communicate with each other and develop a sense of group identity.[50] While value dissimilarity may be positively related to task and relationship conflict, it is negatively related to team involvement.[51] This fact highlights the importance of managing dissimilarity in teams, being open to diversity, and turning conflicts about ideas into positive outcomes.

Functional background is one way to look at dissimilarity in teams. One study of 262 professionals in thirty-seven cross-functional teams found that promoting social identification with functional background helped individuals perform better as team members.[52] Another study of multifunctional management teams in a *Fortune* 100 company found that functional background predicted team involvement.[53] Finally, in a slightly different study of 129 members on twenty multidisciplinary project teams, informational dissimilarity had no adverse effects when there was member task and goal congruence.[54]

Structural Diversity Structural diversity concerns the number of *structural holes*, or disconnections between members, within a work team. One research study examined structural diversity and performance of nineteen teams in a wood-products company. The investigators were interested in demographic diversity among team members as well as the structural diversity, or presence of structural holes, in the teams. Neither race nor gender was a demographic factor that influenced the proportion of structural holes within the teams. However, age diversity significantly improved structural integrity. Hence, greater variance in age within a team leads to more member-to-member connections and fewer member-to-member disconnections.

Are disconnections of team members good or bad for the team? What are the consequences of having more or fewer structural holes between team members? Teams with few structural holes may have problems with creativity, while teams with a high proportion of structural holes may have difficulty coordinating. These observations led the researchers to conclude that there is a curvilinear relationship between structural diversity, or structural integrity, and team performance. The teams with moderate structural diversity achieve the best performance. This research is important because it points out that managers should look at the overall structure and network of relationships within their work teams in addition to the individual characteristics of team members in attempting to achieve the best performance from these teams.[55]

Creativity

Creativity is often thought of in an individual context rather than a team context. However, there is such a thing as team creativity. In a study of fifty-four research and development teams, team creativity scores were explained by aggregation processes across both people and time.[56] In another study of creative behavior, a Korean electronics company found that individual dissimilarity in age and performance, as well as functional diversity within the team, positively affected individual employees' creative behavior.

Some think that the deck is stacked against teams as agents of creativity. Leigh Thompson, a management and organizations professor at Northwestern University, thinks differently and suggests that team creativity and divergent thinking can be enhanced through greater diversity in teams, electronic brainstorming, training facilitators, membership change in teams, electronic brainstorming, and building a playground.[57] These practices can overcome social loafing, conformity, and downward norm setting in teams and organizations. Team members might exercise care in timing the insertion of their novel ideas into the team process so as to maximize the positive impact and benefits.[58]

©iStockphoto.com/gehringj

Empowerment and Self-Managed Teams

To be successful, teams require a culture of empowerment in the organization in which they are implemented. This is especially true of *self-managed teams*, discussed shortly, which are designed to take on responsibilities and address issues traditionally reserved for management.

Empowerment may be thought of as an attribute of a person or of an organization's culture.[59] As an organizational culture attribute, empowerment encourages participation, an essential ingredient for teamwork.[60] *Quality action teams (QATs)* at FedEx are the primary *quality improvement process (QIP)* technique used by the company to engage management and hourly employees in four-to-ten-member problem-solving teams.[61] The teams are empowered to act and solve problems as specific as charting the best route from the Phoenix airport to the local distribution center or as global as making major software enhancements to the online package-tracking system.

Empowerment may give employees the power of a lightning strike, but empowered employees must be properly focused through careful planning and preparation before they strike.[62]

Empowerment Skills

Empowerment through employee self-management is an alternative to empowerment through teamwork.[63] Whether through self-management or teamwork, empowerment requires the development of certain skills if it is to be enacted effectively.

Competence skills are the first set of skills required for empowerment. Mastery and experience in one's chosen discipline and profession provide an essential foundation for empowerment. New employees and trainees should experience only limited empowerment until they demonstrate the capacity to accept more responsibility.

Empowerment also requires certain *process skills*. The most critical process skills include negotiating skills, especially with allies, opponents, and adversaries.[64] Allies are the easiest people to negotiate with because they agree with you about the team's mission and you can trust their actions and behavior. Opponents require a different negotiating strategy; although you can predict their actions and behavior, they do not agree with your concept of the team's mis-

self-managed team

A team that makes decisions that were once reserved for managers.

> To be successful, teams require a culture of empowerment in the organization in which they are implemented.

sion. Adversaries are dangerous, difficult people to negotiate with because you cannot predict their actions or behaviors and they do not agree with your concept of the team's mission.

A third set of empowerment skills involves the development of *cooperative and helping behaviors.*[65] Cooperative people engage in encouraging, helpful behavior to maximize the gains for everyone on the team. The alternative orientations to cooperation are competitive, individualistic, and egalitarian approaches. *Competitive people* are motivated to maximize their personal gains regardless of the expense to other people. This motivation can be very counterproductive to the team. *Individualistic people* are motivated to act autonomously, though not necessarily to maximize their personal gains. They are less prone to contribute to the efforts of the team. *Egalitarian people* are motivated to equalize the outcomes for each team member, which may or may not be beneficial to the team's well-being. Paradoxically, the team members who need the most help often get the least help because helping behaviors are often targeted to the most "expert" team members, a dynamic that actually compromises overall team performance.[66]

Communication skills are a final set of essential empowerment skills.[67] These skills include self-expression skills and skills in reflective listening. Empowerment cannot occur in a team unless members are able to express themselves effectively as well as listen carefully to one another.

Self-Managed Teams

Self-managed teams, also called *self-directed teams* or *autonomous work groups*, are teams that make decisions that were once reserved for managers. Self-managed teams are one way to implement empowerment in organizations. Even though self-managed teams are self-directed, that fact does not negate the influence of managers. In fact, managers have an important role in providing leadership and influence.[68] There is strong support for the use of soft-influence tactics in managers' communication with self-directed teams, which yields more positive results.[69]

A one-year study of self-managed teams suggests that they have a positive impact on employee attitudes but not on absenteeism or turnover.[70] Evaluative research is helpful in achieving a better understanding of this relatively new way of approaching teamwork and the design of work. Such research helps establish expectations for self-managed teams. Nevertheless, there are risks, such as groupthink in self-managed teams, that must be prevented or managed if the team is to achieve full development and function.[71]

It is noteworthy that one evaluation of empowerment, teams, and *Total Quality Management (TQM)* programs found that companies associated with these popular management techniques did not have higher economic performance.[72] Other evaluations of self-managed teams are more positive. Southwest Industries, a high-technology aerospace manufacturing firm, embarked on a major internal reorganization in the early 1990s that included the creation of self-managed teams to fit its high-technology production process. Southwest's team approach resulted in a 30 percent increase in shipments, a 30 percent decrease in lead time, a 40 percent decrease in total inventory, a decrease in machinery downtime, and almost a one-third decrease in production costs.[73] An overall positive history has resulted in U.S.-based multinational corporations increasingly using self-managed teams in their global operations.

LEARNING OUTCOME **8**

Upper Echelons: Teams at the Top

Self-managed teams at the top of the organization—top-level executive teams—are referred to as **upper echelons**. Organizations are often a reflection of these upper echelons.[74] *Upper echelon theory* argues that the background characteristics of the top management team can predict organizational characteristics and set standards for values, competence, ethics, and unique characteristics throughout the organization. Furthermore, upper echelons are one key to the strategic success of the organization.[75] The ability to exert power and influence throughout the entire organization makes the top management team a key to the organization's success. This ability may be compromised if the top team sends mixed signals about teamwork and if executive pay systems foster competition, politics, and individualism.[76]

For example, when Lee Iacocca became CEO at the Chrysler Corporation, his top management team was assembled to bring about strategic realignment within the corporation by building on Chrysler's historical engineering strength. The

dramatic success of Chrysler during the early 1980s was followed by struggle and accommodation during the late 1980s. This raises the question of how long a CEO and the top management team can sustain organizational success.

Hambrick and Fukutomi addressed this question by examining the dynamic relationship between a CEO's tenure and the success of the organization.[77] They found five *seasons* in a CEO's tenure: (1) response to a mandate, (2) experimentation, (3) selection of an enduring theme, (4) convergence, and (5) dysfunction. A summary of each season is shown in Table 9.3 on the next page. All else being equal, the seasons model has significant implications for organizational performance. Specifically, organizational performance increases during a CEO's tenure to a peak, after which performance declines. This relationship is depicted in Figure 9.3 on the next page. The peak has been found to come at about seven years—somewhere in the middle of the executive's seasons. As indicated by the dotted lines in the figure, the peak may be extended, depending on several factors, such as diversity in the executive's support team.

Diversity at the Top

From an organizational health standpoint, diversity and depth in the top management team enhance the CEO's well-being.[78] From a performance standpoint, the CEO's top management team can influence the timing of the performance peak, the degree of dysfunction during the closing season of the CEO's tenure, and the rate of decline in organizational performance. Thus, diversity and heterogeneity in the top management team help sustain high levels of organizational performance at the peak and help maintain the CEO's vitality. A study of 207 U.S. firms in eleven industries found that functional diversity of top management teams had a positive effect on firm performance as the proportion of leaders in the same location increased.[79]

The presence of a "wild turkey" in the top management team can be a particularly positive force. The wild

upper echelon
A top-level executive team in an organization.

The wild turkey is a devil's advocate who challenges the thinking of the CEO and other top executives and provides a counterpoint during debates.

©iStockphoto.com/Eric Isselée

TABLE 9.3 The Five Seasons of a CEO's Tenure

CRITICAL CEO CHARACTERISTICS	1 RESPONSE TO MANDATE	2 EXPERIMENTATION	3 SELECTION OF AN ENDURING THEME	4 CONVERGENCE	5 DYSFUNCTION
COMMITMENT TO A PARADIGM	Moderately strong	Could be strong or weak	Moderately strong	Strong; increasing	Very strong
TASK KNOWLEDGE	Low but rapidly increasing	Moderate; somewhat increasing	High; slightly increasing	High; slightly increasing	High; slightly increasing
INFORMATION DIVERSITY	Many sources; unfiltered	Many sources but increasingly unfiltered	Fewer sources; moderately filtered	Few sources; highly filtered	Very few sources; highly filtered
TASK INTEREST	High	High	Moderately high	Moderately high but diminishing	Moderately low and diminishing
POWER	Low; increasing	Moderate; increasing	Moderate; increasing	Strong; increasing	Very strong; increasing

SOURCE: D. Hambrick and G. D. S. Fukutomi, "The Seasons of a CEO's Tenure," *Academy of Management Review* (1991) 729. Permission conveyed through Copyright Clearance Center, Inc.

turkey is a devil's advocate who challenges the thinking of the CEO and other top executives and provides a counterpoint during debates. If not shouted down or inhibited, the wild turkey helps the CEO and the team sustain peak performance and retard the CEO's dysfunction and decline. For example, former Secretary of State Colin Powell enhanced President George W. Bush's administration by exercising an independent voice. Often taking a more moderate position on policy issues than either the secretary of defense or the vice president, Powell brought variance and value to President Bush's administration.

Leaders must develop communication strategies to bring together team members who are functionally, intellectually, demographically, and temperamentally diverse so that they can act in ways that complement one another. It is out of dissimilarity that strength is developed, and it is out of similarity that connections are built. Therefore, top management should strive for a balance of dissimilarity and similarity within work teams.

We conclude that the leadership, composition, and dynamics of the top management team have an important influence on the organization's performance, leading, in some cases, to a change from having only one CEO to having more than one. Current research has shown a dramatic increase in the number of co-CEO arrangements in both public and private corporations.[80] While more common in Europe than in the United States, a historical U.S. example of a co-CEO arrangement includes a three-member team created by Walter Wriston while he was chairman at Citicorp (now part of Citigroup).

Multicultural Top Teams

Homogeneous groups, in which all members share similar backgrounds, are giving way to *token groups*, in which all

FIGURE 9.3 Executive Tenure and Organizational Performance

SOURCE: D. Hambrick, "The Seasons of an Executive's Tenure", keynote address, the Sixth Annual Texas Conference on Organizations, Lago Vista, Texas, April 1991.

but one member come from the same background; *bicultural groups*, in which two or more members represent each of two distinct cultures; and *multicultural groups*, in which members represent three or more ethnic backgrounds.[81] On the negative side, diversity within a group may increase the uncertainty, complexity, and inherent confusion in group processes, making it more difficult for the group to achieve its full productivity.[82] On the positive side, most organizations report benefits from increased diversity, such as Merck, which attributes its long-term success to its leadership model that promotes diversity. Chairman, president, and CEO Ray Gilmartin values diversity in Merck's top management team because he believes that it sparks innovation when employees with different perspectives work together to offer solutions. Diversities of age and educational specialization within top management teams were found in other studies to have a positive effect on team performance, especially when members needed to partici-

pate in cognitive tasks.[83] A recent study found that the performance of top management teams was greatly increased when the CEO had numerous shared experiences with executives from other companies and cultures.[84] The advantages of culturally diverse groups appear to include the generation of more and better ideas while limiting the risk of groupthink, to be discussed in Chapter 10.

Log in to the **CourseMate** for *ORGB3* at **www.cengagebrain.com** to:

* Review **Key Terms Flash Cards** online

* Play **Beat the Clock** and **Quiz Bowl** to master concepts

* Complete **web quizzes** to prepare for exams

* Watch the video on **Holden Outerwear** and from *Friends with Money* for examples, then test yourself with a quick quiz

* Work through the **"What about You?"** and **Ethical Dilemma** exercises to see how you would handle various situations that organizations face on a daily basis

10

Decision Making by Individuals and Groups

LEARNING OUTCOMES

1 Identify the steps in the decision-making process.

2 Describe various models of decision making.

3 Discuss the individual influences that affect decision making.

4 Explain how groups make decisions.

5 Describe the role culture plays in decision making.

6 Explain how organizations can improve the quality of decisions through participation.

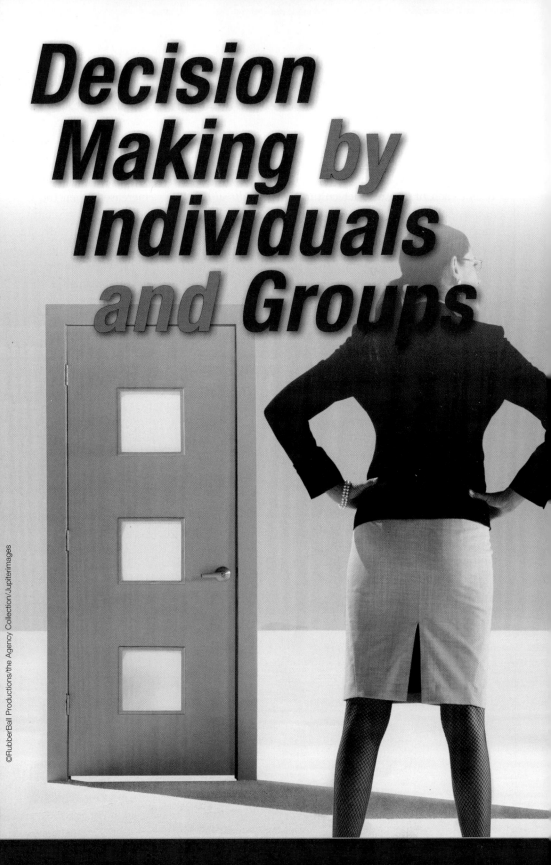

©RubberBall Productions/the Agency Collection/Jupiterimages

" The first step is recognizing the problem; that is, the manager realizes that a decision must be made."

After You Finish
This Chapter
Go to **Page 175**
for **Study Tools**

The Decision-Making Process

Decision making is a critical activity in the lives of managers. The decisions a manager faces can range from very simple, routine matters for which the manager has an established decision rule (**programmed decisions**) to new and complex decisions that require creative solutions (**nonprogrammed decisions**).[1] Scheduling lunch hours for one's work group, for example, is a programmed decision. The manager performs this programmed decision activity on a daily basis, using an established procedure with the same clear goal in mind each time. In contrast, decisions like buying out another company are nonprogrammed, providing a unique, unstructured situation and requiring considerable judgment. Regardless of the type of decision made, it is helpful to understand as much as possible about how individuals and groups make decisions.

Decision making is a process involving a series of steps, as shown in Figure 10.1 on the next page. The first step is recognizing the problem; that is, the manager realizes that a decision must be made. Identifying the real problem is important; otherwise, the manager may be reacting to symptoms rather than dealing with the root cause of the problem. Next, a manager must identify the objective of the decision. In other words, the manager must determine what is to be accomplished by the decision. The third step in the decision-making process is gathering information relevant to the problem. The manager must accumulate sufficient information about why the problem occurred. This involves conducting a thorough diagnosis of the situation and going on a fact-finding mission.

The fourth step is listing and evaluating alternative courses of action. During this step, a thorough "what-if" analysis should be conducted to determine

programmed decision

A simple, routine matter for which a manager has an established decision rule.

nonprogrammed decision

A new, complex decision that requires a creative solution.

FIGURE **10.1** The Decision-Making Process

Recognize the problem and the need for a decision.

↓

Identify the objective of the decision.

↓

Gather and evaluate data and diagnose the situation.

↓

List and evaluate alternatives.

↓

Select the best course of action.

↓

Implement the decision.

↓

Gather feedback.

↓

Follow up.

©Cengage Learning 2013

Decision making can be stressful. Managers must make decisions with significant risk and uncertainty, and often without all of the necessary information. They must trust and rely on others in their decision-making process, yet they are ultimately responsible for the final decision. Sometimes decisions are painful and involve exiting businesses, firing people, and admitting wrong.

Blue Man Group has a history of making effective decisions. Its theatrical productions blend comedy, music, and multimedia in a unique brand of entertainment. It has grown wildly famous and successful by making sound business choices, even though none of the founders has any formal training in music, acting, or business. The group has turned down offers to sell credit cards, soft drinks, breath mints, and paint, all related to the color blue. With each new opportunity, the three founders use the same evaluation: "Okay, that's all good and well, that's a nice thought—but is it Blue Man?" The group has also completed a detailed 132-page operating manual, a task many businesses never complete. Finally, the founders make decisions by unanimous agreement.[2]

the various factors that could influence the outcome. It is important to generate a wide range of options and creative solutions in order to be able to move on to the next step. Next, the manager selects the alternative that best meets the decision objective. If the problem has been diagnosed correctly and sufficient alternatives have been identified, this step is much easier. After the solution is implemented, the situation must then be monitored to see whether the decision met its objective. Consistent monitoring and periodic feedback are essential parts of the follow-up process.

Models and Limits of Decision Making

The success of any organization depends on managers' abilities to make **effective decisions**. An effective decision is timely, is acceptable to the individuals affected by it, and meets the desired objective.[3] This section describes three models of decision making: the rational model, the bounded rationality model, and the Z model. The section will conclude with a discussion of the limits of decision-making techniques.

Rational Model

Rationality refers to a logical, step-by-step approach to decision making with a thorough analysis of alternatives and their consequences. The *rational model* of decision making comes from classic economic theory and assumes the following:

1. The outcome will be completely rational.
2. The decision maker has a consistent system of preferences, which is used to choose the best alternative.
3. The decision maker is aware of all the possible alternatives.
4. The decision maker can calculate the probability of success for each alternative.[4]

In the rational model, the decision maker strives to *optimize*, that is, to select the best possible alternative.

Given the assumptions of the rational model, it is unrealistic. There are time constraints and limits to human knowledge and information-processing capabilities. In addition, a manager's preferences and needs change often. The rational model is thus an ideal that managers strive for in making decisions, and it captures the way a decision should be made, but it does not reflect the reality of managerial decision making.[5]

Bounded Rationality Model

Recognizing the deficiencies of the rational model, Herbert Simon suggested that there are limits on how rational a decision maker can actually be. His decision theory, the *bounded rationality model*, earned a Nobel Prize in economics in 1978. Also referred to as the "administrative man" theory, Simon's theory rests on the idea that there are constraints that force a decision maker to be less than completely rational. The bounded rationality model has four assumptions:

1. Managers select the first alternative that is satisfactory.
2. Managers recognize that their conception of the world is simple.
3. Managers are comfortable making decisions without determining all the alternatives.
4. Managers make decisions by rules of thumb, or heuristics.

Bounded rationality assumes that managers **satisfice**; that is, they select the first alternative that is "good enough," because the costs of optimizing in terms of time and effort are too great.[6] Further, the theory assumes that managers develop shortcuts, called **heuristics**, to make decisions in order to save mental activity. Heuristics are rules of thumb that allow managers to make decisions based on what has worked in past experiences.

Does the bounded rationality model portray the managerial decision process more realistically? Research indicates that it does.[7] One of the reasons managers face limits to their rationality is that they must make decisions under risk and time pressure. The

effective decision
A timely decision that meets a desired objective and is acceptable to those individuals affected by it.

rationality
A logical, step-by-step approach to decision making, with a thorough analysis of alternatives and their consequences.

bounded rationality
A theory that suggests that there are limits to how rational a decision maker can actually be.

satisfice
To select the first alternative that is "good enough," because the costs in time and effort are too great to optimize.

heuristics
Shortcuts in decision making that save mental activity.

Managers often satisfice because of time constraints.

©Polina Lobanova/Shutterstock.com

situation they find themselves in is highly uncertain, and the probability of success is not known.

Z Model

Isabel Briggs Myers, co-creator of the Myers-Briggs Type Indicator, also developed the Z *problem-solving model*, which capitalizes on the strengths of the four separate preferences (Sensing, Intuiting, Thinking, and Feeling). By using the Z problem-solving model, managers can use both their preferences and nonpreferences to make decisions more effectively. The Z model is presented in Figure 10.2. According to this model, good problem solving has four steps:

1. *Examine the facts and details.* Use Sensing to gather information about the problem.

2. *Generate alternatives.* Use Intuiting to develop possibilities.

3. *Analyze the alternatives objectively.* Use Thinking to logically determine the effects of each alternative.

4. *Weigh the impact.* Use Feeling to determine how the people involved will be affected.

Using the Z model can help an individual develop his nonpreferences. Another way to use the Z model is to rely on others to perform nonpreferred activities. For example, an individual who is an NF (Intuition-Feeling person) might want to turn to a trusted NT (Intuition-Thinking person) for help in analyzing alternatives objectively.

Escalation of Commitment

Each decision-making model carries its own unique limits. There is, however, one limitation that they all share: the decision maker's unwillingness to abandon a bad decision. Continuing to support a failing course of action is known as **escalation of commitment**.[8] In situations characterized by escalation of commitment, individuals who make decisions that turn out to be poor choices tend to hold fast to those choices, even when substantial costs are incurred.[9] An example of escalation is the price wars that often occur between airlines. The airlines reduce their prices in response to

escalation of commitment
The tendency to continue to support a failing course of action.

FIGURE 10.2 The Z Problem-Solving Model

Look at the facts and details.
- What are the facts?
- Be specific and realistic.
- List all relevant details.
- Be clear.

Sensing → **Intuition**

What alternatives do the facts suggest?
- Let your imagination run wild.
- Brainstorm.
- Consider various solutions.

Can it be analyzed objectively?
- Consider the consequences of each alternative.
- If you were not involved, what would you suggest?
- What is the cause and effect of each action?

Thinking → **Feeling**

What impact will it have on those involved?
- Is it something you can live with?
- How do you feel about the action?
- What hunches do you have about others' reactions?

SOURCE: From *Type Talk at Work* by Otto Kroeger and Janet Theusen, copyright © 1992 by Janet Theusen and Otto Kroeger. Used by permission of Delacorte Press, an imprint of The Random House Publishing Group, a division of Random House, Inc.

competitors until at a certain stage both airlines are in "no-win" situations. They continue to compete despite the heavy losses they incur. The desire to win is a motivation to continue to escalate, and each airline continues to reduce prices (lose money) based on the belief that the other airline will pull out of the price war.

Another example of escalation of commitment is NASA's enormous International Space Station. Originally estimated to cost $8 billion, the space station has been redesigned five times and remains unfinished. As of 2003, its estimated cost topped $30 billion, and some pundits speculate that the total bill may reach $100 billion for what physicist Robert Park describes as "the biggest technological blunder in history." Despite the station's drain on virtually every other NASA program, it remains a focal point of NASA's work and continues to consume vast resources.[10]

Why does escalation of commitment occur? One explanation is offered by cognitive dissonance theory, as we discussed in Chapter 4. This theory assumes that people dislike inconsistency and that when it exists among their attitudes or between their attitudes and behavior, they strive to reduce the dissonance.[11] Other reasons why people may hang on to a losing course of action are optimism and control. Some people are overly optimistic and overestimate the likelihood that positive things will happen to them. Other people operate under an illusion of control—that they have special skills to control the future that other people don't have.[12] Some individuals "throw good money after bad." They think, "Well, I've invested this much . . . what's a few dollars more?" The closer a project is to completion, the more likely escalation is to occur.[13]

Hanging on to a poor decision can be costly to organizations. While many foreign automakers saw promise in the *green movement* and shifted their development toward hybrid vehicles in 2002, General Motors stuck with a cost-cutting strategy that streamlined its operations and focused on production of SUVs and trucks. Between 2005 and 2008 GM lost $82 billion, and even these losses did not change the ailing company's strategy.[14] In 2009 CEO Rick Wagoner finally attempted to de-escalate, announcing that GM's focus on SUVs and trucks was no longer a viable strategy. It was too late, however, and despite a multibillion-dollar loan from the U.S. government, GM declared bankruptcy.

Recent research on de-escalation found that individuals with higher self-esteem and those who are given an opportunity to affirm an important value are more likely to de-escalate.[15] Organizations can use this information to deal with escalation of commitment in several ways. One method of reducing escalation is to split the responsibility for project decisions by allowing different individuals to make decisions at different project stages. Another way that companies have tried to eliminate escalation of commitment is to closely monitor decision makers.[16] Still another suggestion is to provide individuals with a graceful exit from poor decisions so that their images are not threatened. There can be a reward of some type for those who admit to poor decisions before escalating their commitment to them or having groups make an initial investment decision. This way participants in group decision making may experience a diffusion of responsibility for the failed decision rather than feeling personally responsible; thus, they can pull out of a bad decision without threatening their image.[17]

We have seen that there are limits to how rational a manager can be in making decisions. On reason is that most managerial decisions involve considerable risk, and individuals react differently to risk situations, a subject we address in the next section.

Individual Influences on Decision Making

No decision is made in a vacuum. In many ways, decisions reflect the people who make them, so it is appropriate to examine the individual influences on decision making: comfort with risk, **cognitive style**, personality, intuition, and creativity.

Risk and the Manager

Many decisions involve some element of risk. For managers, decisions regarding hiring, promotions, delegation, acquisitions and mergers, overseas expansions, and new product development are among many that make risk a part of the job. As individuals, managers of course differ in terms of their willingness to take risks—that is, their degree of **risk aversion**. Some choose options that entail fewer risks, preferring familiarity and certainty, while others are *risk takers* and will accept greater potential for loss in decisions as well as tolerating greater uncertainty. Those prone to making risky decisions are more likely to take the lead in group discussions.[18]

Research indicates that women are more risk averse than men and that older, more experienced managers are more risk averse than younger managers. There is also some evidence that successful managers take more risks than unsuccessful managers.[19] However, the tendency to take risks or avoid them is only part of behavior toward risk. Risk taking is influenced not only by an individual's tendency but also by organizational factors. In commercial banks, loan decisions that require the assessment of risk are made every day.

Upper-level managers face a tough task in managing risk-taking behavior. By discouraging lower-level managers from taking risks, they may stifle creativity and innovation. If upper-level managers are going to encourage risk taking, however, they must allow employees to fail without fear of punishment. One way to accomplish this is to consider failure as "enlightened trial and error."[20] The key is establishing a consistent attitude toward risk within the organization.

Obviously, when individuals take risks, losses may occur.

cognitive style
An individual's preferred method for gathering information and evaluating alternatives.

risk aversion
The tendency to choose options that entail fewer risks and less uncertainty.

Suppose an oil producer thinks there is an opportunity to uncover oil by reentering an old drilling site. She gathers a group of investors and shows them the logs, and they chip in to finance the venture. The reentry is drilled to a certain depth, and nothing is found. Convinced they did not drill deep enough, the producer goes back to the investors and requests additional financial backing to continue drilling. The investors consent, and she drills deeper, only to find nothing. She approaches the investors, and after lengthy discussion, they agree to provide more money to drill deeper. Why do decision makers sometimes throw good money after bad? Why do they continue to provide resources to what looks like a losing venture?

Personality, Attitudes, and Values

In addition to all of the individual differences variables (discussed in Chapters 3 and 4)—personality characteristics, attitudes, and values—managers must use both their logic and their creativity to make effective decisions. Most of us are more comfortable using either logic or creativity, and we show that preference in everyday decision making.

Our brains have two lateral halves (Figure 10.3). The right side is the center for creative functions, while the left side is the center for logic, detail, and planning. There are advantages to both kinds of thinking, so the ideal situation is to be

intuition
A fast, positive force in decision making that is utilized at a level below consciousness and involves learned patterns of information.

"brain-lateralized," or to be able to use either logic or creativity or both, depending on the situation.[21] There are ways to develop the side of the brain that you use less often. To develop your right side, or creative side, you can ask "what-if" questions, engage in play, and follow your intuition. To develop the left side, you can set goals for completing tasks and work to attain those goals. For managers, it is important to see the big picture, craft a vision, and plan strategically—all of which require right-brain skills. But it is equally important to be able to understand day-to-day operations and flowchart work processes, which are left-hemisphere brain skills.

Two particular individual influences that can enhance decision-making effectiveness will be highlighted next: intuition and creativity.

Intuition

There is evidence that managers often use their **intuition** to make decisions.[22] Henry Mintzberg, in his work on managerial roles, found that in many cases managers do not appear to use a systematic, step-by-step approach to decision making. Rather, Mintzberg argued, managers make judgments based on "hunches."[23] Daniel Isenberg studied the way senior managers make decisions and found that intuition was used extensively, especially as a mechanism to evaluate decisions made more rationally.[24] Robert Beck studied the way managers at Bank of America made decisions about the future direction of the company following the deregulation of the banking industry. Beck described their use of intuition as an antidote to "analysis paralysis," or the tendency to analyze decisions rather than developing innovative solutions.[25]

Dr. Gary Klein, a renowned cognitive psychologist, has written a book on the power of intuition. Dr. Klein and colleagues insist that skilled decision makers rely on patterns of learned information in making quick and efficient decisions. In a series of studies conducted with the U.S. Navy, firefighters, and the U.S. Army, they found that decision makers normally rely on intuition in unfamiliar, challenging situations. These decisions were superior to those made after careful evaluation of information and potential alternatives.[26]

Just what is intuition? In Jungian theory, intuiting (N) is a preferred method used for gathering data. This is only one way that the concept of intuition has been applied to managerial decision making, but it is perhaps the most widely

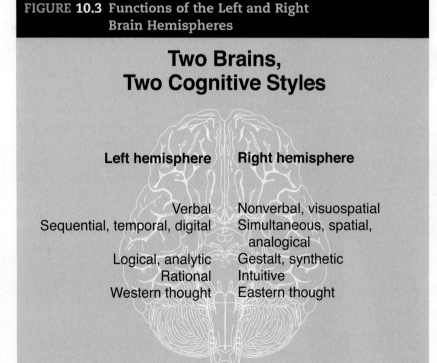

FIGURE 10.3 Functions of the Left and Right Brain Hemispheres

Two Brains, Two Cognitive Styles

Left hemisphere	Right hemisphere
Verbal	Nonverbal, visuospatial
Sequential, temporal, digital	Simultaneous, spatial, analogical
Logical, analytic	Gestalt, synthetic
Rational	Intuitive
Western thought	Eastern thought

SOURCE: Based on ideas from S. P. Springer and G. Deutsch, *Left Brain, Right Brain* (New York: W. H. Freeman and Company, 1993): 272.

researched form of the concept of intuition. There are, however, many definitions of *intuition* in the managerial literature. Chester Barnard, one of the early influential management researchers, argued that intuition's main attributes were speed and the inability of the decision maker to determine how the decision was made.[27] Other researchers have contended that intuition occurs at an unconscious level and that this is why the decision maker cannot verbalize how the decision was made.[28]

Intuition has been variously described as follows:

> The ability to know or recognize quickly and readily the possibilities of a situation.[29]

> Smooth automatic performance of learned behavior sequences.[30]

> Simple analyses frozen into habit and into the capacity for rapid response through recognition.[31]

These definitions share some common assumptions. First, there seems to be a notion that intuition is fast. Second, intuition is used at a level below consciousness. Third, there seems to be agreement that intuition involves learned patterns of information. Fourth, intuition appears to be a positive force in decision making.

The use of intuition may lead to more ethical decisions as intuition allows an individual to take on another's role with ease, and role taking is a fundamental part of developing moral reasoning. You may recall from Chapter 4 the role of cognitive moral development in ethical decision making. One study found a strong link between cognitive moral development and intuition. The development of new perspectives through intuition leads to higher moral growth, and thus to more ethical decisions.[32]

One question that arises is whether managers can be taught to use their intuition. Weston Agor, who has conducted workshops on developing intuitive skills in managers, has attained positive results in organizations such as the city government of Phoenix and entertainment powerhouse Walt Disney Enterprises. After giving intuition tests to more than 10,000 executives, he has concluded that in most cases, higher management positions are held by individuals with higher levels of intuition. But, just as the brain needs both hemispheres to work, Agor cautions that organizations need both analytical and intuitive minds to function at their peak. Lee Iacocca, in his autobiography, spends pages extolling intuition: "To a certain extent, I've always operated by gut feeling."[33] Agor suggests relaxation techniques, using images to guide the mind, and taking creative pauses before making a decision.[34] A review of the research on intuition suggests that although intuition itself cannot be taught, managers can be trained to rely more fully on the promptings of their intuition.[35]

Intuition, with its many definitions, is an elusive concept. Some researchers view "rational" methods as preferable to intuition, yet satisfaction with a rational decision is usually determined by how the decision feels intuitively.[36] Intuition appears to have a positive effect on managerial decision making, but it is not without controversy. Some writers argue that intuition has its place and that instincts should be trusted, but not as a substitute for reason. With new technologies, managers can analyze a lot more information in a lot less time, making the rational method less time consuming than it once was.[37]

Creativity

In some ways, creativity is as elusive a concept as intuition. (We know it when we encounter it and when we feel its absence.) Even though creativity is highly individual, it is also collective. Personal creativity plays a role in the decisions made in organizations every day. For our purposes in this text, we can define **creativity** as a process influenced by individual and organizational factors that results in the production of novel and useful ideas, products, or both.[38]

The four stages of the creative process are preparation, incubation, illumination, and verification.[39] *Preparation* means seeking

Illumination is essential to the creative process.

©iStockphoto.com/ElementalImaging

creativity

A process influenced by individual and organizational factors that results in the production of novel and useful ideas, products, or both.

out new experiences and opportunities to learn, because creativity grows from a base of knowledge. *Incubation* is a process of reflective thought and is often conducted subconsciously. During incubation, the individual engages in other pursuits while the mind considers the problem and works on it. *Illumination* occurs when the individual senses an insight for solving the problem. Finally, *verification* is conducted to determine if the solution or idea is valid. Verification is accomplished by thinking through the implications of the decision, presenting the idea to another person, or trying out the decision. Momentary quieting of the brain through relaxation can increase coherence, or the ability of different parts of the brain to work together.[40] Both individual and organizational influences affect the creative process.

Individual Influences

Several individual variables are related to creativity. One group of factors involves the cognitive processes that creative individuals tend to use. One such cognitive process is *divergent thinking*, meaning the individual's ability to generate several potential solutions to a problem.[41] In addition, associational abilities and the use of imagery are associated with creativity.[42] Unconscious processes such as dreams are also essential cognitive processes related to creative thinking.[43]

Personality factors have also been related to creativity in studies of individuals from several different occupations. These characteristics include intellectual and artistic values, breadth of interests, high energy, concern with achievement, independence of judgment, intuition, self-confidence, and a creative self-image.[44] Tolerance of ambiguity, intrinsic motivation, risk taking, and a desire for recognition are associated with creativity as well.[45] Not surprisingly, people who have a high level of motivation are more creative, since they are more likely to try to think of different ways to get things done. Also, people who are able to see and understand others' perspectives are more creative, since they have skills at seeing situations from more than one viewpoint.[46]

There is evidence that people who are in a good mood are more creative.[47] Positive affect is related to creativity in work teams because being in a positive mood allows team members to explore new ways of thinking.[48] Positive emotions enhance creativity by broadening one's cognitive patterns and resources. These positive emotions initiate thoughts and actions that are novel and unscripted.[49] Moreover, it is

a cyclical process: thinking positively makes us more creative, and being more creative makes us think positively.[50]

Yet, conversely, it has been found that people in negative moods perform better at tasks involving considerable cognitive demands. Apparently, when an individual experiences negative moods or emotions, it is a signal to him that all is not well and thus leads to more attention and vigilance in cognitive activity.

Organizational Influences

The organizational environment in which people work can either support creativity or impede creative efforts. Creativity killers include focusing on how work is going to be evaluated, being closely monitored while you are working, and competing with other people in win–lose situations. In contrast, creativity facilitators include feelings of autonomy, being part of a team with diverse skills, and having creative supervisors and coworkers.[51] High-quality, supportive relationships with supervisors are related to creativity.[52] Plus, high-quality social networks that are cohesive can have a positive impact on creative decision making. Such social networks encourage creative decision making by facilitating shared *sense-making* of relevant information and *consensus building*.[53] In addition, flexible organizational structures and participative decision making have been associated with creativity.

An organization can present impediments to creativity by means of internal political problems, harsh criticism of new ideas, destructive internal competition, and avoidance of risk.[54] Even the physical environment can hamper creativity. Companies like Oticon, a Danish hearing-aid manufacturer, and Ethicon Endo-Surgery, a division of Johnson & Johnson, use open-plan offices that elimi-

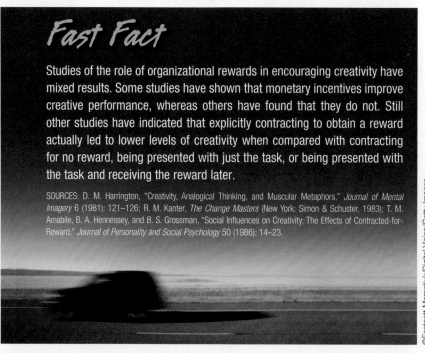

Fast Fact

Studies of the role of organizational rewards in encouraging creativity have mixed results. Some studies have shown that monetary incentives improve creative performance, whereas others have found that they do not. Still other studies have indicated that explicitly contracting to obtain a reward actually led to lower levels of creativity when compared with contracting for no reward, being presented with just the task, or being presented with the task and receiving the reward later.

SOURCES: D. M. Harrington, "Creativity, Analogical Thinking, and Muscular Metaphors," *Journal of Mental Imagery* 6 (1981): 121–126; R. M. Kanter, *The Change Masters* (New York: Simon & Schuster, 1983); T. M. Amabile, B. A. Hennessey, and B. S. Grossman, "Social Influences on Creativity: The Effects of Contracted-for-Reward," *Journal of Personality and Social Psychology* 50 (1986): 14–23.

©Eastcott Momatiuk/Digital Vision/Getty Images

nate walls and cubicles so that employees can interact more frequently. When people mix, ideas mix as well.[55] Organizations can therefore enhance individuals' creative decision making by providing a supportive environment, participative decision making, and a flexible structure.

Individual–Organization Fit Research has indicated that creative performance is highest when there is a match, or fit, between the individual and organizational influences on creativity. When individuals who desire to be creative are matched with an organization that values creative ideas, the result is more creative performance.[56]

A common mistaken assumption regarding creativity is that either you have it or you do not. Research refutes this myth and has shown that individuals can be trained to be more creative.[57] The Disney Institute, for example, features a wide range of programs offered to companies, and one of their best-sellers is creativity training. Part of creativity training involves learning to open up *mental locks* that keep us from generating creative alternatives to a decision or problem. Following are some mental locks that diminish creativity:

> Searching for the "right" answer
> Trying to be logical
> Following the rules
> Avoiding ambiguity
> Striving for practicality
> Being afraid to look foolish
> Avoiding problems outside our own expertise
> Fearing failure
> Believing we are not really creative
> Not making play a part of work[58]

Note that many of these mental locks stem from values within organizations.

Organizations can facilitate creative decision making in many ways. Rewarding creativity, allowing employees to fail, making work more fun, and providing creativity training are a few suggestions. Another way companies can encourage creativity is by exposing employees to new ideas through job rotation. As employees move through different jobs, they can be exposed to different information, projects, and teams, either within or outside the company. Finally, managers can encourage employees to surround themselves with stimuli that they have found to enhance their creative pro-

cesses. These may be music, artwork, books, or anything else that encourages creative thinking.[59]

We have seen that both individual and organizational factors can produce creativity. Another important point to make about creativity is that it means finding problems as well as fixing them. Four different types of creativity in regard to this idea of finding problems have been proposed based on the source of the trigger (internal or external) and the source of the problem (presented versus discovered):

> *Responsive creativity* means responding to a problem that is presented to you by others because it is part of your job.
> *Expected creativity* is discovering problems because the organization expects you to do so.
> *Contributory creativity* is responding to problems presented to you because you want to be creative.
> *Proactive creativity* is discovering problems because you want to be creative.[60]

3M consistently ranks among the top ten in *Fortune's* annual list of most admired corporations. It earned this reputation through innovation. More than one-quarter of 3M's sales are from products less than four years old. Post-It Notes, for example, were created by a worker who wanted little adhesive papers to mark pages in his hymnbook for church service. He thought of another worker who had perfected a light adhesive, and the two spent their free time developing Post-It Notes. 3M has continued its tradition of innovation with Post-It Flags, Pop-Up Tape Strips, and Nexcare Ease-Off Bandages.

3M's products, such as Scotch tape and coatings for flat-panel televisions, benefit from the company's continuous efforts to innovate.

Leaders can play key roles in modeling creative behavior. Sir Richard Branson, founder and chairman of U.K.–based Virgin Group, believes that if you do not use your employees' creative potential, you are doomed to failure. At Virgin Group, the culture encourages risk taking and rewards innovation rather than following rules and regulations. "Analyzing ideas to death" is avoided. Branson says an employee should be able to have an idea in the morning and implement it that afternoon.[61]

LEARNING OUTCOME 4

The Group Decision-Making Process

Managers use groups to make decisions for several reasons. One is **synergy**, which occurs when group members stimulate new solutions to problems through the process of mutual influence and encouragement within the group. Another reason for using a group is to gain commitment to a decision. Groups also bring more knowledge and experience to the problem-solving situation.

Group decisions can sometimes be predicted by comparing the views of the initial group members with the final group decision. These simple relationships are known as **social decision schemes**. One social decision scheme is the *majority-wins rule*, in which the group supports whatever position is taken by the majority of its members. Another scheme, the *truth-wins rule*, predicts that the correct decision will emerge as an increasing number of members realize its appropriateness. The *two-thirds-majority rule* means that the decision favored by two-thirds or more of the members is supported. Finally, the *first-shift rule* states that members support a decision represented by the first shift in opinion shown by a member.

Research indicates that these social decision schemes can predict a group decision as much as 80 percent of the time.[62] Current research is aimed at discovering which rules are used in particular types of tasks. For example, studies indicate that the majority-wins rule is used most often in judgment tasks (that is, when the decision is a matter of preference or opinion), whereas the truth-wins rule predicts decisions best when the task is an intellective one (that is, when the decision has a correct answer).[63]

synergy
A positive force that occurs in groups when group members are stimulated to produce new solutions to problems through the process of mutual influence and encouragement within the group.

social decision schemes
Simple rules used to determine final group decisions.

groupthink
A deterioration of mental efficiency, reality testing, and moral judgment resulting from pressures within the group.

Advantages and Disadvantages of Group Decision Making

Group decision making has advantages and disadvantages. The advantages of group decision making include (1) more knowledge and information through the pooling of group member resources, (2) increased acceptance of and commitment to the decision because the members had a voice in it, and (3) greater understanding of the decision because members were involved in the various stages of the decision process. The disadvantages of group decision making include (1) pressure within the group to conform and fit in, (2) domination of the group by one forceful member or a dominant clique who may ramrod the decision, and (3) the amount of time required because a group makes decisions more slowly than an individual.[64]

Given these advantages and disadvantages, should decisions be made by an individual or a group? Substantial empirical research indicates that effectively making that determination depends on the type of task involved. For judgment tasks requiring an estimate or a prediction, groups are usually superior to individuals because of the breadth of experience that multiple individuals bring to the problem.[65] On tasks that have a correct solution, other studies have indicated that the most competent individual outperforms the group.[66] This finding has been called into question, however. Much of the previous research on groups was conducted in the laboratory, where group members interacted only for short periods of time. Researchers wanted to know how a longer group experience would affect decisions. Their study showed that groups who worked together for longer periods of time outperformed the most competent member 70 percent of the time. As groups gained experience, the best members became less important to the group's success.[67] This study demonstrated that experience in the group is an important variable to consider when evaluating the individual versus group decision-making question.

Given the emphasis on teams in the workplace, many managers believe that groups produce better decisions than individuals, yet the evidence is mixed. More research needs to be conducted in organizational settings to help answer this question.

Limits of Group Decision Making

There are two potential liabilities in group decision making: groupthink and group polarization.

Groupthink One liability of a cohesive group is its tendency to develop the dysfunctional process of **groupthink**. Irving Janis, the originator of this concept, describes groupthink as "a deterioration of mental efficiency, reality testing, and moral judgment" resulting

TABLE 10.1 Symptoms of Groupthink and How to Prevent It

SYMPTOMS OF GROUPTHINK

- *Illusions of invulnerability.* Group members feel that they are above criticism. This symptom leads to excessive optimism and risk taking.
- *Illusions of group morality.* Group members feel they are moral in their actions and therefore above reproach. This symptom leads the group to ignore the ethical implications of their decisions.
- *Illusions of unanimity.* Group members believe there is unanimous agreement on the decisions. Silence is misconstrued as consent.
- *Rationalization.* Group members concoct explanations for their decisions to make them appear rational and correct. The results are that other alternatives are not considered, and there is an unwillingness to reconsider the group's assumptions.
- *Stereotyping the enemy.* Competitors are stereotyped as evil or stupid. This leads the group to underestimate its opposition.
- *Self-censorship.* Members do not express their doubts or concerns about the course of action. This prevents critical analysis of the decisions.
- *Peer pressure.* Any members who express doubts or concerns are pressured by other group members who question their loyalty.
- *Mindguards.* Some members take it upon themselves to protect the group from negative feedback. Group members are thus shielded from information that might lead them to question their actions.

GUIDELINES FOR PREVENTING GROUPTHINK

- Ask each group member to assume the role of the critical evaluator who actively voices objections or doubts.
- Have the leader avoid stating his or her position on the issue prior to the group decision.
- Create several groups that work on the decision simultaneously.
- Bring in outside experts to evaluate the group process.
- Appoint a devil's advocate to question the group's course of action consistently.
- Evaluate the competition carefully, posing as many different motivations and intentions as possible.
- Once consensus is reached, encourage the group to rethink its position by reexamining the alternatives.

SOURCE: From Breckler/Wiggins/Olson. *Social Psychology Alive!*, 1E. © 2008 Nelson Education Ltd. Reproduced by permission. www.cengage.com/permissions

from pressures within the group.[68] One of the conditions that leads to the development of groupthink is high cohesiveness. Cohesive groups tend to favor solidarity because members identify strongly with the group.[69] High-ranking teams that make decisions without outside help are especially prone to groupthink because they are likely to have shared mental models; that is, they are more likely to think alike.[70] Homogeneous groups (ones with little to no diversity among members) are more likely to suffer from groupthink.[71]

Two other conditions that encourage groupthink are (1) having to make a highly consequential decision and (2) time constraints.[72] A highly consequential decision is one that will have a great impact on the group members and on outside parties. Time restraints may cause group members to rush through the decision-making process. Both conditions can influence members to desire concurrence in decisions so much that they fail to evaluate one another's suggestions critically. A group suffering from groupthink shows recognizable symptoms. Table 10.1 presents these symptoms and makes suggestions on how to avoid groupthink.

An incident cited as a prime example of groupthink is the 1986 space shuttle *Challenger* disaster, in which the shuttle exploded, killing all seven crew members. A

The 1986 explosion of the space shuttle *Challenger* is an oft-cited example of groupthink.

presidential commission concluded that flawed decision making was the primary cause of the accident. In 2003, the shuttle *Columbia* exploded over Texas upon reentering the earth's atmosphere, killing all seven crew members. Within days of the *Columbia*

AP Images/NASA

disaster, questions began to surface about the decision-making process that led flight engineers to assume that damage caused to the shuttle upon take-off was minor and to continue the mission. The subsequent investigation of the disaster led observers to note that NASA's decision-making process appears just as flawed in 2003 as it was in 1986, exhibiting all the classic symptoms of groupthink. The final accident report blamed the NASA culture that downplayed risk and suppressed dissent for the decision.[73]

Consequences of groupthink include an incomplete survey of alternatives, failure to evaluate the risks of the preferred course of action, biased information processing, and a failure to work out contingency plans. Furthermore, groupthink may be a contributor to corruption in organizations. Beech-Nut sold millions of dollars of phony apple juice, and investigations indicated that employees were aware that the company had been using cheap concentrate. Employees rationalized their actions by saying that other companies were selling fake juice, and that it was safe to consume. Ultimately, after incurring $25 million in fines and legal costs, the company was almost destroyed.[74]

Table 10.1 presents Janis's guidelines for avoiding groupthink. Many of these suggestions center around ensuring that decisions are evaluated completely, with opportunities for discussion from all group members. This strategy encourages members to evaluate one another's ideas critically. Groups that are educated about the value of diversity tend to perform better as a result. Less successful are groups that are homogenous and not educated about the value of diversity.[75]

Janis has used the groupthink framework to conduct historical analyses of several political and military fiascoes, including the Bay of Pigs invasion, the Vietnam War, and Watergate. One review of the decision situation in the *Challenger* incident proposed that two variables, time and leadership style, are important to include.[76] When a decision must be made quickly, there is more potential for groupthink. Leadership style can either promote groupthink (if the leader makes his or her opinion known up front) or avoid groupthink (if the leader encourages open and frank discussion).

There are few empirical studies of groupthink, and most of these involved students in a laboratory setting. More applied research may be seen in the future, however, as a questionnaire has been developed to measure the constructs associated with groupthink.[77] Janis's work on groupthink has led to several interdisciplinary efforts at understanding policy decisions.[78] The work underscores the

group polarization

The tendency for group discussion to produce shifts toward more extreme attitudes among members.

need to examine multiple explanations for failed decisions. Teams that experience cognitive (task-based) conflict are found to make better decisions than teams that experience affective (emotion-based) conflict. As such, one prescription for managers has been to encourage cognitive conflict while minimizing affective conflict. However, these two forms of conflict can also occur together and more research is needed on how one can be encouraged while minimizing the other.[79]

Group Polarization Another group phenomenon was discovered by a graduate student. His study showed that groups and individuals within the group made riskier decisions and accepted greater levels of risk following a group discussion of the issue. Subsequent studies uncovered another shift—toward caution. Thus, group discussion produced shifts both toward more risky positions and toward more cautious positions.[80] Further research revealed that individual group member attitudes simply became more extreme following group discussion. Individuals who were initially against an issue became more radically opposed, and individuals who were in favor of the issue became more strongly supportive following discussion. These shifts came to be known as **group polarization**.[81]

The tendency toward polarization has important implications for group decision making. Groups whose initial views lean a certain way can be expected to adopt more extreme views following interaction between members. Several ideas have been proposed to explain why group polarization occurs. One explanation is the *social comparison approach*. Prior to group discussion, individuals believe they hold better views than the other members. During group discussion, they see that their views are not so far from average, so they shift to more extreme positions.[82] A second explanation is the *persuasive arguments view*. It contends that group discussion reinforces the initial views of the members, so they take a more extreme position.[83] Both explanations are supported by research. It may be that both processes, along with others, cause the group to develop more polarized attitudes.

In sum, group polarization leads groups to adopt extreme attitudes. In some cases, this can be disastrous. For instance, if individuals are leaning toward a dangerous decision, they are likely to support it more strongly following discussion. A recent study found that after discussing hiring decisions as a group, employers were less accurate in their ratings and were more susceptible both to contrast effects and halo effects.[84]

Both groupthink and group polarization are potential liabilities of group decision making, but several techniques can be used to help prevent or control these two liabilities.

Techniques for Group Decision Making

Once a manager has determined that a group decision approach should be used, he can determine the technique that is best suited to the decision situation. Seven techniques will be briefly summarized: brainstorming, nominal group technique, devil's advocacy, dialectical inquiry, quality circles and quality teams, and self-managed teams.

Brainstorming Brainstorming is a good technique for generating alternatives. The idea behind **brainstorming** is to generate as many ideas as possible, suspending evaluation until all of the ideas have been suggested. Participants are encouraged to build upon the suggestions of others, and imagination is emphasized. One company that benefits from brainstorming is Toyota. Despite its success with the baby-boomer generation, Toyota's executives realized that they were failing to connect with younger buyers who viewed the firm as stodgy. In response, Toyota assembled a group of younger employees to brainstorm new products for this market. The result was Scion, an entirely new line of boxy crossover vehicles aimed at the younger set.[85]

Evidence suggests, however, that group brainstorming is less effective than a comparable number of individuals working alone. This may be because in groups, participants engage in discussions that can make them lose their focus.[86]

Nominal Group Technique A structured approach to decision making that focuses on generating alternatives and choosing one is called **nominal group technique (NGT)**, which involves the following discrete steps:

©Image Source Pink/Jupiterimages

©Stocktrek/Digital Vision/Getty Images

1. Individuals silently list their ideas.
2. Ideas are written on a chart one at a time until all ideas are listed.
3. Discussion is permitted but only to clarify the ideas. No criticism is allowed.
4. A written vote is taken.

NGT is a good technique to use in a situation where group members fear criticism from others.[87]

Devil's Advocacy In the **devil's advocacy** decision method, a group or individual is given the role of critic. This devil's advocate has the task of coming up with the potential problems of a proposed decision. By identifying potential pitfalls in advance, organizations can often avoid costly mistakes in decision making.[88]

---

brainstorming
A technique for generating as many ideas as possible on a given subject while suspending evaluation until all the ideas have been suggested.

nominal group technique (NGT)
A structured approach to group decision making that focuses on generating alternatives and choosing one.

devil's advocacy
A technique for preventing groupthink in which a group or individual is given the role of critic during decision making.

As we discussed in Chapter 9, a devil's advocate who challenges the CEO and top management team can help sustain the vitality and performance of the upper echelon.

Dialectical Inquiry
Dialectical inquiry is essentially a debate between two opposing sets of recommendations. Although it sets up a conflict, it is a constructive approach, because it brings out the benefits and limitations of both sets of ideas.[89] However, when using this technique, it is important to guard against a win–lose attitude and to concentrate on reaching the most effective solution for all concerned. Research has shown that the way a decision is framed (that is, win–win versus win–lose) is very important. A decision's outcome could be viewed as a gain or a loss depending on the way the decision is framed.[90]

Factors in Selecting the Appropriate Technique

Before choosing a group decision-making technique, the manager should carefully evaluate the group members and the decision situation. Only then can the best method for accomplishing the objectives of the group decision-making process be selected. If the goal is generating a large number of alternatives, for example, brainstorming would be a good choice. If group members are reluctant to contribute ideas, the nominal group technique would be appropriate. The need for expert input would be best facilitated by the Delphi technique, which uses a panel of experts. To guard against groupthink, devil's advocacy or dialectical inquiry would be effective. Decisions that concern quality or production would benefit from the advice of quality circles or the empowered decisions of quality teams. Moreover, recent research results suggest that if individuals within a team are made accountable for the process of decision making (rather than the end decision itself), then such teams are more likely to gather diverse information, share information, and eventually make better decisions.[91] Finally, a manager who wants to provide total empowerment to a group should consider self-managed teams.

Special Decision-Making Groups

Even though in organizations many types of groups make collective decisions, quality-oriented groups and self-managed teams have higher levels of involvement and authority in group decision making.

Quality Circles and Quality Teams
A **quality circle** is a small group of employees who work voluntarily on company time, typically one hour per week, to address work-related problems such as quality control, cost reduction, production planning and techniques, and even product design. Quality circles also extend participative decision making into teams. Managers often listen to recommendations from quality circles and implement the suggestions. Involvement in the decision-making process is the primary reward.

Quality circles are not empowered to implement their own recommendations. They operate in parallel fashion to the organization's structure, and they rely on voluntary participation.[92] In Japan, quality circles have been integrated into the organization instead of being added on. This may be one reason for Japan's success with this technique. In contrast, the U.S. experience is not as positive. It has been estimated that 60 to 75 percent of the quality circles in U.S. firms have failed. Reasons for the failures have included a lack of top management support and a lack of problem-solving skills among quality circle members.[93]

Quality teams, in contrast, are included in total quality management and other quality improvement efforts as part of a change in the organization's structure. Quality teams are generated from the top down and are empowered to act on their own recommendations. Whereas qual-

dialectical inquiry
A debate between two opposing sets of recommendations.

quality circle
A small group of employees who work voluntarily on company time, typically one hour per week, to address work-related problems such as quality control, cost reduction, production planning and techniques, and even product design.

quality team
A team that is part of an organization's structure and is empowered to act on its decisions regarding product and service quality.

ity circles emphasize the generation of ideas, quality teams make data-based decisions about improving product and service quality. Various decision-making techniques are employed in quality teams. Brainstorming, flowcharts, and cause-and-effect diagrams help pinpoint problems that affect quality.

Quality circles and quality teams are methods for using groups in the decision-making process. Self-managed teams take the concept of participation one step further.

Self-Managed Teams Another group decision-making method is the use of self-managed teams, which we discussed in Chapter 9. The decision-making activities of self-managed teams are more broadly focused than those of quality circles and quality teams. Self-managed teams make many of the decisions that were once reserved for managers, such as work scheduling, job assignments, and staffing.

Many organizations have claimed success with self-managed teams. At Northern Telecom (now Nortel Networks), revenues rose 63 percent and sales increased 26 percent following the implementation of self-managed teams.[94] Research evidence shows that self-managed teams can lead to higher productivity, lower turnover among employees, and flatter organization structure.[95]

Self-managed teams, like any cohesive group, can fall victim to groupthink. The key to stimulating innovation and better problem solving in these groups is welcoming dissent among members. Dissent breaks down complacency and sets in motion a process that results in better decisions. Team members must know that dissent is permissible so that they won't fear embarrassment or ridicule.[96]

LEARNING OUTCOME 5

Diversity and Culture in Decision Making

Styles of decision making vary greatly among cultures. Many of the dimensions proposed by Hofstede that were presented in Chapter 2 affect decision making. Uncertainty avoidance, for example, can affect the way people view decisions. In the United States, a culture with low uncertainty avoidance, decisions are seen as opportunities for change. In contrast, cultures such as those of Indonesia and Malaysia attempt to accept situations as they are rather than try to change them.[97] Power distance also affects decision making. In more hierarchical cultures, such as India, top-level managers make nearly all decisions. In countries with low power distance, lower-level employees make many decisions. The Swedish culture exemplifies this type.

The individualist/collectivist dimension has implications for decision making. Japan, with its collectivist culture, favors group decisions. The United States has a more difficult time with group decisions because it is an individualistic culture. Time orientation affects the frame of reference of the decision. In China, with its long-term view, decisions are made with the future in mind. In the United States, many decisions are made considering only the short term.

The masculine/feminine dimension can be compared to the Jungian thinking/feeling preferences for decision making. Masculine cultures, as in many Latin American countries, value quick, assertive decisions. Feminine cultures, as in many Scandinavian countries, value decisions that reflect concern for others.

Recent research examining the effects of cultural diversity on decision making has found that when individuals in a group are racially dissimilar, they engage in more open information sharing, encourage dissenting perspectives, and arrive at better decisions than racially similar groups.[98] Other kinds of diversity, such as functional background, have been studied as well. Top management teams that have members who come from a variety of functional backgrounds (for example, marketing, accounting, information systems) engage in greater debate in decision making than top management teams in which the members come from similar backgrounds. This diversity results in better financial performance for the firm.[99] Research also indicates that strategic decision making in firms can vary widely by culture. For example, one such source of variation stems from the differential emphasis placed on environmental scanning in different cultures. Furthermore, strategic decision making might appear rational but is also informed by firm level and national characteristics.[100]

LEARNING OUTCOME 6

Participation in Decision Making

Effective management of people can improve a company's economic performance. Firms that capitalize on this fact share several common practices. Chief among them is participation of employees in decision making.[101] Many companies do this through highly empowered self-managed teams. Even in situations where formal teams are not feasible, decision authority can be handed down to frontline employees who have the knowledge and skills to make a difference. At Hampton Inn hotels, for example, guest services personnel are empowered to do whatever is necessary to make guests happy—without consulting their superiors.

The Effects of Participation

Participative decision making occurs when individuals who are affected by decisions influence the making of those decisions. Participation buffers employees from the negative experiences of organizational politics.[102] Participation in decisions such as how technology is developed has also been found to affect employee's attitudes toward the technology and how they use it.[103] In addition, participative management has been found to increase employee creativity, job satisfaction, and productivity.[104] GE Capital is one company that believes in participation. Each year it holds "dreaming sessions," in which employees from all levels of the company attend strategy and budget meetings to discuss where the company is heading.

As our economy becomes increasingly based on knowledge work and as new technologies make it easier for decentralized decision makers to connect, participative decision making will undoubtedly increase.[105] Consider the city and county of San Francisco, a combined city/county government organization. Needing to adopt a single messaging system to meet the requirements of more than 20,000 employees, it faced a huge challenge in getting all the users to provide input into the decision. Technology helped craft a system that balanced the needs of all the groups involved, and IT planners developed a twenty-eight page spreadsheet to pull together the needs and desires of all sixty departments into a focused decision matrix. Within two years, 90 percent of the users had agreed on and moved to a single system, reducing costs and complexity.[106]

participative decision making
Decision making in which individuals who are affected by decisions influence the making of those decisions.

Foundations for Participation and Empowerment

What conditions must be in place in order for participative decision making to work? The organizational foundations include a supportive organizational culture and a team-oriented work design. A supportive work environment is essential because of the uncertainty within the organization. Lower-level organizational members must be able to make decisions and take action on them. As operational employees are encouraged to take part in making decisions, however, fear, anxiety, or even terror can be created among middle managers in the organization.[107] Thus, senior leadership must create an organizational culture that is supportive and reassuring for these middle managers as the power dynamics of the system change.

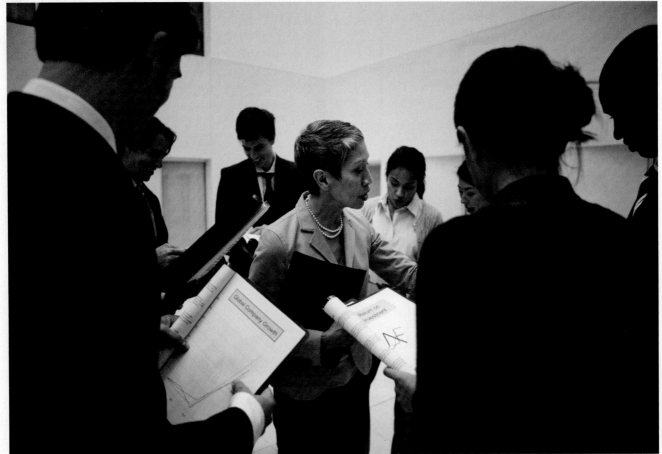

©Ben Bloom/Stone/Getty Images

> *If participative decision making is to work, employees must be able to comprehend how it provides a personal benefit to them.*

A second organizational foundation for participative decision making concerns the design of work. A team-oriented work design is a key organizational foundation because it leads to broader tasks and a greater sense of responsibility. For example, Volvo builds cars using a team-oriented work design in which each person does many different tasks; therefore, each person retains direct responsibility for the finished product.[108] These work designs create a context for effective participation.

The three individual prerequisites for participative decision making are

1. The capability to become psychologically involved in participative activities
2. The motivation to act autonomously
3. The capacity to see the relevance of participation for one's own well-being[109]

First, people must be psychologically equipped to become involved in participative activities if they are to be effective team members. Not all people are so predisposed. For example, Germany has an authoritarian tradition that runs counter to participative decision making at the individual and group levels. As a result, General Motors encountered significant difficulties implementing quality circles in its German plants because workers expected to be directed by supervisors, not to engage in participative problem solving. New initiatives to establish supervisory/worker boards in German corporations are intended to change this authoritarian tradition.

The second individual prerequisite is the motivation to act autonomously. People with dependent personalities are predisposed to be told what to do and to rely on external motivation rather than internal, intrinsic motivation.[110] These dependent people are not often effective contributors to decision making.

Finally, if participative decision making is to work, employees must be able to comprehend how it provides a personal benefit to them. The personal payoff for the individual need not be short term. It may be a long-term benefit that results in workers receiving greater rewards through enhanced organizational profitability.

What Level of Participation?

Participative decision making is complex, and one of the things managers must understand is that employees can be involved in some, or all, of the stages of the decision-making process. For example, employees could be variously involved in identifying problems, generating alternatives, selecting solutions, planning implementations, or evaluating results. Research shows that greater involvement in all five of these stages has a cumulative effect. Employees who are involved in all five processes have higher satisfaction and performance levels. And, all decision processes are not created equal. If employees can't be provided with full participation in all stages, they should be involved in the stages that seem to have the highest payoffs: generating alternatives, planning implementations, and evaluating results.[111] Styles of participation in decision making may need to change as the company grows or as its culture changes.

Log in to the **CourseMate** for *ORGB3* at **www.cengagebrain.com** to:

* Review **Key Terms Flash Cards** online
* Play **Beat the Clock** and **Quiz Bowl** to master concepts
* Complete **web quizzes** to prepare for exams
* Watch the video on **Plant Fantasies** and from *Failure to Launch* for examples, then test yourself with a quick quiz
* Work through the **"What about You?"** and **Ethical Dilemma** exercises to see how you would handle various situations that organizations face on a daily basis

Power and Political Behavior

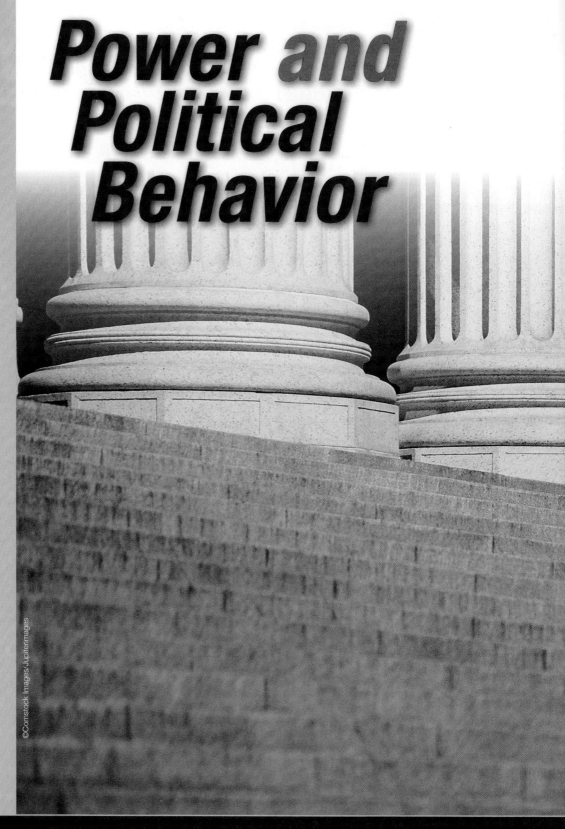

©Comstock Images/Jupiterimages

LEARNING OUTCOMES

1 Describe the concept of power.

2 Identify forms and sources of power in organizations.

3 Describe the role of ethics in using power.

4 Identify symbols of power and powerless-ness in organizations.

5 Define *organizational politics* and understand the role of political skill and major influence tactics.

6 Identify ways to manage political behavior in organizations.

> *Individuals have many forms of power to use in their work settings.*

After You Finish
This Chapter
Go to **Page 191**
for **Study Tools**

The Concept of Power

Power is the ability to influence another person. As an exchange relationship, it occurs in transactions between an agent and a target. The *agent* is the person using the power, and the *target* is the recipient of the attempt to use power.[1] Because power is an ability, individuals can learn to use it effectively, employing either influence or authority or both. **Influence** is the process of affecting the thoughts, behavior, and feelings of another person. **Authority** is the right to influence another person.[2] It is important to understand the subtle differences among these terms. For instance, a manager may have authority but no power. She may have the right, by virtue of her position as boss, to tell someone what to do. But she may not have the skill or ability to influence other people.

In a relationship between the agent and the target, there are many influence attempts that the target will consider legitimate. Working forty hours per week, greeting customers, solving problems, and collecting bills are actions that, when requested by the manager, are considered legitimate by a customer service representative. Requests such as these fall within the employee's **zone of indifference**—the range in which attempts to influence the employee are perceived as legitimate and are acted on without a great deal of thought.[3] The employee accepts that the manager has the authority to request such behaviors and complies with the requests. Some requests, however, fall outside the zone of indifference, so there the manager must work to enlarge the employee's zone of indifference.

power
The ability to influence another person.

influence
The process of affecting the thoughts, behavior, and feelings of another person.

authority
The right to influence another person.

zone of indifference
The range in which attempts to influence a person will be perceived as legitimate and will be acted on without a great deal of thought.

Enlarging the zone is accomplished with power (an ability) rather than with authority (a right).

Suppose the manager asks an employee to purchase a birthday gift for the manager's wife or to overcharge a customer for a service call. The employee may think that the manager has no right to ask these things. These requests fall outside the zone of indifference. They're viewed as extraordinary, and the manager has to operate from outside the authority base to induce the employee to fulfill them. In some cases, no power base is enough to induce the employee to comply, especially if the employee considers the behaviors requested by the manager to be unethical.

LEARNING OUTCOME 2

Forms and Sources of Power in Organizations

Individuals have many forms of power to use in their work settings. Some of them are interpersonal—that is, used in interactions with others. One of the earliest and most influential theories of power comes from John French and Bertram Raven, who tried to determine both the forms and the sources of power managers use to influence other people.

Interpersonal Forms of Power

French and Raven identified five forms of interpersonal power that managers use: reward, coercive, legitimate, referent, and expert power.[4]

reward power
Power based on an agent's ability to control rewards that a target wants.

coercive power
Power that is based on an agent's ability to cause an unpleasant experience for a target.

legitimate power
Power that is based on position and mutual agreement; agent and target agree that the agent has the right to influence the target.

referent power
An elusive power that is based on interpersonal attraction.

expert power
The power that exists when an agent has specialized knowledge or skills that the target needs.

Reward power is power based on an agent's ability to control rewards that a target wants, such as salary increases, bonuses, and promotions. Reward power can lead to better performance, but only as long as the employee sees a clear and strong link between performance and rewards. To use reward power effectively, then, the manager should be explicit about the behavior being rewarded and should make the connection clear between the behavior and the reward.

Coercive power is power that is based on an agent's ability to cause the target to have an unpleas-

ant experience. To coerce someone into doing something means to force the person to do it, often with threats of punishment. Managers using coercive power may verbally abuse employees or withhold support from them.

Legitimate power, which is similar to authority, is power that is based on position and mutual agreement. The agent and target agree that the agent has the right to influence the target. Just because a manager thinks he has the right to influence his employees doesn't mean that he will have legitimate power in their eyes. For legitimate power to be effective, the employees must also believe the manager has the right to tell them what to do. For example, in Native American societies, the chief has legitimate power because tribe members believe in his right to influence the decisions in their lives.

Referent power is an elusive power that is based on interpersonal attraction. The agent has referent power over the target because the target identifies with or wants to be like the agent. Charismatic individuals are often thought to have referent power. Interestingly, the agent need not be superior to the target in any way. People who use referent power well are most often individualistic and respected by the target.

Expert power is the power that exists when an agent has specialized knowledge or skills that the target needs. For expert power to work, three conditions must be in place. First, the target must trust that the expertise given is accurate. Second, the knowledge involved must be relevant and useful to the target. Third, the target's perception of the agent as an expert is crucial. Using easy-to-understand language signals the target that the expert has an appreciation for real-world concerns and increases the target's trust in the expert.[5]

Which type of interpersonal power is most effective? Research has focused on this question since French and Raven introduced their five forms of power. Some of the results are surprising. Reward power and coercive power have similar effects.[6] Both lead to compliance. That is, employees will do what the manager asks them to, at least temporarily, if the manager offers a reward or threatens them with punishment. Reliance on these sources of power is dangerous, however, because it may require the manager to be physically present and watchful in order to apply rewards or punishment when the behavior occurs. Constant surveillance creates an uncomfortable situation for managers and employees and eventually results in a dependency relationship: employees will not work unless the manager is present.

Legitimate power also leads to compliance. When told "Do this because I'm your boss," most employees will comply. However, the use of legitimate power has not been linked to organizational effectiveness or to employee satisfaction.[7] In organizations where managers rely heavily on legitimate power, organizational goals are not necessarily met.

Referent power is linked with organizational effectiveness. It is the most dangerous power, however, because it can be too extensive and intensive in altering the behavior of others. Charismatic leaders need an accompanying sense of responsibility for others. An example of a good use of referent power is Christopher Reeve's power as spokesperson for research on spinal injuries and stem cell research.

Expert power has been called the power of the future.[8] Of the five forms of power, it has the strongest relationship with performance and satisfaction. It is through expert power that vital skills, abilities, and knowledge are passed on within the organization. Employees internalize what they observe and learn from managers they perceive to be experts.

The results on the effectiveness of these five forms of power pose a challenge in organizations. The least effective power bases—legitimate, reward, and coercive—are the ones most likely to be used by managers.[9] Managers inherit these power bases as part of the position when they take a supervisory job. In contrast, the most effective power bases—referent and expert—are ones that must be developed and strengthened through interpersonal relationships with employees. Marissa Mayer, vice president of search products and user experience at Google, is an example of someone with expert power and referent power. Well respected and liked by her colleagues, she is described as someone with a lot of technical knowledge, and she is comfortable in social environments. Her expert power comes from the fact that she has an advanced degree in computer science from Stanford University. Her referent power comes from her ability to connect with people. At thirty-three years old, she has had a very successful career at Google and was recently ranked forty-second on *Fortune*'s fifty most powerful people in the world.[10] Expert power and social networks help CEOs influence their top management teams in ways that are profitable for the firm.

©Ryan Anson/AFP/Getty Images

Steve Jobs used his knowledge of the computer industry to exercise expert power at Apple.

Intergroup Sources of Power

Groups or teams within an organization can also use power from several sources. One source of intergroup power is control of *critical resources*.[11] When one group controls an important resource that another group desires, the first group holds power. Controlling resources needed by another group allows the power-holding group to influence the actions of the less powerful group. This process can continue in an upward spiral. Groups seen as powerful tend to be given more resources from top management.[12]

Groups also have power to the extent that they control **strategic contingencies**—activities that other groups depend on in order to complete their tasks.[13] The dean's office, for example, may control the number of faculty positions to be filled in each department of a college. The departmental hiring plans are thus contingent on approval from the dean's office. In this case, the dean's office controls the strategic contingency of faculty hiring, and thus has power.

Three factors can give a group control over a strategic contingency.[14] One is the *ability to cope with uncertainty*. If a group can help another group deal with uncertainty, it has power. One group that has gained power in recent years in most organizations is the legal department. Faced with increasing government regulations and fears of litigation, many other departments seek guidance from the legal department.

Another factor that can give a group control power is a *high degree of centrality* within the organization. If a group's functioning is important to the organization's success, it has high centrality. The sales force in a computer firm, for example, has power because of its immediate effect on the firm's operations and because other groups (accounting and

strategic contingencies
Activities that other groups depend on in order to complete their tasks.

servicing groups, for example) depend on its activities.

The third factor that can give a group power is *nonsubstitutability*—the extent to which a group performs a function that is indispensable to an organization. A team of computer specialists may be powerful because of its expertise with a system. It may have specialized experience that another team cannot provide.

The strategic contingencies model thus shows that groups hold power over other groups when they can reduce uncertainty, when their functioning is central to the organization's success, and when the group's activities are difficult to replace.[15] The key to all three of these factors, as you can see, is dependency. When one group controls something that another group needs, it creates a dependent relationship—and gives one group power over the other.

LEARNING OUTCOME 3

Using Power Ethically

Managers can work at developing all five forms of power for future use. The key to using them well is to use them ethically, as Table 11.1 shows. Coercive power, for example, requires careful administration if it is to be used in an ethical manner. Employees should be informed of the rules in advance, and any punishment should be used consistently, uniformly, and privately. The key to using all five types of interpersonal power ethically is to be sensitive to employees' concerns and to communicate well.

To French and Raven's five power sources we can add a source that is very important in today's organizations. **Information power** is access to and control over important information. Consider, for example, the CEO's administrative assistant. He has information about the CEO's schedule that people need if they are going to get in to see the CEO. Central to the idea of information power is the person's position within the communication networks in the organization, both formal and informal. Also important is the idea of *framing*, which is the "spin" that managers put on information. Managers not only pass information on to subordinates, they also interpret this information and influence the subordinates' perceptions of it. Information

information power

Access to and control over important information.

TABLE 11.1 Guidelines for the Ethical Use of Power

FORM OF POWER	GUIDELINES FOR USE
Reward Power	Verify compliance. Make feasible, reasonable requests. Make only ethical requests. Offer rewards desired by subordinates. Offer only credible rewards.
Coercive power	Inform subordinates of rules and penalties. Warn before punishing. Administer punishment consistently and uniformly. Understand the situation before acting. Maintain credibility. Fit punishment to the infraction. Punish in private.
Legitimate power	Be cordial and polite. Be confident. Be clear and follow up to verify understanding. Make sure request is appropriate. Explain reasons for request. Follow proper channels. Exercise power consistently. Enforce compliance. Be sensitive to subordinates' concerns.
Referent power	Treat subordinates fairly. Defend subordinates' interests. Be sensitive to subordinates' needs and feelings. Select subordinates similar to oneself. Engage in role modeling.
Expert power	Maintain credibility. Act confident and decisive. Keep informed. Recognize employee concerns. Avoid threatening subordinates' self-esteem.

SOURCE: G. A. Yuki, *Leadership in Organizations*, 1st Edition, © 1981. Reprinted by permission of Pearson Education, Inc., Upper Saddle River, N.J.

power may flow upward from subordinates to managers as well as downward from managers to subordinates. For instance, in manufacturing plants, database operators often control information about plant metrics and shipping performance that is vital to managerial decision making. Information power can also flow laterally. Salespeople convey information from the outside environment (their customers) that is essential for marketing efforts.

Determining whether a power-related behavior is ethical is complicated. One helpful method for establishing criteria in this respect is to ask three questions:[16]

1. *Does the behavior produce a good outcome for people both inside and outside the organization?* This question represents the criterion of *utilitarian outcomes*. The behavior should result in the great-

SCANDAL AT THE FIESTA BOWL

The Fiesta Bowl is a college football game that is held annually and estimated to have an economic impact of more than $200 million. The company that operates the game, however, recently fired its CEO, John Junker, for a series of expenditures that crossed both ethical and legal boundaries. Junker charged the company $1,241 for a lavish night at a strip club. He spent $33,881 of company money for his fiftieth birthday, and $13,086 for an employee wedding. He also used $22,000 of company money to buy gold and silver coins that he gave away as gifts. In addition to these lapses in judgment, Junker had employees of the company make contributions to campaigns of politicians and then reimbursed them with company money, an outright violation of campaign finance laws. When investigators began to probe into company finances, Junker coached witnesses so that they would lie for him and altered documents that were turned in for evidence.

SOURCE: A. Murphy and M. McKnight, "Fiesta Bowl Probe Results in Junker Dismissal, Casts Pall over BCS," *Sports Illustrated* (March 29, 2011), http://sportsillustrated.cnn.com/2011/football/ncaa/03/29/fiesta-bowl-junker/index.html, accessed June 10, 2011.

est good for the greatest number of people. If the power-related behavior serves only the individual's self-interest and fails to help the organization reach its goals, it is considered unethical. A salesperson might be tempted to deeply discount a product in order to make a sale that would win a contest. Doing so would be in her self-interest but would not benefit the organization.

2. *Does the behavior respect the rights of all parties?* This question emphasizes the criterion of *individual rights*. Free speech, privacy, and due process are individual rights that are to be respected, and power-related behaviors that violate these rights are considered unethical.

3. *Does the behavior treat all parties equitably and fairly?* This question represents the criterion of *distributive justice*. Power-related behavior that treats one party arbitrarily or benefits one party at the expense of another is unethical. Granting a day of vacation to one employee in a busy week in which coworkers must struggle to cover for him might be considered unethical.

To be considered ethical, power-related behavior must meet all three criteria. If the behavior fails to meet the criteria, then alternative actions should be considered.

Unfortunately, most power-related behaviors are not easy to analyze. Conflicts may exist among the criteria; for example, a behavior may maximize the greatest good for the greatest number of people but may not treat all parties equitably. Individual rights may need to be sacrificed for the good of the organization. A CEO may need to be removed from power for the organization to be saved. Still, these criteria can be used on a case-by-case basis to sort through the complex ethical issues surrounding the use of power. The ethical use of power is one of the hottest topics in the current business arena due to the abuse of power by top executives such as Bernie Madoff, who was convicted of running a $50 billion Ponzi scheme that financially ruined people and businesses around the world.

Positive versus Negative Power

We turn now to a theory of power that takes a strong stand on the "right" versus "wrong" kind of power to use in organizations. David McClelland has spent a great deal of his career studying the need for power and the ways managers use power. As was discussed in Chapter 5, he believes that there are two distinct faces of power, one negative and one positive.[17] The negative face of power is **personal power**—power used for personal gain. Managers who use personal power are commonly described as "power hungry." Former Illinois

personal power
Power used for personal gain.

Governor Rod Blagojevich allegedly used his power as an elected official to try to sell President Obama's Senate seat in exchange for money, ambassadorships, and even a salary for his wife. People who approach relationships with an exchange orientation often use personal power to ensure that they get at least their fair share—and often more—in the relationship. They are most interested in their own needs and interests. One way to encourage ethical behavior in organizations is to encourage *principled dissent*. This term refers to valid criticism that can benefit the organization rather than mere complaints about working conditions. Much like whistle-blowers, who can serve as checks on powerful people within the organization, dissenters can pinpoint wrongdoings, encourage employee voice in key issues, and create a climate conducive to the ethical use of power.[18]

Individuals who rely on personal power at its extreme might be considered *Machiavellian*—willing to do whatever it takes to get one's own way. Niccolo Machiavelli was an Italian statesman during the sixteenth century who wrote *The Prince*, a guide for acquiring and using power.[19] Among his methods for using power was manipulating others, believing that it was better to be feared than loved. Machiavellians (or high Machs) are willing to manipulate others for personal gain and are unconcerned with others' opinions or welfare.

The positive face of power is **social power**—power used to create motivation or to accomplish group goals. McClelland clearly favors the use of social power by managers. People who approach relationships with a communal orientation focus on the needs and interests of others. In other words, they rely on

social power.[20] McClelland has found that managers who use power successfully have four power-oriented characteristics:

1. *Belief in the authority system.* They believe that the institution is important and that its authority system is valid. They are comfortable influencing and being influenced. The source of their power is the authority system of which they are a part.

2. *Preference for work and discipline.* They like their work and are very orderly. They have a basic value preference for the Protestant work ethic, believing that work is good for a person over and beyond its income-producing value.

3. *Altruism.* They publicly put the company and its needs before their own needs. They are able to do this because they see their own well-being as integrally tied to the company's well-being.

4. *Belief in justice.* They believe justice is to be sought above all else. People should receive that to which they are entitled and that which they earn.

McClelland takes a definite stand on the proper use of power by managers. When power is used for the good of the group, rather than for individual gain, it is positive.

Symbols of Power

Organization charts show who has authority, but they do not reveal much about who has power. Two very different ideas about the symbols of power come from Rosabeth Moss Kanter and Michael Korda.

Kanter's Symbols of Power

Kanter offers a scholarly approach to determining who has power and who feels powerless, providing several characteristics of powerful people in organizations:[21]

1. *Ability to intercede for someone in trouble.* An individual who can pull someone out of a jam has power.

2. *Ability to get placements for favored employees.* Getting a key promotion for an employee is a sign of power.

3. *Exceeding budget limitations.* A manager who can go above budget limits without being reprimanded has power.

4. *Procuring above-average raises for employees.* One faculty member reported that her department head distributed 10 percent raises to the most productive faculty members although the budget allowed for only 4 percent increases. "I don't know how he did it; he must have pull," she said.

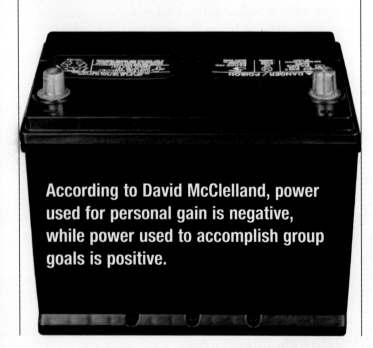

According to David McClelland, power used for personal gain is negative, while power used to accomplish group goals is positive.

©iStockphoto.com/Don Nichols

5. *Getting items on the agenda at meetings.* If a manager can raise issues for action at meetings, it's a sign of power.

6. *Access to early information.* Having information before anyone else does is a signal that a manager is plugged into key sources.

7. *Having top managers seek out their opinion.* When top managers have a problem, they may ask for advice from lower-level managers. The managers they turn to have power.

A theme that runs through Kanter's list is doing things for others—for people in trouble, for employees, for bosses. There is an active, other-directed element in her symbols of power. You can use Kanter's symbols of power to identify powerful people in organizations. They can be particularly useful in finding a mentor who can effectively use power.

Kanter's Symbols of Powerlessness

Kanter also wrote about symptoms of **powerlessness**—a lack of power—in managers at different levels of the organization. First-line supervisors, for example, often display three symptoms of powerlessness: overly close supervision, inflexible adherence to the rules, and a tendency to do the job themselves rather than training their employees to do it. Staff professionals such as accountants and lawyers display different symptoms of powerlessness. When they feel powerless, they tend to resist change and try to protect their turf. Top executives can also feel powerless. They show symptoms such as focusing on budget cutting, punishing others, and using dictatorial, top-down communication. Acting in certain ways can lead employees to believe that a manager is powerless. By making *external attributions* (blaming others or circumstances) for negative events, a manager looks as if she has no power.[22]

Korda's Symbols of Power

Michael Korda offers a semiserious look at some tangible symbols of power: office furnishings, time power, and standing by.[23] Furniture is not just physically useful; it also conveys a message about power. Locked file cabinets are signs that the manager has important and confidential information in the office. A rectangular (rather than round) conference table enables the most important person to sit at the head of the table. The size of one's desk may convey the amount of power, too, as most executives prefer large, expensive desks.

Time power means using clocks and watches as power symbols. Korda says that the biggest compliment a busy executive can pay a visitor is to remove his watch and place it facedown on the desk, thereby communicating "my time is yours." He also notes that the less powerful the executive, the more intricate the watch. Moreover, managers who are really secure in their power wear no watch at all, since they believe nothing important can happen without them. A full calendar is also proof of power. Personal planners are left open on the desk to display busy schedules.

Standing by is a game in which people are obliged to keep their cell phones, pagers, and so forth with them at all times so executives can reach them. The idea is that the more you can impose your schedule on other people, the more power you have. In fact, Korda defines *power* as follows: There are more people who inconvenience themselves on your behalf than there are people on whose behalf you would inconvenience yourself. Closely tied to this is the ability to make others perform simple tasks for you, such as getting your coffee or fetching the mail.

While Kanter's symbols focus on the ability to help others, Korda's symbols focus on status—a person's relative standing in a group based on prestige and having other people defer to him.[24] By identifying powerful people and learning from their modeled behavior, you can learn the keys to power use in the organization.

Political Behavior in Organizations

Like the word *power*, the phrase *politics in organizations* may conjure up negative images. However, **organizational politics** is not necessarily negative; it is the use of power and influence in organizations. Because organizations are arenas in which people have competing interests, effective managers must reconcile competing interests. Organizational politics are central to managing. As people try to acquire power and expand their power base, they use various tactics and strategies. Some are sanctioned (acceptable to the organization); others are not. **Political behavior** refers to actions not officially sanctioned by an organization that are taken to influence others in order to meet one's personal goals.[25] Sometimes personal goals are

powerlessness
A lack of power.

organizational politics
The use of power and influence in organizations.

political behavior
Actions not officially sanctioned by an organization that are taken to influence others in order to meet one's personal goals.

aligned with team or organizational goals, and they can be achieved in support of others' interests. But other times personal goals and the interests of others collide, and individuals pursue politics at the expense of others' interests.[26]

Politics is a controversial topic among managers. Some managers take a favorable view of political behavior; others see it as detrimental to the organization. Some workers who perceive their workplace as highly political actually find the use of political tactics more satisfying and report greater job satisfaction when they engage in political behavior. Some people may therefore thrive in political environments, while others may find office politics distasteful and stressful.[27] It's important to remember, however, that political behavior is not inherently constructive or destructive.[28]

Most people are also amazingly good at recognizing political behavior at all levels of the firm. Employees are not only keenly aware of political behavior at their level but can also spot political behavior at both their supervisor's level and the topmost levels of the organization.[29]

Many organizational conditions encourage political activity. Among them are unclear goals, autocratic decision making, ambiguous lines of authority, scarce resources, and uncertainty.[30] Moreover, even supposedly objective activities may involve politics. One such activity is the performance appraisal process. A study of sixty executives who had extensive experience in employee evaluation indicated that political considerations were nearly always part of the performance appraisal process.[31]

The effects of political behavior in organizations can be quite negative when the political behavior is strategically undertaken to maximize self-interest. If people within the organization are competitively pursuing selfish ends, they're unlikely to be attentive to the concerns of others. As a consequence, the workplace can seem less helpful, more threatening, and more unpredictable. When people focus on their own concerns rather than on organizational goals, we see the negative face of power described earlier by David McClelland as personal power. And when employees view the organization's political climate as extreme, they experience more anxiety, tension, fatigue, and burnout. They are also dissatisfied with their jobs and are more likely to leave.[32]

However, not all political behavior is destructive. Though positive political behavior still involves self-interest, when it is aligned with organizational goals, the self-interest is perceived positively by employees. Political behavior is also viewed positively when it is seen as the only means by which to accomplish something. Job satisfaction and satisfaction with coworkers and supervisors is affected by any kind of political behavior.[33]

Influence Tactics

Influence is the process of affecting the thoughts, behavior, or feelings of another person. That other person could be the boss (upward influence), an employee (downward influence), or a coworker (lateral influence). There are eight basic types of influence tactics. They are listed and described in Table 11.2.[34] Research has shown that the four tactics used most frequently are consultation, rational persuasion, inspirational appeals, and ingratiation. Upward appeals and coalition tactics are used moderately. Exchange tactics are used least often.

Influence tactics are used for *impression management*, which was described in Chapter 3. In impression management, individuals use influence tactics to control others' impressions of them. One way in which people engage in impression management is through image building. Another way is to use impression management to get support for important initiatives or projects.

[Trying to Influence Your Employees? Consider the Relationship.]

Managers have several options in regard to influence, but success may depend on more than which particular tactic is chosen. Recent research indicates that the ways employees view their relationships with their leaders impact the efficacy of the influence tactic. When leaders use ingratiation and employees feel they have good relationships with their supervisors, employees are less likely to resist change. When employees judge their relationships with supervisors to be poor, they are more likely to resist change when ingratiation is used. This holds true as well when leaders employ punishment or tactics that attempt to establish credibility. These findings indicate that before leaders determine how they should influence their followers, they need to consider the relationship. When the relationship is perceived as low quality by the employee, ingratiation, punishment, and legitimating tactics may result in increased resistance.

SOURCE: S. A. Furst and D. M. Cable, "Employee Resistance to Change: Managerial Influence Tactics and Leader–Member Exchange," *Journal of Applied Psychology* 93 (2008); 453–462.

©iStockphoto.com/4x6

TABLE 11.2 Influence Tactics Used in Organizations

TACTICS	DESCRIPTION	EXAMPLES
Pressure	The person uses demands, threats, or intimidation to convince you to comply with a request or to support a proposal.	If you don't do this, you're fired. You have until 5:00 to change your mind, or I'm going without you.
Upward appeals	The person seeks to persuade you that the request is approved by higher management or appeals to higher management for assistance in gaining your compliance with the request.	I'm reporting you to my boss. My boss supports this idea.
Exchange	The person makes an explicit or implicit promise that you will receive rewards or tangible benefits if you comply with a request or support a proposal or reminds you of a prior favor to be reciprocated.	You owe me a favor. I'll take you to lunch if you'll support me on this.
Coalition	The person seeks the aid of others to persuade you to do something or uses the support of others as an argument for you to agree also.	All the other supervisors agree with me. I'll ask you in front of the whole committee.
Ingratiation	The person seeks to get you in a good mood or to think favorably of him or her before asking you to do something.	Only you can do this job right. I can always count on you, so I have another request.
Rational persuasion	The person uses logical arguments and factual evidence to persuade you that a proposal or request is viable and likely to result in the attainment of task objectives.	This new procedure will save us $150,000 in overhead. It makes sense to hire John; he has the most experience.
Inspirational appeals	The person makes an emotional request or proposal that arouses enthusiasm by appealing to your values and ideals or by increasing your confidence that you can do it.	Being environmentally conscious is the right thing. Getting that account will be tough, but I know you can do it.
Consultation	The person seeks your participation in making a decision or planning how to implement a proposed policy, strategy, or change.	This new attendance plan is controversial. How can we make it more acceptable? What do you think we can do to make our workers less fearful of the new robots on the production line?

SOURCE: First two columns from G. Yukl and C. M. Falbe, "Influence Tactics and Objectives in Upward, Downward, and Lateral Influence Attempts," *Journal of Applied Psychology* 75 (1990): 132–140. Copyright © 1990 by the American Psychological Association. Reprinted with permission.

Ingratiation is an example of one tactic often used for impression management. Ingratiation can take many forms, including flattery, opinion conformity, and subservient behavior.[35] *Exchange* is another influence tactic that may be used for impression management. Offering to do favors for someone in an effort to create a favorable impression is an exchange tactic.

Which influence tactics are most effective? It depends on the target of the influence attempt and the objective. Individuals use different tactics for different purposes, and they use different tactics for different people. Influence attempts with subordinates, for example, usually involve assigning tasks or changing behavior. With peers, the objective is often to request help. With superiors, influence attempts are often made to request approval, resources, political support, or personal benefits. *Rational persuasion* and *coalition tactics* are used most often to get support from peers and superiors to change company policy. *Consultation* and *inspirational appeals* are particularly effective for gaining support and resources for a new project.[36] Overall, the most effective tactic in terms of achieving objectives is rational persuasion. *Pressure* is the least effective tactic.

Influence tactics are often used on bosses in order to get the boss to evaluate the employee more favorably or to give the employee a promotion. Two tactics—rational persuasion and ingratiation—appear to work effectively in this way. Employees who use these tactics receive higher performance evaluations than employees who don't.[37] When supervisors believe an employee's motive for doing favors for the boss is simply to be a good citizen, they are likely to reward that employee. However, when the motive is seen as "brownnosing" (ingratiation), supervisors respond negatively.[38] And, as it becomes more obvious that the employee has something to gain by impressing the boss, the likelihood that ingratiation will succeed decreases. So, how does one use ingratiation effectively?

Results from a study conducted among supervisors and subordinates of a large state agency indicate that subordinates with higher scores on political skill used ingratiation regularly and received higher performance ratings, whereas individuals with lower scores on political skill who used ingratiation frequently received lower performance ratings.[39] Additionally, another research study demonstrated that supervisors rated subordinate ingratiation behavior as less manipulative if the subordinate was highly politically skilled.[40] These results indicate that political skill might be one factor that enables people to use ingratiation effectively.

Still, well-disguised ingratiation is hard to resist. Attempts that are not obvious usually succeed in increasing the target's liking for the ingratiator.[41] Most people have trouble remaining neutral when someone flatters them or agrees with them. However, witnesses to the ingratiation are more likely to question the motive behind the flattery or agreement. Observers are more skeptical than the recipients of the ingratiation.

There is evidence that men and women view politics and influence attempts differently. Men tend to view political behavior more favorably than do women. When both men and women witness political behavior, they view it more positively if the agent is of their gender and the target is of the opposite gender.[42] Women executives often view politics with distaste and expect to be recognized and promoted only on the merit of their work. A lack of awareness of organizational politics is a barrier that holds women back in terms of moving into senior executive ranks.[43] Moreover, women may have fewer opportunities to develop political skills because of a lack of mentors and role models and because they are often excluded from informal networks.[44]

Different cultures prefer different influence tactics at work. One study found that American managers dealing with a tardy employee tended to rely on pressure tactics such as "If you don't start reporting on time for work, I will have no choice but to start docking your pay." In contrast, Japanese managers relied on influence tactics that either appealed to the employee's sense of duty ("It is your duty as a responsible employee of this company to begin work on time.") or emphasized a consultative approach ("Is there anything I can do to help you overcome the problems that are preventing you from coming to work on time?").[45]

Influence can also stem from the way a person's personality fits into his work environment. A recent study found that extraverts have more influence in team-oriented work environments, whereas conscientious employees have more influence in environments where individuals work alone on technical tasks.[46]

It is important to note that influence tactics do have some positive effects. When investors form coalitions and put pressure on firms to increase their research and development efforts, it works.[47] However, some influence tactics, including pressure, coalition building, and exchange, can have strong ethical implications. There is a fine line between being an impression manager and being seen as a manipulator.

How can a manager use influence tactics well? First, a manager can develop and maintain open lines of communication in all directions: horizontally, vertically and laterally. Then, the manager can treat the targets of influence attempts—whether managers, employees, or peers—with basic respect. Finally, the manager can understand that influence relationships are reciprocal—they are two-way relationships. As long as the influence attempts are directed toward organizational goals, the process of influence can be advantageous to all involved.

Political Skill

Researchers at Florida State University have generated an impressive body of research on political skill.[48] They have found that political skill is a distinct interpersonal attribute that is important for managerial success. Researchers suggest therefore that political skill should be considered in hiring and promotion decisions. Leaders' political skills have a positive effect on team performance, trust for the leader, and support for the leader.[49] Furthermore, political skill buffers the negative effects of stressors such as role conflict in work settings. This set of research findings points to the importance of developing political skill for managerial success.[50]

So what exactly is **political skill**? It is the ability to get things done through positive interpersonal relationships outside the formal organization. Politically skilled individuals have the ability to accurately understand others and use this knowledge to influence others in order to meet personal or organizational goals. Political skill is made up of four key dimensions; social astuteness, interpersonal influence, networking ability, and sincerity.

Social astuteness refers to the accurate perception and evaluation of social situations. Socially astute individuals manage social situations in ways that present them in the most favorable light. *Interpersonal influence* refers to a subtle and influential personal style that is effective in getting things done. Individuals with interpersonal influence are very flexible in adapting their behavior to differing targets of influence or differing contexts in order to achieve one's goals. *Networking ability* is an individual's capacity to develop and retain diverse and extensive social networks. People who have networking ability are effective in building successful alliances and coalitions, thus making them skilled at negotiation and conflict resolution. Finally, *sincerity* refers to an individual's ability to portray forthrightness and authenticity in all of his or her dealings. Individuals who can appear sincere inspire more confidence and trust, thus making them very successful in influencing other people.[51]

These four dimensions of political skill can each be learned. Several organizations now offer training to help develop their employees' political skill. Political skill is important at all levels of the organization. The most potent cause of failure among top executives is lack of social effectiveness.[52] High self-monitors and politically savvy individuals score higher on an index of political skill, as do individuals who are emotionally intelligent.

Military settings are particularly demanding in their need for leaders who can adapt to changing situations and maintain a good reputation. In such an environment, politically

skilled leaders are seen as more sincere in their motives, can more readily perceive and adapt to work events, and thus build a strong positive reputation among followers. In fact, political skill can be acquired through a social learning process and by having a strong mentor. Such a mentor serves as a role model and helps the protégé navigate organizational politics and learn the informal sources of power and politics in the organization.[53] Individuals who have political skill have been shown to be more likely to engage in OCBs, have more total promotions, have higher perceived career success, and greater life satisfaction.[54]

LEARNING OUTCOME 6

Managing Political Behavior in Organizations

Politics cannot and should not be eliminated from organizations. Managers should, however, take a proactive stance and manage the political behavior that inevitably occurs.[55] The first step in managing political behavior is to recognize it. Some behaviors to watch for include networking, finding key players to support initiatives, making friends with powerful people, bending the rules, and self-promoting. Lesser-used tactics include misinformation, spreading rumors, and blackmailing.[56]

To diffuse these behaviors, open communication is an important tool. Uncertainty tends to increase political behavior, and communication that reduces uncertainty is important. One way to open communication is to clarify the sanctioned and nonsanctioned political behaviors in the organization. For example, managers may want to encourage social power as opposed to personal power.[57]

Another key is to clarify expectations regarding performance. This can be accomplished through the use of specific, quantifiable goals and through the establishment of a clear connection between goal accomplishment and rewards.[58] Participative management is yet another key. Often, people engage in political behavior when they feel excluded from decision-making processes in the organization. By including them, managers will encourage positive input and eliminate behind-the-scenes maneuvering. Also, encouraging

Political skill is the ability to get things done through positive interpersonal relationships outside the formal organization.

©Will Woods/Digital Vision/Getty Images

political skill

The ability to get things done through favorable interpersonal relationships outside formally prescribed organizational mechanisms.

cooperation among work groups is helpful in managing political behavior. Managers can instill a unity of purpose among work teams by rewarding cooperative behavior and by implementing activities that emphasize the integration of team efforts toward common goals.[59]

Managing scarce resources well is also important. An obvious solution to the problem of scarce resources is to increase the resource pool, but few managers have this luxury. However, clarifying the resource allocation process and making the connection between performance and resources explicit can discourage dysfunctional political behavior. Providing a supportive organizational climate allows employees to discuss controversial issues promptly and openly, thus preventing an issue from festering and potentially causing friction among employees.[60]

Managing political behavior at work is important, since the perception of dysfunctional political behavior can lead to job dissatisfaction.[61] When employees perceive that there are dominant interest groups or cliques at work, they are less satisfied with pay and promotions. When they believe that the organization's reward practices are influenced by who you know rather than how well you perform, they are less satisfied.[62] Furthermore, when employees believe that their coworkers are exhibiting increased political behavior, they are less satisfied with their coworkers. Open communication, clear expectations about performance and rewards, participative decision-making practices, work group cooperation, effective management of scarce resources, and a supportive organizational climate can help managers prevent the negative consequences of political behavior.

Managing Up: Managing the Boss

One of the least discussed aspects of power and politics is the relationship between you and your boss. This is a crucial relationship, because your boss is your most important link with the rest of the organization.[63] The employee–boss relationship is one of mutual dependence; you depend on your boss to give you performance feedback, provide resources, and supply critical information. Your boss depends on you for performance, information, and support. Because it's a mutual relationship, you should take an active role in managing it. Too often, the management of this relationship is left to the boss; but if the relationship doesn't meet the employee's needs, chances are

the employee hasn't taken the responsibility to manage it proactively.

Table 11.3 shows the basic steps to take in managing your relationship with your boss. The first step is to try to understand as much as you can about your boss. What are her goals and objectives? What kind of pressures does she face in the job? Many individuals naively expect the boss to be perfect and are disappointed when they find that this is not the case. What are the boss's strengths, weaknesses, and blind spots? Because this is an emotionally charged relationship, it is difficult to be objective; but this is a critical step in forging an effective working relationship. What is the boss's preferred work style? Does she prefer everything in writing or hate detail? Does the boss prefer that you make appointments or is dropping in acceptable? The point is to gather as much information about your boss as you can and to try to put yourself in her shoes.

The second step in managing this important relationship is to assess yourself and your own needs much in the same way you analyzed your boss's. What are your strengths, weaknesses, and blind spots? What is your work style? How do you normally relate to authority figures? Some of us have tendencies toward counterdependence; that is, we rebel against the boss as an authority and view

TABLE 11.3 Managing Your Relationship with Your Boss
Make sure you understand your boss and her context, including: Her goals and objectives.   The pressures on her.   Her strengths, weaknesses, and blind spots.   Her preferred work style.
Assess yourself and your needs, including: Your own strengths and weaknesses.   Your personal style.   Your predisposition toward dependence on authority figures.
Develop and maintain a relationship that: Fits both your boss's and your own needs and styles.   Is characterized by mutual expectations.   Keeps your boss informed.   Is based on dependability and honesty.   Selectively uses your boss's time and resources.

SOURCE: Reprinted by permission of *Harvard Business Review*. From "Managing Your Boss," by J. J. Gabarro and J. P. Kotter (May–June 1993): Page 155.

him as a hindrance to our performance. Or, in contrast, we might take an overdependent stance, passively accepting the employee–boss relationship and treating the boss as an all-wise, protective parent. What is your tendency? Knowing how you react to authority figures can help you understand your interactions with your boss.

Once you have done a careful self-analysis and tried to understand your boss, the next step is to work to develop an effective relationship. Both parties' needs and styles must be accommodated. A fundraiser for a large volunteer organization related a story about a new boss, describing him as cold, aloof, unorganized, and inept. She made repeated attempts to meet with him and clarify expectations, and his usual reply was that he didn't have the time. Frustrated, she almost looked for a new job. "I just can't reach him!" was her refrain. Then she stepped back to consider her boss's and her own styles. Being an Intuitive-Feeling type of person, she prefers constant feedback and reinforcement from others. Her boss, an Intuitive-Thinker type, works comfortably without feedback from others and has a tendency to fail to praise or reward others. She sat down with him and cautiously discussed the differences in their needs. This discussion became the basis for working out a comfortable relationship. "I still don't like him, but I understand him better," she said.

Another aspect of managing the relationship involves working out mutual expectations. One key activity is to develop a plan for work objectives and have the boss agree to it.[64] It is important to do things right, but it is also important to do the right things. Neither party to the relationship is a mind reader, so clarifying the goals is a crucial step. Keeping the boss informed is also a priority. No one likes to be caught off guard.

The employee–boss relationship must be based on dependability and honesty. This means giving and receiving positive and negative feedback. Most of us are reluctant to give any feedback to the boss, but positive feedback is welcomed at the top. Negative feedback, while tougher to initiate, can clear the air. If given in a problem-solving format, it can even bring about a closer relationship.[65]

Finally, remember that your boss is on the same team you are. The golden rule is to make your boss look good, because you expect the boss to do the same for you.

Sharing Power: Empowerment

As modern organizations grow flatter, eliminating layers of management, empowerment becomes more and more important. Jay Conger defines **empowerment** as "creating conditions for heightened motivation through the development of a strong sense of personal self-efficacy."[66] This means sharing power in such a way that individuals learn to believe in their ability to do the job. The driving idea of empowerment is that the individuals closest to the work and to the customers should make the decisions and that this makes the best use of employees' skills and talents. You can empower yourself by developing your sense of self-efficacy.

Four dimensions comprise the essence of empowerment: meaning, competence, self-determination, and impact.[67] *Meaning* is a fit between the work role and the employee's values and beliefs. It is the engine of empowerment through which employees become energized about their jobs. If employees' hearts are not in their work, they cannot feel empowered. *Competence* is the belief that one has the ability to do the job well. Without competence, employees will feel inadequate and lack a sense of empowerment. *Self-determination* is having control over the way one does work. Employees who feel they're just following orders from the boss cannot feel empowered. *Impact* is the belief that one's job makes a difference within the organization. Without a sense of contributing to a goal, employees cannot feel empowered.

Employees need to experience all four of the empowerment dimensions in order to feel truly empowered. Only then will organizations reap the hoped-for rewards from empowerment efforts: employees with increased organizational commitment, better job performance, and reduced job stress.[68]

Empowerment is easy to advocate for but difficult to put into practice. Conger offers some guidelines on how leaders can empower others in the organization. First, managers should express confidence in employees and set high performance expectations. Positive expectations can go a long way toward enabling good performance, as the Pygmalion effect shows (Chapter 3). Second, managers should create opportunities for employees to participate in decision making. This means participation in the forms of both voice and choice. Employees should not just be asked to contribute their opinions about an issue; they should also have a vote in the decision that is made. One method for increasing participation is using *self-managed teams*, which, as discussed in Chapter 9, are the ultimate in empowered teams because they take on decisions and activities that traditionally belong to managers.

Third, managers should remove bureaucratic constraints that stifle autonomy. Often, companies have antiquated rules and policies that prevent employees from managing themselves. An example is a collection agency, where a manager's signature was once required to approve long-term payment arrangements for delinquent customers. Collectors, who spoke directly with customers, were the best judges of whether the payment arrangements were workable, and having to consult a manager made them feel closely supervised and powerless. The rule was dropped, and collections increased. Fourth, managers should set inspirational or meaningful goals. When

empowerment

Sharing power in such a way that individuals learn to believe in their ability to do the job.

individuals feel they "own" a goal, they are more willing to take personal responsibility for it.

Empowerment is a matter of degree. Jobs can be thought of in two dimensions: job content and job context. *Job content* consists of the tasks and procedures necessary for doing a particular job. *Job context* is broader. It is the reason the organization needs the job and includes the way the job fits into the organization's mission, goals, and objectives. These two dimensions are depicted in Figure 11.1, the employee empowerment grid.

Both axes of the grid contain the major steps in the decision-making process. As shown on the horizontal axis, decision-making authority over job content increases in terms of greater involvement in the decision-making process. Similarly, the vertical axis shows that authority over job context increases with greater involvement in that decision-making process. Combining job content and job context authority in this way produces five points that vary in terms of the degree of empowerment.[69]

No Discretion (point A) represents the traditional, assembly-line job—highly routine and repetitive with no decision-making power. Recall from Chapter 7 that if these jobs have a demanding pace and if workers have no discretion, distress will result.

Task Setting (point B) is the essence of most empowerment programs in organizations today. In this case, the worker is empowered to make decisions about the best way to get the job done but has no decision responsibility for the job context.

Participatory Empowerment (point C) represents a situation that is typical of autonomous work groups that have some decision-making power over both job content and job context. Their involvement is in identifying problems, developing alternatives, and evaluating alternatives, but the actual choice of alternatives is often beyond their power. Participatory empowerment can lead to job satisfaction and productivity.

Mission Defining (point D) is an unusual case of empowerment and is seldom seen. Here, employees have power over job context but not job content. An example would be a unionized team that is asked to decide whether their jobs could be better done by an outside vendor. Deciding to outsource would dramatically affect the mission of the company but would not affect job content, which is specified in the union contract. Assuring these employees of continued employment regardless of their decision would be necessary for this case of empowerment.

Self-Management (point E) represents total decision-making control over both job content and job context. It is the ultimate expression of trust. One example is TXI Chaparral Steel (part of Texas Industries), where employees redesign their own jobs to add value to the organization.

Empowerment should begin with job content and proceed to job context. Because the workforce is so diverse, managers should recognize that some employees are more ready for empowerment than others. Hence, managers must diagnose situations and determine the degree of empowerment to extend to employees. Recently, the *man-*

KIVA: EMPOWERING ENTREPRENEURS

With a click of the mouse, anyone can become a microfinance lender to an entrepreneur in Peru or another developing nation. In microfinance, an individual in a developed country makes a microloan to an individual or small business in a country where such resources can go a long way in growing and selling vegetables, making bricks, or raising goats. Kiva, a nonprofit organization founded by Matt and Jessica Flannery in 2005, facilitates these transactions through a website that blends microfinance and social networking. On the site, various microfinance institutions post profiles of qualified entrepreneurs for lenders to browse. Each profile includes a picture of the entrepreneur, a description of the business, and a plan for effective use of the loan. The lender receives updates on how the entrepreneur is doing and when she expects to pay the loan back. Lenders have the option to relend the money, donate it to Kiva's operations, or keep it. Kiva's loans are managed by microfinance institutions with plenty of experience—the default rate is less than 1%, and 98% of the loans are paid back in full. Kiva expects to loan $1 billion within ten years. Bill Clinton and Oprah Winfrey are lenders, as are 495,000 other individuals. The number of entrepreneurs who have been empowered through Kiva exceeds 105,000. One could say that Kiva allows anyone to empower someone—a powerful idea.

SOURCES: http://www.kiva.org; "When Small Loans Make a Big Difference," Forbes.com, June 3, 2008, http://www.forbes.com/2008/06/03/kiva-microfinance-uganda-ent-fin-cx_0603whartonkiva.html, accessed June 30, 2011.

FIGURE **11.1** Employee Empowerment Grid

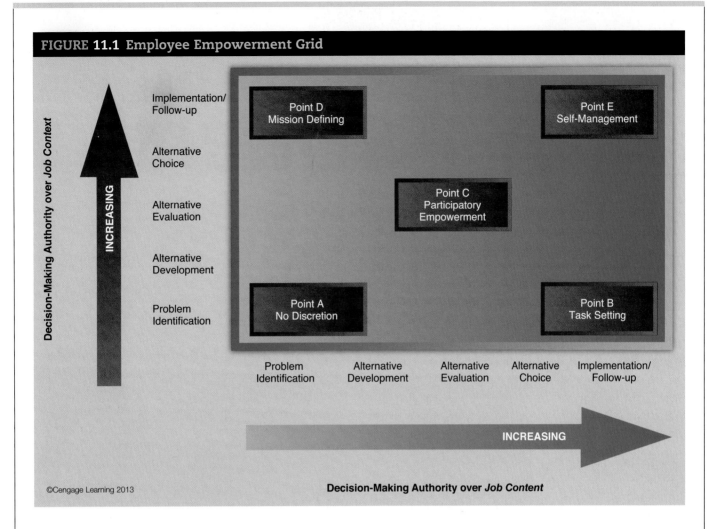

Decision-Making Authority over *Job Context*

INCREASING

- Implementation/Follow-up
- Alternative Choice
- Alternative Evaluation
- Alternative Development
- Problem Identification

Point D
Mission Defining

Point E
Self-Management

Point C
Participatory Empowerment

Point A
No Discretion

Point B
Task Setting

| Problem Identification | Alternative Development | Alternative Evaluation | Alternative Choice | Implementation/Follow-up |

INCREASING

Decision-Making Authority over *Job Content*

©Cengage Learning 2013

agement of change in organizations was identified as another area wherein empowerment can have a strong effect. Empowered employees are more likely to participate in and facilitate change processes in organizations as they feel more committed to the organizations' success.[70] Empowered individuals are also valuable to organizations because they are more motivated, satisfied, and creative.[71]

Unfortunately, the empowerment process carries with it a risk of failure. When you delegate responsibility and authority, you must be prepared to allow employees to fail; and failure is not something most managers tolerate well. At Merck, some say CEO Ray Gilmartin empowered scientists too much and that their failures cost Merck its profitability and reputation as one of *Fortune*'s Most Admired Companies. One example of this empowerment involved a diabetes drug that early research showed caused tumors in mice. Scientists

argued that in spite of early studies showing the drug wasn't viable, research should continue, and it did . . . until the drug was finally axed, costing the company considerably in terms of time and money.[72]

Log in to the **CourseMate** for *ORGB3* at **www.cengagebrain.com** to:

✳ Review **Key Terms Flash Cards** online

✳ Play **Beat the Clock** and **Quiz Bowl** to master concepts

✳ Complete **web quizzes** to prepare for exams

✳ Watch the video on **Barcelona Restaurant Group** and from *Flash of Genius* for examples, then test yourself with a quick quiz

✳ Work through the **"What about You?"** and **Ethical Dilemma** exercises to see how you would handle various situations that organizations face on a daily basis

Leadership and Followership

LEARNING OUTCOMES

1 Discuss the differences between leadership and management and between leaders and managers.

2 Explain the role of trait theory in describing leaders.

3 Describe the role of foundational behavioral research in the development of leadership theories.

4 Describe and compare the four contingency theories of leadership.

5 Discuss the recent developments in leadership theory of leader–member exchange and inspirational leadership.

6 Discuss how issues of emotional intelligence, trust, gender, and servant leadership are informing today's leadership models.

7 Define *followership* and identify different types of followers.

8 Synthesize historical leadership research into key guidelines for leaders.

©Yellow Dog Productions/The Image Bank/Getty Images

"Healthy organizations need both effective leadership and good management."

Leadership in organizations is the process of guiding and directing the behavior of people in the work environment. In the first section, we discuss the ways that leadership differs from *management*. **Formal leadership** is officially sanctioned leadership based on the authority of a formal position. **Informal leadership** is unofficial leadership accorded to a person by other members of the organization. Though one of the most researched topics in organizational behavior, leadership remains one of the least understood social processes in organizations.

LEARNING OUTCOME 1

Leadership versus Management

John Kotter describes leadership and management as two distinct yet complementary systems of action in organizations.[1] Specifically, he believes that effective leadership produces useful change in organizations while good management controls complexity in the organization and its environment.

The *management process* involves (1) planning and budgeting, (2) organizing and staffing, and (3) controlling and problem solving. Done effectively, the management process reduces uncertainty and stabilizes an organization. Alfred P. Sloan's integration and stabilization of General Motors after its early years of growth are an example of good management. In contrast, the *leadership process* involves (1) setting a direction for the organization; (2) aligning people with that direction through communication; and (3) motivating people to action, partly through empowerment and partly through basic need gratification. The leadership process creates uncertainty and change in an organization. Effective leaders not only

leadership
The process of guiding and directing the behavior of people in the work environment.

formal leadership
Officially sanctioned leadership based on the authority of a formal position.

informal leadership
Unofficial leadership accorded to a person by other members of the organization.

After You Finish
This Chapter
Go to **Page 209**
for **Study Tools**

Effective leaders, like Sheryl Sandberg of Facebook, act as enablers of change.

control the future of the organization but also act as enablers of change in organizations. They disturb existing patterns of behaviors, promote novel ideas, and help organizational members make sense of the change process.[2] Sheryl Sandberg, chief operating officer of Facebook, knows about creating change. Since joining the company in 2007, she has helped lead the company to great success by creating an advertising platform that's attracted the world's largest brands.[3]

Abraham Zaleznik proposes that leaders have distinct personalities that stand in contrast to the personalities of managers.[4] Therefore, although both leaders and managers make valuable contributions to an organization, their contributions

leader
An advocate for change and new approaches to problems.

manager
An advocate for stability and the status quo.

are different. Whereas **leaders** agitate for change and new approaches, **managers** advocate stability and the status quo. As a result, there is a dynamic tension between leaders and managers that makes it difficult for each to understand the other. Leaders and managers differ along four separate dimensions of personality: attitudes toward goals, conceptions of work, relationships with other people, and sense of self. The differences between these two personality types are summarized in Table 12.1.

It has been proposed that some people are *strategic leaders* who combine the stability of managers with the visionary abilities of leaders in a synergistic way. The unprecedented success of both Coca-Cola and Microsoft suggests that their leaders, the late Robert Goizueta and Bill Gates, respectively, were strategic leaders.[5]

LEARNING OUTCOME **2**

Early Trait Theories

The first studies of leadership attempted to identify what physical attributes, personality characteristics, and abilities distinguished leaders from other members of a group.[6] The physical attributes that were considered were height, weight, physique, energy, health, appearance, and age. Although this line of research yielded some interesting findings, it provided insufficient evidence for concluding that leaders can be distinguished on the basis of physical attributes.

Leader *personality* characteristics that have been examined include originality, adaptability, introversion–

TABLE 12.1 Leaders and Managers

PERSONALITY DIMENSION	MANAGER	LEADER
Attitudes toward goals	Has an impersonal, passive, functional attitude; believes goals rise out of necessity and reality	Has a personal and active attitude; believes goals arise from desire and imagination
Conceptions of work	Views work as an enabling process that combines people, ideas, and things; seeks moderate risk through coordination and balance	Looks for fresh approaches to old problems; seeks high-risk positions, especially with high payoffs
Relationships with others	Avoids solitary work activity, preferring to work with others; avoids close, intense relationships; avoids conflict	Is comfortable in solitary work activity; encourages close, intense working relationships; is not conflict averse
Sense of self	Is once born; makes a straightforward life adjustment; accepts life as it is	Is twice born; engages in a struggle for a sense of order in life; questions life

SOURCE: Reprinted by permission of *Harvard Business Review*. From "Managers and Leaders: Are They Different?" by A. Zaleznik (January 2004).

extroversion, dominance, self-confidence, integrity, conviction, mood optimism, and emotional control. There is some evidence that leaders may be more adaptable and self-confident than the average group member. With regard to leader *abilities*, attention has been devoted to such constructs as social skills, intelligence, scholarship, speech fluency, cooperativeness, and insight. In this area, there is some evidence that leaders are more intelligent, verbal, and cooperative and have a higher level of scholarship than the average group member.

Nonetheless, these findings are neither strong nor uniform. For each attribute or trait claimed to distinguish leaders from followers, there were always at least one or two studies with contradictory findings. For some, the trait theories are invalid, though interesting and intuitively of some relevance. It is generally agreed that the trait theories have had very limited success in being able to identify universal, distinguishing attributes of leaders.

LEARNING OUTCOME 3

Behavioral Theories

Behavioral theories emerged as a response to the deficiencies of the trait theories. Trait theories attempted to tell us what leaders were like but didn't address how leaders behaved. Three research studies built the foundations of many modern leadership theories: the Lewin, Lippitt, and White studies; the Ohio State studies; and the Michigan studies.

Foundational Behavioral Research

The earliest research on leadership style, conducted by Kurt Lewin and his students, identified three basic styles: autocratic, democratic, and laissez-faire.[7] A leader uses one of these three basic styles when approaching a group of followers in a leadership situation. The specific situation is not an important consideration, because the leader's style does not vary with the situation. The leader with an **autocratic style** uses strong, directive actions to control the rules, regulations, activities, and relationships in the work environment. Followers have little discretionary influence over the nature of the work, its accomplishment, or other aspects of the work environment. The leader with a **democratic style** uses interaction and collaboration with followers to direct work and the work environment. Followers have a high degree of discretionary influence, although the leader has ultimate authority and responsibility. The leader with a **laissez-faire style** entails a hands-off approach. A laissez-faire leader abdicates the authority and responsibility of the position, and this style often results in chaos. Laissez-faire leadership also causes role ambiguity for followers because the leader fails to clearly define goals, respon-

sibilities, and outcomes. It leads to higher interpersonal conflict at work.[8]

The leadership research program at The Ohio State University also measured specific leader behaviors. The initial results suggested that there were two important underlying dimensions of leader behaviors—initiating structure and consideration.[9] **Initiating structure** is leader behavior aimed at defining and organizing work relationships and roles, as well as establishing clear patterns of organization, communication, and ways of getting things done. **Consideration** is leader behavior aimed at nurturing friendly, warm working relationships, as well as encouraging mutual trust and interpersonal respect within the work unit. These two leader behaviors are independent of each other. That is, a leader may be high on both, low on both, or high on one and low on the other.[10]

Finally, studies conducted at the University of Michigan suggest that the leader's style has very important implications for the emotional atmosphere of the

autocratic style
A style of leadership in which the leader uses strong, directive actions to control the rules, regulations, activities, and relationships in the work environment.

democratic style
A style of leadership in which the leader uses interaction and collaboration with followers to direct the work and work environment.

laissez-faire style
A style of leadership in which the leader has a hands-off approach.

initiating structure
Leader behavior aimed at defining and organizing work relationships and roles, as well as establishing clear patterns of organization, communication, and ways of getting things done.

consideration
Leader behavior aimed at nurturing friendly, warm working relationships as well as encouraging mutual trust and interpersonal respect within the work unit.

[**Information Please**]

When Gamal Azia, president of the MGM Grand Hotel and Casino in Las Vegas, set out to increase revenues, the first step he took was to ask all employees to share their thoughts about how to improve the hotel. In one meeting, employees told Azia that they were not given enough information about what was going on in the hotel each day. They didn't know if there were special events or if certain guests had unique needs. Azia heard their comments and took action, requiring that all employees begin their workday with a brief meeting, during which they would be given a thorough rundown of all that was going on.

SOURCE: N. Byrnes, "The Issue: Maintaining Employee Engagement," *BusinessWeek* (January 16, 2009), http://www.businessweek.com/managing/content/jan2009/ca20090116_444132.htm, accessed August 20, 2010.

©iStockphoto.com/Lise Gagne

work environment and, therefore, for the followers who work under that leader. Two styles of leadership were identified: production oriented and employee oriented.[11] A *production-oriented style* leads to a work environment where the focus is on getting things done. The leader in this environment uses direct, close supervision or many written and unwritten rules and regulations to control behavior.

In contrast, an *employee-oriented leadership* style leads to a work environment that focuses on relationships. The leader exhibits less direct, or less close, supervision and establishes fewer written or unwritten rules and regulations for behavior. Employee-oriented leaders display concern for people and their needs.

Taken together, these three groups of studies (the Lewin studies, the Ohio State studies, and the Michigan studies) form the building blocks of many recent leadership theories. What the studies have in common is that two basic leadership styles were identified, with one focusing on *tasks* (autocratic, production oriented, initiating structure) and one focusing on

people (democratic, employee oriented, consideration).

The Leadership Grid: A Contemporary Extension

Robert Blake and Jane Mouton's **Leadership Grid**, originally called the Managerial Grid, was developed with a focus on attitudes.[12] The two underlying dimensions of the grid are labeled Concern for Results and Concern for People. These two attitudinal dimensions are independent of each other, and, in different combinations, they form various leadership styles. Blake and Mouton originally identified five distinct managerial styles, and further development of the grid has led to the seven distinct leadership styles shown in Figure 12.1.

The **organization man manager (5,5)** is a middle-of-the-road leader who has a medium concern for people and production. This leader attempts to balance a concern for people and production without a commitment to either. The **authority-compliance manager (9,1)** has great concern for production and little concern for people. This leader desires tight control in order to get tasks done efficiently and considers creativity and human relations unnecessary. Authority-compliance managers may become so focused on running an efficient organization that they actually use tactics such as bullying. Some authority-compliance managers may intimidate, verbally and mentally attack, and otherwise mistreat subordinates. This form of abuse is quite common, with one in six U.S. workers reporting that they have been bullied by a manager.[13] The inverse position is the **country club manager (1,9)**, who has great concern for people and little concern for production, attempts to avoid conflict, and seeks to be well liked. This leader's goal is to keep people happy through good interpersonal relations, which are more important to her than the task. (This style is not a sound human relations approach but rather a soft Theory X approach.)

The **team manager (9,9)** builds a highly productive team of committed people. This leader works to motivate employees to reach their highest levels of accomplishment, is flexible, is responsive to change, and understands the need for change. The **impoverished manager (1,1)** exerts just enough effort to get by.

Leadership Grid

An approach to understanding a leader's or manager's concern for results (production) and concern for people.

organization man manager (5,5)

A middle-of-the-road leader.

authority-compliance manager (9,1)

A leader who emphasizes efficient production.

country club manager (1,9)

A leader who has great concern for people and little concern for production, attempts to avoid conflict, and seeks to be well liked.

team manager (9,9)

A leader who builds a highly productive team of committed people.

impoverished manager (1,1)

A leader who exerts just enough effort to get by.

FIGURE **12.1** The Leadership Grid

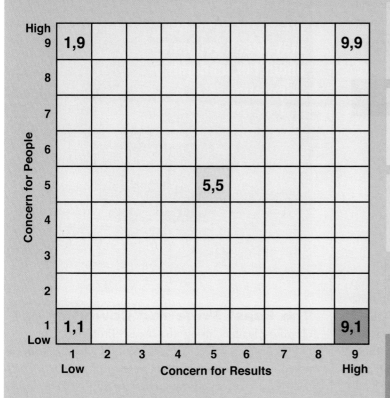

1,9 Country Club Management:
Thoughtful attention to the needs of the people for satisfying relationships leads to a comfortable, friendly organization atmosphere and work tempo.

9,9 Team Management:
Work accomplishment is from committed people; interdependence through a "common stake" in organization purpose leads to relationships of trust and respect.

5,5 Middle-of-the-Road Management:
Adequate organization performance is possible through balancing the necessity to get work out while maintaining morale of people at a satisfactory level.

1,1 Impoverished Management:
Exertion of minimum effort to get required work done is appropriate to sustain organization membership.

9,1 Authority-Compliance Management:
Efficiency in operations results from arranging conditions of work in such a way that human elements interfere to a minimum degree.

Opportunistic Management

In Opportunisitic Management, people adapt and shift to any grid style needed to gain the maximum advantage. Performance occurs according to a system of selfish gain. Effort is given only for an advantage for personal gain.

9+9: Paternalism/Maternalism Management:
Reward and approval are bestowed to people in return for loyalty and obedience; failure to comply leads to punishment.

SOURCE: The Leadership Grid® figure, Paternalism Figure and Opportunism from *Leadership Dilemmas—Grid Solutions,* by Robert R. Blake and Anne Adams McCanse (formerly the Managerial Grid by Robert R. Blake and Jane S. Mouton). Houston: Gulf Publishing Company (Grid Figure: p. 29; Paternalism Figure: p. 30; Opportunism Figure: p. 31). Copyright 1991 by Blake and Mouton, and Scientific Methods, Inc. Reproduced by permission of the owners.

This leader has little concern for people or production, avoids taking sides, and stays out of conflicts; he is often referred to as a laissez-faire leader. Two new leadership styles have been added to these five original leadership styles within the grid. The **paternalistic "father knows best" manager (9+9)** promises reward for compliance and threatens punishment for noncompliance. The **opportunistic "what's in it for me" manager (Opp)** uses whichever style will maximize self-benefit.

It's important to highlight that the grid evaluates the *team manager* (9,9) as the very best style of managerial behavior. This is the basis on which the grid has been used for team building and leadership training in an organization's develop-

paternalistic "father knows best" manager (9+9)
A leader who promises reward and threatens punishment.

opportunistic "what's in it for me" manager (Opp)
A leader who uses whichever style will maximize self-benefit.

ment. As an organizational development method, the grid aims to transform the leader in the organization to lead in the "one best way," which, according to the grid, is the team approach. The team style is one that combines optimal concern for people with optimal concern for results.

SAME BASIC IDEA, VERY DIFFERENT MANIFESTATION

Ohio State	Blake-Mouton
descriptive	normative
nonevaluative	prescriptive
no attitude	attitudinal overtones

LEARNING OUTCOME 4

Contingency Theories

Contingency theories involve the belief that leadership style must be appropriate for the particular situation. By their nature, contingency theories are "if–then" theories: If the situation is x, then the appropriate leadership behavior is y. We examine four such theories, including Fiedler's contingency theory, path–goal theory, normative decision theory, and situational leadership theory.

Fiedler's Contingency Theory

Fiedler's contingency theory of leadership proposes that the fit between the leader's need structure and the favorableness of the leader's situation determines the team's effectiveness in work accomplishment. This theory assumes that leaders are either task oriented or relationship oriented, depending upon how the leaders obtain their primary need gratification.[14] Task-oriented leaders are primarily gratified by accomplishing tasks and getting work done. Relationship-oriented leaders are primarily gratified by developing good, comfortable interpersonal relationships. Accordingly, the effectiveness of both types of leaders depends on the favorableness of their situation. The theory classifies the favorableness of the leader's situation according to the leader's position power, the structure of the team's task, and the quality of the leader–follower relationships.

least preferred coworker (LPC)

The person a leader has least preferred to work with.

task structure

The degree of clarity, or ambiguity, in the work activities assigned to the group.

position power

The authority associated with the leader's formal position in the organization.

leader–member relations

The quality of interpersonal relationships among a leader and the group members.

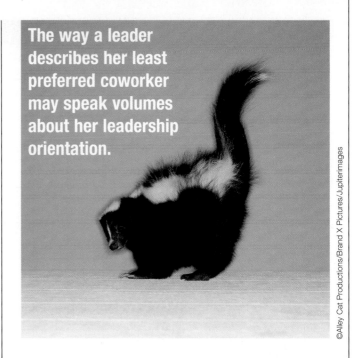

The way a leader describes her least preferred coworker may speak volumes about her leadership orientation.

©Alley Cat Productions/Brand X Pictures/Jupiterimages

The Least Preferred Coworker Fiedler classifies leaders using the Least Preferred Coworker (LPC) Scale, a projective technique in which a leader is asked to choose the person he least prefers to work with (the **least preferred coworker**, or **LPC**).[15] The leader is asked to describe this LPC using sixteen eight-point bipolar adjective sets. Two of these bipolar adjective sets follow (the leader marks the one most descriptive of the LPC):

Efficient : : : : : : : : : Inefficient
Cheerful : : : : : : : : : Gloomy

Leaders who describe their LPC in positive terms (that is, pleasant, efficient, cheerful, and so on) are classified as high LPC, or relationship-oriented, leaders. Those who describe their LPC in negative terms (that is, unpleasant, inefficient, gloomy, and so on) are classified as low LPC, or task-oriented, leaders.

The LPC score is a controversial element in contingency theory.[16] It has been critiqued conceptually and methodologically because it is a projective technique with low measurement reliability.

Situational Favorableness The leader's situation has three dimensions: task structure, position power, and leader–member relations. Based on these three dimensions, the situation is either favorable or unfavorable for the leader. **Task structure** refers to the degree of clarity, or ambiguity, in the work activities assigned to the group. **Position power** refers to the authority associated with the leader's formal position in the organization.

Leader–member relations, the quality of interpersonal relationships among a leader and the group members, is measured by the *Group-Atmosphere Scale*,

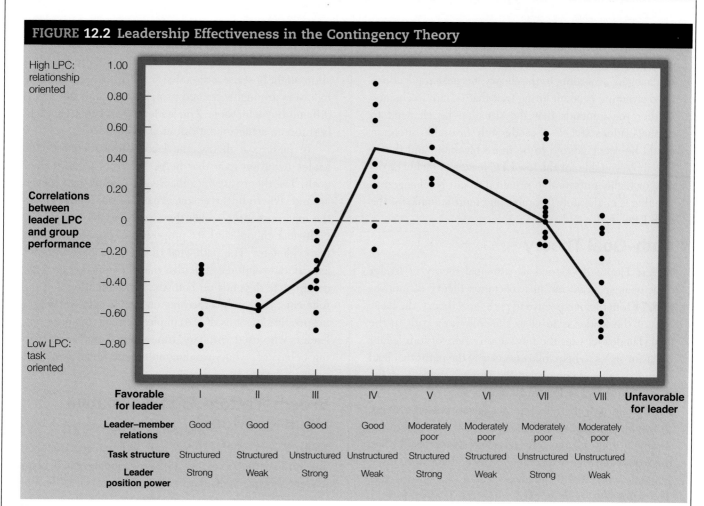

FIGURE 12.2 Leadership Effectiveness in the Contingency Theory

	I	II	III	IV	V	VI	VII	VIII	
Favorable for leader									**Unfavorable for leader**
Leader–member relations	Good	Good	Good	Good	Moderately poor	Moderately poor	Moderately poor	Moderately poor	
Task structure	Structured	Structured	Unstructured	Unstructured	Structured	Structured	Unstructured	Unstructured	
Leader position power	Strong	Weak	Strong	Weak	Strong	Weak	Strong	Weak	

SOURCE: F. E. Fiedler, *A Theory of Leader Effectiveness* (New York: McGraw-Hill, 1964). Reprinted with permission of the author.

composed of nine eight-point bipolar adjective sets. Two of these bipolar adjective sets follow:

Friendly : : : : : : : : : Unfriendly
Accepting : : : : : : : : : Rejecting

A favorable leadership situation, according to Fiedler, is one with a structured task for the work group, strong position power for the leader, and good leader–member relations. In contrast, an unfavorable leadership situation is one with an unstructured task, weak position power for the leader, and moderately poor leader–member relations. Between these two extremes, the leadership situation has varying degrees of moderate favorableness for the leader.

	Favorable	Moderate	Unfavorable
Task structure	Structured		Unstructured
Position power	Strong		Weak
Leader–member relations	Good		Poor

Leadership Effectiveness The contingency theory suggests that low LPC and high LPC leaders are both effective if placed in the right situation.[17] Specifically, low LPC (task-oriented) leaders are most

effective in either very favorable or very unfavorable leadership situations. In contrast, high LPC (relationship-oriented) leaders are most effective in situations of intermediate favorableness. Figure 12.2 shows the nature of these relationships and suggests that leadership effectiveness is determined by the degree of fit between the leader and the situation. Recent research has shown that relationship-oriented leaders encourage team learning and innovation, which helps products get to market faster. This means that most relationship-oriented leaders perform well in leading new product development teams. In short, the right team leader can help get new products out the door faster, while a mismatch between the leader and the situation can have the opposite effect.[18]

What, then, is to be done if there is a misfit? What happens when a low

©iStockphoto.com/Stephen Newman

LPC leader is in a moderately favorable situation or when a high LPC leader is in a highly favorable or highly unfavorable situation? It is unlikely that the leader can be changed, according to the theory, because the leader's need structure is an enduring trait that is hard to change. Fiedler recommends that the situation be changed to fit the leader's style.[19] A moderately favorable situation would be reengineered to be more favorable and therefore more suitable for the low LPC leader. A highly favorable or highly unfavorable situation would be changed to one that is moderately favorable and more suitable for the high LPC leader.

Path–Goal Theory

Robert House developed a path–goal theory of leader effectiveness based on an expectancy theory of motivation.[20] From the perspective of path–goal theory, the basic role of the leader is to clear the follower's path to the goal. The leader uses the most appropriate of four leader behavior styles to help followers clarify the paths that lead them to work and personal goals. The key concepts in the theory are shown in Figure 12.3.

A leader selects from the four leader behavior styles, shown in Figure 12.3, the one that is most helpful to followers at a given time. The directive style is used when the leader must give specific guidance about work tasks, schedule work, and let followers know what is expected. The *supportive style* is used when the leader needs to express concern for followers' well-being and social status. The *participative style* is used when the leader must engage in joint decision-making activities with followers. The *achievement-oriented style* is used when the leader must set challenging goals for followers and show strong confidence in those followers.

In selecting the appropriate leader behavior style, the leader must consider both the followers and the work environment. A number of characteristics are included in Figure 12.3. Let us consider two scenarios. In scenario one, the followers are inexperienced and are working on an ambiguous, unstructured task. The leader in this situation might best use a directive style. In scenario two, the followers are highly trained professionals, and the task is difficult but achievable. The leader in this situation might best use an achievement-oriented style.

In path–goal theory, the leader always chooses the leader behavior style that helps followers achieve their goals. The theory assumes that leaders adapt their behavior and style to fit the characteristics of the followers and the environment in which they work. Actual tests of the path–goal theory and its propositions provide conflicting evidence.[21] The path–goal theory does have intuitive appeal and reinforces the idea that the appropriate leadership style depends on both the work situation and the followers. Research is focusing on which style works best in specific situations. For example, in small organizations, leaders who used visionary, transactional, and empowering behaviors, while avoiding autocratic behaviors, were most successful.[22]

Vroom-Yetton-Jago Normative Decision Model

Victor Vroom, Phillip Yetton, and Arthur Jago developed and refined the normative decision model, which helps leaders and managers determine the appropriate level of employee participation in decision making. The model recognizes the benefits of authoritative, democratic, and consultive styles of leader behavior.[23] Five forms of decision making are described in the model:

> *Decide*. The manager makes the decision alone and either announces it or "sells" it to the group.

> *Consult individually*. The manager presents the problem to the group members individually, gets their input, and then makes the decision.

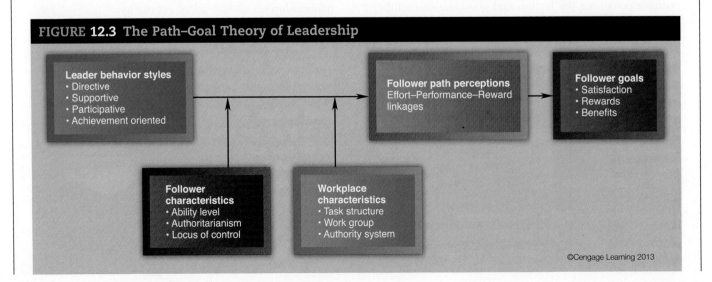

FIGURE **12.3** The Path–Goal Theory of Leadership

Leader behavior styles
• Directive
• Supportive
• Participative
• Achievement oriented

Follower path perceptions
Effort–Performance–Reward linkages

Follower goals
• Satisfaction
• Rewards
• Benefits

Follower characteristics
• Ability level
• Authoritarianism
• Locus of control

Workplace characteristics
• Task structure
• Work group
• Authority system

©Cengage Learning 2013

> *Consult group.* The manager presents the problem to the group members in a meeting, gets their input, and then makes the decision.

> *Facilitate.* The manager presents the problem to the group in a meeting and acts as a facilitator, defining the problem and the boundaries that surround the decision. The manager's ideas are not given more weight than any other group member's ideas. The objective is concurrence.

> *Delegate.* The manager permits the group to make the decision within prescribed limits, providing needed resources and encouragement.[24]

The key to the normative decision model is that a manager should use the decision method most appropriate for a given decision situation. The manager arrives at the proper method by working through matrices like the one in Figure 12.4 on the next page. The factors across the top of the model (decision significance, commitment, leader expertise, and so on) are the situational factors in the normative decision model. This matrix is for decisions that must be made under time pressure, but other matrices are also available. For example, there is a different matrix managers can use when their objective is to develop subordinates' decision-making skills. Although the model offers very explicit predictions as well as prescriptions for leaders, its utility is limited to the leader decision-making tasks.

The Situational Leadership® Model

The Situational Leadership model, developed by Paul Hersey and Kenneth Blanchard, suggests that the leader's behavior should be adjusted to the maturity level of the followers.[25] The model employs two dimensions of leader behavior as used in the Ohio State studies; one dimension is task oriented, and the other is relationship oriented. Follower maturity is categorized into four levels, as shown in Figure 12.5. Follower readiness is determined by the follower's ability and willingness to complete a specific task. Readiness can therefore be low or high depending on the particular task. In addition, readiness varies within a single person according to the task. One

person may be willing and able to satisfy simple requests from customers (high readiness) but less able or willing to give highly technical advice to customers (low readiness). It is important that the leader be able to evaluate the readiness level of each follower for each task. The four styles of leader behavior associated with the four readiness levels are depicted in Figure 12.5 on page 203.

According to the Situational Leadership model, a leader should use a *telling style* (S1) when a follower is unable and unwilling to do a certain task. This style involves providing instructions and closely monitoring performance. As such, the telling style involves considerable task behavior and low relationship behavior. When a follower is unable but willing and confident to do a task, the leader can use the *selling style* (S2), in which there is high task behavior and high relationship behavior. In this case, the leader explains decisions and provides opportunities for the employee to seek clarification or help. Sometimes a follower will be able to complete a task but may seem unwilling or insecure about doing so. In these cases, a *participating style* (S3) is warranted, which involves high relationship but low task behavior. The leader here encourages the follower to participate in decision making. Finally, for tasks in which a follower is able and willing, the leader is able to use a *delegating style* (S4), characterized by low task behavior and low relationship behavior. In this case, follower readiness is high, and low levels of leader involvement (task or relationship) are needed.

One key limitation of the situational leadership model is the absence of central hypotheses that could be tested and would therefore make it a more valid, reliable theory of leadership.[26] However, the theory has intuitive appeal and is widely

Hersey & Blanchard's 4 Styles

Telling (S1)
Selling (S2)
Participating (S3)
Delegating (S4)

©iStockphoto.com/Svetlana Gryankina

FIGURE **12.4** Time-Driven Model

TIME-DRIVEN MODEL

Instructions: The matrix operates like a funnel. You start at the left with a specific decision problem in mind. The column headings denote situational factors that may or may not be present in that problem. You progress by selecting High or Low (H or L) for each relevant situational factor. Proceed down from the funnel, judging only those situational factors for which a judgment is called for, until you reach the recommended process.

Decision Significance	Importance of Commitment	Leader Expertise	Likelihood of Commitment	Group Support	Group Expertise	Team Competence	
H	H	H	H	–	–	–	Decide
			L	H	H	H	Delegate
						L	Consult (Group)
					L	–	Consult (Group)
				L	–	–	Consult (Group)
		L	H	H	H	H	Facilitate
						L	Consult (Individually)
					L	–	Consult (Individually)
				L	–	–	Consult (Individually)
			L	H	H	H	Facilitate
						L	Consult (Group)
					L	–	Consult (Group)
				L	–	–	Consult (Group)
	L	H	–	–	–	–	Decide
		L	–	H	H	H	Facilitate
						L	Consult (Individually)
					L	–	Consult (Individually)
				L	–	–	Consult (Individually)
L	H	–	H	–	–	–	Decide
			L	–	–	H	Delegate
						L	Facilitate
	L	–	–	–	–	–	Decide

SOURCE: Reprinted from *Organizational Dynamics* 28, by V. H. Vroom, "Leadership and the Decision-Making Process," 82–94 (Spring 2000) with permission from Elsevier.

FIGURE 12.5 The Situational Leadership Model

FOLLOWER READINESS			
LOW	**MODERATE**	**MODERATE**	**HIGH**
Unwilling and unable followers	Willing and unable followers	Unwilling but able followers	Willing and able followers

	TELLING	**SELLING**	**PARTICIPATING**	**DELEGATING**
	Give specific instructions and supervise closely	Clarify and explain decisions as needed	Share ideas with followers and facilitate their decision making	Empower followers to make the decisions
Task Behaviors	High	High	Low	Low
Relationship Behaviors	Low	High	High	Low

SOURCE: From Phillips/Gully *Organizational Behavior*, 1e. © 2012 South-Western, a part of Cengage Learning, Inc. Reproduced by permission. www.cengage.com/permissions

used for training and development in corporations. In addition, the theory focuses attention on follower maturity as an important determinant of the leadership process.

LEARNING OUTCOME 5

Recent Leadership Theories

Many newer developments in leadership theory merit discussion here, specifically, leader–member exchange theory and inspirational leadership, which includes transformational, charismatic, and authentic styles.

Leader–Member Exchange

Leader–member exchange theory, or *LMX*, recognizes that leaders may form different relationships with followers. The basic idea behind LMX is that leaders form two groups of followers: in-groups and out-groups. *In-group members* tend to be similar to the leader and are given greater responsibilities, more rewards, and more attention. They work within the leader's inner circle of communication. As a result, in-group members are more satisfied, have lower turnover, and have higher organizational commitment. In contrast, *out-group members* are outside the circle and receive less attention and fewer rewards. They are managed by formal rules and policies.[27]

Research on LMX is supportive. In-group members are more likely to engage in organizational citizenship behavior, while out-group members are more likely to retaliate against the organization.[28] And the type of stress varies according to the group. In-group members' stress comes from the additional responsibilities placed on them by the leader, whereas out-group members' stress comes from being left out of the communication network.[29] One surprising finding is that more frequent communication with the boss may either help or hurt a worker's performance ratings, depending on whether the worker is in the in-group or the out-group. Among the in-group, more frequent communication generally leads to higher performance ratings, while members of the out-group who communicate more often with the superior tend to receive lower performance ratings.[30]

Employees who enjoy more frequent contact with the boss also have a better understanding of what the boss's expectations are. Such agreement tends to lead to better performance by the employee and fewer misunderstandings between employer and employee.[31] In-group members are more likely to support the values of the organization and to become models of appropriate behavior. If the leader, for example, wants to promote safety at work, in-group members are more likely to model safe work practices, which leads to a climate of workplace safety.[32] In-group members may also be more creative. When employees have a positive relationship with their supervisor, it increases their confidence and self-efficacy, which in turn increase creativity.[33]

Employees who enjoy more frequent contact with the boss also have a better understanding of what the boss's expectations are.

Inspirational Leadership

Leadership is an exciting area of organizational behavior, one in which new research is constantly emerging. Three new developments are important to understand. These are transformational leadership, charismatic leadership, and authentic leadership. These three theories can be called *inspirational leadership theories* because in each one, followers are inspired by the leader to perform well.

Transformational Leadership

Transactional leaders, you will recall, are those who use rewards and punishment to strike deals with followers and shape their behavior. In contrast, *transformational leaders* inspire and excite followers to high levels of performance.[34] They rely on their personal attributes instead of their official position to manage followers. There is some evidence that transformational leadership can be learned.[35] Transformational leadership consists of the following four subdimensions: charisma, individualized consideration, inspirational motivation, and intellectual stimulation. We describe *charisma* in detail shortly. *Individualized consideration* refers to how much concern the leader displays for each follower's individual needs and acts as a coach or a mentor. *Inspirational motivation* is the extent to which the leader is able to articulate a vision that is appealing to followers.[36]

Transformational leadership has been shown to increase firm performance. U.S. corporations increasingly operate in a global economy, so there is a greater demand for leaders who can practice transformational leadership by converting their visions into reality and by inspiring followers to perform "above and beyond the call of duty."[37] Howard Schultz, founder and chairman of Starbucks Coffee, is the transformational leader and visionary heart of Starbucks. He has grown his firm from a small specialty coffee bar into one of the best-known brands in the world. However, the flagging global economy may challenge Schultz's abilities to continue to develop the new leaders that helped the firm grow so rapidly in the past.[38]

Transformational leadership is very important for individual followers as well. Transformational leadership that is focused on individuals increases task performance and initiative. Employees who work for a transformational leader are more satisfied, motivated, and perform better than those who do not.[39] Leaders can be both transformational and transactional.[40] However, whereas transformational leadership adds to the effects of transactional leadership, even exceptional transactional leadership cannot substitute for transformational leadership.[41] Transformational leadership is effective because transformational leaders encourage followers to set goals congruent with the followers' own authentic interests and values. As a result, followers see their work as important and their goals as aligned with who they are.[42]

Charismatic Leadership

Steve Jobs, the pioneer behind Apple, has an uncanny ability to create a vision and convince others to become part of it. This was evidenced by Apple's continued overall success despite its major blunders in the desktop computer wars. Jobs's unique ability is so powerful that Apple employees coined a term in the 1980s for it—the *reality-distortion field*. This expression is used to describe the persuasive ability and peculiar charisma of managers like Steve Jobs. His reality-distortion field allows Jobs to convince even skeptics that his plans are worth supporting, no matter how unworkable they may appear. Those close to these kinds of managers become passionately committed to possibly insane projects without regard to the practicality of their implementation or competitive forces in the marketplace.[43]

Charismatic leadership results when a leader uses the force of personal abilities and talents to have profound and extraordinary effects on followers.[44] Some scholars see transformational leadership and charismatic leadership as very similar, but others believe they differ in that charismatic leaders rely heavily on referent power, discussed in Chapter 11, and charismatic leadership is especially effective in times of uncertainty.[45] Charismatic leadership falls to those who are chosen (are born with the "gift" of charisma) or who cultivate that gift. Some say charismatic leaders are born, and others say they are taught.

Charismatic leadership carries with it not only great potential for high levels of achievement and performance on the part of followers but also shadowy risks of destruc-

charismatic leadership

A leader's use of personal abilities and talents in order to have profound and extraordinary effects on followers.

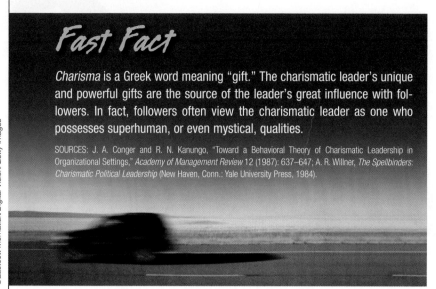

Fast Fact

Charisma is a Greek word meaning "gift." The charismatic leader's unique and powerful gifts are the source of the leader's great influence with followers. In fact, followers often view the charismatic leader as one who possesses superhuman, or even mystical, qualities.

SOURCES: J. A. Conger and R. N. Kanungo, "Toward a Behavioral Theory of Charismatic Leadership in Organizational Settings," *Academy of Management Review* 12 (1987): 637–647; A. R. Willner, *The Spellbinders: Charismatic Political Leadership* (New Haven, Conn.: Yale University Press, 1984).

©Eastcott Momatiuk/Digital Vision/Getty Images

tive courses of action that might harm followers or other people. Several researchers have attempted to demystify charismatic leadership and distinguish its two faces.[46] The ugly face of charisma is revealed in the personalized power motivations of Adolf Hitler in Nazi Germany and David Koresh of the Branch Davidian cult in Waco, Texas. Both men led their followers into struggle, conflict, and death. The brighter face of charisma is revealed in the socialized power motivations of U.S. President Franklin D. Roosevelt. Former presidents Bill Clinton and Ronald Reagan, while worlds apart in terms of their political beliefs, were actually quite similar in their use of personal charisma to inspire followers and motivate them to pursue a specific vision. In each case, followers perceived the leader as imbued with a unique vision for America and unique abilities to lead the country there.

Authentic Leadership Recently, a new form of leadership has started to garner attention thanks to the ethical scandals rocking the business environment. In response to concerns about the potential negative side of inspirational forms of leadership, researchers have called for authentic leadership, which includes transformational, charismatic, or transactional leadership as the situation might demand but only in accordance with the leader's conscious and well-developed sense of values.[47] Because authentic leaders act in ways that are consistent with their value systems, they have a highly evolved sense of moral right and wrong. Their life experiences (which can be labeled "moments that matter") lead to such authentic leadership development, allowing authentic leaders to be their true selves.[48]

Authentic leaders arouse and motivate followers to higher levels of performance by building a workforce characterized by high levels of hope, optimism, resiliency, and self-efficacy.[49] Followers also experience more positive emotions and trust as a result of the authentic leader's transparency and the collective caring climate engendered by such a leader. Researchers contend that this is the kind of leadership embodied by Gandhi, Nelson Mandela, and others like them throughout history. Only time and solid management research will tell if this approach can yield results for organizational leadership.

One recent development in the identification of authentic leaders stems from the arena of emotions. Emotions act as checks on the ugly side of charisma and also provide certain cues to followers. For example, a leader who espouses benevolence (as a value) and does not display compassion (an emotion) might not be very authentic in followers' eyes.[50] Similarly, a leader who displays compassion when announcing a layoff may be seen by followers as more morally worthy and held in high regard.[51]

Despite the warm emotions charismatic leaders can evoke, some charismatic leaders are narcissists who listen only to those who agree with them and do not accept advice from those who disagree.[52] Whereas charismatic leaders with socialized power motivation are concerned about the collective well-being of their followers, charismatic leaders with a personalized power motivation are driven by the need for personal gain and glorification.[53]

Charismatic leadership styles are associated with several positive outcomes. One study reported that firms headed by more charismatic leaders outperformed other firms, particularly in difficult economic times. Perhaps even more important, charismatic leaders were able to raise more outside financial support for their firms than noncharismatic leaders, meaning that charisma at the top may translate to greater funding at the bottom.[54]

LEARNING OUTCOME **6**

Emerging Issues in Leadership

Along with the recent developments in theory, some exciting issues have emerged of which leaders should be aware. These include emotional intelligence, trust, women leaders, and servant leadership.

Emotional Intelligence

It has been suggested that effective leaders possess emotional intelligence, which is the ability to recognize and manage emotion in oneself and in others. In fact, some researchers argue that emotional intelligence is more important for effective leadership than either IQ or technical skills.[55] Emotional intelligence is made up of several competencies, including self-awareness, empathy, adaptability, and self-confidence. While most people gain emotional intelligence as they age, not everyone starts with an equal amount. Fortunately, emotional intelligence can be learned. With honest feedback from coworkers and ongoing guidance, almost any leader can improve emotional intelligence, and with it, the ability to lead in times of adversity.[56]

Emotional intelligence affects the way leaders make decisions. Under high stress, leaders with higher emotional intelligence tend to keep their cool and make better decisions, while leaders with low emotional intelligence make poor decisions and lose their effectiveness.[57] When Joe Torre was manager of the New York Yankees, he got the most out of his team, worked for a notoriously tough boss, and kept his cool. As manager of the Los Angeles Dodgers, he was still a model of emotional intelligence: compassionate, calm under stress, and a great motivator. He advocates "managing against the cycle," which means staying calm when situations are tough, but turning up the heat on players when things are going well.[58]

Trust

Trust, the willingness to be vulnerable to the actions of another, is an essential element in leadership.[59] Trust implies that followers believe that their leader will act with the followers' welfare in mind. Trustworthiness is also one of the competencies in emotional intelligence. Among top management team members, trust facilitates strategy implementation. That means that if team members trust each other, they have a better chance of getting "buy-in" from employees on the direction of the company.[60] And if employees trust their leaders, they will buy in more readily.

Trust in top business leaders may be at an all-time low given the highly publicized failures of many CEOs. Rick Wagoner, CEO of General Motors from 2000 to 2009, lost more money than any CEO in history, yet he continued to express confidence in his company and his strategy. He was fired by the government just before GM went bankrupt.[61] In the midst of the biggest oil spill in history, BP CEO Tony Hayward suggested that the environmental impact of the spill would be "very, very modest" and later complained to reporters that he would like his life back. As people around the Gulf region scrambled for their livelihoods, Hayward took a day off to go yacht racing.

Effective leaders understand both *whom* to trust and *how* to trust. At one extreme, leaders often make the mistake of trusting only a close circle of advisors, listening only to them and gradually cutting themselves off from dissenting opinions. At the opposite extreme, lone-wolf leaders may trust nobody, leading to preventable mistakes. Wise leaders carefully evaluate both the competence and the position of those they trust, seeking out a variety of opinions and input.[62]

Gender and Leadership

An important, emergent leadership question is whether women and men lead differently. Historical stereotypes persist, and people characterize successful managers as having more male-oriented attributes than female-oriented attributes.[63] Although legitimate gender differences may exist, the same leadership traits may be interpreted differently in a man and a woman because of stereotypes. The real issue should be leader behaviors that are not bound by gender stereotypes.

Early evidence shows that women tend to use a more people-oriented style that is inclusive and empowering. Women managers excel in positions that demand strong interpersonal skills.[64] Even though more and more women are assuming positions of leadership in organizations, interestingly, much of what we know about leadership is based on studies that were conducted on men. We need to know more about the ways women lead.

Recent research looks at the phenomenon of the *glass cliff* (as opposed to the *glass ceiling* effect discussed in Chapter 2). The *glass cliff* represents a trend in organizations wherein more women are placed in difficult leadership situations. Women perceive these assignments as necessary to accept due to the difficulty of attaining leadership positions and lack of alternate opportunities combined with male in-group favoritism. On the other hand, men perceive that women are better suited to difficult leadership positions because women are better decision makers.[65]

If employees trust their leaders, they will buy in more readily.

©John Lund/Drew Kelly/Blend Images/Jupiterimages

Servant Leadership

Robert Greenleaf, director of management research at AT&T for many years, believed that leaders should serve employees, customers, and the community, and his essays are the basis for today's view of *servant leadership*. His personal and professional philosophy was that leaders lead by serving others. Other tenets of servant leadership are that work exists for the person as much as the person exists for work, and that servant leaders try to find out the will of the group and lead based on that. Servant leadership leads to higher team performance and increased organizational citizenship behaviors in the organization.[66] Servant leaders consider themselves stewards who regard leadership as a trust and desire to leave the organization in better shape for future generations.[67] Although Greenleaf's writings were completed thirty years ago, many have now been published and are becoming more popular.

Abusive Supervision

Research has investigated not only what makes leaders effective but also negative leadership behaviors. The most common include sexual harassment, physical violence, angry outbursts, public ridicule, taking credit for employees' successes, and scapegoating employees.[68] *Abusive supervision*, as these behaviors are called, is estimated to affect about 13 percent of U.S. workers and leads to many negative consequences. Abused workers report diminished well-being along with increased deviance behavior, problem drinking, psychological distress, and emotional exhaustion.[69] In addition, abusive supervision increases absenteeism and reduces productivity. In fact, the cost of abusive supervision to U.S. corporations has been estimated at $23.8 billion.[70] It is not clear why supervisors abuse others. Some research suggests that injustice experienced by supervisors increases the likelihood that they will, in turn, abuse others. Other studies suggest that abuse stems from the failure of managers to control themselves and handle stress.[71] Abusive supervisors are more likely to direct their aggression toward employees who are very negative, or toward those who appear weak and unwilling or unable to defend themselves.[72]

LEARNING OUTCOME 7

Followership

In contrast to leadership, the topic of **followership** has not been extensively researched. Much of the leadership literature suggests that leader and follower roles are highly differentiated. The traditional view casts followers as passive, whereas a more contemporary view casts the follower

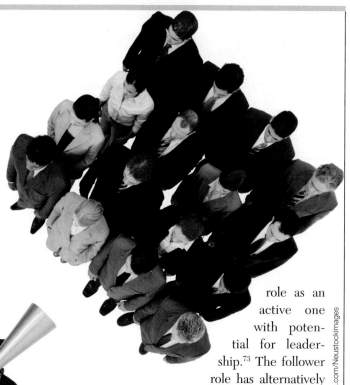

role as an active one with potential for leadership.[73] The follower role has alternatively been cast as one of self-leadership in which the follower assumes responsibility for influencing his own performance.[74] This approach emphasizes the follower's individual responsibility and self-control. Self-led followers perform tasks that are naturally motivating and also do work that must be done but is not naturally motivating. Self-leadership enables followers to be disciplined and effective, essential first steps if one is to become a leader. Organizational programs such as empowerment and self-managed work teams may be used to further activate the follower role.[75]

Types of Followers

Contemporary work environments are ones in which followers recognize their interdependence with leaders and learn to challenge them while at the same time respecting the leaders' authority.[76] Effective followers are active, responsible, autonomous in their behavior, and critical in their thinking without being insubordinate or disrespectful—in essence, they are highly engaged at work.

Effective followers and four other types of followers are identified based on two dimensions: (1) activity versus passivity and (2) independent, critical thinking versus dependent, uncritical thinking.[77] Figure 12.6 on the next page shows these follower types.

Alienated followers think independently and critically, yet are very passive in their behavior. As a result, they become psychologically and emotionally distanced from their leaders. These alienated followers are potentially disruptive and a threat to the health of the organization. *Sheep* are

> **followership**
> The process of being guided and directed by a leader in the work environment.

FIGURE 12.6 Five Types of Followers

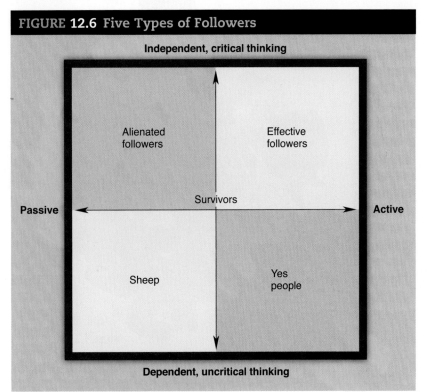

Independent, critical thinking

Alienated followers

Effective followers

Survivors

Passive ← → Active

Sheep

Yes people

Dependent, uncritical thinking

followers who do not think independently or critically and are passive in their behavior. *Yes people* are followers who do not think independently or critically, yet are very active in their behavior. They uncritically reinforce the thinking and ideas of their leaders with enthusiasm, never questioning or challenging the wisdom of the leaders' ideas and proposals. Yes people are the most dangerous to a leader because they are the most likely to give a false positive reaction and give no warning of potential pitfalls. *Survivors* (see the center of the figure) are the least disruptive and the lowest-risk followers in an organization. They perpetually sample the wind, and their motto is "better safe than sorry."

Effective followers are the most valuable to a leader and an organization because of their active contributions. Effective followers share four essential qualities. First, they practice self-management and self-responsibility. A leader can delegate to an effective follower without anxiety about the outcome. Second, they are committed both to the organization and a purpose, principle, or person outside themselves. Effective followers are not self-centered or self-aggrandizing. Third, effective followers invest in their own competence and professionalism and focus their energy for maximum impact. Effective followers look for challenges and ways in which to add to their talents or abilities. Fourth, they are courageous, honest, and credible.

Effective followers might be thought of as self-leaders who do not require close supervision.[78] The notion of *self-leadership*, or *superleadership*, blurs the distinction between leaders and followers. Caring leaders are often able to encourage the development of self-leadership in their employees, creating effective, dynamic followers.

Guidelines for Leadership

Leadership is a key to influencing organizational behavior and achieving organizational effectiveness. When artifacts are eliminated, studies of leadership succession show a moderately strong leader influence on organizational performance.[79] With this said, it is important to recognize that other factors also influence organizational performance. These include environmental factors (such as general economic conditions) and technological factors (such as efficiency).

Corporate leaders play a central role in setting the ethical tone and moral values for their organizations. While many corporate leaders talk about ethics, many never have to actually risk the firm's fortune on an ethical decision. In 1976, when James Burke, head of Johnson & Johnson, challenged his management team to reaffirm the company's historic commitment to ethical behavior, he had no idea he would be asked to demonstrate that commitment in action. But six years later, when poisoned packages of Tylenol appeared on store shelves, Burke did not hesitate to act on what he had pledged. The company pulled the product from the shelves at a cost of $100 million. It also offered a reward for a new design that would revamp the product's packaging. In the end, Tylenol recovered and is once again the leading pain medication in the United States.

Five useful guidelines appear to emerge from the extensive leadership research of the past sixty years:

1. Leaders and organizations should appreciate the unique attributes, predispositions, and talents of each leader. No two leaders are the same, and there is value in this diversity.

2. Although there appears to be no single best style of leadership, there are organizational preferences in terms of style. Leaders should be chosen who challenge the organizational culture, when necessary, without destroying it.

3. Participative, considerate leader behaviors that demonstrate a concern for people appear to enhance the health and well-being of followers in the work environment. This does not imply, however, that a leader must ignore the team's work tasks.

[Lessons Learned at the Top]

Andrea Jung has been CEO of Avon Products, Inc., for over ten years, making her the longest-tenured CEO in the *Fortune* 500. Since she became CEO in 1999, Jung has learned several lessons about both life and business.

According to Jung, one has to reinvent herself before she can reinvent her company. Experience in the job is a good thing, but it can limit the CEO's ability to look at the business from innovative and objective perspectives. To overcome this, Jung fires herself every Friday. This means that she comes in every Monday as if she has just been hired as a new turnaround leader. Jung believes that the skills that lead to success each year become obsolete the following year. To keep up with the fast-paced business world, CEOs must never settle for the comfortable status quo.

Another lesson learned by Jung is that communication is paramount to a flourishing business. Especially in tough times, CEOs and all leaders must be candid about their vision and the reasoning behind difficult decisions. Leaders should frequently communicate face to face—not just over e-mail. This will make the company healthier through trust and respect.

Jung's final lesson is that without the support of the right people, the right vision and strategy mean nothing. Jung spends more than 25 percent of her time in talent development. She believes that businesses must continually grow the best talent because, like her, they will need to reinvent themselves to stay ahead of the game.

SOURCE: "Reinvent Yourself and Your Company," *USA Today* (June 15, 2009): 3B.

©Lew Robertson/Brand X Pictures/Jupiterimages

4. Different leadership situations call for different leadership talents and behaviors. This may result in different individuals taking the leader role according to the specific situation in which the team finds itself.

5. Good leaders are likely to be good followers. Although there are distinctions between their social roles, the attributes and behaviors of leaders and followers may not be as distinct as is sometimes thought.

Log in to the **CourseMate** for *ORGB3* at **www.cengagebrain.com** to:

✳ Review **Key Terms Flash Cards** online

✳ Play **Beat the Clock** and **Quiz Bowl** to master concepts

✳ Complete **web quizzes** to prepare for exams

✳ Watch the video on **Camp Bow Wow** and from *Doomsday* for examples, then test yourself with a quick quiz

✳ Work through the **"What about You?"** and **Ethical Dilemma** exercises to see how you would handle various situations that organizations face on a daily basis

13

Conflict and Negotiation

LEARNING OUTCOMES

1 Describe the nature of conflicts in organizations.

2 Explain the role structural and personal factors play in causing conflict in organizations.

3 Discuss the nature of group conflict in organizations.

4 Describe the factors that influence conflict between individuals in organizations.

5 Describe effective and ineffective techniques for managing conflict.

6 Identify five styles of conflict management.

©iStockphoto.com/Giorgio Fochesato

" Estimates show that managers spend about 21 percent of their time, or one day every week, dealing with conflict. "

After You Finish
This Chapter
Go to **Page 227**
for **Study Tools**

The Nature of Conflicts in Organizations

All of us have experienced conflict of various types, yet we probably fail to recognize the variety of conflicts that occur in organizations. *Conflict* is defined as any situation in which incompatible goals, attitudes, emotions, or behaviors lead to disagreement or opposition between two or more parties.[1] Today organizations may face greater potential for conflict than ever before in history. The marketplace, with its increasing competition and globalization, magnifies differences among people in terms of personality, values, attitudes, perceptions, languages, cultures, and national backgrounds.[2] With the increasing diversity of the workforce comes the potential for incompatibility and conflict.

Importance of Conflict Management Skills for the Manager

Estimates show that managers spend about 21 percent of their time, or one day every week, dealing with conflict.[3] Not surprisingly, then, conflict management skills are a major predictor of managerial success.[4] A critical indicator of a manager's ability to manage conflict is his or her *emotional intelligence (EI)*, which is the power to control one's emotions and perceive emotions in others, adapt to change, and manage adversity. (Conflict management skills may be more a reflection of EI than of IQ.) People who lack emotional intelligence, especially empathy, or the ability to see life from another person's perspective, are more likely to be causes of conflict than managers of conflict.[5]

Functional versus Dysfunctional Conflict

Not all conflict is bad. In fact, some types of conflict encourage new solutions to problems and enhance creativity in the organization. In these cases, managers will want to encourage the conflicts. Thus, the key to conflict management is to stimulate functional conflict and prevent or resolve dysfunctional conflict.

The difficulty, however, is distinguishing between dysfunctional and functional conflicts. The consequences of conflict can be positive or negative, as shown in Table 13.1.

Functional conflict is a healthy, constructive disagreement between two or more people. New ideas, learning, and growth among individuals can result from functional conflict. Such conflict is constructive conflict; individuals can develop a better awareness of themselves and others through it. In addition, functional conflict can improve working relationships because when two parties work through disagreements, they feel they have accomplished something together. By releasing tensions and solving problems in working together this way, they experience improved morale.[6] Functional conflict can lead to innovation and positive change for the organization.[7] Because it tends to encourage creativity among individuals, this positive form of conflict often translates into increased productivity.[8] A key to recognizing functional conflict is that it is often cognitive in origin; that is, it arises from someone challenging old policies or thinking of new ways to approach problems. In fact, managers should work to stimulate this type of conflict when they suspect their group is suffering from groupthink.[9]

Dysfunctional conflict is an unhealthy, destructive disagreement between two or more people. Its danger is that it takes the focus away from the work to be done and places it on the conflict itself and the parties involved. Excessive conflict drains energy that could be used more productively. A key to recognizing a dysfunctional conflict is that its origin is often emotional or behavioral. For example, disagreements that involve personalized anger and resentment directed at specific individuals rather than specific ideas are dysfunctional.[10] Individuals involved in dysfunctional conflict tend to act before thinking, and they often rely on threats, deception, and verbal abuse to communicate. Moreover, dysfunctional conflict can often lead to aggressive acts or retaliation directed at supervisors, peers, subordinates, or even

TABLE 13.1 Consequences of Conflict	
POSITIVE CONSEQUENCES	**NEGATIVE CONSEQUENCES**
• Leads to new ideas • Stimulates creativity • Motivates change • Promotes organizational vitality • Helps individuals and groups establish identities • Serves as a safety valve to indicate problems	• Diverts energy from work • Threatens psychological well-being • Wastes resources • Creates a negative climate • Breaks down group cohesion • Can increase hostility and aggressive behaviors

© Cengage Learning 2013

service providers.[11] In dysfunctional conflict, losses to both parties may exceed any potential gain from the conflict.

Diagnosing Conflict

Diagnosing conflict as functional or dysfunctional is not easy. The manager must look at the issue, the context of the conflict, and the parties involved. Once the manager has diagnosed the type of conflict, he or she can either work to resolve it (if it is dysfunctional) or to stimulate it (if it is functional).

It is easy to make mistakes in diagnosing conflicts. Sometimes task conflict, which is functional, can be misattributed as being personal, and dysfunctional conflict can

Dysfunctional conflict takes the focus of the team way from the work to be done.

©Inmagine/Inspirestock/Jupiterimages

functional conflict

A healthy, constructive disagreement between two or more people.

dysfunctional conflict

An unhealthy, destructive disagreement between two or more people.

follow. Developing trust within the work group can keep this misattribution from occurring.[12] A study of group effectiveness found that decision-making groups made up of friends were able to engage more openly in disagreement than groups made up of strangers, allowing the friends' groups to make more effective decisions. When group members (friends) felt comfortable and trusting enough to express conflicting opinions, optimal performance resulted. But decision-making groups made up of friends and strangers exhibited both high levels of conflict *and* low levels of performance, suggesting that open disagreement in these groups was not helpful. This finding should serve as a cautionary tale for managers trying to apply one country's management style and techniques in another cultural setting.[13]

LEARNING OUTCOME 2

Causes of Conflict in Organizations

Conflict is pervasive in organizations. To manage it effectively, managers should understand its many sources. These can be classified into two broad categories: *structural factors*, which stem from the nature of the organization and the way in which work is organized, and *personal factors*, which arise from differences among individuals. Figure 13.1 summarizes the causes of conflict within each category.

Structural Factors

The causes of conflict related to the organization's structure include specialization, interdependence, common resources, goal differences, authority relationships, status inconsistencies, and jurisdictional ambiguities.

Specialization When jobs are highly specialized, employees become experts at certain tasks. For example, one software company has one specialist for databases, one for statistical packages, and another for expert systems. Highly specialized jobs can lead to conflict, because people have little awareness of the tasks that others perform.

A classic conflict of specialization often occurs between salespeople and engineers. Engineers are technical specialists responsible for product design and quality. Salespeople are marketing experts and liaisons with customers. Salespeople are often accused of making delivery promises to customers that engineers cannot keep because the sales force lacks the technical knowledge necessary to develop realistic delivery deadlines.

Interdependence Work that is interdependent requires groups or individuals to depend on one another to accomplish goals.[14] Depending on other people to get work done is fine when the process works smoothly. When there is a problem, however, it becomes very easy to blame the other party, and conflict escalates. In a garment manufacturing plant, for example, when the fabric cutters get behind in their work, the workers who sew the garments are delayed as well. Considerable frustration may result when the workers at the sewing machines feel their efforts are being blocked by the cutters' slow pace and their pay is affected because they are paid piece-rate.

Common Resources Any time multiple parties must share resources, there is potential for conflict.[15] This potential is enhanced when the shared resources become scarce. For example, managers often share administrative support. Not uncommonly, one administrative assistant supports ten or more managers, each of whom believes his or her work is most important. This puts pressure on the administrative assistant and leads to potential conflicts in prioritizing and scheduling work.

Goal Differences When work groups have different goals, these goals may be incompatible. For example, in one cable television company, the salesperson's goal was to sell as many new installations as possible. This created problems for the service department, because its goal was timely installations. With increasing sales, the

FIGURE 13.1 Causes of Conflict in Organizations

Structural Factors
• Specialization
• Interdependence
• Common resources
• Goal differences
• Authority relationships
• Status inconsistencies
• Jurisdictional ambiguities

Conflict

Personal Factors
• Skills and abilities
• Personalities
• Perceptions
• Values and ethics
• Emotions
• Communication barriers
• Cultural differences

© TongRo Image Stock/Jupiterimages

jurisdictional ambiguity

The presence of unclear lines of responsibility within an organization.

service department's workload became backed up, and orders were delayed. Often these types of conflicts occur because individuals do not have knowledge of another department's objectives.

Authority Relationships A traditional boss–employee relationship is hierarchical in nature, with a boss who is superior to the employee. For many employees, such a relationship is not a comfortable one; they don't like another person having the right to tell them what to do. Some people resent authority more than others, and obviously this creates conflicts. In addition, some bosses are more autocratic than others, compounding the potential for conflict in the relationship. As organizations move toward the team approach and empowerment, there should be less potential for conflict from authority relationships.

Status Inconsistencies Some organizations have a strong status difference between management and nonmanagement workers. Managers may enjoy privileges—such as flexible schedules, reserved parking spaces, and longer lunch hours—that are not available to nonmanagement employees and that may result in resentment and conflict.

Jurisdictional Ambiguities Have you ever called a company with a problem and had your call transferred through several different people and departments? This situation illustrates **jurisdictional ambiguity**—that is, unclear lines of responsibility within an organization.[16] The classic situation here

involves the hardware/software dilemma. You call the company that made your computer, and it informs you that the problem is caused by the software. You call the software division, and it tells you it's the hardware . . . .

Personal Factors

Not all conflicts arise out of structural factors in the organization. Some conflicts arise out of differences among individuals. The causes of conflict that arise from individual differences include skills and abilities, personalities, perceptions, values and ethics, emotions, communication barriers, and cultural differences.

Skills and Abilities Diversity in skills and abilities may be positive for the organization, but it also holds potential for conflict, especially when jobs are interdependent. Experienced, competent workers may find it difficult to work alongside new and unskilled recruits. Workers can become resentful when their new boss, fresh from college, knows a lot about managing people but is unfamiliar with the technology with which they are working.

Personalities Individuals do not leave their personalities at the doorstep when they enter the workplace. Personality conflicts are thus realities in organizations. It is as naïve to expect that you will like all of your coworkers, just as it is naïve to expect that they will all like you.

One personality trait that many people find difficult to deal with is abrasiveness.[17] An abrasive person ignores the interpersonal aspects of work and the feelings of colleagues. These types of people are often achievement oriented and hardworking, but their perfectionist, critical style can leave others feeling unimportant. The working style of abrasive individuals causes stress and strain for those around them.[18]

Perceptions Differences in perception can also lead to conflict. For example, managers and workers may not have a shared perception of what motivates people. In this case, the reward system can create conflicts if managers provide what they *think* employees want rather than what they actually want.

©iStockphoto.com/Josh Rinehults

Values and Ethics Differences in values and ethics can be sources of disagreement. Older workers, for example, value company loyalty and probably would not take a sick day when they were not really ill. Younger workers, valuing mobility, like the concept of "mental health days," or calling in sick to get away from work. This may not be true for all workers, but it illustrates that differences in values can lead to conflict.

Most people have their own sets of values and ethics, although the extent to which they apply these ethics in the workplace varies. Some people have strong desires for approval from others and will work to meet others' ethical standards. Others are relatively unconcerned about approval from others and strongly apply their own ethical standards. Still others operate seemingly without regard to ethics or values.[19] When conflicts about values or ethics do arise, heated disagreement is common because of the personal nature of the differences.

Emotions Conflict is by nature an emotional interaction, and the emotions of the parties involved in conflict play a pivotal role in how they perceive any type of negotiation and therefore how they respond to one another.[20] In fact, emotions are now considered critical elements of negotiation and must be included in an examination of the process and how it unfolds.[21] When negotiators begin to act based on emotions rather than on cognitions, they become much more likely to reach an impasse.[22]

Communication Barriers Communication barriers such as physical separation and language can create distortions in messages, and these can lead to conflict. Another communication barrier is value judgment, in which a listener assigns worth to a message before it is received. For example, suppose a team member is a chronic complainer. When this individual enters the manager's office, the manager is likely to devalue the message before it is even delivered. Conflict can then emerge.

Cultural Differences Although cultural differences are assets in organizations, sometimes they can be sources of conflict. Often, these conflicts stem from a lack of understanding of another culture. In one MBA class, for example, Indian students were horrified when American students challenged the professor. Meanwhile, the American students thought the students from India were too passive. Subsequent discussions revealed that professors in India expect to be treated deferentially and with great respect. While students might challenge an idea vigorously, they would rarely challenge the professor. Diversity training that emphasizes education on cultural differences can make great strides in preventing misunderstandings.

LEARNING OUTCOME **3**

Forms of Group Conflict in Organizations

Conflict in an organization can take on any of several different forms that can mainly be sorted into two core groups: conflicts that occur at the group level and conflicts that occur at the individual level. Conflicts at each level can be further classified as either *inter* or *intra*. It is important to note that the prefix *inter* means "between," whereas the prefix *intra* means "within." Conflict at the group level can occur between organizations (interorganizational), between groups (intergroup), or within a group (intragroup).

Interorganizational Conflict

Conflict that occurs between two or more organizations is called **interorganizational conflict**. Competition can heighten interorganizational conflict. Corporate takeovers, mergers, and

> **interorganizational conflict**
> Conflict that occurs between two or more organizations.

©iStockphoto.com/Chris Gramly

acquisitions can also produce interorganizational conflict. What about the interorganizational conflict between the National Football League's players unions and team owners, which was often characterized as a battle between millionaires and billionaires? The players regularly go on strike to extract more of the profits from the owners, while the owners cry that they are not making a dime.

Intergroup Conflict

When conflict occurs between groups or teams, it is known as **intergroup conflict**. Conflict between groups can have positive effects within each group, such as increased group cohesiveness, increased focus on tasks, and increased loyalty to the group. There are, however, negative consequences as well. Groups in conflict tend to develop an "us against them" mentality whereby each sees the other team as the enemy, becomes more hostile, and decreases its communication with the other group. Groups are even more competitive and less cooperative than individuals. The inevitable outcome is that one group gains and the other group loses.[23]

Competition between groups must be managed carefully so that it does not escalate into dysfunctional conflict. Research has shown that when multiple groups compete for a goal that only one group can achieve, negative consequences like territoriality, aggression, and prejudice toward other groups can result.[24] To prevent these negative results, managers should encourage and reward cooperative behaviors across groups. Some effective ways of doing this include modifying performance appraisals to include assessing intergroup behavior and using an external supervisor's evaluation of intergroup behavior. Group members will be more likely to help other groups when they know that the other group's supervisor will be evaluating their behavior and that they will be rewarded for cooperation.[25] In addition, managers should encourage social interactions across groups so that trust can be developed. Trust allows individuals to exchange ideas and resources with members of other groups and results in innovation when members of different groups cooperate.[26]

Intragroup Conflict

Conflict that occurs within groups or teams is called **intragroup conflict**. Some conflict within a group is functional, since it can help prevent groupthink, as we discussed in Chapter 10.

Even the newest type of teams, virtual teams, is not immune to conflict. The nuances and subtleties of face-to-face communication are often lacking in these teams, and misunderstandings can result. To avoid dysfunctional conflicts, virtual teams should make sure their tasks fit their methods of interacting. Complex strategic decisions may require face-to-face meetings rather than e-mails or threaded discussions. Face-to-face and telephone interactions early on can eliminate later conflicts and allow virtual teams to move on to use electronic communication because trust has been developed.[27]

LEARNING OUTCOME **4**

Individual Conflict in Organizations

As with groups, conflict can occur between individuals (interpersonal) or within a single individual (intrapersonal).

Types of Intrapersonal Conflict

When conflict occurs within an individual, it is called **intrapersonal conflict**. There are several types of intrapersonal conflict, including interrole, intrarole, and person–role conflicts. A *role* is a set of expectations placed on an individual by others.[28] The person occupying the focal role is the *role incumbent*, and the individuals who

intergroup conflict
Conflict that occurs between groups or teams in an organization.

intragroup conflict
Conflict that occurs within groups or teams.

intrapersonal conflict
Conflict that occurs within an individual.

GENERATION CLASH

A n emerging challenge in conflict management is the intergenerational conflict brought about by the diversity in age in the U.S. workforce. Some sources of intergenerational conflict are

- employee benefit packages being designed to appeal more to one age group than another, or

- older employees fearing that younger new hires may take over their jobs.

Organizations should design flexible employee benefit systems that have a broader appeal to a diverse age group and encourage social interaction to reduce these perceived threats and create trust.[29]

place expectations on the person are *role senders*. Figure 13.2 depicts a set of role relationships.

Interrole conflict occurs when a person experiences conflict among the multiple roles in his or her life. One interrole conflict that many employees experience is *work–home conflict*, in which their role as worker clashes with their role as spouse or parent.[30] Work–home conflict can arise from time constraints, strain, and having responsibilities for people in the workplace and at home.[31] This type of conflict has become even more common with the rise of work-at-home professionals and telecommuting, in which the home becomes the office and the boundary between work and family life is blurred.[32] Recently, organizations have been leveraging their use of information technology to gain a competitive edge. This has translated into ambitious and highly involved employees using office communications (e.g., voice mail, e-mail, and so on) even after hours. Such after-hours communication usage is associated with increased work–life conflict as reported by the employee and a significant other.[33] Work–home conflict can have very negative consequences. It reduces personal well-being, decreases organizational citizenship behavior, and increases stress. People also tend to drink more alcohol on days they experience work–home conflict.[34]

Intrarole conflict is conflict within a single role. It often arises when a person receives conflicting messages from role senders about how to perform a certain role. Suppose a manager receives counsel from her

One interrole conflict that many employees experience is work–home conflict.

©Jamie Grill/Corbis

department head that she needs to socialize less with nonmanagement employees. She is also told by her project manager that she needs to be a better team member, and that she can accomplish this by socializing more with other nonmanagement team members. This situation is one of intrarole conflict.

interrole conflict
A person's experience of conflict among the multiple roles in his or her life.

intrarole conflict
Conflict that occurs within a single role, such as when a person receives conflicting messages from role senders about how to perform a certain role.

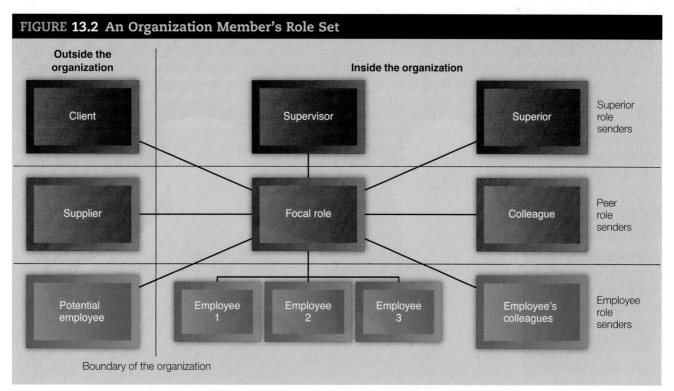

FIGURE **13.2** An Organization Member's Role Set

SOURCE: J. C. Quick, J. D. Quick, D. L. Nelson, and J. J. Hurrell, Jr., *Preventive Stress Management in Organizations* (Washington, DC: American Psychological Association, 1997). Copyright © 1997 by the American Psychological Association. Reprinted with permission.

Person–role conflict occurs when an individual in a particular role is expected to perform behaviors that clash with his personal values.[35] Salespeople, for example, may be required to offer the most expensive item in the sales line first to the customer, even when it is apparent that the customer does not want or cannot afford it. A computer salesman may be required to offer a large, elaborate system to a student he knows is on a tight budget. This may conflict with the salesman's values, and he may experience person–role conflict.

Intrapersonal conflicts can have positive consequences. Often, professional responsibilities clash with deeply held values. A budget shortfall may force you to lay off a loyal, hardworking employee. Your daughter may have a piano recital on the same day your largest client is scheduled to be in town visiting the office. In such conflicts, we often have to choose between right and right; that is, there's no wrong response, only one better than the other. These decisions pose what may be thought of as *defining moments* that challenge individuals to choose between two or more things in which they believe.[36] Character is formed in defining moments because they cause individuals to shape their identities. They help people crystallize their values and serve as opportunities for personal growth.

Managing Intrapersonal Conflict

Intrapersonal conflict can be managed with careful self-analysis and diagnosis of the situation. Three actions in particular can help prevent or resolve intrapersonal conflicts. First, when seeking a new job, you should find out as much as possible about the values of the organization.[37] Many person–role conflicts center around differences between the organization's values and the individual's values. Research has shown that when there is a good fit between the values of the individual and the organization, the individual is more satisfied and committed and is less likely to leave the organization.[38]

Second, *role-analysis* is a good tool for man-

aging intrarole or interrole conflicts.[39] In role analysis, the individual asks the various role senders what they expect of him. The outcomes are clearer work roles and the reduction of conflict and ambiguity.[40] Role analysis is a simple tool that clarifies the expectations of both parties in a relationship and reduces the potential for conflict within a role or between roles.

Third, political skills can help buffer the negative effects of stress that stem from role conflicts. Effective politicians can negotiate role expectations when conflicts occur. All these forms of conflict can be managed. An understanding of the many forms is a first step.

Managing Interpersonal Conflict

Conflict that occurs between two or more individuals, or **interpersonal conflict**, can arise from many individual differences, including personalities, attitudes, values, and perceptions. To manage interpersonal conflict, it is helpful to understand power networks in organizations and defense mechanisms exhibited by individuals when they are in conflict situations.

Power Networks According to W. F. G. Mastenbroek, individuals in organizations are organized into three basic types of power networks.[41] Based on these power relationships, certain kinds of conflict tend to emerge. Figure 13.3 illustrates three basic kinds of power relationships in organizations. The first relationship is *equal versus equal*, in which there is a horizontal balance of power among the parties. An example of this type of relationship would be a conflict between individuals from two different project teams. The behavioral tendency is toward *suboptimization*; that is, the focus is on a win–lose approach to problems, and each party tries to maximize its power at the expense of the other party. Conflict within this type of network can lead to depression, low self-esteem, and other

person–role conflict

Conflict that occurs when an individual in a particular role is expected to perform behaviors that clash with his or her personal values.

interpersonal conflict

Conflict that occurs between two or more individuals.

FIGURE 13.3 Power Relationships in Organizations

Types of power relationships	Behavioral tendencies and problems	Interventions
Equal vs. equal	Suboptimization • Tendency to compete with one another • Covert fighting for positions • Constant friction in border areas	• Defining demarcation lines • Improving coordination procedures • Integrating units • Teaching negotiating skills • Clarifying common interest • Activating central authority
High vs. low	Control versus autonomy • Resistance to change • Motivation problems	• Bureaucratizing power through rules • Using a different style of leadership • Structural and cultural interventions
High vs. middle vs. low	Role conflict, role ambiguity, stress • Concessions, double-talk, and use of sanctions and rewards to strengthen the position	• Improving communication • Clarifying tasks • Horizontalization, vertical task expansion • Teaching power strategies

SOURCE: W. F. G. Mastenbroek, *Conflict Management and Organization Development* (New York: Wiley, 1987). Copyright John Wiley & Sons Limited. Reproduced with permission.

distress symptoms. Interventions such as improving coordination between the parties and working toward common interests can help manage these conflicts.

The second power network is *high versus low*, or a powerful party versus a less powerful party. Conflicts that emerge here take the basic form of the powerful individuals trying to control others, with the less powerful people trying to become more autonomous. Conflict in this network can lead to job dissatisfaction, low organizational commitment, and turnover.[42] Organizations typically respond to these conflicts by tightening the rules. However, the more successful ways of managing these conflicts are to try a different style of leadership, such as a coaching and counseling style, or to change the structure to a more decentralized one.

The third power network is *high versus middle versus low*. This power network illustrates the classic conflicts felt by middle managers. Two particular conflicts are evident for middle managers: *role conflict*, in which conflicting expectations are placed on the manager from bosses and employees, and *role ambiguity*, in which the expectations of the boss are unclear. Improved communication among all parties can reduce role conflict and ambiguity. In addition, middle managers can benefit from training in positive ways to influence others.

Knowing the typical kinds of conflicts that arise in various kinds of relationships can help a manager diagnose conflicts and devise appropriate ways to manage them.

Defense Mechanisms

When individuals are involved in conflict with another human being, frustration often results.[43] Conflicts can often arise within the context of a performance appraisal session. Most people do not react well to negative feedback, as was illustrated in a classic study in which more than 50 percent of employees reacted defensively when given criticism about their work.[44]

When individuals are frustrated, as they often are in interpersonal conflict, they respond by exhibiting *defense mechanisms*.[45] Aggressive mechanisms, such as fixation, displacement, and negativism, are aimed at attacking the source of the conflict. In **fixation**, an individual fixates on the conflict, or keeps up a dysfunctional behavior that obviously will not solve the conflict. An example of fixation occurred in a university where a faculty member became embroiled in a battle with the dean because the faculty member felt he had not received a large enough salary increase. He persisted in writing angry letters to the dean, whose hands were tied because of a low budget allocation to the college. Another aggressive defense mechanism is **displacement**, which means directing anger toward someone who is not the source of the conflict. For example, a manager may respond harshly to an employee after a telephone confrontation with an angry customer. **Negativism** is an aggressive mechanism in which a person responds with pessimism to any attempt at solving a problem. Negativism

fixation

An aggressive mechanism in which an individual keeps up a dysfunctional behavior that obviously will not solve the conflict.

displacement

An aggressive mechanism in which an individual directs his or her anger toward someone who is not the source of the conflict.

negativism

An aggressive mechanism in which a person responds with pessimism to any attempt at solving a problem.

compensation

A compromise mechanism in which an individual attempts to make up for a negative situation by devoting himself or herself to another pursuit with increased vigor.

identification

A compromise mechanism whereby an individual patterns his or her behavior after another's.

rationalization

A compromise mechanism characterized by trying to justify one's behavior by constructing bogus reasons for it.

flight/withdrawal

A withdrawal mechanism that entails physically escaping (flight) or psychologically escaping (withdrawal) a conflict.

conversion

A withdrawal mechanism in which emotional conflicts are expressed in physical symptoms.

fantasy

A withdrawal mechanism that provides an escape from a conflict through daydreaming.

is illustrated by a manager who, when appointed to a committee on which she did not want to serve, made negative comments throughout the meeting.

Compromise mechanisms, such as compensation, identification, and rationalization, are used by individuals to make the best of a conflict situation. **Compensation** is a compromise mechanism in which an individual attempts to make up for a negative situation by devoting himself to another pursuit with increased vigor. Compensation can be seen when a person makes up for a bad relationship at home by spending more time at the office. **Identification** is a compromise mechanism whereby an individual patterns her behavior after another's. One supervisor at a construction firm, not wanting to acknowledge consciously that she was not likely to be promoted,

mimicked the behavior of her boss, even going so far as to buy a car just like the boss's. **Rationalization** is trying to justify one's behavior by constructing bogus reasons for it. Employees may rationalize unethical behavior like padding their expense accounts with the argument that "everyone else does it."

Withdrawal mechanisms are exhibited when frustrated individuals try to flee from a conflict using either physical or psychological means. Flight, conversion, and fantasy are examples of withdrawal mechanisms. Physically escaping a conflict is **flight**. An employee taking a day off after a blowup with the boss is an example. **Withdrawal** may take the form of emotionally leaving a conflict, such as exhibiting an "I don't care anymore" attitude. **Conversion** is a process whereby emotional conflicts become expressed in physical symptoms. Most of us have experienced the conversion reaction of a headache following an emotional exchange with another person. **Fantasy** is a withdrawal mechanism that provides an escape from a conflict through daydreaming. In the Internet age, fantasy as an escape mechanism has found new meaning. A study conducted by International Data Corporation (IDC) showed that 30 to 40 percent of all Internet surfing in the office is nonwork-related and that more than 70 percent of companies have had sex sites accessed from their networks, suggesting that employees' minds aren't always focused on their jobs.[46]

When employees exhibit withdrawal mechanisms, they often pretend to agree with their bosses or coworkers in order to avoid facing an immediate conflict. Many employees fake a positive response this way because the firm informally rewards agreement and punishes

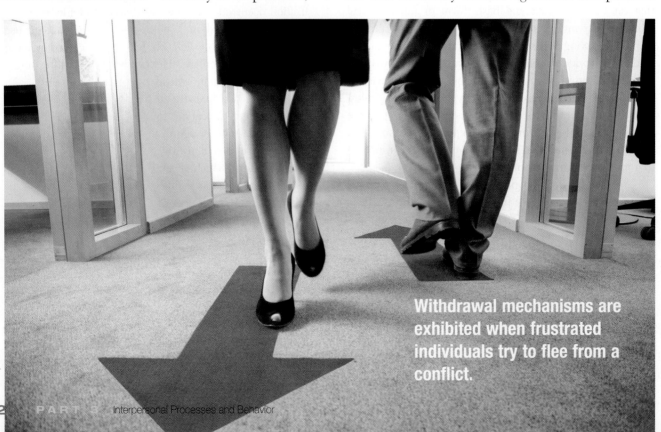

Withdrawal mechanisms are exhibited when frustrated individuals try to flee from a conflict.

dissent. The long-term consequence of withdrawal and faking a positive response is emotional distress for the employee.[47]

Knowledge of these defense mechanisms can be extremely beneficial to a manager. By understanding the ways in which people typically react to interpersonal conflict, managers can be prepared for employees' reactions and help them uncover their feelings about a conflict.

Conflict Management Strategies and Techniques

The overall approach (or strategy) you use in a conflict is important in determining whether the conflict will have a positive or negative outcome. Overall strategies to deal with conflict can be classified as competitive versus cooperative strategies. Table 13.2 on the next page depicts the two strategies and four different conflict scenarios. The *competitive strategy* is founded on assumptions of win–lose and entails dishonest communication, mistrust, and a rigid position from both parties.[48] The *cooperative strategy* is founded on different assumptions: the potential for win–win outcomes, honest communication, trust, openness to risk and vulnerability, and the notion that the whole may be greater than the sum of the parts.

To illustrate the importance of the overall strategy, consider the case of two groups competing for scarce resources. Suppose budget cuts have to be made at an insurance company. The claims manager argues that the sales training staff should be cut because agents are fully trained. The sales training manager argues that claims personnel should be cut because the company is processing fewer claims. This could turn into a dysfunctional brawl, with both sides refusing to give ground. The result would be a win–lose, lose–win, or lose–lose scenario. Personnel cuts could be made in one department or the other, or in both departments. In all three cases, the organization winds up in a losing position with the competitive approach.

Even in such intense conflicts as those over scarce resources, a win–win strategy can lead to an overall win for the organization. In fact, conflicts over scarce resources can be productive if the parties have cooperative goals— a strategy that seeks a winning solution for both parties. To achieve a win–win outcome, the conflict must be approached with open-minded discussion of opposing views. Through open-minded discussion, both parties integrate views and create new solutions that facilitate productivity and strengthen their relationship; the result is feelings of unity rather than separation.[49]

In the example of the conflict between the claims manager and sales training manager, open-minded discussion might reveal that there are ways to achieve

[Quashing Group Conflict]

The type of conflict a group experiences may not impact the group's performance as much as its preferred conflict resolution strategy. Groups tend to fall into one of four strategic categories:

1. **Dual concern**: Groups that work to improve or maintain top performance as well as member satisfaction employ an approach that focuses on concern for the task as well as for integrating the interests of individual team members.
2. **Task focused**: Groups that maintain high performance but experience waning member satisfaction employ a strategy that creates a rules-oriented environment at the expense of integrating individual interests.
3. **Psyche focused**: Poorly performing groups with high member satisfaction completely accommodate individual concerns, avoiding interpersonal conflict, and achieve harmony at the expense of performance.
4. **Zero concern**: Groups that perform poorly and have low member satisfaction lack a conflict management strategy: roles are not clear, and no one identifies or eradicates the source of the problem.

The bottom line? Good performance occurs and team members are satisfied when teams emphasize productivity and integrate the interests of team members while they acknowledge the members who help prevent dysfunctional conflicts.

SOURCE: K. J. Behfar, R. S. Peterson, E. A. Mannix, and W. M. K. Trochim, "The Critical Role of Conflict Resolution in Teams," *Journal of Applied Psychology* 93 (2008): 170–188.

©Masakazu Watanabe/Aflo Foto Agency/Photolibrary

budget cuts without cutting personnel. Sales support might surrender part of its travel budget, and claims might cut overtime. This represents a win–win situation for the company. The budget has been reduced, and relationships between the two departments have been preserved. Both parties have given up something (note the "Win–" in Table 13.2), but the conflict has been resolved with a positive outcome.

You can see the importance of the broad strategy used to approach a conflict. We now move from broad strategies to more specific techniques.

Ineffective Techniques

There are many specific techniques for dealing with conflict. Before turning to techniques that work, it should be recognized that some actions commonly taken in organizations to deal with conflict are not effective.[50]

Nonaction is doing nothing in hopes that the conflict will disappear. Generally, this is not a good technique, because most conflicts do not go away, and the individuals involved in the conflict react with frustration. **Secrecy**, attempting to hide a conflict or an issue that has the potential to create conflict, only creates suspicion. An example is an organizational policy of pay secrecy. In some organizations, discussion of salary is grounds for dismissal. When this is the case, employees suspect that the company has something to hide. **Administrative orbiting** is delaying action on a conflict by buying time, usually by telling the individuals involved that the problem is being worked on or that the boss is still thinking about the issue. Like nonaction, this technique leads to frustration and resentment.

Due process nonaction is a

> ### Effective conflict management techniques include appealing to superordinate goals, expanding resources, changing personnel, changing structure, and confronting and negotiating.

procedure set up to address conflicts that is so costly, time consuming, or personally risky that no one will use it. Some companies' sexual harassment policies are examples of this technique. To file a sexual harassment complaint, detailed paperwork is required, the accuser must go through appropriate channels, and the accuser risks being branded a troublemaker. Thus, the company has a procedure for handling complaints (due process), but no one uses it (nonaction).

Character assassination is an attempt to label or discredit an opponent. Character assassination can backfire and make the individual who uses it appear dishonest and cruel. It often leads to name-calling and accusations by both parties, who both end up losers in the eyes of those who witness the conflict. In 2010, Dana Holgorsen was hired as the head football coach at West Virginia University. The only problem was that the school already had a head coach, Bill Stewart. Holgorsen was hired to serve as an assistant for a year under Stewart and then replace him. This arrangement angered Stewart, who contacted journalists to "dig up dirt" on Holgorsen so that he could use it for character assassination. When this became public knowledge, Stewart resigned from his position.[51]

Effective Techniques

Fortunately, there are effective conflict management techniques. These include appealing to superordinate goals, expanding resources, changing personnel, changing structure, and confronting and negotiating.

Superordinate Goals An organizational goal that is more important to both parties in a conflict than their individual or group goals is a **superordinate goal**.[52] Superordinate goals cannot be achieved by an individual or by one group alone. The achievement of these goals requires cooperation by both parties. One effective technique for resolving conflict is to appeal

---

nonaction

Doing nothing in hopes that a conflict will disappear.

secrecy

Attempting to hide a conflict or an issue that has the potential to create conflict.

administrative orbiting

Delaying action on a conflict by buying time.

due process nonaction

A procedure set up to address conflicts that is so costly, time consuming, or personally risky that no one will use it.

character assassination

An attempt to label or discredit an opponent.

superordinate goal

An organizational goal that is more important to both parties in a conflict than their individual or group goals.

TABLE 13.2 Win–Lose versus Win–Win Strategies			
STRATEGY	**DEPARTMENT A**	**DEPARTMENT B**	**ORGANIZATION**
Competitive	Lose	Lose	Lose
	Lose	Win	Lose
	Win	Lose	Lose
Cooperative	Win–	Win–	Win

© Cengage Learning 2013

to this superordinate goal—in effect, to focus the parties on a larger issue on which they both agree. This helps them realize their similarities rather than their differences.

In the conflict between service representatives and cable television installers that was discussed earlier, appealing to a superordinate goal would be an effective technique for resolving the conflict. Both departments can agree that superior customer service is a goal worthy of pursuit and that this goal cannot be achieved unless cables are installed properly and in a timely manner, and customer complaints are handled effectively. Quality service requires that both departments cooperate to achieve the goal.

Expanding Resources One conflict resolution technique is so simple that it may be overlooked. If the conflict's source is common or scarce resources, providing more resources may be a solution. Of course, managers working with tight budgets may not have the luxury of obtaining additional resources. Nevertheless, it is a technique to be considered. In the example of shared administrative support presented earlier in this chapter, one solution to the conflict among managers over administrative support would be to hire more administrative assistants.

Changing Personnel In some cases, long-running severe conflict may be traced to a specific individual. For example, managers with lower levels of emotional intelligence demonstrate more negative work attitudes, exhibit less altruistic behavior, and produce more negative work outcomes. A chronically disgruntled manager who exhibits low emotional intelligence might not only frustrate his employees but also impede his department's performance. In such cases, transferring or firing an individual could be the best solution, but only after due process.[53]

Changing Structure Another way to resolve a conflict is to change the structure of the organization. One way of accomplishing this is to create an integrator role. An *integrator* is a liaison between groups with very different interests. In severe conflicts, it may be best that the integrator be a neutral third party.[54] Creating the integrator role is a way of opening dialogue between groups that have difficulty communicating.

Using *cross-functional teams* is another way of changing the organization's structure to manage conflict. In the old methods of designing new products in organizations, many departments had to contribute, and delays resulted from difficulties in coordinating the activities of the various departments. Using a cross-functional team made up of members from different departments improves coordination and reduces delays by allowing many activities to be performed at the same time rather than sequentially.[55] The team approach allows members from different departments to work together and reduces the potential for conflict. However, recent research also suggests that such functional diversity can lead to slower informational processing in teams due to differences in members' perceptions of what might be required to achieve group goals. When putting together cross-functional teams, organizations should emphasize superordinate goals and train team members on resolving conflict. One such training technique could involve educating individual members in other functional areas so that everyone on the team can have a shared language.[56] In teamwork, it is helpful to break up a big task so that it becomes a collection of smaller, less complex tasks, and to have smaller teams work on the smaller tasks. This helps to reduce conflict, and organizations can potentially improve the performance of the overall team by improving the outcomes in each subteam.[57]

Confronting and Negotiating Some conflicts require confrontation and negotiation between the parties. Both of these strategies require skill on the part of the negotiator and careful planning before engaging in negotiations. The process of negotiating involves an open discussion of problem solutions, and the outcome often is an exchange in which both parties work toward a mutually beneficial solution.

Negotiation is a joint process of finding a mutually acceptable solution to a complex conflict. There are two major negotiating approaches: distributive

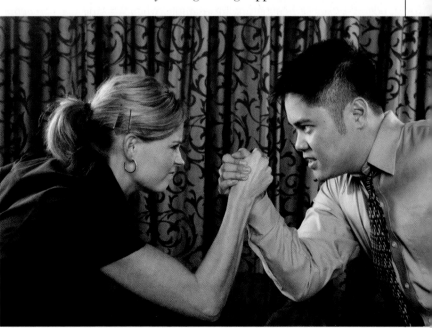

©iStockphoto.com/Lisa Kyle Young

bargaining and integrative negotiation.[58] **Distributive bargaining** is an approach in which the goals of one party are in direct conflict with the goals of the other party. Resources are limited, and each party wants to maximize its share of the resources (get its piece of the pie). It is a competitive, or win–lose, approach to negotiations. Sometimes distributive bargaining causes negotiators to focus so much on their differences that they ignore their common ground. In these cases, distributive bargaining can become counterproductive. The reality is, however, that some situations are distributive in nature, particularly when the parties are interdependent. If a negotiator wants to maximize the value of a single deal and is not worried about maintaining a good relationship with the other party, distributive bargaining may be an option.

In contrast, **integrative negotiation** is an approach in which the parties' goals are not seen as mutually exclusive, but the focus is on both sides achieving their objectives. Integrative negotiation focuses on the merits of the issues and is a win–win approach. (How can we make the pie bigger?) For integrative negotiation to be successful, certain preconditions must be present. These include having a common goal, faith in one's own problem-solving abilities, a belief in the validity of the other party's position, motivation to work together, mutual trust, and clear communication.[59]

Cultural differences in negotiation must be acknowledged. Japanese negotiators, for example, when working with American negotiators, tend to see their power as coming from their role (buyer versus seller). Americans, in contrast, view their power as their ability to walk away from the negotiations.[60] Neither culture understands the other very well, so negotiations can resemble a dance in which one person is waltzing while the other is doing a samba. The collectivism–individualism dimension (discussed in Chapter 2) has a great bearing on negotiations. Americans, with their individualism, negotiate from a position of self-interest; Japanese focus on the good of the group. Cross-cultural negotiations can be more effective if you learn as much about other cultures as possible.

Gender may also play a role in negotiation. There appears to be no evidence that men are better negotiators than women or vice versa. The differences lie in how negotiators are treated. Women are blatantly discriminated against in terms of the offers made to them in negotiations.[61] Gender stereotypes also affect the negotiating process. Women may be seen as accommodating, conciliatory, and emotional (negatives in negotiations), and men may be seen as assertive, powerful, and convincing (positive for negotiations) in accordance with traditional stereotypes. Sometimes, when women feel they're being stereotyped, they exhibit *stereotype reactance*, which is a tendency to display behavior inconsistent with (or even opposite of) the stereotype. This means they become more assertive and convincing. Alternatively, men may "choke" when they're expected to fulfill the stereotype, fearing that they might not be able to live up to it.

Hot Trend: Bossnapping

Top executives in France should watch their backs. Given that the public believes more and more that the only way their needs will be heard is through bossnapping (a play on the word *kidnapping*), incidences of executives being held hostage by workers demanding concessions are becoming more frequent. At the 3M factory at Orleans, employees demanding severance packages for laid-off workers and guarantees of security for the remaining employees held the company's industrial director hostage for more than twenty-four hours until a deal was reached. Sony's CEO and human resources director were held while unions bartered better terms for dismissed workers. Eventually the bossnappers got €13 million added to their redundancy package. Bossnapping may be an illegal tactic, but it certainly seems to be effective.

SOURCES: T. McNicoll, "Sure, Kidnap the Man." *Newsweek* (April 25, 2009). http://www.newsweek.com/id/195092; A. Sage, "Angry French Workers Turn to Bossnapping to Solve Their Problems, *TimesOnline* (April 4, 2009), http://www.timesonline.co.uk/tol/news/world/europe/article6031822.ece.

distributive bargaining

A negotiation approach in which the goals of the parties are in conflict, and each party seeks to maximize its resources.

integrative negotiation

A negotiation approach in which the parties' goals are not seen as mutually exclusive, but the focus is on both sides achieving their objectives.

Conflict Management Styles

Managers have at their disposal a variety of conflict management styles: avoiding, accommodating, competing, compromising, and collaborating. One way of classifying styles of conflict management is to examine the styles' *assertiveness* (the extent to which you want your goals met) and *cooperativeness* (the extent to which you want to see the other party's concerns met).[62] Figure 13.4 graphs the five conflict management styles using these two

FIGURE 13.4 Conflict Management Styles

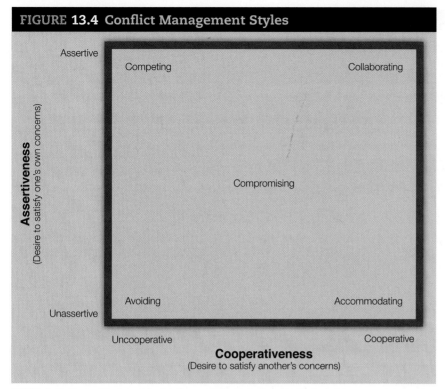

SOURCE: K. W. Thomas, "Conflict and Conflict Management," in M. D. Dunnette, *Handbook of Industrial and Organizational Psychology* (Chicago: Rand McNally, 1976), 900. Used with permission of M. D. Dunnette.

dimensions. Table 13.3 on the next page lists appropriate situations for using each conflict management style.

Avoiding

Avoiding is a style low on both assertiveness and cooperativeness. Avoiding is a deliberate decision to take no action on a conflict or to stay out of a conflict situation. In recent times, Airbus, a European manufacturer of aircraft, has faced massive intraorganizational conflict stemming from major expansions that included French, German, Spanish, and British subsidiaries within the same parent company. Power struggles among executives combined with massive changes in organizational structure are believed to have led to this conflict. Airbus seems to be adopting the avoidance strategy in an effort to let these conflicts subside on their own.[63] Some rela-

tionship conflicts, such as those involving political norms and personal tastes, may distract team members from their tasks, in which case, avoiding may be an appropriate strategy.[64] When the parties are angry and need time to cool down, it may be best to use avoidance. There is a potential danger in using an avoiding style too often, however. Research shows that overuse of this style results in negative evaluations from others in the workplace.[65]

Accommodating

A style in which you are concerned that the other party's goals be met but relatively unconcerned with getting your own way is called accommodating. It is cooperative but unassertive. Appropriate situations for accommodating include times when you find you are wrong, when you want to let the other party have his way so that that individual will owe you similar treatment later, or when the relationship is important. Overreliance on accommodating has its dangers. Managers who constantly defer to others may find that others lose respect for them. In addition, accommodating managers may become frustrated because their own needs are never met, and they may lose self-esteem.[66] Research has also shown that individuals will overestimate the importance of the relationship and accommodate at the expense of actual outcomes. Research has shown that two females involved in conflict or negotiation overuse accommodation more than two males involved in similar situations.[67]

Competing

Competing is a style that is very assertive and uncooperative. You want to satisfy your own interests and are willing to do so at the other party's expense. In an

TABLE 13.3 Uses of Five Styles of Conflict Management

CONFLICT-HANDLING STYLE	APPROPRIATE SITUATION
Competing	1. When quick, decisive action is vital (e.g., emergencies). 2. On important issues for which unpopular actions need implementing (e.g., cost cutting, enforcing unpopular rules, discipline). 3. On issues vital to company welfare when you know you are right. 4. Against people who take advantage of noncompetitive behavior.
Collaborating	1. To find an integrative solution when both sets of concerns are too important to be compromised. 2. When your objective is to learn. 3. To merge insights from people with different perspectives. 4. To gain commitment by incorporating concerns into a consensus. 5. To work through feelings that have interfered with a relationship.
Compromising	1. When goals are important but not worth the effort or potential disruption of more assertive modes. 2. When opponents with equal power are committed to mutually exclusive goals. 3. To achieve temporary settlements to complex issues. 4. To arrive at expedient solutions under time pressure. 5. As a backup when collaboration or competition is unsuccessful.
Avoiding	1. When an issue is trivial or more important issues are pressing. 2. When you perceive no chance of satisfying your concerns. 3. When potential disruption outweighs the benefits of resolution. 4. To let people cool down and regain perspective. 5. When gathering information supersedes immediate decision. 6. When others can resolve the conflict more effectively. 7. When issues seem tangential or symptomatic of other issues.
Accommodating	1. When you find you are wrong—to allow a better position to be heard, to learn, and to show your reasonableness. 2. When issues are more important to others than to yourself—to satisfy others and maintain cooperation. 3. To build social credits for later issues. 4. To minimize loss when you are outmatched and losing. 5. When harmony and stability are especially important. 6. To allow employees to develop by learning from mistakes.

SOURCE: K. W. Thomas, "Toward Multidimensional Values in Teaching: The Example of Conflict Behaviors," *Academy of Management Review* 2 (1977): 309–325. Reproduced by permission of the publisher via Copyright Clearance Center, Inc.

emergency or in situations where you know you are right, it may be appropriate to put your foot down. For example, environmentalists forced Shell Oil Company (part of Royal Dutch/Shell Group) to scrap its plans to build a refinery in Delaware after a bitter "To Hell with Shell" campaign.[68] Relying solely on competing strategies is dangerous, though. Managers who do so may become reluctant to admit when they are wrong and may find themselves surrounded by people who are afraid to disagree with them. As noted earlier, task conflict and relationship conflict could occur together in team settings, although task conflict is seen as functional and relationship conflict as dysfunctional for the team. In a recent study, dyads of participants were exposed to task-based conflict. One of the two members of the dyads was trained on using either the competing conflict-handling style or the collaborative style. Results indicated that

the competing style led to the most relationship conflict, whereas the collaborative style led to the least relationship conflict.[69]

Compromising

The compromising style is intermediate in both assertiveness and cooperativeness, because each party must give up something to reach a solution to the conflict. Compromises are often made in the final hours of union–management negotiations, when time is of the essence. Compromise may be an effective backup style when efforts toward collaboration are not successful.[70]

It is important to recognize that compromises are not optimal solutions. Compromise means partially surrendering one's position for the sake of coming to terms. For this reason, people often inflate their demands when they begin a compromise. A problem with compromise is that the solutions reached may only be temporary, and often compromises do nothing to improve relationships between the parties in conflict.

Collaborating

A win–win style that is high on both assertiveness and cooperativeness is known as collaborating. Working toward it involves an open and thorough discussion of the conflict and arriving at a solution that is satisfactory to both parties. Situations where collaboration may be effective include times when both parties need to be committed to a final solution or when a combination of different perspectives can be formed into a solution. Long-term, collaboration leads to improved relationships and effective performance.[71] Teams that use collaboration effectively view conflict as a mutual problem that needs common consideration to achieve resolution. Understanding this, team members have confidence that other members will work toward mutually beneficial solutions and ultimately generate diverse ideas to facilitate team performance.[72]

Research on the five styles of conflict management indicates that although most managers favor a certain style, they have the capacity to change styles as the situation demands.[73] A study of project managers found that managers who used a combination of competing and avoiding styles were seen as ineffective by the engineers who worked on their project teams.[74]

©iStockphoto.com/Dean Mitchell

Jobs and the Design of Work

LEARNING OUTCOMES

1 Differentiate between *job* and *work*.

2 Discuss the traditional approaches to job design.

3 Identify and describe alternative approaches to job design.

4 Identify and describe contemporary issues facing organizations in the design of work.

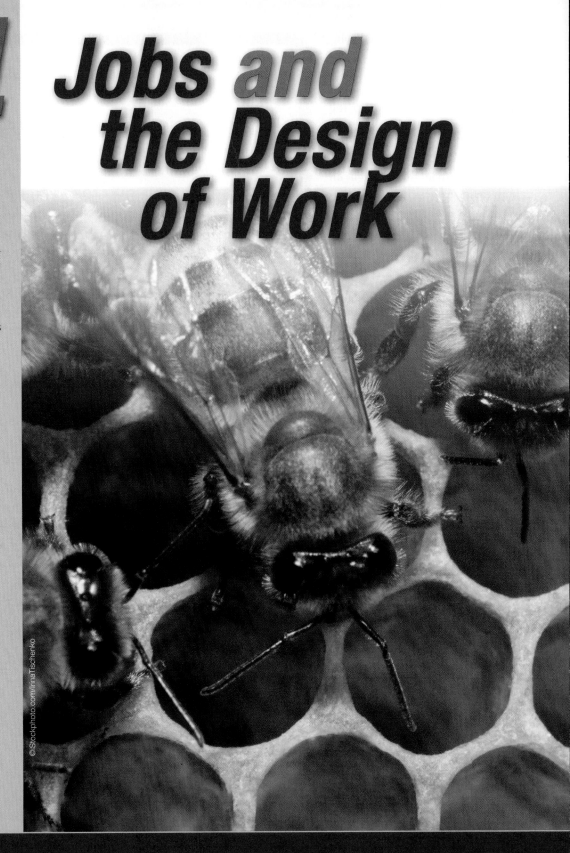

©iStockphoto.com/Irina Tischenko

> **"** It is important to understand and appreciate differences among individuals and cultures with regard to the meaning of work. **"**

After You Finish This Chapter Go to **Page 243** for **Study Tools**

> For all people, work is organized into jobs, and jobs fit into the larger structure of an organization.

Work in Organizations

A **job** can be defined as a set of specified work and task activities that engage an individual in an organization. A job is not the same as an organizational position or a career. *Organizational position* identifies a job in relation to other parts of the organization; *career* refers to a sequence of job experiences over time. A job is also not the same as *work*, at least not in relation to an organization. **Work**, which can be defined as mental or physical activity that has productive results, is organized into jobs. Thus, a *job* is composed of a set of specific tasks, each of which is an assigned piece of *work* to be done in a specific time period.

Work is one important reason organizations exist. Plus, work is an especially important human endeavor, because through work, people become securely attached to reality and securely connected in human relationships. Although *work* has different meanings for different people, from an organization's viewpoint, work is related to the structure of jobs, and jobs fit into the larger structure of an organization. The structure of jobs is the concern of this chapter, and the structure of the organization is the concern of the next chapter. Both chapters emphasize organizations as sets of task and authority relationships through which people get work done.

The Meaning of Work

The **meaning of work** differs from person to person,

job
A set of specified work and task activities that engage an individual in an organization.

work
Mental or physical activity that has productive results.

meaning of work
The way a person interprets and understands the value of work as part of life.

from culture to culture, and from profession to profession.[1] In an increasingly global workplace, it is important to understand and appreciate differences among individuals and cultures with regard to the meaning of work. One study found six patterns people follow in defining *work*, and these help explain the cultural differences in people's motivation to work.[2]

Pattern A people define *work* as an activity in which value comes from performance and for which a person is accountable. It is generally self-directed and devoid of negative affect.

Pattern B people define *work* as an activity that provides a person with positive personal affect and identity. Work contributes to society and is not unpleasant.

Pattern C people define *work* as an activity from which profit accrues to others by its performance and that may be done in various settings other than a working place. Work is usually physically strenuous and somewhat compulsive.

Pattern D people define *work* as primarily a physical activity a person must do that is directed by others and generally performed in a working place. Work is usually devoid of positive affect and is unpleasantly connected to performance.

Pattern E people define *work* as a physically and mentally strenuous activity. It is generally unpleasant and devoid of positive affect.

Pattern F people define *work* as an activity constrained to specific time periods that does not bring positive affect through its performance.

These six patterns were studied in six different countries: Belgium, Germany, Israel, Japan, the Netherlands, and the United States. Table 14.1 summarizes the percentage of workers in each country who defined work according to each of the six patterns. An examination of the table shows that a small percentage of workers in all six countries used either Pattern E or Pattern F to define *work*. Furthermore, there are significant differences among countries in how *work* is defined. In the Netherlands, *work* is defined most positively and with the most balanced personal and collective reasons for doing it. *Work* is defined least positively and with the most collective reason for doing it in Germany and

TABLE 14.1 Work Definition Patterns by Nation

SAMPLE	PATTERN[a]					
	A	**B**	**C**	**D**	**E**	**F**
Total Sample ($N \times 4,950$)	**11%**	**28%**	**18%**	**22%**	**11%**	**12%**
Nation						
Belgium	8%	40%	13%	19%	11%	9%
Germany	8%	26%	13%	28%	11%	14%
Israel	4%	22%	33%	23%	9%	9%
Japan	21%	11%	13%	29%	10%	17%
The Netherlands	15%	43%	12%	11%	9%	9%
United States	8%	30%	19%	19%	12%	11%

Note: X^2 = 680.98 (25 degrees of freedom). P<.0001 Significance level

[a]In Pattern A, work is valued for its performance. The person is accountable and generally self-directed. In Pattern B, work provides a person with positive affect and identity. It contributes to society. In Pattern C, work provides profit to others by its performance. It is physical and not confined to a working place. In Pattern D, work is a required physical activity directed by others and generally unpleasant. In Pattern E, work is physically and mentally strenuous. It is generally unpleasant. In Pattern F, work is constrained to specific time periods. It does not bring positive affect through performance.

SOURCE: From G. W. England and I. Harper, "How Working Is Defined: National Contexts and Demographic and Organizational Role Influences," *Journal of Organizational Behavior* 11 (1990), 253–266. This material is used by permission of John Wiley & Sons, Inc.

Japan. Belgium, Israel, and the United States represent a middle position between these two poles.

In another international study, 5,550 people across ten occupational groups in twenty different countries completed the *Work Value Scales (WVS)*.[3] The WVS is composed of thirteen items measuring various aspects of the work environment, such as responsibility and job security. The study found two common basic work dimensions across cultures: *work content*, measured by items such as "the amount of responsibility on the job," and *job context*, measured by items such as "the policies of my company." This finding suggests that people in many cultures distinguish between the nature of the work itself and elements of the context in which work is done. The idea of two work dimensions supports Herzberg's two-factor theory of motivation (see Chapter 5) and his job enrichment method discussed later in this chapter. Although the meaning of *work* differs among countries, new theorizing about crafting a job also suggests that individual employees can alter work meaning and work identity by changing task and relationship configurations in their work.[4]

Jobs in Organizations

Task and authority relationships define an organization's structure. Jobs, being the basic building blocks of this task–authority structure, are considered the microstructural element to which employees most directly relate. Jobs are usually designed to complement and support other jobs in the organization. Isolated jobs are rare, although one was identified at Coastal Corporation during the early 1970s. Shortly after Oscar Wyatt moved the company from Corpus Christi, Texas, to Houston, Coastal developed organizational charts and job descriptions because the company had grown so large. In the process, it was discovered that the beloved corporate economist reported to no one. Everyone assumed he worked for someone else. Such peculiarities are rare, however.

Jobs in organizations are interdependent and designed to make a contribution to the organization's overall mission and goals. For salespeople to be successful, the production people must be effective. For production people to be effective, the material department must be effective. These interdependencies require careful planning and design so that all of the "pieces of work" fit together into a whole. Suppose an envelope salesperson wants to take an order for 1 million envelopes from John Hancock Financial Services. He must coordinate that order with the production department to establish an achievable delivery date. Failure to incorporate this interdependence into his planning could create conflict, resulting in late delivery to John Hancock.

The central concerns of this chapter are designing work and structuring jobs to prevent such problems and to ensure employee well-being. Inflexible jobs that are rigidly structured have an adverse effect, as they cause stress to employees and limit their career growth. In contrast, so-called smart jobs stimulate learning and growth and thus serve as building blocks for a person's career.[5]

The larger issues in the design of organizations are the competing processes of differentiation and integration (see Chapter 15). *Differentiation* is the process of subdividing and departmentalizing the work of an organization. Jobs result from differentiation, which is necessary because no one can do it all (contrary to the famous statement made by Harold Geneen, former chairman of ITT: "If I had enough arms and legs and time, I'd do it all myself"). Even small organizations must divide work so that each person is able to accomplish a manageable piece of the whole. At the same time that the organization divides up the work, however, it must also integrate those pieces back into a whole. *Integration* is the process of connecting jobs and departments into a coordinated, cohesive whole. For example, if the envelope salesperson coordinates his order from John Hancock with the production manager, the company will meet the customer's expectations because integration will have occurred.

LEARNING OUTCOME 2

Traditional Approaches to Job Design

Failure to differentiate, integrate, or both may result in badly designed jobs, which in turn cause a variety of performance problems in organizations. Good job design helps avoid these problems, improves productivity, and enhances employee well-being. Approaches to job design that were developed during the twentieth century are job enlargement/job rotation, job enrichment, and the job characteristics theory. Each approach offers unique benefits to the organization, the employee, or both, but each also has limitations and drawbacks. Furthermore, an unthinking reliance on a traditional approach can be a serious problem in any company. The later job design approaches were developed to overcome the limitations of traditional job design approaches. For example, job enlargement was intended to overcome the problem of boredom associated with scientific management's narrowly defined approach to jobs.

Scientific Management

Scientific management, an approach to work design first advocated by Frederick Taylor, emphasizes work simplification. **Work simplification** is the standardization and the narrow, explicit specification of task activities for workers.[6] Jobs designed through scientific management have a limited number of tasks, and each task is scientifically designed so that the worker is not required to think or deliberate. According to Taylor, the role of management and the industrial engineer is to calibrate and define each task carefully. The role of the worker is to execute the task. Elements of scientific management, such as time and motion studies,

work simplification
The standardization and the narrow, explicit specification of task activities for workers.

©Corbis/Jupiterimages

No one can do it all.

differential piece-rate systems of pay, and the scientific selection of workers, all focus on the efficient use of labor to the economic benefit of the corporation.

Job Enlargement/ Job Rotation

Job enlargement is a method of job design that increases the number of activities in a job to overcome the boredom of overspecialized work. It is a traditional approach to solving not only the problem of boredom but also the difficulty of coordinating work.[7] **Job rotation**, a variation of job enlargement, exposes a worker to a variety of specialized job tasks over time. Both of these approaches came into being to solve the perceived problems of overspecialization that arose from lack of variety. That is, jobs designed by scientific management were too narrow and limited in the number of tasks and activities assigned to each worker. The lack of variety led to understimulation and underutilization of the worker.

Variety can be increased by adding to a worker's activities by means of job enlargement or by giving a worker different activities by means of job rotation. For example, job enlargement for a lathe operator in a steel plant might include selecting the steel pieces to be turned and performing all of the maintenance

> Job rotation exposes a worker to a variety of specialized tasks over time.

©Martin Barraud/OJO Images/Jupiterimages

work on the lathe in addition to running it. As an example of job rotation, an employee at a small bank might take new accounts one day, serve as a cashier another day, and process loan applications on a third day.

One of the first studies of the problem of repetitive work was conducted at IBM after World War II. The company implemented a job enlargement program during the war and evaluated the effort after six years.[8] The two most important results were a significant increase in product quality and a reduction in idle time, both for people and for machines. Less obvious and measurable benefits were enhanced worker status and improved manager–worker communication. IBM concluded that job enlargement countered the problems of work specialization. A contemporary study in a Swedish electronics assembly plant used physiological measures of muscle tension.[9] Job enlargement had a positive effect on mechanical exposure variability.

A later study examined the effects of mass production jobs on assembly-line workers in the automotive industry.[10] Mass production jobs have six characteristics: mechanically controlled work pace, repetitiveness, minimum skill requirements, predetermined tools and techniques, minute division of the production process, and a requirement for surface mental attention rather than thoughtful concentration. The researchers conducted 180 private interviews with assembly-line workers and found generally positive attitudes toward pay, security, and supervision. They concluded that job enlargement and job rotation would improve other job aspects, such as repetition and a mechanical work pace.

---

job enlargement

A method of job design that increases the number of activities in a job to overcome the boredom of overspecialized work.

job rotation

A variation of job enlargement in which workers are exposed to a variety of specialized jobs over time.

WORK SIMPLIFICATION

A rguments for Work Simplification

1. Work simplification allows workers of diverse ethnic and skill backgrounds to work together in a systematic way, an important factor during the first great period of globalization and immigration to America in the late 1800s.[11]

2. Work simplification leads to production efficiency in the organization and, therefore, to higher profits.

L imitations of Work Simplification

1. Work simplification undervalues the human capacity for thought and ingenuity. Jobs designed through scientific management use only a portion of a person's capabilities. Underutilization makes work boring, monotonous, and understimulating and may cause a variety of work problems.

2. Work simplification tends to treat labor as a means of production, thereby dehumanizing the work force.

Job rotation and **cross-training** programs are variations of job enlargement. Pharmaceutical company Eli Lilly has found that job rotation can be a proactive means for enhancing work experiences for career development and can have tangible benefits for employees in the form of salary increases and promotions.[12] In cross-training, workers are trained in different specialized tasks or activities of different jobs. While job rotation may be common practice for high-potential employees, they should remain in a position long enough to see the consequences of their decisions.[13]

All three kinds of programs—job enlargement, job rotation, and cross-training horizontally—enlarge jobs; that is, the number and variety of an employee's tasks and activities are increased. Graphic Controls Corporation (now a subsidiary of Tyco International) used cross-training to develop a flexible workforce that enabled the company to maintain high levels of production.[14] Many of today's jobs require that employees manage several work activities as part of their normal business day. However, it is important that employees be able to disengage from one task before moving on to another to achieve high levels of performance.[15]

Job Enrichment

Job enrichment is designing or redesigning a job by incorporating motivational factors into it. Whereas job enlargement increases the number of job activities through horizontal loading, job enrichment increases the amount of job responsibility through vertical loading. Both approaches to job design are intended, in part, to increase job satisfaction for employees. A study to test whether job satisfaction results from characteristics of the job or of the person found that an interactionist approach is most accurate and that job redesign can contribute to increased job satisfaction for some employees. Another two-year study found that intrinsic job satisfaction and job perceptions are reciprocally related to each other.[16]

Job enrichment builds on Herzberg's two-factor theory of motivation, which distinguished between motivational and hygiene factors for people at work. Whereas job enlargement recommends increasing and varying the number of activities a person does, job enrichment recommends increasing the recognition, responsibility, and opportunity for achievement. For example, enlarging the lathe operator's job means adding maintenance activities, and enriching the job means having the operator meet with customers who buy the products.

Herzberg believed that only certain jobs should be enriched and that the first step is to select the jobs appropriate for job enrichment.[17] He recognized that some people prefer simple jobs. Once jobs are selected for enrichment, management should brainstorm about possible changes, revise the list to include only specific changes related to motivational factors, and screen out generalities and suggestions that would simply increase activities or numbers of tasks. Those whose jobs are to be enriched should not participate in this process, as doing so would present a conflict of interest.

A seven-year implementation study of job enrichment at AT&T found that approach beneficial.[18] Job enrichment required a big change in management style, and AT&T found that it could not ignore hygiene factors in the work environment just because it was enriching existing jobs. Although the AT&T experience with job enrichment was positive, a critical review of job enrichment did not find that to be the case generally.[19] One problem with job enrichment as a strategy for work design is that it is based on an oversimplified motivational theory. Another problem is the lack of consideration for individual differences among employees. Job enrichment, like scientific management's work specialization and job enlargement/job rotation, is a universal approach to the design of work and thus does not differentiate among individuals.

Job Characteristics Theory

The job characteristics theory, which was initiated during the mid-1960s, is a traditional approach to the design of work that makes a significant departure from the three earlier approaches. It emphasizes the interaction between the individual and specific attributes of the job; therefore, it is a person–job fit model rather than a universal job design model. It originated in a research study of 470 workers in forty-seven different jobs across eleven industries.[20] The study measured and classified relevant task characteristics for these forty-seven jobs and found four core job characteristics: job variety, autonomy, responsibility, and interpersonal interaction. The study also found that core job characteristics did not affect all workers in the same way. A person's values, religious beliefs, and ethnic background influenced how the worker responded to the job. Specifically, workers with rural values and workers with strong religious beliefs preferred jobs high in core characteristics, and workers with urban values and those with weaker religious beliefs preferred jobs low in core characteristics. One study tested the effect of job and work characteristics on employee turnover intentions and found that employees consider both when deciding to leave a company.[21]

Richard Hackman and his colleagues modified the original model by including three critical psychological states of the individual and refining the measurement of core job characteristics. The result is the

cross-training

A variation of job enlargement in which workers are trained in different specialized tasks or activities.

job enrichment

Designing or redesigning a job by incorporating motivational factors into it.

Job Characteristics Model shown in Figure 14.1.[22] The **Job Diagnostic Survey (JDS)**, the most commonly used job design measure, was developed to diagnose jobs by measuring the five core job characteristics and three critical psychological states shown in the model. The core job characteristics stimulate the critical psychological states in the manner shown in Figure 14.1. This results in varying personal and work outcomes, as identified in the figure. A new proposal to modify the job characteristics model suggests that psychological ownership is an important factor in job design.[23]

Hackman and his colleagues say that the five core job characteristics interact to determine an overall *Motivating Potential Score (MPS)* for a specific job. The MPS indicates a job's potential for motivating incumbents. An individual's MPS is determined by the following equation:

$$MPS = \frac{\left[\begin{array}{c}\text{Skill}\\\text{variety}\end{array}\right] + \left[\begin{array}{c}\text{Task}\\\text{identity}\end{array}\right] + \left[\begin{array}{c}\text{Task}\\\text{significance}\end{array}\right]}{3} \times [\text{Autonomy}] \times [\text{Feedback}]$$

The Job Characteristics Model includes *growth need strength* (the desire to grow and fully develop one's abilities) as a moderator. People with high growth need strength respond favorably to jobs with high MPSs, and individuals with low growth need strength respond less favorably to such jobs. The job characteristics theory further suggests that core job dimensions stimulate three critical psychological states according to the relationships specified in the model. These critical psychological states are defined as follows:

1. *Experienced meaningfulness of the work*, or the degree to which the employee experiences the job as one that is generally meaningful, valuable, and worthwhile.

2. *Experienced responsibility for work outcomes*, or the degree to which the employee feels personally accountable and responsible for the results of the work he or she does.

3. *Knowledge of results*, or the degree to which the employee knows and understands, on a continuous basis, how effectively he or she is performing the job.

In one early study, Hackman and Oldham administered the JDS to 658 employees working on sixty-two different jobs in seven business organizations.[24] The JDS was useful for job redesign efforts through one or more of five implementing concepts: (1) combining tasks into larger jobs, (2) forming natural work teams to increase task identity and task significance, (3) establishing relationships with customers, (4) loading jobs vertically with more responsibility, and/or (5) opening feedback channels for the job incumbent. For example, if an automotive mechanic received little feedback on the quality of repair work performed, one redesign strategy would be to solicit customer feedback one month after each repair.

A recent sequence of two studies conducted in Egypt aimed to disaggregate *work autonomy*, an important component in job design theory.[25] Study 1 included 534 employees in two Egyptian organizations. Study 2 involved 120 managers in four organizations. The results indicated

Job Characteristics Model

A framework for understanding person–job fit through the interaction of core job dimensions with critical psychological states within a person.

Job Diagnostic Survey (JDS)

The survey instrument designed to measure the elements in the Job Characteristics Model.

FIGURE **14.1** The Job Characteristics Model

SOURCE: J. R. Hackman and G. R. Oldham, "The Relationship among Core Job Dimensions, the Critical Psychological States, and On-the-Job Outcomes," in *The Job Diagnostic Survey: An Instrument for the Diagnosis of Jobs and the Evaluation of Job Redesign Projects* (New Haven, Conn.: Department of Administrative Services, Yale University, 1974). Reprinted by permission of Greg R. Oldham.

FIVE CORE JOB CHARACTERISTICS DEFINED

1 *Skill variety.* The degree to which a job includes different activities and involves the use of multiple skills and talents of the employee.

2 *Task identity.* The degree to which the job requires completion of a whole and identifiable piece of work—that is, doing a job from beginning to end with a tangible outcome.

3 *Task significance.* The degree to which the job has a substantial impact on the lives or work of other people, whether in the immediate organization or in the external environment.

4 *Autonomy.* The degree to which the job provides the employee with substantial freedom, independence, and discretion in scheduling the work and in determining the procedures to be used in carrying it out.

5 *Feedback from the job itself.* The degree to which carrying out the work activities results in the employee obtaining direct and clear information about the effectiveness of his or her performance.

that separate work method, work schedule, and work criteria autonomy were three separate facets of work autonomy.

An alternative to the Job Characteristics Model is the *Job Characteristics Inventory (JCI)* developed by Henry Sims and Andrew Szilagyi.[26] The JCI primarily measures core job characteristics. It is not as comprehensive as the JDS because it does not incorporate critical psychological states, personal and work outcomes, or employee needs. The JCI does give some consideration to structural and individual variables that affect the relationship between core job characteristics and the individual.[27] One comparative analysis of the JCI and JDS found similarities in the measures and in the models' predictions.[28] The comparative analysis also found two differences. First, the variety scales in the two models appear to have different effects on performance. Second, the autonomy scales in the two models appear to have different effects on employee satisfaction. Overall, the JCI and JDS both support the usefulness of a person–job fit approach to the design of work over the earlier, universal theories.

Engagement Psychological conditions related to job design features are a particular concern of the Job Characteristics Model.[29] One study of more than 200 managers and employees in a Midwestern insurance company found that meaningfulness, safety, and availability were three important psychological conditions that affected employees' **engagement** in their jobs and work roles. When engaged, people employ and express themselves physically, cognitively, and emotionally as they perform their jobs and their work roles. Thus, engagement occurs when organizational members are harnessed to their work roles, and it is important for its positive individual and organizational outcomes. Gallup's Q12 survey was used to improve engagement for a clinical nutrition

group at St. Mary's/Duluth Clinic Health System with successful results.[30] Despite its importance to company success, however, only one-third of employees in a recent study reported that they were engaged in their work.[31]

Full engagement requires the strategic management of one's energy in response to the environment.[32] Being fully engaged in one's work role and job can be highly appropriate and yet demand energy, time, and effort. To achieve balance and afford opportunity for recovery, there is a commensurate need to strategically and appropriately disengage from one's job and work role on a periodic basis. The effective management of energy in response to one's job and work role leads to both high performance and personal renewal. Thus, while the design of work is important, the human spirit's response to job characteristics and work design features is equally important.

LEARNING OUTCOME **3**

Alternative Approaches to Job Design

Because each of the traditional job design approaches has limitations, several alternative approaches have emerged over the past couple of decades. This section examines four alternatives that are in the process of being tried and tested. First, it examines the social information-processing model. Second, it reviews ergonomics and the interdisciplinary framework of Michael Campion and Paul Thayer. Their framework builds on traditional job design approaches. Third, this section examines the international perspectives of the

engagement
The expression of oneself as one performs in work or other roles.

Japanese, Germans, and Scandinavians. Finally, it focuses on the health and well-being aspects of work design. Healthy work enables individuals to adapt, function well, and balance work with private life activities.[33] An emerging fifth approach to the design of work through teams and autonomous work groups was addressed in Chapter 9.

Social Information Processing

The traditional approaches to the design of work emphasize objective core job characteristics. In contrast, the **social information-processing (SIP) model** emphasizes the interpersonal aspects of work design. Specifically, the SIP model says that what others tell us about our jobs is important.[34] The SIP model has four basic premises about the work environment.[35] First, other people provide cues we use to understand the work environment. Second, other people help us judge what is important in our jobs. Third, other people tell us how they see our jobs. Fourth, other people's positive and negative feedback helps us understand our feelings about our jobs. This is very consistent with the dynamic model of the job design process that views it as a social one involving job-holders, supervisors, and peers.[36]

People's perceptions and reactions to their jobs are shaped by information from other people in the work environment.[37] In other words, what others believe about a person's job may be important to understanding the person's perceptions of, and reactions to, the job. This does not mean that objective job characteristics are unimportant; rather, it means that others can modify the way these characteristics affect us. For example, one study of task complexity found that the objective complexity of a task must be distinguished from the subjective task complexity experienced by the employee.[38] Although objective task complexity

may be a motivator, the presence of others in the work environment, social interaction, or even daydreaming may be important additional sources of motivation. The SIP model makes an important contribution to the design of work by emphasizing the importance of other people and the social context of work. For example, relational job design may motivate employees to take prosocial action and make a positive difference in other people's lives.[39] In addition, the relational aspects of the work environment may be more important than objective core job characteristics. Therefore, the subjective feedback of other people about how difficult a particular task is may be more important to a person's motivation to perform than an objective estimate of the task's difficulty.

Ergonomics and Interdisciplinary Framework

Michael Campion and Paul Thayer used **ergonomics** based on engineering, biology, and psychology to develop an interdisciplinary framework for the design of work. Actually, they say that four approaches—the mechanistic, motivational, biological, and perceptual/motor approaches—are necessary because no one approach can solve all performance problems caused by poorly designed jobs. Table 14.2 describes the benefits and limitations of each approach; we will take a closer look at the biological and perceptual/motor approaches below. One ergonomics study of eighty-seven administrative municipal employees found lower levels of upper body pain along with other positive outcomes thanks to the workstation redesign.[40]

The interdisciplinary framework allows the job designer or manager to consider trade-offs and alternatives among the approaches based on desired outcomes. If a manager finds poor performance a problem, for example, the manager should analyze the job to ensure a design aimed at improving performance. The

social information-processing (SIP) model
A model that suggests that the important job factors depend in part on what others tell a person about the job.

ergonomics
The science of adapting work and working conditions to the employee or worker.

> According to the social information-processing model, we should not ignore what our coworkers tell us about our jobs.

©TongRo Image Stock/Jupiterimages

TABLE 14.2 Summary of Outcomes from Various Job Design Approaches

JOB DESIGN APPROACH (DISCIPLINE)	POSITIVE OUTCOMES	NEGATIVE OUTCOMES
MECHANISTIC APPROACH (mechanical engineering)	Decreased training time Higher personnel utilization levels Lower likelihood of error Less chance of mental overload Lower stress levels	Lower job satisfaction Lower motivation Higher absenteeism
MOTIVATIONAL APPROACH (industrial psychology)	Higher job satisfaction Higher motivation Greater job involvement Higher job performance Lower absenteeism	Increased training time Lower personnel utilization levels Greater chance of errors Greater chance of mental overload and stress
BIOLOGICAL APPROACH (biology)	Less physical effort Less physical fatigue Fewer health complaints Fewer medical incidents Lower absenteeism Higher job satisfaction	Higher financial costs because of changes in equipment or job environment
PERCEPTUAL MOTOR APPROACH (experimental psychology)	Lower likelihood of error Lower likelihood of accidents Less chance of mental stress Decreased training time Higher personnel utilization levels	Lower job satisfaction Lower motivation

SOURCE: Reprinted from *Organizational Dynamics*, 15(3), Michael A. Campion, Paul W. Thayer, "Job Design: Approaches, Outcomes, and Trade-offs," Winter/1987. Copyright © 1987, with permission from Elsevier.

emphasizes perception and fine motor skills as opposed to the gross motor skills and muscle strength emphasized in the *mechanistic approach*. The perceptual/motor approach is more likely to be relevant to operational and technical work, such as keyboard operations and data entry jobs, which may tax a person's concentration and attention, than to managerial, administrative, and custodial jobs, which are less likely to strain concentration and attention.

One study using the interdisciplinary framework to improve jobs evaluated 377 clerical, 80 managerial, and 90 analytical positions.[43] The jobs were improved by combining tasks and adding ancillary duties. The improved jobs provided greater motivation for the incumbents and were better from a perceptual/motor standpoint. The jobs were poorly designed from a mechanical engineering standpoint, however, and they were unaffected from a biological standpoint. Again, the interdisciplinary framework considers trade-offs and alternatives when evaluating job redesign efforts. Table 14.2 presents a summary of the positive and negative outcomes of redesign.

International Perspectives on the Design of Work

Each culture has a unique way of understanding and designing work.[44] As organizations become more global and international, an appreciation of the perspectives of others is increasingly important. A study of 2,359 call centers in sixteen countries found that an organization's management strategy and operational context influences variation in work design.[45] The Japanese, Germans, and Scandinavians in particular have distinctive perspectives on the design and organization of work.[46] Each of these cultures has a perspective forged within its unique cultural and economic system, and each is distinct from the approaches used in North America.

The Japanese Approach The Japanese began harnessing their productive energies during the 1950s by

interdisciplinary framework is important because badly designed jobs cause far more performance problems than managers realize.[41]

The *biological approach* to job design emphasizes the person's interaction with physical aspects of the work environment and is concerned with the amount of physical exertion, such as lifting and muscular effort, required by the position. For example, an analysis of medical claims at TXI's Chaparral Steel Company identified lower back pain as the most common physical problem experienced by steel workers and managers alike. As a result, the company instituted an education and exercise program under expert guidance to improve employees' lower back care. Program graduates received back cushions for their chairs with "Chaparral Steel Company" embossed on them.[42]

The *perceptual/motor approach* to job design also emphasizes the person's interaction with physical aspects of the work environment and is based on engineering that considers human factors such as strength or coordination, ergonomics, and experimental psychology. It places an important emphasis on human interaction with computers, information, and other operational systems. This approach addresses how people mentally process information acquired from the physical work environment through perceptual and motor skills. The approach drawing on the product quality ideas of W. Edwards Deming.[47] In addition, the central government became actively involved in the economic resurgence of Japan, and it encouraged companies to conquer industries rather than to maximize profits.[48] Such an industrial policy, built on the Japanese cultural ethic of collectivism, has implications for how work is done. Whereas Frederick Taylor and his successors in the United States emphasized the job of an individual worker, the Japanese system emphasizes the strategic level and encourages collective and cooperative working arrangements.[49] Also, the Japanese emphasize performance, accountability, and other- or self-directedness in defining work, whereas Americans emphasize the positive affect, personal identity, and social benefits of work.

Japanese success with lean production has drawn the attention of managers. **Lean production** methods are similar to the production concept of **sociotechnical systems (STS)**, although there are some differences.[50] In particular, STS gives greater emphasis to (1) teamwork and self-managed and autonomous work groups, (2) the ongoing nature of the design process, and (3) human values in the work process. The approaches are similar, however, in that both differ from Taylor's scientific management and both emphasize job variety, feedback to work groups and teams, support of human resources, and control of production variance close to the point of origin. One three-year evaluation of lean teams, assembly lines, and workflow formalization as lean production practices conducted in Australia found that employees in all lean production groups were negatively affected, with the assembly-line employees experiencing the worst effects.[51]

The German Approach The German approach to work has been shaped by Germany's unique educational system, cultural values, and economic system. The Germans are a highly educated and well-organized people. For example, their educational system has a multitrack design with technical and university alternatives. The German economic system puts a strong emphasis on free enterprise, private property rights, and management–labor cooperation. A comparison of voluntary and mandated management–labor cooperation in Germany found that productivity was superior under voluntary cooperation.[52] The Germans value hierarchy and authority relationships and, as a result, are generally disciplined.[53] Germany's workers are highly unionized, and their discipline and efficiency have enabled Germany to be highly productive while its workers labor substantially fewer hours than do Americans.

The traditional German approach to work design was **technocentric**, an approach that placed technology and engineering at the center of job design decisions. Recently, German industrial engineers have moved to a more **anthropocentric** approach, which places human considerations at the center of job design decisions. The former approach uses a natural scientific process in the design of work, whereas the latter relies on a more humanistic process, as shown in Figure 14.2. In the anthropocentric approach, work is evaluated using the criteria of practicability and worker satisfaction at the individual level and the criteria of endurability and acceptability at the group level. Figure 14.2 also identifies problem areas and disciplines concerned with each aspect of the work design.

The Scandinavian Approach The Scandinavian cultural values and economic system stand in contrast to the German system. The social democratic tradition in Scandinavia has emphasized social concern rather than industrial efficiency. Accordingly, the Scandinavians place great emphasis on a work design

lean production
Using committed employees with ever-expanding responsibilities to achieve zero waste and 100 percent good product, delivered on time, every time.

sociotechnical systems (STS)
Giving equal attention to technical and social considerations in job design.

technocentric
Placing technology and engineering at the center of job design decisions.

anthropocentric
Placing human considerations at the center of job design decisions.

©iStockphoto.com/Orlando Rosu

Scientific approaches of labor sciences	Levels of evaluation of human work	Problem areas and assignment to disciplines
View from natural science — Primarily oriented to individuals ← Primarily oriented to groups ← View from cultural studies ←	Practicability	Technical, anthropometric, and psychophysical problems (ergonomics)
	Endurability	Technical, physiological, and medical problems (ergonomics and occupational health)
	Acceptability	Economical and sociological problems (occupational psychology and sociology, personnel management)
	Satisfaction	Sociopsychological and economic problems (occupational psychology and sociology, personnel management)

SOURCE: H. Luczak, "'Good Work' Design: An Ergonomic, Industrial Engineering Perspective," in J. C. Quick, L. R. Murphy, and J. J. Hurrell, eds., *Stress and Well-Being at Work* (Washington, D.C.: American Psychological Association, 1997). Copyright ©1997 by the American Psychological Association. Reprinted with permission.

model that encourages a high degree of worker control and good social support systems for workers.[54] Lennart Levi believes that circumstantial and inferential scientific evidence provides a sufficiently strong basis for legislative and policy actions for redesigns aimed at enhancing worker well-being. An example of such an action for promoting good working environments and occupational health was Swedish Government Bill 1976/77:149, which stated, "Work should be safe both physically and mentally *but also* provide opportunities for involvement, job satisfaction, and personal development." In 1991, the Swedish Parliament set up the Swedish Working Life Fund to fund research, intervention programs, and demonstration projects in work design. For example, a study of Stockholm police on shift schedules found that going from a daily, counterclockwise rotation to a clockwise rotation was more compatible with human biology and resulted in improved sleep, less fatigue, lower systolic blood pressure, and lower blood levels of triglycerides and glucose.[55] Hence, the work redesign improved the police officers' health.

Work Design and Well-Being

An international group of scholars, including American social scientists, has been concerned about designing work and jobs that are both healthy and productive.[56] Economic and industry-specific upheavals in the United

Scheduling shifts for employees in a clockwise manner (first, second, third) rather than a counterclockwise manner (first, third, second) is more compatible with human biology.

©Rafal Strzechowski/PhotoAlto/Jupiterimages

States during the 1990s led to job loss and unemployment, and the adverse health impact of these factors has received attention.[57] Attention has also been devoted to the effects of specific work design parameters on psychological health.[58] For example, by mixing cognitively challenging and "mindless" work throughout the day, one may reduce pressures from chronic overwork and enhance creativity. In addition, task/job design can be improved by enhancing core job characteristics and not patterning service work after assembly-line work. Frank Landy believes that organizations should redesign jobs to increase worker control and reduce worker uncertainty, while at the same time managing conflict and task/job demands.

Task uncertainty was shown to have an adverse effect on morale in a study of 629 employment security work units in California and Wisconsin.[59] More important, the study showed that morale was better predicted by considering both the overall design of the work unit and the task uncertainty. This study suggests that if one work design parameter, such as task uncertainty, is a problem in a job, its adverse effects on people may be mitigated by other work design parameters. For example, higher pay may offset an employee's frustration with a difficult coworker, or a friendly, supportive working environment may offset frustration with low pay. See Table 14.3 for more information on increasing control, reducing uncertainty, and managing conflict.

LEARNING OUTCOME 4

Contemporary Issues in the Design of Work

A number of contemporary issues related to specific aspects of the design of work have an effect on increasing numbers of employees. Rather than addressing job design or worker well-being in a comprehensive way, these issues—telecommuting, alternative work patterns, technostress, and skill development—address one or another aspect of a job. One study found that employees stay motivated when their work is relationally designed to provide opportunities for respectful contact with those critical to their work.[60] Telecommuting and alternative work patterns such as job sharing can increase flexibility for employees. Companies use these and other approaches to the design of work as ways to manage a growing business while contributing to a better balance of work and family life for employees.

Telecommuting

Telecommuting, as noted in Chapter 2, is when employees work at home or in other locations geographically separate from their company's main location. An estimated 28 million Americans telecommute. Telecommuting may entail working in a combination of home, satellite office, and main office locations. This flexible arrangement is designed to achieve a better fit between the needs of the individual employee and the organization's task demands. Cisco Systems manager Christian Renaud moved from California and began telecommuting from Johnston, Iowa, when he and his wife began their family.

Telecommuting has been around since the 1970s but was slower to catch on than some expected.[61] This was due to confusion and scheduling errors.[62] Actually, with a greater emphasis on managing the work rather than the worker, managers can enhance control, effectively decentralize, and even encourage teamwork through telecommuting. A number of companies, such as AT&T in Phoenix and Verizon Communications, have programs in telecommuting for a wide range of employees. These flexible arrangements help some companies respond to changing demographics and a shrinking labor pool. The Travelers Group (now part of Citigroup) was one of the first companies to try telecommuting and was considered an industry leader in the practice. Because of its confidence in its employees, Travelers reaped significant rewards from telecommuting, including higher productivity, reduced absenteeism, expanded opportunities for workers with disabilities, and an increased ability to attract and retain talent.[63]

Pacific Bell (now part of AT&T) tried telecommuting on a large scale.[64] In 1990, Pacific Bell had 1,500 managers who telecommuted. For example, an information systems designer might work at home four days a week and spend one day a week at the main office location in meetings, work exchanges, and coordination with others. Of

TABLE 14.3 Adjusting Work Design Parameters

Increase control by:	Reduce uncertainty by:	Manage conflict through:
> giving workers the opportunity to control several aspects of the work and the workplace > designing machines and tasks with optimal response times and/or ranges > implementing performance-monitoring systems as a source of relevant feedback to workers	> providing employees with timely and complete information needed for their work > making clear and unambiguous work assignments > improving communication at shift change time > increasing employee access to information sources	> participative decision making > supportive supervisory styles > having sufficient resources available to meet work demands, thus preventing conflict

©Cengage Learning 2013

[Tele-Surveillance]

Though telecommuting helps employees and companies save time and money, it can cause managers anxiety. Since employees are not physically in the office, managers have few ways of keeping track of how employees are spending their working hours. To help solve this problem, a California software company has created oDesk, a program that will take frequent snapshots of a worker's computer screen and record all of their keystrokes and mouse clicks. Using this information, managers can get a better sense of whether an employee is actually working from home or trying to reach the next level on Farmville.

SOURCE: P. Davidson, "Co-Founder of oDesk Helps Employers Monitor Freelancers," *USA Today* (September 13, 2010), http://www.usatoday.com/money/companies/management/entre/2010-09-12-odesk-tsatalos_N.htm.

Alternative Work Patterns

Job sharing is an alternative work pattern in which more than one person occupies a single job. As an alternative to telecommuting and a way of addressing demographic and labor pool concerns, job sharing is found throughout a wide range of managerial and professional jobs as well as production and service jobs. It is not common among senior executives.

The *four-day workweek* is a second type of alternative work schedule. Information systems personnel at the United Services Automobile Association (USAA) in San Antonio, Texas, work four ten-hour days and enjoy a three-day weekend. This arrangement provides the benefit of more time for those who want to balance work and family life through weekend travel. However, the longer workdays may be a drawback for employees with many family or social activities on weekday evenings. Hence, the four-day workweek has both benefits and limitations.

In **flextime**, a third alternative work pattern, employees set their own daily work schedules. Companies in highly concentrated urban areas, such as Houston, Los Angeles, and New York City, may allow employees to set their own daily work schedules as long as they start their eight hours at any thirty-minute interval between 6:00 a.m. and 9:00 a.m. This

3,000 Pacific Bell managers responding to a mail survey, 87 percent said telecommuting would reduce employee stress, 70 percent said it would increase job satisfaction while reducing absenteeism, and 64 percent said it would increase productivity.

However, telecommuting is neither a cure-all nor a universally feasible alternative. A recent study showed that the employees who were most satisfied with telecommuting were those who were comfortable with technology and had more experience within the organization.[65] Many telecommuters feel a sense of social isolation. Some executives are concerned that while telecommuters are more productive, their lack of visibility may hold back their careers. Furthermore, not all forms of work are amenable to telecommuting. For example, firefighters and police officers must be at their duty stations to be successful in their work. Employees for whom telecommuting is not a viable option within a company may feel jealous of those able to telecommute. Thus, telecommuting is a novel, emerging issue with results still to come and be analyzed.

job sharing
An alternative work pattern in which more than one person occupies a single job.

flextime
An alternative work pattern that enables employees to set their own daily work schedules.

arrangement is designed to ease traffic and commuting pressures. It is also responsive to individual biorhythms, allowing early risers to go to work early and nighthawks to work late. Even in companies without formal programs, flextime may be an individual option arranged between supervisor and subordinate. For example, a first-line supervisor who wants to complete a college degree may negotiate a work schedule accommodating both job requirements and course schedules.

Flextime has been applied in numerous ways in work organizations, but may be offered more often to high performers who assure their bosses that work quality and productivity will not suffer.[66] Although flextime can lead to reduced absenteeism, on the cautionary side, one study found that a woman on a flexible work schedule was perceived to have less job–career dedication and less advancement motivation, though no less ability.[67]

Technology at Work

New technologies and electronic commerce are here to stay and are changing the face of work environments, dramatically in some cases. Many government jobs are expected to change, and even disappear, with the advent of e-government using the Internet. The concept involves work being where people are, rather than people moving to where the work is. New technologies make connectivity, collaboration, and communication easy. Critical voice mails and messages can be delivered to and from the central office, a client's office, the airport, the car, or home. Wireless Internet access and online meeting software such as WebEx make it possible for employees to participate in meetings anywhere, any time.

As a force for change, new technology is a double-edged sword that can be used to improve job performance or to create stress. On the positive side, modern technologies are helping to revolutionize the way jobs are designed and the way work gets done. The **virtual office** is a mobile platform of computer, telecommunication, and information technology and services that allows mobile workforce members to conduct business virtually anywhere, anytime. While virtual offices have benefits, they may also lead to a lack of social connection or to **technostress**, which is stress caused by new and advancing technologies, most often information technologies, in the workplace.[68] For example, the widespread use of web forums or blogs as a source for rumors of layoffs may cause feelings of uncertainty and anxiety (technostress). However, the same electronic bulletin boards can be an important source of information and thus reduce uncertainty for workers.

New information technologies enable organizations to monitor employee work performance, even when the employee is not aware of the monitoring.[69] These new technologies also allow organizations to tie pay to performance, because performance is electronically monitored.[70] Three guidelines can help make electronic workplace monitoring, especially of performance, less

virtual office

A mobile platform of computer, telecommunication, and information technology and services.

technostress

The stress caused by new and advancing technologies in the workplace.

stressful: First, workers should participate in the introduction of the monitoring system. Second, performance standards should be seen as fair. Third, performance records should be used to improve performance, not to punish the performer. In the extreme, new technologies that allow for virtual work in remote locations take employees beyond such monitoring.[71]

Skill Development

Problems in work system design are often seen as the source of frustration for those dealing with technostress.[72] However, system and technical problems are not the only sources of technostress in new information technologies. Some experts see a growing gap between the skills demanded by new technologies and the skills possessed by employees in jobs using these technologies.[73] Although technical skills are important and are emphasized in many training programs, the largest sector of the economy is actually service-oriented, and service jobs require interpersonal skills. Managers also need a wide range of nontechnical skills to be effective in their work.[74]

Therefore, any discussion of jobs and the design of work must recognize the importance of incumbent skills and abilities to meet the demands of the work. Organizations must consider the talents and skills of their employees when they engage in job design efforts. The two issues of employee skill development and job design are interrelated. The knowledge and information requirements for jobs of the future are especially high.

Log in to the **CourseMate** for *ORGB3* at **www.cengagebrain.com** to:

* Review **Key Terms Flash Cards** online

* Play **Beat the Clock** and **Quiz Bowl** to master concepts

* Complete **web quizzes** to prepare for exams

* Watch the video on **Camp Bow Wow** and from ***Tyler Perry's Daddy's Little Girls*** for examples, then test yourself with a quick quiz

* Work through the **"What about You?"** and **Ethical Dilemma** exercises to see how you would handle various situations that organizations face on a daily basis

BY THE NUMBERS

6 patterns people follow in defining work

5 core job characteristics

1994 year Aeron chair developed by Don Chadwick and Bill Stumpf of Herman Miller

470 participants in the foundational study of JCM

1970s start of telecommuting

©iStockphoto.com/thesuperph

Organizational Design and Structure

LEARNING OUTCOMES

1 Define *differentiation* and *integration* as organizational design processes.

2 Discuss the basic design dimensions managers must consider in structuring an organization.

3 Describe five structural configurations for organizations.

4 Describe four contextual variables that influence organizational structure.

5 Explain the forces reshaping organizations.

6 Identify and describe emerging organizational structures.

7 Identify factors that can adversely affect organizational structure.

©iStockphoto.com/doram

" *Differentiation and integration are the keys to successful organizational design.* **"**

Organizational design is the process of constructing and adjusting an organization's structure to achieve its business strategy and goals. The design process begins with the organization's goals. These goals are broken into tasks, or pieces of work, as the basis for jobs, as discussed in Chapter 14. Jobs are grouped into departments, and departments are linked to form the **organizational structure**.

Key Organizational Design Processes

Differentiation, which will be defined in more detail shortly, can be described as the design process of breaking organizational goals into tasks. *Integration*, also defined in more detail shortly, can then be considered the design process of linking the tasks together to form a structure that supports goal accomplishment. These two processes are the keys to successful organizational design. The organizational structure is designed to prevent chaos through an orderly set of reporting relationships and communication channels. Understanding the key design processes and organizational structure helps a person understand the larger working environment and may prevent confusion in the organization.

The *organization chart* is the most visible representation of the organization's structure and underlying components. Figure 15.1 is the organizational chart for the World Trade Organization. Most organizations have a series of organization charts showing reporting relationships throughout the system. The underlying components are (1) formal lines of authority and responsibility (the organizational structure designates reporting relationships by the way jobs and departments are grouped) and (2) formal systems of communication, coordination,

organizational design

The process of constructing and adjusting an organization's structure to achieve its business strategy and goals.

organizational structure

The linking of departments and jobs within an organization.

After You Finish This Chapter Go to **Page 261** for **Study Tools**

FIGURE 15.1 Organization

WTO structure

All WTO members may participate in all councils, committees, etc., except Appellate Body, Dispute Settlement panels, Textiles Monitoring Body, and plurilateral committees.

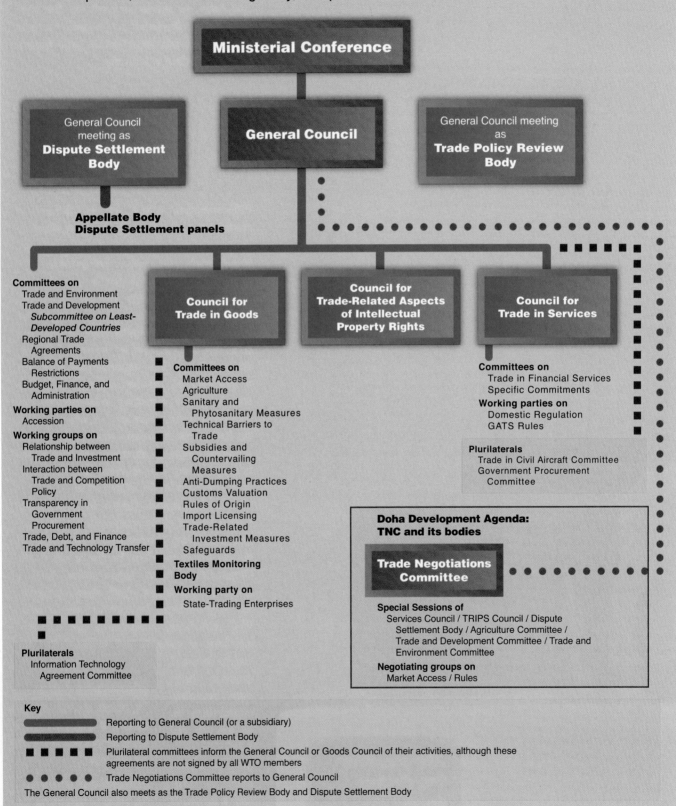

Ministerial Conference

General Council meeting as **Dispute Settlement Body**

General Council

General Council meeting as **Trade Policy Review Body**

Appellate Body
Dispute Settlement panels

Committees on
Trade and Environment
Trade and Development
Subcommittee on Least-Developed Countries
Regional Trade Agreements
Balance of Payments Restrictions
Budget, Finance, and Administration
Working parties on
Accession
Working groups on
Relationship between Trade and Investment
Interaction between Trade and Competition Policy
Transparency in Government Procurement
Trade, Debt, and Finance
Trade and Technology Transfer

Council for Trade in Goods

Council for Trade-Related Aspects of Intellectual Property Rights

Council for Trade in Services

Committees on
Market Access
Agriculture
Sanitary and Phytosanitary Measures
Technical Barriers to Trade
Subsidies and Countervailing Measures
Anti-Dumping Practices
Customs Valuation
Rules of Origin
Import Licensing
Trade-Related Investment Measures
Safeguards
Textiles Monitoring Body
Working party on
State-Trading Enterprises

Committees on
Trade in Financial Services
Specific Commitments
Working parties on
Domestic Regulation
GATS Rules
Plurilaterals
Trade in Civil Aircraft Committee
Government Procurement Committee

Plurilaterals
Information Technology Agreement Committee

Doha Development Agenda: TNC and its bodies

Trade Negotiations Committee

Special Sessions of
Services Council / TRIPS Council / Dispute Settlement Body / Agriculture Committee / Trade and Development Committee / Trade and Environment Committee
Negotiating groups on
Market Access / Rules

Key
Reporting to General Council (or a subsidiary)
Reporting to Dispute Settlement Body
Plurilateral committees inform the General Council or Goods Council of their activities, although these agreements are not signed by all WTO members
Trade Negotiations Committee reports to General Council
The General Council also meets as the Trade Policy Review Body and Dispute Settlement Body

SOURCE: WTO Organization Chart, http://www.wto.org/english/thewto_e/whatis_e/tif_e/org2_e.htm.

and integration (the organizational structure designates the expected patterns of formal interaction among employees).[1]

Differentiation

Differentiation is the process of deciding how to divide the work in an organization.[2] Differentiation ensures that all essential organizational tasks are assigned to one or more jobs and that the tasks receive the attention they need. Many dimensions of differentiation have been considered in organizations. Lawrence and Lorsch found four dimensions of differentiation in one study: (1) manager's goal orientation, (2) time orientation, (3) interpersonal orientation, and (4) formality of structure.[3] Three different forms of differentiation are horizontal, vertical, and spatial.

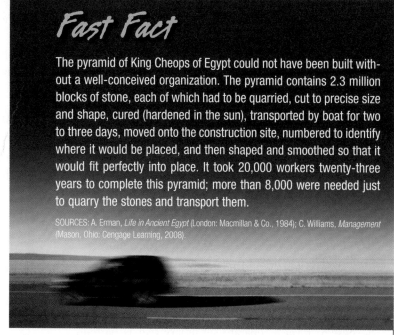

Horizontal Differentiation Horizontal differentiation is the degree of differentiation between organizational subunits and is based on employees' specialized knowledge, education, or training. For example, two university professors who teach specialized subjects in different academic departments are subject to horizontal differentiation. Horizontal differentiation increases with specialization and departmentalization.

Specialization refers to the particular grouping of activities performed by an individual.[4] The degree of specialization, or the division of labor, in the organization gives an indication of how much training is needed for various jobs, what the scope of various jobs is, and what individual characteristics are needed for job holders. Specialization can lead to the development of a specialized vocabulary, as well as other behavioral norms. As the two college professors specialize in their subjects, abbreviations or acronyms take on unique meanings. For example, OB means "organizational behavior" to a professor of management but "obstetrics" to a professor of medicine.

Usually, the more specialized the jobs within an organization, the more departments are differentiated within that organization (in other words, the greater is the *departmentalization*). Departmentalization can be by function, product, service, client, geography, process, or some combination of these. A large organization may departmentalize its structure using some or all of these methods at different levels of the organization. For example, the U.S. Army Reserve changed its departmentalization first from divisional to an operational strategic reserve, then to an operational force structure.[5]

Vertical Differentiation Vertical differentiation is the difference in authority and responsibility in the organizational hierarchy. Vertical differentiation occurs, for example, between a chief executive and a maintenance supervisor. Tall, narrow organizations have greater vertical differentiation, and flat, wide organizations have less vertical differentiation. The height of the organization is also influenced by level of horizontal differentiation and span of control. The *span of control* refers to and defines the number of subordinates a manager can and should supervise.[6]

Tall structures—those with narrow spans of control—tend to be characterized by closer supervision and tighter controls. In addition, the communication becomes more burdensome, since directives and information must be passed through more layers. The banking industry has often had tall structures. *Flat structures*—those with wider spans of control—have simpler communication chains and reduced promotion opportunities due to fewer levels of management. Sears is an example of an organization that has gone to a flat structure.

differentiation
The process of deciding how to divide the work in an organization.

With the loss of more than a million middle management positions, many organizations are now flatter. The degree of vertical differentiation affects organizational effectiveness, but there is no strong evidence that flatter or taller organizations are better.[7] Organizational size, type of jobs, skills and personal characteristics of employees, and degree of freedom must all be considered in determining organizational effectiveness.[8]

Spatial Differentiation Spatial differentiation is the geographic dispersion of an organization's offices, plants, and personnel. A salesperson who works in New York for a company based in Portland experiences spatial differentiation. An increase in the number of locations increases the complexity of organizational design because of spatial differentiation but may be necessary for organizational goal achievement or organizational protection. For example, if an organization wants to expand into a different country, it may be best to form a separate subsidiary that is partially owned and managed by citizens of that country. Few U.S. citizens think of Shell Oil Company as being a subsidiary of Royal Dutch/Shell Group, a company whose international headquarters is in the Netherlands. Spatial differentiation may give an organization political and legal advantages in a country because it is identified as a local company.

Implications of Differentiation Horizontal, vertical, and spatial differentiation indicate the amount of width, height, and breadth an organizational structure needs. Just because an organization is highly differentiated along one of these dimensions does not mean it must be highly differentiated along the others. The university environment, for example, is generally characterized by great horizontal differentiation but relatively little vertical and spatial differentiation. By contrast, a company such as Coca-Cola is characterized by a great deal of all three types of differentiation.

The more structurally differentiated an organization is, the more complex it is.[9] *Complexity* refers to the number of activities, subunits, or subsystems within the organization. Lawrence and Lorsch suggest that an organization's complexity should mirror the complexity of its environment. As the complexity of an organization increases, its need for mechanisms to link and coordinate the differentiated parts also increases. If these links do not exist, the departments or differentiated parts of the organiza-

integration

The process of coordinating the different parts of an organization.

tion can lose sight of the organization's larger mission, and the organization runs the risk of chaos. Chaos is not inevitable, however, as research suggests that environmental complexity may be viewed as a "puzzle" that, if understood correctly, increases competence and increases organizational learning.[10]

Integration

To be effective, organizations must design and build linkage and coordination mechanisms. This process of coordinating the different parts of the organization is known as **integration**. Integration mechanisms are designed to achieve unity among individuals and groups in various jobs, departments, and divisions in the accomplishment of organizational goals and tasks.[11] Effective integration helps keep the organization in a state of *dynamic equilibrium*, a condition in which all the parts of the organization are interrelated and balanced.

To integrate activities up and down the organizational chain of command, a variety of structural devices can be used to achieve *vertical linkages*. These devices include hierarchical referral, rules and procedures, plans and schedules, positions added to the structure of the organization, and management information systems.[12] On an organization chart, the vertical lines indicate these vertical linkages, showing the lines of hierarchical referral up and down the organization. When employees do not know how to solve a problem, they can refer it upward for consideration and resolution. Work that needs to be assigned is usually delegated downward.

Rules and procedures, as well as plans and schedules, provide standing information for employees without direct communication. These vertical integrators, such as an employee handbook, communicate to employees standard information, or information that they can understand on their own. Such integrators allow managers to have wider spans of control because they do not have to inform each employee of what is expected and when it is expected. Vertical integrators encourage managers to use *management by exception*—to make decisions when employees bring problems up the hierarchy. Military organizations depend heavily on vertical linkages, having a well-defined chain of command. Certain duties are expected to be carried out, and proper paperwork is to be in place. In times of crisis, however, much more information is processed, and the proper paperwork becomes secondary to "getting the job done." Vertical linkages help individuals understand their roles in the organization, especially in times of crisis.

©Inspirestock/Jupiterimages

SPEED, SKILL, AND FLEXIBILITY

Cisco Systems' CEO John Chambers recently flattened Cisco's organizational structure, creating an emphasis on horizontal integration and cross-functional teams. While this is a highly complex organizational structure, Chambers believes that an organizational structure based on the concept of the management team provides the company speed, skill, and flexibility. Management teams take various forms, such as councils, boards, and work groups. Cisco management, employees, and senior leaders take part in several of each. The numerous teams at Cisco create a web of integrated structures that enable the right people to make the right decisions. Quick and effective decision making allows Cisco to be agile as a company. Cisco moves quickly into new markets, led by skilled employees engaged in the sectors of the company where they are most effective.

SOURCE: M. Kimes, "Cisco Systems Layers It On," *Fortune* 158 (December 8, 2008): 24.

Adding positions to the hierarchy is used as a vertical integrator when a manager becomes overloaded by hierarchical referral or problems arise in the chain of command. Positions such as "assistant to" may be added, or another level may be added. Such additions often reflect an organization's growth and increasing complexity. This action tends to reduce the span of control, thus allowing more communication and closer supervision.

Generally, the taller the organization, the more vertical integration mechanisms are needed. This is because the chains of command and communication are longer. Additional length requires more linkages to minimize the potential for misunderstandings and miscommunications.

Horizontal integration mechanisms provide the communication and coordination that are necessary for links across jobs and departments in the organization. The need for horizontal integration mechanisms increases as the complexity of the organization increases. These linkages are built into the design of the organization by including liaison roles, task forces, integrator positions, and teams.

A *liaison role* is created when a person in one department or area of the organization has the responsibility for coordinating with another department (for example, a liaison between the engineering and production departments). *Task forces* are temporary committees composed of representatives from multiple departments who assemble to address a specific problem affecting these departments.[13]

A stronger device for integration is to develop a person or department designed to be an *integrator*. In most organizations, the integrator has a good deal of responsibility but not much authority. Such an individual must have the ability to get people together to resolve differences within the perspective of organizational goals.[14]

The strongest method of horizontal integration is through *teams*. Horizontal teams cut across existing lines of organizational structure to create new entities that make organizational decisions. An example of this may occur in product development with the formation of a team that includes marketing, research, design, and production personnel. Ford used such a cross-functional team to develop the Taurus automobile, which was designed to restore the company's market share in the United States. The information exchanged by such a product development team should lead to a product that is acceptable to a wider range of organizational groups, as well as to customers.[15]

The use of these linkage mechanisms varies from organization to organization, as well as within areas of the same organization. In general, the flatter the organization, the more necessary are horizontal integration mechanisms.

LEARNING OUTCOME 2

Basic Design Dimensions

Differentiation, then, is the process of dividing work in the organization, and integration is the process of coordinating work in the organization. From a structural perspective, every manager and organization looks for the best combination of differentiation and integration for accomplishing the goals of the organization. There are many ways to approach this process. One way is to establish a desired level of each structural dimension on a high-to-low continuum and then develop a structure that meets the desired configuration. These structural dimensions include the following:

1. **Formalization:** The degree to which an employee's role is

formalization

The degree to which the organization has official rules, regulations, and procedures.

defined by formal documentation (procedures, job descriptions, manuals, and regulations).

2. **Centralization:** The extent to which decision-making authority has been delegated to lower levels of an organization. An organization is centralized if the decisions are made at the top of the organization and decentralized if decision making is pushed down to lower levels in the organization.

3. **Specialization:** The degree to which organizational tasks are subdivided into separate jobs. The division of labor and the degree to which formal job descriptions spell out job requirements indicate the level of specialization in the organization.

4. **Standardization:** The extent to which work activities are described and performed routinely in the same way. Highly standardized organizations have little variation in the defining of jobs.

5. **Complexity:** The number of activities within the organization and the amount of differentiation needed within the organization.

6. **Hierarchy of authority:** The degree of vertical differentiation through reporting relationships and the span of control within the structure of the organization.[16]

An organization that is high in formalization, centralization, specialization, standardization, and complexity and has a tall hierarchy of authority is said to be highly *bureaucratic*. Bureaucracies are not inherently bad; however, they are often tainted by abuse and red tape. There are cases, however, where centralized structures can be beneficial. For example, one study found that a more centralized structure is effective for increased job satisfaction when perceptions of interactional and procedural justice are present.[17]

An organization that is on the opposite end of each of these continua is very flexible and loose. Control is very hard to implement and maintain in such an organization, but at certain times such a structure is appropriate. The research and development departments in many organizations are often more flexible than other departments in

order to stimulate creativity. An important organizational variable for such flexible structures is trust.

Another approach to the process of accomplishing organizational goals is to describe what is and is not important to the success of the organization rather than worry about specific characteristics. Henry Mintzberg argued that the following questions can guide managers in designing formal structures that fit each organization's unique set of circumstances:

1. How many tasks should a given position in the organization contain, and how specialized should each task be?

2. How standardized should the work content of each position be?

3. What skills, abilities, knowledge, and training should be required for each position?

4. What should be the basis for the grouping of positions within the organization into units, departments, divisions, and so on?

5. How large should each unit be, and what should the span of control be (that is, how many individuals should report to each manager)?

6. How much standardization should be required in the output of each position?

7. What mechanisms should be established to help individuals in different positions and units adjust to the needs of other individuals?

8. How centralized or decentralized should decision-making power be in the chain of authority? Should most of the decisions be made at the top of the organization (centralized) or be made down in the chain of authority (decentralized)?[18]

The manager who can answer these questions has a good understanding of how the organization should implement the basic structural dimensions. These basic design dimensions act in combination with one another and are not entirely independent characteristics of an organization.

Five Structural Configurations

Differentiation, integration, and the basic design dimensions combine to yield various structural configurations. Very early organization structures were often either based on product or function. The *matrix organization* structure merged these two ways of organizing.[19] Mintzberg moved beyond these early approaches and proposed five structural configurations: the simple structure, the machine bureaucracy, the professional bureaucracy, the divisionalized

centralization

The degree to which decisions are made at the top of the organization.

specialization

The degree to which jobs are narrowly defined and depend on unique expertise.

standardization

The degree to which work activities are accomplished in a routine fashion.

complexity

The degree to which many different types of activities occur in the organization.

hierarchy of authority

The degree of vertical differentiation across levels of management.

TABLE 15.1 Five Structural Configurations of Organizations

Structural Configuration	Prime Coordinating Mechanism	Key Part of Organization	Type of Decentralization
Simple structure	Direct supervision	Upper echelon	Centralization
Machine bureaucracy	Standardization of work processes	Technical staff	Limited horizontal decentralization
Professional bureaucracy	Standardization of skills	Operating level	Vertical and horizontal decentralization
Divisionalized form	Standardization of outputs	Middle level	Limited vertical decentralization
Adhocracy	Mutual adjustment	Support staff	Selective decentralization

SOURCE: Mintzberg, Henry, *Structuring of Organizations*, 1st Edition, © 1979. Reprinted by permission of Pearson Education, Inc., Upper Saddle River, N.J.

form, and the adhocracy.[20] Table 15.1 shows the prime coordinating mechanism, the key part of the organization, and the type of decentralization for each of these structural configurations. The five basic parts of the organization, for Mintzberg, are the upper echelon, or strategic apex; the middle level, or middle line; the operating core, where work is accomplished; the technical staff, or technostructure; and the support staff. Figure 15.2 depicts these five basic parts with a small strategic apex, connected by a flaring middle line to a large, flat operating core. Each configuration affects people in the organization somewhat

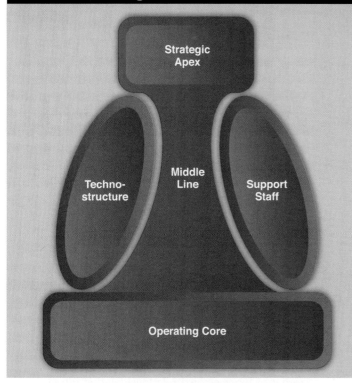

FIGURE 15.2 Mintzberg's Five Basic Parts of an Organization

SOURCE: From H. Mintzberg, *The Structuring of Organizations* (Upper Saddle River, N.J.: Pearson, 1979): 20. Reprinted by permission of Pearson Education, Inc., Upper Saddle River, N.J.

differently, and all organizational structures should support the firm's strategic goals.

Simple Structure

The **simple structure** is a centralized form of organization that emphasizes a small technical and support staff, strong centralization of decision making in the upper echelon, and a minimal middle level. This structure has a minimum of vertical differentiation of authority and minimal formalization. It achieves coordination through direct supervision, often by the chief executive in the upper echelon. An example of a simple structure is a small, independent landscape practice in which one or two landscape architects supervise the vast majority of work with no middle-level managers.

Machine Bureaucracy

The **machine bureaucracy** is a moderately decentralized form of organization that emphasizes a support staff differentiated from the line operations of the organization, limited horizontal decentralization of decision making, and a well-defined hierarchy of authority. The technical staff is powerful in a machine bureaucracy. There is strong formalization through policies, procedures, rules, and regulations. Coordination is achieved through the standardization of work processes. An example of a machine bureaucracy is an automobile assembly plant with routinized operating tasks. The strength of the machine bureaucracy is efficiency of operation in stable, unchanging environments. The weakness of the machine bureaucracy is its slow responsiveness to external changes and to individual employee preferences and ideas.

Professional Bureaucracy

The **professional bureaucracy** is a decentralized form of organization that emphasizes the expertise of the

simple structure
A centralized form of organization that emphasizes a small technical and support staff, strong centralization of decision making in the upper echelon, and a minimal middle level.

machine bureaucracy
A moderately decentralized form of organization that emphasizes support staff differentiated from the line operations of the organization, limited horizontal decentralization of decision making, and a well-defined hierarchy of authority.

professional bureaucracy
A decentralized form of organization that emphasizes the expertise of the professionals in the operating core of the organization.

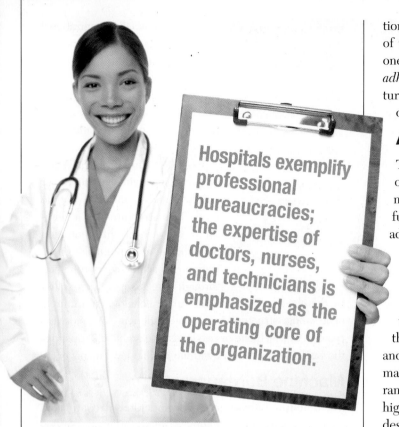

Hospitals exemplify professional bureaucracies; the expertise of doctors, nurses, and technicians is emphasized as the operating core of the organization.

professionals in the operating core of the organization. The technical and support staffs serve the professionals. There is both vertical and horizontal differentiation in the professional bureaucracy. Coordination is achieved through the standardization of the professionals' skills. Examples of organizations where professional bureaucracies can be found are hospitals and universities. The doctors, nurses, and professors are given wide latitude to pursue their work based on professional training and indoctrination through professional training programs. Large accounting firms may also fall into the category of professional bureaucracies.

Divisionalized Form

The **divisionalized form** is a loosely coupled, composite structural configuration composed of divisions, each of which may have its own structural configuration.[21] Each division is designed to respond to the market in which it operates. There is vertical decentralization from the upper echelon to the middle of the organiza-

tion, and the middle level of management is the key part of the organization. This form of organization may have one division that is a machine bureaucracy, one that is an *adhocracy* (discussed next), and one that is a simple structure. The divisionalized organization uses standardization of outputs as its coordinating mechanism.

Adhocracy

The **adhocracy** is a selectively decentralized form of organization that emphasizes the support staff and mutual adjustment among people. It is designed to fuse interdisciplinary experts into smoothly functioning ad hoc project teams. Liaison devices are the primary mechanism for integrating the project teams through a process of mutual adjustment. There is a high degree of horizontal specialization based on formal training and expertise. Selective decentralization of the project teams occurs within the adhocracy. An example of this form of organization is the National Aeronautics and Space Administration (NASA), which is composed of many talented experts who work in small teams on a wide range of projects related to America's space agenda. New high-technology businesses also often select an adhocracy design.

LEARNING OUTCOME **4**

Contextual Variables

The basic design dimensions and the resulting structural configurations play out in the context of the organization's internal and external environments. Four **contextual variables** influence the success of an organization's design: size, technology, environment, and strategy and goals. These variables provide a manager with key considerations for the right organizational design, although they do not determine the structure. The amount of change in the contextual variables throughout the life of the organization influences the amount of change needed in the basic dimensions of the organization's structure.[22] For example, competitive pressures in many industries have led to *outsourcing*, labeled one of the greatest shifts in organization structure in a century.[23]

Size

The total number of employees is the appropriate definition of size when discussing the design of organizational structure. This is logical, because people and their interactions are the building blocks of structure. Other measures, such as net assets, production rates, and total sales, are usually highly correlated with the total number of employees. However, these may not reflect the actual number of interpersonal relationships that are necessary to effectively structure an organization.

Although there is some argument over the degree of influence that size has on organizational structure, there is no argument that it does influence design options. In one study, Meyer found the size of the organization to be the most important of all variables influencing the organization's structure and design, whereas other researchers argue that the decision to expand the organization's business causes an increase in size as the structure is adjusted to accommodate the planned growth.[24] Downsizing is a planned strategy to reduce the size of an organization, and it is often accompanied by related restructuring and revitalization activities.[25]

How much influence size exerts on the organization's structure is not as important as the relationship between size and the design dimensions of structure. In other words, when exploring structural alternatives, the manager needs to know certain facts about designing structures for large versus small organizations. For example, formalization, specialization, and standardization all tend to be greater in larger organizations because they are necessary to control activities within the organization. Larger organizations are more likely to use documentation, rules, written policies and procedures, and detailed job descriptions than to rely on personal observation by the manager. McDonald's has several volumes of manuals that describe how to make all its products, how to greet customers, how to maintain facilities, and so on. This level of standardization, formalization, and specialization helps McDonald's maintain the same quality of product no matter where a restaurant is located. In contrast, at a small, locally owned café, your hamburger and French fries may taste a little different every time you visit—evidence of a lack of standardization.

Formalization and specialization also help a large organization decentralize decision making. Because of the complexity and number of decisions in a large organization, formalization and specialization are used to set parameters for decision making at lower levels. Can you imagine the chaos if the president of the United States, commander-in-chief of all military forces, had to make operational-level decisions in the war on terrorism? By decentralizing decision making, a large organization adds horizontal and vertical complexity, but not necessarily spatial complexity. However, it is more common for a large organization to have more geographic dispersion. For example, the San Diego County Government in California created a regionalized structure to decentralize decision making, share common resources and competencies, and meet its unique client needs.[26]

Hierarchy of authority is another dimension of design related to complexity. As size increases, complexity increases; thus, more levels are added to the hierarchy of authority. This keeps the span of control from getting too large. However, there is a balancing force, because formalization and specialization are added. The more formalized, standardized, and specialized the roles within the organization, the wider the span of control can be.

Technology

An organization's technology is an important contextual variable in determining the organization's structure.[27] Technology is defined as the tools, techniques, and actions used by an organization to transform inputs into outputs.[28] The inputs of the organization include human resources, machines, materials, information, and money. The outputs are the products and services that the organization offers to the external environment. Determining the relationship between technology and structure is complicated, because different departments may employ very different technologies. As organizations become larger, there is greater variation in technologies across units in the organization. Joan Woodward, Charles Perrow, and James Thompson have developed ways to understand traditional organizational technologies.

Woodward introduced one of the best-known classification schemes for technology, identifying three types: unit, mass, or process production. *Unit technology* is small-batch manufacturing technology and, sometimes, made-to-order production. Examples include the arms manufacturer Smith & Wesson and the production of fine furniture. *Mass technology* is large-batch manufacturing technology. Examples include automotive assembly

[**Does Size Matter?**]

Although some have argued that the future belongs to small, agile organizations, others argue that size continues to be an advantage. Yet, to take advantage of size, organizations must become "centerless" corporations with a *global core*.[29] These concepts were pioneered by Booz Allen Hamilton, based on its worldwide technology and management consulting. The global core provides strategic leadership, helps distribute and provide access to the company's capabilities and knowledge, creates corporate identity, ensures access to low-cost capital, and exerts control over the enterprise as a whole.

Technology is an important contextual variable in determining an organization's structure.

©IStockphoto.com/Alvin Burrows

lines and latex glove production. *Process production* is a continuous-production process. Examples include oil refining and beer making. Woodward classified unit technology as the least complex, mass technology as more complex, and process technology as the most complex. The more complex the organization's technology, the more complex the administrative component or structure of the organization needs to be.

Perrow proposed an alternative to Woodward's scheme based on two variables: task variability and problem analyzability. *Task variability* considers the number of exceptions encountered in doing the tasks within a job. *Problem analyzability* examines the types of search procedures followed to find ways to respond to task exceptions. For example, for some exceptions encountered while doing a task, the appropriate response is easy to find. If you are driving down a street and see a sign that says, "Detour—Bridge Out," it is very easy to respond to the task variability, so analyzability is low (i.e., limited analysis is needed). By contrast, when Thomas Edison was designing the first electric light bulb, the problem analyzability was very high for his task.

Perrow went on further to identify the four key aspects of structure that could be modified to technology: (1) the amount of discretion that an individual can exercise to complete a task, (2) the power of groups to control the unit's goals and strategies, (3) the

level of interdependence among groups, and (4) the extent to which organizational units coordinate work using either feedback or planning. Figure 15.3 summarizes Perrow's findings about types of technology and basic design dimensions.[30]

Thompson offered yet another view of technology and its relationship to organizational design. This view is based on the concept of **technological interdependence**, which is the degree of interrelatedness of the organization's various technological elements, and the pattern of an organization's work flows. Thompson's research suggests that greater technological interdependence leads to greater organizational complexity and that the problems of greater complexity may be offset by decentralized decision making.[31]

The research of these three early scholars on the influence of technology on organizational design can be combined into one integrating concept—*routineness* in the process of changing inputs into outputs in an organization. This routineness has a very strong relationship with organizational structure. The more routine and repetitive the tasks of the organization, the higher the degree of formalization that is possible, the more centralized, specialized, and standardized the organization can be, and the more hierarchical levels with wider spans of control that are possible.

Environment

The third contextual variable for organizational design is **environment**. The environment of an organization is most easily defined as anything outside the boundaries of that organization. Different aspects of the environment

technological interdependence
The degree of interrelatedness of the organization's various technological elements.

environment
Anything outside the boundaries of an organization.

FIGURE 15.3 Summary of Perrow's Findings

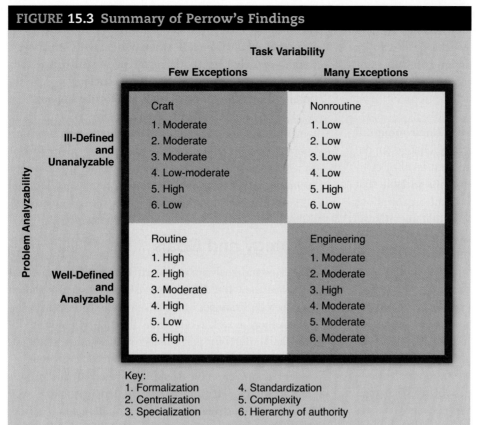

Task Variability

	Few Exceptions	Many Exceptions
Ill-Defined and Unanalyzable	Craft 1. Moderate 2. Moderate 3. Moderate 4. Low-moderate 5. High 6. Low	Nonroutine 1. Low 2. Low 3. Low 4. Low 5. High 6. Low
Well-Defined and Analyzable	Routine 1. High 2. High 3. Moderate 4. High 5. Low 6. High	Engineering 1. Moderate 2. Moderate 3. High 4. Moderate 5. Moderate 6. Moderate

(vertical axis) **Problem Analyzability**

Key:
1. Formalization   4. Standardization
2. Centralization   5. Complexity
3. Specialization   6. Hierarchy of authority

SOURCE: Built from C. Perrow, "A Framework for the Comparative Analysis of Organizations," *American Sociological Review* (April 1967): 194–208.

have varying degrees of influence on the organization's structure. In one study of 318 CEOs between 1996 and 2000, strategic decision speed was found to moderate the relationship between the environment, the structure of an organization, and performance.[32] The general environment includes all conditions that might have an impact on the organization, such as economic factors, political considerations, ecological changes, sociocultural demands, and governmental regulation.

Task Environment When aspects of the general environment become more focused in areas of direct interest to the organization, those aspects become part of the task

environment, or specific environment. The task environment is that part of the environment that is directly relevant to the organization. Typically, this level of environment includes stakeholders such as unions, customers, suppliers, competitors, government regulatory agencies, and trade associations. The *domain* of the organization refers to the area the organization claims for itself with respect to how it fits into its relevant environments. The domain is particularly important because it is defined by the organization, and it influences how the organization perceives and acts within its environments.[33] For example, Walmart and Neiman Marcus both sell clothing, but their domains are very different.

The organization's perceptions of its environment and the actual environment may not be the same. The environment that the manager perceives is the environment that the organization responds to and organizes for.[34] Therefore, two organizations may be in relatively the same environment from an objective standpoint, but if the managers perceive differences, the organizations may enact

task environment

The part of the environment that is directly relevant to the organization.

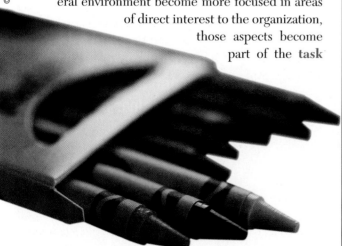

HOW TO DETERMINE ENVIRONMENTAL UNCERTAINTY

Dess and Beard identified three dimensions of environment that should be measured in assessing the degree of uncertainty: capacity, volatility, and complexity.[35] The capacity of the environment reflects the abundance or scarcity of resources. If resources abound, the environment supports expansion, mistakes, or both. In contrast, in times of scarcity, the environment demands survival of the fittest. Volatility is the degree of instability. The airline industry is in a volatile environment. This makes it difficult for managers to know what needs to be done. The complexity of the environment refers to the differences and variability among environmental elements.

©Andrew Bret Wallis/Photodisc/Getty Images

very different structures to deal with this same environment. For example, one company may decentralize and use monetary incentives for managers that lead it to be competitively aggressive, while another company may centralize and use incentives for managers that lead it to be less intense in its rivalry.[36]

Environmental Uncertainty

Environmental uncertainty is the amount and rate of change in the organization's environment. The perceived level of environmental uncertainty is the environmental variable that most influences organizational design. Some organizations have relatively static environments with little uncertainty, whereas others are so dynamic that no one is sure what tomorrow may bring. Binney & Smith, for example, has made basically the same product for more than fifty years with very few changes in the product design or packaging. The environment for its Crayola products is relatively static. In fact, customers rebelled when the company tried to get rid of some old colors and add new ones. In contrast, in the last two decades, competitors in the airline industry have encountered deregulation, mergers, bankruptcies, changes in cost and price structures, changes in customer and employee demographics, and changes in global competition. In such uncertain conditions, fast-response organizations must use expertise coordination practices to ensure that distributed expertise is managed and applied in a timely manner.[37]

The amount of uncertainty in the environment influences the structural dimensions. Burns and Stalker labeled two structural extremes that are appropriate for the extremes of environmental uncertainty—**mechanistic structure** and **organic structure**.[38] The mechanistic and organic structures occupy opposite ends of a continuum of organizational design possibilities. Although the general premise of environmental uncertainty and

structural dimensions has been upheld by research, the organization must make adjustments for the realities of its perceived environment when designing its structure.[39] Some research suggests that the type of structure, either mechanistic or organic, depends on a manager's level of organizational design experience and formal training.[40]

If the organization's environment is uncertain, dynamic, and complex and resources are scarce, the manager needs an organic structure that is better able to adapt to its environment. Such a structure allows the manager to monitor the environment from a number of internal perspectives, thus helping the organization maintain flexibility in responding to environmental changes.[41]

Strategy and Goals

Strategies and goals are the fourth contextual variable that influences how the design dimensions of structure should be enacted. Strategies and goals provide legitimacy to the organization, as well as employee direction, decision guidelines, and criteria for performance.[42] In addition, strategies and goals help the organization fit into its environment.

For example, when Apple introduced its line of personal computers to the market, its strategies were very innovative. The structure of the organization was relatively flat and very informal. Apple had Friday afternoon beer and popcorn discussion sessions, and eccentric behavior was easily accepted. As the personal computer market became more competitive, however, the structure of Apple changed to help it differentiate its products and to help control costs. The innovative strategies and structures devised by Steve Jobs, one of Apple's founders, were no longer appropriate. So the board of directors recruited John Scully, a marketing expert from PepsiCo, to help Apple better compete in the market it had created. In 1996 and

environmental uncertainty
The amount and rate of change in the organization's environment.

mechanistic structure
An organizational design that emphasizes structured activities, specialized tasks, and centralized decision making.

organic structure
An organizational design that emphasizes teamwork, open communication, and decentralized decision making.

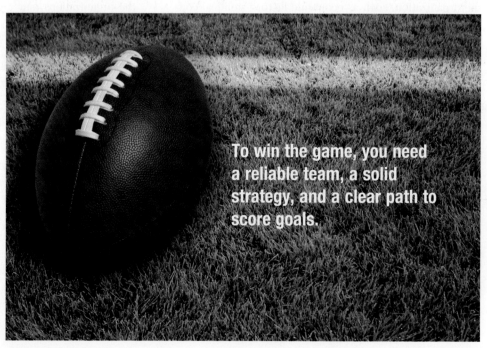

©iStockphoto.com/Dan Thornberg

To win the game, you need a reliable team, a solid strategy, and a clear path to score goals.

1997, Apple reinvented itself again and brought back Jobs to try to restore its innovative edge. After his return, Apple became a major player in the digital music market with its introduction of several models of the iPod and the iPhone.

Limitations exist, however, on the extent to which strategies and goals influence structure. Because the structure of the organization includes the formal information-processing channels in the organization, it stands to reason that the need to change strategies might not be communicated throughout the organization without going through those formal channels. In such a case, the organization's structure influences its strategic choice. Changing the organization's structure might not unlock value but instead drive up costs and difficulties. Therefore, strategic success may hinge on choosing an organization design that works reasonably well, then fine-tuning the structure through a strategic system.[43]

The inefficiency of the structure to perceive environmental changes can even lead to organizational failure. In the airline industry, several carriers failed to adjust quickly enough to deregulation and the highly competitive marketplace. Only those airlines that were generally viewed as lean structures with good information-processing systems have flourished in the turbulent years since deregulation. Examples of how different design dimensions can affect the strategic decision process are listed in Table 15.2.

The four contextual variables—size, technology, environment, and strategy and goals—combine to influence the design process. However, the existing structure of the organization influences how the organization interprets and reacts to information about each of the variables. Each of the contextual variables has management researchers who claim that it is the most important variable in determining the best structural design. Because of the difficulty in studying the interactions of the four contextual dimensions and the complexity of organizational structures, the argument about which variable is most important continues.

What is apparent is that there must be some level of fit between the structure and the contextual dimensions of the organization. The better the fit, the more likely the organization will achieve its short-run goals. In addition, the better the fit, the more likely the organization will process information and design appropriate organizational roles for long-term prosperity, as indicated in Figure 15.4 on the next page.

Forces Reshaping Organizations

Managers and researchers traditionally examine organizational design and structure within the framework of basic design dimensions and contextual variables. In recent decades, though, several forces reshaping organizations are causing managers to go beyond the traditional frameworks to examine ways to make organizations more responsive to customer needs. Some of these forces include shorter organizational life cycles, globalization, and rapid changes in information technology. Together, these forces increase the demands on process capabilities

---

TABLE 15.2 Examples of How Structure Affects the Strategic Decision Process

Formalization

As the level of formalization increases, so does the probability of the following:
1. The strategic decision process will become reactive to crisis rather than proactive through opportunities.
2. Strategic moves will be incremental and precise.
3. Differentiation in the organization will not be balanced with integrative mechanisms.
4. Only environmental crises that are in areas monitored by the formal organizational systems will be acted upon.

Centralization

As the level of centralization increases, so does the probability of the following:
1. The strategic decision process will be initiated by only a few dominant individuals.
2. The decision process will be goal-oriented and rational.
3. The strategic process will be constrained by the limitations of top managers.

Complexity

As the level of complexity increases, so does the probability of the following:
1. The strategic decision process will become more politicized.
2. The organization will find it more difficult to recognize environmental opportunities and threats.
3. The constraints on good decision processes will be multiplied by the limitations of each individual within the organization.

SOURCE: Republished with permission of Academy of Management, from "The Strategic Decision Process and Organizational Structure" (Table), J. Fredrickson, *Academy of Management Review* (1986): 284; permission conveyed through Copyright Clearance Center, Inc.

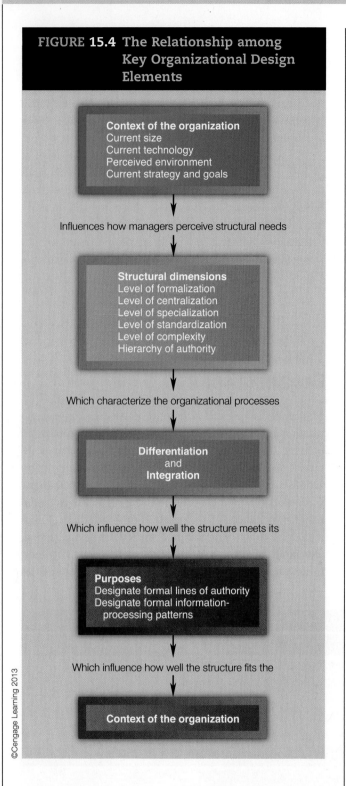

FIGURE 15.4 The Relationship among Key Organizational Design Elements

Context of the organization
Current size
Current technology
Perceived environment
Current strategy and goals

Influences how managers perceive structural needs

Structural dimensions
Level of formalization
Level of centralization
Level of specialization
Level of standardization
Level of complexity
Hierarchy of authority

Which characterize the organizational processes

Differentiation and Integration

Which influence how well the structure meets its

Purposes
Designate formal lines of authority
Designate formal information-processing patterns

Which influence how well the structure fits the

Context of the organization

©Cengage Learning 2013

stages. Usually, researchers think of these stages as **organizational life cycles.** The whole organization has a life cycle that begins at birth, moves through growth and maturity to a stage of decline, and possibly experiences revival.[45]

Organizational subunits may have very similar life cycles. Because of changes in technology and product design, many organizational subunits, especially those that are product based, are experiencing shorter life cycles. Hence, the subunits that compose the organization are changing more rapidly than in the past. These shorter life cycles enable the organization to respond quickly to external demands and changes.

When a new organization or subunit is born, the structure is organic and informal. If the organization or subunit is successful, it grows and matures. This usually leads to formalization, specialization, standardization, complexity, and a more mechanistic structure. If the environment changes, however, the organization must be able to respond. A mechanistic structure is not able to respond to a dynamic environment as well as an organic one. If the organization or subunit does respond, it becomes more organic and revives; if not, it declines and possibly dies. New research suggests that it may be wise to temporarily cycle through mechanistic and organic designs in order to meet the often conflicting demands of organizations.[46]

Shorter life cycles put more pressure on the organization to be both flexible and efficient at the same time. Further, as flexible organizations use design to their competitive advantage, discrete organizational life cycles may give way to a kaleidoscope of continuously emerging, efficiency-seeking organizational designs.[47] The manager's challenge in this context becomes one of creating congruency among various organizational design dimensions to fit continuously changing markets and locations. Many fast-growing organizations face critical transition points through their life cycles that present growth and structural challenges. The organization should attempt to resolve these before moving on to the next phase of growth and development.[48]

Globalization

Another force that is reshaping organizations is the process of globalization, in which organizations operate worldwide rather than in just one country or region. One potential problem with globalization is that corporations can become pitted against sovereign nations when rules and laws conflict across national borders. Also, globalization makes spatial differentiation even more of a reality for organizations. Besides the obvious geographic differences, there may be deep cultural and value-system differences between the various countries that an organization operates in. This adds another type of complexity to the structural design process and necessitates the

within the organization and emerging organizational structures. Thus to retain their health and vitality, organizations must function as open systems that are responsive to their task environment.[44]

Life Cycles in Organizations

Organizations are dynamic entities. As such, they ebb and flow through different

organizational life cycle

The differing stages of an organization's life from birth to death.

creation of integrating mechanisms so that people are able to understand and interpret one another, as well as coordinate with one another.

The choice of structure for managing an international business is generally based on choices concerning the following three factors:

1. *The level of vertical differentiation.* A hierarchy of authority must be created that clarifies the responsibilities of both domestic and foreign managers.

2. *The level of horizontal differentiation.* Foreign and domestic operations should be grouped in such a way that the company effectively serves the needs of all customers.

3. *The degree of formalization, specialization, standardization, and centralization.* The global structure must allow decisions to be made in the most appropriate area of the organization. However, controls must be in place that reflect the strategies and goals of the parent firm.[49]

Changes in Information-Processing Technologies

Many of the changes in information-processing technologies have allowed organizations to move into new product and market areas more quickly. However, just as shorter life cycles and globalization have caused new concerns for designing organizational structures, so has the increased availability of advanced information-processing technologies. New business technologies are increasingly changing and shaping future business processes, initiatives, and organizational designs.[50]

Organizational structures are already feeling the impact of advanced information-processing technologies. More integration and coordination are evident, because managers worldwide can be connected through computerized networks. The basic design dimensions have also been affected as follows:

1. The hierarchy of authority has been flattened.

2. The basis of centralization has been changed. Now managers can use technology to acquire more information and make more decisions, or they can use technology to push information and decision making lower in the hierarchy and thus decrease centralization.

3. Less specialization and standardization are needed, because people using advanced information-processing technologies have more sophisticated jobs that require a broader understanding of how the organization gets work done.[51]

Advances in information processing are leading to knowledge-based organizations that incorporate virtual enterprising, dynamic teaming, and knowledge networking.[52]

Demands on Organizational Processes

Because of the forces reshaping organizations, managers find themselves trying to meet what seem to be conflicting goals: an efficiency orientation that results in on-time

RESTRUCTURING AVON

When Avon, one of the largest cosmetics and perfume companies in the world, needed to reverse decreases in sales and growing losses, it turned to a radical restructuring of its organization. Much of the company's struggles were due to its failures in three key markets—Brazil, Russia, and China. Avon was hurt not only by inventory and supply issues in all three countries, but by allegations from the Chinese government that key company executives had tried to bribe government officials. To restore growth and profit, Avon overhauled its structure, going from six divisions to just two. One division, called the Developing Market Group, will focus on Avon's activities in Latin America, Eastern Europe, Asia Pacific, and China, while the other division will focus its efforts on North America and Western Europe. Through the restructuring, Avon hopes that it will be able to reestablish itself as a strong presence in developing markets all over the world while at the same time stabilizing its growth in developed economies.

SOURCE: E. Byron and P. Ziobro, "Avon Shuffles Managers" *The Wall Street Journal* (February 25, 2011), http://online.wsj.com/article/SB100014240527487034086045761642137978 41714.html.

delivery *and* a quality orientation that results in customized, high-quality goods or services.[53] Traditionally, managers have seen efficiency and customization as conflicting demands.

To meet these conflicting demands, organizations need to become "dynamically stable."[54] To do so, an organization must have managers who see their roles as architects who clearly understand the "how" of the organizing process. Thus, managers must combine long-term thinking with flexible and quick responses that help improve process and know-how. In addition, the organizational structure must help define, at least to some degree, roles for managers who hope to successfully address the conflicting demands of dynamic stability.

LEARNING OUTCOME 6

Emerging Organizational Structures

The demands placed on managers and on process capabilities in turn place demands on structures. Consequently, the emphasis in organizations is shifting to organizing around processes (see Table 15.3). For example, Procter & Gamble increased its level of innovation by creating teams dedicated to conducting market research, developing technology, creating business plans, and testing assumptions for specific projects.[55] This process orientation emerges from the combination of three streams of applied organizational design: high-performance, self-managed teams; managing processes rather than functions; and the evolution of information technology. Information technology and advanced communication

systems have in turn led to *internetworking.* In a study of 469 firms, deeply internetworked firms were found to be more focused and specialized, less hierarchical, and more engaged in external partnering.[56] Three emerging organizational structures associated with these changes are network organizations, virtual organizations, and the circle organization. Virtuality in organizations is often broken down into four interlocking components: geographic dispersion, electronic interdependence, dynamic structure, and national diversity.[57]

Network organizations are weblike structures that contract some or all of their operating functions to other organizations and then coordinate their activities through managers and other employees at their headquarters. Information technology is the basis for building the weblike structure of the network organization and business unit managers that are essential to the success of these systems. This type of organization has arisen in the age of electronic commerce and brought into practice transaction-cost economics, interorganizational collaborations, and strategic alliances. Network organizations can be global in scope.[58]

Virtual organizations are temporary network organizations consisting of independent enterprises. Many dot-coms are virtual organizations designed to come together swiftly to exploit an apparent market opportunity. They may function much like a theatrical troupe that comes together for a "performance."[59] Trust—a complex phenomenon involving ethics, morals, emotions, values, and natural attitudes—can be particularly challenging for virtual organizations. However, trust and trustworthiness are important connective issues in virtual environments. Three key ingredients for the development of trust in virtual organizations are (1) technology that can communicate emotion; (2) a sharing of values, vision, and organizational identity; and (3) a high standard of ethics.[60]

The *circle organization* is a third emerging structure, crafted by Harley-Davidson in its drive to achieve teamwork without teams.[61] The three organizational parts, shown in Figure 15.5, are those that (1) create demand, (2) produce product, and (3) provide support. As the figure indicates, these three parts are linked by the *leadership*

TABLE 15.3 Structural Roles of Managers Today versus Managers of the Future	
Roles of Managers Today	1. Strictly adhering to boss–employee relationships. 2. Getting things done by giving orders. 3. Carrying messages up and down the hierarchy. 4. Performing a prescribed set of tasks according to a job description. 5. Having a narrow functional focus. 6. Going through channels, one by one by one. 7. Controlling subordinates.
Roles of Future Managers	1. Having heirarchical relationships subordinated to functional and peer relationships. 2. Getting things done by negotiating. 3. Solving problems and making decisions. 4. Creating the job by developing entrepreneurial projects. 5. Having broad cross-functional collaboration. 6. Emphasizing speed and flexibility. 7. Coaching their workers.

SOURCE: T. R. Horton, and P. C. Reid (1991). What Fate for Middle Managers?, *Management Review*, 80(1), 22. ©1991. Thomas R. Horton. American Management Association, New York. All rights reserved.

FIGURE 15.5 Harley-Davidson's Circle Organization

Create Demand

Produce Product

Provide Support

Leadership and Strategy Council (LSC)

and strategy council (LSC). The circle organization is a more open system than most and an organic structure for customer responsiveness. One innovation in this organizational scheme is the "circle coach," who possesses acute communication, listening, and influencing skills so as to be highly respected by circle members and the company's president.

Factors That Can Adversely Affect Structure

This chapter has identified the purposes of structure, the processes of organizational design, and the dimensions and contexts that must be considered in structure. In addition, it has looked at forces and trends in organizational design. Two cautionary notes are important for the student of organizational behavior. First, an organizational structure may be weak or deficient if it is out of alignment with its contextual variables, in which case one or more of the following four symptoms appears:

> Decision making is delayed because the hierarchy is overloaded and too much information is being funneled through one or two channels.

> Decision making is of poor quality because information linkages are not providing the correct information to the right person in the right format.

> The organization does not respond innovatively to a changing environment, especially when coordinated effort is lacking across departments.

> A great deal of conflict is evident as some departments work against one another rather than for the strategies and goals of the organization as a whole; the structure is often at fault.

Second, the personality of the chief executive may adversely affect the structure of the organization.[62] Managers' personal, cognitive biases and political ideologies may affect their good judgment and decision making.[63] Five dysfunctional combinations of personality and organization have been identified: the paranoid, the depressive, the dramatic, the compulsive, and the schizoid.[64] Each of these personality–organization constellations can create problems for the people who work in the organization. For example, in a paranoid constellation, people are suspicious of each other, hence distrust in working relationships may interfere with effective communication and task accomplishment. In a depressive constellation, people feel depressed and inhibited in their work activities, which can lead to low levels of productivity and task accomplishment.

Log in to the **CourseMate** for **ORGB3** at **www.cengagebrain.com** to:

❋ Review **Key Terms Flash Cards** online

❋ Play **Beat the Clock** and **Quiz Bowl** to master concepts

❋ Complete **web quizzes** to prepare for exams

❋ Watch the video on **Modern Shed** and from **Rendition** for examples, then test yourself with a quick quiz

❋ Work through the **"What about You?"** and **Ethical Dilemma** exercises to see how you would handle various situations that organizations face on a daily basis

16

Organizational Culture

LEARNING OUTCOMES

1 Identify the three levels of organizational culture and evaluate the roles they play in an organization.

2 Evaluate the four functions of organizational culture within an organization.

3 Explain the relationship between organizational culture and performance.

4 Describe five ways leaders reinforce organizational culture.

5 Describe the three stages of organizational socialization and the ways culture is communicated in each step.

6 Discuss how managers assess their organization's culture.

7 Explain actions managers can take to change organizational culture.

8 Identify the challenges organizations face developing positive, cohesive cultures.

©Flying Colours Ltd/Digital Vision/Jupiterimages

"Organizational cultures are shared, communicated through symbols, and passed down from generation to generation of employees.**"**

The concept of organizational culture has its roots in cultural anthropology. Just as there are cultures in larger human society, there are cultures within organizations. Like societal cultures, they are shared, communicated through symbols, and passed down from generation to generation of employees.

The concept of cultures in organizations was alluded to as early as the Hawthorne studies, which described work group culture. The topic came into its own during the early 1970s, when managers and researchers began to search for keys to survival for organizations in a competitive and turbulent environment. Then, in the early 1980s, several books on corporate culture were published, including Terry Deal and Allan Kennedy's *Corporate Cultures*,[1] William Ouchi's *Theory Z*,[2] and Thomas Peters and Robert Waterman's *In Search of Excellence*.[3] These books found wide audiences, and research began in earnest on the elusive topic of organizational cultures. Executives indicated that these cultures were real and could be managed.[4]

LEARNING OUTCOME **1**

Levels of Organizational Culture

Many definitions of *organizational culture* have been proposed. Most of them agree that there are several levels of culture and that these levels differ in terms of their visibility and their ability to be changed. Culture has been viewed both as what defines the values of the organization and as a toolkit as to how to behave in an organization. As such, culture influences outcomes that an organization desires to achieve, as well as the processes necessary to achieve those outcomes.[5] The definition adopted in this chapter is that **organizational (corporate) culture** is a pattern of basic assumptions that are considered valid and that are taught to new members as the way to perceive, think, and feel in the organization.[6]

> **organizational (corporate) culture**
>
> A pattern of basic assumptions that are considered valid and that are taught to new members as the way to perceive, think, and feel in the organization.

After You Finish This Chapter Go to **Page 276** for **Study Tools**

In his comprehensive book on organizational culture and leadership, Edgar Schein suggests that organizational culture has three levels. His view of culture is presented in Figure 16.1. The levels range from visible *artifacts* and creations to testable *values* to invisible and even preconscious basic *assumptions*. To achieve a complete understanding of an organization's culture, all three levels must be studied.

Artifacts

Symbols of culture in the physical and social work environments are called **artifacts**. They are the most visible and accessible level of culture. The key to understanding culture through artifacts lies in figuring out their meanings. Artifacts are also the most frequently studied manifestation of organizational culture, perhaps because of their accessibility. Examples of the artifacts of culture include personal enactment, ceremonies and rites, stories, rituals, and symbols.[7]

artifacts

Symbols of culture in the physical and social work environments.

The corporate culture of Google is apparent in the offices of Google headquarters located in Mountain View, California. The lobby is replete with lava lamps, pianos, and displays of live searches on the Google search engine from around the world. The hallways house bikes and exercise machines, while office spaces are laid back, with couches and dogs who follow their owners to work.[8] The artifacts at Google reinforce the notion that the company cares about employees and wants them to be creative and comfortable.

The artifacts at Google's offices reinforce the notion that the company cares about its employees.

©Stephen Brashear/Getty Images

Personal Enactment Culture can be understood, in part, through an examination of the behavior of organization members. When this behavior reflects the organization's values, it is called *personal enactment*. In particular, personal enactment by the top managers provides insight into the organization's values. Steve Irby is the founder and CEO of Stillwater Designs, the company that created Kicker audio speakers. He builds trust with his employees by sharing the financial results of the business each month. If monthly sales are higher than sales in the same month of the previous year, Irby will hold a cookout for the employees on the following Friday. What is more, Irby and the general manager always do the cooking.

Eskimo Joe's, a restaurant chain based in Stillwater, Oklahoma, and one of the largest T-shirt sellers in the United States, could probably have become a national franchise years ago. But founder Stan Clark, who began as co-owner of the once tiny bar, says his intent is to become better, not bigger. Clark still meets personally with new hires for the restaurant's serving staff, ensuring that they receive a firm grounding in his philosophy of food and fun.[9]

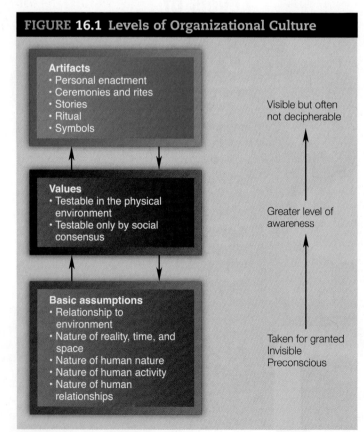

FIGURE 16.1 Levels of Organizational Culture

Artifacts
- Personal enactment
- Ceremonies and rites
- Stories
- Ritual
- Symbols

Values
- Testable in the physical environment
- Testable only by social consensus

Basic assumptions
- Relationship to environment
- Nature of reality, time, and space
- Nature of human nature
- Nature of human activity
- Nature of human relationships

Visible but often not decipherable

Greater level of awareness

Taken for granted
Invisible
Preconscious

SOURCE: From Edgar H. Schein, *Organizational Culture and Leadership: A Dynamic View.* Copyright © 1985 Jossey-Bass, Inc. Reprinted by permission of John Wiley & Sons, Inc.

Modeled behavior is a powerful learning tool for employees, as Bandura's social learning theory demonstrated.[10] As we saw in Chapter 5, individuals learn vicariously by observing others' behavior and patterning their own behavior similarly. In this way, culture can be an important leadership tool. Managerial behavior can clarify what is important and coordinate the work of employees, in effect negating the need for close supervision.[11]

Ceremonies and Rites Relatively elaborate sets of activities that are repeatedly enacted on important occasions are known as organizational ceremonies and rites.[12] These occasions provide opportunities to reward and recognize employees whose behavior is congruent with the values of the company. Ceremonies and rites send a message that individuals who both espouse and exhibit corporate values are heroes to be admired.

The ceremonies also bond organization members together. Southwestern Bell (now part of SBC Communications) emphasized the importance of management training to the company. Training classes were kicked off by a high-ranking executive (a rite of renewal), and completion of the classes was signaled by a graduation ceremony (a rite of passage). Six kinds of rites in organizations have been identified, as shown below.[13]

Berkshire Hathaway, Inc., is an Omaha-based company that owns and operates a number of insurance firms and several other subsidiaries. Chairman and CEO Warren Buffett is known for his business acumen and for ensuring good returns on shareholder investments. Berkshire's annual shareholder meeting is a ceremony of celebration and appears more like a major rock music festival than a corporate meeting. Each meeting starts with a short film poking fun at the CEO and his cantankerous sidekick, Charlie Munger. Susan Lucci starred in the 2008 version and then showed up in person to try jokingly to take Buffett's job. Others who have made cameos include Arnold Schwarzenegger, Donald Trump, and the women of *Desperate Housewives*. In 2007 Jimmy Buffett sang "Margaritaville" at the meeting, with some of the lyrics changed to "wasting away in Berkshire-Hathaway-a-ville!" Bill Gates, who is on the board of directors, often makes it to the meeting and has been seen playing ping-pong with Warren Buffett. More than 20,000 shareholders, employees, and Buffett relatives attend the star-studded event annually.[14]

Stories Some researchers have argued that the most effective way to reinforce organizational values is through stories.[15] As they are retold, stories give meaning and identity to organizations and are especially helpful in orienting new employees. Part of the strength of organizational stories is that the listeners are left to draw their own conclusions—a powerful communication tool.[16]

Some corporate stories even transcend cultural and political boundaries. Visit the website of Walmart China, and you will read the true story of Jeff, a pharmacist in Harrison, Arkansas, a small town deep in the Ozarks. When Jeff received an early morning weekend call telling him that a diabetic patient needed insulin, he quickly opened his pharmacy and filled the prescription.[17] While Arkansas and Beijing are worlds apart, stories such as this

[Rites in Organizations]

Rite	Role	Example
Rites of passage	show that an individual's status has changed	retirement dinners
Rites of enhancement	reinforce the achievement of individuals	awarding certificates to sales contest winners
Rites of renewal	emphasize change in the organization and commitment to learning and growth	opening a new corporate training center
Rites of integration	unite diverse groups or teams within the organization and renew commitment to the larger organization	company functions such as annual picnics
Rites of conflict reduction	dealing with conflicts or disagreements that arise naturally in organizations	grievance hearings and the negotiation of union contracts
Rites of degradation	used to visibly punish persons who fail to adhere to values and norms of behavior	publicly replacing a CEO for unethical conduct or for failure to achieve organizational goals

one help transfer Walmart's corporate "personality" to its new Asian associates. Research by Joanne Martin and her colleagues has indicated that certain themes appear in stories across different types of organizations:[18]

1. *Stories about the boss*. These stories may reflect whether the boss is "human" or how the boss reacts to mistakes.

2. *Stories about getting fired*. Events leading to employee firings are recounted.

3. *Stories about how the company deals with employees who have to relocate*. These stories relate to the company's actions toward employees who have to move—whether the company is helpful and takes family and other personal concerns into account.

4. *Stories about whether lower-level employees can rise to the top*. Often these stories describe a person who started out at the bottom and eventually became the CEO. QuikTrip is well known for promoting from within, one reason it has been voted one of *Fortune*'s 100 Best Companies to Work For seven years running. In fact, two-thirds of QuikTrip's top 100 managers started at entry-level positions in the organization.[19]

5. *Stories about how the company deals with crisis situations*. These stories show how the company overcomes obstacles. Employees at SAS, a software company in North Carolina, love to tell stories of how the company has never once laid off an employee, even during the global recession. Such stories illustrate that even during financial crisis, SAS cares more about employees than about the bottom line.[20]

6. *Stories about how status considerations work when rules are broken*. When Tom Watson, Sr., was CEO of IBM, he was once confronted by a security guard because he was not wearing an ID badge.

These are the themes that can emerge when stories are passed down. The information from these stories serves to guide the behavior of organization members.

To be effective cultural tools, however, stories must be credible. You can't tell a story about your flat corporate hierarchy and then have reserved parking spaces for managers. Stories that aren't backed by reality can lead to cynicism and mistrust.

Effective stories are not only motivational; they can also reinforce culture and create renewed energy. Lucasfilm is the home of director and producer George Lucas and the birthplace of such blockbusters as *Star Wars* and *Indiana Jones*. Stories of the company's legendary accomplishments are used to reinforce the creative culture and to rally the troops. When Gail Currey, former head of the company's digital division, found that her 300 designers were grumbling, she reminded them of how they achieved the special effects for *Forrest Gump* when everyone else said it was impossible and what a hit the film was. The geniuses then headed back to their computers to add to the company's success.[21]

Rituals Everyday, repetitive, organizational practices are rituals. They are usually unwritten, but they send a clear message about "the way we do things around here." While some companies insist that people address each other by their titles and surnames to reinforce a professional image, others prefer that employees operate on a first-name basis—from the top manager on down. Hewlett-Packard values open communication, so its employees address one another by first names only.

Mark Zuckerberg, the founder of Facebook, used to end company meetings with a ritual—pumping his fist into the air and leading employees in a chant of "Domination!" He later replaced this ritual by quoting movie lines aimed at reminding employees that they are engaged in something greater and more meaningful than making money.[22] As everyday practices, rituals reinforce the organizational culture. Insiders who commonly practice the rituals may be unaware of their subtle influence, but outsiders recognize it easily.

Symbols Symbols communicate organizational culture through unspoken messages. They are representative of organizational identity and membership to employees. Some Nike employees proudly display tattoos of the Nike swoosh above their ankles. Symbols are used to build solidarity in the organizational culture.[23]

Personal enactment, rites and ceremonies, stories, rituals, and symbols serve to reinforce the values that are the next level of culture.

Values

Values are the second, deeper, level of culture. They reflect a person's inherent beliefs of what should or should not be. Values are often consciously articulated, both in conversation and in a company's mission statement or annual report. However, there may be a difference between a company's **espoused values** (what the members say they value) and its **enacted values** (values reflected in the way the members actually behave).[24] Values also may be reflected in the behavior of individuals, which is an artifact of culture. One study investigating the gender gap in a Canadian sports organization found that coaches and athletes had come to believe that the inequity between espoused and enacted values was normal, or natural. Some even completely denied it existed even though such inequities were widely prevalent. This was because even though the organization espoused gender equity as a value, its practices did not enact gender equity.[25]

How a firm promotes and publicizes its values may also affect how workers feel about their jobs and themselves. A study of 180 managers evaluated their employers' effectiveness in communicating concern for employees' welfare. Managers in organizations that consistently communicated concern for workers' well-being and that focused on treating employees fairly reported feeling better about themselves and their role in the organization.[26] The lesson? *Treat* employees like valuable team members, and they are more likely to *feel* like valuable team members.

Some organizational cultures are characterized by values that support healthy lifestyle behaviors. When the workplace culture values workers' health and psychological needs, there is enhanced potential for high performance and improved well-being.[27] Clif Bar, the energy bar maker, even has a twenty-two-foot rock-climbing wall in its corporate office.

Assumptions

Assumptions are the deeply held beliefs that guide behavior and tell members of an organization how to perceive situations and people. At the deepest and most fundamental level of an organization's culture, according to Edgar Schein, they are the essence of culture. Assumptions are so strongly held that a member behaving in a fashion that would violate them is unthinkable. Another characteristic of assumptions is that they are often unconscious. Organization members may not be aware of their assumptions and may be reluctant or unable to discuss them or change them.

While unconscious assumptions often guide a firm's actions and decisions, some companies are quite explicit in their assumptions about employees. NetApp, a data storage solution provider, operates under the philosophy that treating employees fairly reduces the need for excessive rules and regulations. For example, NetApp's travel policy is simple: "We are a frugal company, but don't show up dog-tired to save a few bucks."[28] Due in part to its focus on trust and openness, NetApp was named the best company to work for by *Fortune* in 2009.

Functions of Organizational Culture

In an organization, culture serves four basic functions. First, culture provides a sense of identity to members and increases their commitment to the organization.[29] When employees internalize the values of the company, they find their work intrinsically rewarding and identify with their fellow workers. As a result, motivation is enhanced, and employees are more committed.[30]

Second, culture provides a way for employees to interpret the meaning of organizational events.[31] Leaders

espoused values
What members of an organization say they value.

enacted values
Values reflected in the way individuals actually behave.

assumptions
Deeply held beliefs that guide behavior and tell members of an organization how to perceive situations and people.

CLASHING VALUES

 As public debates over healthcare reform swept the United States in the summer of 2009, CEO of Whole Foods Market and self-avowed libertarian John Mackey came under fire from employees and customers alike for vocally opposing a public health insurance plan. Many felt that Mackey's condemnation of universal care undermined the company's otherwise progressive value set, which includes animal welfare, executive pay caps, and organic farming. Though the online news publication *Progressive Review* and several Facebook groups called for a boycott of Whole Foods Market, Mackey has not amended his views on healthcare.

SOURCES: "Rethinking the Social Responsibility of Business," http://www.reason.com/news/show/32239.html; "Whole Foods CEO's Health Care Views Provoke Some Customers to Boycott Store," http://www.foxnews.com/politics/2009/08/15/foods-ceo-provokes-customers-boycottt-store-health-care-view/.

can use organizational symbols such as corporate logos to help employees understand the changing nature of their organizational identity. Sometimes symbols should remain the same to ensure that some things stay constant despite changing conditions. Other times symbols may have to change to reflect the new culture in the organization.

Third, culture reinforces the values of the organization. And, fourth, culture serves as a control mechanism for shaping behavior. Norms that guide behavior are part of culture. Thus, if the norm the company wants to promote is teamwork, then its culture must reinforce that norm. The company's culture must be characterized by open communication, cooperation between teams, and integration of teams.[32] Culture can also be used as a powerful tool to discourage dysfunctional and deviant behaviors in organizations. Norms can send clear messages that certain behaviors are unacceptable.[33]

LEARNING OUTCOME **3**

The Relationship of Culture to Performance

The effects of organizational culture are hotly debated by organizational behaviorists and researchers. It seems that although managers attest strongly to the positive effects of culture in organizations, it is difficult to quantify these effects. John Kotter and James Heskett have reviewed three theories about the relationship between organizational culture and performance and the evidence that either supports or refutes these theories.[34] The three are the strong-culture perspective, the fit perspective, and the adaptation perspective.

The Strong-Culture Perspective

The strong-culture perspective states that organizations with strong cultures perform better than other organizations.[35] A **strong culture** is an organizational culture with a consensus on the values that drive the company and with an intensity that is recognizable even to outsiders. Thus, a strong culture is deeply held and widely shared. It is also highly resistant to change. A good example is IBM, which has a strong culture of conservatism, workforce loyalty, and emphasis on customer service.

Strong cultures are thought to facilitate per-

strong culture
An organizational culture with a consensus on the values that drive the company and with an intensity that is recognizable even to outsiders.

adaptive culture
An organizational culture that encourages confidence and risk taking among employees, has leadership that produces change, and focuses on the changing needs of customers.

formance for three reasons. First, these cultures are characterized by goal alignment; that is, all employees share common goals. Second, strong cultures create a high level of motivation because of the values shared by the members. Third, strong cultures provide control without the oppressive effects of a bureaucracy.

Two perplexing questions about the strong-culture perspective are (1) what can be said about evidence showing that strong economic performance can create strong cultures, rather than the reverse, and (2) what if the strong culture leads the firm down the wrong path? Sears, for example, is an organization with a strong culture, but in the 1980s, it focused inward, ignoring competition and consumer preferences and damaging its performance. Changing Sears's strong but stodgy culture has been a tough task, with financial performance only recently showing an upward trend.[36]

The Fit Perspective

The "fit" perspective argues that a culture is good only if it fits the industry or the firm's strategy. For example, a culture that values a traditional hierarchical structure and stability would not work well in the computer manufacturing industry, which demands fast response and a lean, flat organization. Three particular industry characteristics may affect culture: the competitive environment, customer requirements, and societal expectations.[37]

A study of twelve large U.S. firms indicated that cultures consistent with industry conditions help managers make better decisions. It also indicated that cultures need not change as long as the industry doesn't change. If the industry does change, however, many cultures change too slowly to avoid negative effects on firms' performance.[38]

The fit perspective is useful in explaining short-term performance but not long-term performance. It also indicates that it is difficult to change culture quickly, especially if the culture is widely shared and deeply held. But it doesn't explain how firms can adapt to environmental change.

The Adaptation Perspective

The third theory about culture and performance is the adaptation perspective. Its theme is that only cultures that help organizations adapt to environmental change are associated with excellent performance. An **adaptive culture** is a culture that encourages confidence and risk taking among employees,[39] has leadership that produces change,[40] and focuses on the changing needs of customers.[41] To test the adaptation perspective, Kotter and Heskett interviewed industry analysts about the cultures of twenty-two firms. The contrast between adaptive cul-

©iStockphoto.com/Tomasz Pietryszek

tures and nonadaptive cultures was striking. The results of the study are summarized in Table 16.1.

Adaptive cultures facilitate change to meet the needs of three groups of constituents: stockholders, customers, and employees. Nonadaptive cultures are characterized by cautious management that tries to protect its own interests. Adaptive firms showed significantly better long-term economic performance in Kotter and Heskett's study. Given that high-performing cultures are adaptive ones, it is important to know how managers can develop adaptive cultures.

LEARNING OUTCOME 4

The Leader's Role in Shaping and Reinforcing Culture

According to Edgar Schein, leaders play crucial roles in shaping and reinforcing culture.[42] The five most important elements in managing culture are (1) what leaders pay attention to, (2) how leaders react to crises, (3) how leaders behave, (4) how leaders allocate rewards, and (5) how leaders hire and fire individuals.

What Leaders Pay Attention To

Leaders in an organization communicate their priorities, values, and beliefs through the themes that consistently emerge from their focus. These themes are reflected in what they notice, comment on, measure, and control. If leaders are consistent in their focus, employees receive clear signals about what is important in the organization. If, however, leaders are inconsistent, employees spend a lot of time trying to decipher and find meaning in the inconsistent signals.

How Leaders React to Crises

The way leaders deal with crises communicates a powerful message about culture. Emotions are heightened during a crisis, and learning is intense. Difficult economic times present crises for many companies and illustrate their different values. Some organizations avoid laying off workers at all costs. Others, despite their claim that employees are important, quickly institute major layoffs at the first signal of an economic downturn. Employees may perceive that the company shows its true colors in a crisis and thus pay careful attention to the reactions of their leaders.

How Leaders Behave

Through role modeling, teaching, and coaching, leaders reinforce the values that support the organizational culture. Employees often emulate leaders' behavior and look to the leaders for cues to appropriate behavior. Many companies encourage employees to be more entrepreneurial, using more initiative and innovation. A study showed that if managers want employees to be more entrepreneurial, they must demonstrate such behaviors themselves.[43] This is the case with any cultural value. Employees observe the behavior of leaders to find out what the organization values.

How Leaders Allocate Rewards

To ensure that values are accepted, leaders should reward behavior that is consistent with the values. Some companies, for example, may claim that they use a pay-for-performance system that distributes rewards on the basis of performance. When the time comes for raises, however, the increases are awarded according to length of service with the company. Imagine the feelings of a high-performing newcomer who receives only a tiny raise after hearing company leaders espouse the value of rewarding individual performance.

Some companies may claim to value teamwork. They form cross-functional teams and empower these teams to make important decisions. However,

TABLE 16.1 Adaptive versus Nonadaptive Organizational Cultures		
	ADAPTIVE ORGANIZATIONAL CULTURES	**NONADAPTIVE ORGANIZATIONAL CULTURES**
Core values	Most managers care deeply about customers, stockholders, and employees. They also strongly value people and processes that can create useful change (e.g., leadership up and down the management hierarchy).	Most managers care mainly about themselves, their immediate work group, or some product (or technology) associated with that work group. They value the orderly and risk-reducing management process much more highly than leadership initiatives.
Common behavior	Managers pay close attention to all their constituencies, especially customers, and initiate change when needed to serve their legitimate interests, even if that entails taking some risks.	Managers tend to behave somewhat insularly, politically, and bureaucratically. As a result, they do not change their strategies quickly to adjust to or take advantage of changes in their business environments.

when performance is appraised, the criteria for rating employees focus on individual performance. This sends a confusing signal to employees about the company's culture: Is individual performance valued, or is teamwork the key?

How Leaders Hire and Fire Individuals

A powerful way that leaders reinforce culture is through the selection of newcomers to the organization. With the advent of electronic recruitment practices, applicant perceptions of organizational culture are shaped by what the organization advertises on its recruitment website. Typical perception-shaping mechanisms are organizational values, policies, awards, and goals.[44] Leaders often unconsciously look for individuals who are similar to current organizational members in terms of values and assumptions. Indeed, some companies hire individuals on the recommendation of a current employee. This practice tends to perpetuate the culture because the new employees typically hold similar values to existing employees. Jeffrey Swartz, CEO of Timberland, has a unique way of hiring people. His recruiter calls the applicants in advance, tells them to wear anything they feel passionately about other than Timberland shoes, then sends promising applicants on a day of community service with Timberland executives. Schwartz claims that anyone can be smarter than him in an interview, but service brings out the real person and this is whom he tries to hire.[45]

The way a company fires an employee and the rationale behind the firing also communicates the culture. Some companies deal with poor performers by trying to find a place within the organization where they can perform better and make a contribution. Other companies seem to operate under the philosophy that those who cannot perform are out quickly.

The reasons for terminations may not be directly communicated to other employees, but curiosity leads to speculation. Suppose an employee caught in the act of unethical behavior is simply reprimanded, with no other penalty, even though such behavior is clearly against the organization's values. Other employees may view this as a failure to reinforce the values within the organization.

In summary, leaders play a critical role in shaping and reinforcing organizational culture. Managers need to create a positive culture through what they pay attention to, how they react to crises, how they behave, the way they allocate rewards, and how they hire and fire employees. Transformational leaders create a more adaptive culture, which in turn increases business unit performance.[46]

Organizational Socialization

We have seen that leaders play key roles in shaping an organization's culture. Another process that perpetuates culture is the way it is passed on from generation to generation of employees. Newcomers learn the culture through **organizational socialization**—the process by which newcomers are transformed from outsiders to participating, effective members of the organization.[47] As we saw earlier, cultural socialization begins with the careful selection of newcomers who are likely to reinforce the organizational culture.[48] Once selected, newcomers pass through the socialization process.

The Stages of the Socialization Process

The organizational socialization process is generally described as having three stages: anticipatory socialization, encounter, and change and acquisition. Figure 16.2 presents a model of the process and the key concerns at each stage of it.[49] It also describes the outcomes of the process, which will be discussed in the next section of the chapter.

Anticipatory Socialization The first stage of the socialization process, **anticipatory socialization**, encompasses all of the learning that takes place prior to the newcomer's first day on the job, including the newcomer's expectations. The two key concerns at this stage are realism and congruence.

Realism is the degree to which a newcomer holds realistic expectations about the job and organization. One thing newcomers should receive information about during entry into the organization is the culture. Information about values at this stage can help newcomers begin to construct a scheme for interpreting their organizational

organizational socialization
The process by which newcomers are transformed from outsiders to participating, effective members of the organization.

anticipatory socialization
The first socialization stage, which encompasses all of the learning that takes place prior to the newcomer's first day on the job.

experiences. Later, a deeper understanding of the organization's culture will be possible through time and experience in the organization. Furthermore, a recent study found that when organizations give realistic job previews that not only highlight major stressors but also teach various coping strategies to deal with them, newcomers feel less stressed and report higher levels of adjustment six and nine months post-entry.[50]

There are two types of *congruence* between an individual and an organization: congruence between the individual's abilities and the demands of the job, and the fit between the individual's values and the organization's values. Organizations disseminate information about their values through their web pages, annual reports, and recruitment brochures.[51] *Value congruence* is particularly important for organizational culture. It is also important in terms of newcomer adjustment. Newcomers whose values match the company's values are more satisfied with their new jobs, adjust more quickly, and say they intend to remain with the firm longer.[52]

Encounter The second stage of socialization, **encounter**, is when newcomers learn the tasks associated with the job, clarify their roles, and establish new relationships at work. This stage commences on the first day at work and is thought to encompass the first six to nine months on the new job. Newcomers face task demands, role demands, and interpersonal demands during this period.

Task demands involve the actual work performed. Learning to perform tasks is related to the organization's culture. In some organizations, where creativity is valued, newcomers are given considerable latitude to experiment with new ways to do their job. In others, newcomers are expected to learn the established procedures for their tasks. Early experiences with trying to master task demands can affect employees' entire careers. Auditors, for example, are often forced to choose between being thorough and being fast in completing their work. By pressuring auditors in this way, firms often set themselves up for problems later, when these pressures may lead auditors to make less-than-ethical decisions.

Role demands involve the expectations placed on newcomers. Newcomers may not know exactly what is expected of them (role ambiguity) or may receive conflicting expectations from other individuals (role conflict). The way newcomers approach these demands depends in part on the culture of the organization. Are newcomers expected to operate with considerable uncertainty, or is the manager expected to clarify the newcomers' roles? Some cultures even put newcomers through considerable stress in the socialization process, including humility-inducing experiences, so newcomers will be more open to accepting the firm's values and norms. Long hours, tiring travel schedules, and an overload of work are examples of some socialization practices.

Interpersonal demands arise from relationships at work. Politics, leadership style, and group pressure are interpersonal demands. All of them reflect the values and assumptions that operate within the organization. Most organizations have basic assumptions about the nature of human relationships. For example, the Korean *chaebol* LG Group strongly values harmony in relationships and in society, and its decision-making policy emphasizes unanimity.

In the encounter stage, the expectations formed in anticipatory socialization may clash with the realities of the job. It is a time of facing the task, role, and interpersonal demands of the new job.

Change and Acquisition In the third and final stage of socialization, **change and acquisition**, newcomers begin to master the demands of the job. They become proficient at managing their tasks, clarifying and negotiating

FIGURE **16.2** The Organizational Socialization Process: Stages and Outcomes

Stages of socialization

1. Anticipatory socialization — Realism / Congruence

2. Encounter — Job demands: • Task • Role • Interpersonal

3. Change and acquisition — Mastery

Outcomes of socialization — Performance / Satisfaction / Mutual influence / Low levels of distress / Intent to remain

SOURCE: Reprinted from *Organizational Dynamics*, Autumn 1989, "An Ethical Weather Report: Assessing the Organization's Ethical Climate" by John B. Cullen et al. Copyright © 1989, with permission from Elsevier Science.

encounter
The second socialization stage, in which newcomers learn the tasks associated with the job, clarify their roles, and establish new relationships at work.

change and acquisition
The third socialization stage, in which the newcomer begins to master the demands of the job.

their roles, and engaging in relationships at work. The time when the socialization process is completed varies widely depending on the individual, the job, and the organization. The end of the process is signaled by newcomers being considered by themselves and others as organizational insiders.

Outcomes of Socialization

Newcomers who are successfully socialized should exhibit good performance, high job satisfaction, and the intention to stay with the organization. In addition, they should exhibit low levels of distress symptoms.[53] A high level of organizational commitment is also a mark of successful socialization.[54] This commitment is facilitated throughout the socialization process by the communication of values that newcomers can buy into. Successful socialization is also signaled by mutual influence; that is, the newcomers have made adjustments in the job and organization to accommodate their knowledge and personalities. Newcomers are expected to leave their mark on the organization and not be completely conforming.

When socialization is effective, newcomers understand and adopt the organization's values and norms. This ensures that the company's culture, including its central values, survives. It also provides employees a context for interpreting and responding to things that happen at work, and it ensures a shared framework of understanding among employees.[55] Newcomers adopt the company's norms and values more quickly when they receive positive support from organizational insiders. Sometimes this is accomplished through informal social gatherings.[56]

Socialization is not just the responsibility of the organization and the manager but of the employees as well. Newcomers who are more curious and adaptable adjust to their new jobs more effectively, leading to better performance.[57] Additionally, newcomers who have proactive personalities adjust more effectively to the organization because they are more likely to seek out the information they need to become socialized.[58]

LEARNING OUTCOME **6**

Assessing Organizational Culture

Although some organizational scientists argue for assessing organizational culture with quantitative methods, others say that organizational culture must be assessed with qualitative methods.[59] Quantitative methods, such as questionnaires, are valuable because of their precision, comparability, and objectivity. Qualitative methods, such as interviews and observations, are valuable because of their detail, descriptiveness, and uniqueness.

Two widely used quantitative assessment instruments are the Organizational Culture Inventory (OCI) and the Kilmann-Saxton Culture-Gap Survey. Both assess the behavioral norms of organizational cultures, as opposed to the artifacts, values, or assumptions of the organization.

Organizational Culture Inventory

The OCI focuses on behaviors that help employees fit into the organization and meet the expectations of coworkers. Using Maslow's

©Sean Justice/UpperCut Images/Getty Images

motivational need hierarchy as its basis, it measures twelve cultural styles. The two underlying dimensions of the OCI are task/people and security/satisfaction. There are four satisfaction cultural styles and eight security cultural styles.

A self-report instrument, the OCI contains 120 questions. It provides an individual assessment of culture and may be aggregated to the work group and to the organizational level.[60] It has been used in firms throughout North America, Western Europe, New Zealand, and Thailand, as well as in U.S. military units, the Federal Aviation Administration, and nonprofit organizations.

Kilmann-Saxton Culture-Gap Survey

The Kilmann-Saxton Culture-Gap Survey focuses on what actually happens and on the expectations of others in the organization.[61] Its two underlying dimensions are (1) technical/human orientation and (2) short-term versus long-term time. With these two dimensions, the actual operating norms and the ideal norms in four areas are assessed. The areas are *task support* (short-term technical norms), *task innovation* (long-term technical norms), *social relationships* (short-term human orientation norms), and *personal freedom* (long-term human orientation norms). Significant gaps in any of the four areas are used as a point of departure for cultural change to improve performance, job satisfaction, and morale.

Like the OCI, the Gap Survey, as a self-report instrument, provides an individual assessment of culture and may be aggregated to the work group. It has been used in firms throughout the United States and in not-for-profit organizations.

Triangulation

A study of a rehabilitation center in a 400-bed hospital incorporated **triangulation**—the use of multiple methods to measure organizational culture—to improve inclusiveness and accuracy in measuring the organizational culture.[62] Triangulation has been used by anthropologists, sociologists, and other behavioral scientists to study organizational culture. Its name comes from the navigational technique of using multiple reference points to locate an object. In the rehabilitation center study, the three methods used to triangulate on the culture were (1) obtrusive observations by eight trained observers, which provided an outsider perspective; (2) self-administered questionnaires, which provided quantitative insider information; and (3) personal interviews

with the center's staff, which provided qualitative contextual information.

The study showed that each of the three methods made unique contributions toward the discovery of the rehabilitation center's culture. The complete picture could not have been drawn with just a single technique. Triangulation can lead to a better understanding of the phenomenon of culture and is the best approach to assessing organizational culture.

Changing Organizational Culture

With rapid environmental changes such as globalization, workforce diversity, and technological innovation, the fundamental assumptions and basic values that drive the organization may need to be altered.

Changing an organization's culture is feasible but difficult.[63] One reason for the difficulty is that assumptions—the deepest level of culture—are often unconscious. As such, they are often resistant to confrontation and debate. Another reason for difficulty is that culture is deeply ingrained and behavioral norms and rewards are well learned.[64] In a sense, employees must unlearn the old norms before they can learn new ones. Managers who want to change the culture should look first to the ways culture is maintained. Research among hospitals found that change was welcomed in private hospitals with a collaborative culture whereas it was met with opposition in public hospitals with an autocratic culture.[65]

A model for cultural change that summarizes the interventions managers can use is presented in Figure 16.3 on the next page. In this model, the numbers represent the steps managers can take. There are two basic approaches to changing the existing culture: (1) helping current members buy into a new set of values (steps 1, 2, and 3) or (2) adding newcomers and socializing them into the organization while removing current members as appropriate (steps 4 and 5).[66]

The first step is to change behavior in the organization. Even if behavior does change, however, this change is not sufficient for cultural change to occur. Behavior is an artifact (level 1) of culture. Individuals may

triangulation
The use of multiple methods to measure organizational culture.

change their behavior but not the values that drive it. They may rationalize, "I'm only doing this because my manager wants me to."

Therefore, managers must use step 2, which is to examine the justifications for the changed behavior. Are employees buying into the new set of values, or are they just complying?

The third step, cultural communication, is extremely important. All of the artifacts (personal enactment, stories, rites and ceremonies, rituals, and symbols) must send a consistent message about the new values and beliefs. It is crucial that the communication be credible; that is, managers must live the new values and not just talk about them. Leaders should pay attention to the informal social networks more so than structural positions in leading organizational change. These informal network communication channels combined with employees' values, and beliefs that managers are highly committed to the change effort, can go a long way in making the change a success.[67]

The two remaining steps (4 and 5) involve shaping the workforce to fit the intended culture. First, the organization can revise its selection strategies to more accurately reflect the new culture. Second, the organization can identify individuals who resist the cultural change or who are no longer comfortable with the values in the organization. Reshaping the workforce should not involve a ruthless pursuit of nonconforming employees; it should be a gradual and subtle change that takes considerable time. Changing personnel in the organization is a lengthy process; it cannot be done effectively in a short period of time without considerable problems.

Evaluating the success of cultural change may be best done by looking at behavior. Cultural change can be assumed to be successful if the behavior is intrinsically motivated—that is, on "automatic pilot." If the new behavior were to persist even if rewards were not present, and if the employees have internalized the new value system, then the behavior is probably intrinsically motivated. If employees automatically respond to a crisis in ways consistent with the corporate culture, then the cultural change effort can be deemed successful.

Given the current business environment, managers may want to focus on three particular cultural modifica-

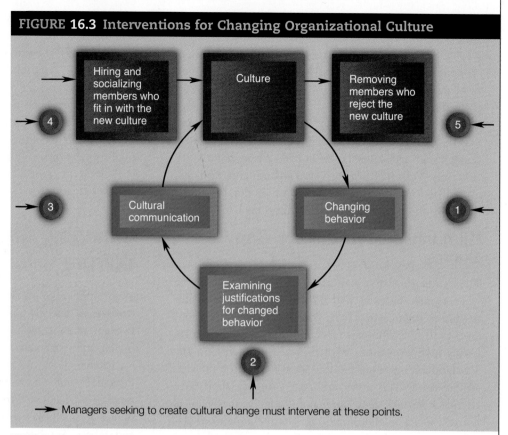

FIGURE 16.3 Interventions for Changing Organizational Culture

Hiring and socializing members who fit in with the new culture

Culture

Removing members who reject the new culture

Cultural communication

Changing behavior

Examining justifications for changed behavior

→ Managers seeking to create cultural change must intervene at these points.

SOURCE: From Vijay Sathe, "How to Decipher and Change Corporate Culture," Chap. 13 in *Gaining Control of the Corporate Culture* (R. H. Kilmann et al., eds.), Fig. 1, p. 245. Copyright © 1985 Jossey-Bass, Inc. Reprinted by permission of John Wiley & Sons, Inc.

tions: (1) support for a global view of business, (2) reinforcement of ethical behavior, and (3) empowerment of employees to excel in product and service quality.

Challenges to Developing a Positive, Cohesive Culture

Developing an organizational culture is challenging in its own right, but certain factors pose additional challenges to managers in their pursuit of positive, cohesive cultures: mergers and acquisitions, globalization, ethics, and empowerment and quality.

Merger or Acquisition

One particular situation that may require cultural change is a merger or acquisition. The blending of two distinct organizational cultures may prove difficult despite good-faith efforts. When established media giant Time Warner merged with free-wheeling Internet firm America Online in 2001, few could have imagined the fireworks that would result as these two "oil and water" firms tried to mix. Typical of the conflicts that followed was a client dinner in which AOL executive Neil Davis horrified Time Warner executives by describing how AOL pre-

Hot Trend: Open Offices

A popular, and effective, way to change an organization's culture is to redesign the office. Intel's headquarters used to be rows and rows of gray cubicles, where employees would work alone. In an effort to increase collaboration and teamwork among employees, however, Intel redesigned over 1 million square feet of space. Gone are cubicles and gray walls, replaced with open spaces filled with conference tables and comfortable chairs where employees can collaborate on projects and help each other come up with great new ideas for the future.

SOURCE: K. Shevory, "Office Work Space Is Shrinking, but That's Not All Bad," *New York Times* (January 18, 2011), http://www.nytimes.com/2011/01/19/realestate/commercial/19space.html, accessed June 21, 2011.

ferred to handle weakened competitors. Taking a steak knife from the table, Davis raised his arm and drove the knife into the table top, explaining, "What we like to do to a competitor that is damaged is drive the knife in their heart." The shocked client ultimately declined to buy ads on AOL, and the entire merger was eventually deemed a multibillion-dollar failure due, at least in part, to the culture clash between the two partners.[68]

Alterations in culture may also be required when an organization employs people from different countries. Research indicates that some organizational cultures actually enhance differences in national cultures.[69] One study compared foreign employees working in a multinational organization with employees working in different organizations within their own countries. The assumption was that the employees from various countries working for the same multinational organization would be more similar than employees working in diverse organizations in their native countries. The results were surprising in that there were significantly greater differences among the employees of the multinational than among managers working for different companies within their native countries. In the multinational, Swedes became more Swedish, Americans became more American, and so forth. It appears that employees enhance their national culture traditions even when working within a single organizational culture.[70] This is more likely to occur when diversity is moderate. When diversity is very high, employees are more likely to develop a shared identity in the organization's culture instead of relying on their own national culture.[71]

Developing a Global Organizational Culture

The values that drive the organizational culture should support a global view of the company and its efforts. Management should embody the shared values and reward employees who support the global view. Finally, the values should be consistent over time. Consistent values

give an organization a unifying theme that competitors may be unable to emulate.[72] Because global corporations suffer from the conflicting pressures of centralization and decentralization, an overarching corporate culture that integrates the decentralized subsidiaries in locations around the world can be an asset in the increasingly competitive global marketplace.

Developing an Ethical Organizational Culture

The culture of an organization can have profound effects on the ethical behavior of organization members.[73] Organizations in which supervisors and top managers act as role models of ethical behavior and create an openness to discuss ethical issues have fewer incidents of unethical behavior.[74] When a company's culture promotes ethical norms, individuals behave accordingly. Thus, managers can encourage ethical behavior by being good role models for employees. They can institute the philosophy that ethical behavior makes good business sense and puts the company in congruence with the larger values of society.[75] Managers can also communicate that rationalizations for unethical behavior are not tolerated.

Trust is another key to managing effectively ethical behavior, especially in cultures that encourage whistle-blowing (as we saw in Chapter 2). Employees must trust that whistle-blowers will be protected, that procedures used to investigate ethical problems will be fair, and that management will take action to solve problems that are uncovered.

Many companies have implemented a code of ethics to help their employees discern right from wrong, but the impact of these codes is not always as positive as might be expected. The implementation of formal ethics guidelines might be expected to improve ethical behavior, yet some studies have shown the exact opposite—institution of formal ethics codes can actually lead to less ethical behavior among employees. There appear to be two main reasons for this: In some cases employees see the code of ethics as simply a management showpiece, leading to cynicism and resentment. In other cases, a heavy reliance on a strict set of rules may reduce the perceived need for employees to think about and be involved in ethical decision making, leading to inferior choices in the long run.[76]

Developing a Culture of Empowerment and Quality

Throughout this book, we have seen that successful organizations promote cultures that empower employees and excel in product and service quality.

Empowerment serves to unleash employees' creativity and productivity, and cultures that emphasize empowerment are preferred by employees. Companies that value empowerment and continuous improvement have cultures that promote high product and service quality.[77] However, to cultivate such a culture, organizations must eliminate traditional hierarchical notions of power. Moreover, it is essential that managers trust their employees. When an organization strives to develop a culture of trust, employees feel accountable for their performance, and thus sales performance and customer service performance improve.[78] The high level of quality of a Harley-Davidson motorcycle is not merely an artifact of better shop practices. The company's management has worked to foster a unique congenial and trusting relationship with its unions, ensuring that continuous improvement is an organizational priority rather than simply the latest management fad. Today's Harley "hog" costs less to produce and is more reliable than any before it, due in large part to the firm's incessant drive to produce a better product.[79] Involving employees in decision making, removing obstacles to their performance, and communicating the value of product and service quality reinforce the values of empowerment and quality in the organizational culture.

Log in to the **CourseMate** for *ORGB3* at **www.cengagebrain.com** to:

* Review **Key Terms Flash Cards** online
* Play **Beat the Clock** and **Quiz Bowl** to master concepts
* Complete **web quizzes** to prepare for exams
* Watch the video on **Camp Bow Wow** and from *Charlie Wilson's War* for examples, then test yourself with a quick quiz
* Work through the **What about You?** and **Ethical Dilemma** exercises to see how you would handle various situations that organizations face on a daily basis

BY THE NUMBERS

3 levels of organizational culture

120 questions on the OCI

6 types of rites in organizations

>20,000 attendees at Berkshire Hathaway's annual meeting

1984 year when AT&T was broken up by the U.S. government

2001 year when Time Warner and AOL merged

©agsandrew/Shutterstock.com

ONE APPROACH.
70 UNIQUE SOLUTIONS.

www.cengage.com/4ltrpress

Career Management

LEARNING OUTCOMES

1 Explain occupational and organizational choice decisions.

2 Identify foundations for a successful career.

3 Explain the career stage model.

4 Explain the major tasks facing individuals in the establishment stage of the career stage model.

5 Identify the issues confronting individuals in the advancement stage of the career stage model.

6 Describe how individuals can navigate the challenges of the maintenance stage of the career stage model.

7 Explain how individuals withdraw from the workforce.

8 Explain how career anchors help form a career identity.

©iStockphoto.com/Andrew Penner

"Whether we approach it as managers or as employees, career management is an integral activity in our lives."

After You Finish
This Chapter
Go to **Page 295**
for **Study Tools**

A **career** is a pattern of work-related experiences that spans the course of a person's life.[1] The two elements in a career are the objective element and the subjective element.[2] The *objective element* of the career is the observable, concrete environment. For example, you can manage a career by getting training to improve your skills. In contrast, the *subjective element* involves your perception of the situation. Rather than getting training (an objective element), you might change your aspirations (a subjective element). Thus, both objective events and the individual's perception of those events are important in defining a career.

Career management is a lifelong process of learning about self, jobs, and organizations, setting personal career goals, developing strategies for achieving the goals, and revising the goals based on work and life experiences.[3] Whose responsibility is career management? It is tempting to place the responsibility solely on individuals, but it is also the organization's duty to form partnerships with individuals in managing their careers. Careers are made up of exchanges between individuals and organizations—in other words, give and take is a part of the relationship between an organization and an individual if a career is involved.

Whether we approach it as managers or as employees, career management is an integral activity in our lives. There are three reasons why it is important to understand careers:

> If we know what to look forward to over the course of our careers, we can take a proactive approach to planning and managing them.

> As managers, we need to understand the experiences of our employees and colleagues as

career
The pattern of work-related experiences that spans the course of a person's life.

career management
A lifelong process of learning about self, jobs, and organizations; setting personal career goals; developing strategies for achieving the goals, and revising the goals based on work and life experiences.

they pass through the various stages of careers over their life spans.

> Career management is good business. It makes good financial sense to have highly trained employees keep up with their fields so that organizations can protect valuable investments in human resources.

Occupational and Organizational Choice Decisions

The time of the fast track to the top of the hierarchical organization is past. Also gone is the idea of lifetime employment in a single organization. Today's environment demands leaner organizations, and the paternalistic attitude that organizations should take care of employees no longer exists. Individuals now take on more responsibility for managing their own careers. So the concept of the career is undergoing a paradigm shift, as shown in Table 17.1. The old career is giving way to a new career characterized by discrete exchange, occupational excellence, organizational empowerment, and project allegiance.[4] Moreover, one recent study found that both individuals and organizations are actively involved in the management of the new career of employees. As such, the new career involves a type of participatory management technique on the part of the individual, but the organization responds to each individual's needs and thus is more flexible in its career development programs.[5]

Discrete exchange occurs when an organization gains productivity while a person gains work experience. It is a short-term arrangement that recognizes that job skills change in value and that renegotiation of the relationship must occur as conditions change. This idea contrasts sharply with the mutual loyalty contract of the old career paradigm in which employee loyalty was exchanged for job security.

Occupational excellence means continually honing skills that can be marketed across organizations. The individual identifies more with the occupation (I am an engineer) than the organization (I am an IBMer). In contrast, the old one-employer focus meant that training was company specific and not meant to prepare the person for future job opportunities. A recent research study that focused on ethnographic data (interviews and stories) was

conducted among software engineers in three European firms and two U.S. firms. The study showed that software engineers did not have much regard for their immediate supervisors, the organization, or formal dress codes. The only thing they did believe in was occupational excellence so that they could be better at what they do. In this regard, the authors of the study note that software engineers represent a unique group in terms of career development and that they fit well within the model of the "new career."[6]

Organizational empowerment means that power flows down to business units and in turn to employees. Employees are expected to add value and help the organization remain competitive by being innovative and creative. The old top-down approach meant that control and strategizing were done only by the top managers, and individual initiative could even be viewed as disloyalty or disrespect.

Project allegiance means that both individuals and organizations are committed to the successful completion of a project. The firm's gain is the project outcome; the individual's gain is experience and shared success. Upon project completion, the project team breaks up as individuals move on to new projects. Under the old paradigm, *corporate allegiance* was paramount, not project allegiance. The needs of projects were overshadowed by corporate policies and procedures. Work groups were long term, and keeping the group together was often a more important goal than project completion.

> " *Organizational empowerment means that power flows down to business units and in turn to employees.*

Preparing for the World of Work

When viewed from one perspective, you might say that we spend our youth preparing for the world of work. Educational and personal life experiences help an individual develop the skills and maturity needed to enter a career. Preparation for work is a developmental process that gradually unfolds over time.[7] As the time approaches for beginning a career, individuals face two difficult decisions: occupational choice and organizational choice.

Occupational Choice

In choosing an occupation, individuals assess their needs, values, abilities, and preferences and attempt to match them with an occupation that provides a fit. Personality plays a role in the selection of occupation. John Holland's theory of occupational choice contends that there are six types of personalities and that each personality is characterized by a set of interests and values.[8]

TABLE 17.1 The New versus Old Career Paradigms

NEW CAREER PARADIGM	OLD CAREER PARADIGM
Discrete exchange means: • explicit exchange of specified rewards in return for task performance • basing job rewards on the current market value of the work being performed • engaging in disclosure and renegotiation on both sides as the employment relationship unfolds • exercising flexibility as each party's interests and market circumstances change	**The mutual loyalty contract meant:** • implicit trading of employee compliance in return for job security • allowing job rewards to be routinely deferred into the future • leaving the mutual loyalty assumptions as a political barrier to renegotiation • assuming employment and career opportunities are standardized and prescribed by the firm
Occupational excellence means: • performance of current jobs in return for developing new occupational expertise • employees identifying with and focusing on what is happening in their adopted occupation • emphasizing occupational skill development over the local demands of any particular firm • getting training in anticipation of future job opportunities; having training lead jobs	**The one-employer focus meant:** • relying on the firm to specify jobs and their associated occupational skill base • employees identifying with and focusing on what is happening in their particular firm • forgoing technical or functional development in favor of firm-specific learning • doing the job first to be entitled to new training: making training follow jobs
Organizational empowerment means: • strategic positioning is dispersed to separate business units • everyone is responsible for adding value and improving competitiveness • business units are free to cultivate their own markets • new enterprise, spinoffs, and alliance building are broadly encouraged	**The top-down firm meant:** • strategic direction is subordinated to "corporate headquarters" • competitiveness and added value are the responsibility of corporate experts • business unit marketing depends on the corporate agenda • independent enterprise is discouraged, and likely to be viewed as disloyalty
Project allegiance means: • shared employer and employee commitment to the overarching goal of the project • a successful outcome of the project is more important than holding the project team together • financial and reputational rewards stem directly from project outcomes • upon project completion, organization and reporting arrangements are broken up	**Corporate allegiance meant:** • project goals are subordinated to corporate policy and organizational constraints • being loyal to the work group can be more important than the project itself • financial and reputational rewards stem from being a "good soldier" regardless of results • social relationships within corporate boundaries are actively encouraged

©Cengage Learning 2013

Holland also states that occupations can be classified using this typology. For example, realistic occupations include mechanic, restaurant server, and mechanical engineer. Artistic occupations include architect, voice coach, and interior designer. Investigative occupations include physicist, surgeon, and economist. Real estate agent, human resource manager, and lawyer are enterprising occupations. Social occupations include counselor, social worker, and member of the clergy. Conventional occupations include word processor, accountant, and data entry operator. Holland's typology has been used to predict career choices with a variety of international participants, including Australians, Germans, Indians, Mexicans, New Zealanders, Pakistanis, South Africans, and Taiwanese.[9]

An assumption that drives Holland's theory is that people choose occupations that match their personalities. People who fit Holland's social types are those who prefer jobs that are highly

©iStockphoto.com/Jarek Szymanski

interpersonal in nature. They may see careers in physical and math sciences, for example, as not affording the opportunity for interpersonal relationships.[10] Therefore, to fulfill the desire for interpersonal work, they may gravitate toward jobs in customer service.

Although personality is a major influence on occupational choice, it is not the only influence. There are a host of other influences, including social class, parents' occupations, economic conditions, and geography.[11] Once a choice of occupation has been made, another major decision individuals face is the choice of organizations. Individuals are often attracted to organizations whose mission matches their passions and values.

Organizational Choice and Entry

There are several theories of how individuals choose organizations, ranging from theories that postulate very logical and rational choice processes to those that offer seemingly irrational processes. *Expectancy theory*, discussed in Chapter 5, can be applied to organizational choice.[12] According to expectancy theory, individuals choose organizations that maximize positive outcomes and avoid negative outcomes. Job candidates calculate the probability that an organization will provide a certain outcome and then compare the probabilities across organizations.

Other theories propose that people select organizations in a much less rational fashion. Job candidates may *satisfice*, that is, select the first organization that meets one or two important criteria and then justify their choice by distorting their perceptions.[13] The method of selecting an organization varies greatly among individuals and may reflect a combination of the expectancy theory and theories that postulate less rational approaches.

Entry into an organization is further complicated by the conflicts that occur between individuals and organizations during the process. Figure 17.1 illustrates these potential conflicts. The arrows in the figure illustrate four types of conflicts that can occur as individuals choose organizations and organizations choose individuals. The first two conflicts

(1 and 2) occur between individuals and organizations. The first is a conflict between the organization's effort to attract candidates and the individual's choice of an organization. The individual needs complete and accurate information to make a good choice, but the organization may not provide it. Since the organization is trying to attract a large number of qualified candidates, it presents itself in an overly attractive way.

The second conflict is between the individual's attempt to attract several organizations and the organization's need to select the best candidate. Individuals want good offers, so they do not disclose their faults. They describe their preferred job in terms of the organization's opening instead of describing a job they would really prefer.

The third and fourth conflicts are conflicts internal to the two parties. The third is a conflict between the organization's desire to recruit a large pool of qualified applicants and the organization's need to select and retain the best candidate. In recruiting, organizations tend to give only positive information, and this sometimes results in mismatches between the individual and the organization. The fourth conflict is internal to the individual; it concerns his or her need to make a good choice from among more than one desirable job offer. This situation can occur when individuals present themselves as overly attractive and consequently receive more job offers than they would have otherwise received, some of which might be a poor fit in terms of their skills and career goals.[14]

The organizational choice and entry process is very complex due to the nature of these conflicts. Partial responsibility for preventing these conflicts rests with the individual. Individuals should conduct thorough research of the organization through published reports and industry analyses. In addition, they should conduct a careful self-analysis and be as honest as possible with organizations to ensure a good match. The job interview process

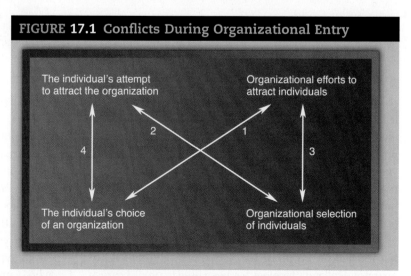

FIGURE **17.1** Conflicts During Organizational Entry

The individual's attempt to attract the organization

Organizational efforts to attract individuals

2

1

4

3

The individual's choice of an organization

Organizational selection of individuals

SOURCE: Figure in L. W. Porter, E. E. Lawler III, and J. R. Hackman, *Behavior in Organizations,* New York: McGraw-Hill, Inc., 1975, p. 134. Reproduced with permission of The McGraw-Hill Companies.

©iStockphoto.com/Douglas Palmer

can be stressful, but also fun if it is engaged properly. Of course, the organization bears part of the responsibility for avoiding a mismatch by conducting an effective job interview.

Realistic Job Previews The conflicts just discussed may result in unrealistic expectations on the part of the candidate. People entering the world of work may expect, for example, that they will receive explicit directions from their boss, only to find that they are left with ambiguity about how to do the job. They may expect that promotions will be based on performance but find that promotions are based mainly on political considerations. Some new hires also expect to be given managerial responsibilities right away, but they rarely are.

Giving potential employees a realistic picture of the job they are applying for is known as a **realistic job preview (RJP)**. When candidates are given both positive and negative information, they can make more effective job choices. Traditional recruiting practices often produce unrealistically high expectations, which produce low job satisfaction, whereas RJPs tend to create expectations that are much closer to reality and thus encourage many candidates to withdraw from further consideration.[15]

Time Warner Cable gives applicants RJPs through videos on its website. In the videos, current Time Warner employees discuss the nature of their jobs and the skills necessary for dealing with the challenges and frustrations that are involved with various jobs within the company.[16] As another example, the Idaho State Police Department's online employment site provides an RJP that begins with these words: "[Y]ou should put aside the images you have seen on television or in the movies and read carefully about the tasks an Idaho State Police Trooper performs."[17] It goes on to provide an exhaustive list of tasks ranging from the exciting (manhunts and serving warrants) to the mundane (inspecting heavy trucks), as well as noting that troopers currently work rotating ten-hour shifts. While the site concludes with a summary of the rewards that accompany the job, it clearly notes that the work is at times tedious and far less glamorous than might be expected.

RJPs can also be thought of as inoculation against disappointment. If new recruits know what to expect in the new job, they can prepare for the experience. Newcomers who are not given RJPs may find that their jobs don't measure up to their expectations. They may then believe that their employer was deceitful in the hiring process, become unhappy and mishandle job demands, and ultimately leave the organization.[18]

Job candidates who receive RJPs view the organization as honest and also have a greater ability to cope with the demands of the job.[19] RJPs perform another important function: uncertainty reduction.[20] Knowing what to expect, both good and bad, gives a newcomer a sense of control that is important to job satisfaction and performance.

With today's emphasis on ethics, organizations need to do all they can to be seen as operating consistently and honestly. Realistic job previews are one way in which companies can provide ethically required information. Ultimately, RJPs result in more effective matches, lower turnover, and higher organizational commitment and job satisfaction.[21] There is much to gain, and little to risk, in providing realistic job information.[22]

In summary, the needs and goals of individuals and organizations can clash during entry into an organization. To avoid potential mismatches, individuals should conduct a careful self-analysis and provide accurate information about themselves to potential

realistic job preview (RJP)
Both positive and negative information given to potential employees about the job they are applying for, thereby giving them a realistic picture of the job.

MONEY TO HIRE?

Organizations need to be diligent in finding a good match for positions because of the costs involved in hiring a new employee. Take for example a position at a telecommunications company in New Jersey. Though the salary is $59,000, the position actually costs the company $74,000. There's $9,561 for health insurance premiums, $153 for life insurance, $56 for federal unemployment coverage, $149 for disability insurance, $300 for workers' compensation, $505 for state unemployment insurance, $856 for Medicare, and $3,661 for Social Security. On top of this, there is the cost of going through applications, conducting interviews, and training the new employee. Because of these costs, organizations should take care to find the right people.

SOURCE: M. P. Fleischer, "Why I'm Not Hiring," *The Wall Street Journal* (August 9, 2010), http://online.wsj.com/article/SB1000142405274870401790457540973377637 2738.html.

employers. They also need to ask appropriate questions. While applicants often focus on asking questions about organizational rewards and not employee contributions, they should seek both in obtaining a realistic job preview.[23] Organizations should present realistic job previews to show candidates both the positive and negative aspects of the job, along with the potential career paths available to the employee.

LEARNING OUTCOME 2

Foundations for a Successful Career

In addition to planning and preparation, building a career takes attention and self-examination. One way you can build a successful career is by becoming your own career coach. Another is by developing your emotional intelligence, which is an important attribute if you want to climb the corporate ladder.

Becoming Your Own Career Coach

The best way to stay employed is to see yourself as being in business for yourself, even if you work for someone else. Know what skills you can package for other employers and what you can do to ensure that your skills are state of the art. Organizations need employees who have acquired multiple skills and are adept at more than one job. Employers want employees who have demonstrated competence in dealing with change.[24] To be successful, think of organizational change not as a disruption to your work but instead as the central focus of your work. You will also need to develop self-reliance, as discussed in Chapter 7, to deal effectively with the stress of change. Self-reliant individuals take an interdependent approach to relationships and are comfortable both giving and receiving support from others.

The people who will be most successful in the new career paradigm are individuals who are flexible, team oriented (rather than hierarchical), energized by change, and tolerant of ambiguity. Those who will become frustrated in the new career paradigm are individuals who are rigid in their thinking and learning styles and who have high needs for control. A commitment to continuous, lifelong learning will prevent you from becoming a professional dinosaur.[25] An intentional and purposeful commitment to taking charge of your professional life will be necessary in managing the new career.

Behaving in an ethical manner, standing by your values, and building a professional image of integrity are also very important. Major corporations such as Google conduct extensive reference checks on their applicants—not just with the references supplied in the application, but also with friends of such references. Behaving ethically is not just a benefit to your job application, since an ethical foundation can also help you withstand pressures that might endanger your career. One study suggests that executives succumb to the temptation of fraud because they feel pressure to keep up with inflated expectations and changes in cultural norms, short-term versus long-term orientations, the composition of the board of directors, and senior leadership in the organization.[26]

Emotional Intelligence and Career Success

Almost 40 percent of new managers fail within the first eighteen months on the job. What are the reasons for the failure? Newly hired managers flame out because they fail to build good relationships with peers and subordinates (82 percent of failures), are confused about what their bosses expect (58 percent of failures), lack internal political skills (50 percent of failures), or are unable to achieve the two or three most important objectives of the new job (47 percent of failures).[27] You'll note that these failures are all due to a lack of interpersonal skills.

In Chapter 13, we introduced the concept of *emotional intelligence (EI)* as an important determinant of conflict management skills. Daniel Goleman argues that emotional intelligence is a constellation of the qualities that mark a star performer at work. These attributes include self-awareness, self-control, trustworthiness, confidence, and empathy, among others. Goleman's belief is that emotional competencies are twice as important to people's success today as raw intelligence or technical know-how. He also

Behaving in an ethical manner, standing by your values, and building a professional image will make you a superstar employee.

argues that the further up the corporate ranks you go, the more important emotional intelligence becomes.[28] Employers, either consciously or unconsciously, look for emotional intelligence during the hiring process. In addition to traditionally recognized competencies such as communication and social skills, interns with higher levels of emotional intelligence are rated as more hireable by their host firms than those with lower levels of EI.[29] Neither gender seems to have cornered the market on EI. Both men and women who can demonstrate high levels of EI are seen as particularly gifted and may be promoted more rapidly.[30]

Emotional intelligence is important to career success in many cultures. A recent study in Australia found that high levels of emotional intelligence are associated with job success. EI improves one's ability to work with other team members and to provide high-quality customer service, and workers with high EI are more likely to take steps to develop their skills. Several U.S. studies have confirmed that high emotional intelligence is an important attribute for the upwardly mobile worker.[31]

The good news is that emotional intelligence can be developed and does tend to improve throughout life. Accordingly, some companies are providing training in emotional intelligence competencies. When American Express began sending managers through an emotional competence training program, it found that trained managers outperformed those who lacked this training. In the year after completing the course, managers trained in emotional competence grew their businesses by an average of 18.1 percent compared to 16.2 percent for those businesses whose managers were untrained.[32]

LEARNING OUTCOME 3

The Career Stage Model

A common way of understanding careers is viewing them as a series of stages through which individuals pass during their working lives.[33] Figure 17.2 presents the career stage model, which will form the basis for our discussion in the remainder of this chapter.[34] The career stage model shows that individuals pass through four stages in their careers: establishment, advancement, maintenance, and withdrawal. It is important to note that the age ranges shown are approximations; that is, the timing of the career transitions varies greatly among individuals.

Establishment is the first stage of a person's career. The activities that occur in this stage center around learn-

ing the job and fitting into the organization and occupation. **Advancement** is a high achievement-oriented stage in which people focus on increasing their competence. The **maintenance** stage finds the individual trying to maintain productivity while evaluating progress toward career goals. The **withdrawal** stage involves contemplation of retirement or possible career change.

Along the horizontal axis in Figure 17.2 are the corresponding life stages for each career stage. These life stages are based on the pioneering research on adult development conducted by Levinson and his colleagues. Levinson conducted extensive biographical interviews to trace the life stages of men and women. He interpreted his research in two books, *The Seasons of a Man's Life* and *The Seasons of a Woman's Life*.[35] Levinson's life stages are characterized by an alternating pattern of stability and transition.[36] Throughout the discussion of career stages that follows, we weave in the transitions of Levinson's life stages. Work and personal life are inseparable, and to understand a person's career experiences, we must also examine the unfolding of the person's personal experiences.

establishment

The first stage of a person's career in which the person learns the job and begins to fit into the organization and occupation.

advancement

The second, high achievement-oriented career stage in which people focus on increasing their competence.

maintenance

The third stage in an individual's career in which the individual tries to maintain productivity while evaluating progress toward career goals.

withdrawal

The final stage in an individual's career in which the individual contemplates retirement or possible career changes.

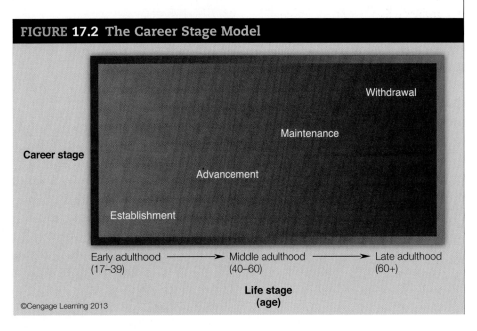

FIGURE 17.2 The Career Stage Model

Career stage

Withdrawal

Maintenance

Advancement

Establishment

Early adulthood (17–39) ⟶ Middle adulthood (40–60) ⟶ Late adulthood (60+)

Life stage (age)

©Cengage Learning 2013

You can see that adult development provides unique challenges for the individual and that there may be considerable overlap between the stages. Now let us examine each career stage in detail.

LEARNING OUTCOME 4

The Establishment Stage

During the establishment stage, the individual begins a career as a newcomer to the organization. This is a period of great dependence on others, as the individual is learning about the job and the organization. The establishment stage usually occurs during the beginning of the early adulthood years (ages eighteen to twenty-five). During this time, Levinson notes, an important personal life transition into adulthood occurs: the individual begins to separate from his or her parents and becomes less emotionally and financially dependent on them. Following this period is a fairly stable time of exploring the adult role and settling down.

The transition from school to work is a part of the establishment stage. Many graduates find the transition to be a memorable experience. The following description was provided by a new graduate who went to work at a large public utility:

> We all tried to one-up each other about jobs we had just accepted . . . bragging that we had the highest salary, the best management training program, the most desirable coworkers, the most upward mobility . . . and believed we were destined to become future corporate leaders. . . . Every Friday after work we met for happy hour to visit and relate the events of the week. It is interesting to look at how the mood of those happy hours changed over the first few months . . . at first, we jockeyed for position in terms of telling stories about how great these new jobs were, or how weird our bosses were. . . . Gradually, things quieted down at happy hour. The mood went from "Wow, isn't this great" to "What in the world have we gotten ourselves into?" There began to be general agreement that business wasn't all it was cracked up to be.[37]

Establishment is thus a time of big transitions in both personal and work life. At work, three major tasks face the newcomer: negotiating effective psychological contracts, managing the stress of socialization, and making a transition from organizational outsider to organizational insider.

Psychological Contracts

A **psychological contract** is an implicit agreement between the individual and the organization that specifies what each is expected to give and receive in the relationship.[38] Individuals expect to receive salary, status, advancement opportunities, and challenging work to meet their needs. Organizations expect to receive time, energy, talents, and loyalty in order to meet their goals. Working out the psychological contract with the organization begins with entry, but the contract is modified as the individual proceeds through the career.

Psychological contracts also exist between individuals.[39] During the establishment stage, newcomers form attachment relationships with many people in the organization. This process of working out effective psychological contracts within each relationship is important. Newcomers need social support in many forms and from many sources. Table 17.2 shows the type of psychological contracts, in the form of social support, that newcomers may work out with key insiders in the organization.

One common newcomer concern, for example, is whose behavior to watch for cues to appropriate behavior. Senior colleagues can provide modeling support by displaying behavior that the newcomer can emulate. This is only one of many types of support that

psychological contract
An implicit agreement between an individual and an organization that specifies what each is expected to give and receive in the relationship.

[**Mending a Breach**]

When an employee's psychological contract with the organization is broken, the employee usually attempts to cope with or resolve the breach. She might do so by retaliating against the organization through absenteeism, neglect of duties, or even more deviant behavior such as theft. A recent study, however, found that conscientious individuals will respond differently than those with low conscientiousness to psychological breaches. While conscientious employees are likely to respond by lowering task performance, nonconscientious employees are more likely to experience a drop in organizational loyalty and job satisfaction. Nonconscientious workers are more likely to withdraw from the organization or quit. It is important that organizations recognize these distinctions. Though psychological breaches should be avoided at all costs, when they are inescapable, organizations need to understand how to intervene to reduce some of the negative impacts. Understanding how different individuals react to psychological breaches may aid in that pursuit.

SOURCE: K. A. Orvis, N. M. Dudley, and J. M. Cortina, "Conscientiousness and Reactions to Psychological Contract Breach," *Journal of Applied Psychology* (2008): 1183–1193.

©Gregor Schuster/Corbis / ©iStockphoto.com/Ed Hidden

TABLE 17.2 Newcomer–Insider Psychological Contracts for Social Support

TYPE OF SUPPORT	FUNCTION OF SUPPORTIVE ATTACHMENTS	NEWCOMER CONCERN	EXAMPLES OF INSIDER RESPONSE/ACTION
Protection from stressors	Direct assistance in terms of resources, time, labor, or environmental modification	What are the major risks/threats in this environment?	*Supervisor* cues newcomer to risks/threats.
Informational	Provision of information necessary for managing demands	What do I need to know to get things done?	*Mentor* provides advice on informal political climate in organization.
Evaluative	Feedback on both personal and professional role performances	How am I doing?	*Supervisor* provides day-to-day performance feedback during first week on new job.
Modeling	Evidence of behavioral standards provided through modeled behavior	Whom do I follow?	Newcomer is apprenticed to *senior colleague.*
Emotional	Empathy, esteem, caring, or love	Do I matter? Who cares if I'm here or not?	*Other newcomers* empathize with and encourage individual when reality shock sets in.

SOURCE: Table from D. L. Nelson, J. C. Quick, and J. R. Joplin, "Psychological Contracting and Newcomer Socialization: An Attachment Theory Foundation," from *Journal of Social Behavior and Personality* 6 (1991): 65. Reprinted with permission.

newcomers need, though. Newcomers should contract with others to receive each of the needed types of support so that they can adjust to the new job. Organizers can also help newcomers form relationships early and should encourage the psychological contracting process between newcomers and insiders. Broken or breached psychological contracts can have detrimental outcomes. When a breach occurs, employees might experience negative emotional reactions that can lead to loss of trust, reduced job satisfaction, lower commitment to the organization, and higher turnover intentions.[40] The influence of a broken psychological contract is often felt even after an employee leaves a job. For example, laid-off employees who feel that a psychological contract breach has occurred are not only unhappy with their former firms but may also be both more cynical and less trusting of their new employers.[41]

LEARNING OUTCOME 5

The Advancement Stage

The advancement stage is a period when many individuals strive for achievement. They seek greater responsibility and authority and strive for upward mobility. Usually around age thirty, an important life transition occurs, leading people to reassess their goals and make changes in their career dreams.[42] The transition at age thirty is followed by a period of stability during which the individual tries to find a role in adult society and wants to succeed in the career. During this stage, several issues are important: exploring career paths, finding a mentor, working out dual-career partnerships, and managing conflicts between work and personal life.

Career Paths and Career Ladders

Career paths are sequences of job experiences along which employees move during their careers.[43] At the advancement stage, individuals examine their career dreams and the paths they must follow to achieve those dreams. For example, suppose a person's dream is to become a top executive in the pharmaceutical industry. She majors in chemistry in college and takes a job with a nationally recognized firm. After she has adjusted to her job as a quality control chemist, she reevaluates her plan and decides that further education is necessary. Now she plans to pursue an MBA degree part time, hoping to

career path

A sequence of job experiences that an employee moves along during his or her career.

gain expertise in management. From there, she hopes to be promoted to a supervisory position within her current firm. If this does not occur within five years, she will consider moving to a different pharmaceutical company. An alternate route would be to try to transfer to a sales position, from which she might advance into management.

The career paths of many women have moved from working in large organizations to starting their own businesses. Currently, there are 10.6 million women-owned firms in the United States, comprising almost half of all privately held firms in the country. What is the motivation for this exodus to entrepreneurship? The main reasons are to seek additional challenge and self-fulfillment and to have more self-determination and freedom.[44]

A **career ladder** is a structured series of job positions through which an individual progresses in an organization. For example, at Southwestern Bell, it is customary to move through a series of alternating line and staff supervisory assignments to advance toward upper management. Supervisors in customer service might be assigned next to the training staff and then rotate back as line supervisors in network services to gain experience in different departments.

Some companies use the traditional concept of career ladders to help employees advance in their careers. Other organizations take a more contemporary approach to career advancement. Sony, for instance, encourages creativity from its engineers by using nontraditional career paths in which people have the freedom to move on to interesting and challenging job assignments without notifying their supervisors. If they join a new project team, their current boss is expected to let them move on. This self-promotion philosophy at Sony is seen as a key to high levels of innovation and creative new product designs.

There has been heightened interest in international assignments in response to globalization and global staffing issues. One problem in this regard has been that most expatriate assignments are not successful. Therefore, organizations have been facing the challenge of properly training and preparing individuals for such assignments. One proposed solution is alternative international work assignments such as commuter work assignments, virtual assignments, short-term assignments, and

so on, which can be used to help individuals gain international work experience in preparation for higher levels in the organization.[45]

Another approach used by some companies to develop skills is the idea of a *career lattice*—an approach to building competencies by moving laterally through different departments in the organization or by moving through different projects. Top management support for the career lattice is essential, because in traditional terms an employee who has made several lateral moves might not be viewed with favor. However, the career lattice approach is an effective way to develop an array of skills to ensure one's employability.[46]

Finding a Mentor

Exploring career paths is one important activity in advancement. Another crucial activity during advancement is finding a mentor. A **mentor** is an individual who provides guidance, coaching, counseling, and friendship to a protégé. Mentors are important to career success because they perform both career and psychosocial functions.[47]

The *career functions* provided by a mentor include sponsorship, facilitating exposure and visibility, coaching, and protection. *Sponsorship* means actively helping the individual get job experiences and promotions. *Facilitating exposure and visibility* means providing opportunities for the protégé to develop relationships with key figures in the organization in order to advance. *Coaching* involves providing advice in both career and job performance. *Protection* is provided by shielding the protégé from potentially damaging experiences. Career functions are particularly important to the protégé's future success. One study found that the amount of career coaching received by protégés was related to more promotions and to higher salaries four years later.[48]

The mentor also performs *psychosocial functions*: role modeling, acceptance and confirmation, counseling, and friendship. *Role modeling* occurs when the mentor displays behavior for the protégé to emulate. Such modeling facilitates social learning. *Acceptance and confirmation* are important to both the mentor and protégé. When the protégé feels accepted by the mentor, it fosters a sense of pride. Likewise, positive regard and appreciation from the junior colleague provide a sense of satisfaction for the mentor. *Counseling* by a mentor helps the protégé explore personal issues that arise and require assistance. *Friendship* is another psy-

career ladder

A structured series of job positions through which an individual progresses in an organization.

mentor

An individual who provides guidance, coaching, counseling, and friendship to a protégé.

©iStockphoto.com/Skip O'Donnell

chosocial function that benefits both mentor and protégé alike.

In effective mentoring relationships, there is regular contact between mentor and protégé that has clearly specified purposes. Mentoring should be consistent with the corporate culture and the organization's goals. Both mentors and protégés alike should be trained in ways to manage the relationship. Mentors should be held accountable and rewarded for their role. They should be perceived (accurately) by protégés as having considerable influence within the organization.[49] While it may be tempting to go after the "top dog" as your mentor, personality compatibility is also an important factor in the success or failure of a mentoring relationship. Thus, mentors who are similar to their protégés in terms of personality traits such as extraversion, and whose expectations are largely met by the relationship are more likely to show interest in continuing the arrangement.[50]

Cigna Financial Advisors takes a proactive approach to integrating new employees. As part of the company's Partnership Program, all new hires work for up to twenty-seven months under the oversight of an experienced, successful mentor. This relationship provides new hires with hands-on instruction in how to sell more effectively, and it increases sales levels for the mentors themselves. Cigna demonstrates its commitment to this approach by hiring no more new producers than it can assign to individual mentors.[51]

Mentoring programs are also effective ways of addressing the challenge of workforce diversity. The mentoring process, however, presents unique problems—including the availability of mentors, issues of language and acculturation, and cultural sensitivity—for minority groups such as Hispanic-Americans. Negative stereotypes can limit minority members' access to mentoring relationships and the benefits associated with mentoring.[52] To address this problem, companies need to take steps to facilitate access to mentors for minority employees.

Mentoring programs may be informal or formal. *Informal mentoring programs* identify pools of mentors and protégés, provide training in the development of effective mentoring and diversity issues, and then provide informal opportunities for the development of mentoring relationships. *Network groups* are another avenue for mentoring. These groups help members identify with a few others who are like them within an organization, build relationships with them, and build social support. Network groups enhance the chance that minorities will find mentors.[53] Lucent Technologies, for example, has several Employee Business Partner groups that serve networking functions, including HISPA for Hispanic Americans, 4A for Asian Americans, ABLE for African Americans, LUNA for Native Americans, and Equal!, for gay, lesbian, and bisexual individuals. These groups serve as links to their respective communities within Lucent. Networks also increase the likelihood that individuals will have more than one mentor, and having multiple mentors has been found to result in greater career success than having only one mentor.[54]

Some companies have *formal mentoring programs*. At PricewaterhouseCoopers (PwC) each intern is assigned both a peer mentor to help with day-to-day questions and an experienced mentor to help with larger issues such as career path development. As an international firm, PwC also employs similar methods overseas. In PwC's Czech Republic operations, a team of two mentors—one of whom is called a "counselor"—fills the same guidance role as the two mentors generally fill for U.S. employees.[55]

Mentoring has had a strong impact in shaping the identities of the Big Four accounting firms. In one study, every partner who was interviewed reported having at least one mentor who played a critical role in his or her attainment of the partnership and beyond. These protégés' work identities were shaped through mentoring, and their work goals, language, and even lifestyles reflected the imperatives of the Big Four firm for which they worked.[56] Protégés were schooled on partners' "hot buttons" (what not to talk about), what to wear, to "tuck in the tie," and not to "cut the grass" without wearing a shirt.

In companies without formal mentoring programs, junior employees are often left to negotiate their own mentoring relationships. The barriers to finding a mentor under these circumstances include lack of access to mentors, fear of initiating a mentoring relationship, and fear that supervisors or coworkers might not approve of the mentoring relationship. Individuals may also be afraid to initiate a mentoring relationship because it might be misconstrued as a sexual advance by the potential mentor or by others. Potential mentors may fear this misinterpretation as well. Some are therefore unwilling to develop a relationship because of their own or the protégé's gender. Women report more of these barriers than men, and individuals who lack previous experience report more barriers to finding a mentor.[57]

There are other gender differences found in mentoring relationships. Male protégés report receiving less

> **In effective mentoring relationships, there is regular contact between mentor and protégé that has clearly specified purposes.**

psychological support than female protégés. Additionally, male mentors report giving more career development support, whereas female mentors report giving more psychological support.[58] Mentoring can be particularly important for women in male-dominated professions. In these environments, women who have male mentors have higher levels of compensation and career progress satisfaction than those without a male mentor.[59] Organizations can encourage junior workers to approach mentors by providing opportunities for them to interact with senior colleagues. The immediate supervisor is not always the best mentor for an individual, so exposure to other senior workers is important. Seminars, multilevel teams, and social events can serve as vehicles for bringing together potential mentors and protégés.

Mentoring relationships go through a series of phases: initiation, cultivation, separation, and redefinition. There is no fixed time length for each phase because each relationship is unique. The *initiation* phase is when the mentoring relationship begins to take on significance for both the mentor and the protégé. In the *cultivation* phase the relationship becomes more meaningful, and the protégé shows rapid progress because of the career support and psychosocial support provided by the mentor. Protégés influence mentors as well. In the *separation* phase the protégé feels the need to assert independence and work more autonomously. Separation can be voluntary, or it can result from an involuntary change (the protégé or mentor may be promoted or transferred). The separation phase can be difficult if it is resisted, either by the mentor (who is reluctant to let go of the relationship) or by the protégé (who resents the mentor's withdrawal of support). Moreover, separation may

dual-career partnership

A relationship in which both people have important career roles.

Hot Trend: Mentoring 2.0

While many mentoring programs involve partnering a young employee with a seasoned veteran, IBM has reinvented the process by using technology. With its web-based BluePages program, IBM allows employees to contact their colleagues all over the world to get advice on countless issues, whether it's preparing for a promotion or dealing with a certain type of customer. When Jocelyn Koh McDowell was looking for advice on how to qualify for a promotion, she used BluePages to connect with Lisa Squires, who supervises a certification program that McDowell needed to complete. Through BluePages, IBM is democratizing the mentoring process and creating a global network that employees can use to learn and teach others.

SOURCE: S. Hamm, "IBM Reinvents Mentoring, via the Web," *Bloomberg Businessweek* (March 12, 2009), http://www.businessweek.com/magazine/content/09_12/b4124057278170.htm.

result from a conflict that disrupts the mentoring relationship rather than proceeding smoothly and naturally.

The *redefinition* phase occurs if separation has been successful. In this phase, the relationship takes on a new identity as the two parties consider each other colleagues or friends. The mentor feels pride in the protégé, and the protégé develops a deeper appreciation for the support from the mentor.

Why are mentors so important? Aside from the support they provide, research shows that mentors are important to the protégé's future success. For example, studies have demonstrated that individuals with mentors have higher promotion rates and higher incomes than individuals who do not have mentors.[60] Professionals who have mentors earn between $5,600 and $22,000 more per year than those who do not.[61] Individuals with mentors are also better decision makers.[62] It is not just the presence of the mentor that yields these benefits. The quality of the relationship is the most important element.[63]

Dual-Career Partnerships

During the advancement stage, many individuals face another transition. They settle into a relationship with a life partner. This lifestyle transition requires adjustment in many respects—learning to live with another person, being concerned with someone besides yourself, dealing with an extended family, and many other demands. The partnership can be particularly stressful if both members are career oriented.

The two-career lifestyle has increased in recent years due in part to the need for two incomes to maintain a preferred standard of living. **Dual-career partnerships** are relationships in which both people have important career roles. This type of partnership can be mutually beneficial, but it can also be stressful. Often these stresses center around stereotypes that providing income is a man's responsibility and taking care of the home is the woman's domain. Thus, men who adhere to traditional gender beliefs may be threatened when the wife's income exceeds their own. However, working women's satisfaction with their marriage is affected by how much the husband helps with child care. Beliefs about who should do what in the partnership complicate the dual-career issue.[64]

One stressor in a dual-career partnership is time pressure. When both partners work outside the home, there may be a time crunch in fitting in work, family, and leisure time. Yet another potential problem is jealousy. When one partner's career blooms before the other's, the partner may feel threatened.[65] Another issue to work out is whose career takes precedence. For example, what happens if one partner is transferred to another city? Must the other partner make a move that might threaten his or her own career in order to be with the partner who was transferred? And who, if anyone, will stay home and take care of a new baby?

Working out a dual-career partnership takes careful planning and consistent communication between the partners. Each partner must serve as a source of social support for the other. In addition, couples may need to turn to other family members, friends, and professionals for support.

Work–Home Conflicts

An issue related to dual-career partnerships that is faced throughout the career cycle but often first encountered in the advancement phase, is the conflict between work and personal life. Such conflict negatively affects an individual's overall quality of life and may even lead to emotional exhaustion. Dealing with customer complaints all day, failed sales calls, or missed deadlines can magnify negative events at home, and vice versa.[66]

Responsibilities at home will likely clash at times with responsibilities at work, so these conflicts must be planned for. Suppose a child gets sick at school. Who will pick up the child and stay home with him? Couples must work together to resolve these conflicts. At Eli Lilly and Co., only 36 percent of workers said it was possible to get ahead in their careers and still devote sufficient time to family. This is surprising, because Lilly has a reputation as one of the world's most family-friendly workplaces.[67] A recent study found that an individual's work–home conflict can lead to unfavorable critique and discouragement of goal attainment by that individual's partner, leading

to mutual feelings of exhaustion and negativity.[68]

Work–home conflicts are particular problems for working women.[69] Women have been quicker to share the provider role than men have been to share responsibilities at home.[70] When working women experience work–home conflict, their performance declines, and they suffer more strain. Work–home conflict is a broad topic. It can be narrowed further into work–family conflict, in which work interferes with family, or family–work conflict, in which family or home life interferes with work.[71] Individuals who believe that men and women should share work and home lives equally experience more guilt from work–home conflict than traditionalists, who tend to feel more guilt when home life interferes with work.[72] Cultural differences arise in these types of conflicts. One study showed that while Americans experience more family–work conflict, Chinese experience more work–family conflict.[73] For example, women in management positions in China were very positive about future advancements and carried a strong belief in their ability to succeed. This, in turn, caused them to reevaluate their personal and professional identities. Such an identity transformation is marked by happiness associated with career advancement, even though many women foresaw emotional costs with such career advancement. This study indicated that female Chinese managers experience work–family conflict in part because the Chinese culture emphasizes close social ties and *guanxi*.[74]

Ways to Manage Work–Home Conflict

To help individuals deal with work–home conflict, companies like Ernst & Young offer **flexible work schedules**, programs that give employees the freedom to set their own hours so that they can attend to personal

> **flexible work schedule**
> A work schedule that allows employees discretion in order to accommodate personal concerns.

©Corbis/Jupiterimages

eldercare
Assistance in caring for elderly parents and/or other elderly relatives.

issues.[75] *Telecommuting* breaks down barriers of time and space by allowing people to work no matter where they are. At Cisco Systems, employees who telecommuted experienced higher productivity, work–life flexibility, and job satisfaction. Furthermore, they reported saving a combined $10.3 million in fuel costs, while the company saved $277 million per year in time and productivity costs.

Company-sponsored child care is another way to help. Companies with on-site day-care centers include Johnson & Johnson, Perdue Farms, and Campbell Soup. Mitchell Gold + Bob Williams, an award-winning furniture maker, believes that treating people right must come first. Its 2,700-square-foot on-site day-care center is education-based rather than activity-based and operates at break-even rates to make it more accessible. The day-care facility was named the county's "Provider of the Year" in 2003.[76] Whereas large companies may offer corporate day care, small companies can also assist their workers by providing referral services for locating the type of child care the workers need. For smaller organizations, this is a cost-effective alternative.[77] At the very least, companies can be sensitive to work–home conflicts and handle them on a case-by-case basis with flexibility and concern.

A program of increasing interest that organizations can provide is **eldercare**. Often workers find themselves part of the so-called sandwich generation. They are expected to care for both their children and their elderly parents. Inclusion in this extremely stressful role is reported more often by women than men.[78] The impact of caring for an aging loved one is often underestimated—17 percent of those who provide such care eventually quit their jobs due to time constraints, and another 15 percent cut back their work hours.[79] Caring for an elderly dependent at home not only creates work–home conflicts for an employee, but also takes a toll on the employee's own well-being and performance at work. This is most often the case if the organization is not one that provides a supportive climate for discussion of eldercare issues.[80] Harvard University has taken steps to help its faculty and staff deal with eldercare issues by contracting with Parents in a Pinch, Inc., a firm that specializes in nanny services and now also offers eldercare.[81]

John Beatrice is one of a growing number of men making work fit their family rather than trying to fit family around career. John remembers his father working most of the night so he could be at John's athletic events during the day, and John wants the same for his family. So while job sharing, flexible scheduling, and telecommuting have traditionally been viewed as meeting the needs of working mothers, John and other men are increasingly taking advantage of such opportunities. In John's case, flexible work hours at Ernst & Young allow him to spend part of his mornings and afternoons coaching a high school hockey team. In John's assessment, flexible work hours actually lead him to work more hours than he would otherwise, and he's happier about doing it. Not surprisingly, John's employer also benefits from the arrangement. After nineteen years, John is more loyal than ever and still loves what he does.[82]

Alternative work arrangements such as flextime, compressed workweeks, work-at-home arrangements, part-time hours, job sharing, and leave options can help employees manage work–home conflicts. Managers must not let their biases get in the way of these benefits. Top managers may be less willing to grant alternative work arrangements to men than to women, to supervisors than

[KPMG Provides Help for the Sandwich Generation]

Many midlife workers find themselves taking care of both their children and their elderly parents. Accounting firm KPMG recognized this precarious position and took steps to address the needs of its sandwiched employees by implementing progressive scheduling practices that promote a healthy work–life balance. Compressed workweeks, flextime, and telecommuting are all available, and if employees' babysitting arrangements fall through, KPMG offers a backup child-care service. KPMG also has a shared-leave program in which employees can donate personal vacation time to colleagues facing family emergencies like sudden illness or the death of a loved one.

Most unique of the new initiatives is the three-part eldercare benefit. First, KPMG provides an online information and referral service that connects employees with aging and health-related resources and facilities. Second, the firm underwrites up to twenty days of facility-based or in-home care for elderly relatives per year. As with the shared-leave program, employees can donate unused care days to colleagues. Third, if an employee needs to take a break from work to plan for eldercare or to tend to an elderly relative, he or she can request a leave of absence or use paid time-off days.

The payoffs for providing such benefits are many. The programs at KPMG led to reduced turnover and an award from Catalyst (the leading nonprofit organization promoting inclusive workplaces for women). Employees reported greater productivity, a boost in morale, and reduced stress and work–home conflict. Certainly, KPMG's novel efforts to accommodate the sandwich generation have proven worthwhile.

SOURCES: http://www.catalyst.org/file/280/difinalpracticekpmg_pdf.pdf; https://web1.lifebenefits.com /MMG/resources/aware_newsletter/aware0408/ef_print.html.

©iStockphoto.com/Kelly Cline

to subordinates, and to employees caring for elderly parents rather than children, but it is important that family-friendly policies be applied fairly.[83]

The Maintenance Stage

Maintenance may be a misnomer for this career stage, because some people continue to grow in their careers, although the growth is usually not at the rate it was earlier. A career crisis at midlife may accompany the midlife transition. A senior product manager at Borden found himself in such a crisis and described it this way: "When I was in college, I had thought in terms of being president of a company. . . . But at Borden I felt used and cornered. Most of the guys in the next two rungs above me had either an MBA or fifteen to twenty years of experience in the food business. My long-term plans stalled."[84]

Some individuals who reach a career crisis are burned out, and a month's vacation will help, according to Carolyn Smith Paschal, who owns an executive search firm. She recommends that companies give employees in this stage sabbaticals instead of bonuses. This would help rejuvenate them. Some individuals, on the other hand, reach the maintenance stage with a sense of achievement and contentment, feeling no need to strive for further upward mobility. Whether the maintenance stage is a time of crisis or contentment, however, there are two issues to grapple with: sustaining performance and becoming a mentor.

Sustaining Performance

Remaining productive is a key concern for individuals in the maintenance stage. This becomes challenging when one reaches a **career plateau**, a point where the probability of moving further up the hierarchy is low. Some people handle career plateauing fairly well, but others may become frustrated, bored, and dissatisfied with their jobs. To keep employees productive, organizations can provide challenges and opportunities for learning. *Lateral moves* are one option. Another option is to involve the employee in *project teams* that provide new tasks and skill development. The key is keeping the work stimulating and involving. Individuals at this stage also need continued affirmation of their value to the organization. They need to know that their contributions are significant and appreciated.[85]

Becoming a Mentor

During maintenance, individuals can make a contribution by sharing their wealth of knowledge and experience with others. Opportunities to be mentors to new employees can keep senior workers motivated and involved in the organization. It is important for organizations to reward mentors for the time and energy they expend. Some employees adapt naturally to the mentor role, but others may need training on how to coach and counsel junior workers.

Maintenance is a time of transition, like all career stages. It can be managed by individuals who know what to expect and plan to remain productive, as well as by organizations that focus on maximizing employee involvement in work. According to Levinson, during the latter part of the maintenance stage, another life transition occurs. The "age-fifty transition" is another time of reevaluating the dream and working further on the issues raised in the midlife transition. Following the age-fifty transition is a fairly stable period. During this time, individuals begin to plan seriously for withdrawing from their careers.

The Withdrawal Stage

The withdrawal stage usually occurs later in life and signals that a long period of continuous employment will soon come to a close. Older workers may face discrimination and stereotyping. They are often viewed by others as less productive, more resistant to change, and less motivated. However, older workers are one of the most undervalued groups in the workforce. They can provide continuity in the midst of change and can serve as mentors and role models to younger generations of employees.

Discrimination against older workers is prohibited under the Age Discrimination in Employment Act (go to eeoc.gov/policy/adea.html to read the provisions of this 1967 act). Organizations should strive to create a culture that values older workers' contributions. With their level of experience, strong work ethic, and loyalty, these workers have much to contribute. In fact, older workers have lower rates of tardiness and absenteeism, are more safety conscious, and are more satisfied with their jobs than are younger workers.[86]

Planning for Change

The decision to retire is an individual one, but the need for planning is universal. A retired sales executive from Boise Cascade said that the best advice is to "plan no unplanned retirement."[87] This means carefully planning not only the transition but also the activities you will be involved in once the transition is made. All options should be open for consideration. One recent trend is to work as a temporary top-level executive. The qualities of a good temporary executive include substantial high-level management experience, financial security that

career plateau
A point in an individual's career at which the probability of moving farther up the hierarchy is low.

allows the executive to choose only assignments that really interest her, and a willingness to relocate.[88] Some individuals at the withdrawal stage find this an attractive option.

Planning for retirement should include not only financial planning but also a plan for psychologically withdrawing from work. The pursuit of hobbies and travel, volunteer work, or more time with extended family can all be part of the plan. The key is to plan early and carefully, as well as to anticipate the transition with a positive attitude and a full slate of desirable activities.

Retirement

There are several retirement trends right now, ranging from early retirement to phased retirement to never retiring. Some adults are choosing a combination of these options, leaving their first career for some time off before reentering the workforce either part time or full time doing something they enjoy. For more and more Americans, the idea of a retirement spent sitting beside the swimming pool sounds, for lack of a better word, boring. Factors that influence the decision of when to retire include company policy, financial considerations, family support or pressure, health, and opportunities for other productive activities.[89]

During the withdrawal stage, the individual faces a major life transition that Levinson refers to as the *late adulthood transition* (ages sixty to sixty-five). One's own mortality becomes a major concern, and the loss of family members and friends becomes more frequent. The person works to achieve a sense of integrity in life—that is, the person works to find the encompassing meaning and value in life.

Retirement need not be a complete cessation of work. Many alternative work arrangements can be considered, and many companies offer flexibility in these options. **Phased retirement** is a popular option for retirement-age workers who want

©iStockphoto.com/Isaac Santillan

to gradually reduce their hours and/or responsibilities. There are many forms of phased retirement, including reduced workdays or workweeks, job sharing, and consulting and mentoring arrangements. Many organizations cannot afford the loss of large numbers of experienced employees at once. In fact, although 50 percent of all U.S. workers are officially retired by age sixty, only 11 percent fully withdraw from work. This means there is an increase in **bridge employment**, which is employment that takes place after a person retires from a full-time position but before the person's permanent withdrawal from the workforce. Bridge employment is related to retirement satisfaction and overall life satisfaction.[90]

Some companies are helping employees transition to retirement in innovative ways. For example, retired individuals can continue their affiliation with the organization by serving as mentors to employees who are embarking on retirement planning or other career transitions. This helps diminish the fear of loss some people have about retirement, because the retiree has an option to serve as a mentor or consultant to the organization.

Lawrence Livermore National Labs (LLNL) employs some of the best research minds in the world. And when these great minds retire from full-time work, they have numerous opportunities to continue contributing. LLNL's retiree program website lists a wide variety of requests, ranging from guiding tours and making phone calls to providing guidance on current research and helping researchers make contact with other researchers.[91] Programs like this one help LLNL avoid the typical knowledge drain that takes place when seasoned veteran employees retire.

Now that you understand the career stage model, you can begin to conduct your own career planning. It is never too early to start.

LEARNING OUTCOME **8**

Career Anchors

Much of an individual's self-concept rests upon a career. Over the course of the career, **career anchors** are developed—self-perceived talents, motives, and values that guide an individual's career decisions.[92] Edgar Schein developed the concept of career anchors based on a twelve-year study of MBA graduates from the Massachusetts Institute of Technology (MIT). Schein found great diversity in the graduates' career histories but great similarities in the way they explained the career decisions they had made.[93] From

phased retirement
An arrangement that allows employees to reduce their hours and/or responsibilities in order to ease into retirement.

bridge employment
Employment that takes place after a person retires from a full-time position but before the person's permanent withdrawal from the workforce.

career anchors
A network of self-perceived talents, motives, and values that guide an individual's career decisions.

extensive interviews with the graduates, Schein developed the five career anchors (see box at right).

Career anchors emerge over time and may be modified by work or life experiences.[94] The importance of knowing your career anchor is that it can help you find a match between you and an organization. For example, individuals with creativity as an anchor may find themselves stifled in bureaucratic organizations. Textbook sales may not be the place for an individual with a security anchor because of the frequent travel and seasonal nature of the business.

FIVE CAREER ANCHORS

1 *Technical/functional competence.* Individuals who hold this career anchor want to specialize in a given functional area (for example, finance or marketing) and become competent. The idea of general management does not interest them.

2 *Managerial competence.* Adapting this career anchor means individuals want general management responsibility. They want to see their efforts have an impact on organizational effectiveness.

3 *Autonomy and independence.* Freedom is the key to this career anchor, and often these individuals are uncomfortable working in large organizations. Autonomous careers such as writer, professor, or consultant attract these individuals.

4 *Creativity.* Individuals holding this career anchor feel a strong need to create something. They are often entrepreneurs.

5 *Security/stability.* Long-term career stability, whether in a single organization or in a single geographic area, fits people with this career anchor. Some government jobs provide this type of security.

BY THE NUMBERS

6 personalities in Holland's typology

10.6 million women-owned businesses in the United States

$10.3 million saved by employees at Cisco in fuel costs by telecommuting

17% of workers responsible for elder-care in their families quit their jobs

11% of retirees fully withdraw from work

Log in to the **CourseMate** for *ORGB3* at **www.cengagebrain.com** to:

✳ Review **Key Terms Flash Cards** online

✳ Play **Beat the Clock** and **Quiz Bowl** to master concepts

✳ Complete **web quizzes** to prepare for exams

✳ Watch the video on **Living Social Escapes** and *Baby Mama* for examples, then test yourself with a quick quiz

✳ Work through the **"What about You?"** and **Ethical Dilemma** exercises to see how you would handle various situations that organizations face on a daily basis

Managing Change

LEARNING OUTCOMES

1 Identify the major external and internal forces for change in organizations.

2 Describe how different types of change vary in scope.

3 Discuss methods organizations can use to manage resistance to change.

4 Explain Lewin's organizational change model.

5 Explain how companies determine the need to conduct an organization development intervention.

6 Discuss the major group-focused techniques for organization development intervention.

7 Discuss the major individual-focused techniques for organization development intervention.

©iStockphoto.com/Steve Debenport

"Organizations are in a state of tremendous turmoil and transition, and all members are affected.""

After You Finish
This Chapter
Go to **Page 312**
for **Study Tools**

Forces for Change in Organizations

Change has become the norm in most organizations. Many American companies have experienced plant closings, failures, mergers and acquisitions, and downsizing. *Adaptiveness, flexibility*, and *responsiveness* are characteristics of organizations that will succeed in meeting the competitive challenges that businesses face.[1] In the past, organizations could succeed by claiming excellence in one area—quality, reliability, or cost, for example—but this is not the case today. The current environment demands excellence in all areas and vigilant leaders. A recent survey of CEOs who were facing crises found that 50 percent of them said they believed problems arrived "suddenly" and that they had not prepared adequately for them. More than 10 percent said they were, in fact, the last to know about problems.[2]

As we saw in Chapter 1, change is what's on managers' minds. The pursuit of organizational effectiveness through downsizing, restructuring, reengineering, productivity management, cycle-time reduction, and other efforts is paramount. Organizations are in a state of tremendous turmoil and transition, and all members are affected. Continued downsizings may have left firms leaner but not necessarily richer. Though downsizing can increase shareholder value by better aligning costs with revenues, firms may suffer from public criticism for their actions. Laying off employees may be accompanied by increases in CEO pay and stock options, linking the misery of employees with the financial success of owners and management.[3]

Organizations must also deal with ethical, environmental, and other social issues. Competition is fierce, and companies can no longer afford to rest on their laurels. Understanding this situation, American Airlines has developed a series of programs to constantly reevaluate and change its operating methods to prevent the company from stagnating. General Electric holds off-site WorkOut sessions with groups of managers and employees, with the goal of making GE a faster, less complex organization that can respond effectively to change. In the WorkOut sessions, employees recommend specific changes, explain why they are needed, and propose ways the changes can be implemented. Top management must make an immediate response: an approval, a disapproval (with an explanation), or a request for more information. The GE WorkOut sessions eliminate the barriers that keep employees from contributing to change.

There are two basic forms of change in organizations. **Planned change** results from a deliberate decision to alter the organization. For example, companies that wish to move from a traditional hierarchical structure to one that facilitates self-managed teams must use a proactive, carefully orchestrated approach. **Unplanned change** is imposed on the organization and is often unforeseen. Changes in government regulations and changes in the economy are two examples. Responsiveness to unplanned change requires tremendous flexibility and adaptability on the part of organizations. Managers must be prepared to handle both planned and unplanned forms of change in organizations.

Forces for change can come from many sources. Some of these are external, arising from outside the company, whereas others are internal, arising from sources within the organization.

External Forces

The four major managerial challenges described throughout the book are major external forces for change: globalization, workforce diversity, technological change, and managing ethical behavior.

Globalization The power players in the global market are the organizations that can capitalize on emerging markets throughout the world. The prime example is China, which has become the second largest economy in the world. Western firms like Nestlé, Procter & Gamble, and Kentucky Fried Chicken are all trying to pick up market share in China. Companies that understand what makes Chinese culture unique are finding success while others, who ignore these elements, are not. Home Depot, for example, has struggled in China because it did not understand that most Chinese people do not have places to store tools and typically hire people to work on their homes rather than doing it themselves. In addition to differences in consumers, companies must negotiate different legal requirements, as the Chinese government is still writing the rule of business.[4] Because global

China, the second largest economy in the world, is a growing market for Western firms.

business implicitly involves multiple governments and legal systems, it carries unique risks not found by firms competing within a single nation.

The United States is but one nation in the drive to open new markets. Japan and Germany are responding to global competition in sufficient ways, and the emergence of the European Union as a powerful trading group will have a profound impact on world markets. By joining with their European neighbors, companies in smaller countries will begin to make major progress in world markets, thus increasing the fierce competition that already exists.

These changes, among others, have led companies to rethink the borders of their markets and to encourage their employees to think globally. Jack Welch, former CEO of GE, was among the first to call for a *borderless company*, in which there are no mental distinctions between domestic and foreign operations or between managers and employees.[5] GE has locations in 160 countries across the globe and has become a truly multinational corporation. The thought that drives the borderless company is that

Fast Fact

The Tata Group, a conglomerate based in India, owns operations in more than eighty countries, including Tetley Tea Company (England), Daewoo Commercial Vehicles (South Korea), Neotel (South Africa), Piaggio Aero Industries (Italy), and Comoplesa Lebrero SA (Spain).

SOURCE: http://www.tata.com/businesses/sectors/index.aspx?sectid=aZ72PXPwpal=.

planned change

Change resulting from a deliberate decision to alter the organization.

unplanned change

Change that is imposed on the organization and is often unforeseen.

RFID

barriers interfere with people working together and should be removed. Globalizing an organization means rethinking the most efficient ways to use resources, disseminate and gather information, and develop people. It requires not only structural changes but also changes in the minds of employees. Microsoft, for example, has become a global leader by acquiring leading software solutions providers across the globe. In 2002, it acquired Navision, a Denmark-based business software solutions provider. By doing so, Microsoft combined the power of Navision's reach in the European markets with its own and now has a strong hold in providing global business solutions in the software industry.[6]

Workforce Diversity Related to globalization is the challenge of workforce diversity. As we have seen throughout this book, workforce diversity is a powerful force for change in organizations. First, increased female participation means that the majority of new workers will be female.[7] In the late 2000s the percentage of female workers in the labor force jumped as men were overwhelmingly represented in recession-related layoffs.[8] Second, the workforce will be increasingly more culturally diverse as a result of globalization and changing U.S. demographics such as the dramatic rise in the participation of African Americans and Hispanic Americans. Third, as the workforce ages, there will be fewer young workers and more middle-aged workers.[9] The global workforce is also diversifying. Following a high-profile bribery scandal (during which many top executives resigned), Siemens, a 160-year-old German technology and equipment firm, moved to represent better the diversity of its 2 million customers. Siemens hired a chief diversity officer who has since launched several programs focusing on mentoring and increasing diversity in the company's previously all-male managerial ranks.[10]

Technological Change Rapid technological innovation is another force for change in organizations, and those who fail to keep pace can quickly fall behind. *Smart tags*, for example, are replacing bar codes for tracking and scanning products. Bar codes are passive identification markers whose stripes are unchangeable, and items must be lined up individually for scanning (like in a grocery store checkout line). Manufacturers are starting to use smart tags, or *radio-frequency identification (RFID)* tags, that are as small as two matches laid side by side, and hold digital memory chips the size of a pinhead.

RFIDs contain a lot more information than bar codes, and users can alter the information on them. As many as fifty tags per second can be read—forty times faster than bar-code scanners. Ford uses RFIDs to track parts. Data such as a unique ID, part type, plant location, and time/date stamps are included on the tag. Because RFIDs are reusable, the long-term costs are about the same as bar codes.[11]

American Express Business Travel Program has gained widespread popularity in the corporate world through technological competition and excellent customer service. It invests in employee engagement, skill training, and leadership development programs. Furthermore, it emphasizes quality of customer care through what it calls the Great Call Experience. Employees are trained on a standard set of protocols to enhance customer satisfaction.[12]

Technological innovations bring about profound change because the innovation process promotes associated changes in work relationships and organizational structures.[13] The team approach adopted by many organizations leads to flatter structures, decentralized decision making, and more open communication between leaders and team members.

Managing Ethical Behavior Recent scandals have brought ethical behavior in organizations to the forefront of public consciousness. Ethical issues, however, are not always public and monumental. Employees face ethical dilemmas in their daily work lives. The need to manage daily ethical behavior has brought about several changes in organizations, most centering around the idea that an organization must create a culture that encourages ethical behavior.

All public companies issue annual financial reports; Gap Inc. has gone a step further by issuing an annual ethical report. The clothing industry is almost synonymous with the use of sweatshops, but what sets Gap apart is its candid admission that none of its 3,000 suppliers fully complies with the firm's ethical code of conduct. Rather than retreat from these problems, Gap has chosen to work with its suppliers to improve conditions overseas. The firm has more than ninety full-time employees charged with monitoring supplier operations around the world.[14] The annual report includes extensive descriptions of workers' activities, including which factories were monitored, violations that were found, and which factories are no longer used by Gap because of the violations. It also addresses media reports critical of Gap and its operations.

Gap tries to improve worker conditions by providing training and encouraging suppliers to develop their own conduct codes. For example, in China it has encouraged lunchtime sessions in which workers are advised of their rights. While most facilities respond positively to these efforts, some don't, and Gap pulled its business from 136 factories it concluded were not going to improve. It also terminated contracts with two factories that had verified use of child labor. Gap's approach to overseas labor offers a model for other garment firms.[15]

Society expects organizations to maintain ethical behavior both internally and in relationships with other organizations, as well as with customers, the environment, and society. These expectations may be informal, or they may come in the form of increased regulation. In addition to the pressure from societal expectations, legal developments, changing stakeholder expectations, and shifting consumer demands can also lead to change.[16] And some companies change simply because others are changing.[17] Other powerful forces for change originate from within the organization.

Internal Forces

Pressures for change that originate inside the organization are generally recognizable by symptoms such as declining effectiveness. A company that experiences its third quarterly loss within a fiscal year undoubtedly experiences a pressure for change. Some companies react by instituting layoffs and massive cost-cutting programs, whereas others look at the bigger picture, view the loss as symptomatic of an underlying problem, and seek out its cause.

A crisis may also stimulate change in an organization. Strikes or walkouts may lead management to change the wage structure. The resignation of a key decision maker may cause the company to rethink the composition of its management team and its role in the organization.

Changes in employee expectations can trigger

incremental change

Change of a relatively small scope, such as making small improvements.

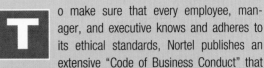

change in organizations as well. A company that hires a group of young newcomers may find that their expectations are very different from those of older workers. One reason for changed expectations is that the workforce is more educated than ever before. Although this has its advantages, workers with more education demand more of employers. Furthermore, today's workers are concerned with career and family balance issues, such as dependent care. And the many sources of workforce diversity hold potential for a host of other differing expectations among employees.

Still another pressure is a change in the work climate that produces a workforce that is lethargic, unmotivated, and dissatisfied. Such symptoms are common in organizations that have experienced layoffs. Workers who have escaped a layoff may grieve for those who have lost their jobs and may find it difficult to continue to be productive. They may fear that they will be laid off as well, and many feel insecure in their jobs.

LEARNING OUTCOME **2**

The Scope of Change

Change can be of a relatively small scope, such as a modification in a work procedure (an **incremental change**). Such changes are a fine-tuning of the organization. For example, Intel and other chip producers must continually upgrade their manufacturing equipment just to stay competitive. Intel's conversion of an Arizona "fab" or chip-making plant from older to newer technology cost $3 billion.[18] While radical

©John Lund/Blend Images/Jupiterimages

change is more exciting and interesting to discuss, most organizational change—and therefore most research on organizational change—has focused on evolutionary (incremental) rather than revolutionary change.[19] Change can also be on a larger scale, such as the restructuring of an organization (a **strategic change**).[20] In strategic change, the organization moves from an old state to a known new state during a controlled period of time. After years of slumping mobile phone sales, particularly in North America, Nokia decided to change its strategy by ditching its own operating system and partnering with Microsoft to develop Windows-based smartphones that can compete with Android-based phones and Apple's iPhone.[21]

The most massive scope of change is **transformational change**, in which the organization moves to a radically different, and sometimes unknown, future state.[22] In transformational change, the organization's mission, culture, goals, structure, and leadership may all change dramatically.[23] Just over a century ago, two successful bicycle makers decided to leave the safety of their business to devote time to building and selling an amazing new invention—the airplane—which transformed travel, warfare, and communications around the world. The Wright brothers transformed not only their bike business but the whole world! Of all the tasks a leader undertakes, many say that changing the form and nature of the organization itself may be the most difficult, an observation supported by research.[24]

One of the toughest decisions faced by leaders is the proper "pace" of change. Some scholars argue that rapid change is more likely to succeed than slower change because it creates momentum,[25] while others argue that these short, sharp changes are actually rare and not experienced by most firms.[26] Still others observe that change in a large organization may occur incrementally in some parts of the firm and quickly in others.[27] In summary, researchers agree that the pace of change is important, but they can't quite agree on which pace of change is most beneficial.

Very little long-term research has looked at change over a significant time period. One twelve-year study looked at change in the structure of Canadian National Sports Organizations (NSOs). It found that within NSOs, radical transition did not always require a fast pace of change. It also found that successful transitions

often involve changing the high-impact elements of an organization (in this case, their decision-making structures) early in the process.[28]

The Change Agent's Role

The individual or group that introduces and manages change in an organization is known as the **change agent**. Change agents can be internal, such as managers or employees who are appointed to oversee the change process. In her book *The Change Masters*, Rosabeth Moss Kanter notes that at companies like Hewlett-Packard and Polaroid, managers and employees alike are developing the needed skills to produce change and innovation in the organization.[29]

Internal change agents have certain advantages in managing the change process. First, they know the organization's history, its political system, and its culture. Then, because they must live with the results of their change efforts, internal change agents are likely to be very careful about managing change. There are disadvantages, however, to using internal change agents. They may be associated with certain factions within the organization, be accused of favoritism, or be too close to the situation to have an objective view of what needs to be done.

Change leaders within organizations tend to be young, between twenty-five and forty. A high number of

strategic change
Change of a larger scale, such as organizational restructuring.

transformational change
Change in which the organization moves to a radically different, and sometimes unknown, future state.

change agent
The individual or group that undertakes the task of introducing and managing a change in an organization.

[GM's Change Agent]

After years of struggle, marked by the low point of a bankruptcy filing and government takeover, General Motors set out to transform itself. At the heart of its change effort is Mary Barra, a 31-year veteran of the company who has been given the responsibility of overseeing changes to the company's vehicle design and development process. Her goal is to create a streamlined, efficient, and speedy process that GM can use to make cars that fit consumer tastes. She also has the responsibility of creating a global platform, so that GM can use a single set of components to produce numerous vehicles all over the world. Finally, she is charged with remaking GM's corporate culture by removing bureaucratic obstacles and giving the engineers freedom to pursue radical designs and communicate with executives.

SOURCE: S. Terlet, "GM's Latest Change Agent Tackles Designs, Red Tape," *The Wall Street Journal* (June 15, 2011), http://online.wsj.com /article/SB10001424052702304665904576383522386471918.html.

AP Images/Paul Sancya

change leaders are women. Also, change agents are more flexible than ordinary general managers and much more people oriented. Using a balance of technical and interpersonal skills, they are tough decision makers who focus on performance results. Plus, they know how to energize people and get them aligned in the same direction. In addition, they have the ability to operate in more than one leadership style and can shift from a team mode to command and control, depending on the situation. Finally, change agents are comfortable with uncertainty.[30]

If change is large scale or strategic in nature, it may require a team of leaders with a variety of skills, expertise, and influence that can work together harmoniously.[31]

External change agents bring an outsider's objective view to the organization. They may be preferred by employees because of their impartiality. External change agents face certain problems, however. Not only is their knowledge of the organization's history limited, but they may also be viewed with suspicion by organization members. External change agents have more power in directing changes if employees perceive them as being trustworthy, possessing important expertise, having a track record that establishes credibility, and being similar to them.[32]

Different change agent competencies are required at different stages of the change process. Leadership, communication, training, and participation have varying levels of impact as the change proceeds, meaning change agents must be flexible in how they work through the different phases of the process.[33] Effective change leaders build strong relationships within their leadership team, between the team and organizational members, and between the team and key environmental players. Maintaining all three relationships simultaneously is quite difficult, so successful leaders are continually "coupling" and "uncoupling" with the different groups as the change process proceeds. Adaptability is a key skill for both internal and external change leaders.[34]

Resistance to Change

People often resist change in a rational response based on self-interest. However, there are countless other reasons people resist change. Many of these center around the notion of *reactance*—that is, a negative reaction that occurs when individuals feel that their personal freedom is threatened.[35] Let us take a look at some expressions of reactance and then at some ways of dealing with it.

Major Reasons People Resist Change

Common reasons people resist change include fear of the unknown, fear of loss, fear of failure, fear of disruption of interpersonal relationships, personality factors, politics, and cultural assumptions and values.

Fear of the Unknown Change often brings with it substantial uncertainty. Employees facing a technological change may resist the change simply because it introduces ambiguity into what was once a comfortable situation for them.

Fear of Loss Some employees may fear losing their jobs with impending change, especially when an advanced technology like robotics is introduced. Employees may also fear losing their status because of change.[36] Computer systems experts, for example, may feel that their expertise will be less appreciated when a more user-friendly networked information system is installed. Another common fear is that changes may diminish the positive qualities the individual enjoys in the job. Computerizing the customer service positions at Southwestern Bell (now part of SBC Communications), for example, threatened the autonomy that representatives previously enjoyed.

Fear of Failure Some employees fear changes because they fear their own failure as a result of those changes. They may question their competence to deal with changes that might mean increased workloads or increased task difficulty. They may also fear that performance expectations will be elevated following the change, and that they might not measure up.[37]

Resistance can also stem from the fear that change will not really take place. In other words, there can be fear of failure on the part of the organization, not the individual. In one large library that was undergoing a major automation effort, employees were doubtful that the vendor could deliver the state-of-the-art system that was promised. In this case, the implementation never became a reality—the employees' fears were well founded.[38]

Fear of Disruption of Interpersonal Relationships Employees may resist change that threatens to limit meaningful interpersonal relationships on the job. Librarians facing the automation effort feared that once the computerized system was implemented, they would not be able to interact as they did when they had to go to another floor of the library to get help finding a resource.

Personality Individuals with an internal locus of control, high growth needs, strong motivation, and a positive outlook are more likely to embrace changes at work.[39] Personality conflicts may impact workers' acceptance of change. A change agent who appears insensitive to employees' concerns and feelings may meet considerable resistance from those who feel that their needs are not being taken into account.

Politics Organizational change may also shift the existing balance of power in the organization. Individuals or groups empowered under the current arrangement may be threatened with losing these political advantages in the advent of change.

Cultural Assumptions and Values Sometimes cultural assumptions and values can be impediments to change, particularly if the assumptions underlying the change are alien to employees. Other times, employees might interpret strategic change initiatives

from the standpoint of the organization's value system and ideologies of the management team. In fact, research indicates that employees pay attention to the informal sense-making process prevalent in organizations and leading top-down change initiatives to fail.[40] This form of resistance can be very difficult to overcome because some cultural assumptions are unconscious. As discussed in Chapter 2, some cultures tend to avoid uncertainty. In Mexican and Greek cultures, for example, change that creates a great deal of uncertainty may be met with great resistance.

We have described several sources of resistance to change, but the reasons for resistance are as diverse as the workforce itself and vary with different individuals and organizations. The challenge for managers is introducing change in a positive manner and managing employee resistance.

Managing Resistance to Change

The traditional view of managing resistance to change was to treat it as something to be overcome, and many organizational attempts to reduce the resistance have only served to intensify it. The contemporary view holds that resistance is simply a form of feedback and that this feedback can be used very productively to manage the change process.[41] In this view, the idea is to manage resistance by planning for it and being ready with a variety of strategies for using the resistance as feedback and helping employees negotiate the transition. Three key strategies

[Resistance Isn't Futile]

Much of the previous research done on resistance to change assumes that those who resist encourage dysfunction. In a recent study, researchers found that resistance to change can in fact be a valuable organizational resource on three levels: existence, engagement, and strengthening.

Existence: While it is often difficult to disseminate new ideas, resistance provides an opportunity to repeat, clarify, and keep a change topic or idea in existence long enough to garner support.

Engagement: Individuals who resist are typically more invested in a change's impact. Change agents should listen to engaged individuals and consider altering the pace, scope or sequencing of the change based on their arguments.

Strengthening: Countering resistance effectively may actually be beneficial to the change process. Resistance can strengthen communication and participation, which often leads to better working relationships.

SOURCE: J. D. Ford, L. W. Ford, and A. D'Amelio, "Resistance to Change: The Rest of the Story," *Academy of Management Review* 33 (2008): 362–377.

©Eric Meola/The Image Bank/Getty Images

for managing resistance to change are communication, participation, and empathy and support.[42]

Communication about impending change is essential if employees are to adjust effectively.[43] The details and, equally important, the rationale of the change should be provided. Accurate and timely information can help prevent unfounded fears and potentially damaging rumors from developing. Conversely, delaying announcements and withholding information can serve to fuel the rumor mill. Open communication in a culture of trust is a key ingredient for successful change.[44] Managers should pay attention to the informal communication networks in an organization because they can serve as power channels for disseminating change-related information.[45] Educating employees on new work procedures and other potential consequences of change is helpful. In addition, both mentors and mentees derive benefits from going through the process of organizational change together. Mentees are assisted by mentors who help them make sense of the change, and mentors experience satisfaction in having helped the mentee through the change process. Another key ingredient that can help employees adjust to change is a supervisor whom they can trust. When employees trust their supervisors, it serves as a social support mechanism and they are more committed to the organization even if they feel they can't control the change process.[46]

There is substantial research support underscoring the importance of *participation* in the change process. Employees must be engaged and involved in order for change to work—as supported by the notion "That which we create, we support." Participation helps employees become involved in the change and establishes a feeling of ownership in the process. Mergers and acquisitions are widely prevalent in the current business environment.

Another strategy for managing resistance is to provide *empathy and support* to employees who have trouble dealing with the change. Active listening is an excellent tool for identifying the reasons behind resistance and for uncovering fears. An expression of concerns about the change can provide important feedback that managers can use to improve the change process. Emotional support and encouragement can help an employee deal with the anxiety that is a natural response to change. Employees who experience severe reactions to change can benefit from talking with a counselor. Some companies provide counseling through their employee assistance plans.

The Hartford Financial Services Group encountered some resistance to change in going global. When the company attempted to enter the lucrative British and Dutch insurance markets through acquisitions, the overseas staff resisted changes suggested by Hartford, such

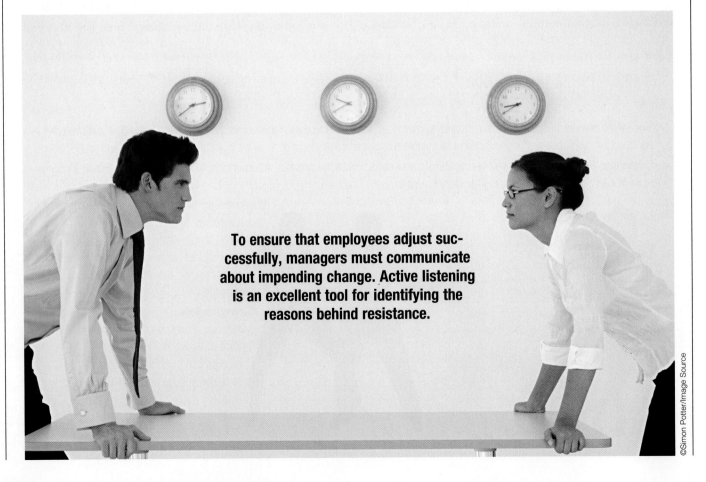

To ensure that employees adjust successfully, managers must communicate about impending change. Active listening is an excellent tool for identifying the reasons behind resistance.

©Simon Potter/Image Source

as using laptops and introducing new financial products. The introduction of such U.S. business practices is often referred to as "economic imperialism" by employees who feel they are being forced to substitute corporate values for personal or national values.

Hartford needed its European staff to understand that they were part of a transnational company. Its solution was to offer a stock ownership plan that tied the personal fortunes of the staff to the company. This gave employees a considerable interest in Hartford's success and helped them identify with the company.[47]

LEARNING OUTCOME 4

Lewin's Model for Managing Change

Kurt Lewin developed a model of the change process that has stood the test of time and continues to influence the way organizations manage planned change. Lewin's model is based on the idea of *force field analysis*.[48] Figure 18.1 shows a force field analysis of a decision to engage in exercise behavior. This model contends that a person's behavior is the product of two opposing forces: One force pushes toward preserving the status quo, and the other force pushes for change. When the two opposing forces are approximately equal, current behavior is maintained. For behavioral change to occur, the forces maintaining the status quo must be overcome. This can be accomplished by increasing the forces for change, by weakening the forces for the status quo, or by a combination of these actions.

Lewin's change model is a three-step process, as shown in Figure 18.2 on the next page. The process begins with **unfreezing**, which is a crucial first hurdle

in the change process. Unfreezing involves encouraging individuals to discard old behaviors by shaking up the equilibrium state that maintains the status quo. Change management literature has long advocated that certain individuals have personalities that make them more resistant to change. However, recent research indicates that only a small portion of a study's respondents (23 percent) displayed consistency in their reactions to three different kinds of change: structural, technological, and office relocation. The majority of respondents (77 percent) reacted differently to these different kinds of change, suggesting that reactions to change might be more situationally driven than was previously thought.[49] Organizations often accomplish unfreezing by eliminating the rewards for current behavior and showing that current behavior is not valued. In essence, individuals surrender by allowing the boundaries of their status quo to be opened in preparation for change.[50]

The second step in the change process is **moving**. In the moving stage, new attitudes, values, and behaviors are substituted for old ones. Organizations accomplish moving by initiating new options and explaining the rationale for the change, as well as by providing training to help employees develop the new skills they need. Employees should be given the overarching vision for the change so that they can establish their roles within the new organizational structure and processes.[51]

Refreezing is the final step in the change process. In this step, new attitudes, values, and behaviors are established as the new status quo. The new ways of operating are cemented in and reinforced. Managers should ensure that the organizational culture and formal reward systems encourage the new behaviors. Changes in the reward structure may be needed to ensure that the organization is not rewarding the old behaviors and merely hoping

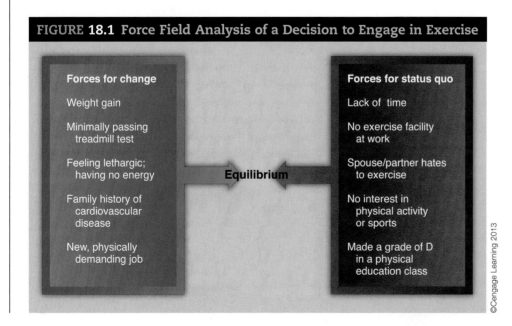

FIGURE **18.1** Force Field Analysis of a Decision to Engage in Exercise

Forces for change

Weight gain

Minimally passing treadmill test

Feeling lethargic; having no energy

Family history of cardiovascular disease

New, physically demanding job

Equilibrium

Forces for status quo

Lack of time

No exercise facility at work

Spouse/partner hates to exercise

No interest in physical activity or sports

Made a grade of D in a physical education class

©Cengage Learning 2013

unfreezing

The first step in Lewin's change model, in which individuals are encouraged to discard old behaviors by shaking up the equilibrium state that maintains the status quo.

moving

The second step in Lewin's change model, in which new attitudes, values, and behaviors are substituted for old ones.

refreezing

The final step in Lewin's change model, in which new attitudes, values, and behaviors are established as the new status quo.

FIGURE 18.2 Lewin's Change Model

©Cengage Learning 2013

Unfreezing	Moving	Refreezing →
Reducing forces for status quo	Developing new attitudes, values, and behaviors	Reinforcing new attitudes, values, and behaviors

and fully. Conversely, organizations whose members' values conflict with the changes may display "superficial conformity," in which members pay lip service to the changes but ultimately revert to their old behaviors.[53]

for the new behaviors. A study by Exxon Research and Engineering showed that framing and displaying a mission statement in managers' offices may eventually change the behavior of 2 percent of the managers. In contrast, changing managers' evaluation and reward systems will change the behavior of 55 percent of the managers almost overnight.[52]

The approach used by Monsanto to increase opportunities for women within the company is an illustration of how to use Lewin's model effectively. First, Monsanto emphasized unfreezing by helping employees debunk negative stereotypes about women in business. This also helped overcome resistance to change. Second, Monsanto moved employees' attitudes and behaviors through diversity training in which differences were emphasized as positive, and supervisors learned ways of training and developing female employees. Third, Monsanto changed its reward system so that managers were evaluated and paid according to how they coached and promoted women, which helped refreeze the new attitudes and behaviors.

One frequently overlooked issue is whether or not the change is consistent with the company's deeply held core values. Value consistency is critical to making a change "stick." Organizations whose members perceive the changes to be consistent with the firm's values adopt the changes much more easily

organization development (OD)

A systematic approach to organizational improvement that applies behavioral science theory and research in order to increase individual and organizational well-being and effectiveness.

LEARNING OUTCOME 5

Determining the Need for Organization Development Interventions

Related to change is the subject of *organization development*, a method that consists of various programs for making organizations more effective. **Organization development (OD)** is defined as a systematic approach to organizational improvement that applies behavioral science theory and research in order to increase individual and organizational well-being and effectiveness.[54] This definition implies certain characteristics. First, as a systematic approach to planned change, OD is a structured cycle of diagnosing organizational problems and opportunities and then applying expertise to them. Second, OD is grounded in solid research and theory. It involves the application of behavioral science knowledge to the challenges that organizations face. Third, OD recognizes the

HOW TO UNFREEZE

R esearch shows that leaders need to take care in how they unfreeze and refreeze their followers because employees will often embellish and retell a leader's stories in ways counterproductive to the change effort. For example, consider a manager who wants to implement change in a sales process. She may attempt to unfreeze the current process by stating it is cumbersome and causes missed sales. Instead of interpreting this explanation to mean that the process needs to be improved upon (as the manager intended), an employee may retell the story stating that the sales department is in jeopardy because of excessive missed sales.

SOURCES: S. Sonenshein, "We're Changing—Or Are We? Untangling the Role of Progressive, Regressive, and Stability Narratives During Strategic Change Implementation," *Academy of Management Journal* 53 (2010): 477–512; W. L. French and C. H. Bell, *Organization Development: Behavioral Science Interventions for Organization Improvement*, 4th ed. (Englewood Cliffs, N.J.: Prentice Hall, 1990); W. W. Burke, *Organization Development: A Normative View* (Reading, Mass: Addison-Wesley, 1987).

©Thinkstock/Jupiterimages

reciprocal relationship between individuals and organizations. It acknowledges that for organizations to change, individuals must change. Finally, OD is goal oriented. It is a process that seeks to improve both individual and organizational well-being and effectiveness.

Prior to deciding on a method of intervention, managers must carefully diagnose the problem they are attempting to address. Diagnosis and needs analysis is a critical first step in any OD intervention. Following this, an intervention method is chosen and applied. Finally, a thorough follow-up of the OD process is conducted. Figure 18.3 presents the OD cycle, a continuous process of moving the organization and its employees toward effective functioning.

Diagnosis and Needs Analysis

Before any intervention is planned, a thorough organizational diagnosis should be conducted. Diagnosis is an essential first step for any organization development intervention.[55] The term *diagnosis* comes from two Greek words, *dia* (through) and *gnosis* (knowledge). Thus, the diagnosis should pinpoint specific problems and areas in need of improvement. Six areas to examine carefully are the organization's purpose, structure, reward system, support systems, relationships, and leadership.[56]

Harry Levinson's diagnostic approach asserts that the process should begin by identifying where the pain (the problem) in the organization is, what it is like, how long it has been happening, and what has already been done about it.[57] Then a four-part, comprehensive diagnosis can begin. The first part of the diagnosis involves achieving an understanding of the organization's history. In the second part, the organization as a whole is analyzed to obtain data about its structure and processes. In the third part, interpretive data about attitudes, relationships, and current organizational functioning are gathered. In the fourth part of the diagnosis, the data are analyzed and conclusions are reached. In each stage of the diagnosis, the data can be gathered using a variety of methods, including observation, interviews, questionnaires, and archival records.

[Do We Need to Change?]

The diagnostic process may yield the conclusion that change is necessary. As part of the diagnosis, it is important to address the following issues:

> What are the forces for change?
> What are the forces preserving the status quo?
> What are the most likely sources of resistance to change?
> What are the goals to be accomplished by the change?

This information constitutes a force field analysis, as discussed earlier in the chapter.

A *needs analysis* is another crucial step in managing change. This is an analysis of the skills and competencies that employees must have to achieve the goals of the change. A needs analysis is essential because interventions such as training programs must target these skills and competencies.

Hundreds of alternative OD intervention methods exist. One way of classifying these methods is by the target of change, which can be the organization, groups within the organization, or individuals.

Group-Focused Techniques for OD Intervention

Some OD intervention methods emphasize changing the organization itself or changing the work groups within the organization rather than targeting the employees as individuals. Intervention methods in this category include survey feedback, management by objectives, product and service quality programs, team building, and process consultation.

Survey Feedback

Survey feedback is a widely used intervention method whereby employee attitudes are solicited using a questionnaire. Once the data are collected, they are analyzed and fed back to the

---

FIGURE 18.3 The Organization Development Cycle

Diagnosis and needs analysis → Intervention → Follow-up → (back to Diagnosis and needs analysis)

©Cengage Learning 2013

survey feedback
A widely used intervention method whereby employee attitudes are solicited using a questionnaire.

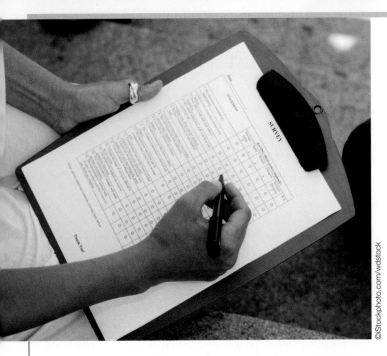
©iStockphoto.com/wdstock

Management by Objectives

As an organization-wide technique, **management by objectives (MBO)** involves joint goal setting between employees and managers. The MBO process includes the setting of initial objectives, periodic progress reviews, and problem solving to remove any obstacles to goal achievement.[59] All these steps are joint efforts between managers and employees.

MBO is a valuable intervention because it meets three needs. First, it clarifies what is expected of employees. This reduces role conflict and ambiguity. Second, MBO provides knowledge of results, an essential ingredient in effective job performance. Finally, MBO provides an opportunity for coaching and counseling by the manager. The problem-solving approach encourages open communication and discussion of obstacles to goal achievement.[60]

Companies that have used MBO successfully include the former Tenneco, Mobil (now part of ExxonMobil), and General Electric. The success of MBO in effecting organizational results hinges on the linking of individual goals to the goals of the organization.[61] MBO programs should be used with caution, however. An excessive emphasis on goal achievement can result in cutthroat competition among employees, falsification of results, and striving for results at any cost.

Product and Service Quality Programs

Quality programs—programs that embed product and service quality excellence in the organizational culture—are assuming key roles in the organization development efforts of many companies. The success or failure of a service company may hinge on the quality of customer service it provides.[62] Even manufacturing companies need high-quality customer service in addition to high-quality products. Toyota Motor Corporation constantly finds ways to integrate cutting-edge technological innovations with the growing pains of global expansion. The famed "Toyota Way" of doing business is focused on two key principles: continuous improvement focused on innovation and respect for people.[63]

Team Building

Team building programs can improve the effectiveness of work groups. Usually they begin with a diagnostic process through which team members identify problems and continue with the team planning actions to resolve those problems. The OD practitioner in team building serves as a facilitator, and the work itself is completed by team members.[64]

Team building is a very popular OD method. A survey of *Fortune* 500 companies indicated that human resource managers considered team building the most successful OD technique.[65] Managers are particularly interested in building teams that can learn. To build *learning teams*,

employees to diagnose problems and plan other interventions. Survey feedback is often used as an exploratory tool and then is combined with some other intervention. The effectiveness of survey feedback in actually improving outcomes (e.g., absenteeism or productivity) increases substantially when this method is combined with other interventions.[58] Furthermore, the effectiveness of this technique is contingent upon trust between management and subordinates, and this can be reinforced through the anonymity and confidentiality of survey responses.

For survey feedback to be an effective method, certain guidelines should be used. Employees must be assured that their responses to the questionnaire will be confidential and anonymous. Feedback should be reported in a group format. Employees must be able to trust that negative repercussions will not result from their responses. Employees should be informed of the purpose of the survey. Failing to do this can set up unrealistic expectations about the changes that might come from the surveys.

In addition, management must be prepared to follow up on the survey results. If some things cannot be changed, the rationale (e.g., prohibitive cost) must be explained to the employees. Without appropriate follow-through, employees will not take the survey process seriously the next time.

management by objectives (MBO)

An organization-wide intervention technique that involves joint goal setting between employees and managers.

quality program

A program that embeds product and service quality excellence in the organizational culture.

team building

An intervention designed to improve the effectiveness of a work group.

members must be encouraged to seek feedback, discuss errors, reflect on successes and failures, and experiment with new ways of performing. Mistakes should be analyzed for ways to improve, and a climate of mutual support should be developed. Leaders of learning teams are good coaches who promote a climate of psychological safety so that team members feel comfortable discussing problems.[66]

One popular technique for team building is the use of outdoor challenges. Participants go through a series of outdoor activities, such as climbing a fourteen-foot wall. Similar physical challenges require the participants to work as a team and focus on trust, communication, decision making, and leadership. GE and Weyerhaeuser use outdoor challenges at the beginning of their team-building courses, and later in the training, team members apply what they have learned to actual business situations.[67] One innovative firm called Teambuilding, Inc, uses rowing as a team-building exercise. It enlisted the services of an Olympic gold medalist, Dan Lyons, to design a seminar focused on team building using rowing as the central organizing theme. This activity encourages participants to practice leadership, communication, goal setting, conflict management, and motivation. GE Healthcare, ING Direct, and Wyeth Corporate Communications have all used this technique for their team-building programs as well.[68] Preliminary studies confirm the idea that team building can improve group processes.[69]

Process Consultation

Pioneered by Edgar Schein, **process consultation** is an OD method that helps managers and employees improve the processes that are used in organizations.[70] The processes most often targeted are communication, conflict resolution, decision making, group interaction, and leadership.

One of the distinguishing features of process consultation is that an outside consultant is used. The role of the

> ## " To build *learning teams*, members must be encouraged to seek feedback, discuss errors, reflect on successes and failures, and experiment with new ways of performing.

consultant is to help employees help themselves. In this way, the ownership of a successful outcome rests with the employees.[71] The consultant guides the organization members in examining the processes in the organization and in refining them. The steps in process consultation are entering the organization, defining the relationship, choosing an approach, gathering data and diagnosing problems, intervening, and gradually leaving the organization.

Process consultation is an interactive technique between employees and an outside consultant, so it is seldom used as a sole OD method. Most often it is used in combination with other OD interventions.

All the preceding OD methods focus on changing the organization or the work group, whereas the following OD methods are aimed at individual change.

LEARNING OUTCOME **7**

Individual-Focused Techniques for OD Intervention

OD efforts that are targeted at individuals include skills training, leadership training and development, executive coaching, role negotiation, job redesign, health promotion programs, and career planning.

This cord is called an andon cord. It runs the length of every Toyota assembly line, and any worker who encounters a quality problem is allowed to pull it and stop the line.

Rui Viera/PA Wire/AP Images

process consultation
An OD method that helps managers and employees improve the processes that are used in organizations.

Skills Training

The key question addressed by **skills training** is "What knowledge, skills, and abilities are necessary to do this job effectively?" Skills training is accomplished either in formal classroom settings or on the job. The challenge is integrating skills training into OD in today's rapidly changing organizational environments. The job knowledge in most positions requires continual updates to keep pace with rapid change.

Leadership Training and Development

Companies invest millions of dollars in **leadership training and development**, a term that encompasses a variety of techniques that are designed to enhance individuals' leadership skills. One popular technique is to send future leaders to off-site training classes. Research shows that this type of education experience can have some impact, but participants' enthusiastic return to work may be short-lived due to the challenges and realities of work life. Classroom learning alone thus has a limited effect on leadership skills.

The best leadership training and development programs combine classroom learning with on-the-job experiences. One way of accomplishing development is through the use of *action learning*, a technique that was pioneered in Europe.[72] In action learning, leaders take on unfamiliar problems or familiar problems in unfamiliar settings. The leaders work on the problems and meet weekly in small groups made up of individuals from different organizations. The outcome of action learning is that leaders learn about themselves through the challenges of their comrades. Other techniques that provide action learning for participants are simulation, business games, role-playing, and case studies.[73]

Eli Lilly has an action-learning program that pulls together eighteen future company leaders and gives them a strategic business issue to resolve. For six weeks, the trainees meet with experts, best-practices organizations, and customers, and then present their recommendations to top brass. One action-learning team was charged with coming up with an e-business strategy; their plan was so good that executives immediately implemented it. At Eli Lilly and other firms, action-learning programs provide developmental experiences for leaders and result in useful initiatives for the company.[74]

Leadership training and development is an ongoing process that takes considerable time and effort. There are no quick fixes. At IBM, managers are held accountable for leadership development. In fact, IBM's managers will not be considered for promotion into senior executive positions unless they have a record of developing leaders. Top management must be committed to the process of leadership training and development if it wants to create a pipeline of high-potential employees to fill leadership positions.[75]

Executive Coaching

Executive coaching is a technique in which managers or executives are paired with a coach in a partnership to help the executive perform more efficiently. Although coaching is usually done in a one-on-one manner, it is sometimes attempted in groups. The popularity of executive coaching has increased dramatically in recent years. The International Coach Federation, a group that trains and accredits executive coaches, doubled its membership in just two years of existence to 7,000 members in thirty-five countries.

Coaching is typically a special investment in top-level managers. Coaches provide another set of eyes and ears and help executives see beyond their own blinders. They elicit solutions and ideas from the client rather than making suggestions. Thus they develop and enhance the talents and capabilities within the client. Many coaching arrangements focus on developing the emotional intelligence of the client executive

©iStockphoto.com/Christopher Hudson

and may use a 360-degree assessment in which the executive, her boss, peers, subordinates, and even family members rate the executive's emotional competencies.[76] This information is then fed back to the executive, and along with the coach, a development plan is put in place.

Good coaches form strong connections with clients, exhibit professionalism, and deliver forthright, candid feedback. The top reasons executives seek out coaches are to make personal behavior changes, enhance their effectiveness, and foster stronger relationships. Does executive coaching pay off? Evidence suggests that successful coaching can result in sustained changes in executives' behavior, increased self-awareness and understanding, and more effective leadership competencies.[77] In one study, for example, executives who worked with executive coaches were more likely to set specific goals, ask for feedback from their supervisors, and were rated as better performers by their supervisors and subordinates when compared to executives who simply received feedback from surveys.[78] Effective coaching relationships depend on a professional, experienced coach, an executive who is motivated to learn and change, and a good fit between the two.

Role Negotiation

Individuals who work together sometimes have differing expectations of one another within the working relationship. **Role negotiation** is a technique whereby individuals meet and clarify their psychological contract, that is, their expectations of each other. The outcome of role negotiation is a better understanding between the two parties. When both parties have a mutual agreement on expectations, there is less ambiguity in the process of working together.

Job Redesign

As an OD intervention method, **job redesign** alters jobs to improve the fit between individual skills and the demands of the job. Chapter 14 outlined several approaches to job design. Many of these methods are used as OD techniques for realigning task demands and individual capabilities or for redesigning jobs to fit new techniques or organizational structures better.

Ford Motor Company has redesigned virtually all of its manufacturing jobs, shifting workers from individual to team-based roles in which they have greater control of their work and can take the initiative to improve products and production techniques. Ford began trying this technique more than a decade ago and found that it not only improved employee job satisfaction but also productivity and product quality.

Another form of job redesign is telecommuting. Companies including American Express, AT&T, and Merrill Lynch have significant numbers of employees who work this way. When AT&T surveyed its managers to assess the impact of telecommuting, 76 percent were happier with their jobs and 79 percent were happier with their careers in general since they began telecommuting.[79]

Health Promotion Programs

As organizations have become increasingly concerned with the costs of distress in the workplace, health promotion programs have become a part of larger OD efforts. In Chapter 7, we examined stress and strain at work. To relieve stress and strain, companies such as AT&T, Caterpillar, Kimberly-Clark, and Johnson & Johnson have successfully integrated health promotion programs into their organizations.

The American Psychological Association recognizes companies for innovative programs that support psychologically healthy work environments. Past winners included *El Nuevo Día* and Green Mountain Coffee Roasters. *El Nuevo Día* is the most popular newspaper in Puerto Rico and offers healthcare benefits to its employees at no cost, after-work fitness programs, and quarterly health publications designed to prevent stress and maintain a healthy lifestyle. Green Mountain

role negotiation

A technique whereby individuals meet and clarify their psychological contract.

job redesign

An OD intervention method that alters jobs to improve the fit between individual skills and the demands of the job.

©iStockphoto.com/Andresr

As organizations have become increasingly concerned with the costs of distress in the workplace, health promotion programs have become a part of larger OD efforts.

Coffee Roasters has yoga, meditation, and physical therapy programs to reduce work-related stress and injury. It pays for 90 percent of healthcare costs of its full-time employees. Furthermore, it reimburses each employee up to $400 per year for participation in wellness programs, health club memberships, or smoking cessation programs.[80]

Although companies have long recognized the importance of maintenance on their machinery, many are only recently learning that their human assets need maintenance as well, and they are supplying that need in the form of employee wellness and health promotion activities. These programs focus on helping employees manage their stress and prevent health problems.

Career Planning

Matching an individual's career aspirations with the opportunities in the organization is career planning. This proactive approach to career management is often part of an organization's development efforts although it is a joint responsibility of organizations and individuals. Certainly career-planning activities benefit both the organization and its individuals. Through counseling sessions, employees identify their skills and skill deficiencies. The organization then can plan its training and development efforts based on this information. In addition, the process can be used to identify and nurture talented employees for potential promotion.

To sum up, managers can choose from a host of organization development techniques to facilitate organizational change. Large-scale changes in organizations require the use of multiple techniques. For example, implementing a new technology

ARE ORGANIZATION DEVELOPMENT EFFORTS EFFECTIVE?

Since organization development is designed to help organizations manage change, it is important to evaluate the effectiveness of these efforts. The success of any OD intervention depends on a host of factors, including the technique used, the competence of the change agent, the organization's readiness for change, and top management commitment. No single method of OD is effective in every instance. Instead, multiple-method OD approaches are recommended because they allow organizations to capitalize on the benefits of several approaches.[81]

Efforts to evaluate OD effects have focused on outcomes such as productivity. One review of more than 200 interventions indicated that worker productivity improved in 87 percent of the cases.[82] We can conclude that when properly applied and managed, organization development programs have positive effects on performance.[83]

like robotics may require simultaneous changes in the structure of the organization, the configuration of work groups, and individual attitudes.

We should recognize at this point that the OD methods just described are means to an end. Programs do not drive change; business needs do. The OD methods are merely vehicles for moving the organization and its employees in a more effective direction.

Log in to the **CourseMate** for *ORGB3* at **www.cengagebrain.com** to:

❋ Review **Key Terms Flash Cards** online

❋ Play **Beat the Clock** and **Quiz Bowl** to master concepts

❋ Complete **web quizzes** to prepare for exams

❋ Watch the video on **Holden Outerwear** and from *Field of Dreams* for examples, then test yourself with a quick quiz

❋ Work through the **"What about You?"** and **Ethical Dilemma** exercises to see how you would handle various situations that organizations face on a daily basis

Notes

Chapter 1

1. H. Schwartz, "The Clockwork or the Snakepit: An Essay on the Meaning of Teaching Organizational Behavior," *Organizational Behavior Teaching Review* 11, No. 2 (1987): 19–26.

2. Rath and Strong Management Consultants, "Creating an Energized Organization," http://www.rathstrong.com/whitepaper_creatingenergized .htm, accessed June 27, 2008.

3. H. G. Barkem, J. A. C. Baum, and E. A. Mannix, "Management Challenges in a New Time," *Academy of Management Journal* 45 (2002): 916–930.

4. K. Lewin, "Field Theory in Social Science: Selected Theoretical Papers" (edited by Dorin Cartwright) (New York: Harper, 1951).

5. N. Schmitt, ed., Industrial/Organizational Section in *Encyclopedia of Psychology* (Washington, D.C.: American Psychological Association, and New York: Oxford University Press, 2000).

6. R. M. Yerkes, "The Relation of Psychology to Military Activities," *Mental Hygiene* 1 (1917): 371–376.

7. R. Lopopolo, "Development of the Professional Role Behaviors Survey (PROBES)," *Physical Therapy* 81 (July 2001): 1317–1327.

8. F. W. Taylor, *The Principles of Scientific Management* (New York: Norton, 1911).

9. E. A. Locke and G. P. Latham, *A Theory of Goal Setting and Task Performance* (Englewood Cliffs, N.J.: Prentice-Hall, 1990).

10. A. L. Wilkins and W. G. Ouchi, "Efficient Cultures: Exploring the Relationship between Culture and Organizational Performance," *Administrative Science Quarterly* 28 (1983): 468–481.

11. M. F. R. Kets de Vries and D. Miller, "Personality, Culture, and Organization," *Academy of Management Review* 11 (1986): 266–279.

12. H. Schwartz, *Narcissistic Process and Corporate Decay: The Theory of the Organizational Ideal* (New York: NYU Press, 1990).

13. J. G. March and H. A. Simon, *Organizations* (New York: Wiley, 1958).

14. H. B. Elkind, *Preventive Management: Mental Hygiene in Industry* (New York: B. C. Forbes, 1931).

15. J. C. Quick, "Occupational Health Psychology: Historical Roots and Future Directions," *Health Psychology* 18 (1999): 82–88.

16. R. Eby and D. Mahone, "How to use ergonomics as a loss control tool," *Risk Management* (March 1, 1991).

17. "Workplace Initiative Reduces Headaches, Neck and Shoulder Pain," *Occupational Health and Safety* (June 10, 2008), http://www .ohsonline.com/articles/64148.

18. B. M. Staw, L. E. Sandelands, and J. E. Dutton, "Threat-Rigidity Effects in Organizational Behavior: A Multilevel Analysis," *Administrative Science Quarterly* 26 (1981): 501–524.

19. D. Kirkpatrick, "The Net Makes It All Easier—Including Exporting U.S. Jobs," *Fortune* (May 26, 2003): 146.

20. C. Crosby, "Quest for Talent Is Driving Evolution in Outsourcing," *Banking Wire* (June 25, 2008): 59.

21. E. V. Brown, Vice President of Global Business Development, Alberto Culver, Inc., "Commencement Address—College of Business Administration, the University of Texas at Arlington" (December 2003).

22. T. Reay, K. Golden-Biddle, and K. Germann, "Legitimizing a New Role: Small Wins and Microprocesses of Change," *Academy of Management Journal* 49 (2006): 977–998.

23. R. L. A. Sterba, "The Organization and Management of the Temple Corporations in Ancient Mesopotamia," *Academy of Management Review* 1 (1976): 16–26; S. P. Dorsey, *Early English Churches in America* (New York: Oxford University Press, 1952).

24. Sir I. Moncreiffe of That Ilk, *The Highland Clans: The Dynastic Origins, Chiefs, and Background of the Clans and of Some Other Families Connected to Highland History,* rev. ed. (New York: C. N. Potter, 1982); D. Shambaugh, "The Soldier and the State in China: The Political Work System in the People's Liberation Army," *Chinese Quarterly* 127 (1991): 527–568.

25. L. L'Abate, ed., *Handbook of Developmental Family Psychology and Psychopathology* (New York: Wiley, 1993); J. A. Hostetler, *Communitarian Societies* (New York: Holt, Rinehart & Winston, 1974).

26. J. M. Lewis, "The Family System and Physical Illness," in *No Single Thread: Psychological Health in Family Systems* (New York: Brunner/Mazel, 1976).

27. D. Katz and R. L. Kahn, *The Social Psychology of Organizations,* 2nd ed. (New York: John Wiley, 1978); H. J. Leavitt, "Applied Organizational Change in Industry: Structural, Technological, and Humanistic Approaches," in J. G. March, ed., *Handbook of Organizations* (Chicago: Rand McNally, 1965): 1144–1170.

28. J. D. Thompson, *Organizations in Action* (New York: McGraw-Hill, 1967).

29. M. Malone, "The Twitter Revolution," *The Wall Street Journal* (April 18, 2009): A11.

30. I. Brat, "Rebuilding after a Catastrophe," *The Wall Street Journal* (May 19, 2008): B1.

31. F. J. Roethlisberger and W. J. Dickson, *Management and the Worker* (Cambridge, Mass.: Harvard University Press, 1939).

32. W. L. French and C. H. Bell, *Organization Development,* 4th ed. (Englewood Cliffs, N.J.: Prentice-Hall, 1990).

33. S. G. Barsade and D. E. Gibson, "Why Does Affect Matter in Organizations?," *Academy of Management Perspectives,* 21 (2007): 36–59.

34. J. P. Kotter, "Managing External Dependence," *Academy of Management Review* 4 (1979): 87–92.

35. H. K. Steensma and D. G. Corley, "Organizational Context as a Moderator of Theories on Firm Boundaries for Technology Sourcing," *Academy of Management Journal* 44 (2001): 271–291.

36. T. B. Lawrence and V. Corwin, "Being There: The Acceptance and Marginalization of Part-Time Professional Employees," *Journal of Organizational Behavior* 24 (2003): 923–943.

37. M. K. Gowing, J. D. Kraft, and J. C. Quick, *The New Organizational Reality: Downsizing, Restructuring and Revitalization* (Washington, D.C.: American Psychological Association, 1998); T. Tang and R. M. Fuller, "Corporate Downsizing: What Managers Can Do to Lessen the Negative Effects of Layoffs," *SAM Advanced Management Journal* 60 (1995): 12–15, 31.

38. L. E. Thurow, *Head to Head: The Coming Economic Battle among Japan, Europe, and America* (New York: William Morrow, 1992).

39. J. E. Patterson, *Acquiring the Future: America's Survival and Success in the Global Economy* (Homewood, Ill.: Dow Jones-Irwin, 1990);

H. B. Stewart, *Recollecting the Future: A View of Business, Technology, and Innovation in the Next 30 Years* (Homewood, Ill.: Dow Jones-Irwin, 1989).

40. D. Ciampa, *Total Quality* (Reading, Mass.: Addison-Wesley, 1992).

41. T. J. Douglas and W. Q. Judge, Jr., "Total Quality Management Implementation and Competitive Advantage: The Role of Structural Control and Exploration," *Academy of Management Journal* 44 (2001): 158–169.

42. American Management Association, *Blueprints for Service Quality: The Federal Express Approach* (New York: American Management Association, 1991); P. R. Thomas, L. J. Gallace, and K. R. Martin, *Quality Alone Is Not Enough* (New York: American Management Association, 1992).

43. J. de Mast, "A Methodological Comparison of Three Strategies for Quality Improvement," *International Journal of Quality & Reliability Management* 21 (2004): 198–213.

44. M. Barney, "Motorola's Second Generation," *Six Sigma Forum Magazine* 1, No. 3 (May 2002): 13.

45. S. Shahabudin, "Six Sigma: Issues and Problems," *International Journal of Productivity and Quality Management* 3 (2008): 145–160.

46. J. A. Edosomwan, "Six Commandments to Empower Employees for Quality Improvement," *Industrial Engineering* 24 (1992): 14–15.

47. G. H. W. Bush, "Remarks at the Presentation Ceremony for the Malcolm Baldrige National Quality Awards" (speech, December 13, 1990).

48. See also the five articles in the Special Research Forum on Teaching Effectiveness in the Organizational Sciences, *The Academy of Management Journal* 40 (1997): 1265–1398.

49. L. Proserpio and D. A. Gioia, "Teaching the Virtual Generation," *Academy of Management Learning & Education* 6 (2007): 69–80.

50. R. M. Steers, L. W. Porter, and G. A. Bigley, *Motivation and Leadership at Work* (New York: McGraw-Hill, 1996).

51. H. Levinson, *Executive Stress* (New York: New American Library, 1975).

52. D. L. Whetzel, "The Department of Labor Identifies Workplace Skills," *Industrial/Organizational Psychologist* 29 (1991): 89–90.

53. D. A. Whetton and K. S. Cameron, *Developing Management Skills,* 3rd ed. (New York: HarperCollins, 1995).

54. U.S. Department of Labor 21st Century Workforce Office, http://www.dol.gov/21cw.

55. C. Argyris and D. A. Schon, *Organizational Learning: A Theory of Action Perspective* (Reading, Mass.: Addison-Wesley, 1978).

56. A. Y. Kolb and D. A. Kolb, "Learning Styles and Learning Spaces: Enhancing Experiential Learning in Higher Education, *Academy of Management Learning & Education* 4 (2005): 193–212.

Chapter 2

1. M. A. Hitt, R. E. Hoskisson, and J. S. Harrison, "Strategic Competitiveness in the 1990s: Challenges and Opportunities for U.S. Executives," *Academy of Management Executive* 5 (1991): 7–22.

2. H. G. Barkem, J. A. C. Baum, and E. A. Mannix, "Management Challenges in a New Time," *Academy of Management Journal* 45 (2002): 916–930.

3. S. C. Harper, "The Challenges Facing CEOs: Past, Present, and Future," *Academy of Management Executive* 6 (1992): 7–25; T. R. Mitchell and W. G. Scott, "America's Problems and Needed Reforms: Confronting the Ethic of Personal Advantage," *Academy of Management Executive* 4 (1990): 23–25.

4. K. Sera, "Corporate Globalization: A New Trend," *Academy of Management Executive* 6 (1992): 89–96.

5. K. Ohmae, *Borderless World: Power and Strategies in the Interlinked Economy* (New York: Harper & Row, 1990).

6. C. A. Bartlett and S. Ghoshal, *Managing across Borders: The Transnational Solution* (Boston: Harvard Business School Press, 1989).

7. F. Warner, "Learning How to Speak to Gen Y," *Fast Company* 72 (July 2003): 36–37.

8. K. R. Xin and J. L. Pearce, "Guanxi: Connections as Substitutes for Formal Institutional Support," *Academy of Management Journal* 39 (1996): 1641–1658.

9. P. S. Chan, "Franchise Management in East Asia," *Academy of Management Executive* 4 (1990): 75–85.

10. H. Weihrich, "Europe 1992: What the Future May Hold," *Academy of Management Executive* 4 (1990): 7–18.

11. E. H. Schein, "Coming to a New Awareness of Organizational Culture," *MIT Sloan Management Review* 25 (1984): 3–16.

12. S. S. Sarwano and R. M. Armstrong, "Microcultural Differences and Perceived Ethical Problems: An International Business Perspective," *Journal of Business Ethics* 30 (2001): 41–56.

13. F. Warner, "Learning How to Speak to Gen Y," *Fast Company* 72 (July 2003): 36–37.

14. R. Sharpe, "Hi-Tech Taboos," *The Wall Street Journal* (October 31, 1995): A1.

15. G. Hofstede, *Culture's Consequences: International Differences in Work-Related Values* (Beverly Hills, Calif.: Sage Publications, 1980). G. Hofstede, "Motivation, Leadership, and Organization: Do American Theories Apply Abroad?" *Organizational Dynamics* (Summer 1980): 42–63.

16. G. M. Spreitzer, M. W. McCall, Jr., and J. D. Mahoney, "Early Identification of International Executive Potential," *Journal of Applied Psychology* 82 (1997): 6–29.

17. M. A. Hitt, L. Bierman, K. Uhlenbruck, and K. Shimizu, "The Importance of Resources in the Internationalization of Professional Service Firms: The Good, the Bad, and the Ugly," *Academy of Management Journal* 49 (2006): 1137–1157.

18. A. J. Michel, "Goodbyes Can Cost Plenty in Europe," *Fortune* (April 6, 1992): 16.

19. G. Hofstede, "Gender Stereotypes and Partner Preferences of Asian Women in Masculine and Feminine Countries," *Journal of Cross Cultural Psychology* 27 (1996): 533–546.

20. G. Hofstede, "Cultural Constraints in Management Theories," *Academy of Management Executive* 7 (1993): 81–94.

21. "IBM Offers Employees New 'Learning Accounts' and Global Training Programs," *InformationWeek* (July 26, 2007).

22. J. Sandberg, "Global-Market Woes Are More Personality Than Nationality," *The Wall Street Journal* (January 29, 2008).

23. L. R. Offerman and M. K. Growing, "Organizations of the Future," *American Psychologist* 45 (1990): 95–108.

24. J. Chatman, J. Polzer, S. Barsade, and M. Neale, "Being Different Yet Feeling Similar: The Influence of Demographic Composition and Organizational Culture on Work Processes and Outcomes," *Administrative Science Quarterly* 43 (1998): 749–780.

25. S. Caudron, "Task Force Report Reveals Coke's Progress on Diversity," *Workforce* 82 (2003): 40, http://www.workforceonline.com/section/03/feature/23/42/44/234246.html.

26. S. Prasso, "Google Goes to India," *Fortune* (October 29, 2007).

27. U.S. Department of Labor, http://stats.bls.gov/data/home.htm.

28. "Degrees Earned by Women," *Indicator* 27 (2008), http://nces.ed.gov/programs/coe/2008/section3/indicator27.asp.

29. Catalyst, *2007 Catalyst Census of Women Corporate Officers and Top Earners of the Fortune 500*, http://catalyst.org/publication/13/2007-catalyst-census-of-women-corporate-officers-and-top-earners-of-the-fortune-500.

30. D. de Lafuente, "The Elite Eight: Pink's Top Companies for Women—2007," *Pink* (August–September 2007): 67–73.

31. U.S. Department of Labor, "Highlights of Women's Earnings in 2005," Report 995 (September 2006): 33; Catalyst, *Catalyst Census of Women Corporate Officers and Top Earners* (2001).

32. A. M. Morrison, R. P. White, E. Van Velsor, and the Center for Creative Leadership, *Breaking the Glass Ceiling: Can Women Reach the Top of America's Largest Corporations?* (Reading, Mass.: Addison-Wesley, 1987).

33. D. E. Arfken, S. L. Bellar, and M. M. Helms, "The Ultimate Glass Ceiling Revisited: The Presence of Women on Corporate Boards," *Journal of Business Ethics* 50 (March 2004): 177–186.

34. D. L. Nelson and M. A. Hitt, "Employed Women and Stress: Implications for Enhancing Women's Mental Health in the Workplace," in J. C. Quick, L. R. Murphy, and J. J. Hurrell, Jr., eds., *Stress and Well-Being at Work* (Washington, D.C.: American Psychological Association, 1992): 164–177.

35. L. L. Martins and C. K. Parsons, "Effects of Gender Diversity Management on Perceptions of Organizational Attractiveness: The Role of Individual Differences in Attitudes and Beliefs," *Journal of Applied Psychology* 92 (2007): 865–875.

36. A. Eyring and B. A. Stead, "Shattering the Glass Ceiling: Some Successful Corporate Practices," *Journal of Business Ethics* 17 (1998): 245–251.

37. Catalyst, *Advancing Women in Business: The Catalyst Guide* (San Francisco: Jossey-Bass, 1998).

38. U.S. Department of Health and Human Services, *Profile of Older Americans* (Washington, D.C.: U.S. Government, 1997).

39. W. B. Johnston, "Global Workforce 2000: The New World Labor Market," *Harvard Business Review* 69 (1991): 115–127.

40. S. Needleman, "The Last Office Perk: Getting Paid to Volunteer," *The Wall Street Journal* (April 29, 2008): D1, D5.

41. J. Li, C. W. L. Chu, K. C. K. Lam, and S. Liao, "Age Diversity and Firm Performance in an Emerging Economy," *Human Resource Management* 50, No. 2 (March–April 2011): 247–270.

42. S. E. Jackson and E. B. Alvarez, "Working through Diversity as a Strategic Imperative," in S. E. Jackson, ed., *Diversity in the Workplace: Human Resources Initiatives* (New York: Guilford Press, 1992), 13–36.

43. "Managing Generational Diversity," *HR Magazine* 36 (1991): 91–92.

44. K. Tyler, "The Tethered Generation," *HR Magazine* (May 2007): 41–46.

45. S. R. Rhodes, "Age-Related Differences in Work Attitudes and Behavior: A Review and Conceptual Analysis," *Psychological Bulletin* 93 (1983): 338–367.

46. B. L. Hassell and P. L. Perrewe, "An Examination of Beliefs about Older Workers: Do Stereotypes Still Exist?" *Journal of Organizational Behavior* 16 (1995): 457–468.

47. U.S. Bureau of the Census, *Population Profile of the United States, 1997* (Washington, D.C.: U.S. Government Printing Office, 1997).

48. W. J. Rothwell, "HRD and the Americans with Disabilities Act," *Training and Development Journal* (August 1991): 45–47.

49. J. J. Laabs, "The Golden Arches Provide Golden Opportunities," *Personnel Journal* (July 1991): 52–57.

50. L. Armstrong, "What Men Say behind Closed Doors," *Working Mother* (June–July 2008): 87–90.

51. J. E. Rigdon, "PepsiCo's KFC Scouts for Blacks and Women for Its Top Echelons," *The Wall Street Journal* (November 13, 1991): A1.

52. P. A. Galagan, "Tapping the Power of a Diverse Workforce," *Training and Development Journal* 26 (1991): 38–44.

53. C. L. Holladay, J. L. Knight, D. L. Paige, and M. A. Quinones, "The Influence of Framing on Attitudes toward Diversity Training," *Human Resource Development Quarterly* 14 (2003): 245–263.

54. R. Thomas, "From Affirmative Action to Affirming Diversity," *Harvard Business Review* 68 (1990): 107–117.

55. T. H. Cox, Jr., *Cultural Diversity in Organizations: Theory, Research and Practice* (San Francisco: Berrett-Koehler, 1994).

56. "Business Ethics 100 Best Corporate Citizens 2004," http://www.business-ethics.com/BE100_2004, accessed June 23, 2008.

57. M. R. Fusilier, C. D. Aby, Jr., J. K. Worley, and S. Elliott, "Perceived Seriousness of Business Ethics Issues," *Business and Professional Ethics Journal* 15 (1996): 67–78.

58. J. S. Mill, *Utilitarianism, Liberty, and Representative Government* (London: Dent, 1910).

59. K. H. Blanchard and N. V. Peale, *The Power of Ethical Management* (New York: Morrow, 1988).

60. A. Smith, *An Inquiry into the Nature and Causes of the Wealth of Nations*, vol. 10 of The Harvard Classics, ed. C. J. Bullock (New York: P. F. Collier & Son, 1909).

61. C. Fried, *Right and Wrong* (Cambridge, Mass.: Harvard University Press, 1978).

62. I. Kant, *Groundwork of the Metaphysics of Morals,* trans. H. J. Paton (New York: Harper & Row, 1964).

63. R. C. Solomon, "Corporate Roles, Personal Virtues: Aristotelean Approach to Business Ethics," *Business Ethics Quarterly* 2 (1992): 317–339; R. C. Solomon, *A Better Way to Think about Business: How Personal Integrity Leads to Corporate Success* (New York: Oxford University Press, 1999).

64. W. Bulkeley, "Email Software Delves into Employees' Contacts," *The Wall Street Journal* (April 21, 2008): B9.

65. D. Kemp, "Employers and AIDS: Dealing with the Psychological and Emotional Issues of AIDS in the Workplace," *American Review of Public Administration* 25 (1995): 263–278.

66. J. J. Koch, "Wells Fargo's and IBM's HIV Policies Help Protect Employees' Rights," *Personnel Journal* (April 1990): 40–48.

67. U.S. EEOC, "Discrimination Because of Sex under Title VII of the 1964 Civil Rights Act as Amended: Adoption of Interim Guidelines—Sexual Harassment," *Federal Register* 45 (1980): 25024–25025.

68. L. F. Fitzgerald, F. Drasgow, C. L. Hulin, M. J. Gelfand, and V. J. Magley, "Antecedents and Consequences of Sexual Harassment in Organizations: A Test of an Integrated Model," *Journal of Applied Psychology* 82 (1997): 578–589.

69. E. Felsenthal, "Rulings Open Way for Sex-Harass Cases," *The Wall Street Journal* (June 29, 1998): A10; S. J. Adler, "Lawyers Advise Concerns to Provide Precise Written Policy to Employees," *The Wall Street Journal* (October 9, 1991): B1.

70. K. T. Schneider, S. Swan, and L. F. Fitzgerald, "Job-Related and Psychological Effects of Sexual Harassment in the Workplace: Empirical Evidence from Two Organizations," *Journal of Applied Psychology* 82 (1997): 401–415.

71. A. M. O'Leary-Kelly, R. L. Paetzold, and R. W. Griffin, "Sexual Harassment as Aggressive Behavior: An Actor-Based Perspective," *Academy of Management Review* 25 (2000): 372–388.

72. L. M. Goldenhar, N. G. Swanson, J. J. Hurrell, Jr., A. Ruder, and J. Deddens, "Stressors and Adverse Outcomes for Female Construction Workers," *Journal of Occupational Health Psychology* 3 (1998): 19–32; C. S. Piotrkowski, "Gender Harassment, Job Satisfaction and Distress among Employed White and Minority Women," *Journal of Occupational Health Psychology* 3 (1998): 33–42.

73. R. A. Posthuma, C. P. Maertz, Jr., and J. B. Dworkin, "Procedural Justice's Relationship with Turnover: Explaining Past Inconsistent Findings," *Journal of Organizational Behavior* 28 (2007): 381–398.

74. D. Fields, M. Pang, and C. Chio, "Distributive and Procedural Justice as Predictors of Employee Outcomes in Hong Kong," *Journal of Organizational Behavior* 21 (2000): 547–562.

75. H. L. Laframboise, "Vile Wretches and Public Heroes: The Ethics of Whistleblowing in Government," *Canadian Public Administration* (Spring 1991): 73–78.

76. S. Covel, "Tours to Fair-Trade Farms Help Coffee Sellers Spread Word," *The Wall Street Journal* (March 11, 2008): B5.

77. D. B. Turban and D. W. Greening, "Corporate Social Performance and Organizational Attractiveness to Prospective Employees," *Academy of Management Journal* 40 (1996): 658–672.

78. R. Walker, "Sex vs. Ethics," *Fast Company* (June 2008): 74–78.

79. R. Nelson, *Technology, Institutions, and Economic Growth* (Cambridge: Harvard University Press, 2005); N. Sandler, "High Tech Puts Israel in the Black," *BusinessWeek Online* (May 14, 2008); http://infotrac-college.thomsonlearning.com/itw/infomark/196/855/37423363w16/purl=rc1_WAD_0_A178998281&dyn=23!xrn_4_0_A178998281?sw_aep=olr_wad, accessed June 24, 2008.

80. C. H. Ferguson, "Computers and the Coming of the U.S. Keiretsu," *Harvard Business Review* 68 (1990): 55–70.

81. J. Collins, *Good to Great: Why Some Companies Make the Leap . . . and Others Don't* (New York: HarperCollins, 2001).

82. J. A. Senn, *Information Systems in Management,* 4th ed. (Belmont, Calif.: Wadsworth, 1990).

83. D. K. Sorenson, O. Bouhaddou, and H. R. Warner, *Knowledge Engineering in Health Informatics* (New York: Springer, 1999).

84. M. T. Damore, "A Presentation and Examination of the Integration of Unlawful Discrimination Practices in the Private Business Sector with Artificial Intelligence" (Thesis, Oklahoma State University, 1992).

85. A. Tanzer and R. Simon, "Why Japan Loves Robots and We Don't," *Forbes* (April 16, 1990): 148–153.

86. E. Fingleton, "Jobs for Life: Why Japan Won't Give Them Up," *Fortune* (March 20, 1995): 119–125.

87. M. Iansitu, "How the Incumbent Can Win: Managing Technological Transitions in the Semiconductor Industry," *Management Science* 46 (2000): 169–185.

88. M. B. W. Fritz, S. Narasimhan, and H. Rhee, "Communication and Coordination in the Virtual Office," *Journal of Management Information Systems* 14 (1998): 7–28.

89. J. Langhoff, "A Telemanager's Index: The Definitive Roundup of Telecommuting Statistics—A Template for Telecommuting Contracts is Provided—Industry Trend or Event," *Home Office Computing* (April 1999), http://findarticles.com/p/articles/mi_m1563/is_4_17/ai_54256828/pg_2?tag=artBody;col1, accessed June 24, 2008.

90. M. Apgar, IV, "The Alternative Workplace: Changing Where and How People Work," *Harvard Business Review* (May–June 1998): 121–136.

91. D. L. Nelson, "Individual Adjustment to Information-Driven Technologies: A Critical Review," *MIS Quarterly* 14 (1990): 79–98.

92. S. Armour, "Hi, I'm Joan and I'm a Workaholic," *USA Today* (May 23, 2007).

93. M. Allen, "Legislation Could Restrict Bosses from Snooping on Their Workers," *The Wall Street Journal* (September 24, 1991): B1–B8.

94. V. Vara, "Pleasing Google's Tech-Savvy Staff: Information Officer Finds Security in Gadget Freedom of Choice," *The Wall Street Journal* (March 18, 2008), http://online.wsj.com/article/SB120578961450043169.html.

95. K. D. Hill and S. Kerr, "The Impact of Computer-Integrated Manufacturing Systems on the First Line Supervisor," *Journal of Organizational Behavior Management* 6 (1984): 81–87.

96. J. Anderson, "How Technology Brings Blind People into the Workplace," *Harvard Business Review* 67 (1989): 36–39.

97. D. L. Nelson and M. G. Kletke, "Individual Adjustment during Technological Innovation: A Research Framework," *Behaviour and Information Technology* 9 (1990): 257–271.

98. D. Mankin, T. Bikson, B. Gutek, and C. Stasz, "Managing Technological Change: The Process Is the Key," *Datamation* 34 (1988): 69–80.

Chapter 3

1. K. Lewin, "Formalization and Progress in Psychology," in D. Cartwright, ed., *Field Theory in Social Science* (New York: Harper, 1951).

2. N. S. Endler and D. Magnusson, "Toward an Interactional Psychology of Personality," *Psychological Bulletin* 83 (1976): 956–974.

3. J. R. Terborg, "Interactional Psychology and Research on Human Behavior in Organizations," *Academy of Management Review* 6 (1981): 561–576.

4. C. Spearman, "General Intelligence: Objectively Determined and Measured," *American Journal of Psychology* 15 (1904): 201–293.

5. F. L. Schmidt and J. Hunter, "General Mental Ability in the World of Work: Occupational Attainment and Job Performance," *Journal of Personality and Social Psychology* 86, No. 1 (2004): 162–173; C. Bertua, N. Anderson, and J. F Salgado, "The Predictive Validity of Cognitive Ability Tests: A UK Meta-Analysis," *Journal of Occupational and Organizational Psychology* 78 (2004): 387–409.

6. T. J. Bouchard, Jr., "Twins Reared Together and Apart: What They Tell Us about Human Diversity," in S. W. Fox, ed., *Individuality and Determinism* (New York: Plenum Press, 1984); R. D. Arvey, T. J. Bouchard, Jr., N. L. Segal, and L. M. Abraham, "Job Satisfaction: Environmental and Genetic Components," *Journal of Applied Psychology* 74 (1989): 235–248.

7. G. Allport, *Pattern and Growth in Personality* (New York: Holt, 1961).

8. R. B. Cattell, *Personality and Mood by Questionnaire* (San Francisco: Jossey-Bass, 1973).

9. J. M. Digman, "Personality Structure: Emergence of a Five-Factor Model," *Annual Review of Psychology* 41 (1990): 417–440.

10. T. A. Judge, J. J. Martocchio, and C. J. Thoresen, "Five-Factor Model of Personality and Employee Absence," *Journal of Applied Psychology* 82 (1997): 745–755.

11. H. J. Bernardin, D. K. Cooke, and P. Villanova, "Conscientiousness and Agreeableness as Predictors of Rating Leniency," *Journal of Applied Psychology* 85 (2000): 232–234.

12. S. E. Seibert and M. L. Kraimer, "The Five-Factor Model of Personality and Career Success," *Journal of Vocational Behavior* 58 (2001): 1–21.

13. T. A. Judge and R. Ilies, "Relationships of Personality to Performance Motivation: A Meta-Analytic Review," *Journal of Applied Psychology* 87 (2002): 797–807.

14. G. M. Hurtz and J. J. Donovan, "Personality and Job Performance: The Big Five Revisited," *Journal of Applied Psychology* 85 (2000): 869–879.

15. S. T. Bell, "Deep-Level Composition Variables as Predictors of Team Performance: A Meta-Analysis," *Journal of Applied Psychology* 92, No. 3 (2007): 595–615.

16. H. Le, I. S. Oh, S. B. Robbins, R. Ilies, E. Holland, and P. Westrick, "Too Much of a Good Thing: Curvilinear Relationships between Personality Traits and Job Performance," *Journal of Applied Psychology* 96 (2011): 113–133.

17. J. F. Salgado, S. Moscoso, and M. Lado, "Evidence of Cross-Cultural Invariance of the Big Five Personality Dimensions in Work Settings," *European Journal of Personality* 17 (2003): S67–S76; C. Rodriguez and T. H. Church, "The Structure and Personality Correlates of Affect in Mexico: Evidence of Cross-Cultural Comparability Using the Spanish Language," *Journal of Cross-Cultural Psychology* 34 (2003): 211–230.

18. H. C. Triandis, "Cultural Influences on Personality," *Annual Review of Psychology* 53 (2002): 133–160.

19. M. Moody, "Adaptive Behavior in Intercultural Environments: The Relationship between Cultural Intelligence Factors and Big Five Personality Traits" (Ph.D. thesis, George Washington University, 2007).

20. M. R. Barrick and M. K. Mount, "The Big Five Personality Dimensions and Job Performance: A Meta-Analysis," *Personnel Psychology* 44 (1991): 1–26.

21. D. D. Clark and R. Hoyle, "A Theoretical Solution to the Problem of Personality-Situational Interaction," *Personality and Individual Differences* 9 (1988): 133–138.

22. D. Byrne and L. J. Schulte, "Personality Dimensions as Predictors of Sexual Behavior," in J. Bancroft, ed., *Annual Review of Sexual Research*, vol. 1 (Philadelphia: Society for the Scientific Study of Sex, 1990).

23. P. Harms, B. Roberts, and D. Wood, "Who Shall Lead? An Integrative Personality Approach to the Study of the Antecedents of Status in Informal Social Organizations," *Journal of Research in Personality* 41 (2007): 689–699.

24. T. A. Judge, E. A. Locke, and C. C. Durham, "The Dispositional Causes of Job Satisfaction: A Core Self-Evaluation Approach," *Research in Organizational Behavior* 19 (1997):151–88.

25. M. Erez and T. A. Judge, "Relationship of Core Self-Evaluations to Goal Setting, Motivation, and Performance," *Journal of Applied Psychology* 86 (2001): 1270–1279; R. F. Piccolo, T. A. Judge, K. Takahashi, N. Watanabe, and E. A Locke, "Core Self-Evaluations in Japan: Relative Effects on Job Satisfaction, Life Satisfaction, and Happiness," *Journal of Organizational Behavior* 26, No. 8 (2005): 965–984.

26. J. B. Rotter, "Generalized Expectancies for Internal vs. External Control of Reinforcement," *Psychological Monographs* 80, No. 609 (1966).

27. M. Erez and T. A. Judge, "Relationship of Core Self-Evaluations to Goal Setting, Motivation and Performance," *Journal of Applied Psychology* 86 (2001): 1270–1279.

28. T. A. Judge and J. E. Bono, "Relationship of Core Self-Evaluations Traits—Self-Esteem, Generalized Self-Efficacy, Locus of Control, and Emotional Stability—With Job Satisfaction and Job Performance: A Meta-Analysis," *Journal of Applied Psychology* 86 (2001): 80–92.

29. Ibid.

30. S. S. K. Lam and J. Shaubroeck, "The Role of Locus of Control in Reactions to Being Promoted and to Being Passed Over: A Quasi Experiment," *Academy of Management Journal* 43 (2000): 66–78.

31. G. Chen, S. M. Gully, J. Whiteman, and R. N. Kilcullen, "Examination of Relationships among Trait-Like Individual Differences, State-Like Individual Differences, and Learning Performance," *Journal of Applied Psychology* 85 (2000): 835–847; G. Chen, S. M. Gully, and D. Eden, "Validation of a New General Self-Efficacy Scale," *Organizational Research Methods* 4 (2001): 62–83.

32. A. Bandura, *Self-Efficacy: The Exercise of Control* (San Francisco: Freeman, 1997).

33. D. R. Avery, "Personality as a Predictor of the Value of Voice," *Journal of Psychology* 137 (2003): 435–447.

34. T. A. Judge and J. E. Bono, "Relationship of Core Self-Evaluations Traits—Self-Esteem, Generalized Self-Efficacy, Locus of Control, and Emotional Stability—With Job Satisfaction and Job Performance: A Meta-Analysis," *Journal of Applied Psychology* 86 (2001): 80–92.

35. B. W. Pelham and W. B. Swann, Jr., "From Self-Conceptions to Self-Worth: On the Sources and Structure of Global Self-Esteem," *Journal of Personality and Social Psychology* 57 (1989): 672–680.

36. A. H. Baumgardner, C. M. Kaufman, and P. E. Levy, "Regulating Affect Interpersonally: When Low Esteem Leads to Greater Enhancement," *Journal of Personality and Social Psychology* 56 (1989): 907–921.

37. J. Schimel, T. Pyszczynski, J. Arndt, and J. Greenberg, "Being Accepted for Who We Are: Evidence That Social Validation of the Intrinsic Self Reduces General Defensiveness," *Journal of Personality and Social Psychology* 80 (2001): 35–52.

38. P. Tharenou and P. Harker, "Moderating Influences of Self-Esteem on Relationships between Job Complexity, Performance, and Satisfaction," *Journal of Applied Psychology* 69 (1984): 623–632.

39. R. A. Ellis and M. S. Taylor, "Role of Self-Esteem within the Job Search Process," *Journal of Applied Psychology* 68 (1983): 632–640.

40. J. Brockner and T. Hess, "Self-Esteem and Task Performance in Quality Circles," *Academy of Management Journal* 29 (1986): 617–623.

41. B. R. Schlenker, M. F. Weingold, and J. R. Hallam, "Self-Serving Attributions in Social Context: Effects of Self-Esteem and Social Pressure," *Journal of Personality and Social Psychology* 57 (1990): 855–863.

42. M. K. Duffy, J. D. Shaw, and E. M. Stark, "Performance and Satisfaction in Conflicted Interdependent Groups: When and How Does Self-Esteem Make a Difference?" *Academy of Management Journal* 43 (2000): 772–782.

43. T. Mussweiler, S. Gabriel, and G. V. Bodenhausen, "Shifting Social Identities as a Strategy for Deflecting Threatening Social Comparisons," *Journal of Personality and Social Psychology* 79 (2000): 398–409.

44. M. Snyder and S. Gangestad, "On the Nature of Self-Monitoring: Matters of Assessment, Matters of Validity," *Journal of Psychology and Social Psychology* 51 (1986): 125–139.

45. G. Toegel, N. Anand, and M. Kilduff, "Emotion Helpers: The Role of High Positive Affectivity and High Self-Monitoring Managers," *Personnel Psychology* 60, No. 2 (2007): 337–365.

46. A. Mehra, M. Kilduff, and D. J. Brass, "The Social Networks of High and Low Self-Monitors: Implications for Workplace Performance," *Administrative Science Quarterly* 46 (2001): 121–146.

47. W. H. Turnley and M. C. Bolino, "Achieving Desired Images while Avoiding Undesired Images: Exploring the Role of Self-Monitoring in Impression Management," *Journal of Applied Psychology* 86 (2001): 351–360.

48. M. Kilduff and D. V. Day, "Do Chameleons Get Ahead? The Effects of Self-Monitoring on Managerial Careers," *Academy of Management Journal* 37 (1994): 1047–1060.

49. A. H. Church, "Managerial Self-Awareness in High-Performing Individuals in Organizations," *Journal of Applied Psychology* 82 (1997): 281–292.

50. C. Douglas and W. L. Gardner, "Transition to Self-Directed Work Teams: Implications of Transition Time and Self-Monitoring for Managers' Use of Influence Tactics," *Journal of Organizational Behavior* 25 (2004): 45–67.

51. A. M. Isen and R. A. Baron, "Positive Affect and Organizational Behavior," in B. M. Staw and L. L. Cummings, eds., *Research in Organizational Behavior,* vol. 12 (Greenwich, Conn.: JAI Press, 1990).

52. D. Watson and L. A. Clark, "Negative Affectivity: The Disposition to Experience Aversive Emotional States," *Psychological Bulletin* 96 (1984): 465–490.

53. R. Ilies and T. Judge, "On the Heritability of Job Satisfaction: The Mediating Role of Personality," *Journal of Applied Psychology* 88 (2003): 750–759.

54. J. M. George, "State or Trait," *Journal of Applied Psychology* 76 (1991): 299–307.

55. J. M. George, "Mood and Absence," *Journal of Applied Psychology* 74 (1989): 287–324.

56. S. Lyubormirsky, L. King, and L. E. Diener, "The Benefits of Frequent Positive Affect: Does Happiness Lead to Success?" *Psychological Bulletin* 131, No. 6 (2005): 803–855.

57. S. Barsade, A. Ward, J. Turner, and J. Sonnenfeld, "To Your Heart's Content: A Model of Affective Diversity in Top Management Teams," *Administrative Science Quarterly* 45 (2000): 802–836.

58. J. M. Crant, "The Proactive Personality Scale and Objective Job Performance among Real Estate Agents," *Journal of Applied Psychology* 80 (1995): 532–537.

59. T. W. H. Ng, L. T. Eby, K. L. Sorensen, and D. C. Feldman, "Predictors of Objective and Subjective Career Success: A Meta Analysis," *Personnel Psychology* 58 (2005): 367–408; D. J. Brown, R. T. Cober, K. Kane, P. E.

Levey, and J. Shalhoop, "Proactive Personality and the Successful Job Search: A Field Investigation with College Graduates," *Journal of Applied Psychology* 91 (2006): 717–726.

60. J. M. Crant and T. S. Bateman, "Charismatic Leadership Viewed from Above: The Impact of Proactive Personality," *Journal of Organizational Behavior* 21 (2000): 63–75.

61. H. Rorschach, *Psychodiagnostics* (Bern: Hans Huber, 1921).

62. C. G. Jung, *Psychological Types* (New York: Harcourt & Brace, 1923).

63. Consulting Psychologists Press, http://www.cpp.com/products/mbti/index.asp, accessed June 30, 2008.

64. R. Benfari and J. Knox, *Understanding Your Management Style* (Lexington, Mass.: Lexington Books, 1991).

65. O. Kroeger and J. M. Thuesen, *Type Talk* (New York: Delacorte Press, 1988).

66. S. Hirsch and J. Kummerow, *Life Types* (New York: Warner Books, 1989).

67. I. B. Myers and M. H. McCaulley, *Manual: A Guide to the Development and Use of the Myers-Briggs Type Indicator* (Palo Alto, Calif.: Consulting Psychologists Press, 1990).

68. G. P. Macdaid, M. H. McCaulley, and R. I. Kainz, *Myers-Briggs Type Indicator: Atlas of Type Tables* (Gainesville, Fla.: Center for Application of Psychological Type, 1987).

69. J. B. Murray, "Review of Research on the Myers-Briggs Type Indicator," *Perceptual and Motor Skills* 70 (1990): 1187–1202; J. G. Carlson, "Recent Assessment of the Myers-Briggs Type Indicator," *Journal of Personality Assessment* 49 (1985): 356–365.

70. A. Thomas, M. Benne, M. Marr, E. Thomas, and R. Hume, "The Evidence Remains Stable: The MBTI Predicts Attraction and Attrition in an Engineering Program," *Journal of Psychological Type* 55 (2000): 35–42.

71. C. Walck, "Training for Participative Management: Implications for Psychological Type," *Journal of Psychological Type* 21 (1991): 3–12.

72. G. Lawrence and C. Martin, *Building People, Building Programs: A Practitioner's Guide for Introducing the MBTI to Individuals and Organizations* (Center for Applications of Psychological Type, 2001); L. Berens, L. Ernst, M. Smith, *Quick Guide to the 16 Personality Types and Teams: Applying Team Essentials™ to Create Effective Teams* (Telos Publications, 2004).

73. J. Michael, "Using the Myers-Briggs Indicator as a Tool for Leadership Development: Apply with Caution," *Journal of Leadership & Organizational Studies* 10 (2003): 68–78.

74. E. C. Webster, *The Employment Interview: A Social Judgment Process* (Schomberg, Canada: SIP, 1982).

75. A. J. Ward, M. J. Lankau, A. C. Amason, J. A. Sonnenfeld, and B. R. Agle, "Improving the Performance of Top Management Teams," *MIT Sloan Management Review* 48, No. 3 (2007): 85–90.

76. N. Adler, *International Dimensions of Organizational Behavior,* 2nd ed. (Boston: PWS-Kent, 1991).

77. L. R. Offerman and M. K. Gowing, "Personnel Selection in the Future: The Impact of Changing Demographics and the Nature of Work," in Schmitt, Borman & Associates, eds., *Personnel Selection in Organizations* (San Francisco: Jossey-Bass, 1993).

78. L. Armstrong, "What Men Say behind Closed Doors," *Working Mother* (June–July 2008): 87–90.

79. J. Park and M. R. Banaji, "Mood and Heuristics: The Influence of Happy and Sad States on Sensitivity and Bias in Stereotyping," *Journal of Personality and Social Psychology* 78 (2000): 1005–1023.

80. M. W. Levine and J. M. Shefner, *Fundamentals of Sensation and Perception* (Reading, Mass.: Addison-Wesley, 1981).

81. R. L. Dipboye, H. L. Fromkin, and K. Willback, "Relative Importance of Applicant Sex, Attractiveness, and Scholastic Standing in Evaluations of Job Applicant Resumes," *Journal of Applied Psychology* 60 (1975): 39–43; I. H. Frieze, J. E. Olson, and J. Russell, "Attractiveness and Income for Men and Women in Management," *Journal of Applied Social Psychology* 21 (1991): 1039–1057.

82. P. Ekman and W. Friesen, *Unmasking the Face* (Englewood Cliffs, N.J.: Prentice-Hall, 1975).

83. J. E. Rehfeld, "What Working for a Japanese Company Taught Me," *Harvard Business Review* (November–December 1990): 167–176.

84. M. W. Morris and R. P. Larrick, "When One Cause Casts Doubt on Another: A Normative Analysis of Discounting in Causal Attribution," *Psychological Review* 102 (1995): 331–355.

85. G. B. Sechrist and C. Stangor, "Perceived Consensus Influences Intergroup Behavior and Stereotype Accessibility," *Journal of Personality and Psychology* 80 (2001): 645–654; A. Lyons and Y. Kashima, "How Are Stereotypes Maintained through Communication? The Influence of Stereotype Sharedness," *Journal of Personality and Social Psychology* 85 (2003): 989–1005.

86. R. Hastings, "The Forgotten Minority: Stereotypes of Asian-Americans Not Only Can Limit Their Workplace Opportunities But Also Can Stifle the Talents They Can Offer Their Employers," *HR Magazine* (July 2007), http://infotrac-college.thomsonlearning.com, accessed June 30, 2008; J. Katz, "How Troublesome are Stereotypes in International Business?," *CAHRS Working Paper Series 1995*, http://digitalcommons.ilr.cornell.edu/cahrswp/193, accessed June 30, 2008.

87. A. Feingold, "Gender Differences in Effects of Physical Attractiveness on Romantic Attraction: A Comparison across Five Research Paradigms," *Journal of Personality and Social Psychology* 59 (1990): 981–993.

88. M. Snyder, "When Belief Creates Reality," *Advances in Experimental Social Psychology* 18 (1984): 247–305.

89. M. Biernat, "Toward a Broader View of Social Stereotyping," *American Psychologist* 58 (2003): 1019–1027.

90. E. Burnstein and Y. Schul, "The Informational Basis of Social Judgments: Operations in Forming an Impression of Another Person," *Journal of Experimental Social Psychology* 18 (1982): 217–234.

91. T. DeGroot and S. Motowidlo, "Why Visual and Vocal Cues Can Affect Interviewers' Judgments and Predict Job Performance," *Journal of Applied Psychology* 84 (1999): 986–993; M. C. L. Greene and L. Mathieson, *The Voice and Its Disorders* (London: Whurr, 1989).

92. R. L. Gross and S. E. Brodt, "How Assumptions of Consensus Undermine Decision Making," *MIT Sloan Management Review* 42 (Winter 2001): 86–94.

93. R. Rosenthal and L. Jacobson, *Pygmalion in the Classroom: Teacher Expectations and Pupils' Intellectual Development* (New York: Holt, Rinehart & Winston, 1968).

94. D. Eden, "Pygmalion without Interpersonal Contrast Effects: Whole Groups Gain from Raising Manager Expectations," *Journal of Applied Psychology* 75 (1990): 394–398.

95. R. A. Giacolone and P. Rosenfeld, eds., *Impression Management in Organizations* (Hillsdale, N.J.: Erlbaum, 1990); J. Tedeschi and V. Melburg, "Impression Management and Influence in the Organization," in S. Bacharach and E. Lawler, eds., *Research in the Sociology of Organizations* (Greenwich, Conn.: JAI Press, 1984), 31–58.

96. A. Colella and A. Varma, "The Impact of Subordinate Disability on Leader–Member Exchange Relationships," *Academy of Management Journal* 44 (2001): 304–315.

97. D. C. Gilmore and G. R. Ferris, "The Effects of Applicant Impression Management Tactics on Interviewer Judgments," *Journal of Management* (December 1989): 557–564; C. K. Stevens and A. L. Kristof, "Making the Right Impression: A Field Study of Applicant Impressions Management during Job Interviews," *Journal of Applied Psychology* 80 (1995): 587–606.

98. S. J. Wayne and R. C. Liden, "Effects of Impression Management on Performance Ratings: A Longitudinal Study," *Academy of Management Journal* 38 (1995): 232–260.

99. R. A. Baron, "Impression Management by Applicants during Employment Interviews: The 'Too Much of a Good Thing' Effect," in R. W. Eder and G. R. Ferris, eds., *The Employment Interview: Theory, Research, and Practice* (Newbury Park, Calif.: Sage Publications, 1989).

100. F. Heider, *The Psychology of Interpersonal Relations* (New York: Wiley, 1958).

101. S. Graham and V. Folkes, *Attribution Theory: Applications to Achievement, Mental Health, and Interpersonal Conflict* (Hillsdale: L. Erlbaum and Associates, 1990).

102. P. D. Sweeney, K. Anderson, and S. Bailey, "Attributional Style in Depression: A Meta-Analytic Review," *Journal of Personality and Social Psychology* 51 (1986): 974–991.

103. P. Rosenthal, D. Guest, and R. Peccei, "Gender Differences in Managers' Causal Explanations for Their Work Performance," *Journal of Occupational and Organizational Psychology* 69 (1996): 145–151.

104. J. Silvester, "Spoken Attributions and Candidate Success in Graduate Recruitment Interviews," *Journal of Occupational and Organizational Psychology* 70 (1997): 61–71.

105. L. Ross, "The Intuitive Psychologist and His Shortcomings: Distortions in the Attribution Process," in L. Berkowitz, ed., *Advances in Experimental Social Psychology* (New York: Academic Press, 1977); M. O'Sullivan, "The Fundamental Attribution Error in Detecting Deception: The Boy-Who-Cried-Wolf Effect," *Personality & Social Psychology Bulletin* 29 (2003): 1316–1327.

106. D. T. Miller and M. Ross, "Self-Serving Biases in the Attribution of Causality: Fact or Fiction?" *Psychological Bulletin* 82 (1975): 313–325.

107. J. R. Schermerhorn, Jr., "Team Development for High-Performance Management," *Training and Development Journal* 40 (1986): 38–41.

108. J. G. Miller, "Culture and the Development of Everyday Causal Explanation," *Journal of Personality and Social Psychology* 46 (1984): 961–978.

109. G. Si, S. Rethorst, and K. Willimczik, "Causal Attribution Perception in Sports Achievement: A Cross-Cultural Study on Attributional Concepts in Germany and China," *Journal of Cross-Cultural Psychology* 26 (1995): 537–553.

Chapter 4

1. A. H. Eagly and S. Chaiken, *The Psychology of Attitudes* (Orlando, Fla.: Harcourt Brace Jovanovich, 1993).

2. M. Pounds, "Bring Positive Attitude to the Workplace Using Praise," *South Florida Sun-Sentinel* (Fort Lauderdale, FL) (September 27, 2007), http://infotrac-college.thomsonlearning.com, accessed July 2, 2008.

3. M. J. Rosenberg, C. I. Hovland, W. J. McGuire, R. P. Abelson, and J. H. Brehm, *Attitude Organization and Change* (New Haven, Conn.: Yale University Press, 1960).

4. L. Festinger, *A Theory of Cognitive Dissonance* (Evanston, Ill.: Row, Peterson, 1957).

5. R. H. Fazio and M. P. Zanna, "On the Predictive Validity of Attitudes: The Roles of Direct Experience and Confidence," *Journal of Personality* 46 (1978): 228–243.

6. A. Tversky and D. Kahneman, "Judgment under Uncertainty: Heuristics and Biases," in D. Kahneman, P. Slovic, and A. Tversky, eds., *Judgment under Uncertainty* (New York: Cambridge University Press, 1982): 3–20.

7. A. Bandura, *Social Learning Theory* (Englewood Cliffs, NJ: Prentice-Hall, 1977).

8. I. Ajzen and M. Fishbein, "Attitude–Behavior Relations: A Theoretical Analysis and Review of Empirical Research," *Psychological Bulletin* 84 (1977): 888–918.

9. B. T. Johnson and A. H. Eagly, "Effects of Involvement on Persuasion: A Meta-Analysis," *Psychological Bulletin* 106 (1989): 290–314.

10. K. G. DeBono and M. Snyder, "Acting on One's Attitudes: The Role of History of Choosing Situations," *Personality and Social Psychology Bulletin* 21 (1995): 629–636.

11. I. Ajzen and M. Fishbein, *Understanding Attitudes and Predicting Social Behavior* (Englewood Cliffs, N.J.: Prentice-Hall, 1980).

12. I. Ajzen, "From Intentions to Action: A Theory of Planned Behavior," in J. Kuhl and J. Beckmann, eds., *Action-Control: From Cognition to Behavior* (Heidelberg: Springer, 1985).

13. I. Ajzen, "The Theory of Planned Behavior," *Organizational Behavior and Human Decision Processes* 50 (1991): 1–33.

14. A. Sagie and M. Krausz, "What Aspects of the Job Have Most Effect on Nurses?" *Human Resource Management Journal* 13 (2003): 46–62.

15. J. Kettle, "Factors Affecting Job Satisfaction in the Registered Nurse," *Journal of Undergraduate Nursing Scholarship*, http://juns.nursing.arizona.edu/Default.htm, accessed July 1, 2008.

16. C. P. Parker, B. B. Baltes, S. A. Young, J. W. Huff, R. A. Altman, H. A. LaCost, and J. E. Roberts, "Relationships between Psychological Climate Perceptions and Work Outcomes: A Meta-Analytic Review," *Journal of Organizational Behavior* 24 (2003): 389–416.

17. E. A. Locke, "The Nature and Causes of Job Satisfaction," in M. Dunnette, ed., *Handbook of Industrial and Organizational Psychology* (Chicago: Rand McNally, 1976).

18. P. C. Smith, L. M. Kendall, and C. L. Hulin, *The Measurement of Satisfaction in Work and Retirement* (Skokie, Ill.: Rand McNally, 1969).

19. R. Ilies and T. A. Judge, "On the Heritability of Job Satisfaction: The Mediating Role of Personality," *Journal of Applied Psychology* 88 (2003): 750–759.

20. T. A. Judge, R. F. Piccolo, N. P. Podsakoff, J. C. Shaw, and B. Rich, "The Relationship between Pay and Job Satisfaction: A Meta-Analysis of the Literature," *Journal of Vocational Behavior* 77 (2010): 157–167.

21. D. J. Weiss, R. V. Davis, G. W. England, and L. H. Lofquist, *Manual for the Minnesota Satisfaction Questionnaire* (Minneapolis: Industrial Relations Center, University of Minnesota, 1967).

22. C. D. Fisher, "Why Do Lay People Believe that Satisfaction and Performance Are Correlated? Possible Sources of a Commonsense Theory," *Journal of Organizational Behavior* 24 (2003): 753–777.

23. M. Christen, G. Iyer, and D. Soberman, "Job Satisfaction, Job Performance, and Effort: A Reexamination Using Agency Theory," *Journal of Marketing* 70 (January 2006): 137–150

24. L. A. Bettencourt, K. P. Gwinner, and M. L. Meuter, "A Comparison of Attitude, Personality, and Knowledge Predictors of Service-Oriented Organizational Citizenship Behaviors," *Journal of Applied Psychology* 86 (2001): 29–41.

25. D. W. Organ, *Organizational Citizenship Behavior: The Good Soldier Syndrome* (Lexington, Mass.: Lexington Books, 1988).

26. P. M. Podsakoff, S. B. Mackenzie, and C. Hui, "Organizational Citizenship Behaviors and Managerial Evaluations of Employee Performance: A Review and Suggestions for Future Research," G. Ferris, ed., in *Research in Personnel and Human Resources Management* (Greenwich, Conn.: JAI Press, 1993): 1–40.

27. K. Lee, and N. J. Allen, "Organizational Citizenship Behavior and Workplace Deviance: The Role of Affect and Cognitions," *Journal of Applied Psychology,* 87, No. 1 (2002): 131–142.

28. O. Christ, R. Van Dick, and U. Wagner, "When Teachers Go the Extra Mile: Foci of Organizational Identification as Determinants of Different Forms of Organizational Citizenship Behavior among Schoolteachers," *British Journal of Educational Psychology* 73 (2003): 329–341.

29. G. L. Blakely, M. C. Andrews, and J. Fuller, "Are Chameleons Good Citizens: A Longitudinal Study of the Relationship between Self-Monitoring and Organizational Citizenship Behavior," *Journal of Business & Psychology* 18 (2003): 131–144.

30. W. H. Bommer, E. W. Miles, and S. L. Grover, "Does One Good Turn Deserve Another? Coworker Influences on Employee Citizenship," *Journal of Organizational Behavior* 24 (2003): 181–196.

31. C. Ostroff, "The Relationship between Satisfaction, Attitudes and Performance: An Organizational Level Analysis," *Journal of Applied Psychology* 77 (1992): 963–974.

32. R. Griffin and T. Bateman, "Job Satisfaction and Organizational Commitment," in C. Cooper and I. Robertson, eds., *International Review of Industrial and Organizational Psychology* (New York: Wiley, 1986).

33. A. R. Wheeler, V. C. Gallagher, R. L. Brouer, and C. J. Sablynski, "When Person-Organization (Mis)Fit and (Dis)Satisfaction Lead to Turnover: The Moderating Role of Perceived Job Mobility," *Journal of Managerial Psychology* 22, No. 2 (2007): 203–219.

34. X. Huang and E. Van De Vliert, "Where Intrinsic Job Satisfaction Fails to Work: National Moderators of Intrinsic Motivation," *Journal of Organizational Behavior* 24 (2003): 133–250.

35. L. Sun, S. Aryee, and K. S. Law, "High-Performance Human Resource Practices, Citizenship Behavior, and Organizational Performance: A Relational Perspective," *Academy of Management Journal* 50 (2007): 558–577.

36. S. L. Robinson, and R. J. Bennett, "A Typology of Deviant Workplace Behaviors: A Multidimensional Scaling Study," *Academy of Management Journal*, 38, No. 2 (1995), 555.; P. D. Dunlop and K. Lee, "Workplace Deviance, Organizational Citizenship Behavior, and Business Unit Performance: The Bad Apples Do Spoil the Whole Barrel," *Journal of Organizational Behavior* 25 (2004): 67–80.

37. M. E. Heilman, and V. B. Alcott, "What I Think You Think of Me: Women's Reactions to Being Viewed as Beneficiaries of Preferential Selection," *Journal of Applied Psychology* 86 (2001): 574–582; M. E. Heilman, C. J. Block, and

P. Stathatos, "The Affirmative Action Stigma of Incompetence: Effects of Performance Information Ambiguity," *Academy of Management Journal* 40, (1997): 603–625.

38. R. T. Mowday, L. W. Porter, and R. M. Steers, *Employee–Organization Linkages: The Psychology of Commitment* (New York: Academic Press, 1982).

39. N. Allen and J. Meyer, "Affective, Continuance, and Normative Commitment to the Organization: An Examination of Construct Validity," *Journal of Vocational Behavior* 49 (1996): 252–276.

40. J. P. Meyer, N. J. Allen, and C. A. Smith, "Commitment to Organizations and Occupations: Extension and Test of a Three-Component Model," *Journal of Applied Psychology* 78 (1993): 538–551.

41. J. P. Curry, D. S. Wakefield, J. L. Price, and C. W. Mueller, "On the Causal Ordering of Job Satisfaction and Organizational Commitment," *Academy of Management Journal* 29 (1986): 847–858; T. N. Bauer, T. Bodner, B. Erdogan, D. M. Truxillo, and J. S. Tucker, "Newcomer Adjustment during Organizational Socialization: A Meta-Analytic Review of Antecedents, Outcomes, and Methods." *Journal of Applied Psychology* 92 (2007): 707–721.

42. B. Benkhoff, "Ignoring Commitment Is Costly: New Approaches Establish the Missing Link between Commitment and Performance," *Human Relations* 50 (1997): 701–726; N. J. Allen and J. P. Meyer, "Affective, Continuance, and Normative Commitment to the Organization: An Examination of Construct Validity," *Journal of Vocational Behavior* 49 (1996): 252–276.

43. M. J. Somers, "Organizational Commitment, Turnover, and Absenteeism: An Examination of Direct and Interaction Effects," *Journal of Organizational Behavior* 16 (1995): 49–58; L. Lum, J. Kervin, K. Clark, F. Reid, and W. Sirola, "Explaining Nursing Turnover Intent: Job Satisfaction, Pay Satisfaction, or Organizational Commitment?" *Journal of Organizational Behavior* 19 (1998): 305–320.

44. F. Stinglhamber and C. Vandenberghe, "Organizations and Supervisors as Sources of Support and Targets of Commitment," *Journal of Organizational Behavior* 24 (2003): 251–270.

45. R. Eisenberger, S. Armeli, B. Rexwinkel, P. D. Lynch, and L. Rhoades, "Reciprocation of Perceived Organizational Support," *Journal of Applied Psychology* 86 (2001): 42–51; J. E. Finegan, "The Impact of Person and Organizational Values on Organizational Commitment," *Journal of Occupational and Organizational Psychology* 73 (2000): 149–169.

46. E. Snape and T. Redman, "Too Old or Too Young? The Impact of Perceived Age Discrimination," *Human Resource Management Journal* 13 (2003): 78–89.

47. J. A. Conger, "The Necessary Art of Persuasion," *Harvard Business Review* 76 (1998): 84–96.

48. J. Cooper and R. T. Croyle, "Attitudes and Attitude Change," *Annual Review of Psychology* 35 (1984): 395–426.

49. B. Martin, D. Wentzel and T. Tomczak, "Effects of Susceptibility to Normative Influence and Type of Testimonial on Attitudes toward Print Advertising," *Journal of Advertising* (Spring 2008), http://infotrac-college.thomsonlearning.com, accessed July 2, 2009.

50. D. M. Mackie and L. T. Worth, "Processing Deficits and the Mediation of Positive Affect in Persuasion," *Journal of Personality and Social Psychology* 57 (1989): 27–40.

51. J. W. Brehm, *Responses to Loss of Freedom: A Theory of Psychological Reactance* (New York: General Learning Press, 1972).

52. D. DeSteno, R. E. Petty, and D. D. Rucker, "Discrete Emotions and Persuasion: The Role of Emotion-Induced Expectancies," *Journal of Personality & Social Psychology* 86 (2004): 43–56.

53. R. Petty, D. T. Wegener, and L. R. Fabrigar, "Attitudes and Attitude Change," *Annual Review of Psychology* 48 (1997): 609–647.

54. P. Brinol and R. E. Petty, "Overt Head Movements and Persuasion: A Self-Validation Analysis," *Journal of Personality and Social Psychology* 84 (2003): 1123–1139.

55. W. Wood, "Attitude Change: Persuasion and Social Influence," *Annual Review of Psychology* 51 (2000): 539–570.

56. A. Ortony, G. L. Clore, and A. Collins, *The Cognitive Structure of Emotions* (Cambridge, England: Cambridge University Press, 1988).

57. R. S. Lazarus, *Emotion and Adaptation* (New York: Oxford University Press, 1991).

58. H. M. Weiss, K. Suckow, and R. Cropanzano, "Effects of Justice Conditions on Discrete Emotions," *Journal of Applied Psychology* 84 (1999): 786–794.

59. P. T. Van Katwyk, S. Fox, P. E. Spector, and E. K. Kelloway, "Using the Job-Related Affective Well-Being Scale to Investigate Affective Responses to Work Stressors," *Journal of Occupational Health Psychology* 52 (2000): 219–230.

60. B. L. Fredrickson, "The Role of Positive Emotions in Positive Psychology: The Broaden-and-Build Theory of Positive Emotions," *American Psychologist* 56 (2001): 218–226.

61. S. S. Kaplan, J. C. Bradley, J. N. Luchman, and D. Haynes, "On the Role of Positive and Negative Affectivity in Job Performance: A Meta-Analytic Investigation," *Journal of Applied Psychology* 94 (2009): 162–178; B. Lawrence and S. L. Robinson, "Ain't Misbehavin: Workplace Deviance as Organizational Resistance," *Journal of Management* 33, No. 3 (2007): 378–394.

62. B. L. Fredrickson and C. Brannigan, "Positive Emotions," in G. Bonnano and T. Mayne, eds., *Emotions: Current Issues and Future Directions* (New York: Guilford Press, 2001): 123–152.

63. D. Watson and L. A. Clark, "Affects Separable and Inseparable: On the Hierarchical Arrangement of Negative Affects," *Journal of Personality and Social Psychology* 62 (1992): 489–505.

64. A. M. Isen and R. A. Baron, "Positive Affect as a Factor in Organizational Behavior," *Research in Organizational Behavior* 13 (1991): 1–53; A. G. Miner and T. M. Glomb, "State Mood, Task Performance, and Behavior at Work: A Within-Persons Approach," *Organizational Behavior and Human Decision Processes* 112 (2010): 43–57.

65. J. M. George, "Mood and Absence," *Journal of Applied Psychology* 74 (1989): 317–324; L. H. Pelled and K. R. Xin, "Down and Out: An Investigation of the Relationship between Mood and Employee Withdrawal Behavior," *Journal of Management* 25 (1999): 875–895.

66. S. G. Barsade, "The Ripple Effect: Emotional Contagion and Its Influence on Group Behavior, *Administrative Science Quarterly* 47 (2007): 644–675.

67. J. E. Dutton, P. J. Frost, M. C. Worline, J. M. Lilius, and J. M. Kanov, "Leading in Times of Trauma," *Harvard Business Review* 80 (2002): 54–61.

68. T. A. Stewart, "The Highway of the Mind," *Harvard Business Review* 82 (2004): 116.

69. J. D. Mayer, P. Salovey, and D. R. Caruso, "Emotional Intelligence: Theory, Findings, and Implications," *Psychological Inquiry* 15 (2004): 197–215.

70. D. L. Joseph and D. A. Newman, "Emotional Intelligence: An Integrative Meta-Analysis and Cascading Modek," *Journal of Applied Psychology* 95 (2010): 54–78.

71. A. R. Hochschild, *The Managed Heart: Commercialization of Human Feeling* (Berkeley: University of California Press, 1983).

72. A. A. Grandey, "When 'The Show Must Go On': Surface Acting and Deep Acting as Determinants of Emotional Exhaustion and Peer-Rated Service Delivery," *Academy of Management Journal* 46 (2003): 86–96; C. M. Brotherridge and A. A. Grandey, "Emotional Labor and Burnout: Comparing Two Perspectives of 'People Work'," *Journal of Vocational Behavior* 60 (2002): 17–39.

73. F. Navran, "Your Role in Shaping Ethics," *Executive Excellence* 9 (1992): 11–12.

74. K. Labich, "The New Crisis in Business Ethics," *Fortune* (April 20, 1992): 167–176.

75. L. S. Paine, *Value Shift: Why Companies Must Merge Social and Financial Imperatives to Achieve Superior Performance* (New York: McGraw-Hill, 2003).

76. D. B. Turban and D. M. Cable, "Firm Reputation and Applicant Pool Characteristics," *Journal of Organizational Behavior* 24 (2003): 733–751.

77. E. A. Lind, J. Greenberg, K. S. Scott, and T. D. Welchans, "The Winding Road from Employee to Complainant: Situational and Psychological Determinants of Wrongful-Termination Claims," *Administrative Science Quarterly* 45 (2000): 557–590.

78. "Stolen Birthrights; Australia's Aborigines," *The Economist* (US) (February 2, 2008), http://infotrac-college.thomsonlearning.com, accessed July 8, 2008; T. Johnston, "Australia Says 'Sorry' to Aborigines for

Mistreatment," *The New York Times* (February 13, 2008), http://www.nytimes.com, accessed July 2, 2008.

79. Miriam Schulman, "Little Brother Is Watching You," Makkula Center for Applied Ethics, http://www.scu.edu/ethics/ publications/iie/v9n2/brother.html, accessed July 1, 2008.

80. M. Oneal, P. Callahan, and E. Osnos, "Mattel Recalls 18 Million Toys," *Chicago Tribune* (August 15, 2007), http://www.chicagotribune.com/business/chi-toysaug15,0,7223810.story.

81. M. S. Baucus and D. A. Baucus, "Paying the Piper: An Empirical Examination of Longer-Term Financial Consequences of Illegal Corporate Behavior," *Academy of Management Journal* 40 (1997): 129–151.

82. J. O. Cherrington and D. J. Cherrington, "A Menu of Moral Issues: One Week in the Life of *The Wall Street Journal*," *Journal of Business Ethics* 11 (1992): 255–265.

83. B. L. Flannery and D. R. May, "Environmental Ethical Decision Making in the U.S. Metal-Finishing Industry," *Academy of Management Journal* 43 (2000): 642–662.

84. K. R. Andrews, "Ethics in Practice," *Harvard Business Review* (September–October 1989): 99–104.

85. M. Rokeach, *The Nature of Human Values* (New York: Free Press, 1973).

86. M. Rokeach and S. J. Ball-Rokeach, "Stability and Change in American Value Priorities, 1968–1981," *American Psychologist* 44 (1989): 775–784.

87. S. P Eisner, "Managing Generation Y," S.A.M. *Advanced Management Journal*, 70, No. 4 (2005): 4–15.

88. M. Henderson and D. Thompson, *Values at Work: The Invisible Threads between People, Performance, and Profit* (Auckland, New Zealand: HarperBusiness, 2003).

89. E. C. Ravlin and B. M. Meglino, "Effects of Values on Perception and Decision Making: A Study of Alternative Work Values Measures," *Journal of Applied Psychology* 72 (1987): 666–673.

90. E. C. Ravlin and B. M. Meglino, "The Transitivity of Work Values: Hierarchical Preference Ordering of Socially Desirable Stimuli," *Organizational Behavior and Human Decision Processes* 44 (1989): 494–508.

91. B. M. Meglino, E. C. Ravlin, and C. L. Adkins, "A Work Values Approach to Corporate Culture: A Field Test of the Value Congruence Process and Its Relationship to Individual Outcomes," *Journal of Applied Psychology* 74 (1989): 424–432.

92. T. A. Judge and R. D. Bretz, Jr., "Effects of Work Values on Job Choice Decisions," *Journal of Applied Psychology* 77 (1992): 261–271.

93. R. H. Doktor, "Asian and American CEOs: A Comparative Study," *Organizational Dynamics* 18 (1990): 46–56.

94. R. L. Tung, "Handshakes across the Sea: Cross-Cultural Negotiating for Business Success," *Organizational Dynamics* (Winter 1991): 30–40.

95. C. Gomez, B. L. Kirkman, and D. L. Shapiro, "The Impact of Collectivism and In-Group/Out-Group Membership on the Evaluation Generosity of Team Members," *Academy of Management Journal* 43 (2000): 1097–1106; J. Zhou and J. J. Martocchio, "Chinese and American Managers' Compensation Award Decisions: A Comparative Policy-Capturing Study," *Personnel Psychology* 54 (2001): 115–145.

96. A. J. Ali and M. Amirshahi, "The Iranian Manager: Work Values and Orientations," *Journal of Business Ethics* 40 (2002): 133–143.

97. R. Neale and R. Mindel, "Rigging Up Multicultural Teamworking," *Personnel Management* (January 1992): 27–30.

98. J. B. Rotter, "Generalized Expectancies for Internal versus External Control of Reinforcement," *Psychological Monographs* 80 (1966): 1–28.

99. L. K. Trevino and S. A. Youngblood, "Bad Apples in Bad Barrels: A Causal Analysis of Ethical Decision-Making Behavior," *Journal of Applied Psychology* 75 (1990): 378–385.

100. H. M. Lefcourt, *Locus of Control: Current Trends in Theory and Research*, 2nd ed. (Hillsdale, N.J.: Erlbaum, 1982).

101. N. Machiavelli, *The Prince*, trans. George Bull (Middlesex, England: Penguin Books, 1961).

102. R. Christie and F. L. Geis, *Studies in Machiavellianism* (New York: Academic Press, 1970).

103. R. A. Giacalone and S. B. Knouse, "Justifying Wrongful Employee Behavior: The Role of Personality in Organizational Sabotage," *Journal of Business Ethics* 9 (1990): 55–61.

104. S. B. Knouse and R. A. Giacalone, "Ethical Decision Making in Business: Behavioral Issues and Concerns," *Journal of Business Ethics* 11 (1992): 369–377.

105. L. Kohlberg, "Stage and Sequence: The Cognitive Developmental Approach to Socialization," in D. A. Goslin, ed., *Handbook of Socialization Theory and Research* (Chicago: Rand McNally, 1969): 347–480.

106. C. I. Malinowski and C. P. Smith, "Moral Reasoning and Moral Conduct: An Investigation Prompted by Kohlberg's Theory," *Journal of Personality and Social Psychology* 49 (1985): 1016–1027; M. Brabeck, "Ethical Characteristics of Whistleblowers," *Journal of Research in Personality* 18 (1984): 41–53; W. Y. Penn and B. D. Collier, "Current Research in Moral Development as a Decision Support System," *Journal of Business Ethics* 4 (1985): 131–136; L. K. Trevino and S. A. Youngblood, "Bad Apples in Bad Barrels: A Causal Analysis of Ethical Decision-Making Behavior," *Journal of Applied Psychology* 75 (1990): 378–385.

107. C. Gilligan, *In a Different Voice: Psychological Theory and Women's Development* (Cambridge, Mass.: Harvard University Press, 1982).

108. S. Jaffee and J. S. Hyde, "Gender Differences in Moral Orientation: A Meta-Analysis," *Psychological Bulletin* 126 (2000): 703–726.

109. G. R. Franke, D. F. Crown, and D. F. Spake, "Gender Differences in Ethical Perceptions of Business Practices: A Social Role Theory Perspective," *Journal of Applied Psychology* 82 (1997): 920–934.

Chapter 5

1. L. W. Porter, G. Bigley, and R. M. Steers, *Motivation and Leadership at Work,* 7th ed. (New York: McGraw-Hill, 2002).

2. J. P. Campbell and R. D. Pritchard, "Motivation Theory in Industrial and Organizational Psychology," in M. D. Dunnette, ed., *Handbook of Industrial and Organizational Psychology* (Chicago: Rand McNally, 1976): 63–130.

3. M. Weber, *The Protestant Ethic and the Spirit of Capitalism* (London: Talcott Parson, tr., 1930).

4. S. Freud, *Civilization and Its Discontents,* trans. and ed. J. Strachey (New York: Norton, 1961).

5. P. D. Dunlop and K. Lee, "Workplace Deviance, Organizational Citizenship Behavior, and Business Unit Performance: The Bad Apples Do Spoil the Whole Barrel," *Journal of Organizational Behavior* 25 (2004): 67–80.

6. K. J. Sweetman, "Employee Loyalty around the Globe," *Sloan Management Review* 42 (2001): 16.

7. B. S. Frey, *Not Just for the Money: An Economic Theory of Personal Motivation* (Brookfield, Vt.: Edgar Elger, 1997).

8. A. Smith, *An Inquiry into the Nature and Causes of the Wealth of Nations,* Vol. 10 of *The Harvard Classics,* C. J. Bullock, ed. (New York: Collier, 1909).

9. J. Jennings, *Less Is More: How Great Companies Use Productivity as a Competitive Tool in Business* (New York: Portfolio, 2002).

10. F. W. Taylor, *The Principles of Scientific Management* (New York: Norton, 1911).

11. Hearings before Special Committee of the House of Representatives to Investigate the Taylor and Other Systems of Shop Management under Authority of House Resolution 90, Vol. 3, 1377–1508 contains Taylor's testimony before the committee from Thursday, January 25, through Tuesday, January 30, 1912.

12. J. Breal, "Secret Sauce," *Fast Company* 115 (May 2007): 61–63.

13. F. J. Roethlisberger, *Management and Morale* (Cambridge, Mass.: Harvard University Press, 1941).

14. L. Van Dyne and J. L. Pierce, "Psychological Ownership and Feelings of Possession: Three Field Studies Predicting Employee Attitudes and Organizational Citizenship Behavior," *Journal of Organizational Behavior* 25 (2004): 439–459.

15. A. H. Maslow, "A Theory of Human Motivation," *Psychological Review* 50 (1943): 370–396.

16. W. James, *The Principles of Psychology* (New York: H. Holt & Co., 1890; Cambridge, Mass.: Harvard University Press, 1983); J. Dewey, *Human Nature and Conduct: An Introduction to Social Psychology* (New York: Holt, 1922); S. Freud, *A General Introduction to Psycho-Analysis: A Course of Twenty-Eight Lectures Delivered at the University of Vienna* (New York: Liveright, 1963); A. Adler, *Understanding Human Nature* (Greenwich, Conn.: Fawcett, 1927).

17. E. E. Lawler, III, and J. L. Suttle, "A Causal Correlational Test of the Need Hierarchy Concept," *Organizational Behavior and Human Performance* 7 (1973): 265–287.

18. N. K. Austin, "The Power of the Pyramid: The Foundation of Human Psychology and, Thereby, of Motivation, Maslow's Hierarchy Is One Powerful Pyramid," *Incentive* 176 (July 2002): 10.

19. D. M. McGregor, *The Human Side of Enterprise* (New York: McGraw-Hill, 1960).

20. D. M. McGregor, "The Human Side of Enterprise," *Management Review* (November 1957): 22–28, 88–92.

21. E. E. Lawler, G. E. Lawford, S. A. Mohrman, and G. E. Ledford, Jr., *Strategies for High Performance Organizations—The CEO Report: Employee Involvement, TQM, and Reengineering Programs in* Fortune *1000 Corporations* (San Francisco: Jossey-Bass, Inc., 1998).

22. J. Boorstin, "No Preservatives. No Unions. Lots of Dough," *Fortune* 148 (September 15, 2003): 127–129.

23. C. P. Alderfer, *Human Needs in Organizational Settings* (New York: Free Press, 1972).

24. B. Schneider and C. P. Alderfer, "Three Studies of Need Satisfactions in Organizations," *Administrative Science Quarterly* 18 (1973): 489–505.

25. H. A. Murray, *Explorations in Personality: A Clinical and Experimental Study of Fifty Men of College Age* (New York: Oxford University Press, 1938).

26. D. C. McClelland, *Motivational Trends in Society* (Morristown, N.J.: General Learning Press, 1971).

27. D. C. McClelland, "Achievement Motivation Can Be Learned," *Harvard Business Review* 43 (1965): 6–24.

28. J. P. Chaplin and T. S. Krawiec, *Systems and Theories of Psychology* (New York: Holt, Rinehart & Winston, 1960); M. Stahl, *Managerial and Technical Motivation: Assessing Needs for Achievement, Power, and Affiliation* (Praeger, 1986).

29. E. A. Ward, "Multidimensionality of Achievement Motivation among Employed Adults," *Journal of Social Psychology* 134 (1997): 542–544.

30. A. Sagie, D. Elizur, and H. Yamauchi, "The Structure and Strength of Achievement Motivation: A Cross-Cultural Comparison," *Journal of Organizational Behavior* 17 (1996): 431–444.

31. D. C. McClelland and D. Burnham, "Power Is the Great Motivator," *Harvard Business Review* 54 (1976): 100–111; J. Hall and J. Hawker, *Power Management Inventory* (The Woodlands, Tex.: Teleometrics International, 1988).

32. S. Schachter, *The Psychology of Affiliation* (Stanford, Calif.: Stanford University Press, 1959).

33. F. Herzberg, B. Mausner, and B. Snyderman, *The Motivation to Work* (New York: Wiley, 1959).

34. F. Herzberg, *Work and the Nature of Man* (Cleveland: World, 1966).

35. J. Marquez, "Winning Women Back," *Workforce Management* 86, No. 7 (2007): 20–21.

36. F. J. Leach and J. D. Westbrook, "Motivation and Job Satisfaction in One Government Research and Development Environment," *Engineering Management Journal* 12 (2000): 3–8.

37. D. L. Nelson and B. L. Simmons, "Health Psychology and Work Stress: A More Positive Approach," in J. C. Quick and L. E. Tetrick, eds., *Handbook of Occupational Health Psychology* (Washington, D.C.: American Psychological Association, 2003): 97–119.

38. K. S. Cameron, J. E. Dutton, and R. E. Quinn, eds., *Positive Organizational Scholarship: Foundations of a New Discipline* (San Francisco: Berrett-Keohler, 2003).

39. J. Loehr and T. Schwartz, "The Making of a Corporate Athlete," *Harvard Business Review* 79 (2001): 120–129.

40. J. Loehr and T. Schwartz, *The Power of Full Engagement: Managing Energy, Not Time, Is the Key to High Performance and Personal Renewal* (New York: Free Press, 2003).

41. G. Kholreiser, "Engaging Employees Crucial for Their Morale," *The Nation* (November 29, 2010), http://www.nationmultimedia.com/2010/11/29/business/Engaging-employees-crucial-for-their-morale-30143355.html, accessed May 12, 2011.

42. P. M. Blau, *Exchange and Power in Social Life* (New York: Wiley, 1964); N. Horster, *Principles of Exchange and Power: Integrating the Theory of Social Institutions and the Theory of Value* (New York: P. Lang, 1997).

43. A. Etzioni, "A Basis for Comparative Analysis of Complex Organizations," in A. Etzioni, ed., *A Sociological Reader on Complex Organizations,* 2nd ed. (New York: Holt, Rinehart & Winston, 1969): 59–76.

44. S. S. Masterson and C. L. Stamper, "Perceived Organizational Membership: An Aggregate Framework Representing the Employee–Organization Relationship," *Journal of Organizational Behavior* 24 (2003): 473–490.

45. L. J. Song, A. S. Tsui, and K. S. Long, "Unpacking Employee Responses to Organizational Exchange Mechanisms: The Role of Social and Economic Exchange Perceptions," *Journal of Management* 35 (2009): 56–93.

46. J. S. Adams, "Inequity in Social Exchange," in L. Berkowitz, ed., *Advances in Experimental Social Psychology,* Vol. 2 (New York: Academic Press, 1965): 267–299; J. S. Adams, "Toward an Understanding of Inequity," *Journal of Abnormal and Social Psychology* 67 (1963): 422–436.

47. J. Nelson-Horchler, "The Best Man for the Job Is a Man," *Industry Week* (January 7, 1991): 50–52.

48. P. D. Sweeney, D. B. McFarlin, and E. J. Inderrieden, "Using Relative Deprivation Theory to Explain Satisfaction with Income and Pay Level: A Multistudy Examination," *Academy of Management Journal* 33 (1990): 423–436.

49. R. C. Huseman, J. D. Hatfield, and E. A. Miles, "A New Perspective on Equity Theory: The Equity Sensitivity Construct," *Academy of Management Review* 12 (1987): 222–234.

50. D. McLoughlin and S. C. Carr, "Equity and Sensitivity and Double Demotivation," *Journal of Social Psychology* 137 (1997): 668–670.

51. K. E. Weick, M. G. Bougon, and G. Maruyama, "The Equity Context," *Organizational Behavior and Human Performance* 15 (1976): 32–65.

52. R. C. Huseman, J. D. Hatfield, and E. W. Miles, "A New Perspective on Equity Theory: The Equity Sensitivity Construct," *The Academy of Management Review* 12 (1987): 222–234.

53. J. Greenberg, "Equity and Workplace Status: A Field Experiment," *Journal of Applied Psychology* 73 (1988): 606–613.

54. J. Greenberg, "Losing Sleep over Organizational Justice: Attenuating Insomniac Reactions to Underpayment Inequity with Supervisory Training in Interactional Justice," *Journal of Applied Psychology* 91 (2006): 58–69.

55. J. Greenberg and B. Alge, "Aggressive Reactions to Workplace Injustice," in R. W. Griffin, A. O'Leary-Kelly, and J. Collins, eds., *Dysfunctional Behavior in Organizations, Vol. 1: Violent Behaviors in Organizations* (Greenwich, CT: JAI, 1998): 119–145.

56. R. A. Cosier and D. R. Dalton, "Equity Theory and Time: A Reformulation," *Academy of Management Review* 8 (1983): 311–319.

57. J. E. Martin and M. W. Peterson, "Two-Tier Wage Structures: Implications for Equity Theory," *Academy of Management Journal* 30 (1987): 297–315.

58. R. J. Sanchez, D. M. Truxillo, and T. N. Bauer, "Development and Examination of an Expectancy-Based Measure of Test-Taking Motivation," *Journal of Applied Psychology* 85 (2000): 739–750.

59. V. H. Vroom, *Work and Motivation* (New York: Wiley, 1964/1970).

60. U. R. Larson, "Supervisor's Performance Feedback to Subordinates: The Effect of Performance Valence and Outcome Dependence," *Organizational Behavior and Human Decision Processes* 37 (1986): 391–409.

61. M. C. Kernan and R. G. Lord, "Effects of Valence, Expectancies, and Goal-Performance Discrepancies in Single and Multiple Goal Environments," *Journal of Applied Psychology* 75 (1990): 194–203.

62. R. J. Sanchez, D. M. Truxillo, and T. N. Bauer, "Development and Examination of an Expectancy-Based Measure of Test-Taking Motivation," *Journal of Applied Psychology* 85 (2000): 739–750.

63. W. VanEerde and H. Thierry, "Vroom's Expectancy Models and Work-Related Criteria: A Meta-Analysis," *Journal of Applied Psychology* 81 (1996): 575–586.

64. E. D. Pulakos and N. Schmitt, "A Longitudinal Study of a Valence Model Approach for the Prediction of Job Satisfaction of New Employees," *Journal of Applied Psychology* 68 (1983): 307–312; F. J. Landy and W. S. Becker, "Motivation Theory Reconsidered," in L. L. Cummings and B. M. Staw, eds., *Research in Organizational Behavior* 9 (Greenwich, Conn.: JAI Press, 1987): 1–38.

65. J. Gibbs, K. Basinger, and D. Fuller, Moral Maturity: Measuring the Development of Sociomoral Reflection (Hillsdale, NJ: L. Erlbaum, 1992).

66. N. J. Adler, *International Dimensions of Organizational Behavior,* 4th ed. (Mason, Ohio: South-Western, 2001).

67. G. Hofstede, "Motivation, Leadership, and Organization: Do American Theories Apply Abroad?" *Organizational Dynamics* 9 (1980): 42–63.

68. G. H. Hines, "Cross-Cultural Differences in Two-Factor Theory," *Journal of Applied Psychology* 58 (1981): 313–317.

69. M. C. Bolino and W. H. Turnley, "Old Faces, New Places: Equity Theory in Cross-Cultural Contexts," *Journal of Organizational Behavior* 29 (2008): 29–50; M. C. Bolino and W. H. Turnley, "Erratum: Old Faces, New Places: Equity Theory in Cross-Cultural Contexts," *Journal of Organizational Behavior* 29 (2008): i.

Chapter 6

1. P. Pavlov, *Conditioned Reflexes* (New York: Oxford University Press, 1927).

2. B. Cannon, "Walter B. Cannon: Reflections on the Man and His Contributions," *Centennial Session,* American Psychological Association Centennial Convention, Washington, D.C., 1992.

3. B. F. Skinner, *The Behavior of Organisms: An Experimental Analysis* (New York: Appleton-Century-Crofts, 1938).

4. B. F. Skinner, *Science and Human Behavior* (New York: Free Press, 1953).

5. F. Luthans and R. Kreitner, *Organizational Behavior Modification and Beyond* (Glenview, Ill.: Scott, Foresman, 1985).

6. A. D. Stajkovic and F. Luthans, "A Meta-Analysis of the Effects of Organizational Behavior Modification on Task Performance, 1975–95," *Academy of Management Journal* 40 (1997): 1122–1149.

7. C. B. Cadsby, F. Song, and F. Tapon, "Sorting and Incentive Effects of Pay for Performance: An Experimental Investigation," *Academy of Management Journal* 50 (2007): 387–405.

8. K. K. Merriman, "Lost in Translation: Cultural Interpretations of Performance Pay," *Compensation and Benefits Review* 42 (2010): 403–410.

9. J. Hale, "Strategic Rewards: Keeping Your Best Talent from Walking Out the Door," *Compensation and Benefits Management* 14 (1998): 39–50.

10. B. F. Skinner, *Contingencies of Reinforcement: A Theoretical Analysis* (New York: Appleton-Century-Crofts, 1969).

11. J. P. Chaplin and T. S. Krawiec, *Systems and Theories of Psychology* (New York: Holt, Rinehart & Winston, 1960).

12. M. Maccoby, J. Hoffer Gittell, and M. Ledeen, "Leadership and the Fear Factor," *Sloan Management Review* 148 (Winter 2004): 14–18.

13. A. Bandura, *Social Learning Theory* (Englewood Cliffs, N.J.: Prentice-Hall, 1977); A. Bandura, "Self-Efficacy: Toward a Unifying Theory of Behavioral Change," *Psychological Review* 84 (1977): 191–215.

14. J. J. Martocchio and E. J. Hertenstein, "Learning Orientation and Goal Orientation Context: Relationships with Cognitive and Affective Learning Outcomes," *Human Resource Development Quarterly* 14 (2003): 413–434.

15. A. Bandura, "Regulation of Cognitive Processes through Perceived Self-Efficacy," *Developmental Psychology* (September 1989): 729–735.

16. J. M. Phillips and S. M. Gully, "Role of Goal Orientation, Ability, Need for Achievement, and Locus of Control in the Self-Efficacy and Goal-Setting Process," *Journal of Applied Psychology* 82 (1997): 792–802.

17. J. C. Weitlauf, R. E. Smith, and D. Cervone, "Generalization Effects of Coping-Skills Training: Influence of Self-Defense Training on Women's Efficacy Beliefs, Assertiveness, and Aggression," *Journal of Applied Psychology* 85 (2000): 625–633.

18. A. D. Stajkovic and F. Luthans, "Social Cognitive Theory and Self-Efficacy: Going beyond Traditional Motivational and Behavioral Approaches," *Organizational Dynamics* (Spring 1998): 62–74.

19. T. M. Amabile and S. J. Kramer, "The Power of Small Wins," *Harvard Business Review* 38, No. 5 (July 8, 2008): 70–80.

20. V. Gecas, "The Social Psychology of Self-Efficacy," *Annual Review of Sociology* 15 (1989): 291–316.

21. E. A. Locke and G. P. Latham, *A Theory of Goal Setting and Task Performance* (Englewood Cliffs, N.J.: Prentice-Hall, 1990).

22. A. D. Stajkovic, E. A. Locke, and E. S. Blair, "A First Examination of the Relationships between Primed Subconscious Goals, Assigned Conscious Goals, and Task Performance," *Journal of Applied Psychology* 91 (2006): 1172–1180.

23. T. O. Murray, *Management by Objectives: A Systems Approach to Management* (Fort Worth, Tex.: Western Company, n.d.).

24. W. T. Brooks and T. W. Mullins, *High Impact Time Management* (Englewood Cliffs, N.J.: Prentice-Hall, 1989).

25. E. A. Locke, "Toward a Theory of Task Motivation and Incentives," *Organizational Behavior and Human Performance* 3 (1968): 157–189.

26. J. C. Quick, "Dyadic Goal Setting within Organizations: Role Making and Motivational Considerations," *Academy of Management Review* 4 (1979): 369–380.

27. D. McGregor, "An Uneasy Look at Performance Appraisal," *Harvard Business Review* 35 (1957): 89–94.

28. J. R. Hollenbeck, C. R. Williams, and H. J. Klein, "An Empirical Examination of the Antecedents of Commitment to Difficult Goals," *Journal of Applied Psychology* 74 (1989): 18–23.

29. R. C. Rodgers and J. E. Hunter, "The Impact of Management by Objectives on Organizational Productivity," unpublished paper (Lexington: University of Kentucky, 1989).

30. E. A. Locke, K. N. Shaw, L. M. Saari, and G. P. Latham, "Goal Setting and Task Performance: 1969–1980," *Psychological Bulletin* 90 (1981): 125–152.

31. D. B. Fedora, W. D. Davis, J. M. Maslync, and K. Mathiesond, "Performance Improvement Efforts in Response to Negative Feedback: The Roles of Source Power and Recipient Self-Esteem," *Journal of Management* 27 (2001): 79–98.

32. J. C. Quick, "Dyadic Goal Setting and Role Stress," *Academy of Management Journal* 22 (1979): 241–252.

33. G. S. Odiorne, *Management by Objectives: A System of Managerial Leadership* (New York: Pitman, 1965).

34. American Management Association, *Blueprints for Service Quality: The Federal Express Approach* (New York: American Management Association, 1991).

35. P. F. Drucker, *The Practice of Management* (New York: Harper & Bros., 1954).

36. R. D. Prichard, P. L. Roth, S. D. Jones, P. J. Galgay, and M. D. Watson, "Designing a Goal-Setting System to Enhance Performance: A Practical Guide," *Organizational Dynamics* 17 (1988): 69–78.

37. C. L. Hughes, *Goal Setting: Key to Individual and Organizational Effectiveness* (New York: American Management Association, 1965).

38. M. E. Tubbs and S. E. Ekeberg, "The Role of Intentions in Work Motivation: Implications for Goal-Setting Theory and Research," *Academy of Management Review* 16 (1991): 180–199.

39. S. Vatave, "Managing Risk," *Supervision* 65 (2004): 6–9.

40. J. R. Hollenbeck and A. P. Brief, "The Effects of Individual Differences and Goal Origin on Goal Setting and Performance," *Organizational Behavior and Human Decision Processes* 40 (1987): 392–414.

41. R. A. Katzell and D. E. Thompson, "Work Motivation: Theory and Practice," *American Psychologist* 45 (1990): 144–153; M. W. McPherson, "Is Psychology the Science of Behavior?" *American Psychologist* 47 (1992): 329–335.

42. E. A. Locke, "The Ideas of Frederick W. Taylor: An Evaluation," *Academy of Management Review* 7 (1982): 15–16; R. M. Yerkes and J. D. Dodson, "The Relation of Strength of Stimulus to Rapidity of Habit-Formation," *Journal of Comparative Neurology and Psychology* 18 (1908): 459–482.

43. F. L. Schmidt and J. Hunter, "General Mental Ability in the World of Work: Occupational Attainment and Job Performance," *Journal of Personality and Social Psychology* 86 (2004): 162–173.

44. R. L. Cardy, *Performance Management: Concepts, Skills, and Exercises* (Armonk, New York, and London, England: M. E. Sharpe, 2004).

45. D. Hartley-Wilkins, "Getting the Best out of Your People: Managing Performance," *Human Resources* (April/May 2010): 26–27.

46. P. Cappelli and N. Rogovsky, "Employee Involvement and Organizational Citizenship: Implications for Labor Law Reform and 'Lean Production,'" *Industrial & Labor Relations Review* 51 (1998): 633–653.

47. L. D. Ordonez, M. E. Schweitzer, A. D. Galinskly, and M. H. Bazerman. "Goals Gone Wild: The Systematic Side Effects of Overprescribing Goal Setting," *Academy of Management Perspectives* 23 (2009): 6–16; E. A. Locke and G. P. Latham, "Has Goal Setting Gone Wild, or Have Its Attackers Abandoned Good Scholarship?" *Academy of Management Perspectives* 23 (2009): 17–23.

48. M. E. Tubbs and M. L. Trusty, "Direct Reports of Motivation for Task Performance Levels: Some Construct-Related Evidence," *Journal of Psychology* 135 (2001): 185–205.

49. S. Ellis, R. Mendel, and M. Aloni-Zohar, "The Effect of Accuracy of Performance Evaluation on Learning from Experience: The Moderating Role of After-Event Reviews," *Journal of Applied Social Psychology* 39, No. 3 (2009): 541–563.

50. R. R. Kilburg, *Executive Coaching: Developing Managerial Wisdom in a World of Chaos* (Washington, D.C.: American Psychological Association, 2000).

51. K. Y. Wilson, "An Analysis of Bias in Supervisor Narrative Comments in Performance Appraisal," *Human Relations* 63 (2010): 1903–1933.

52. H. H. Meyer, E. Kay, and J. R. P. French, "Split Roles in Performance Appraisal," *Harvard Business Review* 43 (1965): 123–129.

53. W. Lam, X. Huang, and E. Snape, "Feedback-Seeking Behavior and Leader-Member Exchange: Do Supervisor-Attributed Motives Matter?" *Academy of Management Journal* 50 (2007): 348–363.

54. W. A. Fisher, J. C. Quick, L. L. Schkade, and G. W. Ayers, "Developing Administrative Personnel through the Assessment Center Technique," *Personnel Administrator* 25 (1980): 44–46, 62.

55. J. S. Goodman, R. E. Wood, and M. Hendrickx, "Feedback Specificity, Exploration, and Learning," *Journal of Applied Psychology* 89 (2004): 248–262.

56. M. B. DeGregorio and C. D. Fisher, "Providing Performance Feedback: Reactions to Alternative Methods," *Journal of Management* 14 (1988): 605–616.

57. G. C. Thornton, "The Relationship between Supervisory and Self-Appraisals of Executive Performance," *Personnel Psychology* 21 (1968): 441–455.

58. A. S. DeNisi and A. N. Kluger, "Feedback Effectiveness: Can 360-Degree Appraisals Be Improved?" *Academy of Management Executive* 14 (2000): 129–140.

59. F. Luthans and S. J. Peterson, "360-Degree Feedback with Systematic Coaching: Empirical Analysis Suggests a Winning Combination," *Human Resource Management* 42 (2003): 243–256.

60. G. Toegel and J. A. Conger, "360-Degree Assessment: Time for Reinvention," *Academy of Management Learning and Education* 2 (2003): 297–311.

61. L. Hirschhorn, "Leaders and Followers in a Postindustrial Age: A Psychodynamic View," *Journal of Applied Behavioral Science* 26 (1990): 529–542.

62. F. M. Jablin, "Superior-Subordinate Communication: The State of the Art," *Psychological Bulletin* 86 (1979): 1201–1222.

63. J. Pfeffer, "Six Dangerous Myths about Pay," *Harvard Business Review* 76 (1998): 108–119.

64. F. L. Giancola, "Examining the Job Itself as a Source of Employee Motivation," *Compensation and Benefits Review* 43 (2011): 23–29.

65. "Six Employee Types Prefer Different Rewards," *HRFocus* 84, No. 4 (April 2007): 12.

66. M. Erez, "Work Motivation from a Cross-Cultural Perspective," in A. M. Bouvy, F. J. R. Van de Vijver, P. Boski, and P. G. Schmitz, eds., *Journeys into Cross-Cultural Psychology* (Amsterdam, Netherlands: Swets and Zeitlinger, 1994): 386–403.

67. G. T. Milkovich and J. M. Newman, *Compensation,* 4th ed. (Homewood, Ill.: Irwin, 1993).

68. T. Taylor, "The Challenge of Project Team Incentives," *Compensation and Benefits Review* 42 (2010): 411–419.

69. J. M. Bardwick, *Danger in the Comfort Zone* (New York: American Management Association, 1991).

70. D. F. Giannetto, "Get Your Money's Worth from Incentives," *Business Performance Management*, 7 (2009): 12.

71. M. J. Martinko and W. L. Gardner, "The Leader/Member Attributional Process," *Academy of Management Review* 12 (1987): 235–249.

72. K. N. Wexley, R. A. Alexander, J. P. Greenawalt, and M. A. Couch, "Attitudinal Congruence and Similarity as Related to Interpersonal

Evaluations in Manager-Subordinate Dyads," *Academy of Management Journal* 23 (1980): 320–330.

73. H. H. Kelley, *Attribution in Social Interaction* (New York: General Learning Press, 1971); H. H. Kelley, "The Processes of Causal Attribution," *American Psychologist* 28 (1973): 107–128.

74. B. Raabe and T. A. Beehr, "Formal Mentoring versus Supervisor and Coworker Relationships: Differences in Perceptions and Impact," *Journal of Organizational Behavior* 24 (2003): 271–293.

75. A. M. Young and P. L. Perrewe, "What Did You Expect? An Examination of Career-Related Support and Social Support among Mentors and Protégés," *Journal of Management* 26 (2000): 611–633.

76. K. Doherty, "The Good News about Depression," *Business and Health* 3 (1989): 1–4.

77. K. E. Kram, "Phases of the Mentor Relationship," *Academy of Management Journal* 26 (1983): 608–625.

78. T. D. Allen, L. T. Eby, M. L. Poteet, E. Lentz, and L. Lima, "Career Benefits Associated with Mentoring for Protégés: A Meta-Analysis," *Journal of Applied Psychology* 89 (2004): 127–136.

79. S.J. Wells, "Choices Flourish at IBM," *HR Magazine* (May 2009): 52–57.

80. K. E. Kram and L. A. Isabella, "Mentoring Alternatives: The Role of Peer Relationships in Career Development," *Academy of Management Journal* 28 (1985): 110–132.

81. J. Greco, "Hey, Coach!" *Journal of Business Strategy* 22 (2001): 28–32.

Chapter 7

1. J. Barling, E. K. Kelloway, and M. R. Frone, eds., *Handbook of Work Stress* (Thousand Oaks, CA: Sage Publications, 2005).

2. M. Blake Hargrove, J. C. Quick, D. L. Nelson, and J. D. Quick. 2011. The Theory of Preventive Stress Management: A 33-Year Review and Evaluation. *Stress and Health,* 27, 182–193.

3. S. Benison, A. C. Barger, and E. L. Wolfe, *Walter B. Cannon: The Life and Times of a Young Scientist* (Cambridge, Mass.: Harvard University Press, 1987).

4. W. B. Cannon, "Stresses and Strains of Homeostasis," *American Journal of the Medical Sciences* 189 (1935): 1–14.

5. W. B. Cannon, *The Wisdom of the Body* (New York: Norton, 1932).

6. R. S. Lazarus, *Psychological Stress and the Coping Process* (New York: McGraw-Hill, 1966).

7. R. Rau, K. Morling, and U. Rosler, "Is There a Relationship between Major Depression and Both Objectively Assessed and Perceived Demands and Control?" *Work and Stress* 24 (2010): 88–106.

8. C. Liu, P. E. Spector, and L. Shi, "Cross-National Job Stress: A Quantitative and Qualitative Study," *Journal of Organizational Behavior* 28 (2007): 209–239.

9. J. Doron, Y. Stephan, C. Maiano, and C. LeScanff, "Motivational Predictors of Coping with Academic Examinations," *The Journal of Social Psychology* 151 (2011): 87–104.

10. J. D. Kammeyer-Mueller, T. A. Judge, and B. A. Scott, "The Role of Core Self-Evaluations in the Coping Process," *Journal of Applied Psychology* 94 (2009): 177–195.

11. D. Katz and R. L. Kahn, *The Social Psychology of Organizations,* 2nd ed. (New York: Wiley, 1978): 185–221.

12. H. Levinson, "A Psychoanalytic View of Occupational Stress," *Occupational Mental Health* 3 (1978): 2–13.

13. P. L. Perrewé, K. L. Zellars, G. R. Ferris, A. M. Rossi, C. J. Kacmar, and D. A. Ralston, "Neutralizing Job Stressors: Political Skill as an Antidote to the Dysfunctional Consequences of Role Conflict," *Academy of Management Journal* 47 (2004): 141–152.

14. T. L. Friedman, *The Lexus and the Olive Tree* (New York: Vintage Anchor, 2000).

15. S. Zuboff, *In the Age of the Smart Machine: The Future of Work and Power* (New York: Basic Books, 1988).

16. D. T. Hall and J. Richter, "Career Gridlock: Baby Boomers Hit the Wall," *Academy of Management Executive* 4 (1990): 7–22.

17. N. P. Podsakoff, J. A. LePine, and M. A. LePine, "Differential Challenge Stressor-Hindrance Stressor Relationships with Job Attitudes, Turnover Intentions, Turnover, and Withdrawal Behavior: A Meta-Analysis," *Journal of Applied Psychology* 92 (2007): 438–454.

18. R. L. Kahn, D. M. Wolfe, R. P. Quinn, J. D. Snoek, and R. A. Rosenthal, *Organizational Stress: Studies in Role Conflict and Ambiguity* (New York: Wiley, 1964).

19. C. Vandenberge, A. Panaciio, K. Bentein, K. Mignonac, P. Roussel, "Assessing Longitudinal Change of and Dynamic Relationships among Role Stressors, Job Attitudes, Turnover Intention, and Well-Being in Neophyte Newcomers," *Journal of Organizational Behavior* 34 (2011): 652–671.

20. L. B. Hammer, T. N. Bauer, and A. A. Grandey, "Work-Family Conflict and Work-Related Withdrawal Behaviors," *Journal of Business and Psychology* 17 (2003): 419–436.

21. M. F. Peterson et al., "Role Conflict, Ambiguity, and Overload: A 21-Nation Study," *Academy of Management Journal* 38 (1995): 429–452.

22. S. Pal and P. O. Saksvik, "Work–Family Conflict and Psychosocial Work Environment Stressors as Predictors of Job Stress in a Cross-Cultural Study," *International Journal of Stress Management* 15, No. 1 (2008): 22–42.

23. A. Skogstad, S. Einarsen, T. Torsheim, M. S. Aasland, and H. Hetland, "The Destructiveness of Laissez-Faire Leadership Behavior," *Journal of Occupational Health Psychology* 12 (2007): 80–92.

24. P. D. Bliese and C. A. Castro, "Role Clarity, Work Overload and Organizational Support: Multilevel Evidence of the Importance of Support," *Work and Stress* 14 (2000): 65–74.

25. P. J. Frost, *Toxic Emotions at Work: How Compassionate Managers Handle Pain and Conflict* (Boston: Harvard Business School Press, 2003).

26. S. Grebner, N. K. Semmer, L. L. Faso, S. Gut, W. Kalin, and A. Elfering, "Working Conditions, Well-Being, and Job-Related Attitudes among Call Centre Agents," *European Journal of Work and Organizational Psychology* 12 (2003): 341–365.

27. M. P. Bell, J. C. Quick, and C. Cycota, "Assessment and Prevention of Sexual Harassment: An Applied Guide to Creating Healthy Organizations," *International Journal of Selection and Assessment* 10 (2002): 160–167.

28. L. T. Hosmer, "Trust: The Connecting Link between Organizational Theory and Philosophical Ethics," *Academy of Management Review* 20 (1995): 379–403; V. J. Doby and R. D. Caplan, "Organizational Stress as Threat to Reputation: Effects on Anxiety at Work and at Home," *Academy of Management Journal* 38 (1995): 1105–1123.

29. R. T. Keller, "Cross-Functional Project Groups in Research and New Product Development: Diversity, Communications, Job Stress, and Outcomes," *Academy of Management Journal* 33 (2001): 547–555.

30. M. F. Peterson and P. B. Smith, "Does National Culture or Ambient Temperature Explain Cross-National Differences in Role Stress? No Sweat!" *Academy of Management Journal* 40 (1997): 930–946.

31. K. K. Gillingham, "High-G Stress and Orientational Stress: Physiologic Effects of Aerial Maneuvering," *Aviation, Space, and Environmental Medicine* 59 (1988): A10–A20.

32. R. S. DeFrank, "Executive Travel Stress: Perils of the Road Warrior," *Academy of Management Executive* 14 (2000): 58–72; M. Westman, "Strategies for Coping with Business Trips: A Qualitative Exploratory Study," *International Journal of Stress Management* 11 (2004): 167–176.

33. R. S. Bhagat, S. J. McQuaid, S. Lindholm, and J. Segovis, "Total Life Stress: A Multimethod Validation of the Construct and Its Effect on Organizationally Valued Outcomes and Withdrawal Behaviors," *Journal of Applied Psychology* 70 (1985): 202–214.

34. J. C. Quick, J. R. Joplin, D. A. Gray, and E. C. Cooley, "The Occupational Life Cycle and the Family," in L. L'Abate, ed., *Handbook of Developmental Family Psychology and Psychopathology* (New York: John Wiley, 1993).

35. S. Shellenbarger, "Work and Family," *The Wall Street Journal* (January 31, 1996): B1.

36. S. A. Lobel, "Allocation of Investment in Work and Family Roles: Alternative Theories and Implications for Research," *Academy of Management Review* 16 (1991): 507–521.

37. G. Porter, "Organizational Impact of Workaholism: Suggestions for Researching the Negative Outcomes of Excessive Work," *Journal of Occupational Health Psychology* 1 (1996): 70–84.

38. J. W. Pennebaker, C. F. Hughes, and R. C. O'Heeron, "The Psychophysiology of Confession: Linking Inhibitory and Psychosomatic

Processes," *Journal of Personality and Social Psychology* 52 (1987): 781–793.

39. J. Loehr and T. Schwartz, "The Making of a Corporate Athlete," *Harvard Business Review* 79 (2001): 120–129.

40. J. D. Quick, R. S. Horn, and J. C. Quick, "Health Consequences of Stress," *Journal of Organizational Behavior Management* 8 (1986): 19–36.

41. R. M. Yerkes and J. D. Dodson, "The Relation of Strength of Stimulus to Rapidity of Habit-Formation," *Journal of Comparative Neurology and Psychology* 18 (1908): 459–482.

42. J. E. McGrath, "Stress and Behavior in Organizations," in M. D. Dunnette, ed., *Handbook of Industrial and Organizational Psychology* (Chicago: Rand McNally, 1976): 1351–1395.

43. T. A. Wright, R. Cropanzano, and D. G. Meyer, "State and Trait Correlates of Job Performance: A Tale of Two Perspectives," *Journal of Business and Psychology* 18 (2004): 365–383.

44. W. B. Cannon, *Bodily Changes in Pain, Hunger, Fear, and Rage* (New York: Appleton, 1915).

45. P. A. Herbig and F. A. Palumbo, "Karoshi: Salaryman Sudden Death Syndrome," *Journal of Managerial Psychology* 9 (1994): 11–16.

46. S. Sauter, L. R. Murphy, and J. J. Hurrell, Jr., "Prevention of Work-Related Psychological Distress: A National Strategy Proposed by the National Institute for Occupational Safety and Health," *American Psychologist* 45 (1990): 1146–1158.

47. R. Cropanzano, D. E. Rupp, and Z. S. Byrne, "The Relationship of Emotional Exhaustion to Work Attitudes, Job Performance, and Organizational Citizenship Behaviors," *Journal of Applied Psychology* 88 (2003): 160–169.

48. A. A. Grandey, "When 'The Show Must Go On': Surface Acting and Deep Acting as Determinants of Emotional Exhaustion and Peer-Rated Service Delivery," *Academy of Management Journal* 46 (2003): 86–96.

49. G. B. Hall, M. F. Dollard, M. R. Tuckey, A. H. Winefield, and B. M. Thompson, "Job Demands, Work–Family Conflict, and Emotional Exhaustion in Police Officers: A Longitudinal Test of Competing Theories," *Journal of Occupational and Organizational Psychology* 83 (2010): 237–250.

50. J. R. B. Halbesleben and W. M. Bowler, "Emotional Exhaustion and Job Performance: The Mediating Role of Motivation," *Journal of Applied Psychology* 92 (2007): 93–106.

51. I. Wylie, "Routing Rust-Out," *Fast Company Magazine* (January 2004): 40, www.fastcompany.com/magazine/78/5things.html.

52. H. Selye, *Stress in Health and Disease* (Boston: Butterworth, 1976).

53. B. G. Ware and D. L. Block, "Cardiovascular Risk Intervention at a Work Site: The Ford Motor Company Program," *International Journal of Mental Health* 11 (1982): 68–75.

54. D. B. Kennedy, R. J. Homant, and M. R. Homant, "Perceptions of Injustice as a Predictor of Support for Workplace Aggression," *Journal of Business and Psychology* 18 (2004): 323–336.

55. N. Bolger, A. DeLongis, R. C. Kessler, and E. A. Schilling, "Effects of Daily Stress on Negative Mood," *Journal of Personality and Social Psychology* 57 (1989): 808–818.

56. B. A. Macy and P. H. Mirvis, "A Methodology for Assessment of Quality of Work Life and Organizational Effectiveness in Behavioral-Economic Terms," *Administrative Science Quarterly* 21 (1976): 212–226.

57. F. K. Cocchiara and J. C. Quick, "The Negative Effects of Positive Stereotypes: Ethnicity-Related Stressors and Implications on Organizational Health," *Journal of Organizational Behavior* 25 (2004): 781–785.

58. J. M. Ivancevich, M. T. Matteson, and E. Richards, "Who's Liable for Stress on the Job?" *Harvard Business Review* 64 (1985): 60–72.

59. *Frank S. Deus v. Allstate Insurance Company*, civil action no. 88-2099, U.S. District Court, Western District of Louisiana.

60. R. S. DeFrank and J. M. Ivancevich, "Stress on the Job: An Executive Update," *Academy of Management Executive* 12 (1998): 55–66.

61. P. Wilson and M. Bronstein, "Employers: Don't Panic about Workplace Stress," *Personnel Today* (November 4, 2003): 10.

62. J. E. Bono and M. A. Vey, "Personality and Emotional Performance: Extraversion, Neuroticism, and Self-Monitoring," *Journal of Occupational Health Psychology* 12 (2007): 177–192.

63. C. S. Troutman, K. G. Burke, and J. D. Beeler, "The Effects of Self-Efficacy, Assertiveness, Stress, and Gender on Intention," *Journal of Applied Business Research* 16 (2000): 63–75.

64. S. E. Taylor, L. C. Klein, G. P. Lewis, T. L. Gruenewald, R. A. R. Burung, and J. A. Updegraff, "Biobehavioral Responses to Stress in Females: Tend-and-Befriend, Not Fight-or-Flight," *Psychological Review* 107 (2000): 411–429.

65. D. L. Nelson and J. C. Quick, "Professional Women: Are Distress and Disease Inevitable?" *Academy of Management Review* 10 (1985): 206–218; T. D. Jick and L. F. Mitz, "Sex Differences in Work Stress," *Academy of Management Review* 10 (1985): 408–420.

66. K. M. Rospenda, K. Fujishiro, C. A. Shannon, and J. A. Richman, "Workplace Harassment, Stress, and Drinking Behavior over Time: Gender Differences in a National Sample," *Addictive Behaviors* 33 (2008): 964–967.

67. L. Verbrugge, "Recent, Present, and Future Health of American Adults," *Annual Review of Public Health* 10 (1989): 333–361.

68. M. D. Friedman and R. H. Rosenman, *Type A Behavior and Your Heart* (New York: Knopf, 1974).

69. L. Wright, "The Type A Behavior Pattern and Coronary Artery Disease," *American Psychologist* 43 (1988): 2–14.

70. J. M. Ivancevich and M. T. Matteson, "A Type A–B Person–Work Environment Interaction Model for Examining Occupational Stress and Consequences," *Human Relations* 37 (1984): 491–513.

71. S. O. C. Kobasa, "Conceptualization and Measurement of Personality in Job Stress Research," in J. J. Hurrell, Jr., L. R. Murphy, S. L. Sauter, and C. L. Cooper, eds., *Occupational Stress: Issues and Developments in Research* (New York: Taylor & Francis, 1988): 100–109.

72. J. K. Ito and C. M. Brotheridge, "Predictors and Consequences of Promotion Stress: A Bad Situation Made Worse by Employment Dependence," *International Journal of Stress Management* 16, No. 1 (2009): 65–85.

73. J. Borysenko, "Personality Hardiness," *Lectures in Behavioral Medicine* (Boston: Harvard Medical School, 1985).

74. J. S. House, K. R. Landis, and D. Umberson, "Social Relationships and Health," *Science* 241 (1988): 540–545.

75. J. Bowlby, *A Secure Base* (New York: Basic Books, 1988).

76. C. Hazan and P. Shaver, "Love and Work: An Attachment-Theoretical Perspective," *Journal of Personality and Social Psychology* 59 (1990): 270–280.

77. J. C. Quick, D. L. Nelson, and J. D. Quick, *Stress and Challenge at the Top: The Paradox of the Successful Executive* (Chichester, England: Wiley, 1990).

78. "Partner Relationship Could Be a Buffer against Work-Related Stress," *Asian News International* (June 24, 2009).

79. J. C. Quick, J. R. Joplin, D. L. Nelson, and J. D. Quick, "Self-Reliance for Stress and Combat" (*Proceedings of the 8th Combat Stress Conference*, U.S. Army Health Services Command, Fort Sam Houston, Texas, September 23–27, 1991): 1–5.

80. J. C. Dvorak, "Baffling," *PC Magazine* 3 (November 4, 2003): 61, http://www.pcmag.com/article2/0,4149,1369270,00.asp.

81. O. Janssen, "How Fairness Perceptions Make Innovative Behavior More or Less Stressful," *Journal of Organizational Behavior* 25 (2004): 201–215; T. A. Judge and J. A. Colquitt, "Organizational Justice and Stress: The Mediating Role of Work–Family Conflict," *Journal of Applied Psychology* 89 (2004): 395–404.

82. K. Hickox, "Content and Competitive," *Airman* (January 1994): 31–33.

83. A. Drach-Zahavy and A. Freund, "Team Effectiveness under Stress: A Structural Contingency Approach," *Journal of Organizational Behavior* 28 (2007): 423–450.

84. R. W. Griffin, A. O'Leary-Kelly, and J. M. Collins, eds., *Dysfunctional Behavior in Organizations: Violent and Deviant Behavior* (Stamford, Conn.: JAI Press, 1998).

85. W. L. French and C. H. Bell, Jr., *Organizational Development: Behavioral Science Interventions for Organization Improvement,* 4th ed. (Englewood Cliffs, N.J.: Prentice-Hall, 1990).

86. M. Macik-Frey, J. C. Quick, and J. D. Quick, "Interpersonal Communication: The Key to Unlocking Social Support for Preventive Stress Management," in C. L. Cooper, ed., *Handbook of Stress, Medicine, and Health,* rev. ed. (Boca Raton, FL: CRC Press).

87. J. C. Quick and C. L. Cooper, *FAST FACTS: Stress and Strain,* 2nd ed. (Oxford, England: Health Press, 2003).

88. M. E. P. Seligman, *Learned Optimism* (New York: Knopf, 1990).

89. F. Griva and F. Anagnostopoulos, "Positive Psychological States and Anxiety: The Mediating Effect of Proactive Coping," *Psychological Reports* 107 (2010): 795–804.

90. F. Luthans, "Positive Organizational Behavior: Developing and Managing Psychological Strengths for Performance Improvement," *Academy of Management Executive* 16 (2002): 57–75.

91. W. T. Brooks and T. W. Mullins, *High-Impact Time Management* (Englewood Cliffs, N.J.: Prentice-Hall, 1989).

92. M. Westman and D. Eden, "Effects of a Respite from Work on Burnout: Vacation Relief and Fade-Out," *Journal of Applied Psychology* 82 (1997): 516–527.

93. C. P. Neck and K. H. Cooper, "The Fit Executive: Exercise and Diet Guidelines for Enhancing Performance," *Academy of Management Executive* 14 (2000): 72–84.

94. M. Davis, E. R. Eshelman, and M. McKay, *The Relaxation and Stress Reduction Workbook,* 3rd ed. (Oakland, Calif.: New Harbinger, 1988).

95. H. Benson, "Your Innate Asset for Combating Stress," *Harvard Business Review* 52 (1974): 49–60.

96. D. Ornish, *Dr. Dean Ornish's Program for Reversing Cardiovascular Disease* (New York: Random House, 1995).

97. J. W. Pennebaker, *Opening Up: The Healing Power of Expressing Emotions* (New York: Guilford, 1997).

98. M. E. Francis and J. W. Pennebaker, "Putting Stress into Words: The Impact of Writing on Physiological, Absentee, and Self-Reported Emotional Well-Being Measures," *American Journal of Health Promotion* 6 (1992): 280–287.

99. Z. Solomon, B. Oppenheimer, and S. Noy, "Subsequent Military Adjustment of Combat Stress Reaction Casualties: A Nine-Year Follow-Up Study," in N. A. Milgram, ed., *Stress and Coping in Time of War: Generalizations from the Israeli Experience* (New York: Brunner/Mazel, 1986): 84–90.

100. D. Wegman and L. Fine, "Occupational Health in the 1990s," *Annual Review of Public Health* 11 (1990): 89–103; J. C. Quick, "Occupational Health Psychology: Historical Roots and Future Directions," *Health Psychology* 17 (1999): 82–88.

101. D. Gebhardt and C. Crump, "Employee Fitness and Wellness Programs in the Workplace," *American Psychologist* 45 (1990): 262–272.

102. T. Wolf, H. Randall, and J. Faucett, "A Survey of Health Promotion Programs in U.S. and Canadian Medical Schools," *American Journal of Health Promotion* 3 (1988): 33–36.

103. S. Weiss, J. Fielding, and A. Baum, *Health at Work* (Hillsdale, N.J.: Erlbaum, 1990).

104. J. B. Bennett, R. F. Cook, and K. R. Pelletier, "Toward an Integrated Framework for Comprehensive Organizational Wellness: Concepts, Practices, and Research in Workplace Health Promotion," in J. C. Quick and L. E. Tetrick, eds., *Handbook of Occupational Health Psychology:* (Washington, D.C.: American Psychological Association, 2003): 69–95.

Chapter 8

1. D. L. Whetzel, "The Department of Labor Identifies Workplace Skills," *The Industrial/Organizational Psychologist* (July 1991): 89–90.

2. M. Macik-Frey, J. C. Quick, and J. D. Quick, "Interpersonal Communication: The Key to Unlocking Social Support for Preventive Stress Management," in C. L. Cooper, ed., *Handbook of Stress, Medicine, and Health,* rev. ed. (Boca Raton, FL: CRC Press), in press.

3. *Richness* is a term originally coined by W. D. Bodensteiner, "Information Channel Utilization under Varying Research and Development Project Conditions" (Ph.D. diss., University of Texas at Austin, 1970).

4. B. Barry and I. S. Fulmer, "The Medium and the Message: The Adaptive Use of Communication Media in Dyadic Influence," *Academy of Management Review* 29 (2004): 272–292.

5. R. Reik, *Listen with the Third Ear* (New York: Pyramid, 1972).

6. E. Rautalinko and H. O. Lisper, "Effects of Training Reflective Listening in a Corporate Setting," *Journal of Business and Psychology* 18 (2004): 281–299.

7. A. G. Athos and J. J. Gabarro, *Interpersonal Behavior: Communication and Understanding in Relationships* (Englewood Cliffs, N.J.: Prentice-Hall, 1978).

8. A. D. Mangelsdorff, "Lessons Learned from the Military: Implications for Management" (Distinguished Visiting Lecture, University of Texas at Arlington, January 29, 1993).

9. D. A. Morand, "Language and Power: An Empirical Analysis of Linguistic Strategies Used in Superior–Subordinate Communication," *Journal of Organizational Behavior* 21 (2000): 235–249.

10. S. Bates, "How Leaders Communicate Big Ideas to Drive Business Results," *Employment Relations Today* 33 (Fall 2006): 13–19.

11. F. Luthans, "Successful versus Effective Real Managers," *Academy of Management Executive* 2 (1988): 127–132.

12. L. E. Penley, E. R. Alexander, I. E. Jernigan, and C. I. Henwood, "Communication Abilities of Managers: The Relationship of Performance," *Journal of Management* 17 (1991): 57–76.

13. J. A. LePine and L. Van Dyne, "Voice and Cooperative Behavior as Contrasting Forms of Contextual Performance: Evidence of Differential Relationships with Big Five Personality Characteristics and Cognitive Ability," *Journal of Applied Psychology* 86 (2001): 326–336.

14. F. M. Jablin, "Superior-Subordinate Communication: The State of the Art," *Psychological Bulletin* 86 (1979): 1201–1222; W. C. Reddin, *Communication within the Organization: An Interpretive Review of Theory and Research* (New York: Industrial Communication Council, 1972).

15. B. Barry and J. M. Crant, "Dyadic Communication Relationships in Organizations: An Attribution Expectancy Approach," *Organization Science* 11 (2000): 648–665.

16. J. Silvester, F. Patterson, A. Koczwara, and E. Ferguson, "'Trust Me . . .': Psychological and Behavioral Predictors of Perceived Physician Empathy," *Journal of Applied Psychology* 92 (2007): 519–527.

17. A. Furhham and P. Stringfield, "Congruence in Job-Performance Ratings: A Study of 360 Degree Feedback Examining Self, Manager, Peers, and Consultant Ratings," *Human Relations* 51 (1998): 517–530.

18. J. W. Gilsdorf, "Organizational Rules on Communicating: How Employees Are—and Are Not—Learning the Ropes," *Journal of Business Communication* 35 (1998): 173–201.

19. D. Tannen, *That's Not What I Mean! How Conversational Style Makes or Breaks Your Relations with Others* (New York: Morrow, 1986); D. Tannen, *You Just Don't Understand* (New York: Ballentine, 1990).

20. D. G. Allen and R. W. Griffeth, "A Vertical and Lateral Information Processing: The Effects of Gender, Employee Classification Level, and Media Richness on Communication and Work Outcomes," *Human Relations* 50 (1997): 1239–1260.

21. K. L. Ashcraft, "Empowering 'Professional' Relationships," *Management Communication Quarterly* 13 (2000): 347–393.

22. G. Hofstede, *Culture's Consequences: International Differences in Work-Related Values* (Beverly Hills, Calif.: Sage Publications, 1980).

23. G. Hofstede, "Motivation, Leadership, and Organization: Do American Theories Apply Abroad?" *Organizational Dynamics* 9 (1980): 42–63.

24. H. Levinson, *Executive* (Cambridge, Mass.: Harvard University Press, 1981).

25. P. Benimadhu, "Adding Value through Diversity: An Interview with Bernard F. Isautier," *Canadian Business Review* 22 (1995): 6–11.

26. M. J. Gannon and Associates, *Understanding Global Cultures: Metaphorical Journeys through 17 Countries* (Thousand Oaks, Calif.: Sage Publications, 1994).

27. T. Wells, *Keeping Your Cool under Fire: Communicating Nondefensively* (New York: McGraw-Hill, 1980).

28. R. D. Laing, *The Politics of the Family and Other Essays* (New York: Pantheon, 1971).

29. H. S. Schwartz, *Narcissistic Process and Corporate Decay: The Theory of the Organizational Ideal* (New York: New York University Press, 1990).

30. W. R. Forrester and M. F. Maute, "The Impact of Relationship Satisfaction on Attribution, Emotions, and Behaviors Following Service Failure," *Journal of Applied Business Research* (2000): 1–45.

31. M. L. Knapp, *Nonverbal Communication in Human Interaction* (New York: Holt, Rinehart & Winston, 1978); J. McCroskey and L. Wheeless, *Introduction to Human Communication* (New York: Allyn & Bacon, 1976).

32. A. M. Katz and V. T. Katz, eds., *Foundations of Nonverbal Communication* (Carbondale, Ill.: Southern Illinois University Press, 1983).

33. M. D. Lieberman, "Intuition: A Social Cognitive Neuroscience Approach," *Psychological Bulletin* (2000): 109–138.

34. E. T. Hall, *The Hidden Dimension* (Garden City, N.Y.: Doubleday Anchor, 1966).

35. E. T. Hall, "Proxemics," in A. M. Katz and V. T. Katz, eds., *Foundations of Nonverbal Communication* (Carbondale, Ill.: Southern Illinois University Press, 1983).

36. R. T. Barker and C. G. Pearce, "The Importance of Proxemics at Work," *Supervisory Management* 35 (1990): 10–11.

37. R. L. Birdwhistell, *Kinesics and Context* (Philadelphia: University of Pennsylvania Press, 1970).

38. K. I. Ruys and D. A. Stapel, "Emotion Elicitor or Emotion Messenger?" *Psychological Science*, 19 (2008): 593–600.

39. M. G. Frank and P. Ekman, "Appearing Truthful Generalizes across Different Deception Situations," *Journal of Personality and Social Psychology* 86 (2004): 486–495.

40. P. Ekman and W. V. Friesen, "Research on Facial Expressions of Emotion," in A. M. Katz and V. T. Katz, eds., *Foundations of Nonverbal Communication* (Carbondale, Ill.: Southern Illinois University Press, 1983).

41. H. H. Tan, M. D. Foo, C. L. Chong, and R. Ng, "Situational and Dispositional Predictors of Displays of Positive Emotions," *Journal of Organizational Behavior* 24 (2003): 961–978.

42. C. Barnum and N. Wolniansky, "Taking Cues from Body Language," *Management Review* 78 (1989): 59.

43. Katz and Katz, *Foundations of Nonverbal Communication*, 181.

44. J. J. Lynch, *A Cry Unheard: New Insights into the Medical Consequences of Loneliness* (Baltimore, MD: Bancroft Press, 2000).

45. J. C. Quick, J. H. Gavin, C. L. Cooper, and J. D. Quick, "Working Together: Balancing Head and Heart," in N. G. Johnson, R. H. Rozensky, C. D. Goodheart, and R. Hammond, eds., *Psychology Builds a Healthy World* (Washington, D.C.: American Psychological Association, 2004): 219–232.

46. J. C. Quick, C. L. Cooper, J. D. Quick, and J. H. Gavin, *The Financial Times Guide to Executive Health* (London, UK: Financial Times–Prentice Hall, 2003).

47. K. M. Wasylyshyn, "Coaching the Superkeepers," in L. A. Berger and D. R. Berger, eds., *The Talent Management Handbook: Creating Organizational Excellence by Identifying, Developing, and Positioning Your Best People* (New York: McGraw-Hill, 2003): 320–336.

48. J. C. Quick and M. Macik-Frey, "Behind the Mask: Coaching through Deep Interpersonal Communication," *Consulting Psychology Journal: Practice and Research* 56 (2004): 67–74.

49. R. Flinn, "Social Media: A New Jury Selection Tool," *Bloomberg Businessweek* (April 21, 2011).

50. B. J. Dunn, "Best Buy's CEO on Learning to Love Social Media," *Harvard Business Review* 88 (December 2010): 43–48.

51. B. Drake and K. Yuthas, "It's Only Words—Impacts of Information Technology on Moral Dialogue," *Journal of Business Ethics* 23 (2000): 41–60.

52. C. Brod, *Technostress: The Human Cost of the Computer Revolution* (Reading, Mass.: Addison-Wesley, 1984).

53. S. Kiesler, "Technology and the Development of Creative Environments," in Y. Ijiri and R. L. Kuhn, eds., *New Directions in Creative and Innovative Management* (Cambridge, Mass.: Ballinger Press, 1988).

54. S. Adams, "Being There," *Forbes* 187 (2011): 94.

55. S. Kiesler, J. Siegel, and T. W. McGuire, "Social Psychological Aspects of Computer-Mediated Communication," *American Psychologist* 39 (1984): 1123–1134.

56. P. Shachaf, "Cultural Diversity and Information and Communication Technology Impacts on Global Virtual Teams: An Exploratory Study," *Information & Management* 45 (2008): 131–142.

Chapter 9

1. J. R. Katzenbach and D. K. Smith, "The Discipline of Teams," *Harvard Business Review* 71 (1993): 111–120.

2. S. S. Webber and R. J. Klimoski, "Crews: A Distinct Type of Work Team," *Journal of Business and Psychology* 18 (2004): 261–279.

3. P. F. Drucker, "There's More than One Kind of Team," *The Wall Street Journal* (February 11, 1992): A16.

4. A. M. Towsend, S. M. DeMarie, and A. R. Hendrickson, "Virtual Teams: Technology and the Workplace of the Future," *Academy of Management Executive* 12 (1998): 17–29.

5. B. L. Kirkman, C. B. Gibson, and D. L. Shapiro, "'Exporting' Teams: Enhancing the Implementation and Effectiveness of Work Teams in Global Affiliates," *Organizational Dynamics* 30 (2001): 12–29.

6. A. Taylor and H. R. Greve, "Superman or the Fantastic Four? Knowledge Combination and Experience in Innovative Teams," *Academy of Management Journal* 49 (2006): 723–740.

7. S. Faraj and A. Yan, "Boundary Work in Knowledge Teams," *Journal of Applied Psychology* 94 (2009): 604–617.

8. P. Shaver and D. Buhrmester, "Loneliness, Sex-Role Orientation, and Group Life: A Social Needs Perspective," in P. Paulus, ed., *Basic Group Processes* (New York: Springer-Verlag, 1985): 259–288.

9. K. L. Bettenhausen and J. K. Murnighan, "The Development and Stability of Norms in Groups Facing Interpersonal and Structural Challenge," *Administrative Science Quarterly* 36 (1991): 20–35.

10. N. Ellemers, S. Pagliaro, M. Barreto, and C. W. Leach, "Is It Better to Be Moral Than Smart? The Effects of Morality and Competence Norms on the Decision to Work at Group Status Improvement," *Journal of Personality and Social Psychology* 95 (2008): 1397–1410.

11. I. Adarves-Yorno, T. Postmes, and S. A. Haslam, "Creative Innovation or Crazy Irrelevance? The Contribution of Group Norms and Social Identity to Creative Behavior," *Journal of Experimental Social Psychology* 43 (2007): 410–416.

12. D. Tjosvold and Z. Yu, "Goal Interdependence and Applying Abilities for Team In-Role and Extra-Role Performance in China," *Group Dynamics: Theory, Research, and Practice* 8 (2004): 98–111.

13. M. S. Cole, F. Walter, and H. Bruch, "Affective Mechanisms Linking Dysfunctional Behavior to Performance in Work Teams: A Moderated Mediation Study," *Journal of Applied Psychology* 93 (2008): 945–958.

14. V. U. Druskat and S. B. Wolff, "Building the Emotional Intelligence of Groups," *Harvard Business Review* 79 (2001): 80–90.

15. I. Summers, T. Coffelt, and R. E. Horton, "Work-Group Cohesion," *Psychological Reports* 63 (1988): 627–636.

16. D. C. Man and S. S. K. Lam, "The Effects of Job Complexity and Autonomy on Cohesiveness in Collectivistic and Individualistic Work Groups: A Cross-Cultural Analysis," *Journal of Organizational Behavior* 24 (2003): 979–1001.

17. Y. Shin and J. N. Choi, "What Makes a Group of Good Citizens? The Role of Perceived Group-Level Fit and Critical Psychological States in Organizational Teams," *Journal of Occupational and Organizational Psychology* 83 (2010): 531–552.

18. K. H. Price, "Working Hard to Get People to Loaf," *Basic and Applied Social Psychology* 14 (1993): 329–344.

19. R. Albanese and D. D. Van Fleet, "Rational Behavior in Groups: The Free-Riding Tendency," *Academy of Management Review* 10 (1985): 244–255.

20. E. Diener, "Deindividuation, Self-Awareness, and Disinhibition," *Journal of Personality and Social Psychology* 37 (1979): 1160–1171.

21. S. Prentice-Dunn and R. W. Rogers, "Deindividuation and the Self-Regulation of Behavior," in P. Paulus, ed., *Psychology of Group Influence* (Hillsdale, N.J.: Erlbaum, 1989): 87–109.

22. B. M. Bass and E. C. Ryterband, *Organizational Psychology*, 2nd ed. (Boston: Allyn & Bacon, 1979).

23. W. G. Bennis and H. A. Shepard, "A Theory of Group Development," *Human Relations* 9 (1956): 415–438.

24. D. L. Fields and T. C. Bloom, "Employee Satisfaction in Work Groups with Different Gender Composition," *Journal of Organizational Behavior* 18 (1997): 181–196.

25. D. C. Lau and J. K. Murnighan, "Demographic Diversity and Faultlines: The Compositional Dynamics of Organizational Groups," *Academy of Management Review* 23 (1998): 325–340.

26. B. Tuckman, "Developmental Sequence in Small Groups," *Psychological Bulletin* 63 (1965): 384–399; B. Tuckman and M. Jensen, "Stages of Small-Group Development," *Group and Organizational Studies* 2 (1977): 419–427.

27. S. T. Bell and J. A. Belohlav, "The Power of 'We': The Effects of Psychological Collectivism on Team Performance over Time," *Journal of Applied Psychology* 96 (2011): 247–262.

28. D. Nichols, "Quality Program Sparked Company Turnaround," *Personnel* (October 1991): 24. For a commentary on Wallace's hard times and subsequent emergence from Chapter 11 bankruptcy, see R. C. Hill, "When the Going Gets Tough: A Baldrige Award Winner on the Line," *Academy of Management Executive* 7 (1993): 75–79.

29. S. Weisband and L. Atwater, "Evaluating Self and Others in Electronic and Face-to-Face Groups," *Journal of Applied Psychology* 84 (1999): 632–639.

30. C. J. G. Gersick, "Time and Transition in Work Teams: Toward a New Model of Group Development," *The Academy of Management Journal* 31 (1988): 9–41.

31. M. Hardaker and B. K. Ward, "How to Make a Team Work," *Harvard Business Review* 65 (1987): 112–120.

32. C. R. Gowen, "Managing Work Group Performance by Individual Goals and Group Goals for an Interdependent Group Task," *Journal of Organizational Behavior Management* 7 (1986): 5–27.

33. K. L. Bettenhausen and J. K. Murnighan, "The Emergence of Norms in Competitive Decision-Making Groups," *Administrative Science Quarterly* 30 (1985): 350–372; K. L. Bettenhausen, "Five Years of Groups Research: What We Have Learned and What Needs to Be Addressed," *Journal of Management* 17 (1991): 345–381.

34. J. E. McGrath, *Groups: Interaction and Performance* (Englewood Cliffs, N.J.: Prentice-Hall, 1984).

35. K. L. Gammage, A. V. Carron, and P. A. Estabrooks, "Team Cohesion and Individual Productivity," *Small Group Research* 32 (2001): 3–18.

36. S. M. Klein, "A Longitudinal Study of the Impact of Work Pressure on Group Cohesive Behaviors," *International Journal of Management* 12 (1996): 68–75.

37. N. Steckler and N. Fondas, "Building Team Leader Effectiveness: A Diagnostic Tool," *Organizational Dynamics* 23 (1995): 20–35.

38. A. Carter and S. Holmes, "Curiously Strong Teamwork," *BusinessWeek* 4023 (February 26, 2007): 90–92.

39. W. R. Lassey, "Dimensions of Leadership," in W. R. Lassey and R. Fernandez, eds., *Leadership and Social Change* (La Jolla, Calif.: University Associates, 1976): 10–15.

40. B. Broysberg and L. Lee, "The Effect of Colleague Quality on Top Performance: The Case of Security Analysts," *Journal of Organizational Behavior* 29 (2008): 1123–1144.

41. J. D. Quick, G. Moorhead, J. C. Quick, E. A. Gerloff, K. L. Mattox, and C. Mullins, "Decision Making among Emergency Room Residents: Preliminary Observations and a Decision Model," *Journal of Medical Education* 58 (1983): 117–125.

42. W. J. Duncan and J. P. Feisal, "No Laughing Matter: Patterns of Humor in the Workplace," *Organizational Dynamics* 17 (1989): 18–30.

43. L. Hirschhorn, *Managing in the New Team Environment*, (Upper Saddle River, N.J.: Prentice-Hall): 521A.

44. G. Chen and R. J. Klimoski, "The Impact of Expectations on Newcomer Performance in Teams as Mediated by Work Characteristics, Social Exchanges, and Empowerment," *Academy of Management Journal* 46 (2003): 591–607.

45. B. Beersma, J. R. Hollenbeck, S. E. Humphrey, H. Moon, D. E. Conlon, and D. R. Ilgen, "Cooperation, Competition, and Team Performance: Toward a Contingency Approach," *Academy of Management Journal* 46 (2003): 572–590.

46. G. Parker, *Team Players and Teamwork* (San Francisco: Jossey-Bass, 1990).

47. N. R. F. Maier, "Assets and Liabilities in Group Problem Solving: The Need for an Integrative Function," *Psychological Review* 74 (1967): 239–249.

48. T. A. Stewart, "The Search for the Organization of Tomorrow," *Fortune* (May 18, 1992): 92–98

49. P. Chattopadhyay, M. Tluchowska, and E. George, "Identifying the Ingroup: A Closer Look at the Influence of Demographic Dissimilarity on Employee Social Identity," *Academy of Management Review* 29 (2004): 180–202.

50. M. M. Stewart and P. Garcia-Prieto, "A Relational Demography Model of Workgroup Identification: Testing the Effects of Race, Race Dissimilarity, Racial Identification, and Communication Behavior," *Journal of Organizational Behavior* 29 (2008): 657–680.

51. E. V. Hobman, P. Bordia, and C. Gallois, "Consequences of Feeling Dissimilar from Others in a Work Team," *Journal of Business and Psychology* 17 (2003): 301–325.

52. A. E. Randel and K. S. Jaussi, "Functional Background Identity, Diversity, and Individual Performance in Cross-Functional Teams," *Academy of Management Journal* 46 (2003): 763–774.

53. J. S. Bunderson, "Team Member Functional Background and Involvement in Management Teams: Direct Effects and the Moderating Role of Power Centralization," *Academy of Management Journal* 46 (2003): 458–474.

54. G. S. Van Der Vegt, E. Van De Vliert, and A. Oosterhof, "Informational Dissimilarity and Organizational Citizenship Behavior: The Role of Intrateam Interdependence and Team Identification," *Academy of Management Journal* 46 (2003): 715–727.

55. F. Balkundi, M. Kilduff, Z. I. Barsness, and J. H. Michael, "Demographic Antecedents and Performance Consequences of Structural Holes in Work Teams," *Journal of Organizational Behavior* 28 (2007): 241–260.

56. A. Pirola-Merlo and L. Mann, "The Relationship between Individual Creativity and Team Creativity: Aggregating across People and Time," *Journal of Organizational Behavior* 25 (2004): 235–257.

57. L. Thompson, "Improving the Creativity of Organizational Work Groups," *Academy of Management Executive* 17 (2003): 96–111.

58. C. Ford and D. M. Sullivan, "A Time for Everything: How the Timing of Novel Contributions Influences Project Team Outcomes," *Journal of Organizational Behavior* 25 (2004): 279–292.

59. K. W. Thomas and B. A. Velthouse, "Cognitive Elements of Empowerment: An 'Interpretive' Model of Intrinsic Task Motivation," *Academy of Management Review* 15 (1990): 666–681.

60. R. R. Blake, J. S. Mouton, and R. L. Allen, *Spectacular Teamwork: How to Develop the Leadership Skills for Team Success* (New York: Wiley, 1987).

61. American Management Association, *Blueprints for Service Quality: The Federal Express Approach,* AMA Management Briefing (New York: AMA, 1991).

62. W. C. Byham, *ZAPP! The Human Lightning of Empowerment* (Pittsburgh, PA: Developmental Dimensions, 1989).

63. F. Shipper and C. C. Manz, "Employee Self-Management without Formally Designated Teams: An Alternative Road to Empowerment," *Organizational Dynamics* (Winter 1992): 48–62.

64. P. Block, *The Empowered Manager: Positive Political Skills at Work* (San Francisco: Jossey-Bass, 1987).

65. V. J. Derlega and J. Grzelak, eds., *Cooperation and Helping Behavior: Theories and Research* (New York: Academic Press, 1982).

66. G. S. Van der Vegt, J. S. Bunderson, and A. Oosterhof, "Expertness Diversity and Interpersonal Helping in Teams: Why Those Who Need the Most Help End Up Getting the Least," *Academy of Management Journal* 49 (2006): 877–893.

67. A. G. Athos and J. J. Gabarro, *Interpersonal Behavior: Communication and Understanding in Relationships* (Englewood Cliffs, N.J.: Prentice-Hall, 1978).

68. C. Douglas and W. L. Gardner, "Transition to Self-Directed Work Teams: Implications of Transition Time and Self-Monitoring for Managers' Use of Influence Tactics," *Journal of Organizational Behavior* 25 (2004): 47–65.

69. C. Douglas, J. S. Martin, and R. H. Krapels, "Communication in the Transition to Self-Directed Work Teams," *Journal of Business Communication* 43 (2006): 295–321.

70. J. L. Cordery, W. S. Mueller, and L. M. Smith, "Attitudinal and Behavioral Effects of Autonomous Group Working: A Longitudinal Field Study," *Academy of Management Journal* 34 (1991): 464–476.

71. G. Moorhead, C. P. Neck, and M. S. West, "The Tendency toward Defective Decision Making within Self-Managing Teams: The Relevance of Groupthink for the 21st Century," *Organizational Behavior and Human Decision Processes* 73 (1998): 327–351.

72. B. M. Staw and L. D. Epstein, "What Bandwagons Bring: Effects of Popular Management Techniques on Corporate Performance, Reputation, and CEO Pay," *Administrative Science Quarterly* 45 (2000): 523–556.

73. R. M. Robinson, S. L. Oswald, K. S. Swinehart, and J. Thomas, "Southwest Industries: Creating High-Performance Teams for High-Technology Production," *Planning Review* 19, published by the Planning Forum (November–December 1991): 10–47.

74. D. C. Hambrick and P. Mason, "Upper Echelons: The Organization as a Reflection of Its Top Managers," *Academy of Management Review* 9 (1984): 193–206.

75. D. C. Hambrick, "The Top Management Team: Key to Strategic Success," *California Management Review* 30 (1987): 88–108.

76. A. D. Henderson and J. W. Fredrickson, "Top Management Team Coordination Needs and the CEO Pay Gap: A Competitive Test of Economic and Behavioral Views," *Academy of Management Journal* 44 (2001): 96–117.

77. D. C. Hambrick and G. D. S. Fukutomi, "The Seasons of a CEO's Tenure," *Academy of Management Review* 16 (1991): 719–742.

78. J. C. Quick, D. L. Nelson, and J. D. Quick, "Successful Executives: How Independent?" *Academy of Management Executive* 1 (1987): 139–145.

79. A. A. Cannella, Jr, J. Park, and H. Lee, "Top Management Team Functional Background Diversity and Firm Performance: Examining the Roles of Team Member Colocation and Environmental Uncertainty," *Academy of Management Journal* 51(2008): 768–784.

80. L. G. Love, "The Evolving Pinnacle of the Corporation: An Explanatory Study of the Antecedents, Processes, and Consequences of Co-CEOs," 2003 (The University of Texas at Arlington).

81. N. J. Adler, *International Dimensions of Organizational Behavior* (Mason, Ohio: South-Western, 2001).

82. I. D. Steiner, *Group Process and Productivity* (New York: Academic Press, 1972).

83. E. Kearney, D. Gebert, and S. C. Voelpel, "When and How Diversity Benefits Teams: The Importance of Team Members' Need for Cognition," *Academy of Management Journal* 52 (2009): 581–598.

84. T. Buyl, C. Boone, W. Hendriks, and P. Matthyssens, "Top Management Team Functional Diversity and Firm Performance: The Moderating Role of CEO Characteristics," *Journal of Management Studies* 48 (2011): 151–176.

Chapter 10

1. H. A. Simon, *The New Science of Management Decision* (New York: Harper & Row, 1960).

2. R. Walker, "Brand Blue," *Fortune* (April 28, 2003): http://www.fortune.com/fortune/smallbusiness/articles/0,15114,426909,00.html.

3. G. Huber, *Managerial Decision Making* (Glenview, Ill.: Scott, Foresman, 1980).

4. H. A. Simon, *Administrative Behavior* (New York: Macmillan, 1957).

5. E. F. Harrison, *The Managerial Decision-Making Process* (Boston: Houghton Mifflin, 1981).

6. R. L. Ackoff, "The Art and Science of Mess Management," *Interfaces* (February 1981): 20–26.

7. R. M. Cyert and J. G. March, eds., *A Behavioral Theory of the Firm* (Englewood Cliffs, N.J.: Prentice-Hall, 1963).

8. B. M. Staw, "Knee-Deep in the Big Muddy: A Study of Escalating Commitment to a Chosen Course of Action," *Organizational Behavior and Human Performance* 16 (1976): 27–44; B. M. Staw, "The Escalation of Commitment to a Course of Action," *Academy of Management Review* 6 (1981): 577–587.

9. B. M. Staw and J. Ross, "Understanding Behavior in Escalation Situations," *Science* 246 (1989): 216–220.

10. T. Freemantle and M. Tolson, "Space Station Had Political Ties in Tow," *Houston Chronicle* (August 4, 2003).

11. L. Festinger, *A Theory of Cognitive Dissonance* (Evanston, Ill.: Row, Peterson, 1957).

12. B. M. Staw, "The Escalation of Commitment: An Update and Appraisal," in Z. Shapira, ed., *Organizational Decision Making* (Cambridge, England: Cambridge University Press, 1997).

13. D. M. Boehne and P. W. Paese, "Deciding Whether to Complete or Terminate an Unfinished Project: A Strong Test of the Project Completion Hypothesis," *Organizational Behavior and Human Decision Processes* 81 (2000): 178–194; H. Moon, "Looking Forward and Looking Back: Integrating Completion and Sunk Cost Effects within an Escalation-of-Commitment Progress Decision," *Journal of Applied Psychology* 86 (2000): 104–113.

14. J. A. Sonnenfeld, "How Rick Wagoner Lost GM," *BusinessWeek* (June 1, 2009), http://www.businessweek.com/managing/content/jun2009/ca2009061_966638.htm.

15. N. Sivanathan, D. C. Molden, A. D. Galinsky, and G. Ku, "The Promise and Peril of Self-Affirmation in the De-Escalation of Commitment," *Organizational Behavior and Human Decision Processes* 107 (2008): 1–14.

16. G. McNamara, H. Moon, and P. Bromiley, "Banking on Commitment: Intended and Unintended Consequences of an Organization's Attempt to Attenuate Escalation of Commitment," *Academy of Management Journal* 45 (2002): 443–452.

17. G. Whyte, "Diffusion of Responsibility: Effects on the Escalation Tendency," *Journal of Applied Psychology* 76 (1991): 408–415.

18. D. van Knippenberg, B. van Knippenberg, and E. van Dijk, "Who Takes the Lead in Risky Decision Making? Effects of Group Members' Risk Preferences and Prototypicality," *Organizational Behavior and Human Decision Processes* 83 (2000): 213–234.

19. K. R. MacCrimmon and D. Wehrung, *Taking Risks* (New York: Free Press, 1986).

20. T. S. Perry, "How Small Firms Innovate: Designing a Culture for Creativity," *Research Technology Management* 28 (1995): 14–17.

21. A. Saleh, "Brain Hemisphericity and Academic Majors: A Correlation Study," *College Student Journal* 35 (2001): 193–200.

22. N. Khatri, "The Role of Intuition in Strategic Decision Making," *Human Relations* 53 (2000): 57–86.

23. H. Mintzberg, "Planning on the Left Side and Managing on the Right," *Harvard Business Review* 54 (1976): 51–63.

24. D. J. Isenberg, "How Senior Managers Think," *Harvard Business Review* 62 (1984): 81–90.

25. R. N. Beck, "Visions, Values, and Strategies: Changing Attitudes and Culture," *Academy of Managment Executive* 1 (1987): 33–41.

26. K. G. Ross, G. A. Klein, P. Thunholm, J. F. Schmitt, and H. C. Baxter, "The Recognition-Primed Decision Model," *Military Review, Fort Leavenworth* 84 (2004): 6–10.

27. C. I. Barnard, *The Functions of the Executive* (Cambridge, Mass.: Harvard University Press, 1938).

28. R. Rowan, *The Intuitive Manager* (New York: Little, Brown, 1986).

29. W. H. Agor, *Intuition in Organizations* (Newbury Park, Calif.: Sage, 1989).

30. Isenberg, "How Senior Managers Think," 81–90.

31. H. A. Simon, "Making Management Decisions: The Role of Intuition and Emotion," *Academy of Management Executive* 1 (1987): 57–64.

32. J. L. Redford, R. H. McPhierson, R. G. Frankiewicz, and J. Gaa, "Intuition and Moral Development," *Journal of Psychology* 129 (1994): 91–101.

33. R. Wild, "Naked Hunch; Gut Instinct Is Vital to Your Business," *Success* (June 1998), http://www.findarticles.com/cf_dls/m3514/n6_v45/20746158/p1/article.jhtml.

34. W. H. Agor, "How Top Executives Use Their Intuition to Make Important Decisions," *Business Horizons* 29 (1986): 49–53.

35. O. Behling and N. L. Eckel, "Making Sense out of Intuition," *Academy of Management Executive* 5 (1991): 46–54.

36. L. R. Beach, *Image Theory: Decision Making in Personal and Organizational Contexts* (Chichester, England: Wiley, 1990).

37. E. Bonabeau, "Don't Trust Your Gut," *Harvard Business Review* 81 (2003): 116–126.

38. L. Livingstone, "Person-Environment Fit on the Dimension of Creativity: Relationships with Strain, Job Satisfaction, and Performance" (Ph.D. diss., Oklahoma State University, 1992).

39. G. Wallas, *The Art of Thought* (New York: Harcourt Brace, 1926).

40. H. Benson and W. Proctor, *The Break-Out Principle* (Scribner: New York, 2003); G. L. Fricchione, B. T. Slingsby, and H. Benson, "The Placebo Effect and the Relaxation Response: Neural Processes and Their Coupling to Constitutive Nitric Oxide," *Brain Research Reviews* 35 (2001): 1–19.

41. M. D. Mumford and S. B. Gustafson, "Creativity Syndrome: Integration, Application, and Innovation," *Psychological Bulletin* 103 (1988): 27–43.

42. T. Poze, "Analogical Connections—The Essence of Creativity," *Journal of Creative Behavior* 17 (1983): 240–241.

43. I. Sladeczek and G. Domino, "Creativity, Sleep, and Primary Process Thinking in Dreams," *Journal of Creative Behavior* 19 (1985): 38–46.

44. F. Barron and D. M. Harrington, "Creativity, Intelligence, and Personality," *Annual Review of Psychology* 32 (1981): 439–476.

45. R. J. Sternberg, "A Three-Faced Model of Creativity," in R. J. Sternberg, ed., *The Nature of Creativity* (Cambridge, England: Cambridge University Press, 1988): 125–147.

46. A. M. Grant and J. W. Berry, "The Necessity of Others Is the Mother of Invention: Intrinsic and Prosocial Motivations, Perspective Taking, and Creativity," *Academy of Management Journal* 54, No. 1 (2011): 73–96.

47. A. M. Isen, "Positive Affect and Decision Making," in W. M. Goldstein and R. M. Hogarth, eds., *Research on Judgment and Decision Making* (Cambridge, England: Cambridge University Press, 1997).

48. G. L. Clore, N. Schwartz, and M. Conway, "Cognitive Causes and Consequences of Emotion," in R. S. Wyer and T. K. Srull, eds., *Handbook of Social Cognition* (Hillsdale, N.J.: Erlbaum, 1994): 323–417.

49. B. L. Frederickson, "What Good Are Positive Emotions?" *Review of General Psychology* 2 (1998): 300–319; B. L. Frederickson, "The Role of Positive Emotions in Positive Psychology," *American Psychologist* 56 (2001): 218–226.

50. T. M. Amabile, S. G. Barsade, J. S. Mueller, and B. M. Staw, "Affect and Creativity at Work," *Administrative Science Quarterly* 50, No. 3 (2005): 367–403.

51. J. Zhou, "When the Presence of Creative Coworkers Is Related to Creativity: Role of Supervisor Close Monitoring, Developmental Feedback, and Creative Personality," *Journal of Applied Psychology* 88 (2003): 413–422.

52. C. Axtell, D. Holman, K. Unsworth, T. Wall, and P. Waterson, "Shopfloor Innovation: Facilitating the Suggestion and Implementation of Ideas," *Journal of Occupational Psychology* 73 (2000): 265–285.

53. B. Kijkuit and J. van den Ende, "The Organizational Life of an Idea: Integrating Social Network, Creativity and Decision-Making Perspectives," *Journal of Management Studies* 44, No. 6 (2007): 863–882.

54. T. M. Amabile, R. Conti, H. Coon, J. Lazenby, and M. Herron, "Assessing the Work Environment for Creativity," *Academy of Management Journal* 39 (1996): 1154–1184.

55. T. Tetenbaum and H. Tetenbaum, "Office 2000: Tear Down the Wall," *Training* (February 2000): 58–64.

56. Livingstone, "Person-Environment Fit."

57. R. L. Firestein, "Effects of Creative Problem-Solving Training on Communication Behaviors in Small Groups," *Small Group Research* (November 1989): 507–521.

58. R. Von Oech, *A Whack on the Side of the Head* (New York: Warner, 1983).

59. A. G. Robinson and S. Stern, *How Innovation and Improvement Actually Happen* (San Francisco: Berrett Koehler, 1997).

60. K. Unsworth, "Unpacking Creativity," *Academy of Management Review* 26 (2001): 289–297.

61. M. F. R. Kets de Vries, R. Branson, and P. Barnevik, "Charisma in Action: The Transformational Abilities of Virgin's Richard Branson and ABBS's Percy Barnevik," *Organizational Dynamics* 26 (1998): 7–21.

62. G. Stasser, L. A. Taylor, and C. Hanna, "Information Sampling in Structured and Unstructured Discussion of Three- and Six-Person Groups," *Journal of Personality and Social Psychology* 57 (1989): 67–78.

63. E. Kirchler and J. H. Davis, "The Influence of Member Status Differences and Task Type on Group Consensus and Member Position Change," *Journal of Personality and Social Psychology* 51 (1986): 83–91.

64. R. F. Maier, "Assets and Liabilities in Group Problem Solving," *Psychological Review* 74 (1967): 239–249.

65. M. E. Shaw, *Group Dynamics: The Psychology of Small Group Behavior,* 3rd ed. (New York: McGraw-Hill, 1981).

66. P. W. Yetton and P. C. Bottger, "Individual versus Group Problem Solving: An Empirical Test of a Best Member Strategy," *Organizational Behavior and Human Performance* 29 (1982): 307–321.

67. W. Watson, L. Michaelson, and W. Sharp, "Member Competence, Group Interaction, and Group Decision Making: A Longitudinal Study," *Journal of Applied Psychology* 76 (1991): 803–809.

68. I. Janis, *Victims of Groupthink* (Boston: Houghton Mifflin, 1972); M. Kostera, M. Proppe, and M. Szatkowski, "Staging the New Romantic Hero in the Old Cynical Theatre: On Managers, Roles, and Change in Poland," *Journal of Organizational Behavior* 16 (1995): 631–646.

69. M. A. Hogg and S. C. Hains, "Friendship and Group Identification: A New Look at the Role of Cohesiveness in Groupthink," *European Journal of Social Psychology* 28 (1998): 323–341.

70. P. E. Jones and H. M. P. Roelofsma, "The Potential for Social Contextual and Group Biases in Team Decision Making: Biases, Conditions, and Psychological Mechanisms," *Ergonomics* 43 (2000): 1129–1152; J. M. Levine, E. T. Higgins, and H. Choi, "Development of Strategic Norms in Groups," *Organizational Behavior and Human Decision Processes* 82 (2000): 88–101.

71. A. L. Brownstein, "Biased Predecision Processing," *Psychological Bulletin* 129 (2003): 545–568.

72. C. P. Neck and G. Moorhead, "Groupthink Remodeled: The Importance of Leadership, Time Pressure, and Methodical Decision-Making Procedures," *Human Relations* 48 (1995): 537–557.

73. J. Schwartz and M. L. Ward, "Final Shuttle Report Cites 'Broken Safety Culture' at NASA," *The New York Times* (August 26, 2003), http://www.nytimes.com/2003/08/26/national/26CND-SHUT.html?ex=10772 53200&en=882575f2c17ed8ff&ei=5070; C. Ferraris and R. Carveth, "NASA and the *Columbia* Disaster: Decision Making by Groupthink?" in *Proceedings of the 2003 Convention of the Association for Business Communication Annual Convention,* http://www.businesscommunication.org/conventions/Proceedings/2003/PDF/03ABC03.pdf.

74. V. Anand, B. E Ashforth, and M. Joshi, "Business as Usual: The Acceptance and Perpetuation of Corruption in Organizations," *Academy of Management Executive* 19 (2005): 9–23.

75. A. C. Homan, D. van Knippenberg, G. A. Van Kleef, and K. W. C. De Dreu, "Bridging Faultlines by Valuing Diversity: Diversity Beliefs, Information Elaboration, and Performance in Diverse Work Groups," *Journal of Applied Psychology* 92, No. 5 (2007):1189–1199.

76. G. Moorhead, R. Ference, and C. P. Neck, "Group Decision Fiascoes Continue: Space Shuttle *Challenger* and a Revised Groupthink Framework," *Human Relations* 44 (1991): 539–550.

77. J. R. Montanari and G. Moorhead, "Development of the Groupthink Assessment Inventory," *Educational and Psychological Measurement* 49 (1989): 209–219.

78. P. Hart, "Irving L. Janis' Victims of Groupthink," *Political Psychology* 12 (1991): 247–278.

79. A. C. Mooney, P. J. Holahan, and A. C. Amason, "Don't Take It Personally: Exploring Cognitive Conflict as a Mediator of Affective Conflict," *Journal of Management Studies* 44, No. 5 (2007): 733–758.

80. J. A. F. Stoner, "Risky and Cautious Shifts in Group Decisions: The Influence of Widely Held Values," *Journal of Experimental Social Psychology* 4 (1968): 442–459.

81. S. Moscovici and M. Zavalloni, "The Group as a Polarizer of Attitudes," *Journal of Personality and Social Psychology* 12 (1969): 125–135.

82. G. R. Goethals and M. P. Zanna, "The Role of Social Comparison in Choice of Shifts," *Journal of Personality and Social Psychology* 37 (1979): 1469–1476.

83. A. Vinokur and E. Burnstein, "Effects of Partially Shared Persuasive Arguments on Group-Induced Shifts: A Problem-Solving Approach," *Journal of Personality and Social Psychology* 29 (1974): 305–315; J. Pfeffer, "Seven Practices of Successful Organizations," *California Management Review* 40 (1998): 96–124.

84. J. K. Palmer and J. M. Loveland, "The Influence of Group Discussion on Performance Judgments: Rating Accuracy, Contrast Effects and Halo," *The Journal of Psychology: Interdisciplinary and Applied* 142 (2008): 117–130.

85. L. Armstrong, "Toyota's Scion: A Siren to Young Buyers?" *BusinessWeek* (March 4, 2002), http://www.businessweek.com/bwdaily/dnflash /mar2002/nf2002034_8826.htm; Edmunds.com, Inc., "Toyota Courts NetGen Youth with Echo Subcompact" (January 1, 1999), http://www .edmunds.com/news/autoshows/articles/44460/page020.html; B. Young, "Mixing It Up: Crossover Vehicles Borrow Best of Cars, SUVs, Trucks," *Los Angeles Times,* http://www.latimes.com/extras/autoleasing/mixing .html.

86. K. Dugosh, P. Paulus, E. Roland, and H. Yang, "Cognitive Stimulation in Brainstorming," *Journal of Personality and Social Psychology* 79 (2000): 722–735.

87. A. Van de Ven and A. Delbecq, "The Effectiveness of Nominal, Delphi and Interacting Group Decision-Making Processes," *Academy of Management Journal* 17 (1974): 605–621.

88. R. A. Cosier and C. R. Schwenk, "Agreement and Thinking Alike: Ingredients for Poor Decisions," *Academy of Management Executive* 4 (1990): 69–74.

89. D. M. Schweiger, W. R. Sandburg, and J. W. Ragan, "Group Approaches for Improving Strategic Decision Making: A Comparative Analysis of Dialectical Inquiry, Devil's Advocacy, and Consensus," *Academy of Management Journal* 29 (1986): 149–159.

90. G. Whyte, "Decision Failures: Why They Occur and How to Prevent Them," *Academy of Management Executive* 5 (1991): 23–31.

91. L. Scholten, D. van Knippenberg, B. A. Nijstad, and K. W. C. De Dreu, "Motivated Information Processing and Group Decision-Making: Effects of Process Accountability on Information Processing and Decision Quality," *Journal of Experimental Social Psychology* 43, No. 4 (2007): 539–552.

92. E. E. Lawler III and S. A. Mohrman, "Quality Circles: After the Honeymoon," *Organizational Dynamics* (Spring 1987): 42–54.

93. T. L. Tang and E. A. Butler, "Attributions of Quality Circles' Problem-Solving Failure: Differences among Management, Supporting Staff, and Quality Circle Members," *Public Personnel Management* 26 (1997): 203–225.

94. J. Schilder, "Work Teams Boost Productivity," *Personnel Journal* 71 (1992): 67–72.

95. L. I. Glassop, "The Organizational Benefits of Teams," *Human Relations* 55 (2002): 225–249.

96. C. J. Nemeth, "Managing Innovation: When Less Is More," *California Management Review* 40 (1997): 59–68.

97. N. Adler, *International Dimensions of Organizational Behavior,* 3rd ed. (Mason, Ohio: South-Western, 1997).

98. K. W. Phillips and D. L. Lloyd, "When Surface- and Deep-Level Diversity Collide: The Effects on Dissenting Group Members," *Organizational Behavior and Human Decision Processes* 99, No. 2 (2006): 143–160.

99. T. Simons, L. H. Pelled, and K. A. Smith, "Making Use of Difference: Diversity, Debate, and Decision Comprehensiveness in Top Management Teams," *Academy of Management Journal* 42, No. 6 (1999): 662–673.

100. S. Elbanna and J. Child, "The Influence of Decision, Environmental and Firm Characteristics on the Rationality of Strategic Decision-Making," *Journal of Management Studies* 44, No. 4 (2007): 561–591.

101. J. Pfeffer, "Seven Practices of Successful Organizations," *California Management Review* 40 (1998): 96–124.

102. L. A. Witt, M. C. Andrews, and K. M. Kacmar, "The Role of Participation in Decision Making in the Organizational Politics–Job Satisfaction Relationship," *Human Relations* 53 (2000): 341–358.

103. J. He and W. R. King, "The Role of User Participation in Information Systems Development: Implications from a Meta-Analysis," *Journal of Management Information Systems* 25 (2008): 301–331.

104. C. R. Leana, E. A. Locke, and D. M. Schweiger, "Fact and Fiction in Analyzing Research on Participative Decision Making: A Critique of Cotton, Vollrath, Froggatt, Lengnick-Hall, and Jennings," *Academy of Management Review* 15 (1990): 137–146; J. L. Cotton, D. A. Vollrath, M. L. Lengnick-Hall, and K. L. Froggatt, "Fact: The Form of Participation Does Matter—A Rebuttal to Leana, Locke, and Schweiger," *Academy of Management Review* 15 (1990): 147–153.

105. T. W. Malone, "Is Empowerment Just a Fad? Control, Decision Making, and Information Technology," *Sloan Management Review* 38 (1997): 23–35.

106. IBM Customer Success Stories, "City and County of San Francisco Lower Total Cost of Ownership and Build on Demand Foundation" (February 3, 2004), http://www-306.ibm.com/software/success/cssdb.nsf/cs/LWRT-5VTLM2?OpenDocument&Site=lotusmandc.

107. T. L. Brown, "Fearful of 'Empowerment': Should Managers Be Terrified?" *Industry Week* (June 18, 1990): 12.

108. P. G. Gyllenhammar, *People at Work* (Reading, Mass.: Addison-Wesley, 1977).

109. R. Tannenbaum and F. Massarik, "Participation by Subordinates in the Managerial Decision-Making Process," *Canadian Journal of Economics and Political Science* 16 (1950): 408–418.

110. H. Levinson, *Executive* (Cambridge, Mass.: Harvard University Press, 1981).

111. R. F. Maier, "Assets and Liabilities in Group Problem Solving," *Psychological Review* 74 (1967): 239–249.

Chapter 11

1. G. C. Homans, "Social Behavior as Exchange," *American Journal of Sociology* 63 (1958): 597–606.

2. R. D. Middlemist and M. A. Hitt, *Organizational Behavior: Managerial Strategies for Performance* (St. Paul, Minn.: West Publishing, 1988).

3. C. Barnard, *The Functions of the Executive* (Cambridge, Mass.: Harvard University Press, 1938).

4. J. R. P. French and B. Raven, "The Bases of Social Power," in D. Cartwright, ed., *Group Dynamics: Research and Theory* (Evanston, Ill.: Row Peterson, 1962); T. R. Hinkin and C. A. Schriesheim, "Development and Application of New Scales to Measure the French and Raven (1959) Bases of Social Power," *Journal of Applied Psychology* 74 (1989): 561–567.

5. K. D. Elsbach and G. Elofson, "How the Packaging of Decision Explanations Affects Perceptions of Trustworthiness," *Academy of Management Journal* 43, No. 1 (2000): 80–89.

6. P. M. Podsakoff and C. A. Schriesheim, "Field Studies of French and Raven's Bases of Power: Critique, Reanalysis, and Suggestions for Future Research," *Psychological Bulletin* 97 (1985): 387–411.

7. M. A. Rahim, "Relationships of Leader Power to Compliance and Satisfaction with Supervision: Evidence from a National Sample of Managers," *Journal of Management* 15 (1989): 545–556.

8. C. Argyris, "Management Information Systems: The Challenge to Rationality and Emotionality," *Management Science* 17 (1971): 275–292; J. Naisbitt and P. Aburdene, *Megatrends 2000* (New York: Morrow, 1990).

9. P. P. Carson, K. D. Carson, E. L. Knight, and C. W. Roe, "Power in Organizations: A Look through the TQM Lens," *Quality Progress* (November 1995): 73–78.

10. Feature "Marissa Mayer: The Talent Scout," *BusinessWeek Online* (June 19, 2006), http://www.businessweek.com/magazine/content/06_25/b3989422.htm; http://money.cnn.com/galleries/2010/fortune/1009/gallery.most_powerful_women.fortune/42.html.

11. J. Pfeffer and G. Salancik, *The External Control of Organizations* (New York: Harper & Row, 1978).

12. T. M. Welbourne and C. O. Trevor, "The Roles of Departmental and Position Power in Job Evaluation," *Academy of Management Journal* 43, No. 4 (2000): 761–771.

13. R. H. Miles, *Macro Organizational Behavior* (Glenview, Ill.: Scott, Foresman, 1980).

14. D. Hickson, C. Hinings, C. Lee, R. E. Schneck, and J. M. Pennings, "A Strategic Contingencies Theory of Intraorganizational Power," *Administrative Science Quarterly* 14 (1971): 219–220.

15. C. R. Hinings, D. J. Hickson, J. M. Pennings, and R. E. Schneck, "Structural Conditions of Intraorganizational Power," *Administrative Science Quarterly* 19 (1974): 22–44.

16. M. Velasquez, D. J. Moberg, and G. F. Cavanaugh, "Organizational Statesmanship and Dirty Politics: Ethical Guidelines for the Organizational Politician," *Organizational Dynamics* 11 (1982): 65–79.

17. D. E. McClelland, *Power: The Inner Experience* (New York: Irvington, 1975).

18. N. Shahinpoor and B. F. Matt, "The Power of One: Dissent and Organizational Life," *Journal of Business Ethics* 74, No. 1 (2007): 37–49.

19. N. Machiavelli, *The Prince,* trans. by G. Bull (Middlesex, England: Penguin Books, 1961).

20. S. Chen, A. Y. Lee-Chai, and J. A. Bargh, "Relationship Orientation as a Moderator of the Effects of Social Power," *Journal of Personality and Social Psychology* 80, No. 2 (2001): 173–187.

21. R. Kanter, "Power Failure in Management Circuits," *Harvard Business Review* (July–August 1979): 31–54.

22. F. Lee and L. Z. Tiedens, "Who's Being Served? 'Self-Serving' Attributions in Social Hierarchies," *Organizational Behavior and Human Decision Processes* 84, No. 2 (March 2001): 254–287.

23. M. Korda, *Power: How to Get It, How to Use It* (New York: Random House, 1975).

24. S. R. Thye, "A Status Value Theory of Power in Exchange Relations," *American Sociological Review* (2000): 407–432.

25. B. T. Mayes and R. T. Allen, "Toward a Definition of Organizational Politics," *Academy of Management Review* 2 (1977): 672–678.

26. M. Valle and P. L. Perrewe, "Do Politics Perceptions Relate to Political Behaviors? Tests of an Implicit Assumption and Expanded Model," *Human Relations* 53 (2000): 359–386.

27. W. A. Hochwarter, "The Interactive Effects of Pro-Political Behavior and Politics Perceptions on Job Satisfaction and Affective Commitment," *Journal of Applied Social Psychology* 33 (2003): 1360–1378.

28. W. A. Hochwarter, "The Interactive Effects of Pro-Political Behavior and Politics Perceptions on Job Satisfaction and Affective Commitment," *Journal of Applied Social Psychology* 33 (2003): 1360–1378.

29. W. A. Hochwarter, K. M. Kacmar, D. C. Treadway, and T. S. Watson, "It's All Relative: The Distinction and Prediction of Political Perceptions across Levels," *Journal of Applied Social Psychology* 33 (2003): 1955–2016.

30. D. A. Ralston, "Employee Ingratiation: The Role of Management," *Academy of Management Review* 10 (1985): 477–487; D. R. Beeman and T. W. Sharkey, "The Use and Abuse of Corporate Politics," *Business Horizons* (March–April 1987): 25–35.

31. C. O. Longnecker, H. P. Sims, and D. A. Gioia, "Behind the Mask: The Politics of Employee Appraisal," *Academy of Management Executive* 1 (1987): 183–193.

32. M. Valle and P. L. Perrewe, "Do Politics Perceptions Relate to Political Behaviors? Tests of an Implicit Assumption and Expanded Model," *Human Relations* 53, No. 3 (2000): 359–386.

33. D. Fedor, J. Maslyn, S. Farmer, and K. Bettenhausen, "The Contribution of Positive Politics to the Prediction of Employee Reactions," *Journal of Applied Social Psychology* 38, No. 1 (2008): 76–96.

34. D. Kipnis, S. M. Schmidt, and I. Wilkinson, "Intraorganizational Influence Tactics: Explorations in Getting One's Way," *Journal of Applied Psychology* 65 (1980): 440–452; D. Kipnis, S. Schmidt, C. Swaffin-Smith, and I. Wilkinson, "Patterns of Managerial Influence: Shotgun Managers, Tacticians, and Bystanders," *Organizational Dynamics* (Winter 1984): 60–67; G. Yukl and C. M. Falbe, "Influence Tactics and Objectives in Upward, Downward, and Lateral Influence Attempts," *Journal of Applied Psychology* 75 (1990): 132–140.

35. G. R. Ferris and T. A. Judge, "Personnel/Human Resources Management: A Political Influence Perspective," *Journal of Management* 17 (1991): 447–488.

36. G. Yukl, P. J. Guinan, and D. Sottolano, "Influence Tactics Used for Different Objectives with Subordinates, Peers, and Superiors," *Groups & Organization Management* 20 (1995): 272–296.

37. C. A. Higgins, T. A. Judge, and G. R. Ferris, "Influence Tactics and Work Outcomes: A Meta-Analysis," *Journal of Organizational Behavior* 24 (2003): 89–106.

38. K. K. Eastman, "In the Eyes of the Beholder: An Attributional Approach to Ingratiation and Organizational Citizenship Behavior," *Academy of Management Journal* 37 (1994): 1379–1391.

39. K. J. Harris, K. M. Kacmar, S. Zivnuska, and J. D Shaw, "The Impact of Political Skill on Impression Management Effectiveness," *Journal of Applied Psychology* 92, No. 1 (2007): 278–285.

40. D. C. Treadway, G. R. Ferris, A. B. Duke, G. L. Adams, and J. B. Thatcher, "The Moderating Role of Subordinate Political Skill on Supervisors' Impressions of Subordinate Ingratiation and Ratings of Subordinate Interpersonal Facilitation," *Journal of Applied Psychology* 92, No. 3 (2007): 848–855.

41. R. A. Gordon, "Impact of Ingratiation on Judgments and Evaluations: A Meta-Analytic Investigation," *Journal of Personality and Social Psychology* 71 (1996): 54–70.

42. A. Drory and D. Beaty, "Gender Differences in the Perception of Organizational Influence Tactics," *Journal of Organizational Behavior* 12 (1991): 249–258.

43. S. Wellington, M. B. Kropf, and P. R. Gerkovich, "What's Holding Women Back?" *Harvard Business Review* (June 2003): 2–4.

44. P. Perrewe and D. Nelson, "Gender and Career Success: The Facilitative Role of Political Skill," *Organizational Dynamics* 33 (2004): 366–378.

45. R. Y. Hirokawa and A. Miyahara, "A Comparison of Influence Strategies Utilized by Managers in American and Japanese Organizations," *Communication Quarterly* 34 (1986): 250–265.

46. C. Anderson, S. E. Spataro, and F. J. Flynn, "Personality and Organizational Culture as Determinants of Influence," *Journal of Applied Psychology* 93 (May 2008): 702–710.

47. P. David, M. A. Hitt, and J. Gimeno, "The Influence of Activism by Institutional Investors on R&D," *Academy of Management Journal* 44, No. 1 (2001): 144–157.

48. G. R. Ferris, P. L. Perrewe, W. P. Anthony, and D. C. Gilmore, "Political Skill at Work," *Organizational Dynamics* 28 (2000): 25–37.

49. D. C. Treadway, W. A. Hochwarter, G. R. Ferris, C. J. Kacmar, C. Douglas, A. P. Ammeter, and M. R. Buckley, "Leader Political Skill and Employee Reactions," *Leadership Quarterly* 15 (2004): 493–513; K. K. Ahearn, G. R. Ferris, W. A. Hochwarter, C. Douglas, and A. P. Ammeter, "Leader Political Skill and Team Performance," *Journal of Management* 30, No. 3 (2004): 309–327.

50. P. L. Perrewé, K. L. Zellars, G. R. Ferris, A. M. Rossi, C. J. Kacmar, and D. A. Ralston, "Neutralizing Job Stressors: Political Skill as an Antidote to the Dysfunctional Consequences of Role Conflict Stressors," *Academy of Management Journal* 47 (2004): 141–152.

51. G. R. Ferris, D. C. Treadway, R. W. Kolodinsky, W. A. Hochwarter, C. J. Kacmar, C. Douglas, and D. D. Frink, "Development and Validation of the Political Skill Inventory," *Journal of Management* 31 (2005): 126–152.

52. G. Ferris, S. Davidson, and P. Perrewé, "Developing Political Skill at Work," *Training* 42 (2005): 40–45.

53. F. R. Blass and G. R. Ferris, "Leader Reputation: The Role of Mentoring, Political Skill, Contextual Learning, and Adaptation," *Human Resource Management* 46, No. 1 (2007): 5–19.

54. S. Y. Todd, K. J. Harris, R. B. Harris, and A. R. Wheeler, "Career Success Implications of Political Skill," *The Journal of Social Psychology* 149, No. 3 (June 2009): 179–204; I. M. Jawahar, J. A. Meurs, G. R. Ferris, and W. A. Hochwarter, "Self-Efficacy and Political Skill as Comparative Predictors of Task and Contextual Performance: A Two-Study Constructive Replication," *Human Performance* 21 (2008): 138–157.

55. K. Kumar and M. S. Thibodeaux, "Organizational Politics and Planned Organizational Change," *Group and Organization Studies* 15 (1990): 354–365.

56. D. Buchanan, "You Stab My back, I'll Stab Yours: Management Experience and Perceptions of Organization Political Behaviour," *British Journal of Management* 19 (March 2008): 49–64.

57. McClelland, *Power*.

58. Beeman and Sharkey, "Use and Abuse of Corporate Politics," 37.

59. C. P. Parker, R. L. Dipboye, and S. L. Jackson, "Perceptions of Organizational Politics: An Investigation of Antecedents and Consequences," *Journal of Management* 21 (1995): 891–912.

60. S. J. Ashford, N. P. Rothbard, S. K. Piderit, and J. E. Dutton, "Out on a Limb: The Role of Context and Impression Management in Selling Gender-Equity Issues," *Administrative Science Quarterly* 43 (1998): 23–57.

61. J. Zhou and G. R. Ferris, "The Dimensions and Consequences of Organizational Politics Perceptions: A Confirmatory Analysis," *Journal of Applied Social Psychology* 25 (1995): 1747–1764.

62. M. L. Seidal, J. T. Polzer, and K. J. Stewart, "Friends in High Places: The Effects of Social Networks on Discrimination in Salary Negotiations," *Administrative Science Quarterly* 45 (2000): 1–24.

63. J. J. Gabarro and J. P. Kotter, "Managing Your Boss," *Harvard Business Review* (January–February 1980): 92–100.

64. P. Newman, "How to Manage Your Boss," *Peat, Marwick, Mitchell & Company's Management Focus* (May–June 1980): 36–37.

65. F. Bertolome, "When You Think the Boss Is Wrong," *Personnel Journal* 69 (1990): 66–73.

66. J. Conger and R. Kanungo, *Charismatic Leadership: The Elusive Factor in Organizational Effectiveness* (New York: Jossey-Bass, 1988).

67. G. M. Spreitzer, M. A. Kizilos, and S. W. Nason, "A Dimensional Analysis of the Relationship between Psychological Empowerment and Effectiveness, Satisfaction, and Strain," *Journal of Management* 23 (1997): 679–704.

68. M. Butts, R. J. Vandenberg, D. M. DeJoy, B. S. Schaffer, and M. G. Wilson, "Individual Reactions to High Involvement Work Processes: Investigating the Role of Empowerment and Perceived Organizational Support," *Journal of Occupational Health Psychology* 14 (April 2009): 122–136.

69. R. C. Ford and M. D. Fottler, "Empowerment: A Matter of Degree," *Academy of Management Executive* 9 (1995): 21–31.

70. M. Holbrook, "Employee Commitment Is Crucial," *Human Resources* (May 2007): 66.

71. X. Zhang and K. M. Bartol, "Linking Empowering Leadership and Employee Creativity: The Influence of Psychological Empowerment, Intrinsic Motivation, and Creative Process Engagement," *The Academy of Management Journal* 53 (2010): 107–128; S. Seibert, G. Wang, and S. Courtright, "Antecedents and Consequences of Psychological and Team Empowerment in Organizations: A Meta-Analytic Review," *The Journal of Applied Psychology* 96, No. 5 (2011): 981–1003.

72. J. Simons, "Merck's Man in the Hot Seat," *Fortune* (February 23, 2004): 111–114.

Chapter 12

1. J. P. Kotter, "What Leaders Really Do," *Harvard Business Review* 68 (1990): 103–111.

2. D. A. Plowman, S. Solansky, T. E Beck, L. Baker, M. Kulkarni, and D. V. Travis, "The Role of Leadership in Emergent, Self-Organization," *Leadership Quarterly* 18, No. 4 (2007): 341–356.

3. B. Stone, "Why Facebook Needs Sheryl Sandberg," *Bloomberg Businessweek* (May 12, 2011), http://www.businessweek.com/magazine /content/11_21/b4229050473695.htm.

4. A. Zaleznik, "HBR Classic—Managers and Leaders: Are They Different?" *Harvard Business Review* 70 (1992): 126–135.

5. W. G. Rowe, "Creating Wealth in Organizations: The Role of Strategic Leadership," *Academy of Management Executive* 15 (2001): 81–94.

6. R. M. Stogdill, "Personal Factors Associated with Leadership: A Survey of the Literature," *Journal of Psychology* 25 (1948): 35–71.

7. K. Lewin, R. Lippitt, and R. K. White, "Patterns of Aggressive Behavior in Experimentally Created 'Social Climates,'" *Journal of Social Psychology* 10 (1939): 271–299.

8. S. D. Sidle, "The Danger of Do Nothing Leaders," *The Academy of Management Perspectives* 21, No. 2 (2007): 75–77.

9. A. W. Halpin and J. Winer, "A Factorial Study of the Leader Behavior Description Questionnaire," in R. M. Stogdill and A. E. Coons, eds., *Leader Behavior: Its Description and Measurement,* research monograph no. 88 (Columbus, Ohio: Bureau of Business Research, The Ohio State University, 1957): 39–51.

10. E. A. Fleishman, "Leadership Climate, Human Relations Training, and Supervisory Behavior," *Personnel Psychology* 6 (1953): 205–222.

11. R. Kahn and D. Katz, "Leadership Practices in Relation to Productivity and Morale," in D. Cartwright and A. Zander, eds., *Group Dynamics, Research and Theory* (Elmsford, NY: Row, Paterson, 1960).

12. R. R. Blake and J. S. Mouton, *The Managerial Grid III: The Key to Leadership Excellence* (Houston: Gulf, 1985).

13. W. Vandekerckhove and R. Commers, "Downward Workplace Mobbing: A Sign of the Times?" *Journal of Business Ethics* 45 (2003): 41–50.

14. F. E. Fiedler, *A Theory of Leader Effectiveness* (New York: McGraw-Hill, 1964).

15. F. E. Fiedler, *Personality, Motivational Systems, and Behavior of High and Low LPC Persons,* tech. rep. no. 70-12 (Seattle: University of Washington, 1970).

16. J. T. McMahon, "The Contingency Theory: Logic and Method Revisited," *Personnel Psychology* 25 (1972): 697–710; L. H. Peters, D. D. Hartke, and J. T. Pohlman, "Fiedler's Contingency Theory of Leadership: An Application of the Meta-Analysis Procedures of Schmidt and Hunter," *Psychological Bulletin* 97 (1985): 224–285.

17. F. E. Fiedler, "The Contingency Model and the Dynamics of the Leadership Process," in L. Berkowitz, ed., *Advances in Experimental and Social Psychology,* vol. 11 (New York: Academic Press, 1978).

18. S. Arin and C. McDermott, "The Effect of Team Leader Characteristics on Learning, Knowledge Application, and Performance of Cross-Functional New Product Development Teams," *Decision Sciences* 34 (2003): 707–739.

19. F. E. Fiedler, "Engineering the Job to Fit the Manager," *Harvard Business Review* 43 (1965): 115–122.

20. R. J. House, "A Path–Goal Theory of Leader Effectiveness," *Administrative Science Quarterly* 16 (1971): 321–338; R. J. House and T. R. Mitchell, "Path–Goal Theory of Leadership," *Journal of Contemporary Business* 3 (1974): 81–97.

21. C. A. Schriesheim and V. M. Von Glinow, "The Path–Goal Theory of Leadership: A Theoretical and Empirical Analysis," *Academy of Management Journal* 20 (1977): 398–405; E. Valenzi and G. Dessler, "Relationships of Leader Behavior, Subordinate Role Ambiguity, and Subordinate Job Satisfaction," *Academy of Management Journal* 21 (1978): 671–678; N. R. F. Maier, *Leadership Methods and Skills* (New York: McGraw-Hill, 1963).

22. J. P. Grinnell, "An Empirical Investigation of CEO Leadership in Two Types of Small Firms," *S.A.M. Advanced Management Journal* 68 (2003): 36–41.

23. V. H. Vroom and P. W. Yetton, *Leadership and Decision Making* (Pittsburgh: University of Pittsburgh, 1973).

24. V. H. Vroom, "Leadership and the Decision-Making Process," *Organizational Dynamics* 28 (2000): 82–94.

25. P. Hersey and K. H. Blanchard, "Life Cycle Theory of Leadership," *Training and Development* 23 (1969): 26–34; P. Hersey, K. H. Blanchard, and D. E. Johnson, *Management of Organizational Behavior: Leading Human Resources,* 8th ed. (Upper Saddle River, N.J.: Prentice-Hall, 2001).

26. B. M. Bass, *Bass and Stogdill's Handbook of Leadership: Theory, Research, and Managerial Applications,* 3rd ed. (New York: Free Press, 1990).

27. G. B. Graen and M. Uhl-Bien, "Relationship-Based Approach to Leadership: Development of Leader–Member Exchange (LMX) Theory of Leadership over 25 Years," *Leadership Quarterly* 6 (1995): 219–247; C. R. Gerstner and D. V. Day, "Meta-Analytic Review of Leader–Member Exchange Theory: Correlates and Construct Issues," *Journal of Applied Psychology* 82 (1997): 827–844; R. C. Liden, S. J. Wayne, and R. T. Sparrowe, "An Examination of the Mediating Role of Psychological Empowerment on the Relations between the Job, Interpersonal Relationships, and Work Outcomes," *Journal of Applied Psychology* 85 (2001): 407–416.

28. J. Townsend, J. S. Phillips, and T. J. Elkins, "Employee Retaliation: The Neglected Consequence of Poor Leader–Member Exchange Relations," *Journal of Occupational Health Psychology* 5 (2000): 457–463.

29. D. Nelson, R. Basu, and R. Purdie, "An Examination of Exchange Quality and Work Stressors in Leader–Follower Dyads," *International Journal of Stress Management* 5 (1998): 103–112.

30. K. M. Kacmar, L. A. Witt, S. Zivnuska, and S. M. Gully, "The Interactive Effect of Leader–Member Exchange and Communication Frequency on Performance Ratings," *Journal of Applied Psychology* 88 (2003): 764–772.

31. A. G. Tekleab and M. S. Taylor, "Aren't There Two Parties in an Employment Relationship? Antecedents and Consequences of Organization–Employee Agreement on Contract Obligations and Violations," *Journal of Organizational Behavior* 24 (2003): 585–608.

32. D. A. Hoffman, S. J. Gerras, and F. P. Morgeson, "Climate as a Moderator of the Relationship between Leader–Member Exchange and Content Specific Citizenship: Safety Climate as an Exemplar," *Journal of Applied Psychology* 88 (2003): 170–178.

33. H. Liao, D. Liu, and R. Loi, "Looking at Both Sides of the Social Exchange Coin: A Social Cognitive Perspective on the Joint Effects of Relationship Quality and Differentiation on Creativity," *Academy of Management Journal* 53 (2010): 1090–1109.

34. J. M. Burns, *Leadership* (New York: Harper & Row, 1978); T. O. Jacobs, *Leadership and Exchange in Formal Organizations* (Alexandria, Va.: Human Resources Research Organization, 1971).

35. B. M. Bass, "From Transactional to Transformational Leadership: Learning to Share the Vision," *Organizational Dynamics* 19 (1990): 19–31; B. M. Bass, *Leadership and Performance beyond Expectations* (New York: Free Press, 1985).

36. P. M. Podsakoff, S. B. MacKenzie, and W. H. Bommer, "Transformational Leader Behaviors and Substitutes for Leadership as Determinants of Employee Satisfaction, Commitment, Trust, and Organizational Citizenship Behaviors," *Journal of Management* 22 (1996): 259–298.

37. W. Bennis, "Managing the Dream: Leadership in the 21st Century," *Training* 27 (1990): 43–48; P. M. Podsakoff, S. B. MacKenzie,

R. H. Moorman, and R. Fetter, "Transformational Leader Behaviors and Their Effects on Followers' Trust in Leader, Satisfaction, and Organizational Citizenship Behaviors," *Leadership Quarterly* 1 (1990): 107–142.

38. MyPrimeTime, Inc., "Great Entrepreneurs—Biography: Howard Schultz, Starbucks," http://www.myprimetime.com/work/ge/schultzbio/index.shtml.

39. X. H. F. Wang, and J. M. Howell, Exploring the Dual-Level Effects of Transformational Leadership on Followers," *Journal of Applied Psychology* 95 (2010): 1134–1144.

40. C. P. Egri and S. Herman, "Leadership in the North American Environmental Sector: Values, Leadership Styles, and Contexts of Environmental Leaders and Their Organizations," *Academy of Management Journal* 43 (2000): 571–604.

41. T. A. Judge and J. E. Bono, "Five-Factor Model of Personality and Transformational Leadership," *Journal of Applied Psychology* 85 (2001): 751–765.

42. J. E. Bono and T. A. Judge, "Self-Concordance at Work: Toward Understanding the Motivational Effects of Transformational Leaders," *Academy of Management Journal* 46 (2003): 554–571.

43. The Jargon Dictionary, "The R Terms: Reality-Distortion Field," http://info.astrian.net/jargon/terms/r/reality-distortion_field.html.

44. R. J. House and M. L. Baetz, "Leadership: Some Empirical Generalizations and New Research Directions," in B. M. Staw, ed., *Research in Organizational Behavior,* vol. 1 (Greenwood, Conn.: JAI Press, 1979): 399–401.

45. D. Waldman, G. G. Ramirez, R. J. House, and P. Puranam, "Does Leadership Matter? CEO Leadership Attributes and Profitability under Conditions of Perceived Environmental Uncertainty," *Academy of Management Journal* 44 (2001): 134–143.

46. J. M. Howell, "Two Faces of Charisma: Socialized and Personalized Leadership in Organizations," in J. A. Conger, ed., *Charismatic Leadership: Behind the Mystique of Exceptional Leadership* (San Francisco: Jossey-Bass, 1988).

47. F. Luthans and B. J. Avolio, "Authentic Leadership: A Positive Development Approach," in K. S. Cameron, J. E. Dutton, and R. E. Quinn, eds., *Positive Organizational Scholarship: Foundations of a New Discipline* (San Francisco: Berrett-Koehler, 2004): 241–261.

48. W. L. Gardner, B. J. Avolio, F. Luthans, D. R. May, and F. O. Walumbwa, "Can You See the Real Me? A Self-Based Model of Authentic Leader and Follower Development," *The Leadership Quarterly* 16 (2005): 343–372.

49. B. J. Avolio, W. L. Gardner, F. O. Walumbwa, F. Luthans, and D. R. May, "Unlocking the Mask: A Look at the Process by Which Authentic Leaders Impact Follower Attitudes and Behaviors," *The Leadership Quarterly* 15 (2004): 801–823.

50. S. Michie and J. Gooty, "Values, Emotions and Authentic Leadership Behaviors: Will the Real Leader Please Stand Up?" *The Leadership Quarterly* 16 (2005): 441–457.

51. S. Michie and D. L. Nelson, "The Effects of Leader Compassion Display on Follower Attributions: Building a Socialized Leadership Image," Paper presented at the *Academy of Management Conference* in Honolulu, Hawaii (2005).

52. M. Maccoby, "Narcissistic Leaders: The Incredible Pros, the Inevitable Cons," *Harvard Business Review* 78 (2000): 68–77.

53. D. Sankowsky, "The Charismatic Leader as Narcissist: Understanding the Abuse of Power," *Organizational Dynamics* 23 (1995): 57–71.

54. F. J. Flynn and B. M. Staw, "Lend Me Your Wallets: The Effect of Charismatic Leadership on External Support for an Organization," *Strategic Management Journal* 25 (2004): 309–330.

55. D. Goleman, "What Makes a Leader?" *Harvard Business Review* 82 (2004): 82–91.

56. D. Goleman, "Never Stop Learning," *Harvard Business Review* 82 (2004): 28–30.

57. C. L. Gohm, "Mood Regulation and Emotional Intelligence: Individual Differences," *Journal of Personality and Social Psychology* 84 (2003): 594–607.

58. J. Useem, "A Manager for All Seasons," *Fortune* (April 30, 2001): 66–72.

59. R. C. Mayer, J. H. Davis, and F. D. Schoorman, "An Integrative Model of Organizational Trust," *Academy of Management Review* 20 (1995): 709–734.

60. R. S. Dooley and G. E. Fryxell, "Attaining Decision Quality and Commitment from Dissent: The Moderating Effects of Loyalty and Competence in Strategic Decision-Making Teams," *Academy of Management Journal* 42 (1999): 389–402.

61. J. Flint, "Why Rick Wagoner Had to Go," *Forbes* (March 30, 2009), http://www.forbes.com/2009/03/30/rick-wagoner-gm-jerry-flint-business-autos-backseat-driver.html.

62. S. A. Joni, "The Geography of Trust," *Harvard Business Review* 82 (2003): 82–88.

63. M. E. Heilman, C. J. Block, R. F. Martell, and M. C. Simon, "Has Anything Changed? Current Characteristics of Men, Women, and Managers," *Journal of Applied Psychology* 74 (1989): 935–942.

64. A. H. Eagly, S. J. Darau, and M. Makhijani, "Gender and the Effectiveness of Leaders: A Meta-Analysis," *Psychological Bulletin* 117 (1995): 125–145.

65. M. K. Ryan, S. A. Haslam, and T. Postmes, "Reactions to the Glass Cliff: Gender Differences in the Explanations for the Precariousness of Women's Leadership Positions," *Journal of Organizational Change Management* 20, No. 2 (2007): 182–197.

66. J. Hu and R. C. Liden, "Antecedents of Team Potency and Team Effectiveness: An Examination of Goal and Process Clarity and Servant Leadership," *Journal of Applied Psychology* 96, No. 4 (2011): 851–862.

67. R. K. Greenleaf, L. C. Spears, and D. T. Frick, eds., *On Becoming a Servant-Leader* (San Francisco: Jossey-Bass, 1996).

68. A. C. H. Schat, M. R. Frone, and E. K. Kelloway, "Prevalence of Workplace Aggression in the U.S. Workforce: Findings from a National Study," in E. K. Kelloway, J. Barling, and J. J. Hurrell, eds., *Handbook of Workplace Violence* (Thousand Oaks, CA:Sage. 2006): 47–89.

69. B. J. Tepper, C. A. Henle, L. S. Lambert, R. A. Giacalone, and M. K. Duffy, "Abusive Supervision and Subordinates' Organization Deviance," *Journal of Applied Psychology* 93 (2008): 721–732; P. A. Bamberger and S. B. Bacharach, "Abusive Supervision and Subordinate Problem Drinking: Taking Resistance, Stress and Subordinate Personality into Account," *Human Relations* 59 (2006): 1–30; B. J. Tepper, "Consequences of Abusive Supervision," *Academy of Management Journal* 43 (2000): 178–190; A. A. Grandey, J. Kern, and M. Frone, "Verbal Abuse from Outsiders Versus Insiders: Comparing Frequency, Impact on Emotional Exhaustion, and the Role of Emotional Labor," *Journal of Occupation Health Psychology* 12 (2007): 63–79.

70. B. J. Tepper, M. K. Duffy, C. A. Henle, and L. S. Lambert, "Procedural Injustice, Victim Precipitation and Abusive Supervision," *Personnel Psychology* 59 (2006): 101–123.

71. S. Thau and M. S. Mitchell, "Self-Gain or Self-Regulation Impairment? Tests of Competing Explanations of the Supervisor Abuse and Employee Deviance Relationship through Perceptions of Distributive Justice," *Journal of Applied Psychology* (in press).

72. B. J. Tepper, "Abusive Supervision in Work Organizations: Review, Synthesis and Research Agenda," *Journal of Management* 33 (2007): 261–289.

73. E. P. Hollander and L. R. Offerman, "Power and Leadership in Organizations: Relationships in Transition," *American Psychologist* 45 (1990): 179–189.

74. H. P. Sims, Jr., and C. C. Manz, *Company of Heros: Unleashing the Power of Self-Leadership* (New York: John Wiley & Sons, 1996).

75. C. C. Manz and H. P. Sims, "Leading Workers to Lead Themselves: The External Leadership of Self-Managing Work Teams," *Administrative Science Quarterly* 32 (1987): 106–128.

76. L. Hirschhorn, "Leaders and Followers in a Postindustrial Age: A Psychodynamic View," *Journal of Applied Behavioral Science* 26 (1990): 529–542.

77. R. E. Kelley, "In Praise of Followers," *Harvard Business Review* 66 (1988): 142–148.

78. C. C. Manz and H. P. Sims, "SuperLeadership: Beyond the Myth of Heroic Leadership," *Organizational Dynamics* 20 (1991): 18–35.

79. G. A. Yukl, *Leadership in Organizations,* 2nd ed. (Upper Saddle River, N.J.: Prentice-Hall, 1989).

Chapter 13

1. Definition adapted from D. Hellriegel, J. W. Slocum, Jr., and R. W. Woodman, *Organizational Behavior* (St. Paul: West, 1992), and from R. D. Middlemist and M. A. Hitt, *Organizational Behavior* (St. Paul, Minn.: West, 1988).

2. D. Tjosvold, *The Conflict-Positive Organization* (Reading, Mass.: Addison-Wesley, 1991).

3. K. Thomas and W. Schmidt, "A Survey of Managerial Interests with Respect to Conflict," *Academy of Management Journal* 19 (1976): 315–318; G. L. Lippitt, "Managing Conflict in Today's Organizations," *Training and Development Journal* 36 (1982): 66–74.

4. M. Rajim, "A Measure of Styles of Handling Interpersonal Conflict," *Academy of Management Journal* 26 (1983): 368–376.

5. D. Goleman, *Emotional Intelligence* (New York: Bantam Books, 1995); J. Stuller, "Unconventional Smarts," *Across the Board* 35 (1998): 22–23.

6. Tjosvold, *The Conflict-Positive Organization*, 4.

7. R. A. Cosier and D. R. Dalton, "Positive Effects of Conflict: A Field Experiment," *International Journal of Conflict Management* 1 (1990): 81–92.

8. D. Tjosvold, "Making Conflict Productive," *Personnel Administrator* 29 (1984): 121–130.

9. I. Janis, *Groupthink*, 2nd ed. (Boston: Houghton Mifflin, 1982).

10. A. C. Amason, W. A. Hochwarter, K. R. Thompson, and A. W. Harrison, "Conflict: An Important Dimension in Successful Management Teams," *Organizational Dynamics* 24 (1995): 25–35.

11. T. L. Simons and R. S. Peterson, "Task Conflict and Relationship Conflict in Top Management Teams: The Pivotal Role of Intergroup Trust," *Journal of Applied Psychology* 85 (2000): 102–111.

12. R. Nibler and K. L. Harris, "The Effects of Culture and Cohesiveness on Intragroup Conflict and Effectiveness," *The Journal of Social Psychology* 143 (2003): 613–631.

13. J. D. Thompson, *Organizations in Action* (New York: McGraw-Hill, 1967).

14. G. Walker and L. Poppo, "Profit Centers, Single-Source Suppliers, and Transaction Costs," *Administrative Science Quarterly* 36 (1991): 66–87.

15. R. Miles, *Macro Organizational Behavior* (Glenview, Ill.: Scott, Foresman, 1980).

16. H. Levinson, "The Abrasive Personality," *Harvard Business Review* 56 (1978): 86–94.

17. J. C. Quick and J. D. Quick, *Organizational Stress and Preventive Management* (New York: McGraw-Hill, 1984).

18. F. N. Brady, "Aesthetic Components of Management Ethics," *Academy of Management Review* 11 (1986): 337–344.

19. J. R. Ogilvie and M. L. Carsky, "Building Emotional Intelligence in Negotiations," *The International Journal of Conflict Management* 13 (2002): 381–400.

20. A. M. Bodtker and R. L. Oliver, "Emotion in Conflict Formation and Its Transformation: Application to Organizational Conflict Management," *International Journal of Conflict Management* 12 (2001): 259–275.

21. D. E. Conlon and S. H. Hunt, "Dealing with Feeling: The Influence of Outcome Representations on Negotiation," *International Journal of Conflict Management* 13 (2002): 35–58.

22. J. Schopler, C. A. Insko, J. Wieselquist, M. Pemberton, B. Witcher, R. Kozar, C. Roddenberry, T. Wildschut, "When Groups Are More Competitive than Individuals: The Domain of the Discontinuity Effect," *Journal of Personality and Social Psychology* 80 (2001): 632–644.

23. M. Sherif and C. W. Sherif, *Social Psychology* (New York: Harper & Row, 1969).

24. M. A. Zarate, B. Garcia, A. A. Garza, and R. T. Hitlan, "Cultural Threat and Perceived Realistic Group Conflict as Dual Predictors of Prejudice," *Journal of Experimental Social Psychology* 40 (2004): 99–105; J. C. Dencker, A. Joshi, and J. J. Martocchio, "Employee Benefits as Context for Intergenerational Conflict," *Human Resource Management Review* 17, No. 2 (2007): 208–220.

25. C. Song, S. M. Sommer, and A. E. Hartman, "The Impact of Adding an External Rater on Interdepartmental Cooperative Behaviors of Workers," *International Journal of Conflict Management* 9 (1998): 117–138.

26. W. Tsai and S. Ghoshal, "Social Capital and Value Creation: The Role of Intrafirm Networks," *Academy of Management Journal* 41 (1998): 464–476.

27. M. L. Maznevski and K. M. Chudoba, "Bridging Space over Time: Global Virtual-Team Dynamics and Effectiveness," *Organization Science* 11 (2000): 473–492.

28. D. L. Nelson and J. C. Quick, "Professional Women: Are Distress and Disease Inevitable?" *Academy of Management Review* 10 (1985): 206–218; D. L. Nelson and M. A. Hitt, "Employed Women and Stress: Implications for Enhancing Women's Mental Health in the Workplace," in J. C. Quick, J. Hurrell, and L. A. Murphy, eds., *Stress and Well-Being at Work: Assessments and Interventions for Occupational Mental Health* (Washington, D.C.: American Psychological Association, 1992).

29. D. Katz and R. Kahn, *The Social Psychology of Organizations*, 2nd ed. (New York: Wiley, 1978).

30. E. C. Dierdorff and J. K. Ellington, "It's the Nature of Work: Examining Behavior-Based Sources of Work–Family Conflict across Occupations," *Journal of Applied Psychology* 93 (2008): 883–892.

31. M. G. Pratt and J. A. Rosa, "Transforming Work–Family Conflict into Commitment in Network Marketing Organizations," *Academy of Management Journal* 46 (2003): 395–418.

32. W. R. Boswell and J. B. Olson-Buchanan, "The Use of Communication Technologies after Hours: The Role of Work Attitudes and Work–Life Conflict," *Journal of Management* 33, No. 4 (2007): 592–610.

33. R. L. Kahn D. M. Wolfe, R. P. Quinn, J. D. Noek, R. A. Rosenthal, *Organizational Stress: Studies in Role Conflict and Ambiguity* (New York: Wiley, 1964).

34. J. R. B. Halbesleben, "A Meta-Analysis of Work Engagement: Relationships with Burnout, Demands, Resources, and Consequences," in A. Bakker and M. Leiter, eds., *Work Engagement: A Handbook of Essential Theory and Research* (New York: Psychology Press, 2010); M. Wang, S. Liu, Y. Zhan, and J. Shi, "Daily Work–Family Conflict and Alcohol Use: Testing the Cross-Level Moderation Effects of Peer Drinking Norms and Social Support," *Journal of Applied Psychology* 95 (2010): 377–386.

35. J. L. Badaracco, Jr., "The Discipline of Building Character," *Harvard Business Review* (March–April 1998): 115–124.

36. B. Schneider, "The People Make the Place," *Personnel Psychology* 40 (1987): 437–453.

37. C. A. O'Reilly, J. Chatman, and D. F. Caldwell, "People and Organizational Culture: A Profile Comparison Approach to Assessing Person-Organization Fit," *Academy of Management Journal* 34 (1991): 487–516.

38. I. Dayal and J. M. Thomas, "Operation KPE: Developing a New Organization," *Journal of Applied Behavioral Science* 4 (1968): 473–506.

39. R. H. Miles, "Role Requirements as Sources of Organizational Stress," *Journal of Applied Psychology* 61 (1976): 172–179.

40. W. F. G. Mastenbroek, *Conflict Management and Organization Development* (Chichester, England: Wiley, 1987).

41. M. R. Frone, "Interpersonal Conflict at Work and Psychological Outcomes: Testing a Model among Young Workers," *Journal of Occupational Health Psychology* 5 (2000): 246–255.

42. K. Thomas, "Conflict and Conflict Management," in M. D. Dunnette, ed., *Handbook of Industrial and Organizational Psychology* (New York: Wiley, 1976).

43. H. H. Meyer, E. Kay, and J. R. P. French, "Split Roles in Performance Appraisal," *Harvard Business Review* 43 (1965): 123–129.

44. T. W. Costello and S. S. Zalkind, *Psychology in Administration: A Research Orientation* (Englewood Cliffs, N.J.: Prentice-Hall, 1963).

45. Snapshot Spy, "Employee Computer & Internet Abuse Statistics," http://www.snapshotspy.com/employee-computer-abuse-statistics.htm; Data sources include U.S. Department of Commerce—Economics and Statistics Administration and the National Telecommunications and Information Administration—Greenfield and Rivet, "Employee Computer Abuse Statistics."

46. P. F. Hewlin, "And the Award for Best Actor Goes to . . . : Facades of Conformity in Organizational Settings," *Academy of Management Review* 28 (2003): 633–642.

47. C. A. Insko, J. Scholper, L. Gaertner, T. Wildschut, R. Kozar, B. Pinter, E. J. Finkel, D. M. Brazil, C. L. Cecil, M. R. Montoya, "Interindividual–Intergroup Discontinuity Reduction through the Anticipation of Future

Interaction," *Journal of Personality and Social Psychology* 80 (2001): 95–111.

48. D. Tjosvold and M. Poon, "Dealing with Scarce Resources: Open-Minded Interaction for Resolving Budget Conflicts," *Group and Organization Management* 23 (1998): 237–255.

49. Miles, *Macro Organizational Behavior;* R. Steers, *Introduction to Organizational Behavior,* 4th ed. (Glenview, Ill.: Harper-Collins, 1991).

50. A. Tyerman and C. Spencer, "A Critical Text of the Sherrif's Robber's Cave Experiments: Intergroup Competition and Cooperation between Groups of Well-Acquainted Individuals," *Small Group Behavior* 14 (1983): 515–531; R. M. Kramer, "Intergroup Relations and Organizational Dilemmas: The Role of Categorization Processes," in B. Staw and L. Cummings, eds., *Research in Organizational Behavior* 13 (1991), 191–228.

51. N. Kercheval, "Dana Holgorsen Becomes West Virginia Coach after Bill Stewart Resigns," *Bloomberg* (June 11, 2011), http://bloomberg.com/news/2011-06-11/dana-holgorsen-becomes-west-virgiinia-coach-after-bill-stewart-resigns.html.

52. A. Carmeli, "The Relationship between Emotional Intelligence and Work Attitudes, Behavior and Outcomes: An Examination among Senior Managers," *Journal of Managerial Psychology* 18 (2003): 788–813.

53. R. Blake and J. Mouton, "Overcoming Group Warfare," *Harvard Business Review* 64 (1984): 98–108.

54. D. G. Ancona and D. Caldwell, "Improving the Performance of New Product Teams," *Research Technology Management* 33 (1990): 25–29.

55. M. A. Cronin and L. R. Weingart, "Representational Gaps, Information Processing and Conflict in Functionally Diverse Teams," *Academy of Management Review* 32, No. 3 (2007): 761–773.

56. C. K. W. DeDreu and L. R. Weingart, "Task versus Relationship Conflict, Team Performance, and Team Member Satisfaction: A Meta-Analysis," *Journal of Applied Psychology* 88 (2003): 741–749.

57. R. J. Lewicki, J. A. Litterer, J. W. Minton, and D. M. Saunders, *Negotiation,* 2nd ed. (Burr Ridge, Ill.: Irwin, 1994).

58. C. K. W. De Dreu, S. L. Koole, and W. Steinel, "Unfixing the Fixed Pie: A Motivated Information-Processing Approach to Integrative Negotiation," *Journal of Personality and Social Psychology* 79 (2000): 975–987.

59. M. H. Bazerman, J. R. Curhan, D. A. Moore, and K. L. Valley, "Negotiation," *Annual Review of Psychology* 51 (2000): 279–314.

60. I. Ayers and P. Siegelman, "Race and Gender Discrimination in Bargaining for a New Car," *American Economic Review* 85 (1995): 304–321.

61. K. W. Thomas, "Conflict and Conflict Management," in M. D. Dunnette, ed., *Handbook of Industrial and Organizational Psychology* (Chicago: Rand McNally, 1976), 900.

62. C. K. W. De Dreu and A. E. M. Van Vianen, "Managing Relationship Conflict and the Effectiveness of Organizational Teams," *Journal of Organizational Behavior* 22 (2001): 309–328.

63. S. Steinberg, "Airbus Workers in France, Germany Strike against Massive Job Cuts," (March 1, 2007). http://www.wsws.org/articles/2007/mar2007/airb-m01.shtml.

64. R. A. Baron, S. P. Fortin, R. L. Frei, L. A. Hauver, and M. L. Shack, "Reducing Organizational Conflict: The Role of Socially Induced Positive Affect," *International Journal of Conflict Management* 1 (1990): 133–152.

65. S. L. Phillips and R. L. Elledge, *The Team Building Source Book* (San Diego: University Associates, 1989).

66. J. R. Curhan, M. A. Neale, L. Ross, and J. Rosencranz-Engelmann, "Relational Accommodation in Negotiation: Effects of Egalitarianism and Gender on Economic Efficiency and Relational Capital," *Organizational Behavior and Human Decision Processes* 107 (2008): 192–205.

67. T. N. Gladwin and I. Walter, "How Multinationals Can Manage Social and Political Forces," *Journal of Business Strategy,* No. 1 (1980): 54–68.

68. L. A. Dechurch, K. L. Hamilton, and C. Haas, "Effects of Conflict Management Strategies on Perceptions of Intragroup Conflict," *Group Dynamics: Theory, Research, and Practice* 11, No. 1 (2007): 66–78.

69. K. W. Thomas, "Toward Multidimensional Values in Teaching: The Example of Conflict Behaviors," *Academy of Management Review* 2 (1977): 484–490.

70. S. Alper, D. Tjosvold, and K. S. Law, "Conflict Management, Efficacy, and Performance in Organizational Teams," *Personnel Psychology* 53 (2000): 625–642.

71. A. Somech, H. S. Desvililya, and H. Lidogoster, " Team Conflict Management and Team Effectiveness: The Effects of Task

Interdependence and Team Identification," *Journal of Organizational Behavior* 30 (2009): 359–378.

72. W. King and E. Miles, "What We Know and Don't Know about Measuring Conflict," *Management Communication Quarterly* 4 (1990): 222–243.

73. J. Barker, D. Tjosvold, and I. R. Andrews, "Conflict Approaches of Effective and Ineffective Project Managers: A Field Study in a Matrix Organization," *Journal of Management Studies* 25 (1988): 167–178.

74. M. Chan, "Intergroup Conflict and Conflict Management in the R&D Divisions of Four Aerospace Companies," *IEEE Transactions on Engineering Management* 36 (1989): 95–104.

Chapter 14

1. J. S. Bunderson and J. A. Thompson, "The Call of the Wild: Zookeepers, Callings, and the Double-Edged Sword of Deeply Meaningful Work," *Administrative Science Quarterly* 54 (2009): 32–57.

2. G. W. England and I. Harpaz, "How Working Is Defined: National Contexts and Demographic and Organizational Role Influences," *Journal of Organizational Behavior* 11 (1990): 253–266.

3. L. R. Gomez-Mejia, "The Cross-Cultural Structure of Task-Related and Contextual Constructs," *Journal of Psychology* 120 (1986): 5–19.

4. A. Wrzesniewski and J. E. Dutton, "Crafting a Job: Revisioning Employees as Active Crafters of Their Work," *Academy of Management Review* 26 (2001): 179–201.

5. D. T. Hall and M. Las Heras, "Reintegrating Job Design and Career Theory: Creating Not Just Good Jobs but *Smart* Jobs," *Journal of Organizational Behavior* 31 (2010): 448–462.

6. F. W. Taylor, *The Principles of Scientific Management* (New York: Norton, 1911).

7. T. Bell, *Out of This Furnace* (Pittsburgh: University of Pittsburgh Press, 1941); J. H. Gittell, D. B. Weinberg, A. L. Bennett, and J. A. Miller, "Is the Doctor in? A Relational Approach to Job Design and the Coordination of Work," *Human Resource Management* 47 (Winter 2008): 729–755.

8. N. D. Warren, "Job Simplification versus Job Enlargement," *Journal of Industrial Engineering* 9 (1958): 435–439.

9. T. Moller, S. E. Mathiassen, H. Franzon, and S. Kihlberg, "Job Enlargement and Mechanical Exposure Variability in Cyclic Assembly Work," *Ergonomics* 47 (2004): 19–40.

10. C. R. Walker and R. H. Guest, *The Man on the Assembly Line* (Cambridge, Mass.: Harvard University Press, 1952).

11. C. R. Walker, "The Problem of the Repetitive Job," *Harvard Business Review* 28 (1950): 54–58.

12. M. A. Campion, L. Cheraskin, and M. J. Stevens, "Career-Related Antecedents and Outcomes of Job Rotation," *Academy of Management Journal* 37 (1994): 1518–1542.

13. H. R. Nalbantian and R. A. Guzzo, "Making Mobility Matter," *Harvard Business Review* (March 2009): 76–84

14. E. Santora, "Keep Up Production through Cross-Training," *Personnel Journal* (June 1992): 162–166.

15. S. Leroy, "Why Is It So Hard to Do My Work? The Challenge of Attention Residue When Switching between Work Tasks," *Organizational Behavior and Human Decision Processes* 109 (2009): 168–181.

16. R. P. Steel and J. R. Rentsch, "The Dispositional Model of Job Attitudes Revisited: Findings of a 10-Year Study," *Journal of Applied Psychology* 82 (1997): 873–879; C. S. Wong, C. Hui, and K. S. Law, "A Longitudinal Study of the Job Perception–Job Satisfaction Relationship: A Text of the Three Alternative Specifications," *Journal of Occupational & Organizational Psychology* 71 (Part 2, 1998): 127–146.

17. F. Herzberg, "One More Time: How Do You Motivate Employees?" *Harvard Business Review* 46 (1968): 53–62.

18. R. N. Ford, "Job Enrichment Lessons from AT&T," *Harvard Business Review* 51 (1973): 96–106.

19. R. J. House and L. A. Wigdor, "Herzberg's Dual-Factor Theory of Job Satisfaction and Motivation: A Review of the Evidence and a Criticism," *Personnel Psychology* 20 (1967): 369–389.

20. A. N. Turner and P. R. Lawrence, *Industrial Jobs and the Worker* (Cambridge, Mass.: Harvard University Press, 1965).

21. D. H. McKnight, B. Phillips, and B. C. Hardgrave, "Which Reduces IT Turnover Intention the Worst: Workplace Characteristics or Job Characteristics?" *Information & Management* 46 (2009): 167–174.

22. J. R. Hackman and G. R. Oldham, "The Relationship among Core Job Dimensions, the Critical Psychological States, and On-the-Job Outcomes," in *The Job Diagnostic Survey: An Instrument for the Diagnosis of Jobs and the Evaluation of Job Redesign Projects* (New Haven, Conn.: Department of Administrative Sciences, Yale University, 1974).

23. J. L. Pierce, I. Jussila, and A. Cummings, "Psychological Ownership within the Job Design Context: Revision of the Job Characteristics Model," *Journal of Organizational Behavior* 30 (2009): 477–496.

24. J. R. Hackman and G. R. Oldham, "Development of the Job Diagnostic Survey," *Journal of Applied Psychology* 60 (1975): 159–170.

25. E. Sadler-Smith, G. El-Kot, and M. Leat, "Differentiating Work Autonomy Facets in a Non-Western Context," *Journal of Organizational Behavior* 24 (2003): 709–731.

26. H. P. Sims, A. D. Szilagyi, and R. T. Keller, "The Measurement of Job Characteristics," *Academy of Management Journal* 19 (1976): 195–212.

27. H. P. Sims and A. D. Szilagyi, "Job Characteristic Relationships: Individual and Structural Moderators," *Organizational Behavior and Human Performance* 17 (1976): 211–230.

28. Y. Fried, "Meta-Analytic Comparison of the Job Diagnostic Survey and Job Characteristic Inventory as Correlates of Work Satisfaction and Performance," *Journal of Applied Psychology* 76 (1991): 690–698.

29. D. R. May, R. L. Gilson, and L. M. Harter, "The Psychological Conditions of Meaningfulness, Safety, and Availability and the Engagement of the Human Spirit at Work," *Journal of Occupational and Organizational Psychology* 77 (2004): 11–37.

30. R. Wagner, "Nourishing Employee Engagement," *Gallup Management Journal* (February 12, 2004): 1–7, http://gmj.gallup.com/content/default.asp?ci=10504.

31. M. Soyars and J. Brusino, "Essentials of Engagement," *T&D* (March 2009): 62–65.

32. J. Loehr and T. Schwartz, *The Power of Full Engagement: Managing Energy, Not Time, Is the Key to High Performance and Personal Renewal* (New York: Free Press, 2003).

33. M. F. R. Kets de Vries, "Creating Authentizotic Organizations: Well-Functioning Individuals in Vibrant Companies," *Human Relations* 54 (2001): 101–111.

34. G. R. Salancik and J. Pfeffer, "A Social Information Processing Approach to Job Attitudes and Task Design," *Administrative Science Quarterly* 23 (1978): 224–253.

35. J. Pfeffer, "Management as Symbolic Action: The Creation and Maintenance of Organizational Paradigms," in L. L. Cummings and B. M. Staw, eds., *Research in Organizational Behavior*, vol. 3 (Greenwich, Conn.: JAI Press, 1981): 1–52.

36. C. Clegg and C. Spencer, "A Circular and Dynamic Model of the Process of Job Design," *Journal of Occupational & Organizational Psychology* 80 (2007): 321–339.

37. J. Thomas and R. Griffin, "The Social Information Processing Model of Task Design: A Review of the Literature," *Academy of Management Review* 8 (1983): 672–682.

38. D. J. Campbell, "Task Complexity: A Review and Analysis," *Academy of Management Review* 13 (1988): 40–52.

39. A. M. Grant, "Relational Job Design and the Motivation to Make a Prosocial Difference," *Academy of Management Review* 32 (2007): 393–417.

40. D. R. May, K. Reed, C. E. Schwoerer, and P. Potter, "Ergonomic Office Design and Aging: A Quasi-Experimental Field Study of Employee Reactions to an Ergonomics Intervention Program," *Journal of Occupational Health Psychology* 9 (2004): 123–135.

41. M. A. Campion and P. W. Thayer, "Job Design: Approaches, Outcomes, and Trade-Offs," *Organizational Dynamics* 16 (1987): 66–79.

42. J. Teresko, "Emerging Technologies," *Industry Week* (February 27, 1995): 1–2.

43. M. A. Campion and C. L. McClelland, "Interdisciplinary Examination of the Costs and Benefits of Enlarged Jobs: A Job Design Quasi-Experiment," *Journal of Applied Psychology* 76 (1991): 186–199.

44. B. Kohut, *Country Competitiveness: Organizing of Work* (New York: Oxford University Press, 1993).

45. D. Holman, S. Frenkel, O. Sorensen, and S. Wood, "Work Design Variation and Outcomes in Call Centers: Strategic Choice and Institutional Explanations," *Industrial and Labor Relations Review* 62 (July 2009): 510–532.

46. J. C. Quick and L. E. Tetrick, eds., *Handbook of Occupational Health Psychology* (Washington, D.C.: American Psychological Association, 2002).

47. W. E. Deming, *Out of the Crisis* (Cambridge, Mass.: MIT Press, 1986).

48. L. Thurow, *Head to Head: The Coming Economic Battle among Japan, Europe, and America* (New York: Morrow, 1992).

49. M. A. Fruin, *The Japanese Enterprise System—Competitive Strategies and Cooperative Structures* (New York: Oxford University Press, 1992).

50. W. Niepce and E. Molleman, "Work Design Issue in Lean Production from a Sociotechnical System Perspective: Neo-Taylorism or the Next Step in Sociotechnical Design?" *Human Relations* 51 (1998): 259–287.

51. S. K. Parker, "Longitudinal Effects of Lean Production on Employee Outcomes and the Mediating Role of Work Characteristics," *Journal of Applied Psychology* 88 (2003): 620–634.

52. E. Furubotn, "Codetermination and the Modern Theory of the Firm: A Property-Rights Analysis," *Journal of Business* 61 (1988): 165–181.

53. H. Levinson, *Executive: The Guide to Responsive Management* (Cambridge, Mass.: Harvard University Press, 1981).

54. B. Gardell, "Scandinavian Research on Stress in Working Life" (Paper presented at the IRRA Symposium on Stress in Working Life, Denver, September 1980).

55. L. Levi, "Psychosocial, Occupational, Environmental, and Health Concepts; Research Results and Applications," in G. P. Keita and S. L. Sauter, eds., *Work and Well-Being: An Agenda for the 1990s* (Washington, D.C.: American Psychological Association, 1992), 199–211.

56. L. R. Murphy and C. L. Cooper, eds., *Healthy and Productive Work: An International Perspective* (London and New York: Taylor & Francis, 2000).

57. R. L. Kahn, *Work and Health* (New York: Wiley, 1981); M. Gowing, J. Kraft, and J. C. Quick, *The New Organizational Reality: Downsizing, Restructuring, and Revitalization* (Washington, D.C.: American Psychological Association, 1998).

58. F. J. Landy, "Work Design and Stress," in G. P. Keita and S. L. Sauter, eds., *Work and Well-Being: An Agenda for the 1990s* (Washington, D.C.: American Psychological Association, 1992): 119–158.

59. C. Gresov, R. Drazin, and A. H. Van de Ven, "Work-Unit Task Uncertainty, Design, and Morale," *Organizational Studies* 10 (1989): 45–62.

60. A. M. Grant, E. M. Campbell, G. Chen, K. Cottone, D. Lapedis, and K. Lee, "Impact and the Art of Motivation Maintenance: The Effects of Contact with Beneficiaries on Persistence Behavior," *Organizational Behavior and Human Decision Processes* 103 (2007): 53–67.

61. Y. Baruch, "The Status of Research on Teleworking and an Agenda for Future Research," *International Journal of Management Review* 3 (2000): 113–129.

62. K. E. Pearlson and C. S. Saunders, "There's No Place Like Home: Managing Telecommuting Paradoxes," *Academy of Management Executive* 15 (2001): 117–128.

63. S. Caudron, "Working at Home Pays Off," *Personnel Journal* (November 1992): 40–47.

64. D. S. Bailey and J. Foley, "Pacific Bell Works Long Distance," *HRMagazine* (August 1990): 50–52.

65. M. Virick, N. DaSilva, and K. Arrington, "Moderators of the Curvilinear Relationship between Extent of Telecommuting and Job and Life Satisfaction; The Role of Performance Outcome Orientation and Worker Type," *Human Relations* 63 (2010): 137–154.

66. S. M. Pollan and M. Levine, "Asking for Flextime," *Working Women* (February 1994): 48.

67. S. A. Rogier and M. Y. Padgett, "The Impact of Utilizing a Flexible Work Schedule on the Perceived Career Advancement Potential of Women," *Human Resource Development Quarterly* 15 (2004): 89–106.

68. S. Zuboff, *In the Age of the Smart Machine: The Future of Work and Power* (New York: Basic Books, 1988).

69. B. A. Gutek and S. J. Winter, "Computer Use, Control over Computers, and Job Satisfaction," in S. Oskamp and S. Spacapan, eds., *People's Reactions to Technology in Factories, Offices, and Aerospace: The*

Claremont Symposium on Applied Social Psychology (Newbury Park, Calif.: Sage, 1990): 121–144.

70. L. M. Schleifer and B. C. Amick, III, "System Response Time and Method of Pay: Stress Effects in Computer-Based Tasks," *International Journal of Human-Computer Interaction* 1 (1989): 23–39.

71. K. Voight, "Virtual Work: Some Telecommuters Take Remote Work to the Extreme," *The Wall Street Journal Europe* (February 1, 2001): 1.

72. G. Salvendy, *Handbook of Industrial Engineering: Technology and Operations Management* (New York: John Wiley & Sons, 2001).

73. D. M. Herold, "Using Technology to Improve Our Management of Labor Market Trends," in M. Greller, ed., "Managing Careers with a Changing Workforce," *Journal of Organizational Change Management* 3 (1990): 44–57.

74. D. A. Whetten and K. S. Cameron, *Developing Management Skills*, 6th ed. (Upper Saddle River, N.J.: Prentice Hall, 2004).

Chapter 15

1. J. Child, *Organization* (New York: Harper & Row, 1984).

2. P. Lawrence and J. Lorsch, "Differentiation and Integration in Complex Organizations," *Administrative Science Quarterly* 12 (1967): 1–47.

3. P. Lawrence and J. Lorsch, *Organization and Environment: Managing Differentiation and Integration*, rev. ed. (Cambridge, Mass.: Harvard University Press, 1986).

4. J. Hage, "An Axiomatic Theory of Organizations," *Administrative Science Quarterly* 10 (1965): 289–320.

5. "The Army Reserve at 100: An Emerging Operational Force," *Army Logistician* (November–December, 2008): 15–16.

6. W. Ouchi and J. Dowling, "Defining the Span of Control," *Administrative Science Quarterly* 19 (1974): 357–365.

7. L. Porter and E. Lawler, III, "Properties of Organization Structure in Relation to Job Attitudes and Job Behavior," *Psychological Bulletin* 65 (1965): 23–51.

8. J. Ivancevich and J. Donnelly, Jr., "Relation of Organization and Structure to Job Satisfaction, Anxiety-Stress, and Performance," *Administrative Science Quarterly* 20 (1975): 272–280.

9. R. Dewar and J. Hage, "Size, Technology, Complexity, and Structural Differentiation: Toward a Theoretical Synthesis," *Administrative Science Quarterly* 23 (1978): 111–136.

10. F. C. Vasoncelos and R. Ramirez, "Complexity in Business Environments," *Journal of Business Research* 64 (2011): 236–241.

11. Lawrence and Lorsch, "Differentiation and Integration," 1–47.

12. J. R. R. Galbraith, *Designing Complex Organizations* (Reading, Mass.: Addison-Wesley-Longman, 1973).

13. W. Altier, "Task Forces: An Effective Management Tool," *Management Review* 76 (1987): 26–32.

14. P. Lawrence and J. Lorsch, "New Managerial Job: The Integrator," *Harvard Business Review* 45 (1967): 142–151.

15. J. Lorsch and P. Lawrence, "Organizing for Product Innovation," *Harvard Business Review* 43 (1965): 110–111.

16. D. Pugh, D. Hickson, C. Hinnings, and C. Turner, "Dimensions of Organization Structure," *Administrative Science Quarterly* 13 (1968): 65–91; B. Reimann, "Dimensions of Structure in Effective Organizations: Some Empirical Evidence," *Academy of Management Journal* 17 (1974): 693–708; S. Robbins, *Organization Theory: The Structure and Design of Organizations*, 3rd ed. (Englewood Cliffs, N.J.: Prentice-Hall, 1990).

17. M. C. Andrews, T. L. Baker, and T. G. Hunt, "The Interactive Effects of Centralization on the Relationship between Justice and Satisfaction," *Journal of Leadership & Organizational Studies* 15 (2008): 135–144.

18. H. Mintzberg, *The Structuring of Organizations* (Englewood Cliffs, N.J.: Prentice-Hall, 1979).

19. J. A. Kuprenas, "Implementation and Performance of a Matrix Organization Structure," *International Journal of Project Management* 21 (2003): 51–62.

20. Mintzberg, *Structuring of Organizations*.

21. K. Weick, "Educational Institutions as Loosely Coupled Systems," *Administrative Science Quarterly* (1976): 1–19.

22. D. Miller and C. Droge, "Psychological and Traditional Determinants of Structure," *Administrative Science Quarterly* 31 (1986): 540;

23. C. B. Clott, "Perspectives on Global Outsourcing and the Changing Nature of Work," *Business and Society Review* 109 (2004): 153–170.

24. M. Meyer, "Size and the Structure of Organizations: A Causal Analysis," *American Sociological Review* 37 (1972): 434–441; J. Beyer and H. Trice, "A Reexamination of the Relations between Size and Various Components of Organizational Complexity," *Administrative Science Quarterly* 24 (1979): 48–64; B. Mayhew, R. Levinger, J. McPherson, and T. James, "Systems Size and Structural Differentiation in Formal Organizations: A Baseline Generator for Two Major Theoretical Propositions," *American Sociological Review* 37 (1972): 26–43.

25. M. Gowing, J. Kraft, and J. C. Quick, *The New Organizational Reality: Downsizing, Restructuring, and Revitalization* (Washington, D.C.: American Psychological Association, 1998).

26. J. Werth and D. Fleming, "Creating a 'Super' Agency in San Diego County," *The Public Manager* (Fall 2008): 21–26.

27. J. Woodward, *Industrial Organization: Theory and Practices* (London: Oxford University Press, 1965).

28. C. Perrow, "A Framework for the Comparative Analysis of Organizations," *American Sociological Review* 32 (1967): 194–208; D. Rosseau, "Assessment of Technology in Organizations: Closed versus Open Systems Approaches," *Academy of Management Review* 4 (1979): 531–542.

29. B. A. Pasternack and A. J. Viscio, *The Centerless Corporation: A New Model for Transforming Your Organization for Growth and Prosperity* (New York: Simon & Schuster, 1999).

30. Perrow, "A Framework for the Comparative Analysis of Organizations," 194–208.

31. J. D. Thompson, *Organizations in Action* (New York: McGraw-Hill, 1967).

32. J. R. Baum and S. Wally, "Strategic Decision Speed and Firm Performance," *Strategic Management Journal* 24 (2003): 1107–1129.

33. Thompson, *Organizations in Action*.

34. H. Downey, D. Hellriegel, and J. Slocum, Jr., "Environmental Uncertainty: The Construct and Its Application," *Administrative Science Quarterly* 20 (1975): 613–629.

35. G. Dess and D. Beard, "Dimensions of Organizational Task Environments," *Administrative Science Quarterly* 29 (1984): 52–73.

36. G. Vroom, "Organizational Design and the Intensity of Rivalry," *Management Science* 52 (2006): 1689–1702.

37. Dess and Beard, "Dimensions of Organizational Task Environments," 52–73.

38. T. Burns and G. Stalker, *The Management of Innovation* (London: Tavistock, 1961); Mintzberg, *Structuring of Organizations*.

39. M. Chandler and L. Sayles, *Managing Large Systems* (New York: Harper & Row, 1971).

40. M. Sanchez-Manzanares, R. Rico, and F. Gil, "Designing Organizations: Does Expertise Matter?" *Journal of Business Psychology* 23 (2008): 87–101.

41. J. Courtright, G. Fairhurst, and L. Rogers, "Interaction Patterns in Organic and Mechanistic Systems," *Academy of Management Journal* 32 (1989): 773–802.

42. R. Daft, *Organization Theory and Design*, 7th ed. (Mason, Ohio: South-Western, 2000).

43. R. S. Kaplan and D. P. Norton, "How to Implement a New Strategy without Disrupting Your Organization," *Harvard Business Review* (March 2006): 100–109.

44. W. R. Scott, *Organizations: Rational, Natural, and Open Systems*, 4th ed. (Upper Saddle River, N.J.: Prentice-Hall, 1997).

45. D. Miller and P. Friesen, "A Longitudinal Study of the Corporate Life Cycle," *Management Science* 30 (1984): 1161–1183.

46. S. Raisch, "Balanced Structures: Designing Organizations for Profitable Growth," *Long Range Planning* 41 (2008): 483–508.

47. M. H. Overholt, "Flexible Organizations: Using Organizational Design as a Competitive Advantage," *Human Resource Planning* 20 (1997): 22–32; P. W. Roberts and R. Greenwood, "Integrating Transaction Cost and Institutional Theories: Toward a Constrained-Efficiency Framework for Understanding Organizational Design Adoption," *Academy of Management Review* 22 (1997): 346–373.

H. Tosi, Jr. and J. Slocum, Jr., "Contingency Theory: Some Suggested Directions," *Journal of Management* 10 (1984): 9–26.

48. G. Davidson, "Organisation Structure: The Life Cycle of an Organization," *New Zealand Management* 56 (2008): 58–60.

49. C. W. L. Hill and G. R. Jones, *Strategic Management Theory,* 5th ed. (Boston: Houghton Mifflin, 2000).

50. F. Hoque, "Designing the Right Kind of Organization," *Baseline* (January/February 2009): 46.

51. Daft, *Organization Theory and Design.*

52. C. M. Savage, *5th Generation Management, Revised Edition: Co-creating through Virtual Enterprising, Dynamic Teaming, and Knowledge Networking* (Boston: Butterworth-Heinemann, 1996).

53. S. M. Davis, *Future Perfect* (Perseus Publishing, 1997).

54. A. Boynton and B. Victor, "Beyond Flexibility: Building and Managing a Dynamically Stable Organization," *California Management Review* 8 (Fall 1991): 53–66.

55. B. Brown and S. D. Anthony, "How P&G Tripled Its Innovation Success Rate," *Harvard Business Review* 89 (June 2011): 64–72.

56. P. J. Brews and C. L. Tucci, "Exploring the Structural Effects of Internetworking," *Strategic Management Journal* 25 (2004): 429–451.

57. C. B. Gibson and J. L. Gibbs, "Unpacking the Concept of Virtuality: Geographic Dispersion, Electronic Dependence, Dynamic Structure, and National Diversity on Team Innovation," *Administrative Science Quarterly* 51 (2006): 451–495.

58. J. Fulk, "Global Network Organizations: Emergence and Future Prospects," *Human Relations* 54 (2001): 91–100.

59. The use of the theatrical troupe as an analogy for virtual organizations was first used by David Mack, circa 1995.

60. E. C. Kasper-Fuehrer and N. M. Ashkanasy, "Communicating Trustworthiness and Building Trust in Interorganizational Virtual Organizations," *Journal of Management* 27 (2001): 235–254.

61. R. Teerlink and L. Ozley, *More than a Motorcycle: The Leadership Journey at Harley-Davidson* (Boston: Harvard Business School Press, 2000).

62. W. A. Cohen and N. Cohen, *The Paranoid Organization and 8 Other Ways Your Company Can Be Crazy: Advice from an Organizational Shrink* (New York: American Management Association, 1993).

63. P. E. Tetlock, "Cognitive Biases and Organizational Correctives: Do Both Disease and Cure Depend on the Politics of the Beholder?" *Administrative Science Quarterly* 45 (2000): 293–326.

64. M. F. R. Kets de Vries and D. Miller, "Personality, Culture, and Organization," *Academy of Management Review* 11 (1986): 266–279.

Chapter 16

1. T. E. Deal and A. A. Kennedy, *Corporate Cultures* (Reading, Mass.: Addison-Wesley, 1982).

2. W. Ouchi, *Theory Z* (Reading, Mass.: Addison-Wesley, 1981).

3. T. J. Peters and R. H. Waterman, *In Search of Excellence* (New York: Harper & Row, 1982).

4. M. Gardner, "Creating a Corporate Culture for the Eighties," *Business Horizons* (January–February 1985): 59–63.

5. S. H. Harrison and K. G. Corley, "Clean Climbing, Carabiners, and Cultural Cultivation: Developing an Open-Systems Perspective of Culture," *Organization Science* 22 (2011): 391–412.

6. Definition adapted from E. H. Schein, *Organizational Culture and Leadership* (San Francisco: Jossey-Bass, 1985): 9.

7. C. D. Sutton and D. L. Nelson, "Elements of the Cultural Network: The Communicators of Corporate Values," *Leadership and Organization Development* 11 (1990): 3–10.

8. See http://www.google.com/corporate/culture.html.

9. J. Pagel, "Eskimo Joe's Getting Older, But Still Fun at 21," *Amarillo Business Journal* (November 20, 1996), http://www.businessjournal.net/entrepreneur1196.html.

10. A. Bandura, *Social Learning Theory* (Englewood Cliffs, N.J.: Prentice-Hall, 1977).

11. J. A. Chatman, "Leading by Leveraging Culture," *California Management Review* 45 (2003): 20–34.

12. J. M. Beyer and H. M. Trice, "How an Organization's Rites Reveal Its Culture," *Organizational Dynamics* 16 (1987): 5–24.

13. H. M. Trice and J. M. Beyer, "Studying Organizational Cultures through Rites and Ceremonials," *Academy of Management Review* 9 (1984): 653–669.

14. K. Rockwood, "Meet the Famous Faces at Berkshire Hathaway's Annual Meeting," *Fast Company* (May 2009), http://www.fastcompany.com/magazine/135/gather-berkshire-hathaway-annual-meeting.html.

15. H. Levinson and S. Rosenthal, *CEO: Corporate Leadership in Action* (New York: *Basic Books,* 1984).

16. V. Sathe, "Implications of Corporate Culture: A Manager's Guide to Action," *Organizational Dynamics* 12 (1987): 5–23.

17. "Wal-Mart Culture Stories—The Sundown Rule," http://www.wal-martchina.com/english/walmart/rule/sun.htm.

18. J. Martin, M. S. Feldman, M. J. Hatch, and S. B. Sitkin, "The Uniqueness Paradox in Organizational Stories," *Administrative Science Quarterly* 28 (1983): 438–453.

19. J. Lofstock, "Aplauding the QuikTrip Culture," http://www.quiktrip.com/aboutqt/news.asp.

20. "No layoffs—ever!" CNNMoney.com (August 12, 2011), http://money.cnn.com/galleries/2010/fortune/1001/gallery.bestcompanies_layoffs.fortune/.

21. B. Durrance, "Stories at Work," *Training and Development* (February 1997): 25–29.

22. J. E. Vascellaro, "Facebook CEO in a Rush to 'Friend' Wall Street," *The Wall Street Journal* (March 3, 2010), http://online.wsj.com/article/SB10001424052748703787304575075942803630712.html?mod=djem_jiewr_HR_domainid.

23. R. Goffee and G. Jones, "What Holds the Modern Company Together?" *Harvard Business Review* (November–December 1996): 133–143.

24. C. Argyris and D. A. Schon, *Organizational Learning* (Reading, Mass.: Addison-Wesley, 1978).

25. L. Hoeber, "Exploring the Gaps between Meanings and Practices of Gender Equity in a Sport Organization," *Gender Work and Organization* 14, No. 3 (2007): 259–280.

26. D. J. McAllister and G. A. Bigley, "Work Context and the Definition of Self: How Organizational Care Influences Organization-Based Self-Esteem," *Academy of Management Journal* 45 (2002): 894–905.

27. M. Peterson, "Work, Corporate Culture, and Stress: Implications for Worksite Health Promotion," *American Journal of Health Behavior* 21 (1997): 243–252.

28. "100 Best Companies to Work For 2009: NetApp," http://money.cnn.com/magazines/fortune/bestcompanies/2009/snapshots/1.html.

29. L. Smircich, "Concepts of Culture and Organizational Analysis," *Administrative Science Quarterly* (1983): 339–358.

30. Y. Weiner and Y. Vardi, "Relationships between Organizational Culture and Individual Motivation: A Conceptual Integration," *Psychological Reports* 67 (1990): 295–306.

31. M. R. Louis, "Surprise and Sense Making: What Newcomers Experience in Entering Unfamiliar Organizational Settings," *Administrative Science Quarterly* 25 (1980): 209–264.

32. T. L. Doolen, M. E. Hacker, and E. M. van Aken, "The Impact of Organizational Context on Work Team Effectiveness: A Study of Production Teams," *IEEE Transactions on Engineering Management* 50 (2003): 285–296.

33. D. D. Van Fleet and R. W. Griffin, "Dysfunctional Organization Culture: The Role of Leadership in Motivating Dysfunctional Work Behaviors," *Journal of Managerial Psychology* 21, No. 8 (2006): 698–708.

34. J. P. Kotter and J. L. Heskett, *Corporate Culture and Performance* (New York: Free Press, 1992).

35. Deal and Kennedy, *Corporate Cultures.*

36. D. R. Katz, *The Big Store* (New York: Viking, 1987).

37. G. G. Gordon, "Industry Determinants of Organizational Culture," *Academy of Management Review* 16 (1991): 396–415.

38. G. Donaldson and J. Lorsch, *Decision Making at the Top* (New York: Basic Books, 1983).

39. R. H. Kilman, M. J. Saxton, and R. Serpa, eds., *Gaining Control of the Corporate Culture* (San Francisco: Jossey-Bass, 1986).

40. J. P. Kotter, *A Force for Change: How Leadership Differs from Management* (New York: Free Press, 1990); R. M. Kanter, *The Change Masters* (New York: Simon & Schuster, 1983).

41. T. Peters and N. Austin, *A Passion for Excellence: The Leadership Difference* (New York: Random House, 1985).

42. Schein, *Organizational Culture and Leadership.*

43. J. A. Pearce II, T. R. Kramer, and D. K. Robbins, "Effects of Managers' Entrepreneurial Behavior on Subordinates," *Journal of Business Venturing* 12 (1997): 147–160.

44. P. W. Braddy, A. W. Meade, and C. M. Kroustalis, "Organizational Recruitment Website Effects on Viewers' Perceptions of Organizational Culture," *Journal of Business and Psychology* 20, No. 4 (2006): 525–543.

45. See http://money.cnn.com/magazines/fortune/fortune_archive/2006/01/23/8366992/index.htm.

46. A. Xenikou and M. Simosi, "Organizational Culture and Transformational Leadership as Predictors of Business Unit Performance," *Journal of Managerial Psychology* 21, No. 6 (2006): 566–579.

47. D. C. Feldman, "The Multiple Socialization of Organization Members," *Academy of Management Review* 6 (1981): 309–318.

48. R. Pascale, "The Paradox of Corporate Culture: Reconciling Ourselves to Socialization," *California Management Review* 27 (1985): 26–41.

49. D. L. Nelson, "Organizational Socialization: A Stress Perspective," *Journal of Occupational Behavior* 8 (1987): 311–324.

50. J. Fan and J. P. Wanous, "Organizational and Cultural Entry: A New Type of Orientation Program for Multiple Boundary Crossings," *Journal of Applied Psychology* 93 (2008): 1390–1400.

51. D. M. Cable, L. Aiman-Smith, P. W. Mulvey, and J. R. Edwards, "The Sources and Accuracy of Job Applicants' Beliefs about Organizational Culture," *Academy of Management Journal* 43 (2000): 1076–1085.

52. J. Chatman, "Matching People and Organizations: Selection and Socialization in Public Accounting Firms," *Administrative Science Quarterly* 36 (1991): 459–484.

53. D. L. Nelson, J. C. Quick, and M. E. Eakin, "A Longitudinal Study of Newcomer Role Adjustment in U.S. Organizations," *Work and Stress* 2 (1988): 239–253.

54. N. J. Allen and J. P. Meyer, "Organizational Socialization Tactics: A Longitudinal Analysis of Links to Newcomers' Commitment and Role Orientation," *Academy of Management Journal* 33 (1990): 847–858.

55. T. N. Bauer, E. W. Morrison, and R. R. Callister, "Organizational Socialization: A Review and Directions for Future Research," *Research in Personnel and Human Resources Management* 16 (1998): 149–214.

56. D. M. Cable and C. K. Parsons, "Socialization Tactics and Person–Organization Fit," *Personnel Psychology* 54 (2001): 1–23.

57. S. H. Harrison, D. M. Sluss, and B. E. Ashforth, "Curiosity Adapted the Cat: The Role of Trait Curiosity in Newcomer Adaption," *Journal of Applied Psychology* 96 (2011): 211–220; M. Wang, Y. Zhan, E. McCune, and D. Truxillo, "Understanding Newcomers' Adaptability and Work-Related Outcomes: Testing the Mediating Roles of Perceived P-E Fit Variables," *Personnel Psychology* 64 (2011): 163–189.

58. A. M. Saks, J. A. Gruman, and H. Cooper-Thomas, "The Neglected Role of Proactive Behavior and Outcomes in Newcomer Socialization," *Journal of Vocational Behavior* 79 (2011): 36–46.

59. D. M. Rousseau, "Assessing Organizational Culture: The Case for Multiple Methods," in B. Schneider, ed., *Organizational Climate and Culture* (San Francisco: Jossey-Bass, 1990).

60. R. A. Cooke and D. M. Rousseau, "Behavioral Norms and Expectations: A Quantitative Approach to the Assessment of Organizational Culture," *Group and Organizational Studies* 12 (1988): 245–273.

61. R. H. Kilmann and M. J. Saxton, *Kilmann-Saxton Culture-Gap Survey* (Pittsburgh: Organizational Design Consultants, 1983).

62. W. J. Duncan, "Organizational Culture: 'Getting a Fix' on an Elusive Concept," *Academy of Management Executive* 3 (1989): 229–236.

63. P. Bate, "Using the Culture Concept in an Organization Development Setting," *Journal of Applied Behavior Science* 26 (1990): 83–106.

64. K. R. Thompson and F. Luthans, "Organizational Culture: A Behavioral Perspective," in B. Schneider, ed., *Organizational Climate and Culture* (San Francisco: Jossey-Bass, 1990).

65. S. Seren and U. Baykal, "Relationships between Change and Organizational Culture in Hospitals," *Journal of Nursing Scholarship* 39, No. 2 (2007): 191–197.

66. V. Sathe, "How to Decipher and Change Corporate Culture," in R. H. Kilman et al., *Managing Corporate Cultures* (San Francisco: Jossey-Bass, 1985).

67. M. E. Johnson-Cramer, S. Parise, and R. L. Cross, "Managing Change through Networks and Values," *California Management Review* 49(3) (2007): 85–109.

68. C. Yang, "Merger of Titans, Clash of Cultures," *BusinessWeek Online* (July 14, 2003), http://www.businessweek.com/magazine/content/03_8/b3841042_mz005.htm.

69. N. J. Adler, *International Dimensions of Organizational Behavior,* 2nd ed. (Boston: PWS Kent, 1991).

70. A. Laurent, "The Cultural Diversity of Western Conceptions of Management," *International Studies of Management and Organization* 13 (1983): 75–96.

71. P. C. Earley and E. Mosakowski, "Creating Hybrid Team Cultures: An Empirical Test of Transnational Team Functioning," *Academy of Management Journal* 43 (2000): 26–49.

72. D. Lei, J. W. Slocum, Jr., and R. W. Slater, "Global Strategy and Reward Systems: The Key Roles of Management Development and Corporate Culture," *Organizational Dynamics* 19 (1990): 27–41.

73. L. K. Trevino and K. A. Nelson, *Managing Business Ethics: Straight Talk about How to Do It Right* (New York: John Wiley & Sons, 1995).

74. M. Kaptein, "Understanding Unethical Behavior by Unraveling Ethical Culture," *Human Relations* (in press).

75. A. Bhide and H. H. Stevenson, "Why Be Honest if Honesty Doesn't Pay?" *Harvard Business Review* (September–October 1990): 121–129.

76. A. Pater and A. van Gils, "Stimulating Ethical Decision Making in a Business Context: Ethics of Ethical and Professional Codes," *European Management Journal* 21 (December 2003): 762–772.

77. J. R. Detert, R. G. Schroeder, and J. J. Mauriel, "A Framework for Linking Culture and Improvement Initiatives in Organizations," *Academy of Management Review* 25 (2000): 850–863.

78. S. D. Salamon and S. L. Robinson, "Trust that Binds: The Impact of Collective Felt Trust on Organizational Performance," *Journal of Applied Psychology* 93 (2008): 593–601.

79. R. Bruce, "A Case Study of Harley-Davidson's Business Practices," http://stroked.virtualave.net/casestudy.shtml.

Chapter 17

1. J. H. Greenhaus, *Career Management* (Hinsdale, Ill.: CBS College Press, 1987).

2. D. T. Hall, *Careers in Organizations* (Pacific Palisades, Calif.: Goodyear, 1976).

3. Greenhaus, *Career Management;* T. G. Gutteridge and F. L. Otte, "Organizational Career Development: What's Going on out There?" *Training and Development Journal* 37 (1983): 22–26.

4. M. B. Arthur, P. H. Claman, and R. J. DeFillippi, "Intelligent Enterprise, Intelligent Careers," *Academy of Management Executive* (November 1995): 7–22.

5. M. Lips-Wiersma and D. T. Hall, "Organizational Career Development Is Not Dead: A Case Study on Managing the New Career during Organizational Change," *Journal of Organizational Behavior* 28, No. 6 (2007): 771–792.

6. D. Jemielniak, "Managers as Lazy, Stupid Careerists?" *Journal of Organizational Change Management* 20, No. 4 (2007): 491–508.

7. D. E. Super, *The Psychology of Careers* (New York: Harper & Row, 1957); D. E. Super and M. J. Bohn, Jr., *Occupational Psychology* (Belmont, Calif.: Wadsworth, 1970).

8. J. L. Holland, *The Psychology of Vocational Choice* (Waltham, Mass.: Blaisdell, 1966); J. L. Holland, *Making Vocational Choices: A Theory of Careers* (Englewood Cliffs, N.J.: Prentice-Hall, 1973).

9. F. T. L. Leong and J. T. Austin, "An Evaluation of the Cross-Cultural Validity of Holland's Theory: Career Choices by Workers in India," *Journal of Vocational Behavior* 52 (1998): 441–455.

10. C. Morgan, J. D. Isaac, and C. Sansone, "The Role of Interest in Understanding the Career Choices of Female and Male College Students," *Sex Roles* 44 (2001): 295–320.

11. J. K. Hellerstein and M. S. Morrill, "Dads and Daughters: The Changing Impact of Fathers on Women's Occupational Choices," *Journal of Human Resources* 46, No. 2 (2011): 333–372; S. H. Osipow, *Theories of Career Development* (Englewood Cliffs, N.J.: Prentice-Hall, 1973).

12. J. P. Wanous, T. L. Keon, and J. C. Latack, "Expectancy Theory and Occupational/Organizational Choices: A Review and Test," *Organizational Behavior and Human Performance* 32 (1983): 66–86.

13. P. O. Soelberg, "Unprogrammed Decision Making," *Industrial Management Review* 8 (1967): 19–29.

14. J. P. Wanous, *Organizational Entry: Recruitment, Selection, and Socialization of Newcomers* (Reading, Mass.: Addison-Wesley, 1980).

15. S. L. Premack and J. P. Wanous, "A Meta-Analysis of Realistic Job Preview Experiments," *Journal of Applied Psychology* 70 (1985): 706–719.

16. http://www.timewarnercable.com/corporate/about/careers.

17. Idaho State Police, "Realistic Job Preview," http://www.isp.state.id.us/hr/trooper_info/realistic_job.html.

18. P. W. Hom, R. W. Griffeth, L. E. Palich, and J. S. Bracker, "An Exploratory Investigation into Theoretical Mechanisms Underlying Realistic Job Previews," *Personnel Psychology* 41 (1998): 421–451.

19. J. A. Breaugh, "Realistic Job Previews: A Critical Appraisal and Future Research Directions," *Academy of Management Review* 8 (1983): 612–619.

20. G. R. Jones, "Socialization Tactics, Self-Efficacy, and Newcomers' Adjustment to Organizations," *Academy of Management Journal* 29 (1986): 262–279.

21. M. R. Buckley, D. B. Fedor, J. G. Veres, D. S. Wiese, and S. M. Carraher, "Investigating Newcomer Expectations and Job-Related Outcomes," *Journal of Applied Psychology* 83 (1998): 452–461.

22. M. R. Buckley, D. B. Fedor, S. M. Carraher, D. D. Frink, and D. Marvin, "The Ethical Imperative to Provide Recruits Realistic Job Previews," *Journal of Managerial Issues* 9 (1997): 468–484.

23. A. De Vos and C. Freese, "Sensemaking During Organizational Entry: Changes in Newcomer Information Seeking and the Relationship with Psychological Contract Fulfillment," *Journal of Occupational and Organizational Psychology* 84 (2011): 288–314.

24. P. Buhler, "Managing in the '90s," *Supervision* (July 1995): 24–26.

25. D. T. Hall and J. E. Moss, "The New Protean Career Contract: Helping Organizations and Employees Adapt," *Organizational Dynamics* (Winter 1998): 22–37.

26. S. A. Zahra, R. L. Priem, and A. A. Rasheed, "Understanding the Causes and Effects of Top Management Fraud," *Organizational Dynamics* 36, No. 2 (2007): 122–139.

27. A. Fisher, "Don't Blow Your New Job," *Fortune* (June 22, 1998): 159–162.

28. D. Goleman, *Working with Emotional Intelligence* (New York: Bantam, 1998); A. Fisher, "Success Secret: A High Emotional IQ," *Fortune* (October 26, 1998): 293–298.

29. M. L. Maynard, "Emotional Intelligence and Perceived Employability for Internship Curriculum," *Psychological Reports* 93 (December 2003): 791–792.

30. K. V. Petrides, A. Furnham, and G. N. Martin, "Estimates of Emotional and Psychometric Intelligence," *Journal of Social Psychology* 144 (April 2004): 149–162.

31. C. Chermiss, "The Business Case for Emotional Intelligence," *The Consortium for Research on Emotional Intelligence in Organizations* (2003), http://www.eiconsortium.org/research/business_case_for_ei.htm; L. M. Spencer, Jr. and S. Spencer, *Competence at Work: Models for Superior Performance* (New York: John Wiley & Sons, 1993); L. M. Spencer, Jr., D. C. McClelland, and S. Kelner, *Competency Assessment Methods: History and State of the Art* (Boston, MA: Hay/McBer, 1997).

32. Chermiss, "The Business Case for Emotional Intelligence."

33. J. O. Crites, "A Comprehensive Model of Career Adjustment in Early Adulthood," *Journal of Vocational Behavior* 9 (1976): 105–118; S. Cytrynbaum and J. O. Crites, "The Utility of Adult Development in Understanding Career Adjustment Process," in M. B. Arthur, D. T. Hall, and B. S. Lawrence, eds., *Handbook of Career Theory* (Cambridge: Cambridge University Press, 1989): 66–88.

34. D. E. Super, "A Life-Span, Life-Space Approach to Career Development," *Journal of Vocational Behavior* 16 (1980): 282–298; L. Baird and K. Kram, "Career Dynamics: Managing the Superior/Subordinate Relationship," *Organizational Dynamics* 11 (1983): 46–64.

35. D. J. Levinson, *The Seasons of a Man's Life* (New York: Knopf, 1978); D. J. Levinson, *The Seasons of a Woman's Life* (New York: Knopf, 1996).

36. D. J. Levinson, "A Conception of Adult Development," *American Psychologist* 41 (1986): 3–13.

37. D. L. Nelson, "Adjusting to a New Organization: Easing the Transition from Outsider to Insider," in J. C. Quick, R. E. Hess, J. Hermalin, and J. D. Quick, eds., *Career Stress in Changing Times* (New York: Haworth Press, 1990): 61–86.

38. J. P. Kotter, "The Psychological Contract: Managing the Joining Up Process," *California Management Review* 15 (1973): 91–99.

39. D. M. Rousseau, "New Hire Perceptions of Their Own and Their Employers' Obligations: A Study of Psychological Contracts," *Journal of Organizational Behavior* 11 (1990): 389–400; D. L. Nelson, J. C. Quick, and J. R. Joplin, "Psychological Contracting and Newcomer Socialization: An Attachment Theory Foundation," *Journal of Social Behavior and Personality* 6 (1991): 55–72.

40. H. Zhao, S. Wayne, B. Glibkowski, and J. Bravo "The Impact of Psychological Breach on Work-Related Outcomes," *Personnel Psychology* (2007): 647–680.

41. S. D. Pugh, D. P. Skarlicki, and B. S. Passell, "After the Fall: Layoff Victims' Trust and Cynicism in Reemployment," *Journal of Occupational and Organizational Psychology* 76 (June 2003): 201–212.

42. Levinson, "A Conception of Adult Development," 3–13.

43. J. W. Walker, "Let's Get Realistic about Career Paths," *Human Resource Management* 15 (1976): 2–7.

44. E. H. Buttner and D. P. Moore, "Women's Organizational Exodus to Entrepreneurship: Self-Reported Motivations and Correlates," *Journal of Small Business Management* 35 (1997): 34–46; Center for Women's Business Research Press Release, "Privately Held, 50% or More Women-Owned Businesses in the United States," 2004, http://www.nfwbo.org/pressreleases/nationalstatetrends/total.htm.

45. D. G. Collings, H. Scullion, and M. J. Morley, "Changing Patterns of Global Staffing in the Multinational Enterprise: Challenges to the Conventional Expatriate Assignment and Emerging Alternatives," *Journal of World Business* 42, No. 2 (2007): 198–213.

46. B. Filipczak, "You're on Your Own," *Training* (January 1995): 29–36.

47. K. E. Kram, *Mentoring at Work: Developmental Relationships in Organizational Life* (Glenview, Ill.: Scott, Foresman, 1985).

48. C. Orpen, "The Effects of Mentoring on Employees' Career Success," *Journal of Social Psychology* 135 (1995): 667–668.

49. J. Arnold and K. Johnson, "Mentoring in Early Career," *Human Resource Management Journal* 7 (1997): 61–70.

50. B. P. Madia and C. J. Lutz, "Perceived Similarity, Expectation–Reality Discrepancies, and Mentors' Expressed Intention to Remain in the Big Brothers/Big Sisters Programs," *Journal of Applied Social Psychology* 34 (March 2004): 598–622.

51. "A Guide to the Mentor Program Listings," *Mentors Peer Resources,* http://www.mentors.ca/mentorprograms.html.

52. B. R. Ragins, "Diversified Mentoring Relationships in Organizations: A Power Perspective," *Academy of Management Review* 22 (1997): 482–521.

53. R. Friedman, M. Kan, and D. B. Cornfield, "Social Support and Career Optimism: Examining the Effectiveness of Network Groups among Black Managers," *Human Relations* 51 (1998): 1155–1177.

54. S. E. Seibert, M. L. Kraimer, and R. C. Liden, "A Social Capital Theory of Career Success," *Academy of Management Journal* 44 (2001): 219–237.

55. PricewaterhouseCoopers Czech Republic, "Graduate Recruitment—FAQs," http://www.pwcglobal.com/cz/eng/car-inexp/main/faq.html.

56. M. A. Covaleski, M. W. Dirsmuth, J. B. Heian, and S. Samuel, "The Calculated and the Avowed: Techniques of Discipline and Struggles over Identity in Big Six Public Accounting Firms," *Administrative Science Quarterly* 43 (1998): 293–327.

57. B. R. Ragins and J. L. Cotton, "Easier Said than Done: Gender Differences in Perceived Barriers to Gaining a Mentor," *Academy of Management Journal* 34 (1991): 939–951; S. D. Phillips and A. R. Imhoff, "Women and Career Development: A Decade of Research," *Annual Review of Psychology* 48 (1997): 31–43.

58. Ibid.

59. A. Ramaswami, G. F. Dreher, R. Bretz, and C. Wiethoff, "Gender, Mentoring and Career Success: The Importance of Organizational Context," *Personnel Psychology* 63, No. 2 (2010): 385–405.

60. W. Whiteley, T. W. Dougherty, and G. F. Dreher, "Relationship of Career Mentoring and Socioeconomic Origin to Managers' and Professionals'

Early Career Progress," *Academy of Management Journal* 34 (1991): 331–351; G. F. Dreher and R. A. Ash, "A Comparative Study of Mentoring among Men and Women in Managerial, Professional, and Technical Positions," *Journal of Applied Psychology* 75 (1990): 539–546; T. A. Scandura, "Mentorship and Career Mobility: An Empirical Investigation," *Journal of Organizational Behavior* 13 (1992): 169–174.

61. G. F. Dreher and T. H. Cox, Jr., "Race, Gender and Opportunity: A Study of Compensation Attainment and Establishment of Mentoring Relationships," *Journal of Applied Psychology* 81 (1996): 297–309.

62. D. D. Horgan and R. J. Simeon, "Mentoring and Participation: An Application of the Vroom-Yetton Model," *Journal of Business and Psychology* 5 (1990): 63–84.

63. B. R. Ragins, J. L. Cotton, and J. S. Miller, "Marginal Mentoring: The Effects of Type of Mentor, Quality of Relationship, and Program Design on Work and Career Attitudes," *Academy of Management Journal* 43 (2000): 1177–1194.

64. R. T. Brennan, R. C. Barnett, and K. C. Gareis, "When She Earns More than He Does: A Longitudinal Study of Dual-Earner Couples," *Journal of Marriage and Family* 63 (2001): 168–182.

65. F. S. Hall and D. T. Hall, *The Two-Career Couple* (Reading, Mass.: Addison-Wesley, 1979).

66. J. S. Boles, M. W. Johnston, and J. F. Hair, Jr., "Role Stress, Work–Family Conflict and Emotional Exhaustion: Inter-Relationships and Effects on Some Work-Related Consequences," *Journal of Personal Selling and Sales Management* 17 (1998): 17–28.

67. B. Morris, "Is Your Family Wrecking Your Career? (And Vice Versa)," *Fortune* (March 17, 1997): 70–80.

68. Ibid.

69. D. L. Nelson, J. C. Quick, M. A. Hitt, and D. Moesel, "Politics, Lack of Career Progress, and Work/Home Conflict: Stress and Strain for Working Women," *Sex Roles* 23 (1990): 169–185.

70. L. E. Duxbury and C. A. Higgins, "Gender Differences in Work–Family Conflict," *Journal of Applied Psychology* 76 (1991): 60–74.

71. R. G. Netemeyer, J. S. Boles, and R. McMurrian, "Development and Validation of Work–Family Conflict and Family–Work Conflict Scales," *Journal of Applied Psychology* 81 (1996): 400–410.

72. B. Livingston and T. A. Judge, "Emotional Responses to Work-Family Conflict: An Examination of Gender Role Orientation among Working Men and Women," *Journal of Applied Psychology* (2008): 207–216.

73. N. Yang, C. C. Chen, J. Choi, and Y. Zou, "Sources of Work–Family Conflict: A Sino–U.S. Comparison of the Effects of Work and Family Demands," *Academy of Management Journal* 43 (2000): 113–123.

74. A. Iris Aaltion and H. Jiehua Huang, "Women Managers' Careers in Information Technology in China: High Flyers with Emotional Costs?" *Journal of Organizational Change Management* 20, No. 2 (2007): 227–244.

75. See http://www.ehow.com/info_7737471_companies-great-benefits.html.

76. Mitchell Gold Co., "Day Care," http://www.mitchellgold.com/daycare.asp.

77. D. Machan, "The Mommy and Daddy Track," *Forbes* (April 6, 1990): 162.

78. E. M. Brody, M. H. Kleban, P. T. Johnsen, C. Hoffman, and C. B. Schoonover, "Work Status and Parental Care: A Comparison of Four Groups of Women," *Gerontological Society of America* 27 (1987): 201–208; J. W. Anastas, J. L. Gibson, and P. J. Larson, "Working Families and Eldercare: A National Perspective in an Aging America," *Social Work* 35 (1990): 405–411.

79. Cincinnati Area Senior Services, "Corporate Elder Care Program," http://www.senserv.org/elder.htm.

80. E. E. Kossek, J. A. Colquitt, and R. A. Noe, "Caregiving Decisions, Well-Being, and Performance: The Effects of Place and Provider as a Function of Dependent Type and Work–Family Climates," *Academy of Management Journal* 44 (2001): 29–44.

81. Harvard University Office of Human Resources, "Work/Life Support Services—Elder Care Resources," http://atwork.harvard.edu/worklife/eldercare/.

82. M. Richards, "'Daddy Track' Is Road Taken More Often," *The Morning Call* (July 28, 2004), http://www.mcall.com/business/local/all-daddyjul28,0,1869593.story?coll=all-businesslocal-hed.

83. L. J. Barham, "Variables Affecting Managers' Willingness to Grant Alternative Work Arrangements," *Journal of Social Psychology* 138

(1998): 291–302; J. Kaplan, "Hitting the Wall at Forty," *Business Month* 136 (1990): 52–58.

84. K. E. Kram, "Phases of the Mentoring Relationship," *Academy of Management Review* 26 (1983): 608–625.

85. B. Rosen and T. Jerdee, *Older Employees: New Roles for Valued Resources* (Homewood, Ill.: Irwin, 1985).

86. J. W. Gilsdorf, "The New Generation: Older Workers," *Training and Development Journal* (March 1992): 77–79.

87. J. F. Quick, "Time to Move On?" in J. C. Quick, R. E. Hess, J. Hermalin, and J. D. Quick, eds., *Career Stress in Changing Times* (New York: Haworth Press, 1990): 239–250.

88. D. Machan, "Rent-an-Exec," *Forbes* (January 22, 1990): 132–133.

89. S. Kim and D. C. Feldman, "Working in Retirement: The Antecedents of Bridge Employment and Its Consequences for Quality of Life in Retirement," *Academy of Management Journal* 43 (2000): 1195–1210.

90. E. Daspin, "The Second Midlife Crisis," *The Baltimore Sun* (originally published in *The Wall Street Journal*) (May 10, 2004), http://www.baltimoresun.com/business/bal-crisis051004,0,614944.story?coll=bal-business-headlines.

91. Lawrence Livermore Retiree Program, "Tasks Requested by Lab Programs," http://www.llnl.gov/aadp/retiree/tasks.html.

92. E. Schein, *Career Anchors* (San Diego: University Associates, 1985).

93. G. W. Dalton, "Developmental Views of Careers in Organizations," in M. B. Arthur, D. T. Hall, and B. S. Lawrence, eds., *Handbook of Career Theory* (Cambridge: Cambridge University Press, 1989): 89–109.

94. D. C. Feldman, "Careers in Organizations: Recent Trends and Future Directions," *Journal of Management* 15 (1989): 135–156.

Chapter 18

1. M. A. Verespej, "When Change Becomes the Norm," *Industry Week* (March 16, 1992): 35–38.

2. P. Mornell, "Nothing Endures but Change," *Inc.* 22 (July 2000): 131–132, http://www.inc.com/magazine/20000701/19555.html.

3. H. J. Van Buren, III, "The Bindingness of Social and Psychological Contracts: Toward a Theory of Social Responsibility in Downsizing," *Journal of Business Ethics* 25 (2000): 205–219.

4. "The Mystery of the Chinese Consumer," *The Economist* (July 7, 2011), http://www.economist.com/node/18928514?story_id=189285148.

5. See http://www.tata.com/htm/Grou-_MnA_YearWise.htm.

6. See http://www.microsoft.com/presspass/Press/2002/Jul02/07-11NavisionAcquisitionPR.mspx.

7. L. R. Offerman and M. Gowing, "Organizations of the Future: Changes and Challenges," *American Psychologist* (February 1990): 95–108.

8. J. Goudreau "Overworked, Overextended and Overstressed," *Time* (August 26, 2009), http://www.forbes.com/2009/08/26/household-responsibility-husband-wife-forbes-woman-time-equality.html.

9. W. B. Johnston, "Global Work Force 2000: The New World Labor Market," *Harvard Business Review* (March–April 1991): 115–127.

10. H. Brown, "Diversity Does Matter," *ForbesWoman Q&A* (July 21, 2009), http://www.forbes.com/2009/07/21/diversity-jill-lee-business-forbes-woman-q-and-a-competitive.html.

11. G. Bylinsky, "Hot New Technologies for American Factories," *Fortune* (June 26, 2000): 288A–288K.

12. See http://home3.americanexpress.com/corp/pc/2007/axiom.asp.

13. R. M. Kanter, "Improving the Development, Acceptance, and Use of New Technology: Organizational and Interorganizational Challenges," in *People and Technology in the Workplace* (Washington, D.C.: National Academy Press, 1991): 15–56.

14. Gap Inc. press release, "Gap Inc. Joins the Ethical Trading Initiative," *CSRwire* (April 28, 2004), http://www.csrwire.com/article.cgi/2683.html.

15. "Gap Inc. 2003 Social Responsibility Report," *Gap Inc.* (September 17, 2004), http://ccbn.mobular.net/ccbn/7/645/696/index.html.

16. S. A. Mohrman and A. M. Mohrman, Jr., "The Environment as an Agent of Change," in A. M. Mohrman, Jr., et al., eds., *Large-Scale Organizational Change* (San Francisco: Jossey-Bass, 1989), 35–47.

17. T. D'Aunno, M. Succi, and J. A. Alexander, "The Role of Institutional and Market Forces in Divergent Organizational Change," *Administrative Science Quarterly* 45 (2000): 679–703.

18. M. Jarman, "Intel Opens 'Leading-Edge Fab': Plant to Build Most Powerful Chips," *The Arizona Republic* (October 21, 2007), http://www.azcentral.com/arizonarepublic/business/articles/1021biz-intel1021.html.

19. Q. N. Huy, "Emotional Balancing of Organizational Continuity and Radical Change: The Contribution of Middle Managers," *Administrative Science Quarterly* 47 (March 1, 2002): 31–69.

20. D. Nadler, "Organizational Frame-Bending: Types of Change in the Complex Organization," in R. Kilmann and T. Covin, eds., *Corporate Transformation* (San Francisco: Jossey-Bass, 1988): 66–83.

21. P. Olson, "Nokia and Microsoft announce strategic partnership," *Forbes* (February 11, 2011), http://blogs.forbes.com/parmyolson/2011/02/11/nokia-and-microsoft-announce-strategic-partnership/.

22. L. Ackerman, "Development, Transition, or Transformation: The Question of Change in Organizations," *OD Practitioner* (December 1986): 1–8.

23. T. D. Jick, *Managing Change* (Homewood, Ill.: Irwin, 1993): 3.

24. J. M. Bloodgood and J. L. Morrow, "Strategic Organizational Change: Exploring the Roles of Environmental Structure, Internal Conscious Awareness, and Knowledge," *Journal of Management Studies* 40 (2003): 1761–1782.

25. D. Miller and M. J. Chen, "Sources and Consequences of Competitive Inertia. A Study of the U.S. Airline Industry," *Administrative Science Quarterly* 39 (1994): 1–23.

26. S. L. Brown and K. M. Eisenhardt, "The Art of Continuous Change: Linking Complexity Theory and Time-Paced Evolution in Relentlessly Shifting Organizations," *Administrative Science Quarterly* 42 (1997): 1–34.

27. J. Child and C. Smith, "The Context and Process of Organizational Transformation: Cadbury Ltd. In Its Sector," *Journal of Management Studies* 12 (1987): 12–27.

28. J. Amis, T. Slack, and C. R. Hinings, "The Pace, Sequence, and Linearity of Radical Change," *Academy of Management Journal* 47 (2004): 15–39.

29. R. M. Kanter, *The Change Masters* (New York: Simon & Schuster, 1983).

30. J. R. Katzenbach, *Real Change Leaders* (New York: Times Business, 1995).

31. J. L. Denis, L. Lamothe, and A. Langley, "The Dynamics of Collective Leadership and Strategic Change in Pluralistic Organizations," *Academy of Management Journal* 44 (2001): 809–837.

32. M. Beer, *Organization Change and Development: A Systems View* (Santa Monica, Calif.: Goodyear, 1980): 78.

33. K. Whalen-Berry and C. R. Hinings, "The Relative Effect of Change Drivers in Large-Scale Organizational Change: An Empirical Study," in W. Passmore and R. Goodman, eds., *Research in Organizational Change and Development* 14 (New York: JAI Press, 2003): 99–146.

34. Denis et al., "The Dynamics of Collective Leadership and Strategic Change in Pluralistic Organizations."

35. J. W. Brehm, *A Theory of Psychological Reactance* (New York: Academic Press, 1966).

36. J. A. Klein, "Why Supervisors Resist Employee Involvement," *Harvard Business Review* 62 (1984): 87–95.

37. B. L. Kirkman, R. G. Jones, and D. L. Shapiro, "Why Do Employees Resist Teams? Examining the 'Resistance Barrier' to Work Team Effectiveness," *International Journal of Conflict Management* 11 (2000): 74–92.

38. D. L. Nelson and M. A. White, "Management of Technological Innovation: Individual Attitudes, Stress, and Work Group Attributes," *Journal of High Technology Management Research* 1 (1990): 137–148.

39. S. Elias, "Employee Commitment in Times of Change: Assessing the Importance of Attitudes Toward Organizational Change," *Journal of Management* 35 (2009): 37–55; J. B. Avey, T. S. Wernsing, and F. Luthans, "Can Positive Employees Help Positive Organizational Change? Impact of Psychological Capital and Emotions on Relevant Attitudes and Behaviors," *Journal of Applied Behavioral Science* 44 (2008): 48–70.

40. T. Diefenbach, "The Managerialistic Ideology of Organisational Change Management," *Journal of Organizational Change Management* (20), No. 1 (2007): 126–144.

41. D. Klein, "Some Notes on the Dynamics of Resistance to Change: The Defender Role," in W. G. Bennis, K. D. Benne, R. Chin, and K. E. Corey, eds., *The Planning of Change*, 3rd ed. (New York: Holt, Rinehart & Winston, 1969), 117–124.

42. T. G. Cummings and E. F. Huse, *Organizational Development and Change* (St. Paul, Minn.: West, 1989).

43. N. L. Jimmieson, D. J. Terry, and V. J. Callan, "A Longitudinal Study of Employee Adaptation to Organizational Change: The Role of Change-Related Information and Change-Related Self Efficacy," *Journal of Occupational Health Psychology* 9 (2004): 11–27.

44. N. DiFonzo and P. Bordia, "A Tale of Two Corporations: Managing Uncertainty during Organizational Change," *Human Resource Management* 37 (1998): 295–303.

45. J. de Vries, C. Webb, and J. Eveline, "Mentoring for Gender Equality and Organisational Change," *Employee Relations* 28, No. 6 (2006): 573–587.

46. P. Neves and A. Caetano, "Social Exchange Processes in Organizational Change: The Roles of Trust and Control." *Journal of Change Management* 6, No. 4 (2006): 351–364.

47. M. Hickins, "Reconcilable Differences," *Management Review* 87 (1998): 54–58.

48. K. Lewin, "Frontiers in Group Dynamics," *Human Relations* 1 (1947): 5–41.

49. C. Bareil, A. Savoie, and S. Meunier, "Patterns of Discomfort with Organizational Change," *Journal of Change Management* 7(1) (2007):13–24.

50. W. McWhinney, "Meta-Praxis: A Framework for Making Complex Changes," in A. M. Mohrman, Jr., et al., eds., *Large-Scale Organizational Change* (San Francisco: Jossey-Bass, 1989), 154–199.

51. M. Beer and E. Walton, "Developing the Competitive Organization: Interventions and Strategies," *American Psychologist* 45 (1990): 154–161.

52. B. Bertsch and R. Williams, "How Multinational CEOs Make Change Programs Stick," *Long Range Planning* 27 (1994): 12–24.

53. J. Amis, T. Slack, and C. R. Hinings, "Values and Organizational Change," *Journal of Applied Behavioral Science* 38 (2002): 356–385.

54. W. L. French and C. H. Bell, *Organization Development: Behavioral Science Interventions for Organization Improvement*, 4th ed. (Englewood Cliffs, N.J.: Prentice-Hall, 1990); W. W. Burke, *Organization Development: A Normative View* (Reading, Mass.: Addison-Wesley, 1987).

55. A. O. Manzini, *Organizational Diagnosis* (New York: AMACOM, 1988).

56. M. R. Weisbord, "Organizational Diagnosis: Six Places to Look for Trouble with or without a Theory," *Group and Organization Studies* (December 1976): 430–444.

57. H. Levinson, *Organizational Diagnosis* (Cambridge, Mass.: Harvard University Press, 1972).

58. J. Nicholas, "The Comparative Impact of Organization Development Interventions," *Academy of Management Review* 7 (1982): 531–542.

59. G. Odiorne, *Management by Objectives* (Marshfield, Mass.: Pitman, 1965).

60. E. Huse, "Putting in a Management Development Program that Works," *California Management Review* 9 (1966): 73–80.

61. J. P. Muczyk and B. C. Reimann, "MBO as a Complement to Effective Leadership," *Academy of Management Executive* (May 1989): 131–138.

62. L. L. Berry and A. Parasuraman, "Prescriptions for a Service Quality Revolution in America," *Organizational Dynamics* 20 (1992): 5–15.

63. T. A. Stewart, and A. P. Raman, "Lessons from Toyota's Long Drive," *Harvard Business Review* 85, No. 7/8 (2007): 74–83.

64. W. G. Dyer, *Team Building: Issues and Alternatives*, 2nd ed. (Reading, Mass.: Addison-Wesley, 1987).

65. E. Stephan, G. Mills, R. W. Pace, and L. Ralphs, "HRD in the *Fortune* 500: A Survey," *Training and Development Journal* (January 1988): 26–32.

66. A. Edmondson, "Psychological Safety and Learning Behavior in Work Teams," *Administrative Science Quarterly* 44 (1999): 350–383.

67. M. Whitmire and P. R. Nienstedt, "Lead Leaders into the '90s," *Personnel Journal* (May 1991): 80–85.

68. See http://www.teambuildinginc.com/services4_teamconcepts.htm; http://www.teambuildinginc.com/services5.htm.

69. E. Salas, T. L. Dickinson, S. I. Tannenbaum, and S. A. Converse, *A Meta-Analysis of Team Performance and Training, Naval Training System Center Technical Reports* (Orlando, Fla.: U.S. Government, 1991).

70. E. Schein, *Its Role in Organization Development,* vol. 1 of *Process Consultation* (Reading, Mass.: Addison-Wesley, 1988).

71. H. Hornstein, "Organizational Development and Change Management: Don't Throw the Baby Out with the Bath Water," *Journal of Applied Behavioral Science* 37 (2001): 223–226.

72. R. W. Revans, *Action Learning* (London: Blonde & Briggs, 1980).

73. I. L. Goldstein, *Training in Organizations,* 3rd ed. (Pacific Grove, Calif.: Brooks/Cole, 1993).

74. J. A. Conger and R. M. Fulmer, "Developing Your Leadership Pipeline," *Harvard Business Review* 81 (2003): 76–84.

75. D. A. Ready and J. A. Conger, "Why Leadership Development Efforts Fail," *MIT Sloan Management Review* 44 (2003): 83–89.

76. M. Jay, "Understanding How to Leverage Executive Coaching," *Organization Development Journal* 21 (2003): 6–13; D. Goleman, R. Boyaysis, and A. McKee, *Primal Leadership: Learning to Lead with Emotional Intelligence* (Harvard Business School Press, 2004).

77. K. M. Wasylyshyn, "Executive Coaching: An Outcome Study," *Consulting Psychology Journal* 55 (2003): 94–106.

78. J. W. Smither, M. London, R. Flautt, Y. Vargas, and I. Kucine, "Can Working with an Executive Coach Improve Multisource Feedback Ratings over Time? A Quasi-Experimental Field Study," *Personnel Psychology* 56 (2003): 23–44.

79. "Occupational Stress and Employee Stress," *American Psychological Association* (June 6, 2004), http://www.psychologymatters.org/karasek .html.

80. American Psychological Association, "Psychologically Healthy Workplace Awards," http://apahelpcenter.mediaroom.com/file.php/mr _apahelpcenter/spinsite_docfiles/134/phwa_magazine_2007.pdf.

81. A. M. Pettigrew, R. W. Woodman, and K. S. Cameron, "Studying Organizational Change and Development: Challenges for Future Research," *Academy of Management Journal* 44 (2001): 697–713.

82. R. A. Katzell and R. A. Guzzo, "Psychological Approaches to Worker Productivity," *American Psychologist* 38 (1983): 468–472.

83. Goldstein, *Training in Organizations.*

Index

A

Ability diversity, 26
Abusive supervision, 207
Acceptance in mentorships, 288–289
Accommodation (conflict management), 225, 226
Achievement, need for, 79, 88
Achievement as value, 69
Achievement-oriented leadership style, 200
Achilles' heel phenomenon, 115
Acquisitions and organizational culture, 274–275
Action learning, 310
Adams, Stacy, 85–87
Adaptive cultures, 268–269, 298
Addiction, 114
Adhocracy, 251, 252
Adjourning stage, 148
Adkins, Joyce, 118
Adler, Alfred, 77
Administrative orbiting (conflict management), 222
Administrative science. *See* Management
Advancement stage of career, 285, 287–293
Aerobic exercises, 121
Affect
    as component of attitude, 55–56
    creativity and, 166
    job satisfaction and, 59–60
    OCBs and, 61
Affective commitment, 62
Affiliation, need for, 79–80
Age
    of change agents, 301
    changes in, of labor force, 299
    discrimination, 293
    values and, 68
Age Discrimination in Employment Act (1967), 293
Age diversity, 25–26
Age-fifty transition, 293
Agents, defined, 177
Agor, Weston, 165
Agreeableness, as personality trait, 39

AIDS, as ethical workplace issue, 29–30
Air France, 69
Airbus, 225
Alcon Laboratories, 23, 27
Alderfer, Clayton, 78
Alienated followers, 207
Alienated relationships, 84
Allegiance in career, 280, 281
Allport, Gordon, 38
Allstate, 115
America Online (AOL), 274–275
American Airlines, 99, 297
American Apparel, 31
American Express
    Business Travel Program, 299
    family-friendly policies, 79
    gender diversity, 24
    telecommuting, 311
American Psychological Association, 311
Americans with Disabilities Act (1992), 26, 29
Amgen, 76
Amygdala hijacks, 64
Anheuser-Busch, 33
Anthro, 5
Anthropocentric approach (job design), 238, 239
Anthropology, 5
Anticipatory socialization, 270–271
AOL, 274–275
Apple
    customer satisfaction, 10
    leadership, 204
    organizational structure changes, 256–257
Appointments, global cultural differences, 21
Appraisals. *See* Evaluations
Aristotle, 29
Armstrong World Industries, 46
Artifacts (corporate), 264
Artistic occupations, 281
Artistic personality, 282
Assembly-line work, 232, 240
Assertiveness, 224
Assessments. *See* Evaluations
Assets, intangible, 34

Assigned groups, 147
Assumptions (corporate), 267
AstraZeneca, 130
Atlantic Richfield (ARCO), 30
AT&T
    health promotion program, 311
    informal groups, 147
    job enrichment, 233
    MBTI use, 46
    telecommuting, 33, 240, 311
Attachment theory, 117
Attitude–behavior link, 57–58
Attitudes
    ABC model, 55–57
    decision making and, 164
    described, 55
    formation, 57–59
    of leaders, 196–198
    persuasion and change in, 63–64
    social perception and, 48
    at work, 58
Attractiveness and attitude change, 63
Attribution theory, 52–53, 103–104
Authentic leadership, 205
Authority, defined, 177
Authority-compliance managers, 196, 197
Authority issues, 146
Authority relationships, 214
Autocratic style of leadership, 195
Autonomous work groups, 154–155
Autonomy
    as career anchor, 295
    as job characteristic, 234–235
    need for, 80
    work design and, 240
Avoidance (conflict management), 225, 226
Avon Products, Inc., 209, 259
Azia, Gamal, 195

B

Baby boomers
    values, 68
    in workforce, 25, 26

Baby boomlet, 26
Baby bust generation, 26, 68
Bandura, Albert, 94–95, 265
Bank of America, 164
Bar codes, 299
Barnard, Chester, 165
Barnes, Brenda, 45
Barra, Mary, 301
Beard, D., 255
Beatrice, John, 292
Beck, Robert, 164
Beech-Nut, 170
Behavioral costing guidelines, 114
Behavioral intent, 56
Behavioral learning models
    classical conditioning, 91–92
    operant conditioning, 92
    reinforcement theory, 92–94
Behavioral measures, 43–47
Behavioral norms, 148–149
Behavioral problems, 114
Bell Canada, 34
Benefits programs, 76
Bennis, Warren, 146
Benson, Herbert, 121
Berkshire Hathaway, Inc., 265
Biases, attributional, 53
Bible, 29
Bicultural groups, 157
Big Five personality classification, 38–39, 43
Binney & Smith, 267
Biological approach (job design), 237
BJ Services Company, 95, 102
Black & Decker, 5
Blagojevich, Rod, 182
Blake, Robert, 196–198
Blanchard, Kenneth, 201–202
Blankfein, Lloyd, 178
Blood, Milton, 75
Blue Man Group, 160
BlueLight.com, 32
BluePages program, 290
Booz Allen Hamilton, 253
Borderless companies, 298–299
Bossnapping, 224
Bounded rationality model of decision making, 161–162
BP, 152, 206
Brain hemisphere function, 164–165
Brainstorming, 171
Branch Davidian culture, 205
Branson, Sir Richard, 168
Bridge employment, 294
Briggs, Katherine, 43
British Airways, 121
Brown, Eric, 6
Buffet, Jimmy, 265
Buffett, Warren, 45, 265

Bureaucracies, 250
Burke, James, 66, 208
Burnout, 113–114, 293
Burns, T., 256
Bush, George H. W., 12
Bush, George W., 156

C

Calculated relationships, 84
Campbell Soup, 292
Campion, Michael, 236–237
Canadian National Sports Organizations (NSOs), 301
Cannon, Walter B., 91, 107, 108, 113
Capacity of environment, 255
Career, defined, 279
Career anchors, 294–295
Career functions, 288
Career ladders, 288
Career lattices, 288
Career management
    advancement stage, 285, 287–293
    becoming own coach, 284
    defined, 279
    dual-career partnerships, 290–291
    emotional intelligence and, 284–285
    establishment stage, 285, 286–287
    maintenance stage, 285, 293
    mentors and, 288–290, 293
    new versus old paradigms, 280–281
    occupational choice, 280–282
    organizational choice and entry, 282–283
    paths and ladders, 287–288
    preparation for work world, 280
    realistic job previews, 284
    withdrawal stage, 285, 293–294
    work–home conflicts and, 291–293
Career paths, 287–288
Career planning, 312
Career plateaus, 293
Career stage model
    advancement, 285, 287–293
    establishment, 285, 286–287
    maintenance, 285, 293
    withdrawal, 285, 293–294
Caribou Coffee, 9
Carnegie Mellon University, 35
Caterpillar, 7, 311
Cattell, Raymond, 38
Centrality, degree of, 179–180
Centralization, 250, 259
Ceremonies (corporate), 265
Challenge, defined, 3
Challenger disaster, 169, 170
Challengers (in groups/teams), 152

Chambers, John, 249
Change
    acquisition and, 271–272
    adjusting to technological, 35
    agent's role, 301–302
    behavior in times of, 5–6
    characteristics needed for successful, 297
    defined, 3
    external forces, 298–300
    internal forces, 300–301
    Lewin model, 305–306
    networks for social, 18
    as opportunity creator, 9–13
    organization development interventions, 306–312
    organizational behavior management, 12
    persuasion and attitude and, 63–64
    resistance to, 302–305
    scope of, 300–301
    workforce diversity and, 28
Change agents, 301–302
The Change Masters (Kanter), 301
Chaparral Steel Company, 4, 237
Character assassination, 222
Character theories of ethics, 29
Charismatic leadership, 204–205
Chrysler, 155
Churchill, Winston, 6
Cigna Financial Advisors, 289
Circle coaches, 261
Circle organizations, 260–261
Cisco Systems
    organizational structure, 249
    telecommuting, 240, 292, 295
Civility and communication, 132
Clark, Stan, 264
Classical conditioning, 91–92
Clif Bar, 267
Clinton, Bill, 190, 205
Clockwork metaphor, 3
Coaching
    becoming own, 284
    executive, 310–311
    in feedback, 99, 100
    healing dialogue model, 137
    in mentoring, 105, 288
Coalition tactics, 185
Coastal Corporation, 230–231
Coca-Cola
    ethnic diversity, 24
    leadership, 194
    organizational structure, 247
    as transnational organization, 17
"Code of Business Conduct" (Nortel), 62, 300
Coercive power, 178, 179, 180
Cognition, in ABC model, 56, 61
Cognitive appraisal approach to stress, 108

Cognitive dissonance, 56–57
Cognitive functioning and emotions, 64
Cognitive learning theories, 95
Cognitive moral development, 70–72
Cognitive process, 87–88
Cognitive routes to persuasion, 63–64
Cognitive structure and social perception, 48
Cognitive style, 163–164, 166
Cohesiveness and workforce diversity, 28
Collaboration (conflict management), 226, 227
Collaborators (in groups/teams), 152, 275
Collectivism
    decision making and, 173
    expectancy theory and, 88
    individualism versus, 20
    job design and, 238
    negotiations and, 224
    values, 69
Columbia disaster, 169–170
Comfort zones, 134–135
Committed relationships, 84
Common resources, 213
Communication
    barriers and gateways, 130–131, 215
    change and, 304
    civility and incivility, 132–134
    clues to lying, 137
    conflict and, 215
    cultural, 274
    by effective managers, 129–130
    face-to-face, 209
    FAME method, 130
    Internet, 32
    interpersonal, 125–129
    language use, 126, 129, 131
    managing political behavior with, 187
    nonverbal, 134–136, 138
    positive, healthy, 136–137
    skills and teams, 154
    social media use, 137
    social perception and, 49
    technologies, 138–140
    workforce diversity and problems, 28
    written, 137
Communicative disease, 136
Communicators (in groups/teams), 152
Communicators, defined, 125
Compensation (compromise mechanism), 220
Compensation awards, 115
Competence in empowerment, 189
Competence norms, 145
Competence skills, 154
Competition
    as change driver, 9
    conflict management and, 225–226
    global, 9–11, 17
Competitive people, 154

Competitive strategy (conflict management), 221
Complexity, 247, 250, 253
Complexity of environment, 255
Comprehensive health programs, 122
Compromise (conflict management), 226–227
Compromise mechanisms, 220
Conaty, William J., 100
Concern for others as value, 69
Confessions, 122
Confidentiality, 30
Confirmation in mentorships, 288–289
Conflict
    causes, 213–215
    defense mechanisms, 219–221
    defined, 211
    diagnosing, 212–213
    dual-career partnerships, 290–291
    functional versus dysfunctional, 211–212
    intergenerational, 216
    intergroup, 216
    interorganizational, 215–216
    interpersonal, 218–221
    interrole, 217
    intragroup, 216
    intrapersonal, 216–218
    intrarole, 217
    management time spent on, 211
    organizational entry and, 282
    reduction through rites, 265
    work–home, 291–293
Conflict management
    competitive strategy, 221
    cooperative strategy, 221
    effective techniques, 222–224
    in groups, 221
    ineffective techniques, 222
    styles, 224–227
    work design and, 240
Conger, Jay, 189
Congruence, 271
Conscientiousness, as personality trait, 39
Consensus, as informational cue, 103
Consensus building, 166–167
Consequential theories of ethics, 28
Consideration (leadership behavior), 195
Consistency as informational cue, 103
Consultations, 185
Continental Airlines, 121
Contingency theories of leadership, 198–201
Continuance commitment, 62
Continuous reinforcement, 93
Contributions in exchange relationships, 84–85
Contributors (in groups/teams), 152
Contributory creativity, 167
Control Data Services, Inc., 9

Conventional developmental level, 71
Conventional occupations, 281
Conventional personality, 282
Conversion, 220
Cooper, Kenneth, 121
Cooperative and helping behaviors, 154
Cooperative strategy (conflict management), 221
Cooperative teamwork skills, 151
Cooperativeness, 224
Coping methods
    emotion-focused, 108
    problem-focused, 108
    regressive, 116
    transformational, 116
Core feelings, 128
Core self-evaluations (CSEs), 40, 41
Coronary-prone behavior, 116
Corporate allegiance, 280, 281
Corporate culture. *See* Organizational culture
Corporate Cultures (Deal and Kennedy), 263
Costs of new employees, 283
Counseling
    by mentors, 105, 288–289
    as performance feedback, 99, 100
Counterdependence, 117
Country club managers, 196, 197
Crayola products, 267
Creativity, 165–168
    as career anchor, 295
    diversity and, 27
    team, 153
Crier, Catherine, 132
Crises, leader's reaction to, 269
Critical-incident technique, 82
Critical resources, control of, 179
Critical thinking, 13–14
Cross-cultural motivation, 20
Cross-functional teams, 223, 249
Cross-training programs, 233
Cultivation phase in mentoring, 290
Cultural differences, 19–20
    achievement and, 79
    attitudes and, 20–23, 57
    attribution error and, 53
    comfort zones, 135
    communication barriers, 131
    conflict and, 215
    decision making and, 173
    global guide, 21
    group/team effectiveness, 147, 152–153
    job design, 237–239
    job satisfaction and, 61
    meaning of work and, 229–230
    mentoring programs and, 289
    motivation and, 88
    negotiations and, 21, 224
    nonverbal communication, 134, 136

organizational culture and, 275
political behavior, 186
reward systems, 101, 102
social perception and, 47
stress, 108, 111
understanding, 19–20
values, 69
work–home conflicts, 291
Cultural intelligence, 39
Cultural relativism, 29
Culture
artifacts of, 264
change and, 303
definition of, 263
See also Organizational culture
Currey, Gail, 266

D

Data, 126
Davis, Neil, 274–275
Day-care facilities, 292
Deal, Terry, 263
Decision making
attitudes and values and, 164
bounded rationality model, 161–162
creativity and, 165–168
diversity and culture in, 173
employee involvement, 276
escalation of commitment, 162–163
factors adversely affecting, 261
individual influences, 166
individual-organization fit, 167–168
intuition and, 164–165
organizational influences, 166–167, 257
participation in, 173–175
personality type and, 95, 164
process, 159–160
rational model, 161
risk aversion and taking, 163–164
under time pressures, 202
in Vroom-Yetton-Jago model, 200–201
Z problem-solving model, 162
See also Group decision making
Deep acting, 65
Defense mechanisms, 219–221
Defensive communication, 132–133
Deficiency in performance measurement, 98
Defining moments, 218
Delegating leadership style, 201, 203
Delphi technique, 172
Demands, in exchange relationships, 84
Deming, W. Edwards, 238
Democratic style of leadership, 195
Department of Defense (DOD), 32
Department of Labor, 14

Departmentalization, 247
Depressive constellation, 261
Dess, G., 255
Deus, Frank, 115
Devil's advocacy, 171–172
Dewey, John, 77
Diagnosis (in OD), 307
Dialectical inquiry, 172
Diet, 121–122
Differentiation, 231, 245, 247–248, 259
Directive leadership style, 200
Disabled individuals
devices for, 27, 35
other-enhancing by, 51
in workforce, 26
Discounting principle, 49
Discrete exchange, 280, 281
Discrimination, 27, 33
Disney Institute, 167
Displacement, 219
Display rules, 65
Dispositions, 40
Distinctiveness as informational cue, 103
Distress, 82, 107, 113–115
Distributive bargaining, 224
Distributive justice, 30, 181
Divergent thinking, 166
Diversity
decision making and, 173
ethnic diversity, 23–24
group/team effectiveness, 152–153
group/team formation, 147
organizational culture and, 275
social perception and, 47
structural, 153
types of, in workforce, 23–28, 299
in upper echelons, 155, 156–157
valuing, 26–27
See also Cultural differences; Gender differences
Divisionalized form, 251, 252
Domain, 255
Dominant defensiveness, 133
Dow Chemical, 17
Dow Jones Sustainability Index, 69
Downsizing, 29, 253
Dreaming sessions, 174
Dress, global cultural differences, 21
DriveSavers, 118
Drucker, Peter, 97
Dual-career partnerships, 290–291
Dual concern, 221
Due process nonaction (conflict management), 222
Dunn, Brian J., 137
Dynamic equilibrium, 248
Dynamic stability, 260
Dysfunctional turnover, 115

Dysfunctional versus functional conflict, 211–212

E

Earnings, 24, 290
Eastern Airlines, 150
Eastman Kodak, 8
Economy (U.S.), size and sectors, 9
Edison, Thomas, 254
Effective decisions, 161
Effective followers, 208
Efficiency, 5
Egalitarian people, 154
Ego-ideal, 108
El Neuvo Dia, 311
Elaboration likelihood model of persuasion, 63–64
Eldercare, 292, 295
Elderly, discrimination against, 293
Eli Lilly and Co., 233, 291, 310
Emergency response, 108
Emergent groups, 147
Emotion-focused coping, 108
Emotional contagion, 64
Emotional dissonance, 65, 111
Emotional exhaustion, 113
Emotional intelligence (EI)
career success and, 284–285
leaders and, 205–206, 211
overview of, 65
Emotional labor, 65
Emotional stability, as personality trait, 39
Emotional toxins, 111
Emotions, 64–66
change and, 302–304
conflict and, 215
creativity and, 166
leaders and, 205
Empathy of supervisors, 129, 304
Employee assistance programs (EAPs), 122
Employee-oriented leadership, 196
Empowerment
components, 189
organizational culture and, 275–276
organizational structure and, 280, 281
role of management, 189–191
self-managed teams and, 154–155
Enacted values, 267
Encounter, 271
Endorsements and attitude change, 63
Energy recovery, 84
Engagement in jobs, 235
Engineering, 4–5
Enterprising occupations, 281
Enterprising personality, 282
Environment, 38

Environmental uncertainty, 267
Environmentalism and greenwashing, 65
Equal Employment Opportunity Commission, 30
Equal versus equal power network, 218–219
Equitability in performance measurement, 101
Equity theory, 84–85
ERG theory, 78
Ergonomics, 5, 236–237
Ernst & Young, 25
Escalation of commitment, 162–163
Eskimo Joe's, 264
Espoused values, 267
Establishment stage of career, 285, 286–287
Ethical behavior
    company codes, 31–32, 60, 62, 300
    conflicts and, 215
    employee rights, 29–30
    factors influencing, 67–72
    frequency of misconduct, 71
    gender differences, 72
    global perspective, 70
    globalization and, 70, 299–300
    as group norm, 145
    organizational culture and, 275
    organizational justice, 30–31
    organization's performance and, 66–67
    person–role conflicts and, 110–111
    procedural justice, 30–31
    sexual harassment, 30
    social responsibility, 31
    in use of power, 180–182
    whistle-blowing, 31
    workplace issues, 29–32, 67
Ethicon Endo-Surgery, 166–167
Ethics, theories of, 28–29
Ethnic diversity, 23–24, 27, 289
Etzioni, Amitai, 84
European Union, 18
Eustress, 82–83, 112–113
Evaluation systems, 87
Evaluations
    accuracy, 98–99, 101
    core self-, 41
    goal-setting and, 97
    of organizational culture, 272–273
    performance management and, 97–98
    of personality, 42–47
    self-esteem and, 41
    self-performance, 98
Exchange relationships, 84–85
Exchanges, 185
Executive coaching, 310–311
Executives. See Leaders/leadership; Managers/management
Existence need, 78
Expanding resources, 223

Expatriate managers, 19, 20
Expectancy, 87
Expectancy theory, 282
Expectation theory, 87–88
Expected creativity, 167
Experience, openness to, 39
Expert power, 178, 179, 180
Expert systems, 33
Expertise and attitude change, 63
Expressiveness of supervisors, 129
External attributions, 52, 103–104, 183
External change agents, 302
External theories of motivation, 75
Externals (locus of control), 41, 70
Extinction, 94
Extraversion, 39, 115
Extraversion/Introversion, 43, 44, 45
Extreme workers, 34–35
ExxonMobil, 46, 308
Eye behavior, 128, 136

F

Facebook
    etiquette, 140
    leadership, 194
    rituals, 266
    use of, 137, 139
Facial behavior, 128, 136
Facilitating exposure and visibility, 288
Failure, learning from, 6
Failure and change, 302
Fairness as value, 69
False-consensus effect, 51
FAME (Focus, Articulate, Model, and Engage) method of communication, 130
Familiarity and social perception, 48
Family organizations, 6
Fantasy, 220
FedEx
    goal-setting, 97
    performance appraisal, 101
    quality action teams, 154
Feedback
    defined, 126
    goal setting and, 96
    job design and, 236
    from job itself, 235
    performance, 96, 99–101
    response to negative, 219
    survey, 307–308
Feelers, decision making by, 95
Feeling, in messages, 126, 127
Feeling/Thinking, 44–45
Femininity, 22, 173
Fiedler's contingency theory, 198–200
Fiesta Bowl, 181

Fight-or-fight response, 108
First-impression error, 50
First impressions, 50
First-shift rule, 168
Fisher, George, 12
Fit cultures, 268
Five-state model of group development, 147–148
Fixation, 219
Fixed interval reinforcement, 93
Fixed ratio reinforcement, 93
Flannery, Jessica, 190
Flannery, Matt, 190
Flat structures, 247–248, 299
Flexibility, 284, 298
Flexibility exercises, 121
Flexibility in performance measurement, 101
Flextime/flexible work schedules, 56, 241–242, 291–293
Flight (withdrawal mechanism), 220
Followership, 207–208
Force field analysis, 305
Ford Motor Company
    cost of stress-related illnesses, 114
    cross-functional teams, 249
    job redesign, 311
    use of new technology, 299
Formal leadership, defined, 193
Formal mentoring programs, 289
Formal organization, 7–8
Formalization, 249–250, 253, 259
Forming stage, 147
Four-way ethics test, 31
Framing information, 180
Free riding, 146
French, John, 178
Freud, Sigmund, 75–76, 77
Friendship in mentorships, 288–289
Fukutomi, G. D. S., 155
Full engagement, 83–84
Functional turnover, 115
Functional versus dysfunctional conflict, 211–212
Fundamental attribution error, 53

G

Gaddafi, Muammar al-, 136
Galleon Group, 61
Gandhi, 205
Gap Inc., 299–300
Gates, Bill, 45, 194, 265
GE Capital, 174
GE Healthcare, 309
GE Medical Systems Groups (GEMS), 22
GeekDesk, 5

Gender differences
    attribution, 52
    communication barriers, 130–131
    decision-making, 44
    ethical behavior, 72
    group formation and, 147
    Kohlberg model of moral development, 72
    leadership and, 206
    mentoring and, 289–290
    negotiations and, 224
    political behavior, 186
    responses to stress, 115–116
    risk taking, 163
    values in organizational culture and, 267
Gender diversity, 24–25
Gender harassment, 30
Geneen, Harold, 144, 231
General Electric (GE)
    change mechanisms, 297–298, 308
    as multinational corporation, 298
    performance feedback, 99
    Six Sigma philosophy, 10
    talent management, 100
    team building, 309
General mental ability (GMA), 38
General Motors (GM)
    corporate decay, 5
    escalation of commitment, 163
    stabilization under Sloan, 193
    transformational change, 301
    trustworthiness of leadership, 206
Generation X, 26, 68
Generation Y, 26, 68
Gerdau Ameristeel, 101
German approach (job design), 238
Gersick, Connie, 148
Gestalt school of thought, 95
Gifts, global cultural differences, 21
Gilligan, Carol, 72
Gilmartin, Ray, 157, 191
Glass ceiling, 24–25
Glass cliff, 206
Global Citizens Portfolio (IBM), 22
Global competition, 9–11, 17
Global core, 253
Global Leadership Program (GEMS), 22
Globalization
    career ladders and, 288
    development of global organizational culture, 275
    ethical behavior and, 299–300
    international activity versus, 17
    labor competition, 17
    layoffs and, 29
    organizational change and, 298–299
    organizational reshaping and, 258–259

staff resistance, 304–305
Globoforce, 102
Goal differences, 213–214, 268
Goal setting
    aggressive, 96
    central ingredients, 97
    characteristics of effective, 95–96
    conflict and, 213–214
    described, 95
    functions, 96–97
    organizational design and, 245
    politics and, 183–184
    stress and, 119, 121
    Taylor and, 5
Goffer, Amit, 27
Gofstede, Gert, 19
Goizueta, Robert, 194
Goldman Sachs Group, 178
Goleman, Daniel, 284–285
Good as moral value, 28
Google
    artifacts of culture, 264
    reference checks on applicants, 284
    stress naps, 121
    technology use, 34
Goolsby Leadership Academy, 147
Government sectors, 9
GP³ method of time management, 120–121
Grant, Jody, 151
Graphic Controls Corporation, 233
Great Call Experience, 299
Greatest good, 28
Green architecture, 171
Green Mountain Coffee Roasters, 311–312
Greenleaf, Robert, 207
Greenwashing, 65
Gross domestic product (U.S.), 9
Group-Atmosphere Scale, 198
Group behavior, 145–146
Group cohesion, 145–146, 149
Group decision making
    advantages, 168
    disadvantages, 168–170
    reasons for, 168
    special groups, 172–173
    techniques, 171–172
Group polarization, 170
Groups
    characteristics of mature, 148–150
    conflict and, 216
    conflict management, 221
    described, 143
    development of, 147–148
    formation, 146–147
    See also Work teams
Groupthink, 168–170
Growth need, 78

Growth need strength, 234
Guanxi, 18

H

Hackman, Richard, 233–234
Hall, Edward, 135
Hallmark Cards, 152
Hambrick, D. C., 155
Hampton Inns, 173
Hardee's Food Systems, 118
Harley-Davidson, 260–261, 276
Harris, Paul, 31
Hartford Financial Services Groups, 304–305
Harvard University, 292
Hawthorne studies, 8
Hayward, Tony, 206
HCL Technologies, 127
Healing dialogue, 137
Health
    communicative disease, 136
    job design and, 239–240
    office work dangers to, 109, 111
    personality and, 39
    programs, 122, 311–312
    See also Stress
Hearst, 121
Heredity and personality, 38
Hersey, Paul, 201–202
Herzberg, Frederick, 80–82, 230, 233
Heskett, James, 268–269
Heuristics, 161
Hewlett-Packard
    MBTI use, 46
    rituals, 266
    workforce diversity, 27
Hierarchy of authority, 250, 253
High versus low power network, 219
High versus middle versus low power network, 219
Hirschhorn, Larry, 144–145
Hitler, Adolf, 205
HIV/AIDS, as ethical workplace issue, 29–30
H&M, 18
Hofstede, Geert, 19, 20, 23, 173
Holgorsen, Dana, 222
Holland, John, 280–282, 295
Home demands, 112
Home Depot, 298
Homeostatic approach to stress, 108
Homogeneous groups, 156
Honesty as value, 69
Honeywell, 46
Horizontal differentiation, 247, 259
Horizontal integration mechanisms, 249
Hospitals, TQM practices, 10

Hostile jokes, 133
House, Robert, 200
Hsieh, Tony, 58, 139
HTC, 10
Human behavior, 3–6
Hygiene factors, 81, 82
Hyundai, 96

I

Iacocca, Lee, 155
IBM
    gender diversity, 25
    Global Citizens Portfolio, 22
    goal-setting, 5
    job enlargement, 232
    leadership development, 310
    mentoring, 105, 290
    Process Quality Management, 148
    response to competition, 9
    social responsibility, 31
    stories about, 266
    strong culture of, 268
    telecommuting, 33
Idaho State Police Department, 283
Identification, 220, 267
Illumination stage of creativity, 166
Impact in empowerment, 189
Impoverished managers, 196, 197
Impression management, 51–52, 184
In-group members, 201, 203
In Search of Excellence (Waterman), 263
Incentive programs, 76, 77
Incivility and communication, 132
Incremental change, 300–301
Incubation stage of creativity, 166
Independence as career anchor, 295
Individual differences
    challenge of, 37
    locus of control, 40–41, 70
Individual distress, 113–114
Individual rights, 181
Individualism
    collectivism versus, 20
    decision making and, 173
    expectancy theory and, 88
    job design and, 238
    negotiations and, 224
    values, 69
Individualistic people, 154
Individualized consideration, 204
Inequity theory, 85–87
Influence, defined, 177, 184
Influence tactics, 184–186
Informal leadership, defined, 193
Informal mentoring programs, 289
Informal organization, 7–8

Information
    dissemination by management, 130
    dissemination of misleading, 133
    used in messages, 126
Information communication technology (ICT)
    effect on behavior, 138–140
    effect on health, 109–111, 242–243
    mentoring programs, 290
    organizational design and structure and, 259, 260
Information databases, 138
Information power, 180
ING Direct, 309
Ingratiation, 185, 186
Initiating structure, 195
Initiation phase in mentoring, 290
Innovation and workforce diversity, 27
Inputs, defined, 7
Inspirational appeals, 185
Inspirational leadership theories, 204–205
Inspirational motivation, 204
Instrumental values, 68, 69
Instrumentality, 87
Intangible assets, 34
Integrated involvement, 145
Integration, 231, 245, 248–249
Integrative approach, 40
Integrative negotiations, 224
Integrators, 152, 223, 249
Intel, 274–275, 300–301
Intellectual property, as intangible asset, 34
Intentions and social perception, 49
Interactional psychology, 37–38
Interdependence, 213
Interdependent behavior, 117
Intergenerational conflicts, 216
Intergroup conflicts, 216
Intermittent reinforcement, 93
Internal attributions, 52, 103, 104
Internal change agents, 301
Internal theories of motivation, 75
Internals (locus of control), 40–41, 70
International Coach Federation, 310
International executives, competencies needed, 19
International Space Station, 162
Internet, 32
Internetworking, 260
Interorganizational conflicts, 215–216
Interpersonal communication
    importance of, 125
    model, 125–126
    reflective listening, 126–129
Interpersonal conflicts, 218–221
Interpersonal demands, 111, 271
Interpersonal influence, 187
Interpersonal issues, 146
Interrole conflicts, 110, 217

Intimate space, 135
Intragroup conflicts, 216
Intrapersonal conflicts, 216–218
Intrarole conflicts, 110, 217
Intrinsic motivation, 80
Introversion/Extraversion, 43, 44, 45
Intuition, 164–165
Intuition/Sensing, 44
Intuitors, learning by, 95
Invalidity in performance measurement, 98, 99, 101
Investigative occupations, 281
Investigative personality, 282
Invisible hand, 76
Irby, Steve, 264
Isenberg, Daniel, 164
Ivancevich, John M., 95

J

J. Willard Marriott Award of Excellence, 92
J.A. Counter & Associates, 242
Jago, Arthur, 200–201
James, William, 4, 77
Janis, Irving, 168–169, 170
Japanese approach (job design), 237–238
Job Characteristics Inventory (JCI), 235
Job characteristics theory, 233–234
Job choice, factors influencing, 69
Job content, 190
Job context, 190, 230
Job Descriptive Index (JDI), 59
Job Diagnostic Survey (JDS), 234
Job enlargement, 232–233
Job enrichment, 233
Job performance. *See* Performance
Job redesign, 119, 311
Job rotation, 232–233
Job satisfaction, 58–60
    accurate prediction, 87
    group formation and, 147
    MPS and, 234
    OCBs and, 61
    organizational commitment and, 62
    organizational culture and, 267
    organizational political climate and, 184
    organizational socialization and, 272
    shareholder returns and, 83
Job sharing, 241
Job strain model, 119
Jobs, Steve, 204, 256, 257
Jobs and design of work
    autonomy in, 234–235
    biological approach, 237
    core characteristics, 235
    culture and approach, 237–239
    defined, 229

engagement, 235
ergonomics, 236–237
flexibility, 231
flextime, 241–242
health and, 239–240
job characteristics theory, 233–234
job enlargement, 232–233
job enrichment, 233
job rotation, 232–233
job sharing, 241
mechanistic approach, 237
motivational approach, 237
in organizations, 230–231
parameter adjustments, 240
perceptual/motor approach, 237
redesign, 119
scientific management, 231–232
skill development, 243
social information processing (SIP)
    model, 236
technology and, 242–243
telecommuting, 240–241
Johnson & Johnson
    day-care facilities, 292
    decision making, 166–167
    ethics code, 32, 60, 145, 208
    health program, 5, 122, 311
    personnel selection methods, 4
    Tylenol recall, 60
Joint Ethics Regulation (DOD), 32
Judging/Perceiving, 43, 45
Jung, Andrea, 209
Jung, Carl, 43, 95, 164–165
Junker, John, 181
Jurisdictional ambiguities, 214
Just Coffee Cooperative, 31

K

Kahn, L., 6
Kahn, Robert, 108
Kant, Immanuel, 29
Kanter, Rosabeth Moss, 182–183, 301
Karoshi, 113
Katz, D., 6
Kelley, Harold, 103
Kenexa, 83
Kennedy, Allan, 263
Kentucky Fried Chicken (KFC), 18, 27, 298
Kilmann-Saxton Culture-Gap Survey, 272, 273
Kimberly-Clark, 311
Kinesics, 136
Kiva, 190
Klein, Gary, 164
Kmart, 32
Kohlberg, Lawrence, 70–72
Koran, 29

Korda, Michael, 183
Koresh, David, 205
Kotter, John, 193, 268–269
KPMG, 292
Krafcik, John, 96
Kraft Foods, 118

L

Labeling, 133
Laissez-faire style of leadership, 195
Landy, Frank, 240
Late adulthood transition, 294
Lateral (career) moves, 293
Latham, Gary, 95
Law of effect, 92
Lawrence, 247
Lawrence Livermore National Labs (LLNL),
    294
Layoffs, global differences, 29
Lazarus, Richard, 108
Leader–member exchange theory (LMX), 201,
    203
Leader–member relations, 198–199
Leaders/leadership
    abusive, 207
    attitudes of, 196–198
    behavioral aspects, 12
    behavioral theories, 195–198
    change and, 301–302
    contingency theories, 198–201, 203
    defined, 193, 194
    early trait theories, 194–195
    effective, 193–194, 199
    emotional intelligence and, 64, 205–206
    followers and, 207–208
    gender differences, 206
    guidelines, 208–209
    inspirational theories, 204–205
    introverts, examples of, 45
    leader-member exchange theory, 201,
        203
    management versus, 193–194
    problematic personality-organization
        constellations, 261
    role in organizational culture, 269–270
    servant, 207
    styles, 195–196
    trust and, 206
    See also Managers/management
Leadership, training and development, 310
Leadership and strategy councils (LSCs), 261
Leadership Grid, 196–198
Lean production, 238
Learned optimism, 120
Learning
    behavioral models, 91–94

    cognitive models, 95
    described, 91
    personality functions and, 95
    social models, 94–95
Learning teams, 309
Least preferred coworker (LPC), 198–200
Leavitt, H. J., 6
Legitimate power, 178, 179, 180
Leisure activities and stress, 121
Letters, 137
Levi, Lennart, 239
Levinson, Daniel J., 285, 293, 294
Levinson, Harry, 108, 307
Lewin, Kurt, 4, 37, 195, 305–306
LG Group, 271
Liaison role, 249
LinkedIn, 140
"Live for Life Program," 5
Locke, Edwin, 95
Locus of control, 40–41, 70
Loehr, Jim, 83–84
Lorenzo, Frank, 150
Lorsch, J., 247
Loss, fear of, and change, 302
Loss of individuality, 146
Louisiana Office of Motor Vehicles, 113
Lucasfilm, 266
Lucci, Susan, 265
Lucent Technologies, 289
Luthans, Frederick, 92, 94–95
Lying, clues to, 137
Lynch, James, 136, 137
Lyons, Dan, 309

M

Machiavelli, Niccolò, 70, 182
Machiavellianism, 70, 182
Machine bureaucracy, 251
Macik-Frey, Marilyn, 137
Mackey, John, 78, 267
Madoff, Bernie, 181
Maintenance functions, 150, 151
Maintenance stage of career, 285, 293
Majority-wins rule, 168
Malcolm Baldrige National Quality Award, 12
Management by exception, 248
Management by objectives (MBO), 96, 97,
    308
Management of change, 190–191
Management process, 193
Managerial competence (career anchor), 295
Managerial Grid, 196–198
Managers/management
    characteristics, 39, 182, 194–195
    circle coaches, 261
    communication skills, 129–130

competencies needed by international, 19

conflicting demands on, 259–260

dealing with conflict, 211–213

defined, 5, 194

ESTJ type, 45

executive coaching for, 310–311

hierarchy of authority, 250

interventions for organizational culture change, 273–274

intuition and, 165

leadership versus, 193–194

methods to increase workers' commitment, 62

modeling behavior of, 264–265

organizational politics and, 183–184

role of, in empowerment, 189–191

self-monitoring and, 42

teams, 249

technology and, 34–35

trust in employees, 276

upper echelons, 155–157

See also Leaders/leadership; Organizational structure

Managing up, 188–189

Mandela, Nelson, 205

Manifest needs, 79, 80

Manuals, 137

Manufacturing sector, 9

March, J. G., 5

Marketing and workforce diversity, 27

Marriott International, 92

Martin, Joanne, 266

Masculinity, 22, 173

Maslach, Christina, 113–114

Maslow, Abraham, 77–78, 273

Mass production jobs, 232, 240

Mass technology, 253–254

Mastenbroek, W. F. G., 218–219

Matrix organization structure, 250–251

Mattel, 67

Mayer, Marissa, 179

McClelland, David, 78–80, 181–182

McDonald's, 26, 253

McDowell, Jocelyn Koh, 290

McGrath, Joseph, 112

McGregor, Douglas, 78

McJOBS, 26

Meaning in empowerment, 189

Mechanistic approach (job design), 237

Mechanistic structure, 256

Medical approach to stress, 108

Meetings, having good, 149

Memorandums (memos), 137

Mental locks, 167

Mentors/mentoring

career management and, 288–290, 293

change and, 288, 304

coaching and counseling in, 104–105

Merck & Company

empowerment, 191

ethical behavior, 28

upper echelon diversity, 157

Mergers and organizational culture, 274–275

Merrill Lynch, 311

Messages, defined, 126

MetroNap Energy Pods, 121

MGM Grand Hotel and Casino, 195

Microchips, 35

Microcultural differences, 19

Microfinance, 190

Microsoft

leadership, 194

as multinational corporation, 299

strategic change, 301

video game market, 9

Militaristic approach, 108

Military organizations, 6, 32

Mill, John Stuart, 28

Millenials, 26

Miller Brewing Company, 76

Minnesota Multiphasic Personality Inventory (MMPI), 43

Minnesota Satisfaction Questionnaire (MSQ), 59

Mintzberg, Henry, 164, 250–251

Mission, 148

Mitchell Gold + Bob Williams, 292

Mobil Chemical, 65

Modeled behavior, 264–265

Modeling, 57

Monsanto, 306

Mood and social perception, 48

Moods, 64, 65

Moore Rubell Yudell (MRY), 171

Moral maturity, 88

Morality norms, 145

Motivating Potential Score (MPS), 234

Motivation

burnout and, 114

defined, 75

factors, 80–82

goal-setting and, 96–97

increase in intrinsic, 80

work dimensions and, 230

Motivation and behavior

cultural differences, 79

external incentives, 76–77

internal needs, 75–76

Motivation and behavior theories

equity theory, 84–87

ERG of Alderfer, 78

eustress, 82–83

expectancy of Vroom, 87–88

inequity theory of Adams, 85

manifest needs of Murray, 78, 80

need hierarchy of Maslow, 77–78

needs of McClelland, 78–80

positive energy and full engagement, 83–84

two-factor of Herzberg, 80–82, 230, 233

X and Y of McGregor, 77, 78

Motivational approach (job design), 237

Motivations programs, 87

Motorola

Be Cool team, 144

customer satisfaction, 10

ethnic diversity, 24

Six Sigma philosophy, 10

Mouton, Jane, 196–198

Moving (Lewin change model), 305

Multicultural groups, 157

Multinational organizations, 17, 275

Multitasking, 140

Munger, Charlie, 265

Murray, Henry, 78

Murray Thematic Apperception Test (TAT), 79

Mutual loyalty contract, 280, 281

Myers, Isabel Briggs, 43, 162

Myers-Briggs Type Indicator® (MBTI), 43–47

N

NAFTA (North American Free Trade Agreement), 18–19

Naps, 121

National Aeronautics and Space Agency (NASA)

corporate decay, 5

escalation of commitment, 162

flawed decision making, 169–170

organizational structure, 252

Twitter usage, 7

Natural liberty, 28

Navision, 299

Nayar, Vineet, 127

Need for achievement, 79

Need for affiliation, 79–80

Need for autonomy, 80

Need for power, 79

Need hierarchy, 77–78, 273

Need theories of motivation, 76

Needs analysis (in OD), 307

Negative affect/affectivity, 42

Negative consequences, 92, 93

Negative reinforcement, 93

Negativism, 219–220

Negotiations, 21, 223–224

Neiman Marcus, 255

NEO Personality Inventory, 43

Nestlé, 298

NetApp, 267

Netflix, 76

NetJets, 50
Network groups, 289
Network organizations, 260
Networking ability, 187
Networks for social change, 18
Newsweek, 121
Nike, 266
Nintendo, 9
Noise and stress, 112
Nokia, 152, 301
Nominal group technique (NGT), 171
Nonaction (conflict management), 222
Nonadaptive cultures, 268–269
Nondefensive communication, 132, 133–134
Nonprogrammed decisions, 159
Nonsubstitutability, 180
Nonverbal communication, 49, 134–136, 138
Normative commitment, 62
Normative decision model, 200–201
Norming stage, 148
Norms of behavior, 145
Nortel Networks, 62, 173, 300
North American Free Trade Agreement (NAFTA), 18–19
Northern Telecom, 173
Northwest Airlines, 9
Novia, Jack, 70

Objective element (of career), 279
Objective knowledge, 13–14
Occupational excellence, 280, 281
ODesk, 241
Official groups, 147
Ogilvy & Mather, 152
Oldham, Greg R., 234
One-way communication, 128–129
Online retailing, 32
Open systems, 6–7
Openness to experience, as personality trait, 39
Operant conditioning, 92
Opportunistic "what's in it for me" managers, 197
Opportunities, 3, 9–13
Optimism, learned, 120
Optimization, in decision making, 161
Organic structure, 256
Organization chart, 245–247
Organization development (OD)
    evaluation of effectiveness, 312
    group-focused techniques, 307–309
    individual-focused techniques, 309–312
    needs determination, 306–307
Organization man managers, 196, 197

Organizational behavior, 3–5
Organizational behavior modification (OBM), 92
Organizational citizenship behaviors (OCBs), 60–62, 64, 98, 146
Organizational commitment, 62
Organizational context, 6–7
Organizational culture
    anthropology and, 5, 263
    artifacts, 264
    assessing, 272–273
    assumptions in, 267
    ceremonies and rites, 265
    changing, 273–274
    defined, 263
    empowerment and, 275–276
    functions, 267–268
    job performance and, 268–269
    leader's role, 269–270
    learning, 270–272
    levels, 263–267
    mergers/acquisitions and, 274–275
    personal enactment, 264
    quality of products and service and, 275–276
    rituals, 266
    stories, 265–266
    symbols, 266
    values, 267
Organizational Culture Inventory (OCI), 272–273
Organizational design
    basic dimensions, 249–250
    forces reshaping, 257–260
    goals and, 245
Organizational empowerment, 280, 281
Organizational flexibility and workforce diversity, 28
Organizational Health Centers (OHCs), 118
Organizational justice, 30–31
Organizational life cycles, 258
Organizational politics
    change and, 303
    described, 183
    management and, 183–184
    managing political behavior, 187–191
    managing up, 188–189
    political skill, 186–187
    tactics, 184–186
Organizational socialization, 270–272
Organizational stress/distress, 114–115, 121
Organizational structure
    configurations, 250–252
    contextual variables, 252–257
    described, 245
    differentiation, 247–248
    dimensions, 249–251
    emerging, 260–261

environment, 254–256
factors adversely affecting, 261
forces reshaping, 257–260
integration, 248–249
organization chart and, 245–247
size, 252–253
strategy and goals, 256–257
technology, 253–254
Organizational wellness, 122
Ornish, Dean, 122
Other-enhancing, 51
Oticon, 166–167
Ouchi, William, 263
Out-group members, 203
Outputs, defined, 7
Outside consultants, use of, 309
Outsourcing, 6, 252
Overdependence, 117

Pacific Bell, 240–241
Pacific Gas and Electric (PG&E), 33
Panic, Milan, 30
Paralanguage, 136
Paranoid constellation, 261
Parents in a Pinch, Inc., 292
Park, Robert, 162
Participating leadership style, 201, 203
Participation in change, 304
Participation problems, 114–115
Participative decision making, 174, 187–188
Participative leadership style, 200
Paschal, Carolyn Smith, 293
Passive-aggressive behavior, 133
Paternalistic "father knows best" managers, 197
Path-goal theory, 200
Pavlov, Ivan, 91
People, defined, 6
Perceiving/Judging, 43, 45
Perceptions and conflict, 214
Perceptual/motor approach (job design), 237
Perdue Farms, 292
Perez, Bill, 150
Performance
    attribution theory, 103–104
    causes of poor, 102–103
    correcting poor, 104–105
    decrements, 115
    defining, 98
    feedback, 96, 99–101
    group cohesion and, 145–146, 149
    mood and, 64
    organizational culture and, 268–269
    organizational socialization and, 272
    predicting, 97

rewarding, 101–102
stress and, 112–113
as task accomplishment, 97
Performance appraisal. *See* Evaluations
Performance management, 97–98
Performance norms, 145
Performance planning systems, 87
Performing stage, 148
Perpetual screens, defined, 125–126
Perrewé, Pam, 109
Perrow, Charles, 254, 255
Person, in interactional psychology, 38
Person–environment fit approach to stress, 108
Person–organization fit, 61
Person–role conflicts, 110–111, 218
Personal attributions, 103, 104
Personal enactment, 264
Personal factors in conflict, 214–215
Personal freedom, 273
Personal power, 181–182
Personality
   application of theories, 43–44, 46
   attitude–behavior link and, 58
   change and, 303
   characteristics in organizations, 40–42
   characteristics of leaders and managers, 194–195, 261
   conflict and, 214
   decision making and, 164
   defined, 38
   determinants, 38
   hardiness, 116
   integrative approach, 40
   measurement tools, 42–47
   occupation choice and, 280, 281–282, 295
   trait theory, 38–39
Personalized power, 79
Personnel changes, 223
Persuasion and attitude change, 63–64
Persuasive arguments view, 170
Persuasiveness of supervisors, 130
Pessimism, 120
Petro Kazakstan, 131
Phased retirement, 294
Physical appearance and social perception, 48–49, 51
Physical demands, 111
Physical exercise, 121
Pillsbury Company, 67
PizzaBot, 35
Planned change, 298
Planning
   goal-setting and, 97
   for retirement, 293–294
   stress and, 121
Polarization, 170

Political behavior, 183–184
Political skill, 186–187
Politics in organizations. *See* Organizational politics
Polyphasic activity, 140
Position power, 198, 199
Positive affect, 42
Positive competitive teamwork skills, 151–152
Positive consequences, 92, 93
Positive energy and full engagement, 83–84
Positive organizational behavior (POB), 82, 120
Positive reinforcement, 92, 93
Positive stress, 82–83, 112–113
Post-Its, 167
Powell, Colin, 156
Power
   concept, 177–178
   distribution, 20, 173
   ethical use, 180–182
   forms, 178–179
   intergroup sources, 179–180
   in language of communication, 129
   need for, 79
   positive versus negative, 181–182
   relationship types, 218–219
   symbols, 182–183
Power distance, 20, 173
Power-napping, 83
Power networks, 218–219
Power of the future, 179
Power plays, 133
Powerlessness, 183
Praise and stress, 121
Prejudice, 26–27
Premoral developmental level, 71
Preparation stage of creativity, 165–166
Pressure, 185
Prestige and group cohesion, 150
Preventive stress management, 117–120
PricewaterhouseCoopers (PwC), 289
Primary effect, 50
Primary prevention, 117, 120
The Prince (Machiavelli), 70, 182
Principled developmental level, 71
Principled dissent, 182
Prioritization and stress, 121
Privacy rights, 32–33, 34, 67
Private sector, 9
Proactive creativity, 167
Proactive personality, 42
Problem analyzability, 254, 255
Problem-focused coping, 108
Problem solving and diversity, 28
Procedural justice, 30–31
Process, described, 39
Process consultation, 309

Process production, 254
Process skills, 154
Process theories of motivation, 75
Proctor & Gamble, 260, 298
Production-oriented leadership, 196
Productivity
   job satisfaction and, 58, 59
   as performance measure, 5
   technology and, 76
Professional bureaucracy, 251–252
Programmed decisions, 159
Progression hypothesis, 77
Project allegiance, 280, 281
Project teams, 293
Projection and social perception, 51
Projective tests, 42–43
Protection in mentorships, 288
Protestant ethic, 75
Proxemics, 134–135
Psyche focused, 221
Psychoanalysis, 76
Psychoanalytic approach to stress, 108
Psychological contracts, 285–287
Psychological intimacy, 145
Psychological Types (Jung), 43
Psychology, 4
Psychosocial functions, 288–289
Punctuated equilibrium model of group development, 148
Punishment, 93–94
Pygmalion effect, 51, 189
Pyramids, building of, 247

Qualitative goals, 95
Quality, 10–12
Quality action teams (QATs), 154
Quality circles, 172–173
Quality improvement process, 154
Quality programs, 308
Quality teams, 172–173
Quick, James Campbell, 137
Quick, Jonathan D., 79
QuikTrip, 266

Radio-frequency identification (RFID) tags, 299
Rational model of decision making, 161
Rational persuasion, 185
Rationality, 161
Rationalization, 220
Raven, Bertram, 178
Reactance, 302

Reagan, Ronald, 137, 205
Realism, 270–271
Realistic job previews (RJPs), 284
Realistic occupations, 281
Realistic personality, 282
Reality-distortion field, 204
Receivers, defined, 125
Redefinition phase in mentoring, 290
Reeve, Christopher, 179
Referent power, 178, 179, 180
Reflective listening
    clarification of implicit, 128
    contact affirmation, 127
    eye contact, 128
    one-way versus two-way, 128–129
    paraphrasing, 127–128
    reasons for use, 126–127
    reflection of core feelings, 128
    silence during, 128
Refreezing (Lewin change model), 305–306
Regression hypothesis, 78
Regressive coping, 116
Reinforcement theory, 92–94
Reinvention, 35
Relatedness need, 78
Relational job design, 236
Relationship-oriented leaders, 198, 199
Relationships
    alienated, 84
    authority, 214
    calculated, 84
    change and, 303, 304
    committed, 84
    exchange, 84–85
    leaders and, 188–189, 198–199
    role, 216–217
    social, 273
    stress-strain, 115–117
Relaxation training, 121
Religious organizations, 6
Renaud, Christian, 240
Reports, 137
Resource expansion, 223
Resource sharing, 213
Responsive creativity, 167
Responsiveness in performance
    measurement, 101
Retention methods, 57
Retirement, 293–294, 295
Returnships, 45
ReWalk, 27
Reward power, 178, 179, 180
Rewards
    allocation, 269–270
    strategic, 92
Rhodes, Rocky, 112
Richness of mediums, 126
Risk aversion, 163

Risk takers/taking, 22, 163
Rites (corporate), 265
Rituals (corporate), 266
Robotics, 33
Rohrshach ink blot test, 43
Role, 216
    ambiguity, 111, 219
    conflicts, 110, 219
    demands, 271
    incumbent, 216
    modeling in mentorships, 288–289
    negotiation, 119, 311
    relationships, 216–217
    senders, 217
    stress, 97, 110–111
Roosevelt, Franklin D., 205
Rosensweig, Dan, 149
Rotary International, 31
Routineness, 254
ROWE (Results Only Work Environment), 242
Royal Dutch/Shell Group, 247
Rudd, Kevin, 66
Rule-based theories of ethics, 29
Rust-out, 114

S

Sabbaticals, 293
Sandberg, Sheryl, 194
Sandwich generation, 292
Sanger-Harris, 95
Sara Lee Corp., 45
Sarbanes-Oxley Act (2002), 31
SAS, 266
Satellite offices, 34
Satisficing, 161, 282
S.C. Johnson, 76
Scandinavian approach (job design), 238–239
Schein, Edgar, 19, 264, 267, 269, 294–295, 309
Schultz, Howard, 204
Schwarzenegger, Arnold, 265
Schwartz, H., 5
Sciencetech, 9
Scientific management, 76, 231–232
Scully, John, 256–257
Sears, 247, 268
The Seasons of a Man's Life (Levinson, D.), 285
The Seasons of a Woman's Life (Levinson, D.), 285
Seating dynamics, 135
Secondary prevention, 117–118, 120
Secrecy (conflict management), 222
Security/stability (career anchor), 295
Segal, Jonathan, 101
Selection interview and social perception, 47

Selective perception, 49–50
Self-concept and social perception, 48
Self-determination in empowerment, 189
Self-directed teams, 154–155
Self-efficacy, 41, 94–95
Self-enhancing, 51
Self-esteem, 41–42, 63, 133
Self-evaluations, 40
Self-fulfilling prophecies and social
    perception, 51
Self-image, 108
Self-interest, 28, 76, 77
Self-leadership, 208
Self-managed teams, 154–155, 172, 173, 189
Self-monitoring, 42, 58
Self-performance evaluations, 98
Self-reliance, 117, 284
Self-report questionnaires, 43
Self-serving bias, 53
Selling leadership style, 201, 203
Semel, Terry, 59
Sensing/Intuition, 44
Sensitivity of supervisors, 129
Sensors, learning by, 95
Separation phase in mentoring, 290
Servant leadership, 207
Service sector, 9
Sexual coercion, 30
Sexual harassment, 30
Shareholder returns and job satisfaction, 83
Sheep (followers), 207–208
Shell Oil Company, 226, 247
Shepard, Herbert, 146
Siemens, 299
Silence during communication, 128
Silent generation, 25–26
Simon, H. A., 5
Simon, Herbert, 161
Simple structure, 251
Sims, Henry, 235
Sincerity, 187
Situation, in interactional psychology, 38
Situational attributions, 103–104
Situational cues and social perception, 49
Situational Leadership model, 201, 203
Six Sigma, 10–11, 12
Skill development, 13, 14, 243
Skill variety, 235
Skills
    conflict and, 214
    effective management communication, 129–130
    essential workplace, 14
    team, 151–152, 154
    training, 310
Skinner, B. F., 91–92
Skoglund, Linda, 242

Sloan, Alfred P., 193
SMART (Specific, Measurable, Attainable, Realistic, and Time-bound) goals, 95–96
Smart tags, 299
Smartphones, 138
Smith, Adam, 28, 76
Smith, Fred, 101
Smith & Wesson, 253
Smyth, Michael, 67
Snake pit metaphor, 3
Social astuteness, 187
Social comparison approach, 170
Social constraints, 58
Social decision schemes, 168
Social distance zone, 135
Social exchange, 84–87
Social information processing (SIP) model, 236
Social learning, 57
Social learning theories, 94–95, 265
Social loafing, 146
Social media use, 137–140
Social occupations, 281
Social perception
    barriers to, 49–52
    influences on, 46–49
Social personality, 282
Social power, 182
Social reinforcement, 94–95
Social relationships, 273
Social responsibility, 31
Social status and group cohesion, 150
Social support systems, 119, 120, 287
Socialized power, 79
Sociology, 4
Sociotechnical systems (STS), 238
Sokol, Dave, 50
Solomon, Robert, 29
Sony, 9, 224
Southwest Airlines, 9
Southwest Industries, 155
Southwestern Bell, 265, 288, 302
Span of control, 247
Spatial differentiation, 248
Spearman, Charles, 38
Specialization, 213, 247, 250, 253, 259
Spielberg, Steven, 45
Sponsorship, 288
Squires, Lisa, 290
St. Mary's/Duluth Clinic Health System, 235
Stajkovic, Alexander, 94–95
Stalker, G., 256
Stamping in, 57
Standardization, 250, 259
Standing by and power, 183
Starbucks, 9, 204
Status
    inconsistencies and conflict, 214

personality and, 40
    self-esteem and, 41
    symbols of power and, 183
Status structure, 150
Stereotypes/stereotyping
    as communication barriers, 131
    reactance, 224
    social perception and, 50
Stewart, Bill, 222
Stillwater Designs, 264
Stories (corporate), 265–266
Storming stage, 147
Strain, 107
Strategic change, 301
Strategic contingencies, 179–180
Strategic leaders, 194
Stress
    basic definitions, 107
    bodily effects, 123
    cognitive appraisal approach, 108
    decision making and, 160
    gender differences in responses, 115–116
    goals and, 97
    homeostatic/medical approach, 108
    individual distress, 113–114
    individual prevention, 120–122
    naps, 121
    new technologies and, 242–243
    organizational distress, 114–115
    performance feedback and, 99
    person-environment fit approach, 108
    personality hardiness, 116
    physiology, 108
    positive, 82–83, 112–113
    prevention, 117–120
    psychoanalytic approach, 108
    related illness, 114
    responses, 109, 115–116
    self-reliance, 117
    sources, 107, 109–112
    types A and B behavior patterns, 116
    violence and, 118
Stress audits, 111
Stress–strain relationship, 115–117
Stressors, 107
Strong cultures, 268
Strong situations, 40
Structural diversity, 153
Structural holes, 153
Structure
    conflict and, 214, 223
    defined, 7
    of work teams, 151
Subjective element (of career), 279
Suboptimization, 218
Subordinate defensiveness, 133
Substance abuse, 114

Superleadership, 208
Superordinate goals, 222–223
Supportive leadership style, 200
Surface acting, 65
Surveillance of employees, 32–33, 34
Survey feedback, 307–308
Survivors (followers), 208
Sustainability values, 69
Swartz, Jeffrey, 270
Sweatshops, 111
Symbolic rehearsal, 57
Symbols (corporate), 266
Synergy, 168
Szilagyi, Andrew, 235

T

Talent management, 100
Tall structures, 247, 249
Talmud, 29
Targets, defined, 177
Task
    accomplishment, 97
    defined, 6
    demands, 110, 271
    environment, 255–256
    focused groups, 221
    forces, 249
    functions, 150–151
    goal-setting and performance, 96–97
    identity, 235
    innovation, 273
    issues, 146
    significance, 235
    structure, 198, 199
    support, 273
    uncertainty, 240
    variability, 254, 255
Task-oriented leaders, 198, 199
Task-specific self-efficacy, 41, 94
Tata Group, 298
Taylor, Frederick W., 4–5, 76, 97, 231–232, 238
Team building
    decision making and, 175
    as OD technique, 308–309
    as stress preventer, 118, 119
Team managers, 196, 197–198
Teambuilding, Inc., 309
Teamwork
    benefits, 118, 119, 144–145
    change and, 299
    empowerment and, 154–155
    skills, 151–152, 154
Technical/functional competence (career anchor), 295
Technocentric approach (job design), 238

Technological interdependence, 254
Technology
    as change agent, 299
    classification, 253–254
    de-engineering, 33
    defined, 7, 32
    effect on behavior, 138–140
    effect on health, 109–111, 242–243
    innovation in workplace, 32–35
    mentoring programs, 290
    organizational structure and, 253–254,
      259, 260
    productivity and, 76
    reinvention and, 35
Technostress, 242–243
Tele-surveillance, 241
Telecommuting, 33–34, 240–241, 292, 295,
    311
Telling leadership style, 201, 203
Tenneco, 308
Terminal values, 68, 69
Territorial space, 134–135
Tertiary prevention, 118, 120
Testimonials and attitude change, 63
Thayer, Paul, 236–237
Theory of equity, 84–85
Theory of inequity, 85–87
Theory X, 77, 78
Theory Y, 77, 78
Theory Z (Ouchi), 263
Thinkers, decision making by, 95
Thinking/Feeling, 44–45
Thompson, J. D., 7
Thompson, James, 254
Thompson, Leigh, 153
Thought, in messages, 126
360-degree feedback, 100
3M
    bossnapping at, 224
    creativity at, 167
    as transnational organization, 17
Throughputs, defined, 7
Thurow, Lester, 10
Timberland, 66, 270
Time management, 120–121
Time orientation, 22, 173
Time power, 183
Time Warner, 121, 274–275, 283
Token groups, 156–157
Torre, Joe, 206
Total quality, 10
Total quality management (TQM), 10, 11, 155
Toyota Motor Corporation
    decision making at, 171
    quality program, 308
    TQM practices, 10
Trait theory, 38–39
Transactional leadership, 204

Transformational change, 301
Transformational coping, 116
Transformational leadership, 204
Transnational organizations, 17, 275
Travelers Group, 240
Tri-mentoring, 105
Triangulation, 273
True assessments, 98
Trump, Donald, 265
Trustworthiness
    attitude change and, 63
    of employees, 276
    of leaders, 206
    virtual organizations, 260
Truth-wins rule, 168
Tuckman, Bruce, 147
Twitter
    etiquette, 140
    use of, 7, 137, 139
Two-factor theory of motivation, 80–82, 230,
    233
Two-thirds-majority rule, 168
Two-way communication, 128–129
Tylenol recall, 60
Type A behavior pattern, 116
Type B behavior pattern, 116

U

Uncertainty
    coping with, 179
    reducing in job design, 240
Uncertainty avoidance, 22, 173
Unfreezing (Lewin change model), 305, 306
Union management strife, 8
Unit technology, 253
United Services Automobile Association
    (USAA), 241
Unknown, fear of, and change, 302
Unofficial groups, 147
Unplanned change, 298
Unreliability in performance measurement,
    98, 99, 101
Unwanted sexual attention, 30
Upper echelon theory, 155
Upper echelons, 155–157
Upward appeals, 185
U.S. Air Force, 118
U.S. Army Reserve, 247
U.S. Steel, 8
Utilitarianism, 28, 180–181

V

Valeant Pharmaceuticals International, 30
Valence, 87

Valero Energy, 4
Validity in performance measurement, 98,
    99, 101
Value congruence, 271
Values
    change and, 303, 306
    conflicts and, 215
    decision making and, 164
    development of global organizational
      culture and, 275
    good as ultimate, 28
    influence on ethical behavior, 68
    in organizational culture, 267
    work, 68–69
Variable interval reinforcement, 93
Variable ratio reinforcement, 93
Verbal communication and social perception,
    49
Verification stage of creativity, 166
Verizon Communications, 240
Vertical differentiation, 247–248, 259
Vertical linkages, 248
Video game market, 9
Violence, 118
Virgin Group, 168
Virtual offices, 34, 242
Virtual organizations, 260
Virtual teams, 143–144, 152
Virtue ethics, 29
Volatility of environment, 255
Volvo, 175
Vroom, Victor, 87–88, 200–201
Vroom-Yetton-Jago normative decision model,
    200–201

W

Wagoner, Rick, 163, 206
Wallace Supply Company, 148
Walmart, 255, 265–266
Walsh, Jackie, 83
Walters, Barbara, 136
Wasylyshyn, Karol, 137
Waterman, Robert, 263
Watson, Tom, Sr., 266
Weak organ hypothesis, 115
Weak situations, 40
Weaker sex stereotypes, 115
Weber, Max, 75
Welch, Jack, 298
Weldon, Bill, 60
Wellness programs, 5
Wells Fargo, 30
Western Company of North America, 95, 102
Weyerhaeuser, 5, 309
Whistle-blowing, 31, 275
Whole Foods Market, 267

Wii, 9
Wild turkeys, 155–156
Winfrey, Oprah, 190
Withdrawal, 220
Withdrawal mechanisms, 220–221
Withdrawal stage of career, 285, 293–294
Wm. Wrigley Jr. Company, 150
Women
    businesses owned, 24, 295
    career paths of, 287
    as change agents, 301–302
    glass ceiling, 24–25
    glass cliff, 206
    increased opportunities at Monsanto, 306
    number in labor force, 24, 299
    positions held, 24
    work–home conflicts, 291
    See also Gender differences
Woodward, Joan, 253–254
Work
    attitudes, 58
    autonomy, 234–235
    content, 230
    defining, 229–230
    dimensions of, 230
    meaning of, 229–230

    simplification, 231, 232
    values, 68–69
Work–home conflicts, 217, 291
Work teams
    benefits, 144–145
    collaboration and physical space, 275
    cross-functional, 223, 249
    described, 143–144
    factors influencing effectiveness, 144, 151–153
    horizontal integration and, 249
    learning, 309
    management, 249
    project, 293
    self-managed, 154–155, 172, 189
    task and maintenance functions, 150–151
    upper echelons, 155–157
    virtual, 143–144, 152
Work Value Scales (WVS), 230
Workaholism, 112
Working Together (Alcon), 27
WorkOut sessions, 297–298
Workplace deviance behaviors (WDBs), 61–62
World Trade Organization (WTO), 10, 246
Worlds Apart, 83

Wrigley, Bill, 150
Wriston, William, 156
Wyatt, Oscar, 230–231
Wyeth Corporate Communications, 309

Y

Yahoo!, 59
Yelo, 121
Yerkes-Dodson law, 112–113
Yes people, 208
Yetton, Phillip, 200–201
YouTube, 140

Z

Z problem-solving model of decision making, 162
Zalenik, Abraham, 194
Zappos.com, 58, 139
Zero concern, 221
Zones of indifference, 177–178
Zuckerberg, Mark, 266

WHY CHOOSE?

Every 4LTR Press solution comes complete with a visually engaging textbook in addition to an interactive eBook. Go to CourseMate for ORGB to begin using the eBook. Access at **www.cengagebrain.com**

...izational Behavior and Opportunity

...organizational behavior.

...behavior is individual behavior and group dynamics in organizations. The foundation of organizational behavior is human behavior, so the study of OB involves understanding ...onal value systems and examining the exter...onal behavior has grown out of contributions ...logy, management, and medicine.

To help you succeed, we have designed a review card for each chapter.

Key Terms

Here, you'll find the key terms and definitions in the order they appear in the chapter.

opportunities
Favorable times or chances for progress and advancement.

change
The transformation or modification of an organization and/or its stakeholders.

challenge
The call to competition, contest, or battle.

organizational behavior
The study of individual behavior and group dynamics in organizations.

psychology
The science of human behavior.

sociology
The science of society.

engineering
The applied science of energy and matter.

anthropology
The science of human learned behavior.

management
The study of overseeing activities and supervising people in organizations.

...ng positively in times of change.

Change is an opportunity when one has a positive attitude, asks questions, listens, and is committed to succeed. People in change situations often ... rigid and reactive, rather than open and responsive. This behavior works well in ... e of gradual, incremental change. However, rigid a... significant change.

In this column, you'll find summary points that give an overview of important concepts.

3 Identify the impor...

Organizations are open sy... task. The organization as a system also has an external task environment composed of different constituents, such as suppliers, customers, and federal regulators. The organization system takes inputs, converts them into throughputs, and delivers outputs to its task environment.

4 Describe the formal and informal elements of an organization.

Organization... ...ganization is the official, l... ...ganizations in logical and ra... elements of t... nization deve...

Flip to Assess
Flip the card over for a self-assessment that helps you explore how the chapter concepts relate to you personally.

5 Identify ... ...n the economy.

The United States has the largest economy in the world. It is composed of manufacturing ...vice organizations, privately owned companies, and nonprofit organizations; ...ur national well-being. Understanding a variety of organizations will help you ...appreciation for your own organization and for others in the world of private ...ses and nonprofit organizations.

How to Use This Card

1. Look over the card to preview the new concepts you'll be introduced to in the chapter.
2. Read the chapter to fully understand the material.
3. Go to class (and pay attention).
4. Review the card one more time to make sure you've registered the key concepts.
5. Don't forget, this card is only one of many ORGB learning tools available to help you succeed in your organizational behavior course.

...e opportunities that change creates for organizational behavior.

...challenges that managers face are driven by international competition and ...ds. Managers in this environment must be aware of the risks associated ...nd the marginalization of part-time workers. Organizations also face regular ...areas o... ...on.

structure
The systems of communication, authority and roles, and workflow.

formal organization
The official, legitimate, and most visible part of the system.

7 Demonstrate t... the study of org...

Prepare for Exams
When it's time to prepare for exams, use the card and the technique to the left to ensure successful study sessions.

Although organizational b... nizational behavior. Rathe... in learning. To enrich your study of organizational behavior, take the learning style inventory on the back of this card.

informal organization
The unofficial and less visible part of the system.

Hawthorne studies
Studies conducted during the 1920s and 1930s that suggested the importance of the informal organization.

objective knowledge
Knowledge that results from research and scientific activities.

skill development
The mastery of abilities essential to successful functioning in organizations.

Learning organizational behavior involves the following:

©Cengage Learning 2013

What about You? Learning Style Inventory

Directions: This 24-item survey is not timed. Answer each question as honestly as you can. Place a check on the appropriate line after each statement.

	OFTEN	SOMETIMES	SELDOM
1. Can remember more about a subject through the lecture method with information, explanations, and discussion.	___	___	___
2. Prefer information to be written on the chalkboard, with the use of visual aids and assigned readings.	___	___	___
3. Like to write things down or to take notes for visual review.	___	___	___
4. Prefer to use posters, models, or actual practice and some activities in class.	___	___	___
5. Require explanations of diagrams, graphs, or visual dire...			___
6. Enjoy wor...			
7. Am skillfu... making g...			___
8. Can tell if... pairs of s...			___
9. Remembe... several ti...			___
10. Can unde...			___
11. Do better at academic subjects by listening to lectures and tapes.	___	___	___
12. Play with coins or keys in pockets.	___	___	___
13. Learn to spell better by repeating the word out loud than by writing the word on paper.	___	___	___
14. Can better understand a news development by reading about it in the paper than by listening to the radio.	___	___	___
15. Chew gum, smoke, or snack during studies.	___	___	___
16. Feel the best way to remember is to picture it in my head.	___	___	___
17. Learn spelling by "finger spelling" words.	___	___	___
18. Would rather listen to a good lecture or speech than read about the same material in a textbook.	___	___	___
19. Am good at working and solving jigsaw puzzles and mazes.	___	___	___
20. Grip objects in hands during learning period.	___	___	___
21. Prefer listening to the news on the radio rather than reading about it in the newspaper.	___	___	___
22. Obtain information on an interesting subject by reading relevant materials.	___	___	___
23. Feel comfortable touching others, hugging, hand-shaking, etc.	___	___	___
24. Follow oral directions better than written ones.	___	___	___

> ### What about You?
> Each chapter has unique self-assessment tools to help you gain a better sense of how to apply the concepts from the chapter to your personal experience.

Scoring Procedures:

Score 5 points for each OFTEN, 3 points for each SOMETIMES, and 1 point for each SELDOM.

Visual Preference Score: 5 points each for questions 2 + 3 + 7 + 10 + 14 + 16 + 19 + 22 = ___

Auditory Preference Score: 5 points each for questions 1 + 5 + 8 + 11 + 13 + 18 + 21 + 24 = ___

Tactile Preference Score: 5 points each for questions 4 + 6 + 9 + 12 + 15 + 17 + 20 + 23 = ___

SOURCE: Adapted from J. N. Gardner and A. J. Jewler, *Your College Experience: Strategies for Success, Third Concise Edition* (Belmont, CA: Wadsworth/ITP, 1998), 62–63; E. Jensen, *Student Success Secrets*, 4th ed. (Hauppauge, NY: Barron's, 1996), 33–36.

Chapter 1 Organizational Behavior and Opportunity

1. Define *organizational behavior*. What is its focus?
2. Identify the four action steps for responding positively to change.
3. What is an organization? What are its four system components? Give an example of each.
4. Briefly describe the elements of the formal and the informal organization. Give examples of each.
5. Describe how competition and total quality are affecting organizational behavior.

Chapter 2 Challenges for Managers

1. What are Hofstede's five dimensions of cultural differences that affect work attitudes?
2. What are the primary sources of diversity in the U.S. workforce?
3. What are the potential benefits and problems of diversity?
4. What are some of the ethical challenges encountered in organizations?
5. Describe the difference between distributive and procedural justice.

Chapter 3 Personality, Perception, and Attribution

1. What are individual differences, and why should managers understand them?
2. Define *personality* and describe its origins.
3. Describe two theories of personality and explain what each contributes to our knowledge of personality.
4. What factors influence social perception? What are the barriers to social perception?
5. Describe the errors that affect the attribution process.

Chapter 4 Attitudes, Emotions, and Ethics

1. Discuss cultural differences in job satisfaction and organizational commitment.
2. Define *values*. Distinguish between instrumental values and terminal values.
3. What is the relationship between values and ethics?
4. How does locus of control affect ethical behavior?
5. What is Machiavellianism, and how does it relate to ethical behavior?

Chapter 5 Motivation at Work

1. What are the five categories of motivational needs described by Maslow? Give an example of how each can be satisfied.
2. What are the Theory X and Theory Y assumptions about people at work? How do they relate to the hierarchy of needs?
3. What three manifest needs does McClelland identify?
4. How do hygiene and motivational factors differ?
5. What are two new ideas in motivation that managers are using?

Chapter 6 Learning and Performance Management

1. Define the terms *learning*, *reinforcement*, *punishment*, and *extinction*.
2. What are the differences in the way introverted and extraverted and intuitive and sensing people learn?
3. What are the five characteristics of well-developed goals?
4. What are the benefits of 360-degree feedback?
5. What are the two possible attributions of poor performance? What are the implications of each?

Chapter 7 Stress and Well-Being at Work

1. Define *stress, distress,* and *strain.*
2. Describe four approaches to understanding stress.
3. What are the four changes associated with the stress response?
4. What is a nonwork demand? How does it affect an individual?
5. What are primary prevention, secondary prevention, and tertiary prevention?

Chapter 8 Communication

1. What are the three defining features of reflective listening?
2. What are the four levels of verbal response in reflective listening?
3. What are the five communication skills of effective supervisors and managers?
4. Describe dominant and subordinate defensive communication.
5. What is communicative disease?

Chapter 9 Work Teams and Groups

1. What is the difference between a group and a team?
2. What are the components of Tuckman's Five-Stage Model?
3. Describe the four characteristics of mature groups.
4. Describe five task and five maintenance functions that effective work teams must perform.
5. What are the benefits and potential drawbacks of self-managed teams?

Chapter 10 Decision Making by Individuals and Groups

1. List and describe Jung's four cognitive styles.
2. What are the individual and organizational influences on creativity?
3. What are the individual and organizational foundations of empowerment and teamwork?
4. Describe the advantages and disadvantages of group decision making.
5. Describe the symptoms of groupthink, and identify actions that can be taken to prevent it.

Chapter 11 Power and Political Behavior

1. What are the five types of power according to French and Raven? What are their effects?
2. What is information power?
3. What are the intergroup sources of power?
4. What are the four power-oriented characteristics of the best managers?
5. What are the symbols of power according to Kanter?

Chapter 12 Leadership and Followership

1. Define leadership and followership.
2. Distinguish between formal leadership and informal leadership.
3. Define transformational, charismatic, and authentic leadership.
4. Describe the differences between autocratic and democratic work environments. How do they differ from a laissez-faire workplace?
5. Define initiating structure and consideration as leader behaviors.

Chapter 13 Conflict and Negotiation

1. Discuss the differences between functional and dysfunctional conflict.
2. Identify the structural and personal factors that contribute to conflict.
3. Discuss the four major forms of conflict in organizations.
4. What defense mechanisms do people use in interpersonal conflict?
5. Identify five styles of conflict management.

Chapter 14 Jobs and the Design of Work

1. Describe six patterns of working that have been studied in different countries.
2. Describe four traditional approaches to the design of work in America.
3. What are the salient features of the social information-processing (SIP) model of job design?
4. How do the Japanese, German, and Scandinavian approaches to work differ from one another and from the American approach?
5. What are five emerging issues in jobs and the design of work?

Chapter 15 Organizational Design and Structure

1. Define differentiation and integration.
2. Describe the six basic dimensions of organizational design.
3. Identify four forces that are reshaping organizations today.
4. Discuss the nature of emerging organizational structures.
5. List four symptoms of structural weakness.

Chapter 16 Organizational Culture

1. Explain the three levels of organizational culture.
2. Describe five artifacts of culture and give an example of each.
3. Explain three theories about the relationship between organizational culture and performance.
4. Contrast adaptive and nonadaptive cultures.
5. Describe the three stages of organizational socialization. How is culture communicated in each stage?

Chapter 17 Career Management

1. What is a realistic job preview, and why is it important?
2. What are psychological contracts?
3. What stressors are associated with socialization?
4. What are the career functions provided by a mentor?
5. What are the two key issues to deal with during the maintenance career stage?

Chapter 18 Managing Change

1. What are the major external and internal forces for change in organizations?
2. Contrast incremental, strategic, and transformational change.
3. Name the four behavioral reactions to change.
4. Describe force field analysis and its relationship to Lewin's change model.
5. What is organization development? Why is it undertaken by organizations?

Key Terms

opportunities
Favorable times or chances for progress and advancement.

change
The transformation or modification of an organization and/or its stakeholders.

challenge
The call to competition, contest, or battle.

organizational behavior
The study of individual behavior and group dynamics in organizations.

psychology
The science of human behavior.

sociology
The science of society.

engineering
The applied science of energy and matter.

anthropology
The science of human learned behavior.

management
The study of overseeing activities and supervising people in organizations.

medicine
The applied science of healing or treating diseases to enhance an individual's health and well-being.

task
An organization's mission, purpose, or goal for existing.

people
The human resources of an organization.

technology
The tools, knowledge, and/or techniques used to transform inputs into outputs.

structure
The systems of communication, authority and roles, and workflow.

formal organization
The official, legitimate, and most visible part of the system.

>> In Review

Organizational Behavior and Opportunity

1 Define *organizational behavior.*

Organizational behavior is individual behavior and group dynamics in organizations. The foundation of organizational behavior is human behavior, so the study of OB involves understanding workers' behavior in terms of their history and personal value systems and examining the external factors to which a person is subject. Organizational behavior has grown out of contributions from psychology, sociology, engineering, anthropology, management, and medicine.

2 Identify four action steps for responding positively in times of change.

Change is an opportunity when one has a positive attitude, asks questions, listens, and is committed to succeed. People in change situations often become rigid and reactive, rather than open and responsive. This behavior works well in the face of gradual, incremental change. However, rigid and well-learned behavior may be counterproductive responses to significant change.

3 Identify the important system components of an organization.

Organizations are open systems composed of people, structure, and technology committed to a task. The organization as a system also has an external task environment composed of different constituents, such as suppliers, customers, and federal regulators. The organization system takes inputs, converts them into throughputs, and delivers outputs to its task environment.

4 Describe the formal and informal elements of an organization.

Organizations have formal and informal elements within them. The formal organization is the official, legitimate, and most visible part that enables people to think of organizations in logical and rational ways. The informal organization is unofficial and less visible. The informal elements of the organization are often points of diagnostic and intervention activities in organization development.

5 Identify factors that contribute to the diversity of organizations in the economy.

The United States has the largest economy in the world. It is composed of manufacturing organizations, service organizations, privately owned companies, and nonprofit organizations; all contribute to our national well-being. Understanding a variety of organizations will help you develop a greater appreciation for your own organization and for others in the world of private business enterprises and nonprofit organizations.

6 Describe the opportunities that change creates for organizational behavior.

The changes and challenges that managers face are driven by international competition and customer demands. Managers in this environment must be aware of the risks associated with downsizing and the marginalization of part-time workers. Organizations also face regular challenges in the areas of globalization, workforce diversity, ethics and character, and technological innovation.

7 Demonstrate the value of objective knowledge and skill development in the study of organizational behavior.

Although organizational behavior is an applied discipline, a student is not "trained" in organizational behavior. Rather, one is "educated" in organizational behavior and is a coproducer in learning. To enrich your study of organizational behavior, take the learning style inventory on the back of this card.

>>

informal organization
The unofficial and less visible part of the system.

Hawthorne studies
Studies conducted during the 1920s and 1930s that suggested the importance of the informal organization.

objective knowledge
Knowledge that results from research and scientific activities.

skill development
The mastery of abilities essential to successful functioning in organizations.

Learning organizational behavior involves the following:

Learning Activity

Mastery of basic objective knowledge

↓

Development of specific skills and abilities

↓

Application of knowledge and skills

©Cengage Learning 2013

What about You? Learning Style Inventory

Directions: This 24-item survey is not timed. Answer each question as honestly as you can. Place a check on the appropriate line after each statement.

	OFTEN	SOMETIMES	SELDOM
1. Can remember more about a subject through the lecture method with information, explanations, and discussion.	___	___	___
2. Prefer information to be written on the chalkboard, with the use of visual aids and assigned readings.	___	___	___
3. Like to write things down or to take notes for visual review.	___	___	___
4. Prefer to use posters, models, or actual practice and some activities in class.	___	___	___
5. Require explanations of diagrams, graphs, or visual directions.	___	___	___
6. Enjoy working with my hands or making things.	___	___	___
7. Am skillful with and enjoy developing and making graphs and charts.	___	___	___
8. Can tell if sounds match when presented with pairs of sounds.	___	___	___
9. Remember best by writing things down several times.	___	___	___
10. Can understand and follow directions on maps.	___	___	___
11. Do better at academic subjects by listening to lectures and tapes.	___	___	___
12. Play with coins or keys in pockets.	___	___	___
13. Learn to spell better by repeating the word out loud than by writing the word on paper.	___	___	___
14. Can better understand a news development by reading about it in the paper than by listening to the radio.	___	___	___
15. Chew gum, smoke, or snack during studies.	___	___	___
16. Feel the best way to remember is to picture it in my head.	___	___	___
17. Learn spelling by "finger spelling" words.	___	___	___
18. Would rather listen to a good lecture or speech than read about the same material in a textbook.	___	___	___
19. Am good at working and solving jigsaw puzzles and mazes.	___	___	___
20. Grip objects in hands during learning period.	___	___	___
21. Prefer listening to the news on the radio rather than reading about it in the newspaper.	___	___	___
22. Obtain information on an interesting subject by reading relevant materials.	___	___	___
23. Feel comfortable touching others, hugging, hand-shaking, etc.	___	___	___
24. Follow oral directions better than written ones.	___	___	___

Scoring Procedures:
Score 5 points for each OFTEN, 3 points for each SOMETIMES, and 1 point for each SELDOM.

Visual Preference Score: 5 points each for questions 2 + 3 + 7 + 10 + 14 + 16 + 19 + 22 = ___

Auditory Preference Score: 5 points each for questions 1 + 5 + 8 + 11 + 13 + 18 + 21 + 24 = ___

Tactile Preference Score: 5 points each for questions 4 + 6 + 9 + 12 + 15 + 17 + 20 + 23 = ___

SOURCE: Adapted from J. N. Gardner and A. J. Jewler, *Your College Experience: Strategies for Success, Third Concise Edition* (Belmont, CA: Wadsworth/ITP, 1998), 62–63; E. Jensen, *Student Success Secrets*, 4th ed. (Hauppauge, NY: Barron's, 1996), 33–36.

Challenges for Managers

1 Describe the factors that affect organizations competing in the global economy.

Globalization suggests that the world is free from national boundaries. In transnational organizations, the global viewpoint supersedes national issues; organizations operate across long distances and employ a multicultural mix of workers. Social and political issues affect global operations and strategy development.

2 Explain how cultural differences form the basis of work-related attitudes.

Individualistic cultures emphasize and encourage individual achievement, whereas collectivist cultures view group loyalty and unity as paramount. Other factors affecting work-related attitudes are power distance, uncertainty avoidance, masculinity versus femininity, and time orientation. Developing cross-cultural sensitivity training, cultural task forces, and global human resource management is critical to success.

3 Describe the challenges and positive influences diversity brings to today's business environment.

Diversity encompasses all forms of differences among individuals, including culture, gender, age, ability, religion, personality, social status, and sexual orientation. The benefits of diversity are human talent, marketing, creativity and innovation, problem solving, and flexibility. Potential problems are resistance to change, lack of cohesiveness, communication, conflicts, and decision making.

4 Discuss the role of ethics, character, and personal integrity in the organization.

Ethical theories help us understand, evaluate, and classify moral arguments; make decisions; and defend conclusions about what is right and wrong. Ethical theories can be classified as consequential, rule based, or character.

5 Explain five issues that pose ethical dilemmas for managers.

Organizations experience a variety of ethical and moral dilemmas such as employee rights, sexual harassment, organizational justice, whistle-blowing, and social responsibility. Managers can use ethical theories to guide them through moral choices and ethical decisions.

6 Describe the effects of technological advances on today's workforce.

Technological advances have prompted alternative work arrangements, improved working conditions, increased skilled jobs, and brought disadvantaged individuals into the workforce. They have also generated stress, workaholism, and fear of being replaced by technology or being displaced into jobs of lower skill levels.

Key Terms

transnational organization
An organization in which the global viewpoint supersedes national issues.

guanxi
The Chinese practice of building networks for social exchange.

expatriate manager
A manager who works in a country other than her or his home country.

individualism
A cultural orientation in which people belong to loose social frameworks, and their primary concern is for themselves and their families.

collectivism
A cultural orientation in which individuals belong to tightly knit social frameworks and depend strongly on extended families or clans.

power distance
The degree to which a culture accepts unequal distribution of power.

uncertainty avoidance
The degree to which a culture tolerates ambiguity and uncertainty.

masculinity
A cultural orientation in which assertiveness and materialism are valued.

femininity
A cultural orientation in which relationships and concern for others are valued.

time orientation
Whether a culture's values are oriented toward the future (long-term orientation) or toward the past and present (short-term orientation).

diversity
All forms of difference among individuals, including culture, gender, age, ability, religion, personality, social status, and sexual orientation.

>>

glass ceiling
A transparent barrier that keeps women from rising above a certain level in organizations.

consequential theory
An ethical theory that emphasizes the consequences or results of behavior.

rule-based theory
An ethical theory that emphasizes the character of the act itself rather than its effects.

character theory
An ethical theory that emphasizes the character, personal virtues, and intent of the individual.

distributive justice
The fairness of outcomes that individuals receive in an organization.

procedural justice
The fairness of the process by which outcomes are allocated in an organization.

whistle-blower
An employee who informs authorities of the wrongdoings of her or his company or coworkers.

social responsibility
The obligation of an organization to behave ethically in its social environment.

technology
The intellectual and mechanical processes used by an organization to transform inputs into products or services that meet its goals.

expert system
A computer-based application that uses a representation of human expertise in a specialized field of knowledge to solve problems.

robotics
The use of robots in organizations.

telecommuting
Electronically transmitting work from a home computer to the office.

reinvention
The creative application of new technology.

What about You? Planning for a Global Career

Think of a country you would like to work in, do business in, or visit. Find out about its culture, using Hofstede's dimensions as guidelines. You can use a variety of sources to accomplish this, particularly your school library, government offices, faculty members, or others who have global experience. Answer the following questions:

1. Is the culture individualistic or collectivist?

2. Is the power distance high or low?

3. Is uncertainty avoidance high or low?

4. Is the country masculine or feminine in its orientation?

5. Is the time orientation short term or long term?

6. How did you arrive at your answers to the first five questions?

7. How will these characteristics affect business practices in the country you chose to investigate?

What about You? How Much Do You Know about Sexual Harassment?

Indicate whether you believe each statement below is true (T) or false (F).

_____ **1.** Sexual harassment is unprofessional behavior.
_____ **2.** Sexual harassment is against the law in all fifty states.
_____ **3.** Sexual advances are a form of sexual harassment.
_____ **4.** A request for sexual activity is a form of sexual harassment.
_____ **5.** Verbal or physical conduct of a sexual nature may be sexual harassment.
_____ **6.** Sexual harassment occurs when submission to sex acts is a condition of employment.
_____ **7.** Sexual harassment occurs when submission to or rejection of sexual acts is a basis for perrformance evaluation.
_____ **8.** Sexual harassment occurs when behavior interferes with an employee's performance or creates an intimidating, hostile, and offensive environment.
_____ **9.** Sexual harassment may include physical contact of a sexual nature, such as touching.
_____ **10.** Sexual harassment requires that a person have the intent to harass, harm, or intimidate.

Scoring

All of the items are true except item 10, which is false. While somewhat ambiguous, sexual harassment is defined in the eyes of the beholder. Give yourself 1 point for each correct answer. Scores can range from 0 (poorly informed about sexual harassment) to 10 (well informed about sexual harassment). This score reflects how much you know about sexual harassment. If your score was less than 5, you need to learn more about sexual harassment.

SOURCE: See W. O'Donohue, ed., *Sexual Harassment* (Boston: Allyn & Bacon, 1997) for theory, research and treatment. See http://www.eeoc.gov/stats/harass.html for the latest statistics.

Chapter 3

Personality, Perception, and Attribution

1 Describe individual differences and explain why they are important in understanding organizational behavior.

Individual differences are skills, abilities, personalities, perceptions, attitudes, emotions, and ethics. To understand human behavior, we must know something about the person and something about the organization, work group, personal life situation, job characteristics, and environmental influences.

2 Articulate key personality traits and explain how they influence behavior in organizations.

Personality is an individual difference that lends consistency to a person's behavior. Two major theories, integrative approach and trait theory, state that personality affects attitude, performance, attendance, motivation, satisfaction, commitment, and occupational success at work.

3 Discuss how personality theories may be applied in organizations.

Managers assess the personalities of their organizations' members with projective tests, behavioral measures, and self-report questionnaires. These tests give practical insight into the personality and psychological traits of workers such as decision-making skills, management style, thought processes, diversity, and tolerance.

4 Define *social perception* and explain the factors that affect it.

Social perception is the process of interpreting information about another person. Management perceptions are affected by familiarity with the target, attitude, mood, and cognitive structure. The target's physical appearance, communication skills, and perceived intentions as well as characteristics of the situation influence perception. In an organization, virtually all management activities rely on perception.

5 Identify five common barriers to social perception and explain the difficulties they cause.

In organizations, expectations of an individual affect both the manager's behavior toward the individual and the individual's response. Five barriers to social perception are selective perception, stereotyping, first-impression error, projection, and self-fulfilling prophecies. Understanding social perception in organizations may lead to favorable performance evaluations, salary increases, and help individuals compete for jobs.

6 Explain the attribution process and how attributions affect managerial behavior.

Attribution theory explains how we pinpoint the causes of our own behavior (and performance) and that of others. Attribution theory has many applications in the workplace. We can attribute events to an internal source of responsibility or an external source. In other words, when we succeed, we take credit for it (internal source); when we fail, we blame the situation on other people (external source).

Key Terms

individual differences
The way in which factors such as skills, abilities, personalities, perceptions, attitudes, values, and ethics differ from one individual to another.

interactional psychology
The psychological approach to understanding human behavior that involves knowing something about the person and about the situation.

personality
A relatively stable set of characteristics that influence an individual's behavior.

trait theory
A personality theory that advocates breaking down behavior patterns into a series of observable traits in order to understand human behavior.

integrative approach
The broad theory that describes personality as a composite of an individual's psychological processes.

strong situation
A situation that overwhelms the effects of individual personalities by providing strong cues for appropriate behavior.

locus of control
An individual's generalized belief about internal control (self-control) versus external control (control by the situation or by others).

general self-efficacy
An individual's general belief that he or she is capable of meeting job demands in a wide variety of situations.

self-esteem
An individual's general feeling of self-worth.

self-monitoring
The extent to which people base their behavior on cues from other people and situations.

positive affect
An individual's tendency to accentuate the positive aspects of herself or himself, other people, and the world in general.

>>

negative affect

An individual's tendency to accentuate the negative aspects of himself or herself, other people, and the world in general.

projective test

A personality test that elicits an individual's response to abstract stimuli.

behavioral measures

Personality assessments that involve observing an individual's behavior in a controlled situation.

self-report questionnaire

A common personality assessment that involves an individual's responses to a series of questions.

Myers-Briggs Type Indicator® (MBTI) instrument

An instrument developed to measure Carl Jung's theory of individual differences.

Extraversion

Being energized by interaction with other people.

Introversion

Being energized by spending time alone.

Sensing

Gathering information through the five senses and focusing on what actually exists.

Intuition

Gathering information through a "sixth sense" and focusing on what could be.

Thinking

Making decisions in a logical, objective fashion.

Feeling

Making decisions in a personal, value-oriented way.

Judging

Preferring closure and completion in making decisions.

Perceiving

Preferring to explore many alternatives with flexibility and spontaneity.

social perception

The process of interpreting information about another person.

discounting principle

The assumption that an individual's behavior is accounted for by the situation.

selective perception

The tendency to select information that supports our individual viewpoints while discounting information that threatens our viewpoints.

What about You? What's Your Locus of Control?

Below is a short scale that can give you an idea of your locus of control. For each of the four items, circle the choice with which you most strongly agree.

1. **a.** Becoming a success is a matter of hard work; luck has little or nothing to do with it.
   b. Getting a good job depends mainly on being in the right place at the right time.
2. **a.** The average citizen can have an influence on government decisions.
   b. This world is run by the few people in power, and there is not much the little guy can do about it.
3. **a.** As far as world affairs are concerned, most of us are the victims of forces we can neither understand nor control.
   b. By taking an active part in political and social affairs, people can control world events.
4. **a.** With enough effort, we can wipe out political corruption.
   b. People have difficulty controlling the things politicians do in office.

Scoring Key:

The internal locus of control answers are: 1a, 2a, 3b, 4a.

The external locus of control answers are: 1b, 2b, 3a, 4b.

Determine which category you circled most frequently using this key. This gives you an approximation of your locus of control.

SOURCES: T. Adeyemi-Bello, "Validating Rotter's Locus of Control Scale with a Sample of Not-for-Profit Leaders," *Management Research News* 24 (2001): 25–35; J. B. Rotter, "Generalized Expectancies for Internal vs. External Locus of Control of Reinforcement," *Psychological Monographs* 80, No. 609 (1966).

stereotype

A generalization about a group of people.

first-impression error

Forming lasting opinions about an individual based on initial perceptions.

projection

Overestimating the number of people who share our own beliefs, values, and behaviors.

self-fulfilling prophecy

Allowing expectations about people to affect our interaction with them in such a way that those expectations are fulfilled.

impression management

The process by which individuals try to control the impressions others have of them.

attribution theory

A theory that explains how individuals pinpoint the causes of their own and others' behavior.

fundamental attribution error

The tendency to make attributions to internal causes when focusing on someone else's behavior.

self-serving bias

The tendency to attribute one's own successes to internal causes and one's failures to external causes.

Attitudes, Emotions, and Ethics

1 Explain the ABC model of an attitude.

Attitudes are closely linked to behavior and are an integral part of the world of work. Attitudes are a response to an entity (person, object, situation, or issue) on an affective, cognitive, or behavioral basis. People prefer consistency between attitudes and behavior. Disruption causes tension, which motivates individuals to change attitudes or behavior to maintain consistency. The tension produced by a conflict between attitudes and behavior is *cognitive dissonance.*

2 Describe how attitudes are formed.

Attitudes are learned. Influences on attitudes are direct experience and social learning. Culture also plays a definitive role in attitude development. Attitude–behavior correspondence depends on five things: attitude specificity, attitude relevance, timing of measurement, personality factors, and social constraints. Attitudes affect work behavior. Demanding jobs over which employees have little control negatively affect their work attitudes. A positive psychological climate can generate positive attitudes and good performance.

3 Identify sources of job satisfaction and commitment.

Job satisfaction is a pleasurable or positive emotional state resulting from the appraisal of one's job or job experiences. It has been treated as a general attitude and as satisfaction with five specific dimensions of the job: pay, the work itself, promotion opportunities, supervision, and coworkers. Rewards are key to influencing both job satisfaction and work performance if valued by employees and tied directly to performance.

4 Distinguish between organizational citizenship and workplace deviance behaviors.

Individuals who identify strongly with the organization are more likely to perform *organizational citizenship behavior*—behavior above and beyond the call of duty. A misfit between an individual's and the organization's values is called a lack of person–organization fit. Dissatisfied workers are likely to skip work and quit jobs. *Workplace deviance behavior* is a result of negative attitudes and consists of counterproductive behavior that violates organizational norms and harms others or the organization.

5 Identify the characteristics of the source, target, and message that affect persuasion.

Through persuasion, one individual (the source) tries to change the attitude of another person (the target). Three major characteristics of the source affect persuasion: expertise, trustworthiness, and attractiveness. Targets with low self-esteem or in a good mood are easier to persuade. Individuals with extreme attitudes or high self-esteem are more resistant. The elaboration likelihood model proposes that persuasion occurs either through a central route or peripheral route, differentiated by the amount of elaboration, scrutiny, or motivation in the message.

6 Discuss the definition and importance of emotions at work.

Emotions are mental states including feelings, physiological changes, and the inclination to act and are normal parts of human functioning and decision making. Positive emotions that travel through a work group produce cooperation and task performance. The opposite also occurs when negative emotions destroy morale and performance.

Key Terms

attitude
A psychological tendency expressed by evaluating something with a degree of favor or disfavor.

affect
The emotional component of an attitude.

cognitive dissonance
A state of tension produced when an individual experiences conflict between attitudes and behavior.

social learning
The process of deriving attitudes from family, peer groups, religious organizations, and culture.

job satisfaction
A pleasurable or positive emotional state resulting from the appraisal of one's job or job experiences.

organizational citizenship behavior (OCB)
Behavior that is above and beyond the call of duty.

workplace deviance behavior (WDB)
Any voluntary counterproductive behavior that violates organizational norms and causes some degree of harm to organizational functioning.

organizational commitment
The strength of an individual's identification with an organization.

affective commitment
Organizational commitment based on an individual's desire to remain in an organization.

continuance commitment
Organizational commitment based on the fact that an individual cannot afford to leave.

normative commitment
Organizational commitment based on an individual's perceived obligation to remain with an organization.

Glossary terms (left column)

emotions
Mental states that include feelings, physiological changes, and the inclination to act.

emotional contagion
A dynamic process through which the emotions of one person are transferred to another, either consciously or unconsciously, through nonverbal channels.

ethical behavior
Acting in ways consistent with one's personal values and the commonly held values of the organization and society.

values
Enduring beliefs that a specific mode of conduct or end state of existence is personally or socially preferable to an opposite or converse mode of conduct or end state of existence.

instrumental values
Values that shape the acceptable behaviors that can be used to achieve some goal or end state.

terminal values
Values that influence the goals to be achieved or the end states of existence.

Machiavellianism
A personality characteristic involving one's willingness to do whatever it takes to get one's own way.

cognitive moral development
The process of moving through stages of maturity with regard to making ethical decisions.

---

7 Contrast the effects of individual and organizational influences on ethical behavior.

Ethical behavior is behavior that is consistent with one's personal values and the commonly held values of the organization and society. Firms with better reputations attract more applicants, creating a larger hiring pool, and evidence suggests that respected firms can choose higher-quality applicants. Unethical behavior by employees can affect individuals, work teams, and even the organization.

8 Identify the factors that affect ethical behavior.

Factors that influence an individual's ethical behavior are values, locus of control, *Machiavellianism* (one's willingness to do whatever it takes to get one's own way), and an individual's level of *cognitive moral development.* Organizations can offer guidance by encouraging ethical behavior through codes of conduct, ethics committees, ethics communication systems, training, norms, modeling, and rewards and punishments.

What about You? Assess Your Job Satisfaction

Think of the job you have now or a job you've had in the past. Indicate how satisfied you are with each aspect of your job below, using the following scale:

**1 Extremely dissatisfied   2 Dissatisfied   3 Slightly dissatisfied   4 Neutral
5 Slightly satisfied   6 Satisfied   7 Extremely satisfied**

1. The amount of job security I have.
2. The amount of pay and fringe benefits I receive.
3. The amount of personal growth and development I get in doing my job.
4. The people I talk to and work with on my job.
5. The degree of respect and fair treatment I receive from my boss.
6. The feeling of worthwhile accomplishment I get from doing my job.
7. The chance to get to know other people while on the job.
8. The amount of support and guidance I receive from my supervisor.
9. The degree to which I am fairly paid for what I contribute to this organization.
10. The amount of independent thought and action I can exercise in my job.
11. How secure things look for me in the future in this organization.
12. The chance to help other people while at work.
13. The amount of challenge in my job.
14. The overall quality of the supervision I receive on my work.

Scoring

Now, compute your scores for the facets of job satisfaction.

Pay satisfaction:
Q2 + Q9 = ____ Divided by 2: ____

Security satisfaction:
Q1 + Q11 = ____ Divided by 2: ____

Social satisfaction:
Q4 + Q7 + Q12 = ____ Divided by 3: ____

Supervisory satisfaction:
Q5 + Q8 + Q14 = ____ Divided by 3: ____

Growth satisfaction:
Q3 + Q6 + Q10 + Q13 = ____ Divided by 4: ____

Scores on the facets range from 1 to 7. (Scores lower than 4 suggest there is room for change.)

This questionnaire is an abbreviated version of the Job Diagnostic Survey, a widely used tool for assessing individuals' attitudes about their jobs. Compare your scores on each facet to the following norms for a large sample of managers.

Pay satisfaction: 4.6   Security satisfaction: 5.2   Social satisfaction: 5.6
Supervisory satisfaction: 5.2   Growth satisfaction: 5.3

How do your scores compare? Are there actions you can take to improve your job satisfaction?

SOURCE: *Work Redesign* by Hackman/Oldham, © 1980. Reprinted by permission of Pearson Education, Inc., Upper Saddle River, N.J.

Chapter 5

Motivation at Work

Key Terms

motivation
The process of arousing and sustaining goal-directed behavior.

psychoanalysis
Sigmund Freud's method for delving into the unconscious mind to better understand a person's motives and needs.

self-interest
What is in the best interest of and benefit to an individual.

Theory X
A set of assumptions managers might apply to individuals who are motivated by lower order needs.

Theory Y
A set of assumptions managers might apply to individuals who are motivated by higher order needs.

ERG theory
A theory that organizes human needs into the categories of existence, relatedness, and growth.

manifest needs
Learned or acquired needs that are easily perceived.

need for achievement
A manifest need that concerns excellence, competition, challenging goals, persistence, and overcoming difficulties.

need for power
A manifest need that concerns the desire to influence others, change people or events, and make a difference in life.

need for affiliation
A manifest need to establish and maintain warm, close, intimate relationships with other people.

motivation factor
A work condition that satisfies the need for psychological growth.

1 Define *motivation* and articulate different views of how individuals are motivated at work.

Motivation is the process of arousing and sustaining goal-directed behavior. Motivation theories may be broadly classified into internal, process, and external theories. A comprehensive approach to understanding motivation, behavior, and performance must consider three elements of the work situation—the individual, the job, and the work environment—and how these elements interact.

2 Explain Maslow's hierarchy of needs and its two main modifications.

Douglas McGregor used Maslow's need theory to explain motivation. McGregor's Theory X assumptions are appropriate for employees motivated by lower order needs—physiological and safety needs. Theory Y assumptions apply to employees motivated by higher order needs—social, esteem, and self-actualization. Clayton Alderfer's ERG theory of motivation grouped human needs into three basic categories: existence, relatedness, and growth. He explains both progressive need gratification and regression when people face frustration.

3 Discuss how the needs for achievement, power, and affiliation influence an individual's behavior in the workplace.

David McClelland identified three learned or acquired needs, called manifest needs. The *need for achievement* encompasses excellence, competition, challenging goals, persistence, and overcoming difficulties. The *need for power* includes the desire to influence others, the urge to change people or events, and the wish to make a difference in life. The *need for affiliation* means an urge to establish and maintain warm, close, intimate relationships with others.

4 Describe the two-factor theory of motivation.

Frederick Herzberg's two-factor theory examined experiences that satisfied or dissatisfied people at work. Motivation factors relate to job satisfaction; hygiene factors relate to job dissatisfaction. Motivation factors are responsibility, achievement, recognition, advancement, and the work itself. Hygiene factors are company policy and administration, technical supervision, salary, interpersonal relations with one's supervisor, working conditions, salary, and status. Excellent hygiene factors result in employees being *not dissatisfied.*

5 Explain two new ideas in human motivation.

Positive organizational scholarship links eustress to investing in strengths, finding positive meaning in work, displaying courage and principled action, and drawing on positive emotions at work. A second idea, by Jim Loehr, centers on positive energy and full engagement. This approach suggests that individuals do not need to be activated by fulfilling unmet needs but are already activated by their own physical, emotional, mental, and spiritual energy.

6 Describe the role of inequity in motivation.

Equity theory is a social exchange process theory of motivation that focuses on the individual–environment interaction. Individuals and organizations want an equitable arrangement for both members of the relationship. Inequity occurs when a person receives more, or less, than the person believes is deserved based on effort and/or contribution.

7 Describe the expectancy theory of motivation.

Vroom's expectancy theory of motivation focuses on personal perceptions of the performance process. The key constructs in the expectancy theory of motivation are *valence*, *expectancy*, and *instrumentality.* Valence is the value or importance one places on a particular reward. Expectancy is the belief that effort leads to performance. Instrumentality is the belief that performance is related to rewards.

Glossary

hygiene factor
A work condition that generates dissatisfaction due to discomfort or pain.

eustress
Healthy, normal stress.

inequity
A situation in which a person perceives that he or she is receiving less than he or she is giving or is giving less than he or she is receiving.

equity sensitive
An individual who prefers an equity ratio equal to that of his or her comparison other.

benevolent
An individual who is comfortable with an equity ratio less than that of his or her comparison other.

entitled
An individual who is comfortable with an equity ratio greater than that of his or her comparison other.

valence
The value or importance one places on a particular reward.

expectancy
The belief that effort leads to performance.

instrumentality
The belief that performance is related to rewards.

moral maturity
The measure of a person's cognitive moral development.

---

8 Describe the cultural differences in motivation.

Most motivation theories in use today have been developed by and about Americans. When researchers have examined the universality of these theories, they have found that the studies did not replicate the results found in the United States due to cultural differences.

What about You? How Strong Is Your Protestant Work Ethic?

Rate the following statements from 1 (for *disagree completely*) to 6 (for *agree completely*).

_____ **1.** When the workday is finished, people should forget their jobs and enjoy themselves.

_____ **2.** Hard work makes us better people.

_____ **3.** The principal purpose of a job is to provide people with the means for enjoying their free time.

_____ **4.** Wasting time is as bad as wasting money.

_____ **5.** Whenever possible, a person should relax and accept life as it is rather than always striving for unreachable goals.

_____ **6.** A good indication of a person's worth is how well she does her job.

_____ **7.** If all other things are equal, it is better to have a job with a lot of responsibility than one with little responsibility.

_____ **8.** People who "do things the easy way" are the smart ones.

Scoring

_____ Total your score for the pro-Protestant work ethic items (2, 4, 6, and 7).

_____ Total your score for the non-Protestant work ethic items (1, 3, 5, and 8).

A pro-Protestant work ethic score of 20 or over indicates you have a strong work ethic; 15–19 indicates a moderately strong work ethic; 9–14 indicates a moderately weak work ethic; 8 or less indicates a weak work ethic.

A non-Protestant work ethic score of 20 or over indicates you have a strong non-work ethic; 15–19 indicates a moderately strong non-work ethic; 9–14 indicates a moderately weak non-work ethic; 8 or less indicates a weak non-work ethic.

SOURCE: M. R. Blood, "Work Values and Job Satisfaction," *Journal of Applied Psychology* 53 (1969): 456–459. Copyright © 1969 by the American Psychological Association. Reprinted with permission.

What about You? What's Important to Employees?

There are many possible job rewards that employees may receive. Listed below are ten possible job reward factors. Rank these factors three times. First, rank them as you think the average employee would rank them. Second, rank them as you think the average employee's supervisor would rank them for the employee. Finally, rank them according to what you consider important. Your instructor has normative data for 1,000 employees and their supervisors that will help you interpret your results and place the results in the context of Maslow's need hierarchy and Herzberg's two-factor theory of motivation.

Employee	Supervisor	You	
_____	_____	_____	**1.** job security
_____	_____	_____	**2.** full appreciation of work done
_____	_____	_____	**3.** promotion and growth in the organization
_____	_____	_____	**4.** good wages
_____	_____	_____	**5.** interesting work
_____	_____	_____	**6.** good working conditions
_____	_____	_____	**7.** tactful discipline
_____	_____	_____	**8.** sympathetic help with personal problems
_____	_____	_____	**9.** personal loyalty to employees
_____	_____	_____	**10.** sense of inclusivity

SOURCE: "Crossed Wires on Employee Motivation," *Training and Development* 49 (1995): 59–60. American Society for Training and Development. Reprinted with permission. All rights reserved.

Chapter 6

Learning and Performance Management

Key Terms

learning
A change in behavior acquired through experience.

classical conditioning
Modifying behavior by pairing a conditioned stimulus with an unconditioned stimulus to elicit an unconditioned response.

operant conditioning
Modifying behavior through the use of positive or negative consequences following specific behaviors.

positive consequences
Results of a behavior that a person finds attractive or pleasurable.

negative consequences
Results of a behavior that a person finds unattractive or aversive.

reinforcement
A strategy to cultivate desirable behavior by either bestowing positive consequences or withholding negative consequences.

punishment
A strategy to discourage undesirable behavior by either bestowing negative consequences or withholding positive consequences.

extinction
A strategy to weaken a behavior by attaching no consequences to it.

task-specific self-efficacy
An individual's internal expectancy to perform a specific task effectively.

goal setting
The process of establishing desired results that guide and direct behavior.

management by objectives (MBO)
A goal-setting program based on interaction and negotiation between employees and managers.

1 Describe behavioral theories of learning.

The behaviorist approach to learning assumes that observable behavior is a function of its consequences. Behaviorists argue that learning stems from classical and operant conditioning. *Classical conditioning* is the process of modifying behavior so that pairing a conditioned stimulus with an unconditioned stimulus elicits an unconditioned response. *Operant conditioning* is the process of modifying behavior by following specific behaviors with positive or negative consequences. Reinforcement enhances desirable behavior, while punishment and extinction diminish undesirable behavior.

2 Describe social and cognitive theories of learning.

The social learning theory occurs when we observe other people and model their behavior. Central to the theory is the notion of *task-specific self-efficacy,* an individual's beliefs and expectancies about his or her ability to perform a task effectively. In the cognitive theory, the personality functions of intuition, sensing, thinking, and feeling have learning implications. Each person has a preferred mode of gathering, evaluating, and making decisions about information.

3 Explain how goal setting can be used to direct learning and performance.

Goal setting is the process of establishing desired results that guide and direct behavior. Goals often increase employee effort and motivation, which in turn improve task performance. Goal setting also reduces the role of stress associated with conflicting and confusing expectations because it clarifies the task–role expectations for employees. The third major function of goal setting is improving the accuracy and validity of performance evaluation.

4 Define *performance* and identify the tools used to measure it.

Performance is most often called task accomplishment. *Performance management* is a process of defining, measuring, appraising, providing feedback on, and improving performance. Performance appraisals give employees feedback on performance, identify the employees' developmental needs, and influence promotion and reward decisions, demotion and termination decisions, and information about selection and placement decisions. Electronic performance-monitoring systems, goal setting, and MBO are performance appraisal methods.

5 Explain the importance of performance feedback and how it can be delivered effectively.

Good performance appraisal systems develop people, enhance careers, and boost individual and team achievements in an organization. Effective performance appraisal systems have five key characteristics: validity, reliability, responsiveness, flexibility, and equitability. The supervisor must establish mutual trust, be vulnerable and open to challenge, and be a skilled, empathetic listener who encourages employees to discuss their aspirations.

6 Identify ways managers can reward performance.

Performance rewards can be pay, rewards, trust, fun, and meaningful work. Individual reward systems foster autonomous, independent behavior; and encourage creativity, problem solving, and distinctive contributions. At the individual level, these include skill-based and pay-for-knowledge systems. Team reward systems encourage cooperation, joint efforts, and the sharing of information and expertise. At the group level, gain-sharing plans emphasize collective cost reduction by allowing workers to share in the gains achieved by reducing production costs.

>>

performance management
A process of defining, measuring, appraising, providing feedback on, and improving performance.

performance appraisal
The evaluation of a person's performance.

360-degree feedback
A process of self-evaluation and evaluations by a manager, peers, direct reports, and possibly customers.

consensus
An informational cue indicating the extent to which peers in the same situation behave in a similar fashion.

distinctiveness
An informational cue indicating the degree to which an individual behaves the same way in other situations.

consistency
An informational cue indicating the frequency of behavior over time.

mentoring
A work relationship that encourages development and career enhancement for people moving through the career cycle.

7 List several strategies for correcting poor performance.

Harold Kelley's attribution theory aims to explain behavior based on shared perceptions and attitudes between supervisors and employees. Internal attributions might include low effort, lack of commitment, or lack of ability. External attributions might include equipment failure or unrealistic goals. Supervisors may express personal concern, reprimand the employee, or provide training. They may provide coaching, counseling, mentoring, or refer the employee to trained professionals.

What about You? How Do You Correct Poor Performance?

At one time or another, each of us has had a poor performance of some kind. It may have been a poor test result in school, a poor presentation at work, or a poor performance in an athletic event. Think of a poor performance event that you have experienced and work through the following three steps.

Step 1. Briefly describe the specific event in some detail. Include why you label it a poor performance (bad score? someone else's evaluation?).

Step 2. Analyze the poor performance.
    a. List all the possible contributing causes to the poor performance. Be specific, such as the room was too hot, you did not get enough sleep, you were not told how to perform the task, etc. You might ask other people for possible ideas, too.
        1. _____
        2. _____
        3. _____
        4. _____
        5. _____
        6. _____
        7. _____
    b. Is there a primary cause for the poor performance? What is it?

Step 3. Plan to correct the poor performance.

Develop a step-by-step plan of action that specifies what you can change or do differently to improve your performance the next time you have an opportunity. Include seeking help if it is needed. Once your plan is developed, look for an opportunity to execute it.

Chapter 7

Key Terms

stress
The unconscious preparation to fight or flee that a person experiences when faced with any demand.

stressor
The person or event that triggers the stress response.

distress
The adverse psychological, physical, behavioral, and organizational consequences that may arise as a result of stressful events.

strain
Distress.

homeostasis
A steady state of bodily functioning and equilibrium.

ego-ideal
The embodiment of a person's perfect self.

self-image
How a person sees himself or herself, both positively and negatively.

workaholism
An imbalanced preoccupation with work at the expense of home and personal life satisfaction.

participation problem
A cost associated with absenteeism, tardiness, strikes and work stoppages, and turnover.

performance decrement
A cost resulting from poor quality or low quantity of production, grievances, and unscheduled machine downtime and repair.

compensation award
An organizational cost resulting from court awards for job distress.

Type A behavior pattern
A complex of personality and behavioral characteristics, including competitiveness, time urgency, social status insecurity, aggression, hostility, and a quest for achievements.

>> In Review

Stress and Well-Being at Work

1 Define *stress, distress,* and *strain.*

Stress, or the stress response, is the unconscious preparation to fight or flee experienced when faced with any demand. A *stressor,* or demand, is the person or event triggering the stress response. *Distress* or *strain* refers to adverse psychological, physical, behavioral, and organizational consequences that may occur as a result of stressful events.

2 Compare four different approaches to stress.

There are four principal approaches to stress. Walter B. Cannon developed the homeostatic/medical approach because he believed stress resulted when an external, environmental demand upset the *homeostasis.* Richard Lazarus's cognitive appraisal approach saw stress as a result of a person–environment interaction, yet emphasized cognitive appraisal in classifying persons or events as stressful. Robert Kahn's person–environment fit approach claimed that confusing and conflicting expectations of social roles create stress. Harry Levinson's psychoanalytic approach believed the *ego-ideal* and the *self-image* interact to cause stress.

3 Explain the psychophysiology of the stress response.

The stress response begins with the release of chemical messengers, primarily adrenaline, into the bloodstream. These messengers activate the sympathetic nervous system and endocrine (hormone) system to trigger mind–body changes to prepare the person for fight or flight. As the body responds, the person shifts from a neutral posture to an offensive posture.

4 Identify work and nonwork causes of stress.

Major categories of work demands that cause stress are role conflict, role ambiguity, task demands, role demands, interpersonal demands, and physical demands. Nonwork demands may broadly be identified as home demands from an individual's personal life environment and personal demands that are self-imposed.

5 Describe the consequences of stress.

Positive stress can create *eustress,* while negative stress, or distress, can erode morale and performance. Three forms of individual distress are: *psychological distress, medical illnesses,* and *behavioral problems.* The symptoms of *organizational stress* are: low morale, dissatisfaction, communication breakdowns, and disruption of working relationships. Three major costs of *organizational distress* are: participation problems, performance decrements, and compensation awards.

6 Discuss individual factors that influence a person's response to stress and strain.

Individual differences, such as gender and Type A behavior pattern, enhance vulnerability to strain under stressful conditions. Other individual differences, such as personality hardiness and self-reliance, reduce vulnerability to strain under stressful conditions.

7 Identify the stages and elements of preventive stress management for individuals and organizations.

The three stages of prevention are primary, secondary, and tertiary prevention. *Primary prevention* is intended to reduce, modify, or eliminate the demand or stressor causing stress. *Secondary prevention* is intended to alter or modify the individual's or the organization's response to a demand or stressor. *Tertiary prevention* is intended to heal individual or organizational symptoms of distress and strain.

>>

personality hardiness
A personality characterized by commitment, control, and challenge and, hence, resistant to distress.

transformational coping
A way of managing stressful events by changing them into less subjectively stressful events.

self-reliance
A healthy, secure, interdependent pattern of behavior related to how people form and maintain supportive attachments with others.

counterdependence
An unhealthy, insecure pattern of behavior that leads to separation in relationships with other people.

overdependence
An unhealthy, insecure pattern of behavior that leads to preoccupied attempts to achieve security through relationships.

preventive stress management
An organizational philosophy according to which people and organizations should take joint responsibility for promoting health and preventing distress and strain.

primary prevention
The stage in preventive stress management designed to reduce, modify, or eliminate the demand or stressor causing stress.

secondary prevention
The stage in preventive stress management designed to alter or modify the individual's or the organization's response to a demand or stressor.

tertiary prevention
The stage in preventive stress management designed to heal individual or organizational symptoms of distress and strain.

What about You? Are You Self-Reliant?

Each of the following questions relates to how you form relationships with people at work, at home, and in other areas of your life. Read each statement carefully and rate each on a scale from 0 (strongly disagree) to 5 (strongly agree) to describe your degree of disagreement or agreement with the statement. *Answer all 15 questions.*

Am I Overstressed?

____ **1.** It is difficult for me to delegate work to others.
____ **2.** Developing close relationships at work will backfire on you.
____ **3.** I avoid depending on other people because I feel crowded by close relationships.
____ **4.** I am frequently suspicious of other people's motives and intentions.
____ **5.** Asking for help makes me feel needy, and I do not like that.
____ **6.** It is difficult for me to leave home or work to go to the other.
____ **7.** People will always be there when I need them.
____ **8.** I regularly and easily spend time with other people during the workday.
____ **9.** I trust at least two other people to have my best interests at heart.
____ **10.** I have a healthy, happy home life.
____ **11.** I need to have colleagues or subordinates close in order to feel secure about my work.

Scoring

Follow the instructions to determine your score for each subscale of the Self-Reliance Inventory. *Note: Question 6 is used twice in scoring.*

Self-Reliance/Counterdependence

Step 1: Total your responses to Questions 1–6 ___
Step 2: Total your responses to Questions 7–10 ___
Step 3: Subtract your Step 2 total from 20 (20 – ___) = ___
Step 4: Add your results in Steps 1 and 3 ___

Self-Reliance/Overdependence

Step 5: Total your responses to Questions 6 and 11–15 ___
A score lower than 16 in Step 4 or Step 5 indicates self-reliance on that particular subscale. A score higher than 20 in Step 4 suggests possible counterdependence, and a score higher than 20 in Step 5 suggests possible overdependence.

SOURCE: Adapted from J. C. Quick, D. L. Nelson, and J. D. Quick, "The Self-Reliance Inventory," in J. W. Pfeiffer, ed., *The 1991 Annual: Developing Human Resources* (San Diego: Pfeiffer & Co., 1991), 149–161.

Chapter 8

>> In Review

Communication

Key Terms

communication
The evoking of a shared or common meaning in another person.

interpersonal communication
Communication between two or more people in an organization.

communicator
The person sending a message.

receiver
The person accepting a message.

perceptual screen
A window through which one interacts with others. It influences the quality, accuracy, and clarity of the communication.

message
The thoughts and feelings that the communicator is attempting to evoke in the receiver.

feedback
Information fed back that completes two-way communication.

language
The words, their pronunciations, and the methods of combining them used and understood by a group of people.

data
Uninterpreted and unanalyzed elements of a message.

information
Data that have been interpreted, analyzed, and have meaning to some user.

richness
The ability of a medium to convey meaning to a receiver.

reflective listening
Carefully listening to a message and immediately repeating it back to the speaker.

two-way communication
An interactive form of communication in which there is an exchange of thoughts, feelings, or both.

1 Describe the interpersonal communication process and the role of listening in the process.

Interpersonal communication is reflective, objective, and perceptual. The conceptual and emotional component of messages is affected by verbal and nonverbal communication and is key to understanding and verifying the message. Reflective listening enables the listener to understand the communicator's meaning, reduce perceptual distortions, and overcome interpersonal barriers that lead to communication failures.

2 Describe the five communication skills of effective supervisors.

Five communication skills that distinguish "good" from "bad" supervisors include being expressive speakers, empathetic listeners, persuasive leaders, sensitive people, and informative managers.

3 Explain five communication barriers and the gateways through them.

Barriers to communication in the workplace are physical separation, status differences, gender differences, cultural diversity, and language. Awareness and recognition are the first steps to overcoming barriers. Other gateways are recognizing differences in gender-specific conversation style, understanding cultural differences, and avoiding technical terms and jargon.

4 Distinguish between civility and incivility, and defensive and nondefensive communication.

Civility is communication that respects the integrity and dignity of the individual. It carries the potential to avoid hurt feelings, prevent harm and damage to working relationships, and contribute to well-being in the workplace. *Incivility* is communication that respects the integrity and dignity of the individual. It can create a barrier between people and jar emotions, though the consequences of incivility depend on its source. *Defensive communication* includes aggressive and angry communication as well as passive, withdrawing communication. *Nondefensive communication* is an assertive, direct, powerful form of communication.

5 Explain the impact of nonverbal communication.

Most meaning in a message is conveyed nonverbally. *Nonverbal communication* includes all elements of communication, such as gestures and the use of space, that do not involve words or language. The four basic kinds of nonverbal communication that managers need to understand and read are proxemics, kinesics, facial and eye behavior, and paralanguage.

6 Explain positive, healthy communication.

James Lynch suggests that heartfelt communication may be equally or more important than cognition in the communication process. According to Lynch, positive, healthy communication is exemplified by trust and truthfulness, core values and beliefs, strong ethical character, personal integrity, openness, and simplicity in communication.

7 Identify how new communication technologies and social media affect the communication process.

Technologies such as cell phones, e-mail, voice mail, faxes, computers, and informational databases provide instant exchange of volumes of information and render geographic boundaries and time zones irrelevant. Lack of personal interaction and nonverbal cues alter the social context of exchange and remove organizational barriers. The potential for information overload, constant accessibility to work, and multitasking also affects behavior.

>>

one-way communication
Communication in which a person sends a message to another person and no feedback, questions, or interaction follows.

barriers to communication
Factors that distort, disrupt, or even halt successful communication.

gateways to communication
Openings that break down communication barriers.

civility
Communication and behavior that respect the integrity and dignity of the individual.

incivility
Discourteous communication and rude behavior that are disrespectful, hurtful, or injurious.

defensive communication
Messages that are aggressive, malevolent, passive, or withdrawn.

nondefensive communication
Messages that are assertive, direct, and powerful.

nonverbal communication
All elements of communication that do not involve words or language.

proxemics
The study of an individual's perception and use of space.

territorial space
Bands of concentric space radiating outward from the body.

kinesics
The study of body movement and posture.

communicative disease
Loneliness and social isolation resulting from the absence of heartfelt communication in relationships.

information communication technology (ICT)
An extensive category of new developments in interpersonal communication that allow fast, even immediate, access to information.

What about You? Test Your Verbal Incivilities

Common everyday incivilities are those behaviors that are thought of as rude or inconsiderate. Incivilities generally fall into one of two categories: physical or verbal.

Think about the range of interpersonal communications in which you participate on a weekly basis. In the first column, indicate how often you have experienced any of these behaviors. In the second column, indicate how often you have engaged in any of these behaviors.

Behavior

Others	You	
_____	_____	Use of inappropriate language (swearing, making sexual remarks)
_____	_____	Display of verbal aggression (using abusive or threatening language)
_____	_____	Use of mobile phones in an inappropriate way (answering calls during funerals, church services, meetings, interviews, or other similar social settings)

Look at the number of marks in the "You" column. If you notice a lot of marks, consider making a conscience effort to reduce or eliminate these uncivil behaviors altogether.

SOURCE: Adapted from T. Phillips and P. Smith, "Everyday Incivility: Towards a Benchmark," *The Sociological Review* 51 (2003): 85–105.

FIGURE 8.2 Zones of Territorial Space in U.S. Culture

Zone a, **intimate space:** spouses, significant others, family members, and others with whom one has an intimate relationship
Zone b, **personal distance:** friends
Zone c, **social distance:** business associates and acquaintances
Zone d, **public distance:** strangers

©iStockphoto.com/Andreas Rodriguez

Chapter 9

Key Terms

group
Two or more people with common interests, objectives, and continuing interaction.

work team
A group of people with complementary skills who are committed to a common mission, performance goals, and approach for which they hold themselves mutually accountable.

teamwork
Joint action by a team of people in which individual interests are subordinated to team unity.

psychological intimacy
Emotional and psychological closeness to other team or group members.

integrated involvement
Closeness achieved through tasks and activities.

norms of behavior
The standards that a work group uses to evaluate the behavior of its members.

group cohesion
The "interpersonal glue" that makes members of a group stick together.

social loafing
The failure of a group member to contribute personal time, effort, thoughts, or other resources to the group.

loss of individuality
A social process in which individual group members lose self-awareness and its accompanying sense of accountability, inhibition, and responsibility for individual behavior.

status structure
The set of authority and task relations among a group's members.

task function
An activity directly related to the effective completion of a team's work.

>> In Review

Work Teams and Groups

1 Define *group* and *work team*.

A *group* is two or more people having common interests, objectives, and continuing interaction. A *work team* is a group of people with complementary skills who are committed to a common mission, performance goals, and approach for which they hold themselves mutually accountable.

2 Explain the benefits organizations and individuals derive from working in teams.

Teams are very useful in performing work that is complicated, complex, interrelated, and/or more voluminous than one person can handle. Teams combine the knowledge, talent, skills, and abilities of individual members and integrate effort for task accomplishment. On an individual level, members benefit from psychological intimacy and achieving integrated involvement.

3 Identify the factors that influence group behavior.

Group norms of cooperative behavior facilitate team performance and effectiveness. *Group cohesion* can enhance job satisfaction and improve productivity. Social loafing—member failure to contribute time, effort, thoughts, or other resources to a group—may negate the group's efforts and achievements. With loss of individuality, members may lose their sense of accountability, inhibition, and responsibility for individual behavior.

4 Describe how groups form and develop.

Groups, formal and informal, go through stages of development to become mature and productive units. Mature groups work through the necessary interpersonal, task, and authority issues to achieve at high levels. According to this group development model, a group addresses three issues: interpersonal issues, task issues, and authority issues.

Forming → Storming → Norming → Performing → Adjourning

©Cengage Learning 2013

5 Explain how task and maintenance functions influence group performance.

Effective groups carry out various task functions to perform work successfully and do maintenance functions to ensure member satisfaction and a sense of team spirit. Teams that successfully fulfill these functions afford members the potential for the social benefits of psychological intimacy and integrated involvement.

6 Discuss the factors that influence group effectiveness.

Work team effectiveness in the new team environment requires management's attention to both work team structure and work team process. In addition to how the team is structured and what the team does, diversity and creativity are two areas with significant impact on team performance.

7 Describe how empowerment relates to self-managed teams.

Empowerment, an organizational attribute, encourages participation, an essential ingredient for teamwork. Empowered *self-managed teams*, designed to take on responsibilities and address issues traditionally reserved for management, succeed through development of competence skills, process skills, communication skills, and cooperative and helping behaviors.

maintenance function
An activity essential to effective, satisfying interpersonal relationships within a team or group.

self-managed team
A team that makes decisions that were once reserved for managers.

upper echelon
A top-level executive team in an organization.

8 Explain the importance of upper echelons and top management teams.

Self-managed teams at the top of the organization are referred to as *upper echelons*. Organizations are often a reflection of these upper echelons. Upper echelon theory argues that background characteristics of the top management team can predict organizational characteristics and set standards for values, competence, ethics, and unique characteristics throughout the organization.

What about You? How Much Diversity Is on Your Team?

This exercise allows you to explore the level of diversity on your team. Listed below are words that describe a variety of individual differences in the workplace.

Categories and Types of Diversity

Surface-Level
Social-category differences
- Race
- Ethnicity
- Gender
- Age
- Religion
- Sexual orientation
- Physical abilities

Differences in values or beliefs
- Cultural background
- Ideological beliefs

Personality differences
- Cognitive style
- Affective disposition
- Motivational factors

Organizational- or community-status differences
- Tenure or length of service
- Position title

Differences in social and network ties
- Work-related ties
- Friendship ties
- Community ties
- In-group memberships

Deep-Level
Differences in knowledge or skills
- Education
- Functional knowledge
- Information or expertise
- Training
- Experience
- Abilities

Think about the level of diversity you have on your team.
1. Which of the above-listed attributes are in your team?
2. What attributes contribute to team effectiveness/performance?
3. What diversity characteristics need to be added to your team to make it more effective?

SOURCE: Adapted from E. Mannix and M. A. Neale, "What Differences Make a Difference?" *Psychological Science in the Public Interest* 6 (2005): 31–55.

Chapter 10

Decision Making by Individuals and Groups

Key Terms

programmed decision
A simple, routine matter for which a manager has an established decision rule.

nonprogrammed decision
A new, complex decision that requires a creative solution.

effective decision
A timely decision that meets a desired objective and is acceptable to those individuals affected by it.

rationality
A logical, step-by-step approach to decision making, with a thorough analysis of alternatives and their consequences.

bounded rationality
A theory that suggests that there are limits to how rational a decision maker can actually be.

satisfice
To select the first alternative that is "good enough," because the costs in time and effort are too great to optimize.

heuristics
Shortcuts in decision making that save mental activity.

escalation of commitment
The tendency to continue to support a failing course of action.

cognitive style
An individual's preferred method for gathering information and evaluating alternatives.

risk aversion
The tendency to choose options that entail fewer risks and less uncertainty.

intuition
A fast, positive force in decision making that is utilized at a level below consciousness and involves learned patterns of information.

1 Identify the steps in the decision-making process.

The decision-making process involves *programmed decisions* and *nonprogrammed decisions*. The first step is recognizing the problem or realizing a decision must be made. Second, the objective of the decision is identified. The third step is gathering information relevant to the problem. The fourth step is listing and evaluating alternative courses of action. Finally, the manager selects the alternative that best meets the decision objective.

2 Describe various models of decision making.

The *rational model* of decision making contends that the decision maker is completely rational in his or her approach. *Bounded rationality* theory suggests that constraints force decision makers to be less rational and assumes that managers satisfice and develop heuristics. The *Z problem-solving model* capitalizes on the strengths of four separate preferences (Sensing, Intuiting, Thinking, and Feeling), allowing managers to use preferences and nonpreferences to make decisions.

3 Discuss the individual influences that affect decision making.

Decisions reflect the people who make them. The individual influences that affect decision making are comfort with risk, cognitive style, personality, intuition, and creativity.

4 Explain how groups make decisions.

Group decisions are utilized for several reasons: to achieve *synergy*, to gain commitment to a decision, and to maximize knowledge and experience in problem-solving situations. Seven techniques utilized in group decisions are brainstorming, nominal group technique, devil's advocacy, dialectical inquiry, quality circles and quality teams, and self-managed teams.

5 Describe the role culture plays in decision making.

Styles of decision making vary greatly among cultures and affect the way people view decisions. The dimensions proposed by Hofstede in Chapter 2 that affect decision making are: uncertainty avoidance, power distance, individualism/collectivism, time orientation, masculinity/femininity, cultural diversity, functional background, and strategic decision making.

6 Explain how organizations can improve the quality of decisions through participation.

Participative decision making can include employees identifying problems, generating alternatives, selecting solutions, planning implementations, and/or evaluating results. Participative management can increase employee creativity, job satisfaction, and productivity, and improve a company's economic performance.

creativity

A process influenced by individual and organizational factors that results in the production of novel and useful ideas, products, or both.

synergy

A positive force that occurs in groups when group members are stimulated to produce new solutions to problems through the process of mutual influence and encouragement within the group.

social decision schemes

Simple rules used to determine final group decisions.

groupthink

A deterioration of mental efficiency, reality testing, and moral judgment resulting from pressures within the group.

group polarization

The tendency for group discussion to produce shifts toward more extreme attitudes among members.

brainstorming

A technique for generating as many ideas as possible on a given subject while suspending evaluation until all the ideas have been suggested.

nominal group technique (NGT)

A structured approach to group decision making that focuses on generating alternatives and choosing one.

devil's advocacy

A technique for preventing groupthink in which a group or individual is given the role of critic during decision making.

dialectical inquiry

A debate between two opposing sets of recommendations.

quality circle

A small group of employees who work voluntarily on company time, typically one hour per week, to address work-related problems such as quality control, cost reduction, production planning and techniques, and even product design.

quality team

A team that is part of an organization's structure and is empowered to act on its decisions regarding product and service quality.

participative decision making

Decision making in which individuals who are affected by decisions influence the making of those decisions.

What about You?   Which Side of Your Brain Do You Favor?

There are no "right" or "wrong" answers to this questionnaire. It is more of a self-assessment than a test. Do not read the questions more than once. Don't overanalyze. Simply circle "a" or "b" to indicate which answer is more typical of you.

1. Typically, when I have a problem to solve,
   a. I make a list of possible solutions, prioritize them, and then select the best answer.
   b. I "let it sit" for a while or talk it over with someone before I attempt to reach a solution.
2. When I sit with my hands clasped in my lap (FOLD YOUR HANDS THAT WAY RIGHT NOW BEFORE GOING ON, THEN LOOK AT YOUR HANDS), the thumb that is on top is
   a. my right thumb.
   b. my left thumb.
3. I have hunches
   a. sometimes, but do not place much faith in them.
   b. frequently and I usually follow them.
4. If I am at a meeting or lecture, I tend to take extensive notes.
   a. True
   b. False
5. I am well organized, have a system for doing things, have a place for everything and everything in its place, and can assimilate information quickly and logically.
   a. True
   b. False
6. I am good with numbers.
   a. True
   b. False
7. Finding words in a dictionary or looking up names in a telephone book is something I can do easily and quickly.
   a. True
   b. False
8. If I want to remember directions or other information,
   a. I make notes.
   b. I visualize the information.
9. I express myself well verbally.
   a. True
   b. False
10. To learn dance steps or athletic moves,
    a. I try to understand the sequence of the steps and repeat them mentally.
    b. I don't think about it; I just try to get the feel of the game or the music.

Interpretation:

- Four, five, or six "a" answers indicate lateralization—an ability to use either hemisphere easily and to solve problems according to their nature rather than according to a favored manner.
- One, two, or three "a" answers indicate right-hemisphere dominance; corresponding traits include inventiveness, creativity, innovation, risk taking, whimsy, and an ability to see the "big picture."
- Seven, eight, or nine "a" answers indicate a left-hemisphere dominance—a tendency toward attention to detail, the use of logic, and traits of thoroughness and accuracy.

SOURCE: "Which Side of the Brain Do You Favor?" in *Quality Driven Designs* (San Francisco: Pfeiffer/Jossey-Bass, 1992). Copyright 1992 Pfeiffer/Jossey-Bass. Reprinted by permission of Jossey-Bass, Inc., a subsidiary of John Wiley & Sons, Inc.

Chapter 11

>> In Review

Power and Political Behavior

1 Describe the concept of power.

Power is the ability to influence others. Influence is the process of affecting the thoughts, behavior, and feelings of others. Authority is the right to influence others. Power is an exchange relationship.

2 Identify forms and sources of power in organizations.

Power in organizations can be categorized simply as interpersonal or intergroup. French and Raven's five forms of interpersonal power are reward, coercive, legitimate, referent, and expert power. Information power is another form of interpersonal power. Intergroup power derives from control of critical resources and of strategic contingencies. To have control over contingencies, a group must be able to cope with uncertainty, have a high degree of centrality, and perform a function indispensable to the organization.

3 Describe the role of ethics in using power.

The key to using all of these types of power well is to use them ethically. McClelland believes personal power is negative and social power is positive. That is, when power is used for the good of the group rather than for individual gain, the power is positive.

4 Identify symbols of power and powerlessness in organizations.

Two theorists examine symbols of power: Rosabeth Moss Kanter's list of symbols is grounded in doing things for others: for people in trouble, for employees, for bosses. There is an active, other-directed element in her symbols. Michael Korda's list focuses on status and whether there are more people for whom you would inconvenience yourself than people who would inconvenience themselves for you.

5 Define *organizational politics* and understand the role of political skill and major influence tactics.

Organizational politics is an inevitable feature of work life. Political behavior consists of actions not officially sanctioned that are taken to influence others in order to meet personal goals. Managers should take a proactive role in managing politics. Political skill is the ability to get things done through favorable interpersonal relationships outside formally prescribed organizational mechanisms.

6 Identify ways to manage political behavior in organizations.

To manage political behavior in their employees, managers can: use open communication; clarify expectations regarding employee performance; use participative management techniques; encourage cooperation among work groups; manage scarce resources well; and provide a supportive organizational climate. Individuals must also manage up—that is, manage the boss. The biggest trump to political behavior is empowerment.

What about You?   Are You Self-Empowered?

Circle the option that best describes how you usually are in each of the following situations:

1. If someone disagrees with me in a class or a meeting, I
   a. immediately back down.
   b. explain my position further.
2. When I have an idea for a project, I
   a. typically take a great deal of time to start it.

   b. get going on it fairly quickly.
3. If my boss or teacher tells me to do something that I think is wrong, I
   a. do it anyway, telling myself he or she is "the boss."
   b. ask for clarification and explain my position.

Key Terms

power
The ability to influence another person.

influence
The process of affecting the thoughts, behavior, and feelings of another person.

authority
The right to influence another person.

zone of indifference
The range in which attempts to influence a person will be perceived as legitimate and will be acted on without a great deal of thought.

reward power
Power based on an agent's ability to control rewards that a target wants.

coercive power
Power that is based on an agent's ability to cause an unpleasant experience for a target.

legitimate power
Power that is based on position and mutual agreement; agent and target agree that the agent has the right to influence the target.

referent power
An elusive power that is based on interpersonal attraction.

expert power
The power that exists when an agent has specialized knowledge or skills that the target needs.

strategic contingencies
Activities that other groups depend on in order to complete their tasks.

information power
Access to and control over important information.

personal power
Power used for personal gain.

>>

social power
Power used to create motivation or to accomplish group goals.

powerlessness
A lack of power.

organizational politics
The use of power and influence in organizations.

political behavior
Actions not officially sanctioned by an organization that are taken to influence others in order to meet one's personal goals.

political skill
The ability to get things done through favorable interpersonal relationships outside formally prescribed organizational mechanisms.

empowerment
Sharing power in such a way that individuals learn to believe in their ability to do the job.

4. When a complicated problem arises, I usually tell myself I
   a. can take care of it.
   b. will not be able to solve it.
5. When I am around people of higher authority, I often
   a. feel intimidated and defer to them.
   b. enjoy meeting important people.
6. As I awake in the morning, I usually feel
   a. alert and ready to conquer almost anything.
   b. tired and have a hard time getting myself motivated.
7. During an argument, I
   a. put a great deal of energy into "winning."
   b. try to listen to the other side and see if we have any points of agreement.
8. When I meet new people, I
   a. always wonder what they are "really" up to.
   b. try to learn what they are about and give them the benefit of the doubt until they prove otherwise.
9. During the day, I often
   a. criticize myself on what I am doing or thinking.
   b. think positive thoughts about myself.
10. When someone else does a great job, I
    a. find myself picking apart that person and looking for faults.
    b. often give a sincere compliment.
11. When I am working in a group, I try to
    a. do a better job than the others.
    b. help the group function more effectively.
12. If someone pays me a compliment, I typically
    a. try not to appear boastful and I downplay the compliment.
    b. respond with a positive "thank you" or similar response.
13. I like to be around people who
    a. challenge me and make me question what I do.
    b. give me respect.
14. In love relationships, I prefer the other person to
    a. have his/her own selected interests.
    b. do pretty much what I do.
15. During a crisis, I try to
    a. resolve the problem.
    b. find someone to blame.
16. After seeing a movie with friends, I
    a. wait to see what they say before I decide whether I liked it.
    b. am ready to talk about my reactions right away.
17. When work deadlines are approaching, I typically
    a. get flustered and worry about completion.
    b. buckle down and work until the job is done.
18. If a job comes up I am interested in, I
    a. go for it and apply.
    b. tell myself I am not qualified enough.
19. When someone treats me unkindly or unfairly, I
    a. try to rectify the situation.
    b. tell other people about the injustice.
20. If a difficult conflict situation or problem arises, I
    a. try not to think about it, hoping it will resolve itself.
    b. look at various options and may ask others for advice before I figure out what to do.

Scoring:
Score one point for each of the following circled: 1b, 2b, 3b, 4a, 5b, 6a, 7b, 8b, 9b, 10b, 11b, 12b, 13a, 14a, 15a, 16b, 17b, 18a, 19a, 20b.

Analysis of Scoring

16–20: You are a take-charge person and generally make the most of opportunities. When others tell you something cannot be done, you may take this as a challenge and do it anyway. You see the world as an oyster with many pearls to harvest.

11–15: You try hard, but sometimes your negative attitude prevents you from getting involved in productive projects. Many times you take responsibility, but there are situations in which you look to others to take care of problems.

0–10: You complain too much and are usually focused on the "worst case scenario." To you the world is controlled by fate, and no matter what you do, it seems to get you nowhere, so you let other people develop opportunities. You need to start seeing the positive qualities in yourself and in others and see yourself as the "master of your fate."

Chapter 12

Leadership and Followership

Key Terms

leadership
The process of guiding and directing the behavior of people in the work environment.

formal leadership
Officially sanctioned leadership based on the authority of a formal position.

informal leadership
Unofficial leadership accorded to a person by other members of the organization.

leader
An advocate for change and new approaches to problems.

manager
An advocate for stability and the status quo.

autocratic style
A style of leadership in which the leader uses strong, directive actions to control the rules, regulations, activities, and relationships in the work environment.

democratic style
A style of leadership in which the leader uses interaction and collaboration with followers to direct the work and work environment.

laissez-faire style
A style of leadership in which the leader has a hands-off approach.

initiating structure
Leader behavior aimed at defining and organizing work relationships and roles, as well as establishing clear patterns of organization, communication, and ways of getting things done.

consideration
Leader behavior aimed at nurturing friendly, warm working relationships as well as encouraging mutual trust and interpersonal respect within the work unit.

1 Discuss the differences between leadership and management and between leaders and managers.

Leadership is the process of guiding and directing behavior of people in the work environment. The management process reduces uncertainty and stabilizes an organization. *Leaders* agitate for change and new approaches; in contrast, *managers* advocate stability and the status quo. They differ along four separate dimensions of personality: attitudes toward goals, conceptions of work, relationships with other people, and sense of self.

2 Explain the role of trait theory in describing leaders.

The first studies of leadership attempted to identify what physical attributes, personality characteristics, and abilities distinguished leaders from other members of a group. The trait theories have had very limited success in being able to identify the universal, distinguishing attributes of leaders.

3 Describe the role of foundational behavioral research in the development of leadership theories.

Behavioral theories address how leaders behave. The Lewin, Lippitt, and White studies identified three basic leadership styles: autocratic, democratic, and laissez-faire. Ohio State University measured specific leader behaviors—initiating structure and consideration. The University of Michigan studies suggested two styles of leadership: employee oriented and production oriented.

4 Describe and compare the four contingency theories of leadership.

Fiedler's contingency theory proposes that the fit between the leader's need structure and the favorableness of the leader's situation determine the team's effectiveness in work accomplishment. The role of the leader in path–goal theory is to clear the follower's path to the goal. In normative decision theory, leaders and managers determine the appropriate level of employee participation in decision making, and the Situational Leadership theory suggests that the leader's behavior should be adjusted to the maturity level of the followers.

5 Discuss the recent developments in leadership theory of leader–member exchange and inspirational leadership.

With leader–member exchange theory (LMX), leaders form *in-groups* whose members work within the leader's inner circle and *out-groups* whose members are outside the circle. In-group members receive greater responsibilities, more rewards, and more attention. Inspirational leadership theories—*transformational leadership*, *charismatic leadership*, and *authentic leadership*—can result in positive, productive member behavior because followers are inspired by the leader to perform well.

6 Discuss how issues of emotional intelligence, trust, gender, and servant leadership are informing today's leadership models.

All workers must be aware of emerging leadership issues such as emotional intelligence, trust, women leaders, and servant leadership. These trait studies can affect leaders' decision-making skills, strategy implementation, and ability to build organizational citizenship behaviors. For women as leaders, the focus is shifting to behaviors and style rather than gender stereotypes.

>>

Leadership Grid
An approach to understanding a leader's or manager's concern for results (production) and concern for people.

organization man manager (5,5)
A middle-of-the-road leader.

authority-compliance manager (9,1)
A leader who emphasizes efficient production.

country club manager (1,9)
A leader who has great concern for people and little concern for production, attempts to avoid conflict, and seeks to be well liked.

team manager (9,9)
A leader who builds a highly productive team of committed people.

impoverished manager (1,1)
A leader who exerts just enough effort to get by.

paternalistic "father knows best" manager (9+9)
A leader who promises reward and threatens punishment.

opportunistic "what's in it for me" manager (Opp)
A leader who uses whichever style will maximize self-benefit.

least preferred coworker (LPC)
The person a leader has least preferred to work with.

task structure
The degree of clarity, or ambiguity, in the work activities assigned to the group.

position power
The authority associated with the leader's formal position in the organization.

leader–member relations
The quality of interpersonal relationships among a leader and the group members.

charismatic leadership
A leader's use of personal abilities and talents in order to have profound and extraordinary effects on followers.

followership
The process of being guided and directed by a leader in the work environment.

7 Define *followership* and identify different types of followers.

The follower role has alternatively been cast as one of self-leadership in which the follower assumes responsibility for influencing his or her own performance. Five types of followers are *effective*, *alienated*, *sheep*, *yes people*, and *survivors*. They are identified based on two dimensions: (1) activity versus passivity and (2) independent, critical thinking versus dependent, uncritical thinking.

8 Synthesize historical leadership research into key guidelines for leaders.

Leaders and organizations appreciate the unique attributes, predispositions, and talents of each leader. Leaders challenge the organizational culture, when necessary, without destroying it. Participative, considerate leader behaviors demonstrate a concern for people. Different leadership situations call for different leadership talents and behaviors. Good leaders are likely to be good followers.

What about You? Are You an Effective Follower?

To determine whether you are an effective follower, read the text section on "Types of Followers," and work through the following four steps. Answer each question in the four steps yes or no.

Step 1. Self-Management and Self-Responsibility
_____ Do you take the initiative at work?
_____ Do you challenge the system at work when appropriate?
_____ Do you ask questions when you need more information?
_____ Do you successfully bring your projects to completion?

Step 2. Commitment beyond Yourself
_____ Are you committed to your boss's and company's success?
_____ Is there a higher purpose in life that you value deeply?
_____ Are there principles that you will not compromise?
_____ Is there a person at work or elsewhere you admire greatly?

Step 3. Self-Development
_____ Do you attend a professional development class annually?
_____ Do you have a program of self-study or structured learning?
_____ Do you take at least one class each semester in the year?
_____ Have you identified new skills to learn for your job?

Step 4. Courage and Honesty
_____ Have you disagreed with your boss twice this year?
_____ Have you taken two unpopular positions at work this year?
_____ Have you given critical feedback to someone, kindly?
_____ Have you taken one risk at work to do a better job?

Scoring:
Count the number of "yes" answers in Steps 1 through 4: _____
If you have ten to sixteen "yes" answers, this would suggest that you are an effective follower. If you have seven or fewer "yes" answers, this may suggest that you fall into one of the other four categories of followers.

SOURCE: R. E. Kelley, "In Praise of Followers," *Harvard Business Review* (November–December 1988), http://hbr.org/1988/11/in-priase-of-followers/ar/1. Reprinted by permission of Harvard Business Review. Copyright © 1988 by Harvard Business School Publishing Corporation; all rights reserved.

Chapter 13

Conflict and Negotiation

1 Describe the nature of conflicts in organizations.

Conflict is defined as any situation in which incompatible goals, attitudes, emotions, or behaviors lead to disagreement or opposition between two or more parties. *Functional conflict* is a healthy, constructive disagreement between two or more people. *Dysfunctional conflict* is an unhealthy, destructive disagreement between two or more people.

2 Explain the role structural and personal factors play in causing conflict in organizations.

Conflict can be classified into categories: *structural factors* and *personal factors*. Structural factors include specialization, interdependence, common resources, goal differences, authority relationships, status inconsistencies, and jurisdictional ambiguities. The causes of conflict that arise from individual differences include skills and abilities, personalities, perceptions, values and ethics, emotions, communication barriers, and cultural differences.

3 Discuss the nature of group conflict in organizations.

Interorganizational conflict occurs between two or more organizations. Conflict occurring between groups or teams is known as *intergroup conflict*. Possible positive effects include increased group cohesiveness, task focus, and group loyalty. Possible negative consequences include extreme competition, hostility, and decreased communication between groups. *Intragroup conflict* is within groups or teams and can serve to avoid groupthink.

	GROUP	**INDIVIDUAL**
INTER	interorganizational	interpersonal > power networks > defense mechanisms > compromise mechanisms
INTRA	intragroup	intrapersonal > interrole > intrarole > person–role conflict

4 Describe the factors that influence conflict between individuals in organizations.

Intrapersonal conflict occurs within an individual. Tips for managing intrapersonal conflict are to analyze and match your values with the organization's, understand expectations, and develop political skills. Conflict between two or more people, or *interpersonal conflict*, can arise from individual differences. To manage interpersonal conflict, it is helpful to understand power networks in organizations, defense mechanisms exhibited by individuals, and ways to cope with difficult people.

5 Describe effective and ineffective techniques for managing conflict.

Effective conflict management techniques include appealing to superordinate goals, expanding resources, changing personnel, changing structure, and confronting and negotiating. Ineffective techniques include nonaction, secrecy, administrative orbiting, due process nonaction, and character assassination.

Key Terms

functional conflict
A healthy, constructive disagreement between two or more people.

dysfunctional conflict
An unhealthy, destructive disagreement between two or more people.

jurisdictional ambiguity
The presence of unclear lines of responsibility within an organization.

interorganizational conflict
Conflict that occurs between two or more organizations.

intergroup conflict
Conflict that occurs between groups or teams in an organization.

intragroup conflict
Conflict that occurs within groups or teams.

intrapersonal conflict
Conflict that occurs within an individual.

interrole conflict
A person's experience of conflict among the multiple roles in his or her life.

intrarole conflict
Conflict that occurs within a single role, such as when a person receives conflicting messages from role senders about how to perform a certain role.

person–role conflict
Conflict that occurs when an individual in a particular role is expected to perform behaviors that clash with his or her personal values.

interpersonal conflict
Conflict that occurs between two or more individuals.

fixation
An aggressive mechanism in which an individual keeps up a dysfunctional behavior that obviously will not solve the conflict.

displacement
An aggressive mechanism in which an individual directs his or her anger toward someone who is not the source of the conflict.

negativism
An aggressive mechanism in which a person responds with pessimism to any attempt at solving a problem.

compensation
A compromise mechanism in which an individual attempts to make up for a negative situation by devoting himself or herself to another pursuit with increased vigor.

identification
A compromise mechanism whereby an individual patterns his or her behavior after another's.

rationalization
A compromise mechanism characterized by trying to justify one's behavior by constructing bogus reasons for it.

flight/withdrawal
A withdrawal mechanism that entails physically escaping (flight) or psychologically escaping (withdrawal) a conflict.

conversion
A withdrawal mechanism in which emotional conflicts are expressed in physical symptoms.

fantasy
A withdrawal mechanism that provides an escape from a conflict through daydreaming.

nonaction
Doing nothing in hopes that a conflict will disappear.

secrecy
Attempting to hide a conflict or an issue that has the potential to create conflict.

administrative orbiting
Delaying action on a conflict by buying time.

due process nonaction
A procedure set up to address conflicts that is so costly, time consuming, or personally risky that no one will use it.

character assassination
An attempt to label or discredit an opponent.

superordinate goal
An organizational goal that is more important to both parties in a conflict than their individual or group goals.

---

6 Identify five styles of conflict management.

Managers have at their disposal a variety of conflict management styles: avoiding, accommodating, competing, compromising, and collaborating. One way of classifying styles of conflict management is to examine the styles' assertiveness (the extent to which you want your goals met) and cooperativeness (the extent to which you want to see the other party's concerns met).

What about You? Assess Your Team's Conflict

Think of a team you're a member of or one you were part of in the past. Answer the following eight questions regarding that team.

1. How much emotional tension was there in your team?

No tension				Lots of tension
1	2	3	4	5

2. How much conflict of ideas was there in your team?

No idea conflict			Lots of idea conflict	
1	2	3	4	5

3. How often did people get angry while working in your team?

Never				Often
1	2	3	4	5

4. How different were your views on the content of your project?

Very similar views			Very different views	
1	2	3	4	5

5. How much were personality clashes evident in your team?

No clashes evident			Personality clashes very evident	
1	2	3	4	5

6. How much did you talk through disagreements about your team projects?

Never talked through disagreements		Always talked through disagreements		
1	2	3	4	5

7. How much interpersonal friction was there in your team?

No friction				Lots of friction
1	2	3	4	5

8. How much disagreement was there about task procedure in your team?

No disagreement about procedure		Lots of disagreement about procedure		
1	2	3	4	5

Total for items 2, 4, 6, and 8 = ___ indicating task conflict.
Total for items 1, 3, 5, and 7 = ___ indicating relationship conflict.

- Did your team experience higher relationship or task conflict?
- What actions can you take to better manage task conflict? Relationship conflict?
- Was there an absence of both, or either, types of conflict in your team? What does this indicate?

SOURCE: Adapted from K. Jehn, "A Multimethod Examination of the Benefits and Detriments of Intragroup Conflict," *Administrative Science Quarterly* 40 (1995): 256–282.

---

distributive bargaining
A negotiation approach in which the goals of the parties are in conflict, and each party seeks to maximize its resources.

integrative negotiation
A negotiation approach in which the parties' goals are not seen as mutually exclusive, but the focus is on both sides achieving their objectives.

Chapter 14

Jobs and the Design of Work

Key Terms

job
A set of specified work and task activities that engage an individual in an organization.

work
Mental or physical activity that has productive results.

meaning of work
The way a person interprets and understands the value of work as part of life.

work simplification
The standardization and the narrow, explicit specification of task activities for workers.

job enlargement
A method of job design that increases the number of activities in a job to overcome the boredom of overspecialized work.

job rotation
A variation of job enlargement in which workers are exposed to a variety of specialized jobs over time.

cross-training
A variation of job enlargement in which workers are trained in different specialized tasks or activities.

job enrichment
Designing or redesigning a job by incorporating motivational factors into it.

Job Characteristics Model
A framework for understanding person–job fit through the interaction of core job dimensions with critical psychological states within a person.

Job Diagnostic Survey (JDS)
The survey instrument designed to measure the elements in the Job Characteristics Model.

engagement
The expression of oneself as one performs in work or other roles.

1 Differentiate between *job* and *work*.

A *job* is an employee's specific work and task activities in an organization. *Work* is effortful, productive activity resulting in a product or a service. A job is composed of a set of specific tasks, each of which is an assigned piece of work to be done in a specific time period. Work is an especially important human endeavor because it has a powerful effect in binding a person to reality.

2 Discuss the traditional approaches to job design.

Good job design differentiates and integrates tasks, improves productivity, and enhances employee well-being. Approaches to job design that were developed during the twentieth century are job enlargement/job rotation, job enrichment, and the job characteristics theory. Each approach offers unique benefits to the organization, the employee, or both, but each also has limitations and drawbacks.

3 Identify and describe alternative approaches to job design.

Several alternative approaches to job design have emerged over the past couple of decades: the social information-processing model; ergonomics and the interdisciplinary framework of Michael Campion and Paul Thayer; the international perspectives of the Japanese, Germans, and Scandinavians; and the health and well-being aspects of work design. Healthy work enables individuals to adapt, function well, and balance work with private life activities.

JOB DESIGN APPROACH (DISCIPLINE)	POSITIVE OUTCOMES	NEGATIVE OUTCOMES
MECHANISTIC APPROACH (mechanical engineering)	Decreased training time Higher personnel utilization levels Lower likelihood of error Less chance of mental overload Lower stress levels	Lower job satisfaction Lower motivation Higher absenteeism
MOTIVATIONAL APPROACH (industrial psychology)	Higher job satisfaction Higher motivation Greater job involvement Higher job performance Lower absenteeism	Increased training time Lower personnel utilization levels Greater chance of errors Greater chance of mental overload and stress
BIOLOGICAL APPROACH (biology)	Less physical effort Less physical fatigue Fewer health complaints Fewer medical incidents Lower absenteeism Higher job satisfaction	Higher financial costs because of changes in equipment or job environment
PERCEPTUAL MOTOR APPROACH (experimental psychology)	Lower likelihood of error Lower likelihood of accidents Less chance of mental stress Decreased training time Higher personnel utilization levels	Lower job satisfaction Lower motivation

SOURCE: Reprinted from *Organizational Dynamics*, 15(3), Michael A. Campion, Paul W. Thayer, "Job Design: Approaches, Outcomes, and Trade-offs," Winter/1987. Copyright © 1987, with permission from Elsevier.

social information-processing (SIP) model

A model that suggests that the important job factors depend in part on what others tell a person about the job.

ergonomics

The science of adapting work and working conditions to the employee or worker.

lean production

Using committed employees with ever-expanding responsibilities to achieve zero waste and 100 percent good product, delivered on time, every time.

sociotechnical systems (STS)

Giving equal attention to technical and social considerations in job design.

technocentric

Placing technology and engineering at the center of job design decisions.

anthropocentric

Placing human considerations at the center of job design decisions.

job sharing

An alternative work pattern in which more than one person occupies a single job.

flextime

An alternative work pattern that enables employees to set their own daily work schedules.

virtual office

A mobile platform of computer, telecommunication, and information technology and services.

technostress

The stress caused by new and advancing technologies in the workplace.

---

4 Identify and describe contemporary issues facing organizations in the design of work.

Contemporary job design issues include telecommuting, alternative work patterns, technostress, and skill development. Work is relationally designed to provide opportunities and increase flexibility for employees. Companies use these and other approaches to the design of work as ways to manage a growing business while contributing to a better balance of work and family life for employees.

What about You? Is Your Work Environment a Healthy One?

To determine whether your work environment is a healthy one, read the text section on "Work Design and Well-Being" on pages 239–240, then complete the following four steps. Answer each question in the five steps "yes" or "no."

Step 1. Control and Influence

_____ Do you have influence over the pace of your work?
_____ Are system response times neither too fast nor too slow?
_____ Do you have a say in your work assignments and goals?
_____ Is there an opportunity for you to comment on your performance appraisal?

Step 2. Information and Uncertainty

_____ Do you receive timely information to complete your work?
_____ Do you receive complete information for your work assignments?
_____ Is there adequate planning for changes that affect you at work?
_____ Do you have access to all the information you need at work?

Step 3. Conflict at Work

_____ Does the company apply policies clearly and consistently?
_____ Are job descriptions and task assignments clear and unambiguous?
_____ Are there adequate policies and procedures for the resolution of conflicts?
_____ Is your work environment an open, participative one?

Step 4. Job Scope and Task Design

_____ Is there adequate variety in your work activities and/or assignments?
_____ Do you receive timely, constructive feedback on your work?
_____ Is your work important to the overall mission of the company?
_____ Do you work on more than one small piece of a big project?

Scoring

Count the number of "yes" answers in Steps 1 through 4: _____

If you have ten to sixteen "yes" answers, this suggests that your work environment is a psychologically healthy one.

If you have seven or fewer "yes" answers, this may suggest that your work environment is not as psychologically healthy as it could be.

Chapter 15

>> In Review

Organizational Design and Structure

1 Define *differentiation* and *integration* as organizational design processes.

Differentiation is the design process of breaking the organizational goals into tasks. Three different forms of differentiation are horizontal, vertical, and spatial. *Integration* is the design process of linking the tasks together to form a structure that supports goal accomplishment. Vertical linkage devices include hierarchical referral, rules and procedures, plans and schedules, added positions, and management information systems. The horizontal linkages are liaison roles, task forces, integrator positions, and teams.

2 Discuss the basic design dimensions managers must consider in structuring an organization.

Basic design dimensions combine to yield various structural configurations. Structural dimensions include the following: formalization, centralization, specialization, standardization, complexity, and hierarchy of authority. Levels of structural dimensions determine bureaucratic (high) or flexible and loose (low) organizations. Henry Mintzberg's alternative approach is to describe what is and is not important to the success of the organization and design structures that fit each organization's unique set of circumstances.

TABLE 15.1 Five Structural Configurations of Organizations			
Structural Configuration	**Prime Coordinating Mechanism**	**Key Part of Organization**	**Type of Decentralization**
Simple structure	Direct supervision	Upper echelon	Centralization
Machine bureaucracy	Standardization of work processes	Technical staff	Limited horizontal decentralization
Professional bureaucracy	Standardization of skills	Operating level	Vertical and horizontal decentralization
Divisionalized form	Standardization of outputs	Middle level	Limited vertical decentralization
Adhocracy	Mutual adjustment	Support staff	Selective decentralization

SOURCE: H. Mintzberg, *Structuring of Organizations*, 1st Edition, ©1979. Reprinted by permission of Pearson Education, Inc., Upper Saddle River, N.J.

3 Describe five structural configurations for organizations.

Henry Mintzberg proposed five structural configurations: the simple structure, the machine bureaucracy, the professional bureaucracy, the divisionalized form, and the adhocracy. The five basic parts of the organization, for Mintzberg, are the upper echelon, and/or strategic apex; the middle level, or middle line; the operating core; the technical staff, or technostructure; and the support staff. The organization's goals and levels of differentiation, integration, and formalization determine the structural configuration.

4 Describe four contextual variables that influence organizational structure.

Four variables influence the success of an organization's design: size, technology, environment, and strategy and goals. These variables provide a manager with key considerations for the right organizational design. The amount of change in the contextual variables throughout the life of the organization influences the amount of change needed in the basic dimensions of the organization's structure.

Key Terms

organizational design
The process of constructing and adjusting an organization's structure to achieve its business strategy and goals.

organizational structure
The linking of departments and jobs within an organization.

differentiation
The process of deciding how to divide the work in an organization.

integration
The process of coordinating the different parts of an organization.

formalization
The degree to which the organization has official rules, regulations, and procedures.

centralization
The degree to which decisions are made at the top of the organization.

specialization
The degree to which jobs are narrowly defined and depend on unique expertise.

standardization
The degree to which work activities are accomplished in a routine fashion.

complexity
The degree to which many different types of activities occur in the organization.

hierarchy of authority
The degree of vertical differentiation across levels of management.

simple structure
A centralized form of organization that emphasizes a small technical and support staff, strong centralization of decision making in the upper echelon, and a minimal middle level.

machine bureaucracy
A moderately decentralized form of organization that emphasizes a support staff differentiated from the line operations of the organization, limited horizontal decentralization of decision making, and a well-defined hierarchy of authority.

>>

professional bureaucracy
A decentralized form of organization that emphasizes the expertise of the professionals in the operating core of the organization.

divisionalized form
A loosely coupled, composite structural configuration composed of divisions, each of which may have its own structural configuration.

adhocracy
A selectively decentralized form of organization that emphasizes the support staff and mutual adjustment among people.

contextual variables
A set of four characteristics that influence the success of an organization's design: size, technology, environment, and strategy and goals.

technological interdependence
The degree of interrelatedness of the organization's various technological elements.

environment
Anything outside the boundaries of an organization.

task environment
The part of the environment that is directly relevant to the organization.

environmental uncertainty
The amount and rate of change in the organization's environment.

mechanistic structure
An organizational design that emphasizes structured activities, specialized tasks, and centralized decision making.

organic structure
An organizational design that emphasizes teamwork, open communication, and decentralized decision making.

organizational life cycle
The differing stages of an organization's life from birth to death.

5 Explain the forces reshaping organizations.

Several forces reshaping organizations are causing managers to go beyond the traditional frameworks and to examine ways to make organizations more responsive to customer needs. Some of these forces include shorter organizational life cycles, globalization, and rapid changes in information technology. These forces together increase the demands on process capabilities within the organization and emerging organizational structures. To successfully retain their health and vitality, organizations must function as open systems that are responsive to their task environment.

6 Identify and describe emerging organizational structures.

Network organizations are weblike structures that contract some or all of their operating functions to other organizations and then coordinate their activities through managers and other employees at their headquarters. Virtual organizations are temporary network organizations consisting of independent enterprises. The circle organization, crafted by Harley-Davidson in its drive to achieve teamwork without teams, is a more open system and an organic structure for customer responsiveness.

7 Identify factors that can adversely affect organizational structure.

If organizational structure is out of alignment with its contextual variables, one or more of the following symptoms appears: delayed decision making, low-quality decision making, nonresponse to changing environment, and interdepartmental conflict. Also, managers' personal cognitive biases and political ideologies affect their good judgment and decision-making abilities and may adversely affect the structure of the organization.

What about You? Managers of Today and the Future

Are the roles for managers in your organization more oriented toward today or toward the future? (If you do not work, think of an organization where you have worked or talk with a friend about managerial roles in his or her organization.)

Step 1. Reread Table 15.3 at the end of the chapter and check which orientation (today or future) predominates in your organization for each of the following seven characteristics:

	Today	Future
1. Boss–employee relationships.		
2. Getting work accomplished.		
3. Messenger versus problem solver.		
4. Basis for task accomplishment.		
5. Narrow versus broad functional focus.		
6. Adherence to channels of authority.		
7. Controlling versus coaching subordinates.		

Step 2. Examine the degree of consistency across all seven characteristics. Could the organization make one or two structural changes to achieve a better alignment of the manager's role with today or with the future?

Step 3. Identify one manager in your organization who fits very well into the organization's ideal manager's role. What does this manager do that creates a good person–role fit?

Step 4. Identify one manager in your organization who does not fit very well into the organization's ideal manager's role. What does this manager do that creates a poor person–role fit?

Organizational Culture

1 Identify the three levels of organizational culture and evaluate the roles they play in an organization.

Organizational culture is a pattern of basic assumptions considered valid and taught to new members as the way to perceive, think, and feel in the organization. *Artifacts* are cultural symbols in the physical and social work environments, such as personal enactment, ceremonies and rites, stories, rituals, and symbols. Deeper level *values* reflect inherent beliefs, and *assumptions* guide behavior and tell members of an organization how to perceive situations and people.

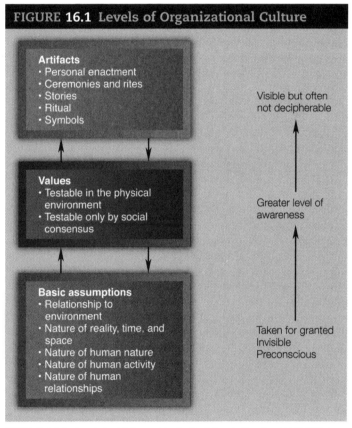

FIGURE 16.1 Levels of Organizational Culture

Artifacts
- Personal enactment
- Ceremonies and rites
- Stories
- Ritual
- Symbols

Visible but often not decipherable

Values
- Testable in the physical environment
- Testable only by social consensus

Greater level of awareness

Basic assumptions
- Relationship to environment
- Nature of reality, time, and space
- Nature of human nature
- Nature of human activity
- Nature of human relationships

Taken for granted
Invisible
Preconscious

SOURCE: E. Schein, *Organizational Culture and Leadership: A Dynamic View.* Copyright © 1985 Jossey-Bass, Inc. Reprinted by permission of John Wiley & Sons, Inc.

2 Evaluate the four functions of organizational culture within an organization.

Organizational culture serves four basic functions. First, culture provides a sense of identity to members and increases commitment to the organization. Second, culture provides a way for employees to interpret the meaning of organizational events. Third, culture reinforces the values in the organization. Finally, culture serves as a control mechanism for shaping behavior.

3 Explain the relationship between organizational culture and performance.

A *strong-culture* organization acts with a consensus on the values that drive the company and with an intensity that is recognizable even to outsiders. The "fit" perspective (*fit culture*) argues that a culture is good only if it fits the industry or the firm's strategy. Three particular industry characteristics may affect culture: the competitive environment, customer requirements, and societal expectations. An *adaptive culture* is a culture that encourages confidence and risk taking among employees, has leadership that produces change, and focuses on the changing needs of customers.

Key Terms

organizational (corporate) culture
A pattern of basic assumptions that are considered valid and that are taught to new members as the way to perceive, think, and feel in the organization.

artifacts
Symbols of culture in the physical and social work environments.

espoused values
What members of an organization say they value.

enacted values
Values reflected in the way individuals actually behave.

assumptions
Deeply held beliefs that guide behavior and tell members of an organization how to perceive situations and people.

strong culture
An organizational culture with a consensus on the values that drive the company and with an intensity that is recognizable even to outsiders.

adaptive culture
An organizational culture that encourages confidence and risk taking among employees, has leadership that produces change, and focuses on the changing needs of customers.

organizational socialization
The process by which newcomers are transformed from outsiders to participating, effective members of the organization.

anticipatory socialization
The first socialization stage, which encompasses all of the learning that takes place prior to the newcomer's first day on the job.

encounter
The second socialization stage, in which newcomers learn the tasks associated with the job, clarify their roles, and establish new relationships at work.

>>

change and acquisition
The third socialization stage, in which the newcomer begins to master the demands of the job.

triangulation
The use of multiple methods to measure organizational culture.

4 Describe five ways leaders reinforce organizational culture.

Leaders play a critical role in shaping and reinforcing organizational culture. Managers need to create a positive culture through what they pay attention to how they react to crises, how they behave, how they allocate rewards, and how they hire and fire employees. Transformational leaders create a more adaptive culture, which in turn increases business unit performance.

5 Describe the three stages of organizational socialization and the ways culture is communicated in each step.

Newcomers are transformed from outsiders to participating, effective members of the organization through *organizational socialization.* Three stages in the socialization process are *anticipatory socialization, encounter,* and *change and acquisition.* Through positive effective socialization, newcomers understand and adopt values and norms ensuring the company's culture and central values survive. Results can be good performance, high job satisfaction, and the intention to stay with the organization.

6 Discuss how managers assess their organization's culture.

Both qualitative and quantitative methods can be used to assess organizational culture. The Organizational Culture Inventory (OCI) and the Kilmann-Saxton Culture-Gap Survey are quantitative tools. In the hopes of generating a more accurate assessment of organizational culture, managers combine multiple instruments, a practice called *triangulation.*

7 Explain actions managers can take to change organizational culture.

Managers can use two approaches to change organizational culture: help current members buy into a new set of values, or add newcomers and socialize them into the organization and remove current members appropriately. Managers must send consistent messages about the new values and beliefs, provide credible communication, and live the new values. Cultural change can be assumed to be successful if new behavior is intrinsically motivated.

8 Identify the challenges organizations face developing positive, cohesive, cultures.

Achieving a positive, cohesive corporate culture may be difficult in mergers, acquisitions, and globalization due to possible conflicts between organizations and cultural diversity on a geographic level. Developing an ethical culture requires management modeling, promoting ethical norms, and trust. Developing a culture of empowerment and quality involves including employees in decision making, removing obstacles to their performance, and reinforcing the value of product and service.

What about You? Analyzing the Three Levels of Culture

Select an organization you respect. Analyze its culture using the following dimensions.
The artifacts of _____'s culture are as follows:

Personal enactment:
Rites and ceremonies:
Stories:
Rituals:
Symbols:

The values embedded in _____'s culture are as follows:
The assumptions of _____'s culture are as follows:

1. On what information did you base your analysis?
2. How complete is your view of this organization's culture?

Chapter 17

Key Terms

career
The pattern of work-related experiences that spans the course of a person's life.

career management
A lifelong process of learning about self, jobs, and organizations; setting personal career goals; developing strategies for achieving the goals, and revising the goals based on work and life experiences.

realistic job preview (RJP)
Both positive and negative information given to potential employees about the job they are applying for, thereby giving them a realistic picture of the job.

establishment
The first stage of a person's career in which the person learns the job and begins to fit into the organization and occupation.

advancement
The second, high achievement-oriented career stage in which people focus on increasing their competence.

maintenance
The third stage in an individual's career in which the individual tries to maintain productivity while evaluating progress toward career goals.

withdrawal
The final stage in an individual's career in which the individual contemplates retirement or possible career changes.

psychological contract
An implicit agreement between an individual and an organization that specifies what each is expected to give and receive in the relationship.

career path
A sequence of job experiences that an employee moves along during his or her career.

career ladder
A structured series of job positions through which an individual progresses in an organization.

>> In Review

Career Management

1 Explain occupational and organizational choice decisions.

Today most workers no longer work in one organization for the length of their working lives. The new career model is characterized by discrete exchange, occupational excellence, organizational empowerment, and project allegiance. When building a career, individuals first select an occupation that meets their needs, values, abilities, and preferences.

2 Identify foundations for a successful career.

Two foundations for a successful career are becoming your own career coach and developing your emotional intelligence. To become your own career coach, you must acquire multiple skills, develop self-reliance, and cultivate a flexible, team-oriented attitude. Emotional competencies are of equal or greater importance than technical skills.

3 Explain the career stage model.

The career stage model shows that individuals pass through four stages in their careers: establishment, advancement, maintenance, and withdrawal. Timing of career transitions varies greatly among individuals.

4 Explain the major tasks facing individuals in the establishment stage of the career stage model.

Establishment is the first stage of a person's career. The activities that occur in this stage center around learning the job and fitting into the organization and occupation. Individuals in this stage begin to work out their psychological contract with the organization and form attachment relationships with coworkers.

5 Identify the issues confronting individuals in the advancement stage of the career stage model.

Advancement is a high achievement-oriented stage in which people focus on increasing their competence. A hallmark of this stage is the exploration of career paths, or sequences of job experiences along which employees move during their careers. Some companies use career lattices that move employees laterally through the organization in an attempt to build diverse skills. A mentor provides numerous sponsorship, facilitating, and psychosocial functions for the protégé. Dual-career partnerships are common now and can lead to work–home conflicts.

6 Describe how individuals can navigate the challenges of the maintenance stage of the career stage model.

The *maintenance* stage finds the individual trying to maintain productivity while evaluating progress toward career goals. Individuals sustain their performance and continue to grow, although at a slower rate. Individuals in this stage may also become mentors.

7 Explain how individuals withdraw from the workforce.

The *withdrawal* stage involves contemplation of retirement or possible career change. Increasingly, individuals in this stage are opting for phased retirement, which is a gradual cessation of work. To help workers at this stage of their careers, organizations should provide opportunities for continued involvement with the organization, such as mentoring to other employees making career transitions.

8 Explain how career anchors help form a career identity.

Career anchors are self-perceived talents, motives, and values that guide an individual's career decisions. Five main anchors are technical/functional competence, managerial competence, autonomy and independence, creativity, and security/stability.

>>

mentor

An individual who provides guidance, coaching, counseling, and friendship to a protégé.

dual-career partnership

A relationship in which both people have important career roles.

flexible work schedule

A work schedule that allows employees discretion in order to accommodate personal concerns.

eldercare

Assistance in caring for elderly parents and/or other elderly relatives.

career plateau

A point in an individual's career at which the probability of moving farther up the hierarchy is low.

phased retirement

An arrangement that allows employees to reduce their hours and/or responsibilities in order to ease into retirement.

bridge employment

Employment that takes place after a person retires from a full-time position but before the person's permanent withdrawal from the workforce.

career anchors

A network of self-perceived talents, motives, and values that guide an individual's career decisions.

What about You? What's Your EI at Work?

Answering the following twenty-five questions will allow you to rate your social skills and self-awareness.

EI, the social equivalent of IQ, is complex in no small part because it depends on some pretty slippery variables—including your innate compatibility, or lack thereof, with the people who happen to be your coworkers. But if you want to get a rough idea of how your EI stacks up, this quiz will help.

As honestly as you can, estimate how you rate in the eyes of peers, bosses, and subordinates on each of the following traits, on a scale of 1 to 4, with 4 representing strong agreement, and 1, strong disagreement.

_____ 1. I usually stay composed, positive, and unflappable even in trying moments.

_____ 2. I can think clearly and stay focused on the task at hand under pressure.

_____ 3. I am able to admit my own mistakes.

_____ 4. I usually or always meet commitments and keep promises.

_____ 5. I hold myself accountable for meeting my goals.

_____ 6. I'm organized and careful in my work.

_____ 7. I regularly seek out fresh ideas from a wide variety of sources.

_____ 8. I'm good at generating new ideas.

_____ 9. I can smoothly handle multiple demands and changing priorities.

_____ 10. I'm results-oriented, with a strong drive to meet my objectives.

_____ 11. I like to set challenging goals and take calculated risks to reach them.

_____ 12. I'm always trying to learn how to improve my performance, including asking advice from people younger than I am.

_____ 13. I readily make sacrifices to meet an important organizational goal.

_____ 14. The company's mission is something I understand and can identify with.

_____ 15. The values of my team—or of our division or department, or the company—influence my decisions and clarify the choices I make.

_____ 16. I actively seek out opportunities to further the overall goals of the organization and enlist others to help me.

_____ 17. I pursue goals beyond what's required or expected of me in my current job.

_____ 18. Obstacles and setbacks may delay me a little, but they don't stop me.

_____ 19. Cutting through red tape and bending outdated rules are sometimes necessary.

_____ 20. I seek fresh perspectives, even if that means trying something totally new.

_____ 21. My impulses or distressing emotions don't often get the best of me at work.

_____ 22. I can change tactics quickly when circumstances change.

_____ 23. Pursuing new information is my best bet for cutting down on uncertainty and finding ways to do things better.

_____ 24. I usually don't attribute setbacks to a personal flaw (mine or someone else's).

_____ 25. I operate from an expectation of success rather than a fear of failure.

A score below 70 indicates a problem. If your total is somewhere in the basement, don't despair: EI is not unimprovable. "Emotional intelligence can be learned, and in fact we are each building it, in varying degrees, throughout life. It's sometimes called maturity," says Daniel Goleman. "EI is nothing more or less than a collection of tools that we can sharpen to help ensure our own survival."

SOURCE: A. Fisher, "Success Secret: A High Emotional IQ." Reprinted from the October 26, 1998, issue of *Fortune* by special permission; copyright 1998, Time Inc. All rights reserved.

Chapter 18

Key Terms

planned change
Change resulting from a deliberate decision to alter the organization.

unplanned change
Change that is imposed on the organization and is often unforeseen.

incremental change
Change of a relatively small scope, such as making small improvements.

strategic change
Change of a larger scale, such as organizational restructuring.

transformational change
Change in which the organization moves to a radically different, and sometimes unknown, future state.

change agent
The individual or group that undertakes the task of introducing and managing a change in an organization.

unfreezing
The first step in Lewin's change model, in which individuals are encouraged to discard old behaviors by shaking up the equilibrium state that maintains the status quo.

moving
The second step in Lewin's change model, in which new attitudes, values, and behaviors are substituted for old ones.

refreezing
The final step in Lewin's change model, in which new attitudes, values, and behaviors are established as the new status quo.

organization development (OD)
A systematic approach to organizational improvement that applies behavioral science theory and research in order to increase individual and organizational well-being and effectiveness.

>> In Review

Managing Change

1 Identify the major external and internal forces for change in organizations.

When organizations are in a state of turmoil and transition, all members are affected. *External* forces that demand change are globalization, workforce diversity, technological change, and managing ethical behavior. *Internal* pressures for change are generally recognizable: declining effectiveness, crisis, changes in employee expectations, and a changed work climate. Adaptiveness, flexibility, and responsiveness are characteristics of the organizations that will succeed in meeting the challenges of change.

2 Describe how different types of change vary in scope.

Change can be of a relatively small scope, such as a modification in a work procedure (an *incremental change*) or of a larger scale, such as the restructuring of an organization (a *strategic change*). The most massive scope of change is *transformational change*, in which the organization moves to a radically different, and sometimes unknown, future state. One of the toughest decisions faced by leaders is the "pace" of change. Researchers agree that pace is important; however, they can't agree on which pace of change is most beneficial.

3 Discuss methods organizations can use to manage resistance to change.

The contemporary view holds that resistance is simply a form of feedback and that this feedback can be used very productively to manage the change process. Three key strategies for managing resistance to change are communication, participation, and empathy and support.

4 Explain Lewin's organizational change model.

Lewin's model, the idea of force field analysis, contends that a person's behavior is the product of two opposing forces; one force pushes toward preserving the status quo and the other force pushes for change. Lewin's change model is a three-step process: *unfreezing*—encouraging individuals to discard old behaviors, *moving*—new attitudes, values, and behaviors are substituted for old ones, and *refreezing*—new attitudes, values, and behaviors are established as the new status quo.

5 Explain how companies determine the need to conduct an organization development intervention.

Organization development (OD) is a systematic approach to organizational improvement. The first step, the diagnosis, should pinpoint specific problems and areas in need of improvement. Six areas to examine carefully are the organization's purpose, structure, reward system, support systems, relationships, and leadership. A needs analysis then determines the skills and competencies that employees must have to achieve the goals of the change.

6 Discuss the major group-focused techniques for organization development intervention.

Some OD intervention methods emphasize changing the organization itself or changing the work groups within the organization. Intervention methods in this category include survey feedback, management by objectives, product and service quality programs, team building, and process consultation. All the preceding OD methods focus on changing the organization or the work group.

>>

survey feedback
A widely used intervention method whereby employee attitudes are solicited using a questionnaire.

management by objectives (MBO)
An organization-wide intervention technique that involves joint goal setting between employees and managers.

quality program
A program that embeds product and service quality excellence in the organizational culture.

team building
An intervention designed to improve the effectiveness of a work group.

process consultation
An OD method that helps managers and employees improve the processes that are used in organizations.

skills training
Increasing the job knowledge, skills, and abilities that are necessary to do a job effectively.

leadership training and development
A variety of techniques that are designed to enhance individuals' leadership skills.

executive coaching
A technique in which managers or executives are paired with a coach in a partnership to help them perform more efficiently.

role negotiation
A technique whereby individuals meet and clarify their psychological contract.

job redesign
An OD intervention method that alters jobs to improve the fit between individual skills and the demands of the job.

---

7 Discuss the major individual-focused techniques for organization development intervention.

Managers have a host of organization development techniques to facilitate organizational change. Development efforts include skills training, leadership training and development, executive coaching, role negotiation, job redesign, health promotion programs, and career planning. Success depends on techniques used, competence of the change agent, the organization's readiness for change, and top management commitment. Programs do not drive change; business needs do.

What about You? Tolerance for Ambiguity

Read each of the following statements carefully. Then rate each of them in terms of the extent to which you either agree or disagree with the statement using the following scale:

Completely Disagree		Neither Agree nor Disagree			Completely Agree	
1	2	3	4	5	6	7

Place the number that best describes your degree of agreement or disagreement in the blank to the left of each statement.

_____ 1. An expert who doesn't come up with a definite answer probably doesn't know much.

_____ 2. I would like to live in a foreign country for a while.

_____ 3. The sooner we all acquire similar values and ideals, the better.

_____ 4. A good teacher is one who makes you wonder about your way of looking at things.

_____ 5. I like parties where I know most of the people more than ones where all or most of the people are complete strangers.

_____ 6. Teachers or supervisors who hand out vague assignments give a chance for one to show initiative and originality.

_____ 7. A person who leads an even, regular life in which few surprises or unexpected happenings arise really has a lot to be grateful for.

_____ 8. Many of our most important decisions are based upon insufficient information.

_____ 9. There is really no such thing as a problem that can't be solved.

_____ 10. People who fit their lives to a schedule probably miss most of the joy of living.

_____ 11. A good job is one where what is to be done and how it is to be done are always clear.

_____ 12. It is more fun to tackle a complicated problem than to solve a simple one.

_____ 13. In the long run, it is possible to get more done by tackling small, simple problems rather than large and complicated ones.

_____ 14. Often the most interesting and stimulating people are those who don't mind being different and original.

_____ 15. What we are used to is always preferable to what is unfamiliar.

Scoring: For even-numbered questions, add the total points.
For odd-numbered questions, use reverse scoring and add the total points.
Your score is the total of the even- and odd-numbered questions.

Norms Using the Tolerance for Ambiguity Scale

Basis: The survey asks fifteen questions about personal and work-oriented situations with ambiguity. You were asked to rate each situation on a scale from 1 (tolerant) to 7 (intolerant). (Alternating questions have the response scale reversed.) The index scores the items. A perfectly tolerant person would score 15 and a perfectly intolerant person 105. Scores between 20 and 80 are reported, with means of 45. The responses to the even-numbered questions with 7 minus the score are added to the response for the odd-numbered questions.

SOURCE: "Tolerance for Ambiguity" from D. Marcic, *Organizational Behavior: Experiences and Cases* (St. Paul, MN: West Publishing, 1992), 339–340. Adapted from Paul Nutt. Used with permission.